Objects and Materials

There is broad acceptance across the humanities and social sciences that our deliberations on the social need to take place through attention to practice, to object-mediated relations, to non-human agency and to the affective dimensions of human sociality. This *Companion* focuses on the objects and materials found on the stage, and asks: what matters about objects?

Objects and Materials explores the providing succinct summary accounts of contemporary scholarship, along with new research investigating the capacity of objects to shape, unsettle and exceed expectations. Original chapters from more than 40 international, interdisciplinary contributors array of objects and materials to ask what the terms of collaborations with objects and are, and to consider how these collaborations become integral to our understanding complex, relational dynamics that fashion social worlds.

Objects and Materials will be to students and scholars across the social sciences and humanities, including in sociology, theory, science and technology studies, history, anthropology, archaeology, gender and women's studies, geography, cultural studies, politics and international relations, and p

Penny Harvey is Professor of Anthropology at the University of Manchester and Director of CRESC, the ESRC Centre on Socio-Cultural Change.

Eleanor Conlin Casella is Historical Archaeology at the University of Manchester.

Gillian Evans is a Lecturer in Anthropology at the University of Manchester.

Hannah Knox is a Research at CRESC, the ESRC Centre for Research on Socio-Cultural Change at the University Manchester.

Christine McLean is a Senior Lecturer at the Manchester Business School, University of Manchester.

Elizabeth B. Silva is Professor of Sociology at the Open University.

Nicholas Thoburn is a Senior Lecturer in Sociology at the University of Manchester.

Kath Woodward is Professor of Sociology

Culture, Economy and the Social

A new series from CRESC – the ESRC Centre for Research on Socio-Cultural Change

Editors
Professor Tony Bennett, Social and Cultural Theory, University of Western Sydney; Professor Penny Harvey, Anthropology, Manchester University; Professor Kevin Hetherington, Geography, Open University

Editorial Advisory Board
Andrew Barry, University of Oxford; Michel Callon, Ecole des Mines de Paris; Dipesh Chakrabarty, The University of Chicago; Mike Crang, University of Durham; Tim Dant, Lancaster University; Jean-Louis Fabiani, Ecoles de Hautes Etudes en Sciences Sociales; Antoine Hennion, Paris Institute of Technology; Eric Hirsch, Brunel University; John Law, The Open University; Randy Martin, New York University; Timothy Mitchell, New York University; Rolland Munro, Keele University; Andrew Pickering, University of Exeter; Mary Poovey, New York University; Hugh Willmott, University of Cardiff; Sharon Zukin, Brooklyn College City University New York/Graduate School, City University of New York

The *Culture, Economy and the Social* series is committed to innovative contemporary, comparative and historical work on the relations between social, cultural and economic change. It publishes empirically-based research that is theoretically informed, that critically examines the ways in which social, cultural and economic change is framed and made visible, and that is attentive to perspectives that tend to be ignored or side-lined by grand theorising or epochal accounts of social change. The series addresses the diverse manifestations of contemporary capitalism, and considers the various ways in which the 'social', 'the cultural' and 'the economic' are apprehended as tangible sites of value and practice. It is explicitly comparative, publishing books that work across disciplinary perspectives, cross-culturally, or across different historical periods.

The series is actively engaged in the analysis of the different theoretical traditions that have contributed to the development of the 'cultural turn' with a view to clarifying where these approaches converge and where they diverge on a particular issue. It is equally concerned to explore the new critical agendas emerging from current critiques of the cultural turn: those associated with the descriptive turn for example. Our commitment to interdisciplinarity thus aims at enriching theoretical and methodological discussion, building awareness of the common ground that has emerged in the past decade, and thinking through what is at stake in those approaches that resist integration to a common analytical model.

Series titles include:

The Media and Social Theory (2008)
Edited by David Hesmondhalgh and
Jason Toynbee

Culture, Class, Distinction (2009)
Tony Bennett, Mike Savage, Elizabeth Bortolaia
Silva, Alan Warde, Modesto Gayo-Cal and
David Wright

Material Powers (2010)
Edited by Tony Bennett and Patrick Joyce

The Social after Gabriel Tarde: Debates
and Assessments (2010)
Edited by Matei Candea

Cultural Analysis and Bourdieu's
Legacy (2010)
Edited by Elizabeth Silva and Alan Ward

Milk, Modernity and the Making of the
Human (2010)
Richie Nimmo

Creative Labour: Media Work in Three
Cultural Industries (2010)
Edited by David Hesmondhalgh and
Sarah Baker

Migrating Music (2011)
Edited by Jason Toynbee and Byron Dueck

Sport and the Transformation of
Modern Europe: States, Media and
Markets 1950–2010 (2011)
Edited by Alan Tomlinson, Christopher Young and
Richard Holt

Inventive Methods: The Happening of the
Social (2012)
Edited by Celia Lury and Nina Wakeford

Understanding Sport: A Socio-Cultural
Analysis (2012)
John Horne, Alan Tomlinson, Garry Whannel and
Kath Woodward

Shanghai Expo: An International Forum on
the Future of Cities (2012)
Edited by Tim Winter

Diasporas and Diplomacy: Cosmopolitan
Contact Zones at the BBC World Service
(1932–2012) (2012)
Edited by Marie Gillespie and Alban Webb

Making Culture, Changing Society (2013)
Tony Bennett

Interdisciplinarity: Reconfigurations
of the Social and Natural Sciences (2013)
Edited by Andrew Barry and Georgina Born

Objects and Materials: A Routledge
Companion (2014)
Edited by Penny Harvey, Eleanor Conlin Casella,
Gillian Evans, Hannah Knox, Christine McLean,
Elizabeth B. Silva, Nicholas Thoburn and
Kath Woodward

Rio de Janeiro: Urban Life through the
Eyes of the City (forthcoming)
Beatriz Jaguaribe

Devising Consumption: Cultural
Economies of Insurance, Credit and
Spending (forthcoming)
Liz Mcfall

Unbecoming Things: Mutable Objects and
the Politics of Waste (forthcoming)
Nicky Gregson and Mike Crang

Centre for Research on
Socio-Cultural Change

Objects and Materials

A Routledge Companion

*Edited by Penny Harvey, Eleanor Conlin Casella,
Gillian Evans, Hannah Knox, Christine McLean,
Elizabeth B. Silva, Nicholas Thoburn and
Kath Woodward*

LONDON AND NEW YORK

First published 2014
by Routledge
2 Park Square, Milton Park, Abingdon, Oxfordshire OX14 4RN

Simultaneously published in the USA and Canada
by Routledge
711 Third Avenue, New York, NY 10017

First issued in paperback 2014

Routledge is an imprint of the Taylor & Francis Group, an informa business

British Library Cataloguing in Publication Data
A catalogue record for this book is available from the British Library

Library of Congress Cataloging in Publication Data
Objects and materials: a Routledge companion / edited by Penny Harvey,
Eleanor Conlin Casella, Gillian Evans, Hannah Knox, Christine McLean,
Elizabeth B. Silva, Nicholas Thoburn and Kath Woodward.
   pages cm
Includes bibliographical references and index.
1. Material culture. 2. Ceremonial objects. 3. Art objects. I. Harvey, Penelope,
GN406.O28 2013
930.1–dc23   2012049615

ISBN 978-0-415-67880-3 (hbk)
ISBN 978-1-138-89941-4 (pbk)
ISBN 978-0-203-09361-0 (ebk)

Typeset in Bembo
by Cenveo Publisher Services

Contents

Contents

Contents

Illustrations

Figures

Table

Contributors

Mario Biagioli is Professor of STS, Law, and History at the University of California at Davis. He is the author of *Galileo Courtier* (Chicago, 1994) and *Galileo's Instruments of Credit* (Chicago, 2007) and the co-editor of *Scientific Authorship* (Routledge, 2002), *The Science Studies Reader* (Routledge, 1999) and *Making and Unmaking Intellectual Property* (Chicago, 2011).

Helen Brookfield works in a supported housing department of a housing association. She also provides support to higher education students with a range of emotional, cognitive, social and learning needs. Her research interests include adoption issues, in particular the experiences of adopters, parenting children with histories of trauma, neglect and abuse; the effects of early trauma and abuse on cognitive, emotional and social development; the effects of prenatal exposure to alcohol and drugs and mental health issues and the effects of trauma on memory.

Steven D. Brown is Professor of Social and Organizational Psychology at the University of Leicester. He is author of *The Social Psychology of Experience: Studies in Remembering and Forgetting*, with David Middleton (2005, Sage); *Psychology without Foundations: History, Philosophy and Psychosocial Theory*, with Paul Stenner (2009, Sage) and *Vital Memory: Ethics, Affect and Agency*, with Paula Reavey (forthcoming, Routledge).

Matei Candea is a Lecturer in Social Anthropology at the University of Cambridge. He is the author of *Corsican Fragments: Difference, Knowledge and Fieldwork* (Indiana University Press, 2010) and editor of *The Social After Gabriel Tarde: Debates and Assessments* (Routledge, 2010). His current research focuses on human–animal relations in scientific research.

Eleanor Conlin Casella is Professor of Historical Archaeology at the University of Manchester. She is the author of numerous books, most recently *The Archaeology of Institutional Confinement* (University Press of Florida, 2007) and *The Alderley Sandhills Project: An Archaeology of Community Life* (University of Manchester Press, 2010). She has also recently co-edited *The Archaeology of Colonialism: Intimate Encounters and Sexual Effects* (Cambridge University Press, 2011).

Patricia Ticiento Clough is Professor of Sociology and Women's Studies, at Queens College and the Graduate Center of the City University of New York. Her books include *Autoaffection* (University of Minnesota Press, 2000), *The End(s) of Ethnography* (Second Edition, Peter Lang Inc., 1998), *Feminist Thought: Desire, Power and Academic Discourse* (Blackwell, 1994), *Beyond Biopolitics: Essays in the Governance of Life and Death*, with Craig Willse (eds) (Duke University Press, 2011) and *The Affective Turn: Theorizing the Social*, with Jean Halley (Duke University Press, 2007).

Karina Croucher has recently completed a British Academy Postdoctoral Fellowship at the University of Manchester. She is author of *Death and Dying in the Neolithic Near East* (Oxford Univeristy Press, 2012).

Tim Dant is Professor of Sociology at Lancaster University and is the author of a number of books including *Materiality and Society* (McGraw Hill, 2005) and the forthcoming *Television and the Moral Imaginary* (Palgrave Macmillan). His current research is focused on moral materialism.

Maurits W. Ertsen is Associate Professor of Irrigation at Delft University of Technology in the Netherlands. He is one (of two) main editors of *Water History*. His recent book is *Locales of Happiness* (VSSD, 2010) on irrigation in the Netherlands East Indies.

Gillian Evans is a Lecturer in Social Anthropology at the University of Manchester. Her research focuses on various aspects of socioeconomic change in post-industrial Britain. In 2006, she published an ethnographic monograph entitled *Educational Failure and Working Class White Children in Britain* (Palgrave Macmillan, 2007). Her new book entitled *London's Olympic Legacy* is in preparation. It is an analysis of the planning and evolution of urban change in the East End of London.

Karen Exell is a Lecturer in Museum Studies for UCL Qatar at Hamad bin Khalifa University in Doha. An Egyptologist by background, her publications include *Soldiers, Sailors and Sandalmakers* (Golden House Publications, 2009) and she is co-editor of the forthcoming *Egypt: Ancient Histories and Modern Archaeologies* (Cambria Press, 2013). Her current research explores heritage and identity in Qatar and the wider Gulf region.

Matthew Fuller works at the Centre for Cultural Studies, Goldsmiths, University of London. His books include *Media Ecologies: Materialist Energies in Art and Technoculture* (MIT, 2007) and with Andrew Goffey, *Evil Media* (MIT, 2012).

Andrew Goffey is Associate Professor in Critical Theory and Cultural Studies at Nottingham University. He is co-author, with Matthew Fuller, of *Evil Media* (MIT, 2012), co-editor of *The Guattari Effect* (Continuum, 2011) and translator of numerous works of French philosophy.

Sarah Green is Professor of Social and Cultural Anthropology at the University of Helsinki. She is the author of *Notes from the Balkans* (Princeton UP, 2005) and *Urban Amazons* (Macmillan, 1997). She is currently researching the circulation of money in the Aegean region.

Alexandra Hall is Lecturer in Politics at the University of York. She is the author of *Border Watch: Cultures of Immigration, Detention and Control* (Pluto Press, 2012), an ethnography of the everyday experience of security in an immigration removal centre.

Graham Harman is Professor of Philosophy and Associate Provost for Research Administration at the American University in Cairo. He is the author of numerous books, most recently *Weird Realism: Lovecraft and Philosophy* (Zero Books, 2012).

Penny Harvey is Professor of Social Anthropology at the University of Manchester and Director of CRESC, the ESRC Centre for Research on Socio-Cultural Change. Together with Jeanette

Edwards and Peter Wade she co-edited *Technologized Images, Technologized Bodies* (Berghahn, 2010) and *Anthropology and Science: Epistemologies in Practice* (Berg, 2007). She is currently working on technical knowledge, regulatory practice and the regional state in Peru.

Martin Holbraad teaches in the Anthropology Department of University College London, where he co-runs the Cosmology, Religion, Ontology and Culture Research Group (CROC). He has conducted fieldwork on Afro-Cuban religion and socialism in Havana since 1998. He is the author of *Truth in Motion: The Recursive Anthropology of Cuban Divination* (Chicago, 2012) and co-editor of *Thinking through Things: Theorising Artefacts Ethnographically* (Routledge, 2007) and 'Technologies of the Imagination' (special issue of *Ethnos*, 2009).

Hannah Knox is a Research Fellow at CRESC, the ESRC Centre for Research on Socio-Cultural Change at the University of Manchester. Her research explores the place of engineering, expertise and contemporary knowledge practices in the making of material worlds.

Susanne Küchler is Professor of Anthropology and Material Culture at University College London. She has conducted ethnographic fieldwork in Papua New Guinea and Eastern Polynesia over the past 25 years, studying creativity, innovation and futurity in political economies of knowledge from a comparative perspective. Her more recent work on the history of the take-up, in the Pacific, of cloth and clothing as 'new' material and 'new' technology has focused on the epistemic nature of materials and its role in long-term social change. Over the past five years, she has extended the comparative remit of this research to science-based materials innovation, com-modification and consumption.

John Law is a Professor of Sociology in the Faculty of Social Sciences at the Open University. In addition to authoring *Aircraft Stories: Decentering the Object in Technoscience* (Duke University Press, 2002), he has a wide range of publications in the areas of non-coherent methods; people, technologies and animals; biosecurity, agriculture and disaster; and alternative knowledge spaces.

Marc Lenglet is a Lecturer at the European Business School Paris, and Head of the Management, Strategy Systems Department. With interests in phenomenology and anthropology, his research focus is on the compliance function and the dissemination of norms within financial practices.

Marianne Elisabeth Lien is Professor of Social Anthropology at the University of Oslo. She is the author of *Marketing and Modernity* (Berg, 1997), and co-editor of *The Politics of Food* (Berg, 2004) and *Holding Worlds Together* (Berghahn, 2007).

Celia Lury is Director of the Centre for Interdisciplinary Methodologies at the University of Warwick. She has published on brands, consumer culture and the global culture industry. Recent publications include *Inventive Methods*, co-edited with Nina Wakeford (Routledge, 2012).

Maryon McDonald is a Fellow in Social Anthropology and Director of Studies at Robinson College, University of Cambridge. She has recently co-edited *Social Bodies*, with Helen Lambert (Berghahn, 2009) and authored various book chapters on the subject of organ donation and bioethics.

Adrian Mackenzie (Centre for Social and Economic Aspects of Genomics, Lancaster University) researches in the area of technology, science and culture. His books include

Transductions: Bodies and Machines at Speed (Continuum, 2002/6) and *Wirelessness: Radical Empiricism in Network Cultures* (MIT Press, 2010).

Chris McLean is a Senior Lecturer in Manchester Business School at the University of Manchester. She has recently co-edited *Imagining Organizations: Performative Imagery in Business and Beyond* (Routledge, 2012) as well as publications in the area of organizing, images and performativity within the newspaper printing industry and mental health care.

Noortje Marres is Senior Lecturer in Sociology and Director of the Centre for the Study of Invention and Social Process at Goldsmiths, University of London. She convenes the MA/MSc Digital Sociology and is the author of *Material Participation: Technology, the Environment and Everyday Publics* (Palgrave, 2012).

Jonathan Mendel is Lecturer in Human Geography at the University of Dundee. His work focuses on security, policing, networks and conflict.

Mike Michael is a Professor in Sociology at the University of Sydney. He is author of several books including *Technoscience and Everyday Life* (Open University Press, 2006), and has published many articles in such areas as biomedical innovation and culture; publics and science; and materiality and sociality.

Chandra Mukerji is Professor of Communication and Science Studies at the University of California, San Diego. Her books include *Territorial Ambitions and the Gardens of Versailles* (Cambridge, 1997), *A Fragile Power: Scientists and the State* (Princeton, 1990) and *Impossible Engineering: Technology and Territoriality on the Canal de Midi* (Princeton, 2009).

Peter Oakley is Research Lead for the School of Materials at the Royal College of Art. His research interests include a focus on the social impact of new materials/production technologies and materials sourcing in the luxury goods sector.

Robert Oppenheim is Associate Professor of Asian Studies and Anthropology at the University of Texas at Austin. He is the author of *Kyongju Things: Assembling Place* (University of Michigan, 2008), as well as several articles.

Morten Axel Pedersen is Associate Professor at the Department of Anthropology, University of Copenhagen. He works on shamanic cosmology and the postsocialist city. His latest book is *Not Quite Shamans: Spirit Worlds and Political Lives in Northern Mongolia* (Cornell, 2011).

Griselda Pollock is Professor of the Social and Critical Histories of Art at the University of Leeds. She is author of numerous books, most recently including *Encounters in the Virtual Feminist Museum* (Routledge, revised 2007), *Psychoanalysis and the Image* (Wiley-Blackwell, 2006) and *After-affects/After-images: Trauma and Aesthetic Transformation* (Manchester University Press, 2013). In addition, she is co-editor of *Art as Compassion: Bracha L. Ettinger* (Asa Publishers, 2011).

Paula Reavey is a Reader in Psychology at London South Bank University. Recent works include two co-edited volumes, with Sam Warner, *New Feminist Stories of Child Sexual Abuse: Sexual Scripts* (Routledge, 2003) and with Janice Haaken, *Dangerous Dialogues* and *Memory*

Matters: Contexts for Understanding Sexual Abuse Recollections (Psychology Press, 2009), an edited volume, *Visual Psychologies: Using and Interpreting Images in Qualitative Research* (Routledge, 2011) and a co-authored book, with John Cromby and Dave Harper, *Psychology, Mental Health and Distress* (Palgrave, 2012).

Marsha Rosengarten is a Reader in Sociology at Goldsmiths, University of London. She is the author of *HIV Interventions: Biomedicine and the Traffic between Information and Flesh* (University of Washington Press, 2009) in addition to a wide range of publications addressing a variety of issues relating to biomedicine, pharmaceuticals and HIV.

Elizabeth B. Silva is Professor of Sociology at the Open University. Her recent publications include special issues of *Cultural Sociology* on 'Fields, Boundaries and Social Inequalities' (co-edited, June, 2013) and *Poetics* on 'Cultural Capital: Histories, Limits and Prospects' (co-edited, December, 2011). Other work includes *Cultural Analysis and Bourdieu's Legacy* (co-edited, Routledge, 2010) and *Culture, Class, Distinction* (co-authored, Routledge, 2009). Her most recent sole authored book is *Technology, Culture, Family: Influences on Home Life* (Palgrave, 2010).

Kathleen Stewart is Professor of Anthropology at the University of Texas at Austin. Her publications include *Ordinary Affects* (Duke University Press, 2007) and *A Space on the Side of the Road* (Princeton University Press, 1996).

Nicholas Thoburn is Senior Lecturer in Sociology at the University of Manchester. He has published on media aesthetics, political theory and social movements. He is the author of *Deleuze, Marx and Politics* (Routledge, 2003), among other publications.

Soumhya Venkatesan is a Lecturer in Social Anthropology at the University of Manchester. She is author of *Craft Matters: Artisans, Development and the Indian Nation* (Orient Blackswan, 2009).

Kath Woodward is Professor of Sociology at the Open University, UK. Her recent publications include *Planet Sport* (Routledge, 2012), *Why Feminism Matters* (Palgrave Macmillan, 2009) and *Boxing, Masculinity and Identity* (Routledge, 2006).

Acknowledgements

This book has emerged from many conversations and engagements and it would be a lengthy task to tease out all the ideas and encouragements that are enfolded in the pages of this collection. An intellectual curiosity in the relational complexity and serendipity of how things come into being has been the driving force behind this project, making us all too aware of how difficult it is to fully acknowledge those people, things and circumstances that have helped us on the way. We have thus opted to acknowledge the very basic contexts that sustained the project, in the expectation that the individual chapters will open up the wider intellectual and personal networks that have fed our enthusiasms and energized our work. Our editorial collective is firmly located in CRESC, the ESRC Centre for Research on Socio-Cultural Change. We have benefited from generous funding from the UK Economic and Social Research Council, and from the support of our many colleagues at the Open University and the University of Manchester who have become our close collaborators over the past nine years. We have also benefited directly from the RCUK fellowship scheme, which brought Gillian Evans to CRESC. CRESC was founded by Mike Savage, Karel Williams and Tony Bennett, and it was thanks to them that our research centre was based on a very open approach to sociocultural change. The funding model encouraged us both to concentrate resources in research posts and to find ways to draw on the energies and interests of academics from across the two lead universities that were 'bought out', or as we preferred to express it, 'bought in' to CRESC, in order to keep our research agendas broad, while also providing some basic funding for academic colleagues who were interested in what we were trying to do. It has been a rich and rewarding experience. It is also a logistical challenge, for which we received great administrative support in the arrangement of workshops and residential meetings, and all the accounting and feedback procedures required to sustain the enterprise. We would particularly like to thank Josine Opmeer, Bussie Awosanya, Stacey Vigars, Susan Hogan and Karen Ho for all they have done for us over the years. Kevin Hetherington and Tony Bennett, Penny's co-editors on the CRESC book series *Culture, Economy and the Social*, were supportive of our unusual editorial arrangements, aware of the importance that we place on collaborative work within CRESC. We are also grateful to Gerhard Boomgaarden for trusting us to collaborate rather than fragment. Emily Briggs and Emily Davies have overseen the process of coordinating our disparate formats. Their care and attention have coaxed this volume into production.

1

Objects and materials

An introduction

Penny Harvey and Hannah Knox

Objects and materials – collaborative relations

The array of objects and materials with which we open this *Companion* volume (see Figure 1.1) deliberately echoes the imaginary encyclopedic listing that Foucault draws from the work of Borges to show how things become intelligible through the relations that surround them. An encyclopedia, traditionally, does the job of revealing what a thing is by mustering and representing the relations deemed most relevant, and thus most useful to readers. Borges was working in the opposite direction. His fantastical encyclopedia revealed the unsettling effects of things grouped as if there were connections, when those connections are unfathomable to the reader. The effect was to undo the certainties, the habitual modes of classification, and to open things up to strange alternative possibilities. Foucault's (1970: xxiii) interest in *The Order of Things* was to track back through Western intellectual history to reveal that the apparent certainties and stabilities of the modern social sciences were a mere 'wrinkle in our knowledge', a recent invention of the modern *episteme*.

Our introduction does not claim, nor does it aim, to provide an integrative overview or an account of a twenty-first-century episteme. Rather, it builds on the incidental nature of the objects and materials presented in this volume to uncover some of the preoccupations and philosophical questions regarding the heuristic promise of objects and materials in the contemporary social sciences and humanities. The chapters gathered here suggest that there is a general agreement across the humanities and social sciences that *things* are relational, that subject/object distinctions are produced through the work of differentiation, and that any specific material form or entity with edges, surfaces, or bounded integrity is not only provisional but also potentially transformative of other entities. At the same time, our array of objects holds no categorical promise. It is rather a set of empirical starting points for exploring just what the nature of such material or object relations might be, how differentiation occurs, and what the implications might be for seeing objects in terms of their transformative potential. All the objects and materials listed in Figure 1.1 are drawn from the work of our contributors. They are things that provoked reflections on the insistent presence of object forms in everyday life. And they open us to what objects and materials, separately and/or together, can draw attention to, or teach us about the worlds in which they appear.

Figure 1.1 Some of the objects and materials addressed in the *Companion*

This *Companion* thus sets out to accompany those who are interested in exploring how objects and materials actively participate in the worlds that we research or otherwise engage as artists, practitioners and/or activists. Our primary objective is to interrogate the terms of our collaborations with objects and materials and to consider how these become integral to how we engage one another.

From the beginning, our approach to bringing this book into being has been as an exercise in interdisciplinary engagement. Our editorial collective grew out of a particular experiment in cross–disciplinary social science, which has, since 2006, gone under the name of CRESC: the Economic and Social Research Council (ESRC)–funded Centre for Research on Socio–Cultural Change. Within CRESC, different research groupings have emerged and each has worked in its own particular way. We have not systematically compared or drawn together our diverse disciplinary approaches to a common topic. Objects and materials were not our starting point. Rather, we came together as a group of people with a general interest in issues of politics and cultural value. Our presence in CRESC suggested an openness to other ways of working, but at the same time, we each continued to work on these themes in our own way. The objects of our research focus were diverse. Periodically, we came together and listened to what others were absorbed by, we read each other's work, and took up suggestions of what to read. We began a reading group on Deleuze, we organized seminars on topics of common interest, and slowly the mutual influences grew until (at one of our annual residential meetings) we realized that a powerful common preoccupation was how to approach the presence of objects and materials at a time when, theoretically at least, the self-evidence of such things was overtly in question. We recognized that there were important differences in the way we were approaching the challenges posed by objects and materials. But we were reluctant to explain such differences in purely disciplinary terms. The differences seemed to have as much to do with the specificity of our empirical concerns as they did with the overlapping theoretical and analytical approaches that we brought to our work. We thus set about choosing, each from our own perspective, who we would like to introduce each other to: to read, to talk and listen to. The invited contributors to two key events in 2009, became the core of this collection.[1]

Our model of interdisciplinary engagement thus did not focus primarily on specific disciplinary histories and preoccupations. We were already in an intellectual space in which the objects and materials that engaged us were challenging any easy disciplinary containment. Working within the explicitly interdisciplinary space of CRESC, we were all reading across established canons and all looking for ideas and approaches from a variety of sources.

This is not to say that our awareness of disciplinary tendencies was not important. Rather, we approached disciplines not as contained collectivities, but as particular, institutionalized gatherings of conceptual resources, as intellectual spaces where particular theories, philosophies and empirical findings shape research questions and the ways in which scholars go about answering them. We were interested in how disciplines change over time, diversifying, fragmenting but also consolidating around particular concerns and interests. It is for this reason that we have chosen not to rehearse here any specific history of disciplinary configuration. Instead, in this introduction we draw attention to the ways in which a collection such as this shows that although different disciplinary histories shape the ways in which scholars apprehend the empirical, they can never fully account for the routes that specific research trajectories will take. Patterns can be found, and they can be disrupted. Rather than taking our lead from a teleology of disciplinary thought, we start instead with the engagements with objects and materials as they appear in this volume.

Objects and materials – similarities and differences

There is no *a priori* resolution in this volume as to the nature of the distinction between objects and materials or the relationship between them. For some authors, the distinction between objects and materials is fundamental to their argument. Others treat the terms as more or less synonymous. Some authors work with a strong distinction between things and objects, others are more concerned to distinguish objects from artefacts. Some focus on processes of materialization and the material condition or materiality. Some allow materials to take pride of place. Still others are drawn to conceptual objects.

It is perhaps useful at this stage to note that it is the category of the 'object' that emerges as particularly contentious for our authors. The reader will find materials, things, artefacts and concepts deployed across the range of contributions (and they can be tracked through the index). But these terms are all far less controversial than the category of the 'object'. Materials and artefacts are generally understood in terms of a distinction between matter and a fabricated form. Materials are consistently used to refer to the constituent fabric of things, whereas artefacts denote specific constructions. Similarly, those who choose to talk about things rather than objects are connecting to a well-rehearsed and influential philosophical debate stemming initially from the rejection of the Kantian distinction between the thing as perceived by human beings, the passive object of human appropriation, and the thing as subject of its own movements and capacities, existing independently of human beings, unknowable and autonomous. There is a general agreement amongst our contributors that the value of the 'thing' concept in contemporary scholarship derives from an interest in attending to how things act back on the world, manifesting resistances, capacities, limits and potential, and thereby challenging the normative subject/object dichotomy. Concepts can also, in this sense, manifest thing-like qualities, which several authors explore. But although some authors are at times concerned about the objective qualities of concepts, the conceptual nature of abstract ideas is not particularly brought into question, although they materialize in unexpected ways in different contributions.

Where the trouble starts is with objects. And it is perhaps objects above all that reveal the need for a *Companion* guide to their diverse permutations. Objects are sites of intellectual dispute: there is no agreement on what objects are. Are they active or passive? Are they living or inanimate? Are they complete or in process? Are they material or immaterial? Do they shut you out or invite you in? In this volume, it seems that objects can be all these things. This confusion or profusion is exciting to think with and about. Indeed, the force of this debate appears to offer the potential to shed light not just on objects themselves but on broader questions about why objects have become so contentious in the current moment.

Objects and materials: why now?

Objects and materials do seem to have gained a particularly powerful purchase in the contemporary social sciences and humanities. A number of encyclopedias, readers and edited collections have been published in recent years that provide an introduction to the place of objects and materials in different disciplines, including anthropology, archaeology, sociology, and across the social sciences and humanities more generally (Graves-Brown 2000; Buchli 2002; Latour and Weibel 2005; Meskell 2005; Miller 2005; Tilley 2006; Henare *et al.* 2007; Candlin and Guins 2009; Cooper *et al.* 2009; Hicks and Beaudry 2010).

In the recent *Object Reader* (Candlin and Guins 2009), Grosz explains the current interest in objects by suggesting that they seem to straddle a 'great divide' in philosophical approaches, allowing people to think in concrete terms about what is implied by the move from the Enlightenment traditions of Kant and Descartes to the thinking of those 'pragmatist philosophers who put the questions of action, practice, and movement at the center of ontology. What these disparate thinkers share in common is little else but an understanding of the *thing as question*, as provocation, incitement, or enigma' (Grosz 2009: 125). Grosz associates philosophers as diverse as Nietzsche, Peirce, James, Bergson, Rorty and Deleuze in this philosophical move, which suggests that they in turn were motivated by provocations from beyond philosophy, from a world where developments in science and technology were blatantly disturbing established paradigms. Sloterdijk has written of how the use of poison gas in World War I reconfigured military awareness of where danger might lurk, the previously abstract atmospheric conditions becoming a source of threat and potential harm, in turn preconfiguring new types of warfare in which the enemy is unseen, and potentially unidentifiable by traditional means (Sloterdijk 2009). Biotechnologies, to cite another example, opened new questions about life itself (Franklin 2007), and research in cellular technologies developed techniques that depended on 'making cells live differently in time, in order to harness their productive or reproductive capacities' (Landecker 2007: 212). Technological changes also provoked the law to assert new forms of ownership. Strathern (1995a), for example, discusses a case brought to the Supreme Court of Justice in California in which a surrogate mother seeks to claim 'ownership' of the child to which she has given birth. Social studies of science and technology have repeatedly shown how material processes actively participate in the formation of philosophical and political constructs.

We cite several examples here to emphasize that we are not trying to produce a singular narrative that signals linear epochal change. We are simply wanting to point out how many contemporary objects destabilize object categories. We could add many more examples of objects emerging from specific sites of innovation, such as: the linking of biology, computer sciences and cognitive sciences; advances in theoretical physics; the importance of virtuality in contemporary art and design; the design paradigm itself as it emerges via synthetic chemistry to produce new smart materials; the new markets and trading possibilities that have enabled the development of knowing capitalism, and have driven financial booms and collapse; the possibilities for mass production and mass consumption (for global branding and commodity circulation, and the forces of nostalgia for the non-modern that in turn becomes another commodity). Computing is central to these new configurations, as is the rise in awareness of systems and networks, and of the interconnectivity (planned and unplanned, consequential and inconsequential) of all things. These relational paradigms combined with the increase in the volume and rhythms of informational circulation, storage and retrieval underpin many contemporary concerns: with climate change, pollution, food security, population trends and movements, and political and financial futures.

There are, moreover, other things that entities conceived as overtly relational draw attention to. Synthetic objects, and all those objects that are explicitly informational, such as those driven by algorithms that have the dynamic capacity for self-transformation, have provoked scholars from many different backgrounds to revisit objects that have been there all along. Thus, it is that this *Companion to Objects and Materials* sets out to reintroduce archaeological artefacts, political tools (coins, records, patents), infrastructures, human bodies, carved statues, and domestic technologies alongside dynamic data objects, synthetic pharmaceuticals, driverless cars and digital models. Overall, we are less interested in whether objects are 'new' or 'old', and agree with Edgerton's warnings of misplaced futurism (Edgerton 2008). What we are more interested in is how contemporary conjunctures render objects problematic in new ways, and provoke us to look again at familiar things: patent law, mummified bodies, ontological differences, technological artefacts, animal behaviour, financial systems. Although these things have some kind of 'object'-ive continuity through time, their histories and effects at different times have sometimes been so radically different that we might even argue that they are not the same 'things' at all.

The capacity of seemingly stable objects to radically change over time is a key preoccupation of many of the contributors to this volume, and perhaps one of the central reasons why all of the pieces gathered in this collection are focused on the possibilities afforded by a relational understanding of objects and materials. An awareness of the paradoxical way in which objects both seem to change and endure through time requires a form of analysis that draws attention to the way in which objects are constituted by, participate in and push at the limits of particular relational configurations. One effect of this attention to the relational properties of objects, is to introduce the relation as itself a particular kind of analytic object. The relation accompanies all our objects and materials, is intrinsic to all our contributions, and central to the ways in which objects, materials, artefacts, things and concepts are variously configured by our authors. Some celebrate these relations, and work to make them explicit. Others experiment with forms of narrative description to evoke the relational properties of objects that cannot be easily explicated. Some are even worried that the contemporary enchantment with relations threatens what they value most about objects, namely their capacity to stand alone. It is to these relational concerns that we now turn.

Relational affordances

In this section, our aim is to locate the chapters in relation to a broader theoretical conversation about the relational dynamics of objects and materials. Whereas the relation accompanies all of the objects and materials presented in this *Companion*, the kind of relations that objects are understood to partake in varies in relation to specific objects, materials and the theoretical arguments put forward by different authors. Although this variety is highly generative analytically, it also risks having the effect of destabilizing objects and materials to such an extent that it becomes difficult to compare their appearances across the chapters. Without attempting to explain away the productive tension that the variety of relational approaches to objects produces, then, we offer in what follows an alignment of this variety of object-relations into three broad categories. We identify these as (1) relations between objects, (2) objects and materials as relations, and (3) excessive objects. These three kinds of relations are not easily reducible to discrete theoretical traditions or to particular thinkers. Nor do they neatly demarcate the different chapters presented here. Nonetheless, they do seem to lie at the heart of many of the discussions, questions, analytical choices and political objectives that the contributors to this book are pursuing. Our hope is that by addressing each category of relation in turn, this introduction will provide a navigational device that will assist in drawing lines of association across what at first might have appeared a disparate and disconnected array of objects and materials.

Relations between objects

As we have argued above, a general awareness of relational thinking in the humanities and the social sciences has made it commonplace to think in terms of how objects become meaningful, useful, or in some way significant via their relations with other entities. Take, for example, this book. We might want to approach the book as an object that participates in relationships with other things. From this perspective, we could trace how the book connects or mediates relations between authors, publishers and readers, but also paper, ink, computers and printers, and even more abstract 'things' such as ideas, memories, images and expectations. In such studies of material culture, each such relation can be taken as a point of departure for tracking further webs of relations, allowing us to trace what have come to be known as the social lives of things, in which objects, like persons, have particular biographies of circulation (Appadurai 1986; Kopytoff 1986).

Equally, in a particular project, such as the production of a book, we could take any of these related objects as elements that actively propel the process. No longer simply objects in a passive sense, institutions, technologies and artefacts play an active role in bringing our book into being. The book would not exist without the involvement of publishing houses and their key distributors, bookshops, libraries, postal services, printing firms, computers, websites, software systems, Kindles and iPads, cardboard and paper. Latour (1988) referred to these helpers (human and non-human) as 'allies' in his concern to highlight the active force of material things. The agency of things, in this respect, requires no intention or human-like quality, it simply refers to the ways in which specific material configurations are actively engaged in shaping relations and in that sense are social actors. Thus, for example, he describes how the concrete 'sleeping policeman' compels drivers to slow down in residential areas, the Berlin key ensures that residents lock the door behind them or the automated door closer guarantees that drafts are avoided (Latour 1991; Latour 1992) (that is, as long as it does not break down). Such breakdowns are of course also part of social life, and another dimension within which objects make and are made by their relations with other entities (Graham and Thrift 2007).

Once we start to attend to the relations that specific objects engage in, we also become attuned to the way in which objects acquire different significance under different sets of relational conditions (Thomas 1991; Miller 2009; Miller 2011; Miller and Woodward 2012). Thus for our contributing authors, this book may be a more or less significant achievement as part of a personal history of academic and social reproduction. For people who buy the book, it may hold the promise of answering particular questions. It may also of course serve more unexpected purposes: a doorstop, for example.

In a different theoretical vein, we also want to acknowledge the relations that objects themselves appear to call forth. James Gibson discussed the ways in which objects shape relations by reference to their affordances, that is, the particular qualities of things through which an object lends itself to specific relational possibilities according to whether it is hard or soft, sharp or blunt, liquid or solid, pliable, malleable or rigid. However, as Ingold (2011) has recently pointed out, Gibson oscillated between two different ways of approaching object relations. On the one hand, he seemed to propose the relational dynamic as mutually constitutive, with things and persons formed in processes of engagement; but yet he also writes about more stable relations between preexisting objective entities. That is, Gibson tried to have it both ways, as shown by the following passage:

> An important fact about the affordances of the environment is that they are in a sense objective, real, and physical, unlike values and meanings, which are often supposed to be subjective, phenomenal and mental. But, actually, an affordance is neither an objective property nor a subjective property; or it is both if you like. An affordance cuts across the dichotomy of subjective-objective and helps us to understand its inadequacy. It is equally a fact of the environment and a fact of behaviour. It is both physical and psychical, yet neither. An affordance points both ways, to the environment and to the observer.
>
> *(Gibson 1979: 129, cited in Ingold 2011: 78)*

For Ingold, in his sympathetic adaptation of Gibson's insights, it is the sense of the prefigured 'object' that gets in the way. Rather than approach the world as a place filled with such things, which humans perceive as external to themselves, and then build relationships to those things according to their specific qualities (or affordances), he suggests that we might think instead of how the life-worlds of persons and things are entangled from the start. Thus, rather than attending to how persons relate to things, we might think instead of environments as spaces of action and experience in and through which persons and things take on significance, uses, possibilities in relations of mutual specification. What something is, what its qualities are, is then figured as an outcome not a precondition.

In the first section of the book, on *Material qualities*, some of these possibilities are explicitly addressed, and the themes resonate through other sections, particularly in the final section on *Becoming object*. However, at this point, we find that we have reached the limits of our discussion of relations between objects, or what from now on we will refer to as 'extensive relations'. The tracing of extensive relations between objects reveals objects as active participants in social networks. However, the limits to this approach concern the ways in which the objects themselves, although engaged as fully social, nonetheless tend to be understood as singular and stable.

They move and engage but do not otherwise transform themselves. Other approaches to which we now turn are more concerned with how it is that objects and materials can come to seem so stable. Starting from an interest in the intrinsic multiplicity of things, those who approach objects and materials in this way are more likely to ask how it is that objects and materials can achieve this sense of stablity. It is to this aspect of relationality that we turn in the following section, moving from a focus on relations between objects to an understanding of objects as relations (Strathern 1995b).

Objects and materials as relations

Asking what things are made of is the most basic question to pose with respect to objects and materials from some disciplinary perspectives. Archaeological research, for example, has traditionally started from an analysis of material composition, but so too would research into things where their chemical properties are active and in question, or indeed the investigation of all kinds of objects and materials that are known to be unstable, to transform or mutate. Anthropologists have frequently drawn attention to the way in which some people routinely question what things are, secure in the knowledge that outer form or appearance is no guarantor of inner substance. In the Peruvian Andes, for example, malign forces are said to disguise themselves in human forms, which the cautious would do well to be alert to. It is difficult to tell the difference between a human and a spirit body, and people look out for small signs of non-human composition, a straw waist, or a fleshy crown hidden under a human-style hat (Harvey 2001).

Understandings of material composition may thus be important in specific circumstances, and more importantly the things we are told or shown by those we engage in the course of our research may well indicate significant ontological differences to which we might wish to attend. However, our understanding of objects and materials as relations is not primarily directed at this notion of material composition, and still less at the correlate understanding of 'objects' as detached units of volume or containment. On the contrary, we are interested in moving beyond the categorical distinctions between insides and outsides that the container metaphor holds us to, in order to explore in a more open way how entities, conceived as collectives, can manifest continuity in time and space, despite the mutations in form that living process necessarily entails. We find it useful to call the relations that go into making objects in this way, 'intensive relations'. Drawing attention to intensive relations allows for an increased sensitivity to ontological instability and the related sense of ontological multiplicity that encourages a move away from a preoccupation with ontological difference per se.

This topic animates the discussion of many of the objects and materials that our authors attend to in the chapters that follow: such multiple, mutating objects include waste matter, stone carvings, human cadavers, biodigital objects, brands, money, algorithms, fish, meerkats and many more. Scholars of science and technology studies have invested considerable energy in explicating the intrinsic multiplicity of things, and in looking at the practices through which mutating entities can appear stable, and multiple entities can appear singular. Annemarie Mol's account of how atherosclerosis is made to cohere as a singular medical condition is the subject of her renowned work on ontological multiplicity (Mol 2003). Fieldwork in a Dutch hospital revealed how fragile this disease object was in practice, meaning different things to different people, manifesting as divergent conditions, and thus drawing forth and enacting a whole range of different relations. Living with atherosclerosis in this framing involves not simply living with 'a disease', but living within the networks of persons and things where what atherosclerosis is, is never settled but constantly under negotiation. Mol sets out to explore in this case what she needs to understand in order to grasp how atherosclerosis can be both singular and multiple. In the STS (science, technology and society) approach advocated by authors such as Mol, Law, Haraway and Latour, there is no assumption of any meaningful distinction between human subjects and non-human objects; indeed, the human and the non-human are taken as axiomatically entangled. All entities in this respect are ontologically heterogeneous. Haraway expresses this condition with her trademark verve:

> I think we learn to be worldly from grappling with, rather than generalizing from, the ordinary. I am a creature of the mud, not the sky. I am a biologist who has always found edification in the amazing abilities of slime to hold things in touch and to lubricate passages for living beings and their parts. I love the fact that human genomes can be found in only 10 percent of all the cells that occupy the mundane space I call my body; the other 90 percent of the cells are filled with the genomes of bacteria, fungi, protists, and such, some of which play in a symphony necessary to my being alive at all, and some of which are hitching a ride and doing the rest of me, of us, no harm.
>
> *(Haraway 2008: 3–4).*

Thus while our previous focus on relations between objects (extensive relations), might encourage the analyst to bring context into view, this focus on intensive relations, or on objects as relations, encourages us to think about the ways in which entities are never unitary or stable. Their intrinsic multiplicity implies constant work of care and repair if things are to hold some integrity even when changing. This also implies processes of decay or growth, the possibility of unexpected outcomes or the sudden activation of relational dynamics which were not previously apprehended. These uncertain relational dynamics are the subject of our third relational configuration: that of the excessive relation or relational happening.

However, to conclude this section, we return briefly to our example of the book you are currently reading. In what sense is this book ontologically multiple and unstable? How is it transforming and mutating, when it actually seems to be unexciting in this particular respect? To enliven the book, and to become aware of its intensive relations requires attention to the practices through which it comes to appear so stable. The fact that this book exists at all is already a manifestation of the relationship between readers, authors and a publishing company (with all the relational entities contained in each of these entities), and in a more distributed sense we should also fold in our areas of empirical concerns and the theories and traditions we each draw on. These relations might not appear to be that different to the ones described previously: contextual relations that include relations with publishers, authors, readers, printers, distributors, paper makers, etc. But the shift of focus to intensive relations is a shift to thinking about how all these distributed relations come together: how they materialize as a book; how the book enfolds these relations, exists only through them, and in that sense exists differently depending on the practices through which any particular person is engaged in the process.

Our exploration of intensive and extensive relations has enabled us to clarify that the objects and materials to which we refer in this *Companion* are variously assembled. The reader should now expect the objects and materials discussed within these pages to defy any straightforward distinction between subjects and objects, and look forward to meeting things that mutate, travel and unsettle. In the final section of the introduction, we look in more detail at how an attention to intensive relations comes to reveal the ontological instability of things. For as suggested above, the notion of ontological instability points us towards the limits of what we can know (for sure) about the things we study. This dynamic engagement with uncertainty and with the unknowable, or the barely known, is what we turn to in the following section.

Excessive objects

There is a persistent unease in many of the chapters of this volume, regarding the degree to which objects and materials are amenable to descriptive closure. There is, it seems, an important quality to the relations we have just described that cannot be captured through the work of mapping these relations as either extensive or intensive, but which is nonetheless essential to understanding these relations and the politics of their effects. As we have seen, an attention to the intensive relations through which objects come into being, necessarily produces the object as ontologically highly unstable. Objects appear not just as socially entangled or materially and socially constituted, but also as crystallizations of histories, projections into the future, powerful forbears of that which is to come and painful reminders of that which has been. It is perhaps unsurprising then, that the authors of the chapters in this volume frequently find themselves struggling with a certain quality of being in the objects and materials that they address, which appears to escape the describable or representative dimensions of the objects that they are concerned with. The power of objects and materials that our contributors have chosen to attend to often appear to exceed that which can be explained through attention to either the relations that are established between things, or the tracing of the relations that brought them into being. Instead objects draw out questions of a certain quality that constantly escapes their description, of the complexity that always accompanies them, and of event-like nature of their presence in particular situations.

For those who take a pragmatic approach to understanding objects in terms of the extensive and intensive relations that we have described so far, excess poses a problem. Some approaches attempt to contain the apparently excessive qualities of the relational object by explaining excess as a containable side-effect of the relations that they aim to describe. We might look to the externalities of economics as an example of this kind of excess (Callon, 1998). Excess in this mode becomes the new ground, which a desire for descriptive containment then attempts to colonize. In contrast, others choose to see excess as the limits of their (social) science. For Latour, excess exists in the figure of 'plasma' (Latour, 2005). For positivist natural science, it must lie in entities such as god, spirit and magic that are not generally considered understandable through experimental method. However, what is striking about many of the contributions to this volume is the desire not to stop at the point where the excessive qualities of objects rear their heads but rather to find ways of holding on to the importance of the excessive qualities of objects. Rather than trying to relocate these excesses via practices of categorization, or denoting them as outside the purview of social science, many of the chapters in this volume make an explicit attempt to hold on to that quality of the object that cannot be captured by the mapping of relations in the intensive or extensive modes or the reduction of object effects to the descriptive closure of human interpretation. We term these relations, which escape relational mapping in this way, 'excessive relations'.

An example of attention to the excessive quality of an object occurred during the writing of this introduction, when one of the editors of this edition recounted a story she had been told by a friend. The friend had been alone at home when she had heard the footsteps of an intruder at the bottom of the stairs. Grabbing the nearest heavy item, she took hold of her husband's thesis and hid behind the door ready to assail the burglar with the heavy tome. On recounting the incident later to her husband, the friend commented that he had been less disturbed by the trauma of the possible burglary than the fact that she had chosen to defend herself with his PhD. He was horrified at the idea that his thesis, on which he had lavished so much care, over so many years, could be used as a weapon. As an object, at the moment of the event, the thesis stood for more than the relations that went into its production or the nexus of relations in which it now circulates. The mutual specification of heavy book, scared woman and potential burglar had, indeed, transformed the thesis into a potential weapon; however, it was a weapon that could not entirely shed its symbolic status as a work of scholarly endeavour. It is this quality of in-betweenness or irresolution that the idea of 'excessive' relationship aims to draw attention to. Similarly as readers pick up and flick through this volume, we cannot imagine how the ghosts of past thinkers and the spirit of the objects and materials that they will encounter in this book may produce unexpected juxtapositions, uncanny coincidences or unsettling reactions that cannot be explained through a descriptive stabilization of relations.

For several of the contributors, the language of 'affect' offers a powerful way of attending to this tense awareness of instability, which it is difficult to capture through 'normal' social scientific description. The work of Gilles Deleuze has been hugely influential in providing a theoretical resource for our authors, in exploring those qualities of relations that resist or escape the representational tendencies of social science. Deleuze's (2005) analysis of Francis Bacon's oeuvre (cited by Woodward in Chapter 9), for example, depends not so much on mapping the artwork as a network of constitutive relations in the vein of Alfred Gell (1998), but instead articulates the relational effect of the artwork in terms of what Deleuze terms a 'logic of sensation', with a focus on the force of relations of shape, form and non-form for accounting for the power of Bacon's art. It is this attention to force, to sensation and to the rhythmic qualities of the artwork that allows us to reconceive of the painting less as an object defined through constitutive or contextual relations and rather as an 'event'. Deleuze explicates the eventual qualities of the artwork, by dwelling on the power of form and non-form to act dynamically to produce sensation. In this respect, Deleuze moves the analysis of the artwork from a form of cartographic description to a topological invocation, which stresses the sensory intensities of the work rather than its 'meaning'.

Law and Mol's (2002) writing on complexity offers a helpful articulation of a broader preoccupation with how social analysis can deal with the complexity that defines the world(s) in which we live in a way that neither reduces that complexity through representational techniques of simplification, nor attempts the potential folly of tracking the entirety of all the complex relations that constitute the kinds of objects that we address in this book. Law and Mol are not writing about affect, although their analysis of complexity is helpful for thinking about the techniques available for keeping some of the more affective qualities of objects in view, and the politics entailed in doing so. They explicitly disavow themselves either of an interest in what we have called extensive relations 'As you read this, where are you? Are you sitting at a desk or on a sofa, on an aircraft perhaps, or on a train', or intensive relations 'how many versions did this text go through, and what was added or deleted along the way', in favour of the question 'how might a text be where it is while also acknowledging that it is not everywhere – how might a text make room for whatever it also necessarily leaves out' (2002: 6).

Law and Mol find a provisional resolution to the problem of complexity in three ways. First, they appeal to the value of non-systematized lists, not unlike the collection of objects with which we began this introduction. This suggestion is reminiscent of another thinker who has been influential for many of our authors: Walter Benjamin. Benjamin was also interested in the possibilities of the collection, although as Thoburn's chapter shows, his preoccupation was more with the question of how to wrench objects from their utilitarian position within capitalist social relations, rather than dealing with the problem of complexity as such.

Second, Law and Mol suggest the use of empirical cases, with the proviso that the case is conceived not as an illustration of a general principle but as something that might 'seduce the reader into continuing to read … may act as an irritant, destabilizing expectations' and 'may act allegorically, which means that they may tell not just about what they are manifestly telling but also about something else, something that may be hard to tell directly' (2002: 15). Given this description, the chapters collected in this volume might usefully be thought of as a series of cases, whilst many of the chapters construct their own narrative precisely by bringing a number of discrete cases into contact with one another in a way that generates analytical surprises for the reader.

Finally, Law and Mol make a case for walking, as a 'mode of covering space that provides no overview'. Like Ingold's argument for a 'dwelling perspective', Law and Mol suggest that walking is a way of drawing out the dynamics of encounter, which are key to understanding. As the case of the thesis used as a weapon shows, the notion of encounter offers the possibility of evoking some of those more affective dynamics associated with object relations, or what Law and Mol would call those 'other possibilities', which necessarily disappear in the act of creating a comprehensive understanding of the object of enquiry.

Returning for the last time to the figure of the book, these analyses, which draw attention to the object as an unstable encounter, work to open up a sensibility to dynamics that would conventionally escape a descriptive account of a book as representational form. The temporal quality of, for example, the torpidity of boredom or the thrill of a new idea would be seen to inhere neither in the content of the text nor in the mind of the person reading the book but might rather be found in what Deleuze might call the 'becoming' of the book/reader assemblage.

This generative potential of objects and materials as moments of becoming, which focuses on the part that they play in bringing into being new social formations is another dimension of what we have termed the 'excessive'. The moment of becoming appears as an important limit to the possibility of defining or describing object relations. In an effort to escape some of the commitments entailed by attempts to describe objects in terms of either their intensive and excessive forms of description, many of our authors draw on artists, whose creative and embodied engagement with materials provides inspiration for thinking about the coemergence of human, social and material formations, and for exploring the limits of each of these categories. Others find that their engagements with objects require experimental and performative modes of description in order to access the particular qualities that would be erased by more conventional forms of academic writing.

In addition, the issue of the emergent co-becoming of social and material worlds raises key questions within the volume about the relationship between the excessive qualities of objects and materials and their temporal dimensions, in particular in relation to the way in which objects index traumatic memories, or hold out the uncertain promise of an as-yet unforeseeable future. Objects are not just a way of describing the past through the relations via which they have been made, nor are they simply a means of constituting the present through the relations that they forge, but in many contributions they also seem to have a virtual potential, orienting people and things towards an undefined and yet pressing sense of future. At the same time, the terminology of ghosts and haunting appears as a powerful language for alluding to the invisible, the silent, and that which escapes the materiality or the presence of objects and materials. Haunting seems to connect the past, present and future: the resonating past comes to haunt in the present; meanwhile, the unresolved or troubling relations in the practices of the present are always at risk of producing the grounds for future ghosts to appear.

In each of these cases, the excessive capacity of objects works to push the social sciences and the humanities into new spaces of description, and into new forms of conceptualization. Via their excessive qualities, objects and materials have the effect of drawing forth creative attempts to do justice to that which cannot be subsumed within the cartographic imaginaries of relational connectivity. What is perhaps most exciting for many of the contributors to this book is that the excessive or evental qualities of objects and materials, like the extensive and intensive relations we outlined above, draw out new dimensions of object-politics. Given the difficulty, however, of explicating the politics of affect and the excessive in the conventional language of social science, the objects we find in this volume repeatedly challenge us to engage with a broader question about where the empirical space of social science is thought to be and what place objects, materials, things and concepts might play in forming and reforming the shape of the empirical and its relationship to politics.

Theory and the empirical

Almost without exception, the chapters in this volume are driven by a specific engagement with the empirical, drawing heavily on primary research to attend to cases of phenomena in flux, and attempting to draw out relational insights through the description of complex and emergent patterns of more or less material relations. As we have seen, there are certain philosophical influences that recur in these chapters and that appear particularly useful for the authors in making sense of the empirical relations that they are exploring. At the same time, as we have shown above, the way in which the theoretical is brought to bear on the empirical is uneven and complex.

We suggest that this is in part to do with the way in which particular methodologies have become part of the dynamics by which different disciplinary configurations set out to answer specific questions. Archaeologists, for example, work closely with materials in the course of excavation, in ways that make them highly attentive to the possibilities of both the narrative capabilities of matter, and the limits to the capacity of matter to produce theoretical insights. Ethnographic methods, in contrast, have tended to draw the attention of anthropologists and sociologists to an encounter with the complexity and emergence of social relations not only between humans but including non-humans of different kinds. Within anthropology, the discipline which claims ethnography as the core methodological tool out of which it is able to generate theoretical analyses, the spaces and subject-matter of ethnographic attention have shifted radically in recent years (e.g., analyses of science, technology, global processes, post-identity politics, mobility, multisited ethnography). Sociological traditions of ethnographic research continue to engage the question of how inequalities are forged and perpetuated by looking to theories of how power operates within human societies. Nevertheless, new empirical conditions such as those generated by digital technologies, transactional data, and processes of securitization destabilize the self-evidence of concepts such as race, class and gender leaving the question hanging for some, as to what kind of empirical sociology is appropriate for a world which is increasingly characterized by uncertainty, instability and flux and in which there is ever more scepticism of the value of a search for overarching and enduring theories of 'society' as an object in its own right (Adkins and Lury 2009).

As new empirical situations pose challenging questions for the social sciences and humanities then, we are increasingly forced to recognize that a turn to materiality and objects in the quest to develop new methods and theories is not merely an academic thought experiment. The desire to find non-epochal answers to material transformations is simultaneously driven by a sense of urgency that acknowledges that proceeding as if there were a separation between theoretical and empirical knowledge is untenable. Crises of security, territory and population, to recall Foucault (2007), manifested in events such as the financial crisis since 2008, the global 'war on terror' (Massumi 2005; Amoore 2009) and the ongoing threat of anthropogenic climate change (Serres 1991; Latour 2004) impinge on our capacity to theorize the world in which we live, driving the search for new epistemological paradigms and political theories capable of addressing the problems that we face (Bennett 2010; Coole and Frost 2010; Connolly 2011). Retaining the teachings of post-structuralism, but returning to the question of the material dimensions of social and political life, people working in diverse disciplinary traditions are asking how can we both exercise a critique of human-induced crises and retain an openness to the tension that lies between the excessive, intensive and excessive forms of relationality which we have explored here.

The most important lesson to be drawn from the contributors to this volume is that material relations are highly political inasmuch as they condition the nature of action in the world and of future forms of intervention. This volume will not provide simple answers to these complex issues, but we hope it will in one way or another become a participant in the ongoing question of how to think and act in a world where our forms of thought and action are always tied up with complex material experiments and the formation and deformation of objects.

Introducing the sections

Because of the diverse and overlapping interests of these chapters, we have grouped the chapters according to five themes that emerged from our attempts to understand the key questions preoccupying our contributors. All of the chapters engage, to a greater or lesser extent, with the three relational problematics that we have outlined in this introduction, but they do so for different purposes and with different questions in mind.

The first section is titled *Material qualities.* Here, we have drawn together a set of chapters that we see as most explicitly engaging the question of what role material qualities play in constituting social worlds. In these chapters, we encounter a range of objects, from living and dead bodies to deified statues, canals, water, artworks, synthetic plastics and smart materials. In contrast to classificatory knowledge practices that class materials according to measurable and definable properties, this section alerts us to the qualities of materials, be they numerical, tactile, physical or aesthetic, and to the ways in which they are both made by and make social relations. The material qualities section draws attention in particular to the relational surfaces of materials: the moment of contact between objects; to the action potential that materials contain and their capacity to constrain and condition social relations; to the ways in which materials participate in processes of political transformation in a process we refer to as 'transforming states', and to the fragility of the material world. In drawing together these chapters around the question of material qualities, we aim to provide a series of competing and sometimes contradictory explanations for how social and material dynamics are interrelated. Our hope is that the dissonances and contradictions that we find between the papers can provide a generative starting point for thinking about the ways in which materials are capable of both instantiating and destabilizing relations in complex and often surprising ways.

In the section on *Affective objects* we bring together a set of chapters that collectively attempt to articulate an understanding of the materiality of emotive relationships. The chapters provide a series of compelling and empirically rich accounts of emotive relations that are established and destabilized through the presence of objects and material relations, such as a battered child's toy, an inherited pen or a broken jaw. Although the chapters each provide their own analysis of the particular role that objects and materials play in the constitution of affect, all of the chapters engage the issue of how objects participate in modes of communication or transportation across space and time. Thus we find discussions in these chapters of the relationship between the viscerality of presence and the virtuality of memory and representation, the invisibility of the mundane as it relates to the moment of spectacle, and the link between the transience of a fleeting object and the sedimentation of meaning through processes of repetition and encounter. Collectively, the chapters provide a rich analysis of a perennial problematic of Western philosophy, namely the relationship between human subjectivity and material objectivity, or mind and matter. Resisting the temptation to fall on either side of this divide, the chapters offer new and often experimental forms of description and analysis that attempt to circumvent the conditions of knowledge production and analysis that tends towards the reproduction of the mind/matter dualism. The chapters in this section often mirror the ephemerality of affect and the capacity of affective objects to point to 'unfinished business' by leaving open the space for an ongoing discussion of how objects and materials participate in the making and breaking of emotionally charged sociality.

The section titled *Unsettling objects* opens up the concept of the object to an array of entities that might, at first glance, not appear to be objects at all. Starting from the position that objects are not defined through some shared material substance, but are rather the effect of a relational othering (the object is that which is not me [unless I am seen from the perspective of another, in which case 'I' potentially become an object too]), these chapters open up the discussion of object–relations to include such entities as ghosts, shamans, commodities, programming code, powder, spirits and earthworms. Ironically, perhaps, the most elusive of the uncertain objects we encounter in this section is Graham Harman's ontological 'object' considered as a problem of philosophical speculation. Like the ontological object discussed in Harman's chapter, each of the objects described in this section are discussed in terms of their capacity to unsettle the conventional concepts of the social sciences and humanities. The uncertainty that these objects seem to produce is turned to analytical ends to rethink the conceptual repertoire we have at our disposal for understanding why objects unsettle or, at times, to tame these objects into more settled conceptual spaces. These objects draw the authors to consider such issues as the place of sensory perception in social relations, the role of distraction and the cultivation of attention in forming relations with the world around us, the cumulative dynamics of knowledge as it pertains to processes of understanding and misunderstanding, and to the role of processes of decay, digestion and renewal in the constitution of the world which we inhabit.

In the section on *Interface objects*, we have brought together a set of chapters that pay particular attention to the way in which objects become constituted through moments of encounter. Building on the metaphor of the interface, each of the chapters in this section explore how objects of different kinds (money, models, cars, kettles, brands) emerge through the work that they do in conjoining fields or entities of different kinds. Interfaces are shown in each of these chapters to be highly dynamic. Whereas on the one hand they bring fields of activity together, they also work to transform these fields in the process of their enactment. Moreover, at the same time as bringing together particular activities or materialities, they also produce new divisions, setting up the conditions of possibility for imagining the kinds of futures that might be desired and the outcomes that need to be avoided. They are, in this sense, intensive sites of change. What each of the chapters show in their own ways, however, is how change at the interface is not a generic conceptual phenomenon but is highly specific. In all of the chapters, change is shown to occur under the weight of specific administrative, legal, technical and material constraints. Indeed, what these chapters show is that it is precisely in the moment of encounter between diverse systems of ordering that both the potential and the threat associated with transformation comes into view.

Our final section, *Becoming object*, extends this focus on transformation by bringing together those chapters that work most explicitly with the issue of how objects and materials participate in processes of change. This section starts not from the idea that objects produce change, but instead asks what difference it would make to consider objects and materials themselves as manifestations of process, movement, emergence and becoming. The chapters in this section make productive use of some key conceptual metaphors that help us to imagine the morphological and material dynamics of change. Much inspiration is taken from the topological relationships through which matter might be understood to transform itself. Linear notions of temporal change are replaced by terms such as swarms, generativity, repetition, the archi-textural, the choreographic, networks, relational matrices and lash-ups, to rethink the material dynamics of a terrorist threat, the behaviour of meerkats or the qualities of place. The contribution of these chapters is to turn these distributed collections of material and object relations into an analytical resource in order to provide a radical reevaluation of the valency of objects and the possibility of identifying the agentive qualities of change.

Note

1 These events were a workshop on '*Materialising the Subject*', and the CRESC annual conference on the theme of '*Objects. What Matters?*'.

Bibliography

Adkins, L. and Lury, C. (2009) 'Introduction: What Is the Empirical?', *European Journal of Social Theory: Special Issue: What is the Empirical?*, 12(1): 5–20.

Amoore, L. (2009) 'Lines of Sight: On the Visualization of Unknown Futures', *Citizenship Studies*, 13(1): 17–30.

Appadurai, A. (1986) *The Social Life of Things: Commodities in Cultural Perspective*, Cambridge; New York: Cambridge University Press.

Bennett, J. (2010) *Vibrant Matter: A Political Ecology of Things*, Durham, NC: Duke University Press.

Borges, J. L. and Di Giovanni, N. T. (1973) *A Universal History of Infamy*, London: Allen Lane.

Buchli, V. (2002) *The Material Culture Reader*, Oxford: Berg.

Callon, M. (1998) *The Laws of the Markets*, Oxford: Blackwell.

Candlin, F. and Guins, R. (2009) *The Object Reader*, Abingdon, Oxon; New York: Routledge.

Collier, S. J. (2011) *Post-Soviet Social: Neoliberalism, Social Modernity, Biopolitics*, Princeton: Princeton University Press.

Connolly, W. E. (2011) *A World of Becoming*, Durham, NC: Duke University Press.

Coole, D. H. and Frost, S. (2010) *New Materialisms: Ontology, Agency, and Politics*, Durham, NC: Duke University Press.

Cooper, G., King, A. S. and Rettie, R. (2009) *Sociological Objects: Reconfigurations of Social Theory*, Aldershot: Ashgate.

Deleuze, G. (2005) *Francis Bacon: The Logic of Sensation*, London: Continuum.

Edgerton, D. (2008) *The Shock of the Old: Technology and Global History Since 1900*, London: Profile.

Foucault, M. (1970) *The Order of Things: An Archaeology of the Human Sciences*, London: Routledge.

Foucault, M. (2007) *Security, Territory, Population: Lectures at the Collège De France, 1977–1978*, Houndmills, Basingstoke, Hampshire; New York: Palgrave Macmillan.

Franklin, S. (2007) *Dolly Mixtures: The Remaking of Genealogy*, Durham, NC: Duke University Press; Chesham: Combined Academic [distributor].

Gell, A. (1998) *Art and Agency: Towards a New Anthropological Theory*, Oxford: Clarendon.

Graham, S. and Thrift, N. (2007) 'Out of Order: Understanding Repair and Maintenance', *Theory, Culture and Society*, 24(3): 1–25.

Graves-Brown, P. (2000) *Matter, Materiality and Modern Culture*, London: Routledge.

Grosz, E. (2009) The Thing in *The Object Reader*, F. Candlin and R. Gains, Eds. London and New York: Routledge: 2009.

Haraway, D. J. (2003) *The Companion Species Manifesto: Dogs, People, and Significant Otherness*, Chicago, Ill.: Prickly Paradigm; Bristol: University Presses Marketing.

Haraway, D. J. (2008) *When Species Meet*, Minneapolis, Minn.: University of Minnesota Press; Bristol: University Presses Marketing [distributor].

Harvey, P. (2001) Landscape and Commerce: Creating Contexts for the Exercise of Power in *Contested Landscapes: Movement, Exile and Place*, B. Bender and M. Winer, Eds. Oxford: Berg: 197–210.

Henare, A.J.M., Holbraad, M. and Wastell, S. (2007) *Thinking through Things: Theorising Artefacts Ethnographically*, London; New York: Routledge.

Hicks, D. and Beaudry, M. C. (2010) *The Oxford Handbook of Material Culture Studies*, Oxford: Oxford University Press.

Ingold, T. (2011) *Being Alive: Essays on Movement, Knowledge and Description*, London: Routledge.

Joyce, P. (2013) *The State of Freedom: Making the Liberal Leviathan, Britain since 1800*, Cambridge: Cambridge University Press.

Kopytoff, I. (1986) The Cultural Biography of Things: Commoditization as Process in *The Social Life of Things: Commodities in a Cultural Perspective*, A. Appadurai, Ed. Cambridge: Cambridge University Press: 64–91.

Landecker, H. (2007) *Culturing Life: How Cells Became Technologies*, Cambridge, MA; London: Harvard University Press.

Latour, B. (1988) *The Pasteurization of France*, Cambridge, MA; London: Harvard University Press.

Latour, B. (1991) The Berlin Key or How to Do Things with Words in *Matter, Materiality and Modern Culture*, P. M. Graves-Brown, Ed. London: Routledge: 10–21.

Latour, B. (1992) Where Are the Missing Masses? The Sociology of a Few Mundane Artifacts in *Shaping Technology/Building Society: Studies in Sociotechnical Change*, W. Bijker and J. Law, Eds. Cambridge, MA: MIT Press.

Latour, B. (2004) *Politics of Nature: How to Bring the Sciences into Democracy*, Cambridge, MA; London: Harvard University Press.

Latour, B. (2005) *Reassembling the Social: An Introduction to Actor-Network Theory*, Oxford: Oxford University Press.

Latour, B. and Weibel, P. (2005) *Making Things Public. Atmospheres of Democracy*, Cambridge, MA; London: MIT Press.

Law, J. and Mol, A. (2002) *Complexities: Social Studies of Knowledge Practices*, Durham, NC; London: Duke University Press.

Massumi, B. (2005) *The Future Birth of the Affective Fact*, Genealogies of Biopolitics [conference proceedings].

Meskell, L. (2005) *Archaeologies of Materiality*, Malden, MA; Oxford: Blackwell.

Miller, D. (2005) *Materiality*, Durham, NC: Duke University Press; Chesham: Combined Academic [distributor].

Miller, D. (2008) *The Comfort of Things*, Cambridge: Polity.

Miller, D. (2009) *Anthropology and the Individual: A Material Culture Perspective*, Oxford: Berg.

Miller, D. (2011) *Tales from Facebook*, Cambridge: Polity.

Miller, D. and Woodward, S. (2012) *Blue Jeans: The Art of the Ordinary*, Berkeley, CA; London: University of California Press.

Mol, A. (2003) *The Body Multiple: Ontology in Medical Practice*, Durham, NC; London: Duke University Press.

Serres, M. (1991) *The Natural Contract*, Ann Arbor: University of Michigan Press.

Sloterdijk, P. (2009) *Terror from the Air*, Los Angeles, CA: Semiotext(e).

Strathern, M. (1995a) *Shifting Contexts: Transformations in Anthropological Knowledge*, London; New York: Routledge.

Strathern, M. (1995b) *The Relation: Issues in Complexity and Scale*, Cambridge: Prickly Pear Press.

Thomas, N. (1991) *Entangled Objects: Exchange, Material Culture, and Colonialism in the Pacific*, Cambridge, MA; London: Harvard University Press.

Tilley, C.Y. (2006) *Handbook of Material Culture*, London: Sage.

Part I
Material qualities
Introduction

Gillian Evans

Relational surfaces

In 2007, Tim Ingold argued against the fashion in anthropology for a focus on an unspecified abstract materiality. He was inspired by psychologist James Gibson's tripartite division of the inhabited environment into medium, substances and surfaces. This enabled Ingold to spell out and call for a more pragmatic and ethnographically grounded study of 'the life-world', in which life is not understood as the exclusive preserve of humanity but is the condition of the environment such that surfaces are seen, on close inspection, to be what make possible the formation and transformation of relational interfaces between an infinite variety of substances and the various mediums of habitation: air, water, etc.

Ingold railed against the use of the term materiality to create an unanalysed, blind alley of mystifying contradistinction between 'thing-ness' and human mind (as the condition of subjectivity), and argued (after theorist of design David Pye, 1968) for a renewed focus on material properties: the stuff with which things are made (as relational qualities) and as the intuitive bedrock for the interactive, unpredictable and poetic emergence of human being:

> The properties of materials are objective and measurable. They are *out there*. The qualities on the other hand are subjective: they are *in here*: in our heads [bodies]. They are [embodied] ideas of ours. They are part of that private view of the world which artists each have within them. We each have our own view of what stoniness is.
>
> *(Pye 1968: 45–47; original emphasis, cited in Ingold 2007)*

Ingold's polemic about material qualities is directly relevant to and therefore serves as an opening provocation for the chapters collected in this part of the book. For example, artist Helen Barff describes her skin as a shifting membrane whose aliveness and tactility of touch makes possible an intimate and sensitive relationship with the non-human materials and forms of the world outside her own body. One gets a very real sense that through her attempts to grasp the world (to come to terms with it through her hands), Barff is working out/sculpting art-objects as a way of also exploring the possibilities and limits of her own being. It becomes clear through Barff's reflections on her practice that human skin and non-human materials and objects are usefully thought of as relational surfaces. Through the process of reaching out, touching, holding, working and grasping with her hands and thereby bringing herself into bodily, active relation with material surfaces and object forms, Barff also discovers, in contradistinction to the stuff of the world, her self as a particular kind of sculptural type and worldly entity too. Embodied, fleshy, with a surface of responsive, living skin, Barff is preoccupied with the human form, its shape: with hands that can feel and touch delicately and seize and hold firmly. It is through what her skin and hands encounter on the outside of herself that Barff experiences, moment to moment, both the edge of her being and the emerging, changing feeling of what it is like to exist in and to be of and in contact with the edges of things in the world.[1]

Action potentials

Reaching out, relating and adapting to what exists outside of herself, bringing it within her grasp, Barff is aware that an inner world of experience arises through her bodily action, with internalized conscious reflection, comprehension of her actions, and exterior verbalization happening only later.[2] Instinctively, Barff searches the world of objects, crafting and differentiating her relations with it as she goes, and she describes as 'magical' the surprising journey into materials (concrete, latex, felt and silicone). She marvels at her exploration of the unique qualities of materials, what they make possible in the world, their promise in terms of human exploitation (what she can do with them) and their resistance to her desire to do with them as she pleases. Barff's art practice, as a journey of constant discovery, helps us to understand materials and objects as relational surfaces and sets of action potentials.

Another example of how humans accommodate to, work with and surmount the limits of potential for human action of particular materials is Maurits Ertsen's work on water resources. He describes irrigation systems as illustrative of a more general point, which is that despite human determination, ingenuity and complex tool use (as an attempt to harness the world and get it under control) humans simply cannot do as they please, because the material qualities of the environing world are largely constitutive of and structure what becomes possible as human action. Comparing and contrasting three case studies from the USA, Peru and Argentina, Ertsen outlines the different ways in which irrigation systems have been used by humans as a means for gaining control over water as a vital resource and powerful feature of the natural environment. He contradicts the general assumption that irrigation systems are passive artefacts, as if their material properties do not matter or do not influence human actions, and he shows how the physical shape of irrigation systems actually constrains and enables human actions in particular ways. He explains how human actions and the behaviour of flowing water through canals and structures together create spatial and temporal patterns of water flows. In turn, these flow patterns are likely to provoke new actions at individual and/or collective level with these same canals and structures. Irrigation systems are, therefore, both the outcome of and medium for human action. Ertsen shows how, for those groups disadvantaged by their geographic position relative to water flow, the social imperative to overcome material disadvantage requires the capacity for social compensation in the form of political organization. Once humans deploy and attempt to harness particular kinds of materials (i.e. make them the basis for experimentation with specific kinds of actions), then spatiality and temporality are revealed, experientially, as material qualities too.

Transforming states

Similarly, Chandra Mukerji's chapter illustrates a more general point about material deployment, which is that in addition to certain kinds of spatial and temporal effects, political consequence is always the intended or unintended outcome of the attempt to reorganize 'figured worlds'. If human collective relations are constituted through and substantiated in the particular arrangement and possibilities of material things, then it makes sense that for humans to purposefully disrupt the order of things is to potentially disturb the structure and organization of social life. She explains that although social analysts readily agree that material relations are important to the development of political states/nations, few routinely entertain the idea that artefacts themselves have a significant role in shaping political regimes. She describes how the effectiveness of top-down material management by states is often explicitly denied and questioned by many contemporary archaeologists, but as she shows here, objects and material practices can indeed have subtle and enduring political importance for state formation and reformation.

Mukerji analyses the material association of France with Rome, and shows how a forceful process of material reordering was used for political effect during state formation under Louis XIV. In seventeenth-century France, the state was not yet a powerful institution and was struggling for authority against the clergy and nobility who dominated French politics. Mukerji's case study shows how state policies of material change were a means of side-stepping patrimonial politics, using evocations of Rome's worldly power to justify new state activism. Her work usefully allows us to think of material entities not just as relational surfaces or action potentials, or indeed as aesthetic possibilities, but also as transforming states, and this applies as much to grand political projects of nation formation and reformation as it does, for example, to the more everyday relationship between a workman and his tools or the intimacy of connection between a concert violinist and her instrument. The state of being of the violin and the state of being of the soloist are mutually constituted and transformed in the moment of action.

Absent from Mukerji's historical account but present as a force of contestation in Penny Harvey's chapter about state action in contemporary Peru are the voices that dissent loudly as the state attempts to reconfigure material arrangements for urban living. This is important because it shows that state projects of material change not only imply the bringing into being of a new political order, as Mukerji's chapter shows, but also that such orders are in fact difficult to implement in practice and fragile with respect to the vested interests who do not take too kindly to disruption. Taking as her case study the problem of the disposal of solid waste in the city of Cusco, Harvey shows how the Peruvian state constitutes itself as 'neoliberal' in so far as the power to act is both decentralized and privatized. She describes how an attempt is made to locate the resolution of the chronic problem of solid waste disposal in an artful articulation of independent technical experts and local-level stakeholders. However, this eliciting of the 'neoliberal' subject as a person capable of acting as client to state service provision leads to the undermining of expertise as an independent expression of objective assessment. Ironically, this results in calls on the one hand for even more distributed solutions, which take account both of municipal desires to capitalize on the profitability of waste recycling, and, on the other, in a generalized demand that rather than stand off, the state needs to act more forcefully, to make itself more manifest as a regulatory body.

At the heart of this controversy over waste disposal is not only the question of the changing form of the nation state as it makes itself manifest through its material projects but also the question of who should profit from what waste declares (its instability) as it becomes a problem in the urban environment. What Harvey's case study of waste reminds us of, as does Casella and

Croucher's later chapter in a different way, is that all things exist in a transforming state. What then becomes interesting are the ways in which the relational possibilities of materials change over time. Harvey shows, for example, how the material qualities of all the different kinds of plastic as it decomposes are unique relative to other materials and that specialist plastic recycling endeavours are developing as small-scale initiatives to adapt to this potential. It is the instability of matter, which, in this case, becomes the foundation of an economy built on the transforming use-value of things in flux.

Technical proficiency

Ingold (2007) describes a life-world of substances, mediums and relational surfaces as a moving trajectory, a permanent condition of possibility and flux:

> Like all other creatures, human beings do not exist on the 'other side' of materiality but swim in an ocean of materials. Once we acknowledge our immersion, what this ocean reveals to us is not the bland homogeneity of different shades of matter but a flux in which materials of the most diverse kinds – through the process of admixture and distillation, of coagulation and dispersal, and of evaporation and precipitation – undergo continual generation and transformation. The forms of things, far from having been imposed from without upon an inert substrate, arise and are borne along – as indeed we are too – within this current of materials. As with the Earth itself, the surface of every solid is but a crust, the more or less ephemeral congelate of a generative movement.
>
> *(Ingold 2007: 7)*

The 'generative movement' out of which new relations are brought into being and new forms arise is, in Ingold's account, the source of human imagining/ideas that are revealed as the aftereffect of practical, bodily engagement/interfacing in and with the 'ocean of materials'. Usefully, this allows us to think of world–body–mind or life–world as a material continuum in flux, with mental concepts dethroned from their transcendent subjective position and carefully posited as simply the outcome and not the source of human being in the world.[3]

Social anthropologist Soumhya Venkatesan, in contrast, takes issue with Ingold's fundamentalist approach to material qualities. She does not see all human crafting as an emerging, experimental process with inspiration about form arising from the interfacing process itself. Venkatesan's chapter focuses on stone carvers in Tamilnadu, southeastern India and the transformation of the granite carvings, through ritual practice, into embodiments of deities. Her ethnography shows that stone carvers must follow strict rules about what form the sculpture must take for each deity to meet the criteria of the god ordered by clients. In this sense, then, the form of the object to be made is very much preconceived and the task of the stone carver is technical in terms of following the manuals of formation, rather than artistic in the sense of exploratory imagining. The importance of the task of the carver, in terms of his technical proficiency at producing the right sculpture, is underlined by the vagaries of the ritual process through which gods must be harnessed, encouraged to enter into and inhabit the sculpture. If the sculptor were to follow the flight of his imagination as it encounters the material qualities of the granite, the form produced might compromise the ritual specialists' understanding of what needs to be in place for the deity to become embodied in the stone.

This is not to say that carvers are not aware of the material qualities of the stone, or that they have not had to embody years of skilled practice in order to work effectively with it. On the contrary, stone carvers are careful to differentiate between granite and other kinds of stone and between the granite that is of the right quality for the bodily form of the carving and that which is only good enough for the plinth, which will support it. Venkatesan's support for Ingold's missive, that anthropologists pay attention to materials and the details of the process in and through which humans interface with them, produces, then, not a reinforcement, in this case, of Ingold's poetic, romantic account of what happens at the surface of things. Rather, a more pragmatic return of the primacy or at least equality of the conceptualizing subject is proposed as the moving force behind the production of new forms and admixtures in the world. Mukerji's chapter, too, reveals with dramatic effect how humans can exhibit a pragmatic and purposeful preconceptualization of what needs to be made to materialize in the world. Arguably, this restores to anthropological accounts of embodiment and skilled practice equity of consideration for mental concepts/representations not as transcendent achievements, but as points on a continuum of consciousness, which includes body–mind–world, and which sees creativity as a continuous two-way process between material qualities and thoughtful imaginings. Furthermore, an anthropological insistence on continuing to work out and specify what are our uniquely human attributes and which make possible the invention and production of an endless stream of new things in the world restores a depth to subjectivity that risks becoming nothing more than a surface when materials take centre stage.

Fragile substance

Also contradicting the idea that the form of a thing is necessarily the emergent outcome of the qualities of the materials humans choose to work with, the chapter by Küchler and Oakley examines the extent to which humans can impose what they intend on materials or are necessarily constrained by a process of adaptation to what materials make possible. These authors focus on the invention of new synthetic materials and describe how with the advent of vulcanized rubber and then synthetic polymers, design became less constrained by the qualities of materials and more about the pragmatics of how to produce, artificially, materials to order. This is achieved through molecular alteration with minimal physical effort and massive commercial success, such that materials themselves come to be both the object of manufacture and design and nodes in a transforming matrix of relational classifications and use values. Küchler and Oakley describe the radical implications of this development, for our understanding of both materials and human being. Just as Helen Barff and Tim Ingold's reflections allow us to think of world–body–mind or life–world as a material continuum in flux, with mental concepts dethroned from their transcendent subjective position and carefully posited as simply the outcome and not the source of human being in the world, Küchler and Oakley, in a mirror reversal, force us to have to think of the intrinsic qualities of materials as overthrown by human ingenuity. This unsettles any kind of aesthetic or poetic bargain with a world suddenly rendered more plastic and product of our preconceived intervention than we could ever have imagined:

> The challenge to the integrity of materials that plastics entailed was brilliantly captured by Roland Barthes in his now classic description of watching the manufacture of plastic objects in *Mythologies* (1972). For Barthes, plastic epitomized the dissolution of the material in that it 'hardly exists as substance', but is sublimated as movement and infinite transformation at the same time as it appears to replace all other substances.
>
> *(Barthes 1972: 97) (Küchler and Oakley, this volume)*

What these 'new' materials and allied technologies impress upon us, Küchler and Oakley argue, is 'a new kind of object ontology, which replaces the management of diverse preexisting physical tendencies with limitless physical transformation' and that supersedes the idea of the intrinsic material properties of things with the notion of fragile substance, always open to technological reconstruction.

Reaching a similar conclusion, but from a very different vantage point, Casella and Croucher argue that processes of decay are an intrinsic quality of materials of all kinds. Even the most durable of materials is fragile in the face of the duration of time. As archaeologists, they are not looking into the future, at the becoming reality of science fiction–type materials, but rather, looking back, not only at what processes of decay tell us about what artefacts are made of, but also at what made-objects recovered from the past can allow us to imagine about object-mediated human relations and experiences. Even the very act of retrieving and preserving artefacts from archaeological remains creates a contemporary matrix of relationality for those items and the intervention is always political, as is the question of which things to preserve and which to allow to decay, now that everything worth looking at is exposed to the corrosive environment of the present time. Like Ertsen, Casella and Croucher consider the spatial implications of specific material deployments in particular environments, for example, in the excavated site of the Ross Female Prison and its nursery ward in Tazmania. The careful tracing of the addition of wooden floorboards to an original structure allows the archaeological team to consider and then to discover what may have fallen through those floorboards. This leads to the locating of artefacts that may well have mediated the relationship between mothers and children who were physically separated from each other, but remained somehow still in communication. The imagining of a maternal bond indexed in found objects speaks of the affective quality of inanimate artefacts and also speaks something of the temporal moment in which objects are enmeshed and, to varying degrees, preserved. It is this possibility of entering into a deeply meaningful, emotion-laden relationship with objects that posits a kind of equivalence: an equality between object being and human being in a state of mutual 'coemergence'. This reminds us that as much as human form embodies the effects of the materials it must adapt to as environment, humans also inhere in and make the world fleshy (Merleau-Ponty 1962).

Notes

1 Human flesh is, one might say, worldly in its dependence on and inseparability from the historically specific objects and material relations that make possible culturally specific lives. For example, hunters in the interior jungle regions of Sumatra among the Orang Rimba hunter–gatherers must learn to run fast and balance skilfully in the slippery tropical forest environment. The accommodation of hunters' bodies to the specificity of these material surroundings leads to the development of extremely hard skin on the bottom of men's feet. This becomes so thick that is functions like a natural shoe (Elkholy 2010).

2 This tallies with theory and evidence in genetic epistemology. Piaget (1971), for example, argues that the foundation of human thought is sensorimotor action such that bodily intelligence, developed through reaching out to and making sense of the world in early childhood, becomes the empirical basis for all future achievements of symbolic thought and representation in language. It makes sense to argue that the same can also be true of new knowledge seeking, even in adulthood. See also Toren (1999) for a phenomenological and anthropological perspective on and argument for the necessity of a commitment to genetic epistemology.

3 This is reminiscent of the architects-as-foam-cutters in the work of actor-network-theorist Albena Yaneva (2009); the Koolhaas architectural team that Yaneva studied do not preconceive the building that is to be designed, but rather fashion it out of what Ingold might call an 'admixture': a combination of what designers' modelling foam makes it possible for architects to craft/imagine-as-they-go-along and the action potential spoken by the limits of an extant built environment in New York city.

Bibliography

Barthes R. (1972) Mythologies. New York: Farrar, Strauss and Giroux.

Elkholy R. (2010) Being and Becoming in the World: embodiment and experience among the Orang Rimba of Sumatra, PhD Thesis, University of Manchester.

Gibson J. (1986) The Ecological Approach to Visual Perception. London: Routledge.

Heidegger M. (1962) Being and Time. Oxford: Blackwell.

Ingold T. (2007) Materials Against Materiality. *Archaeological Dialogues*, 14 (1): 1–16.

Latour B. (1988) The Pasteurisation of France. Massachusetts: Harvard University Press.

Law J. (2011) Emergent Aliens: on salmon, nature and their enactment. *Ethnos*, 65 (1): 65–87.

Merleau-Ponty M. (1962) The Phenomenology of Perception. London: Routledge and Kegan Paul.

Piaget J. (1971) Genetic Epistemology. New York: WW Norton & Co Inc.

Pye D. (2000 [orig.1964]) The Nature and Aesthetics of Design: ecology, culture and human intention. New York: Oxford University Press.

Toren C. (1999) Mind, Materiality and History. London: Routledge.

Yaneva A. (2009) The Making of a Building: a pragmatist approach to architecture. Oxford: Peter Lang AG.

2

An interview with artist Helen Barff[1]

Gillian Evans

Objects for me take on personalities, they become almost like my children, they are creatures and the resulting work becomes an object that is a being, so, it is projecting my own
being onto them, making them something I can relate to.

G: Is it true to say that to some extent your work explores found objects?

H: Yes, I work with objects, found objects or quite often I have an idea what object I would
like to work with so either found or hunted out. I think the interest in objects is an interest in
the human interaction with objects and seeing them as anthropomorphic beings, as things
[beings] in their own right. It is also about collecting, having collections or series of things and
indexing them through making work from them.

G: And when you say found objects or when you go on a hunting expedition how important
is the found-ness or hunted out-ness of the objects?

H: I have hardly ever used a new object – I like an object with a history to it – an object that
is shaped by its history is very important. The shape of it tells its story, or its history has determined its shape, if you see what I mean. It might be a piano with scratches on it or it might be
a thing washed up by the Thames, which has been shaped by the river. With the latter I found
a specific site, for example a beach in Greenwich, and went there to collect whatever I found,
it is to do with the location of the object in that case. I then document or index that location
through the objects that are found there. So, those objects are unexpected. With other objects,
the larger objects like the car, piano or the boat the important thing is to hunt for an object with
a history, so it wouldn't be a new shiny piano, it had to be an old piano that had the story
included in it.

G: The way the object embodies its history, it is not just about human shaping of it?

H: No, it could be a weathering like the things in the Thames – the tides or what being in
water has done to them. Or my collections of stones; I've collected stones from sites all around,
wherever I've been really, there the stones are shaped for thousands of years by their location.

G: And when you find an object that interests you, is the thing that interests you immediately
the material trace of the history or is it the material quality of the thing itself or both?

H: Both, the material traces on it and the sculptural form of it as well. At the moment, I am
working with found or bought clothes and again, they are all second hand, from charity shops,

27

found or donated things. So, have signs of human use. I am thinking that I would like to do something, but I don't know what yet, with old furniture. But the shape of the objects is very important too – the form. There are two different categories of things – the things in the Thames from a geographical location [which are a surprise] and the furniture, the clothes, the car – things that I'd kind of chosen.

G: It's almost archaeological in a way, like you're excavating history, but in different ways?

H: Yes, I see the Thames objects or stones as a sort of index of a site or place.

G: And with the found objects where you are looking at say, human influence, do you see that as a human index there, in the way that by the Thames what you find there indexes the place?

H: Yes, I guess I do, but some histories are more traceable than others, for example an old piano which has the trace of people, but it is anonymous. In the Thames you can often trace and see where [the object's] been weathered by the water. Or there will be a whole site where there are loads of rusty old nails and it's because there has been a ship building yard there so, there is human influence too. Other objects you've no idea how they got there, so there is a human index, but it's anonymous or forgotten.

G: And that preoccupation with the history of effects – where has that come from in your work? Have you always had that, is that something you have always been fascinated about or is that something that's come about over time?

H: No, I think it has always been there, maybe in a different way though. It's an interest in the traces of things, traces and memories on things, which relates to drawing as well, a drawing could be said to be an imprint, a memory, a trace, an event, a happening or an idea and I think that scratches on an old object are a similar idea so it's [the preoccupation with the history of effects] always been there, but just maybe in different formats.

G: So, the leaving of a trace is quite similar there? So, in terms of your found objects and your hunting sites and locations, have you come to be obsessed with certain materials like rocks or cars, pianos or do you just find that you remain open or do you go through phases?

H: I go through phases with different objects. But yes, I can get a bit obsessed, especially with the material I end up working with, concrete or felt or rubber.

G: Oh, in the next phase [after having found something]?

H: Yes.

G: Ok, so just tell me a bit about that, you've done the initial finding, hunting, then what happens?

H: I always have to live with the object for a bit before I do anything. It's strange, it has to sit for a bit, but this stage usually involves wider research into the object and its history or use. Also research into materials I will use to create the work, so there's the subject matter research and then the material research. It's very important that I use materials that relate to the materiality of the object.

So with the piano, I ended up using felt because felt is used inside pianos and with the buoys they were very rubbery so I used latex, silicone and other types of rubber. So, that's how I start using materials with the object. With concrete it started in a perverse way because I started working with the Thames and was interested in all these floating boats and things washed up by the river and then I wanted to reverse it and take something that normally floats and cast it out of concrete.

G: Something that I'm really intrigued in about your work, you say you have to live with the object for a while. What is that about?

H: It is almost like a kind of getting to know, it sits there and I look at it, draw it, photograph it, look at it, it's sort of a getting to know the object, thinking about it, rather than jumping in and pouring concrete all over it straight away. I haven't thought about it that much, but I know that's what I do, they kind of sit there.

G: But when you say that it is important for there to be some continuity between the materiality of the object and the materials you are going to use, why is that so important?

H: I think it is to do with the closeness to the object. All the work that I've made is to do with the contact with the object. Between the material that I'm using and the object there is always direct contact between the two. There has to be a physical closeness between them and they have to relate to each other. I also use paper to make pencil rubbings or drawings of objects, as a way of getting to know the object. When investigating the object I am interested in investigating what it is made from, so then I will start using similar materials.

G: So, it is like a continuous exploration, sort of getting to know and then beginning to work with, can you give me an example [of the process], what about the piano?

H: The piano is the first in a trajectory of work that has followed a similar pattern. I had this idea that I wanted to work with a piano and found an old piano in a junk shop. I played the piano [as a child], I mean I wasn't great, but I saw this analogy between drawing and the piano because they are both about a sensitivity of touch.

The piano keyboard is sensitive to pressure as is drawing, I wanted to bring these two things together. Again, I had this settling in time with the piano. It was really old, totally out of tune, it had keys missing and I made these funny sound recordings of me playing this piano. I made drawings and rubbings, I didn't know what the results were going to be. There must be a judgment in a way: is this a finished artwork or not? Has this worked in some way or not? This is a question of whether it goes beyond what it is, whether it says something more than the object.

One of the things I did was put black paper inside the piano and effectively using the keyboard as a typewriter, by putting chalk on the piano hammers and playing the piano. It created lines of chalk dots or splodges where the piano hammers were hitting the paper, so recording the

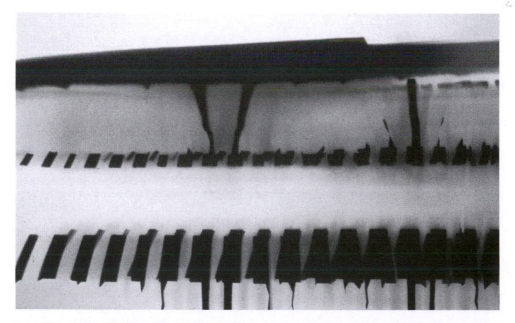

Figure 2.1 Helen Barff: *Fairy Lights inside a Piano (detail),* 2000, photographic paper, 50 x 150 cm

Figure 2.2 Helen Barff: *Piano*, 1999, felt, dust, rust and glue, 9 m x 150 cm

sense of touch I mentioned. I also put photographic paper inside the piano and some lights, which cast shadows of the piano hammers onto the paper. Then I used felt because of felt being a material used inside the piano and being a sound absorbent material, as if it might hold all the sounds the piano had ever made.

So, I ended up wrapping the entire piano inside and out in a huge piece of felt. I bought manufactured felt though subsequently I made my own felt. I wrapped the entire piano then covered the whole thing in water and glue and wall paper paste and let it dry and shrink onto the piano. I pulled it off and I had this massive nine metre long print of the inside and outside of the piano. And I guess this was the first instance, of getting the inside and outside of [the object] and subsequently everything has come after that.

Because I captured the duration of my playing the piano as a single image (with the photographic and chalk artwork), I then became interested in how time can be turned into a single image and I started doing train journeys into a single image using a pinhole camera and then the car, which again started off about trying to catch a single journey and then became about the car as a thing [in itself].

G: Can you tell me more about what comes after the 'getting to know the object' stage?

H: The next stage is making samples, choosing what material I might work with and there might be a bit of trial and error in that. If it is a new material I try out samples, if, say, I was going to coat the object in rubber, trying out different rubbers in different sections. Like with the piano before wrapping the entire thing in felt, I took out some internal bits of the piano and tried wrapping them in felt first.

Figure 2.3 Helen Barff: *Tethered Boat*, 2009, tracing paper, tape, metal frame and light, 80 x 130 x 300 cm

G: And, in going from the 'getting to know' to the 'material sample' experiments, what are you aiming to do?

H: It probably varies with the different objects. I think in a lot of cases I don't particularly know what I am aiming to do because I am led by the materials. I have an idea and an object, but it is all to do with the hands. I feel like I think with my hands when I am working with objects or materials. The initial idea is why I am interested in that object, so with the boat, it was about a vessel that holds. I was interested in the fact that it holds people, has an inside and an outside, its size and shape and that it has a poetic-ness to it. And so, I have an idea which I might want to portray, but once I start working with the materials it can lead in different directions. The materials don't necessarily do what you think they are going to do, it's a very tactile process and it can change, which is great.

G: That's the exciting part?

H: Yes, so you often end up making something different to what you thought you were going to be making.

G: So, what you end up making quite often surprises you?

H: Yes, and you learn something. Although I know the recurring themes in my work and they always tend to come out, but not always as expected. With the clothes I wanted to cast the inside and the outside of clothes, trying to get the idea of a continual inside–outside space. So far what has come out is these very solid sculptures because of the material I was using.

G: And that inside outside space is a recurring theme in your work. Can you try and describe to me what you are exploring in that?

Figure 2.4   *A Möbius strip* © Helen Barff 2011

H: It is again to do with the sense of touch. Touch is a 3D sense, so, when you look at things, you see just one side of them, but touch enables you to go around and inside and out as well. It relates to the human body – always there is an inside and outside – there is no separation between the two, they are a continual space. I think that is where the interest in boats and vessels came from – that the inside and outside, the continual tactile surface, go in and out of each other, there is not a separation – like the Möbius strip. That relates to the human skin as it is also a continual surface, no start or finish.

I think a lot of what I do goes back in my mind to a series of drawings I did years ago. I tried to draw around my body, but you can't because if you try to draw around your body you will always get to a point where you are stuck because you can't draw around the hand you are drawing with and you can't step outside your own body in order to see your body as whole. You can never see your entire edges, you are stuck inside your edges so you can't see them as complete, as whole. I think that is what I am trying to do with a lot of the objects. It is because you can see an object as whole [unlike your self] although also, it becomes an extension of your body as well, but you can see this object. You can trace it with your hands as a 3D object in a way you can't with your own body, so I am projecting that need or want to see my entire edges onto an object. I think what I am often doing is covering an object, say for example entirely in latex or rubber, then turning that covering inside out so you are left with a trace of the entire object. This becomes a substitute for the impossibility of turning myself inside out so, and seeing my own entire edges.

Then there's also the inside your head or imaginative interior space, or even just your breath that goes in and out of your body. That's also continuous space. Where do those start and finish? There is no separation between the two. There's a continuous movement. Breath is a good analogy because it continually goes in and out and there is no …

G: No edge?

H: You feel like, I guess it all comes back to the body and your own experience of the body as not a self-contained entity, that you are always this shifting membrane, that there isn't a clear inside or outside.

G: Yes, I have a fascination for the way in which being human and being a certain kind of human is so intimately bound up with object interactions. How can you tell where the materiality

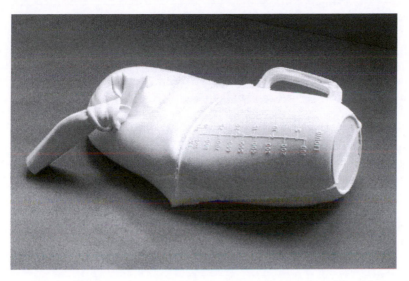

Figure 2.5   Helen Barff: *The Inside and Outside of a Jug*, 2008, silicone rubber filled with water, 20 x 15 x 40 cm

of flesh ends and object begins? Think about the violinist or pianist, their whole being is wrapped up with a particular kind of object. What is distinct about the being of the human as distinct from the being of the object?

H: That is one of the questions. By using objects we are projecting onto the object what is different about this object. A lot goes back to drawing. The pencil becomes an extension, a tool [for being]. You don't learn by looking at it, you learn by using it as an extension of yourself.

G: So, it's through getting to know objects and what they allow you to do that you come to know what your inside is in any moment, not as a fixed thing …

H: You don't find a conclusion, it's continuous.

G: What's fascinating about this is that you never know what journey any materials might aid you in, so it's not as if the inside preexists and you're looking to project it out it, it is a coemerging …

H: Yes, definitely, that describes it.

G: Have you read much Heidegger?

H: I came across it through an interest in how we use tools. I was interested in collecting and using hand-held tools.

G: Can you remember what Heidegger you read?

H: It was to do with learning, I think how children learn through doing things, the tactility of things, doing something with your hands rather than just looking at it.

G: Or at least both.

H: Yes, it has to be both, not one or the other. When I was working with stones I covered them all with felt. In response to their tactility someone told me about this German word, the way I translated it in my head is 'hand-ability' – it sits in your hand, is comfortable in the hand, is the right size for the hand. The idea of it links with Heidegger, the tool has to be hand size.

G: So, there is a commensurability between the form of the body and the form of the object.

H: I find that very interesting – that these objects I work with are all human size. They all fit-in-your-hand or they are a car that you fit in, there is this compatibility and the same particularity with tools – they have to be body compatible and become extensions of the body to be useful objects.

G: Because of the sheer fascination with the range of materials available in the world, does it lead you to reflect on what kind of material flesh is? There tends to be an assumption that material is the stuff of the world and we are something other than material because we are not objects we are subjects, but actually flesh is a kind of material as well, do you think of it as a kind of material as well?

H: Yes and no, because like, drawing around my body, I think of my body as a physical thing that I could potentially work with and it could therefore potentially become an object in itself. I have drawn around Louis [Helen's six-month-old son] as well, so he temporarily became an object. But I don't think of the skin as being material to be manipulated like rubber or concrete. I am very interested in the tactility of the skin, I've read and thought about it because the sense of touch is so important, but I've never thought about using skin as the material as such.

G: And do you ever think of it as a living material? I have found it harder to think of the body, especially my own living body, as a form of material in the world.

H: It is almost like I think of the body, the entire body as a sculptural form, as a shape rather than a material.

G: But this is definitely material to you: concrete, latex?

H: It is really difficult, though, because these materials don't exist as tactile materials unless my skin is tactile material too. There has to be the contact between the two. In a way they are equivalent; if my skin wasn't tactile that contact wouldn't exist, so in a way, so skin has to be material as well.

G: It's just the living, the aliveness of the skin that is different. And when you speak about an object being an anthropomorphic being, what is the being sense of the object for you?

H: Objects for me take on personalities, they become almost like my children, they are creatures and the resulting work becomes an object that is a being, so it is projecting my own being onto them, making them something I can relate to. And a means of understanding or negotiating with the world.

G: It feels like an entering into a relation with, which is always an intimate process.

H: I definitely see the clothes casts that I am working on becoming creatures, they become a family.

G: Just coming back to the inside outside theme and the continuous space, I remember we spoke before about topology, had you come across that term, were you already thinking about that?

H: I had come across it somewhere. A book I was reading mentioned the topology of the skin (Connor 2003) and got me interested in that relation to the Möbius strip, that it's a continual thing. And the idea of the inside outside being a continuous space, this relates to the Klein bottle, where the inside and the outside of the bottle is a continuous space [surface] almost like a further development of the Möbius strip.

G: It is an easier-to-grasp example

H: A bodily version

G: Yes, you almost want one to play with one – to touch one.

H: I've tried to make one when I started working with clothes. The Klein bottle describes almost too perfectly what I am interested in, in the clothes as a continuous space inside and outside that relates to the body. I've tried to make one, it hasn't worked, but I'll maybe try again sometime. I've tried to make it by deconstructing a jacket, in fact I tried to make one from scratch as well, stitching and reconstructing it as a Klein bottle, but it didn't really work it just looked like a blob, you couldn't see the inside and outside. It worked as a process of investigation for me, but not as a final result.

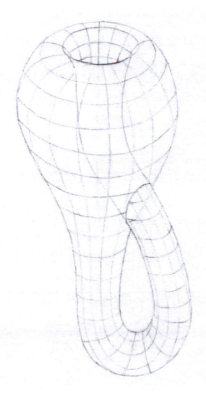

Figure 2.6   A Klein bottle © Helen Barff 2011

G: Can you give me an example of when the material sampling phase has really surprised you and taken you in a direction where just working with what the material allows you to do, limits you or has taken you in a surprising direction because you can't do what you want with it?

H: The felt stones would be one example because I never intended to cover stones in felt – I had all these collections of stones and I was also interested in felt because of working with the piano. I wanted to try making felt around something 3D and solid so, covering or encasing the entire thing in felt. I just picked up a stone because I had loads of them. I didn't know it was going to work or what was going to happen but they eventually became an entire, unexpected big piece of artwork.

G: When you are working with the material, asking: what is this material making possible, how did you arrive at latex as the right material for something?

H: I started collecting buoys and they are so rubbery, I was using felt, but this was not the right material so, I started using latex and other rubbery materials to cast these things.

G: And how did you arrive at latex, was it because it was compatible with the material of the buoy itself?

H: Yes, and also silicone, so different types of rubber, but latex is more versatile and stronger. You can coat it onto the object like a skin, building up layers. It picks up incredible detail.

G: What was the concrete like to use?

H: Concrete is another example where I had to learn what was possible with it. I filled a buoy with concrete and then peeled the buoy off, so casting the inside of the buoy. I didn't

Figure 2.7 Helen Barff: *Stones II*, 2004, stones and felt, various sizes

know that it would pick up the detail in the way it does, like plaster. I had used plaster before, but concrete works quite differently in that it takes a long time to set and needs a particular way of working. I also cast the inside of all those shoes – that was just trying to test the material – they are samples in a way. It was just trying to learn: what can I put this concrete in? So, I will fill loads of shoes to see what happens.

G: And were they found shoes?

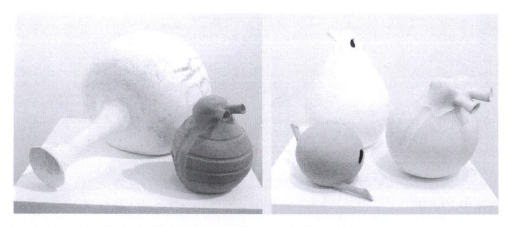

Figure 2.8 Helen Barff: *Inside Out Buoys*, 2009, coloured latex, various sizes

Figure 2.9   Helen Barff: *Upside-down Buoy (detail)*, 2008, ceiling height x 20 x 20 cm

H: Some were found shoes and some were charity shop. I started working with shoes in South Africa. I was on a residency there, I began thinking that I would find an old boat to work with, but couldn't find one because people didn't throw away boats. Second-hand boats had a higher value or there was the other end of the scale – million-pound boats, yachts. So I ended up using shoes almost like, they were small boats or vessels, but also because there were lots of shoes around for some reason. The place I was staying in Cape Town had loads of old discarded shoes lying around.

I guess with all sculptural material I don't know what is going to happen with it, it is a learning thing. I started off drawing and all these processes come from my relation to drawing. Or rather my particular frustration with it – if I am drawing that bottle, the paper I am drawing on is here and the bottle over there. I'm always doing this: I am looking at that [the bottle] and then looking at this [the paper], there's always a gap between the two, I call it a blind gap. In this gap, I am retaining the information, what the bottle looks like and putting it onto paper. Working in direct contact with sculptural materials is trying to close that gap so that the bottle then comes into contact with the paper.

G: A bit like your photographic work where you started putting the objects directly onto the silver paper to close that gap?

H: Yes, that was the stage between drawing and more and more sculptural work, closing the gap by placing the object directly onto the photographic paper. Then that was still not enough because I wanted to wrap the entire object so that every surface of a 3D object was covered. There is a surprise or new discovery at every stage.

G: So you are always looking for the wrapping potential of materials and their tracing potentials?

Figure 2.10   Helen Barff: *Things from the Thames,* Photogram, 2005, 30 x 30 cm

Figure 2.11   Helen Barff: *Styloid*, 2010, plaster, 20 x 10 x 10 cm

H: Yes, I guess materials that can be used in direct contact with particular objects. It's good to discover a new material, it still almost seems magic.

G: Your work at the moment, what are you working on?

H: I am still casting the inside of clothes. I am starting to focus it more so that it is not so general, for a solo show. Maybe just certain clothes – shirts, pockets and bras.

G: The concrete ones?

H: Yes, the idea is that some will hang on the wall rather than sit on the floor.

The idea behind these was related to the skin. I've talked about the inside–outside space of the clothes.

G: In trying to experiment with the inside–outside space of the clothes and the body-liness, is there something about the relationship between the skin and the clothes?

H: Oh yes, also casting the inside space of things you don't see, it's revealing the hidden space. It's that and trying to cast the space or the contact that you have between your clothes and your body. All the time I guess I'm trying to turn the edges inside out.

G: Just like the clothes that you are wearing edge you, they edge you, they give you an edge by being on you?

H: Yes, and by turning them inside-out I'm attempting to reveal those edges. That direct contact is important again, and that my choice of materials is one that picks up the edges as closely as possible. I started using plaster because I knew it would entirely fill every space inside the clothes. Also because I was thinking about them kind of growing out of the floor or the wall so I wanted them to be an architectural material so, they relate to the space of the room, which is a new kind of thing for me.

G: Thinking about the materiality of the space they are going to appear in?

H: Yes, because I was thinking about buildings having an inside and outside too. That is what is emerging at the moment. The working title for the exhibition is *Flock*. I wanted a descriptive word to describe them, they are anthropomorphic and like a group of beings so, at the moment it is called *Flock* but that might change.

Note

1 Helen Barff is an artist living and working in London. She graduated from Goldsmiths College in Fine Art and Art History BA (hons) in 1999 and completed an MA in Drawing at Camberwell College of Art in 2004. Since then she has exhibited in various locations in the UK and internationally.

Bibliography

Connor, S. (2003) *The Book of Skin*. London: Reaktion Books.

3

A poor workman blames his tools or how irrigation systems structure human actions

Maurits W. Ertsen

Introduction

In the Phoenix region of Arizona in the USA, extensive remains of irrigation networks can be found. Water from the Salt and Gila Rivers enabled farming of dry land in the desert area. The irrigation systems were created by the Hohokam civilization and were in operation between 700 and 1450 AD. Typically, different villages can be associated with different canal systems, suggesting that individual villages were at least partially economically and politically independent of each other. However, Hohokam canals also link multiple settlements, which must have meant that villages were or became dependent on each other when irrigation developed.

How these systems may have functioned is still under study (for example, Abbott 2003; Howard 2006; Howard 1993; Nelson *et al.* 2010; Peeples *et al.* 2006; Woodson 2010). Conflicts between villages and users may have arisen, but because the systems were in operation for such a long time, cooperation is more likely to have been the norm. Discussions on volume, availability and scheduling of water and canal control must have been frequent, but somehow arrangements must have been produced to run the irrigation systems. There are only limited material remains of canals, structures and settlements, which means that it is not possible to uncover all the arrangements in full detail. However, because the material properties of irrigation systems do matter at all times, as I argue in this chapter, it should be possible to reconstruct Hohokam irrigation reality in considerable detail.

The Hohokam are not the only ancient civilization that used irrigation as an important means to sustain their society. Because irrigation is related to the development of the earliest larger-scale human civilizations, its relation to human society has been well studied (Marcus and Stanish 2006; Scarborough 2003; Scarborough and Isaac 1993). The best-known debate relates to the formation of ancient civilizations. Although he was certainly not the first to stress the importance of irrigation and water control in societal development, Wittfogel was the first to develop a general theory about this. A crucial argument of Wittfogel (1957; see also Worster 1985) is that large-scale irrigation requires mass labour, which must be coordinated and disciplined, subordinated to a directing authority. Small-scale irrigation farming also involves a high intensity of cultivation on irrigated fields, but Wittfogel preserves central control for situations in which large quantities of water have to be manipulated. Many ancient systems are located in arid plains with a single, large river running through them. Within such an agricultural landscape, water is the natural variable par excellence, but one basic assumption of Wittfogel's is that larger-scale irrigation development (such as that of the Hohokam) required use (and control) of mass labour.

Until today, many scholars studying the development of large irrigation works have assumed, in the spirit of Wittfogel, that these were always constructed in one phase, requiring a strong institution (a central state) to supervise and organize such massive work. However, it is likely that larger systems are the result of many smaller-scale actions over a longer period. The result of a series of smaller actions through a longer time frame might be that the need for strong central authority would be less automatic. Therefore, when considering irrigation, 'large-scale' does not necessarily mean 'strong central authority' (Hunt and Hunt 1976; Hunt 1988).

Irrigation systems are generally regarded as important means to control natural environments. They are also generally conceptualized as passive artefacts. However, the physical shape of irrigation systems constrains and enables human actions. Human actions and the properties of moving water together create spatial and temporal patterns of water flows, which in turn provoke new actions at individual or collective level. Human actions (e.g., cooperating and conflicting over manipulation of irrigation gates, sharing of water) shape reality, but the ways in which the system passes water flows through the irrigation infrastructure (the hydraulics of the system) constrain the set of possible actions.

Irrigation as agricultural practice is as much about manipulating water flows in short periods of hours and days as it is about balancing water volumes over periods of months or even seasons. People fight over water today, which hampers cooperation tomorrow or next year. It should not be a surprise that (given that in human society control of knowledge, possessions and power is typically skewed) the outcome of this water competition is socially stratified. In many irrigation systems, water is unevenly distributed. Water management roles are actually power roles, which are directly linked to control of production. In irrigation, social relationships are shaped and changed when agents struggle with and upon artefacts (Van der Zaag 1992). Power is not something hidden, negative or obscure; it is expressed daily in the capacity to achieve outcomes successfully through enrolment of resources (Giddens 1984). Results of such short-term actions build up over time, affecting complete societies on larger temporal and spatial scales. In other words, irrigation systems are both outcome of and medium for human actions.

In this chapter, I do not provide an answer to the question of how the Hohokam irrigation systems functioned (what decisions were made and what patterns of water use were created) but I discuss three case studies of irrigation systems in Latin America (two modern and one ancient) to show what types of issues need to be understood to make sense of the Hohokam irrigation systems. In doing so, I discuss the intricate relations between humans and irrigation infrastructure. I have discussed these case studies in earlier published works (Ertsen 2010a,b; Ertsen and Van der Spek 2009; Ertsen and Van Nooijen 2009), but this chapter allows me to integrate them within one text to show how relations between water users within the systems differ, despite the similar hydraulic properties of the irrigation infrastructure.

Arequipa, Peru

The city of Arequipa is the capital of the province with the same name in south Peru. The irrigation system in Arequipa is managed by three organizations: the *Administración Técnica del Distrito Riego* (ATDR), the *Junta de Usuarios*, and several *Comisiones de Regantas*. The irrigation system in Arequipa is under the jurisdiction of the Chili department of the ATDR, a governmental organization. The ATDR regulates the daily discharge of the river Chili in consultation with other stakeholders, and is concerned with conflict management within the irrigation system. The area supervised by the ATDR is divided into two districts each managed by a *Junta de Usuarios* (*Chili zona Regulado* and *Chili zona no Regulado*). The district *Chili zona Regulado* is divided into fifteen *Comisiones de Regantas*. A *Comisión* consists of farmers from the region and external employees. The main tasks of a *Comisión* are water allocation and maintenance of canals at secondary and tertiary level. Furthermore the *Comisión* is concerned with conflict management within the tertiary block. *Comisiones de Regantas* have two water guards to check all water structures within the area. Technical problems are directly transferred to the *Junta de Usuarios*.

I discuss three *Comisiones de Regantas* in more detail: Acequia Alta Cayma, Zamácola and Alto Cural. The three *Comisiones* cover approximately 2600 hectares (ha), which represents 35 per cent of the total irrigated areas in the district *Chili zona Regulado*. With approximately 2100 water users, the average plot size in the area is about 1.2 ha. However, differences between *Comisiones* are considerable. Average field size in Alta Cayma is about 0.5 ha, whereas Zamácola and Alto Cural have average areas of 2.2 and 2.3 ha, respectively. The *Comisiones* receive their irrigation water from the river Chili through a shared main canal. This Canal Madre Zamácola starts at the river Chili, then runs along Acequia Alta Cayma, through Zamácola and ends up at the head of Alto Cural. The average discharge at the inlet of Canal Madre Zamácola is approximately 4.2 cubic metres per second (m³/s). Between Acequia Alta Cayma and Zamácola an off-take is located, which retrieves 1.5 m³/s for the preparation of domestic water. This leaves approximately 2.7 m³/s for irrigation, which is about 1 litre per second (l/s) per hectare.

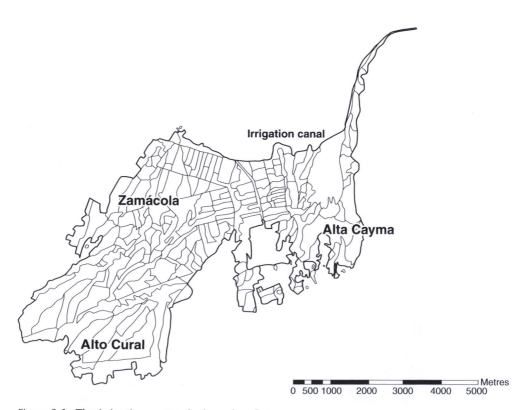

Figure 3.1 The irrigation system in Arequipa, Peru

Table 3.1 Properties of the different *Comisiones de Regantes*

	Average field size	Actual discharges
Alta Cayma	0.5 ha	1.2 litres per second per ha
Zamácola	2.2 ha	1.2 litres per second per ha
Alto Cural	2.3 ha	0.6 litres per second per ha

However, when looking at actual discharges, Acequia Alta Cayma and Zamácola receive two times more water per hectare than downstream Alto Cural: about 1.2 l/s per hectare compared with 0.6 l/s per hectare. The water availability of Acequia Alta Cayma is relatively stable, because it is not influenced by actions of fellow water users. Furthermore, discharges through its two orifices used as intakes are less influenced by changing conditions upstream compared with Zamácola and Alto Cural. If needed, Acequia Alta Cayma users can change the discharges in their secondary canals: when conditions change, water users can manipulate the orifices to their benefit. In Zamácola, proportional water division structures divide the discharge upstream of the structure proportionally to the secondary canals. This means that any increase or decrease in the flows in Canal Madre will be noticed in the secondary canals immediately, because the proportional structures cannot be adjusted (at least not in a legal way). Orifices bring water from secondary canals to field canals, through intermittent flow according to a rotation scheme. Zamácola's water availability is influenced by the actions of water users in Acequia Alta Cayma, but even when Acequia Alta Cayma consumes as much water as possible regarding its canal capacities, enough water remains for Zamácola to irrigate. In contrast, the downstream area Alto Cural totally depends on the actions of Acequia Alta Cayma and Zamácola. Because of the low hydraulic flexibility of the subirrigation system, the water availability of Alto Cural is uncertain.

As can be expected, economic benefits are not equally spread either. Although Acequia Alta Cayma has the benefit of ample water supply, its small plot sizes make profitable agricultural practices less possible. The small plot sizes are probably caused by a long history of inheritance. Because Alta Cayma is by far the oldest system, probably predating the Spanish conquest, this fragmentation process would have been long. Because of a low profitability from their small plots, most farmers in Alta Cayma perform other activities, and do not give top priority to their agricultural practices. Furthermore, land use in Acequia Alta Cayma is changing rapidly. Plots are sold for urbanization. In Zamácola, farmers are generally satisfied with the water availability and the way it is allocated, although sometimes they encounter water shortages, especially from August to October. Some farmers in Zamácola have constructed their own farm reservoirs to deal with unpredictable water availability. Apparently, there is enough water available on average to construct these devices. Because the reservoirs are paid for by the farmers, it indicates that farmers have enough resources to install them. The main problem in the downstream area Alto Cural is the lack of irrigation water. The current configuration of the irrigation infrastructure, both in terms of hydraulic behaviour of the canals and in terms of the downstream position, results in water supply being inadequate to meet the water needs of Alto Cural. In Alto Cural, the lack of irrigation water may translate into farmers not willing to organize, because there is nothing to organize for, even though they have on average the largest plots and youngest irrigation system.

Thus, although the three *Comisiones de Regantas* operate in the same legal context and share the same main canal, the way the *Comisiones* and their water users are organized varies considerably. There appears to be a relation between the way irrigation is managed and the position of a *Comisión* along the canal. The upstream farmers in Alta Cayma have the greatest and most reliable

43

water supply, but also experience a disincentive to farm because their fields are relatively small and the value of land for urbanization outweighs the potential gains from farming. In Alta Cayma, profitability is low and farmers appear to be unwilling to participate in irrigation organization. Acequia Alta Cayma has a surplus of irrigation water at all times anyway, which may not give an incentive for collective organization (Uphoff *et al.* 1990). For farmers in downstream Alto Cural, low agricultural profitability is due to the lack of irrigation water. Their fields are the largest within the canal area and, therefore, have the potentially highest gain from farming, but they have the least and most unreliable water supply. As argued by Levine (1980) and Keller (1986), such water scarcity may lead to unwillingness to participate. In Zamácola, which is between the upstream and the downstream, profitability is relatively high and farmers participate in projects initiated by the *Comisión de Regantas*. Water availability of Zamácola is sufficient on average, which means that the available volume for a season is ensured, but when water is actually delivered through the canal is unpredictable in time. The total volume is more or less secure, but the actual daily flows are less predictable, which may lead to a niche for an effect of organization regarding water distribution (Uphoff *et al.* 1990). As a response, farmers have invested in farm reservoirs, which store the volume and make farmers less dependent on short-term flows.

Santiago del Estero, Argentina

The province of Santiago del Estero, Argentina, is located in the western border of the Gran Chaco. Annual precipitation (mainly summer rains between November and April) ranges from 500 mm to 850 mm. Although small compared with Argentina's major river the Río Parana, the two rivers in the region are the sources for life in Santiago del Estero, because they allowed development of agricultural and pastoral activities. The Río Salado has succeeded in reaching the Río Parana and thus the sea, but our focus in this chapter is on the other river, the Río Dulce, which flows into the salt-lake La Mar Chiquita. From the Dulce River, the irrigation area known as the *Proyecto Río Dulce* (PRD) currently includes an irrigable area of 122,000 ha in a command area of 350,000 ha. Irrigation in the region has a long history. In 1577, the Spanish built their first canal in Santiago del Estero. In 1583, this had a length of 5 km. In 1680, an irrigation register was established (Michaud 1942). Before 1968, the irrigation infrastructure provided two or three irrigation turns for each farmer in late spring and summer, when water levels in the Río Dulce were sufficiently high. The building of a reservoir in 1968, the Embalse de Río Hondo, has shaped the potential for irrigation all year round. The Río Dulce region shows an extreme subdivision of farm sizes, with a dominance of smaller farms. The mean farm (*finca*) in the PRD has an area of 10 ha, usually consisting of several smaller plots (*lotes*), which do not necessarily have to be in the same place. The larger farms in the PRD area are located at the tails of the irrigation canals, and partly outside the irrigated area.

Water from the Río Dulce is diverted in the irrigation system through the main canal La Matriz, which brings water to several secondary canals, including Canal San Martin, the focus in these paragraphs. The modern Canal San Martin is the main canal on the right bank of the Río Dulce, serving an irrigated area of about 19,000 ha. Water is diverted to the canal from the main canal Matriz through a siphon under the river. The official capacity of the canal is about 10 m^3/s; in practice, 5 to 6 m^3/s is diverted into the canal. The total canal grid in the area amounts to some 152 km. Canal San Martin is lined for the first 38 km; its length is a little over 60 km. In the original design, off-takes are equipped with structures suggesting demand management, but Canal San Martin does not have the storage capacity usually associated with such management. The lined part of the canal includes three sliding gates, which are used as cross-regulators. Each regulator has an emergency overflow side-weir directly upstream. In daily practice, demand management is not practised. Off-takes are managed through a simple open or closed routine, in line with the general water distribution arrangement, in which farmers are allowed to irrigate once a month.

The hydraulic layout appears to be a potentially large disadvantage for downstream users. Manipulation of cross-regulators could easily result in lower discharges downstream, especially because overflows caused by such manipulations would be spilled out of the canal and thus no longer be available for downstream uses. Maintenance of the canal is important. Officially, the entire PRD system is closed for one month per year to clean and repair canals, usually in May. The San Martin area is a particular case in terms of maintenance. The canal side slopes are lined with concrete slabs, but the canal bed is lined with stones. Water plants can easily grow on the canal bed, which they do abundantly. To remove the plants Canal San Martin is emptied several times during the irrigation season. The fierce summer sun kills the water plants, which are flushed away the next time the canal is operated. If not properly maintained, increased canal roughness will result in higher water levels, causing the spillways to discharge more, resulting in less water available downstream. Canal maintenance in the upstream canal sections is thus vital for downstream farmers to secure water delivery to their farms. Another way to influence the downstream flow is to manipulate the cross-regulators. When the sliding gates of the cross-regulators are lowered, downstream discharges obviously decrease too.

However, in practice, the downstream farmers in the San Martin area irrigate more than their upstream colleagues. Upstream farmers irrigate on average three to four times per year, whereas farmers downstream take water during six to eight turns. They sometimes irrigate a larger area than officially allowed (Prieto 2006). Downstream farmers are clearly able to arrange irrigation matters in their favour, despite their potentially disadvantaged position in the tail of a canal with a hydraulic behaviour favouring upstream users. Nevertheless, downstream irrigators have managed to increase their control over irrigation water flows. The downstream farmers in San Martin are large farmers, with farm sizes up to thousands of hectares, and much political influence. The ability and the need of these farmers to arrange matters in their favour is shown by what happened in 1991, when it became clear that budget problems by federal and provincial authority government threatened regular irrigation management. In this uncertain situation, the *Asociación de Productores Agropecuarios Zona IV*, the new farmer organization in the San Martin area, was established to secure water distribution within the canal area. The *Asociación* was controlled by the large farmers. Through investing their labour and money, larger farmers appropriated the San Martin canal, when in their view the scheme management was unable to guarantee water delivery and maintenance.

This increase in control is not something that can be taken for granted. The hydraulic reality of the irrigation system requires continuous efforts from downstream irrigators to maintain, let alone increase, their control. As we have seen in the Arequipa case, farmers in downstream Alto Cural were unable to do so. In the San Martin reality, the hierarchy predicted by gravity was countered by social structures, with powerful downstream farmers succeeding in exercising power over the canal to ensure sufficient water. The key to explaining the difference between San Martin and Alto Cural is economic and social power of farmers, expressed in political influence and farm size.

Pampa de Chapparí, Peru

Despite its arid environment, ancient civilizations have prospered on the Peruvian coast. The rivers flowing from the Andean mountains to the west provide the fertile coastal valleys with irrigation water. The valleys are oases, and exploitation of their agricultural potential depends on irrigation, although some small, highly productive areas do not require irrigation (Kosok 1965; Netherly 1984). Irrigation canals diverted (part of) the water available in the rivers. Some canals had two intakes, with one being used when the water level in the river was low; the river water level was probably raised to divert water into the canal by means of stone and brush weirs (Netherly 1984). These weirs were built in the river to guide part of the river flow into the canal. Such diversion systems are still being applied in Peru and many other regions worldwide. They are relatively cheap in terms of money and (usually) labour, although they need regular replacement, because they may be washed away during floods. Peruvian conveyance canals could be long and often required aqueducts to pass small side valleys. Sometimes canals were cut into rock in order to maintain the gradient. Canals were frequently stone-lined; others became lined with the clay sediments in the irrigation water settling in the canal (Kosok 1965; Netherly 1984).

The Pampa de Chaparrí, located on the north coast of Peru close to the city of Chiclayo, received its water from the Río Chancay. The irrigation system of the Pampa de Chaparrí was used between 900 and 1532 AD by the Sicán, Chimú and Inca civilizations (Hayashida 2006). In the sixteenth century, the system was abandoned. Apart from the Pampa de Chaparrí, two other areas downstream were irrigated from the Río Chancay. Furthermore, water from the Río Chancay was diverted to the Río La Leche through the Pampa de Chaparrí main canal and the Río Sanjon. It is not unlikely that this diversion to the Río La Leche carried water only when water availability in the Río Chancay was high and excess water was not used in the Pampa de Chaparrí. Téllez and Hayashida (2004) discuss how canals and walled fields on the Pampa may have been constructed with organized labour replacing taxes. Water on the Pampa was distributed through the Racarumi canal system. The Racarumi I canal is the main canal conveying water from the river through an intake about 10 km to the east of Chongoyape. No fields have been found along this canal before it reaches the Pampa. From the main canal, three distribution canals diverted water to some 3300 ha (Hayashida 2006).

Inflows into the canal system of the Pampa de Chaparrí were highly dependent on water levels in the Río Chancay. Given the strong fluctuations within months, water levels in the canal may have fluctuated considerably within shorter time frames. This difference in water level could have been considerable, and would have strong implications for flow distribution within the system. As water storage at system level seems to be absent, buffering water demand and water availability would have been impossible. How ancient Peruvian irrigation systems like the Pampa de Chaparrí were managed is unclear, but permanent gates or diversions have not been found in ancient irrigation canals on the north coast. Distribution structures were probably temporary and constructed of earth, stones, sticks and brush. After building a temporary barrier, cutting a breach in the canal bank upstream of the barrier would be sufficient to irrigate fields. Permanent distribution sluices were introduced by the Spanish colonizers (Netherly 1984).

There is some evidence available through aerial photographs of the Pampa de Chaparrí indicating three areas with properties that can be attributed to their respective position within the irrigation system. Each area is characterized by differences in layout of fields and canals and is associated with different management practices (Hayashida 2006). Hydraulic modelling results suggest that water availability associated with the hydraulic behaviour of the canal system is strongly linked to these different layouts. Upstream in the canal system, a 900-ha area shows a highly regular canal system. It could be either a single, large plot or a series of identical plots in strips. As discussed by Netherly (1984), such upstream fields may have received most water and thus been able to produce two crops a year. With water available, it would have been possible to invest in canal infrastructure. In the upstream area, centralized management, perhaps state production, may have been the case. In contrast, the area most downstream on the Pampa would not have received water from the canal system. This area has an appearance of a patchwork of varied plots and some minor canals (Hayashida 2006). However, the presence of fields does suggest that agriculture was practised in this area, which would have been unlikely if crops only depended on rain, which is basically zero. Layouts of fields and canals suggest that canal water was less important, which is reason to assume that groundwater may have been used as a source in this area, in line with the different types of irrigated fields given by Netherly (1984). Groundwater in the downstream of the Pampa may even have been fed by excess irrigation in the upstream area. These lower areas may have been managed by farmers for their own support. In the area between these clear upstream and downstream areas, layouts of canals and fields are variable in shape, but still regular. In line with the reasoning above (and the Arequipa case), this may indicate a reasonably predictable water supply. This case shows that a downstream location in an irrigation system need not necessarily equate to insufficient water availability or less reliable flows of water for farmers, although the water may not become available through the canal system itself. In a way, downstream farmers may have benefited from high water use by upstream farmers, because this may have fed the groundwater flows that the downstream depended upon.

Discussion

Although I have only discussed a few selected case studies, it is clear that there are many different ways in which irrigation networks can take shape and that social implications of and interventions in the structure of irrigation systems may vary from case to case. Just think of the terraced rice fields from Asia, the large-scale irrigated plains of the western USA or the small irrigated gardens in several west African countries to realize that the typical irrigation system does not exist. It is therefore not possible (at least not within this chapter) to assume which irrigation network model would be suited to explain the Hohokam canal systems. Nevertheless, in all irrigation systems similar issues need to be solved, all involving social and material arrangements in time and space. Any irrigation system needs a source for its water. Many irrigation systems divert their water directly from rivers, although diversion from natural and artificial lakes occurs too. To divert water from a river, some kind of intake structure is needed. From the intake structure, one or more canals bring the water into the irrigation area. Often, division structures are used to manage water flows from one canal into another. In such a way, an irrigated area has a certain hierarchy of canals, with larger canals bringing water to diversion structures, with smaller canals branching off from this structure to bring water to designated areas. Water arriving at fields is somehow spread over the fields. There are several ways to do this, including applying furrows or small basins. Drainage often includes existing streams, with small drains collecting water from fields flowing to larger drains flowing back to the river and/or out of the irrigated area. As we have seen from the Pampa case, excess drainage water can be used by irrigators downstream.

Whatever the exact result, irrigation links water, humans and infrastructure in producing a water transformation process. In canal irrigation, fields downstream along a canal are potentially at the mercy of the area upstream. If people upstream decide to close the tap, people downstream have serious problems. The Arequipa case is a clear example of a hierarchical irrigation system, with downstream users being in a less favourable position in terms of water availability. The Arequipa irrigation canals and other objects are the material and spatial reality within which social interaction shapes spatial patterns of water flows and related actions through time. At the same time, social interactions intervene in the material and spatial reality. The Argentinean case does show that even in canal systems with a clear higher vulnerability of downstream users, these same users can exercise strong control over the canal, because of their economic power. The Pampa situation suggests that within a clear upstream–downstream pattern in terms of water control and availability within the canal system, downstream users may still be able to profit from the capacity of the irrigation system to redistribute water within the natural environment (compare with Carlstein 1982).

Ultimately, water availability in a canal system is the result of hydraulic properties and human actions together. Water distribution, canal management and hydraulic properties are complex issues, and conclusions are not as straightforward as it seems in terms of upstream or downstream relations, but it is clear that canal irrigation is potentially hierarchical in nature (Ertsen and Van Nooijen 2009; Lansing *et al.* 2009). How this hierarchy worked out in the case of Hohokam needs to be studied further, but the Hohokam social production of irrigated space-time (as in any irrigation society) will not have been 'a smooth and automatic process in which social structure is stamped out, without resistance or constraint, onto the landscape. [...] Spatiality must be socially reproduced, and this reproduction process presents a continuing source of struggle, conflict and contradiction' (Soja 1985: 97). Even though gravity irrigation systems do enforce upstream–downstream dependencies, the outcome (whether the upstream or the downstream 'wins') is the result of social struggle and/or negotiations. The production of irrigated space-time is both the medium and the outcome of social actions and relationships (Soja 1985: 94); hydraulic infrastructure in irrigation systems can be conceptualized as structures in the way Giddens and Sewell define them: structures are medium and outcome of social practices through everyday actions, in which routines are an important phenomenon (see Giddens 1984; Sewell 2005).

Bibliography

Abbott, D. (2003) *Centuries of decline during the Hohokam Classic Period at Pueblo Grande*, Tucson: University of Arizona Press.

Carlstein, T. (1982) *Time resources, society and ecology. On the capacity for human interaction in space and time, Volume 1: pre-industrial societies*, London: Allen and Unwin.

Ertsen, M. W. (2010a) 'Structuring properties of irrigation systems. Understanding relations between humans and hydraulics through modeling', *Water History*, 2: 165–183.

Ertsen, M. W. (2010b) 'An irrigated landscape in Argentina', *Landscape Archaeology and Ecology*, 8: 47–56.

Ertsen, M. W. and Van der Spek, J. (2009) 'Modeling an irrigation ditch opens up the world. Hydrology and hydraulics of an ancient irrigation system in Peru', *Physics and Chemistry of the Earth*, 34: 176–191.

Ertsen, M. W. and Van Nooijen, R. (2009) 'The man swimming against the stream knows the strength of it. Hydraulics and social relations in an Argentinean irrigation system', *Physics and Chemistry of the Earth*, 34: 2000–2008.

Giddens, A. (1984) *The constitution of society: outline of the theory of structuration*, Cambridge: Polity Press.

Hayashida, F.M. (2006) 'The Pampa de Chaparrí: water, land, and politics on the north coast of Peru', *Latin American Antiquity*, 13: 243–263.

Howard, J.B. (1993) 'A paleohydraulic approach to examining agricultural intensification in Hohokam irrigation systems', in: Scarborough, V. L. and Isaac, B. (eds) *Economic aspects of water management in the prehispanic New World*, Santa Fe, NM: SAR Press.

Howard, J.B. (2006) 'Hohokam irrigation communities: a study of internal structure, external relationships and sociopolitical complexity', unpublished thesis, Arizona State University.

Hunt, R. (1988) 'Size and the structure of authority in canal irrigation systems', *Journal of Anthropological Research*, 44: 335–355.

Hunt, R.C. and Hunt, E. (1976) 'Canal irrigation and local social organization', *Current Anthropology*, 17: 389–411.

Keller, J. (1986) 'Irrigation system management', in: Nobe, K.C. and Sampath, R.K. (eds) *Irrigation in development countries*, Boulder, CO: Westview Press.

Kosok, P. (1965) *Life, land, and water in ancient Peru*, New York: Long Island University Press.

Lansing, J.S., Cox, M.P., Downey, S.S., Janssen, M.A. and Schoenfelder, J.W. (2009) 'A robust budding model of Balinese water temple networks', *World Archaeology*, 41: 112–133.

Levine, G. (1980) 'The relationship of design, operation and management', in: Coward, E.W. (ed) *Irrigation and agricultural development in Asia: Perspectives from the social sciences*, Ithaca, NY: Cornell University Press.

Marcus, J. and Stanish, C. (eds.) (2006) *Agricultural Strategies*, Los Angeles, CA: Cotsen Institute of Archaeology.

Michaud, C. (1942) *Regadios en Santiago del Estero y en particular en la zona del Río Dulce*, Santiago del Estero: Gobierno de Santiago del Estero.

Nelson, M.C., Kintigh, K., Abbott, D.R. and Anderies, J.M. (2010) 'The cross-scale interplay between social and biophysical context and the vulnerability of irrigation-dependent societies: archaeology's long-term perspective', *Ecology and Society*, 3: 31.

Netherly, P.J. (1984) 'The management of late Andean irrigation systems on the north coast of Peru', *American Antiquity*, 49: 227–254.

Peeples, M.A., Barton, C.M. and Schmich, S. (2006) 'Resilience lost: intersecting land use and landscape dynamics in the prehistoric southwestern United States', *Ecology and Society*, 2: 22.

Prieto, D. (2006) 'Modernization and the evolution of irrigation practices in the Río Dulce Irrigation Project', unpublished thesis, Wageningen University.

Scarborough, V.L. (2003) *The flow of power. Ancient water systems and landscape*, Santa Fe, NM: SAR Press.

Scarborough, V.L. and Isaac, B. (eds) (1993) *Economic aspects of water management in the prehispanic New World*, Greenwich: Research in Economic Anthropology.

Sewell, W.H. (2005) *Logics of history. Social theory and social transformation*, Chicago, IL: Chicago Studies in Practices of Meaning.

Soja, E. (1985) 'The spatiality of social life: towards a transformative retheorisation', in: Gregory, D. and Urry, J. (eds) *Social relations and spatial structures*, London: Macmillan.

Téllez, S. and Hayashida, F. (2004) Campos de Cultivo Prehispánicos en la Pampa de Chaparrí, *Boletín de Arqueología PUCP*, 8: 373–390.

Uphoff, N., Wickramasinghe, M.I. and Wijayaratna, C.M. (1990) '"Optimum" participation in irrigation management: issues and evidence from Sri Lanka', *Human Organization*, 49: 26–40.

Van der Zaag, P. (1992) 'The material dimension of social practice in water management. Factors influencing the operational flexibility of three farmer-managed irrigation systems in Mexico', in: Diemer, G. and Huibers, F. (eds) *Irrigators and engineers*, Amsterdam: Thesis Publishers.

Wittfogel, K. (1957) *Oriental despotism. A comparative study of total power*, New Haven, CT: Yale University Press.

Woodson, M.K. (2010) 'The social organization of Hohokam irrigation in the Middle Gila River Valley, Arizona', unpublished thesis, Arizona State University.

Worster, D. (1985) *Rivers of empire: Water, aridity, and the growth of the American West*, Oxford and New York: Oxford University Press.

4

The material construction of state power

Artifacts and the new Rome

Chandra Mukerji

Although social analysts readily agree that material relations are important to the development of states, few routinely entertain the idea that artifacts themselves have a significant role in shaping political regimes. The effectiveness of top-down material management by states is explicitly denied by Scott (1998), and questioned by many contemporary archeologists (Tilley *et al.* 2006). But as I show here, objects and material practices can indeed have subtle and enduring political importance for states (Watenpaugh 2004, Feldman 2010). The question is how. To consider this problem, I analyze the material association of France with Rome, and how it was used for political effect during state formation under Louis XIV. In seventeenth-century France, the state was not yet a powerful institution and was struggling for authority against the clergy and nobility, who dominated French politics. State policies of material change were a means of side-stepping patrimonial politics, using evocations of Rome's worldly power to justify new state activism.

By legend, the 'Sun King' consolidated power around his person in the late seventeenth century, claiming *l'état c'est moi*, but in fact, the movement of power into the administration could not simply be an act of royal will. It entailed a change of political imagination and practice that was achieved by drawing material associations between France and Rome (Apostolidès 1981, Marin 1981). Rome was an ideal of military empire attractive to Louis XIV, but less obviously and more importantly, the empire provided examples of material practices to control the flow of power. The French state studied and copied these techniques of governance, using legal documents to reduce noble autonomy in matters of law, establishing academies to produce art in imitation of Rome, and initiating projects of infrastructural engineering like those of the ancient empire. Through these practices of material mimesis, the administration under Louis XIV made France culturally more Roman, gave the government new powers, and reoriented French politics around the pursuit of empire in the name of Rome.

Importantly, the state was able to create material links between France and Ancient Rome by employing non-nobles with antiquarian expertise or tacit knowledge of material practices. These agents of the state were generally men without the social rank to serve as noble officers of the crown (Mukerji 2011). As they took positions in or contracts with the administration, many entered the government as Weberian (Weber *et al.* 1978) servants of standing, performing circumscribed duties and exercising an impersonal authority at odds with the personal power of noble office holders. The state provided not only income but new sources of dignity for people of talent. The academies recruited notable artisans as artists; the royal library honored the skills of antiquarian collectors; and infrastructural projects made heroes of financiers and engineers. State power, in turn, was increased by organizing these experts to orchestrate politically transforming Roman revival.

In the patrimonial system up to this time, the French king was traditionally a weak ruler; the Church and nobility had enormous authority and independence from the crown. The king had no obvious means to control them, leaving him dependent on their largesse (Machiavelli and Donno 1966). But the monarch had rights over his kingdom as territory, which gave him material powers that proved key to French state formation. The administration could engage in logistical activities, controlling the material world in ways that the clergy and nobility could not. Nobles (the most obvious political rivals of the king) depended for their social dignity and privileges on eschewing material activities like production and trade. In contrast, the state could legitimately create new manufactures, sponsor art, and make territorial improvements, and used this power to make France more like Rome (Mukerji 1994). The Church, on the other hand, often set up manufactures, made money, and created lavish displays of art, architecture, and treasure, but it could not match the military and territorial reach of the king. That is why the French state had distinct logistical powers with which to transform the material world and reorient French politics around classical revival (Mukerji 1997, 2009a, 2010).

Logistical power, as I use the term (Mukerji 2010), should be distinguished from the exercise of power through social relations of domination or control of legitimate violence in the Weberian tradition (Weber *et al.* 1978). Logistical power works through the material order, creating the cultural context of collective life that gives social practices meaning and animates political logics. Because logistical power is normally wielded by those who already have strategic power, logistical activity usually seems an outgrowth of social relations of power. But dominating people for political effect or using the material world for political advantage are fundamentally different modes of exercising power (Mukerji 2010).

Logistics started to become important to politics in the early modern period in England, the Netherlands, and Venice as well as France. This was partly because timber supplies started to dwindle as ship-building for trade and war became key to power, and land became more important as engineers developed new methods of creating communication infrastructure and building fortresses. Territorial management started to affect international competition among states, spurring governments to become interested in natural and technical expertise.

Appuhn (2009) has shown for the Venetian Republic that the perceived need for reliable sources of wood for ship-building, lagoon repair, and firewood impelled the Venetians to capture and manage forests on the mainland. This, in turn, spurred them to recruit into the administration experts in forest management and to create archives of forestry records to manage their trees. The result was a new bureaucracy of nascent technocrats inside the administration.

Jean-Baptiste Colbert, minister of the treasury and navy and superintendent of the king's households under Louis XIV, also turned to logistical power, focusing at first, like Venice, on French timber reserves. But Colbert soon used material management more broadly to redefine public administration itself. He revived Roman methods of governance, using infrastructure, art and legal archives to engage in politics outside patrimonial traditions (Mukerji 2010).

These activities seemed innocent enough as forms of cultural mimesis in a humanist age, but Colbert used these evocations of Rome to expand the purview and institutional efficacy of the state. He assembled legal documents explicitly to limit the power of the clergy and nobility; he commissioned new infrastructure to take control of French land from the nobility and to undermine the power of quasiautonomous trading cities; he also founded academies as a way to bypass the productive and pedagogical power of guilds. Using paper, precious metals, stone, paint, earth, and timber as tools of political change, Colbert replaced social relations of power with new methods of impersonal rule (Soll 2009, Gerbino 2010, Mukerji 2010). The state gained new authority not by investing power in the body of the king at all but quite the opposite: investing it in artifacts used in the name of Rome. *L'état c'est moi* became a legend of French royal authority because it fitted the king's political ambitions and fed British fears of French despotism (Lough 1985).

Colbert's assignment of scholars, technical experts, artists, artisans, financiers, and laborers to state projects and institutions could have threatened the administration's political legitimacy (Nietzsche 1990:147–190), but the minister gave his new appointees particular duties, not personal authority of office. Members of academies and scholars in the libraries in principle pursued their own agendas, but in fact were governed carefully. Meanwhile, entrepreneurs, engaged in construction projects, gained contracts only for limited work. Constrained and empowered in strict ways, these agents became Weber's (Weber *et al.* 1978:957) 'servants' of standing with contingent authority in relation to prescribed duties. In this capacity, they engaged in acts of logistical government, creating artifacts and exercising material powers outside the restrictions of the patrimonial order as a means of reviving the glory of Gaul.

To show how the state gained power by material means, I focus on an unlikely set of political objects: legal records, coins, and infrastructural projects used for reviving the Gallic legacy. They defined a new heritage and destiny for the kingdom in competition with the feudal conception of spiritual pursuit that had been the taken-for-granted foundation of French patrimonial politics. Allusions to Rome justified dreams of secular success and military prowess, including the French drive to empire. So, evocations of Rome did important political work. And things (legal records, coins, public monuments, and an infrastructure 'worthy' of Rome) became tools of political transformation (Mukerji 2009c, 2011).

Mitchell (2005), Stern (1999), Feldman (2010), Watenpaugh (2004), Turner (2012), and Hosler (1994), among others, have already made strong cases that aesthetic objects can exercise power, and Latour (2004) has persuasively argued that artifacts can serve as 'things', drawing people together around issues of political concern. Becker and Clark (2001) and Joyce (2009) have also argued that paperwork and files should be included as material tools of modern governance. And Leone (2005, Leone and Silberman, 1995) has shown that the material competences of subjugated groups (Scott's (1985) weapons of the weak) can be used as tools of the strong. At the same time, Holland *et al.* (1998) have shown that materialized imaginaries can shape political reasoning, pointing to the power of material mimesis to transform not only political practices, but also collective desires.

Legal archives

Rome was famous not just for its legal code but also for its use of legal records to set precedents. Legal archives were designed to prevent powerful nobles from exercising arbitrary power or usurping legal authority for private purposes; decisions were meant to follow a paper trail. Colbert readily embraced this practice because he did not have the power to reform the legal system, but he could collect documents to set precedents and place new constraints on noble officials (Stein 1999, Soll 2009).

Colbert began collecting legal paperwork as part of his forest reform. As minister of the treasury and navy, Colbert was certainly interested in studying French forests to assess the state of the kingdom's timber reserves (particularly of trees appropriate for ship-building), but he also knew that estate holders who had been charged with managing French forests were misusing them and covering their tracks by withholding documents (Froidour 1899:9–19, Mukerji 2007, 2009a:26–27). So, the minister charged his foresters not only to measure the forests and make notes on their condition but also to collect legal documents pertaining to land rights and offices.

Legal papers, particularly about land, were not easy to obtain in this period because they were not public records and had political value worth guarding. Noble families held land and offices in perpetuity, so they acquired legal authority, rights, and lands through complex patterns of birth, death, marriage, and descent that made family documents important to the exercise of power. For this reason, family papers were often kept secret and controlled locally (Kettering 1986, Lanham 2002:13–16, 251–252, Bourgain and Hubert 2005:331–334, Lemarchand 2010). Landholders could hide illegal practices and exaggerate their rights to parcels by keeping records of official transactions out of public view (Mousnier 1979:627–656, Murat 1980:143–147, Beik 1985:18–49, 77–97, Kettering 1988:152, 169, 225, 227).

The Church kept many legal records, including documents of their own actions and offices, and the birth and death records of noble families. But land transfers (and the powers pertaining to them) had to be verified and maintained by notaries. Notaries were themselves officials and in many towns were important people who prided themselves on the independence of their archives (Dolan 1998:49–69). Still, noble families also served as patrons to *notaires* and used the privacy of notarial archives to keep their abuses of power and privilege out of public view (Froidour 1672:9–23, Mousnier 1979:627–656, Murat 1980:143–147, Beik 1985:18–49, 77–97, Kettering 1988:152, 169, 225, 227, Mukerji 2007: 16–19).

In the face of this system of documentation that was so easy to abuse, Colbert started to build his own legal archives, acquiring and copying records with which to supervise French land use practices. His foresters created legal dossiers, including plans of each parcel of woods, assessments of forest trees and their condition, interview data about abuses to the forest, and historical maps of the region. They also gathered family and official documents related to land claims and rights, which gave the administration broader knowledge about patterns of land control by the French nobility and clergy.

Colbert's foresters were non-noble functionaries, not men of rank. They filled out forms and made maps with standard *arpent* chains. But they had authority to request legal documents even from those of noble blood, because that was part of their official duties. And they produced a set of dossiers used to bring legal proceedings against landholders who had abused the forests and to make visible to the state future disregard of forestry regulations (Froidour 1899:18–19, compare with Murat 1980:143–147, Mukerji 2007).

Louis de Froidour was Colbert's most trusted forestry official and a servant of the state in the Weberian sense. He was deeply attached to his duties and saw his work as service, protecting assets that belonged to the king. He knew how forests were managed both for good and bad. He respected good stewardship, protecting peasant communities that were treating their forests well. And he had an eye for the illegal uses of forests that nobles were prone to try, including their use of royal forests as their own. He was disdainful of nobles who tried to misrepresent themselves to the king, so he was relentless in getting family papers to check their rights. Even threatened with violence, he built up state dossiers and made them legal records (Froidour 1899:15–19).

Colbert also assembled historical documents pertaining to royal authority to constrain the legal power of the Church and nobility in relation to the king. For this, he called upon antiquarian and legal experts, who had the skill to collect and interpret historical legal documents accurately and convincingly. He hired as his personal librarian, Etienne Baluze, a respected scholar who assembled a compendium of legal papers from the period of Charlemagne in his book, the *Histoire des capitulaires des Rois François* (Murat 1980:180, Soll 2009:101–103, Baluze

[1677] 1755). Baluze contended that the *capitulaires* firmly established that the French king was meant to govern both secular and sacred affairs within the kingdom (Stein 1999:41–42).The inalterable powers of the king, Baluze argued, were later usurped by high nobles, seigneurs and the Church, leaving the monarchy weak in France. But legal precedent from Carolingian times showed that the French king had been and should be the final authority in his lands (Baluze [1677] 1755:ij–xiv). In this way, Baluze used humanist forms of legal reasoning that had been previously honed by the Church to make the argument for subordinating the Church and nobility in France to the king (Soll 2009:25–35, 108–113).

Again, Colbert tapped the expertise of those outside the nobility to acquire powers for the state. Baluze was a scholar: part of an intellectual infrastructure of books and people that Colbert used to dominate the Republic of Letters and control the terms of political debate. Soll (2009:143–150) says that Baluze was not in a position to make personal judgments about the political value of the documents he collected for Colbert. Instead, he supplied legal extracts to the minister, drawing on what became the largest collection of legal documents in Europe. Baluze could have no personal power in French politics, but what he did was enormously powerful. By gathering and interpreting such a large collection of legal papers, he provided Colbert with an intellectual asset that the king's adversaries could not easily match (Soll 2009:101–113, 143–52).

Coins and medals

If Colbert used books and documents to control the Republic of Letters and legal debate, he used art and artifacts to constitute France's aesthetic position as heir to Rome. Perhaps surprisingly, coins or medals were key items. Coins collected from the ancient world carried portraits of political leaders and images of historical events from the classical world. They constituted an inheritance for France from the ancient world that was studied and copied by the administration to relate France to Rome.

Colbert collected small antiquities for scholars appointed to the *Académie Royale des Inscriptions et Médailles* or his *petite académie* of advisors who advised him on the cultural programs for the regime (Barret-Kriegel 1988:178–192, Berger 1993:145). The academy consisted of a small group of respected but mainly bourgeois men with antiquarian expertise (Jean Chapelain, François Charpentier, l'abbé de Bourzeix, l'abbé de Cassgnes, and later as secretary, Charles Perrault) (Barret-Kriegel 1988:171). As the name of the academy suggests, they oversaw and studied a growing collection of small antiquities: coins, medals, engraved stones, small statues, and the like. They also met in the royal library, where they could study the growing collection of ancient manuscripts to interpret the small antiquities.

Small antiquities appealed to humanists because there were lots of them, they were easy to trade, and they provided evidence of events and people from the classical world. The Romans themselves had engaged in medal and coin collection, acquiring ancient Greek coins as well as striking new commemorative medals (Zanker 1988:54–65, 240–243). The *petite académie* simply picked up these practices as part of antiquarian study and used ancient coins as precedents to design new medals and other artifacts to celebrate the reign of Louis XIV.

Schnapper *et al.* (2005:285–287) argue that Louis XIV was unusual in having such a large collection of medals, but the king was particularly fond of them. He claimed to use them to instruct himself in classical history. The monarch liked the collection so much he often showed them off as treasures to visitors, placing the cabinet containing coins and medals between the grand staircase and his apartments, where visitors passed and he would see them every day (Verlet 1985:230–231). Celebrating military prowess and political achievements with medals and coins perhaps made particular sense to a king whose interests lay in war, empire, treasure, and glory.

The bulk of the royal collection of medals and coins came from the king's uncle, Gaston d'Orleans, who left the monarch a huge inventory of antiquities on his death (Soll 2009,127–128). Antiquarian scholarship and collecting had been humanist activities shared by both noble and non-noble scholars alike. And Colbert turned to both groups not only to compose his *petite académie* but also to increase the collection of small antiquities. For example, Colbert called upon the chevalier d'Arvieux, a nobleman with diplomatic duties in the eastern Mediterranean, to try to locate coin collections for the king. D'Arvieux in turn, employed one *sieur* Vaillant to find coins and other antiquities in North Africa. We know this because on 1 February 1675, d'Arvieux wrote to Colbert from Algiers upset that Vaillant had been captured on a foreign vessel along with other Frenchmen (Colbert 1979,V:372–373).

There were other equally vexed attempts at collection by men who were clearly scholars and not noblemen. Daniel Huet in his memoirs wrote about his ill-fated effort to acquire medals and coins for Colbert. Huet was an antiquarian without noble background, who, on locating a collection of rare coins and medals belonging to a family that had lost its fortune, sought and gained Colbert's permission to buy the collection for the king. Huet became Colbert's agent in this deal, but the rarest of the pieces that he acquired were secretly stolen en route to Paris. The embarrassed Huet offered to compensate the minister for the loss, but Colbert refused, taking the remaining collection for his own cabinet (Colbert 1979:lvi–lvii). Collecting coins and medals was a dangerous and difficult business that Colbert could do well only by turning to experts, whatever their rank, to join in the search. But with non-nobles like Huet, Colbert assigned specific duties and responsibilities and did not give them the personal power to act without official review.

Not only did Colbert help the king acquire ancient medals with the help of non-nobles but he also had new ones struck by artisans to celebrate the achievements of Louis XIV. The events for commemoration and content of the coins were debated by the *petite académie*, but the coins were designed by master engravers. The most famous of the coin and medal designers included Jean Varin, Thomas Bernard, and François Chéron. Varin was from the north of France or Flanders, a master artisan who came to Paris in 1625, and was assigned in 1629 as a *conducteur de la Monnaie du Moulin*. He was raised in rank as an engraver of medals and coins, finally becoming the engraver of the king's seal and a member of the academy of painting and sculpture (Jacquiot and Musée de la monnaie [France] 1970:79–80). Thomas Bernard was an engraver who entered the king's service while still young and from 1685 to 1688 famously engraved stamps to produce a history of the reign of Louis XIV in gold medals (Jacquiot and Musée de la monnaie [France] 1970:95). François Chéron was also an engraver from France, but one who did not find ready patronage from the crown in France. So, he went to Rome to work for the pope, and studied with local engravers until he perfected their techniques (Jacquiot and Musée de la monnaie [France] 1970:119–120). When Chéron returned to Paris, he was a perfect candidate for making medals resembling those of Rome, old and new, and to honor his aesthetic abilities, he was appointed to the academy of painting and sculpture (Jacquiot and Musée de la monnaie [France] 1970:127–128). All these engravers brought artisans' skills into government service to build a living heritage for France with small artifacts that had long historical reach (Jacquiot and Musée de la monnaie [France] 1970:79–136).

The arts and architecture

In establishing academies, Colbert not only could honor artisans of talent but also could build an institutional capacity for connecting France with Rome through aesthetics. The academy, like the library, was an institutional form that could be traced back to the Ancients, and it was also an institution that accepted members without noble rank simply on the basis of their abilities. This brought their expertise into Colbert's purview, and turned art into a powerful tool of politics in France (Goldstein 2008). We can see how this worked by focusing on the *Académie d'Architecture*.

Colbert appointed as the first head of the academy of architecture, François Blondel, a man without noble rank who was a respected mathematician and antiquarian, with strong political ambitions and abilities. Blondel developed a French version of classicism that was true to aesthetic principles of the Ancients, but was appropriate to French taste. For this task, he assembled in the academy architects with antiquarian knowledge to debate classical principles of design and determine how these principles should be properly followed in France. He developed a set of precise rules, and gained a reputation for dogmatism from his peers in the academy for his strictness. He nonetheless taught the rules to French architecture students, and used them to vet projects financed by the state. Although he ridiculed French Renaissance architecture for its use of contrasting masses and ornate decorations, he still championed the French taste for large windows and light interior spaces, and in this way, produced principles of French neoclassicism that remained in force into the eighteenth century (Gerbino 2010:60–65).

The *Académie d'Architecture* exercised enormous power through aesthetic regulation. By developing and enforcing new rules of design, it displaced local architects and artisans who had worked in the French Renaissance tradition. Parisian builders and architects in particular had previously exercised an autonomy that Colbert found distasteful. He solved the problem by encouraging Blondel to condemn their aesthetics and replace their tastes and techniques with ones taught by the academy to a new generation. In this, the *Académie d'Architecture* served as a disciplinary arm of the state as much as a site of aesthetic control (Goubert 1974:205–208, Colbert 1979,V:384–385).

Blondel then instructed Parisians in French neoclassical tastes by displaying them in a set of arches he built as gates to the city of Paris after the medieval walls to the city were razed. The Porte Saint Denis was the most important of the arches, and the only one Blondel was able to design entirely on his own. It was modeled on the arch of Titus from Ancient Rome, and celebrated French military victories in the Netherlands, symbolically aligning French military power with that of the ancient empire. The front of the arch was decorated with obelisks as tributes to those who died in battle. Part monument, part memorial, the Porte Saint Denis linked the dead and the living with a style that was itself dead and living. It suggested immortality for the classical tradition and for a tradition of military heroism still alive in French culture (Gerbino 2010:43–47).

The gates were icons of Rome, but served French habits, too. They were set in an avenue of trees (not a road but a garden promenade) circling much of the northern boundary of Paris. These parks gave Parisians a place to walk after dinner, as was their custom. Blondel hoped that in passing the new city gates while they strolled through the trees, Parisians would cultivate a taste for classical architecture (Gerbino 2010:71–77). The Porte Saint Denis succeeded so well that it became the favored location for the king to promenade with the people of the city, where the mantle of Rome and French heritage were aligned in architecture (Gerbino 2010:77–84).

Blondel was not from a noble family, but a mathematician with a background in fortress design who had gained the attention of the king by becoming his son's mathematics tutor. He was a political creature who enjoyed life at court, but did not have the rank to gain personal power. So, he became a client of Colbert, working to make France aesthetically heir to Rome. An able mathematician, he became a member of the academy of science, writing on subjects from architectural proportions to Roman calendars (Blondel, 1682, Blondel and Patte 1771). But most importantly for his position as director of the academy, he developed careful rules for connecting France to Rome, which explicitly undermined those who did not share this vision (Gerbino 2010:65–70).

Infrastructure

Developing extensive and technically sophisticated infrastructure was another material means of equating France with Rome that the administration pursued under Colbert. It was also a way to reduce noble power over land, and to erode the power of cities that had traditional autonomy. As minister of the navy, Colbert was particularly interested in designing new ports on the Atlantic for colonial trade and fortifying existing ports on the Mediterranean to defend them from pirates. The Romans had developed ports along coasts where no natural harbors existed. So, new ports could serve France both as practical infrastructure and demonstrations that the French had the skill to pick up the technical mantel of Rome (Konvitz 1978:73–89, Mukerji 2009a:110–111).

The man whom Colbert sent to search for sites to build new ports was the Chevalier de Clerville, a nobleman who directed fortress engineering for the state. Clerville suggested building ports at Brest, Lorient, Rochefort and Sète. Sète could rival Marseilles on the Mediterranean and Rochefort could take trade away from La Rochelle on the Atlantic. Colbert employed for these projects (and comparable infrastructural work elsewhere) local architects, civil engineers, artisans and laborers under the careful supervision of officers of the crown. This structure gave the minister greater administrative capacity to control French lands as well as the new infrastructure itself (Konvitz 1978:73–89, Degage 1987:47–52).

The most famous engineering project of the period and one repeatedly associated with Rome was the Canal du Midi. This waterway was first meant to accommodate naval vessels, allowing French ships to reach the Atlantic from the Mediterranean without passing Gibraltar, but this goal had to be abandoned because the canal could not be made wide enough in the mountains. Still, the Canal du Midi was celebrated as worthy of the Romans, facilitating the movement of vessels between the two seas (Rolt 1973, Mousnier 1985, Mukerji 2009a).

Languedoc was famous for its dissidents and difficult to administer by the crown, because many of the nobles there were Huguenots and believed that they should not submit to the authority of a Catholic king. Locals had actively resisted the forest reform and some continued to attack tax farmers (Devèze 1962:234–235, Mukerji 2007:22–23, 2009a:17–18). Running a large canal through the heart of Languedoc was an act of power that undermined the autonomy of this region's elites by following material precedents set by Rome.

The Canal du Midi also brought non-noble expertise into the material construction of France-as-Rome. The canal was not technically feasible according to the formal knowledge of engineering in the period. Educated engineers like the Chevalier de Clerville did not know enough hydraulics to understand exactly how to build it. Peasants knew more. They designed and maintained irrigation systems and built water supplies for mills. The most sophisticated hydraulic engineers of the period were peasant women from the Pyrenees, who were developing water systems for domestic purposes in former Roman bath colonies. Their knowledge of hydraulics was classical in provenance, but understood by them as common sense. Some of these women came to work as laborers on the Canal du Midi, and brought this expertise to the project. Because of their skills, they ended up perfecting the complex water supply system, and threading the canal along contours through the mountains that surveyors at that time could not even accurately measure. In the end, the Canal du Midi made France more like Rome by employing non-noble experts who helped establish the administration's capacity to exercise logistical power like Rome (Mukerji 2008, 2009b).

The figured world of France-as-Rome and the French state

The result of this logistical work was a new 'figured world' of power (Holland *et al.* 1998). France was aligned with the Roman Empire with a built environment that silently pointed back to Rome and with medals and coins that circulated as icons of classical culture. The heritage of Gaul was made a living tradition by French artists, engineers, artisans, and peasants. The line between Ancient Gaul and Louis XIV's France was blurred by material means, legitimating new administrative activism in imitation of Rome. This figured world was built by experts employed by the state as 'servants of standing', who worked in new government institutions like academies or did contract work. They joined forces against the clergy and nobility and brought to French government new tools of impersonal rule: material means of political change. The administration used logistics to shift French political identity away from feudal culture and toward a humanist one that celebrated the worldly successes of Rome and suggested a new destiny for France as heir to the ancient empire.

Bibliography

Apostolidès, J.M. (1981) *Le roi-machine: spectacle et politique au temps de Louis XIV,* Paris: Editions de Minuit.

Appuhn, K.R. (2009) *A forest on the sea: environmental expertise in Renaissance Venice,* Baltimore: Johns Hopkins University Press.

Baluze, E. ([1677] 1755) *Histoire des Capitulaires des Rois François,* Paris: La Haye.

Barret-Kriegel, B. (1988). *Les académies de l'histoire,* 1st ed., Paris: Presses Universitaires de France.

Becker, P. and Clark, W. (2001) *Little tools of knowledge: historical essays on academic and bureaucratic practices,* Ann Arbor: University of Michigan Press.

Beik, W. (1985) *Absolutism and society in seventeenth-century France: state power and provincial aristocracy in Languedoc,* Cambridge: Cambridge University Press.

Berger, R.W. (1993) *The Palace of the Sun: the Louvre of Louis XIV,* University Park, PA: Pennsylvania State University.

Blondel, F. (1682) *Histoire du calendrier romain qui contient son origine et les divers changemens qui lui sont arrivez,* Paris: L'Autheur et N. Langlois.

Blondel, J.F. and Patte, P. (1771) *Cours d'architecture, ou, Traité de la décoration, distribution et construction des bâtiments: contenant les leçons données en 1750, et les années suivants,* Paris: Desaint.

Bourgain, P. and Hubert, M.C. (2005) *Le latin médiéval,* Turnhout, Belgium: Brepols.

Colbert, J.B. (1979) *Lettres, instructions et mémoires de Colbert: publiés d'après les ordres de l'empereur, sur la proposition de Son Excellence M. Magne, ministre secrétaire d'état des finances,* Nendeln: Kraus Reprint.

Degage, A. (1987) Un Nouveau port en Languedoc (de la fin du XVIe siècle au début du XVIIIe, in J. Sagnes (ed.) *Histoire de Sète,* Toulouse: Privat, 47–52.

Devèze, M. (1962) *La Grande Réformation des Forêts Royales sous Colbert, 1661–1680,* Nancy: École Nationale des Eaux et Forêts.

Dolan, C. (1998) *Le notaire, la famille et la ville,* Toulouse: Presses Universitaires de Mirail.

Feldman, M. (2010) Object Agency? Spatial Perspective, Social Relations, and the Stele of Hammurabi, in S. Steadman and J. Ross (eds) *Agency and identity in the Ancient Near East,* London: Equinox, 149–65.

Froidour, L.D. (1672). *Lettre à Monsievr Barrillon Damoncourt ... contenant la relation et la description des travaux qui se font en Languedoc, pour la commvnication des deux mers,* Toulouse: I.D. Camvsat.

Froidour, L.D. (1899) *Les Pyrenées centrales au XVIIe siècle; lettres écrites ... à M. de Héricourt ... et à M. de Medon,* Auch: Impr. et lithographie G. Foix.

Gerbino, A. (2010) *François Blondel: architecture, erudition, and the scientific revolution,* London; New York: Routledge.

Goldstein, C. (2008) *Vaux and Versailles: the appropriations, erasures, and accidents that made modern France,* Philadelphia, PA: University of Pennsylvania Press.

Goubert, P. (1974) *The ancien régime: French society, 1600–1750,* New York: Harper and Row.

Holland, D.C., Lachicotte, W., Skinner, D. and Cain, C. (1998) *Identity and agency in cultural worlds,* Cambridge, MA: Harvard University Press.

Hosler, D. (1994) *The sounds and colors of power: the sacred metallurgical technology of ancient West Mexico,* Cambridge, MA: MIT Press.

Jacquiot, J. and Musée De La Monnaie (France) (1970) *La Médaille au temps de Louis XIV. [Exposition à l'Hôtel de la Monnaie, janvier–mars 1970],* Paris: Impr. Nationale.

Joyce, P. (2009) Filing the Raj: political technologies of the Imperial British state, in T. Bennett and P. Joyce (eds) *Material powers: essays beyond cultural materialism,* London: Routledge.

Kettering, S. (1986) *Patrons, brokers, and clients in seventeenth-century France,* New York: Oxford University Press.

Kettering, S. (1988) The Historical Development of Political Clientelism, *Journal of Interdisciplinary History,* 18, 419–447.

Konvitz, J.W. (1978) *Cities and the sea: port city planning in early modern Europe,* Baltimore: The Johns Hopkins University Press.

Lanham, C.D. (2002) *Latin grammar and rhetoric: from classical theory to medieval practice,* London, New York: Continuum.

Latour, B. (2004) Why Has Critique Run out of Steam? From Matters of Fact to Matters Of Concern, *Critical Inquiry,* 30, 225–248.

Lemarchand, Y. (2010) Chiffres de finance, in M.-L. Legay (ed.) *Dictionnaire historique de la comptabilité publique 1500–1850,* Rennes: Presses Universitaires de Rennes.

Leone, M.P. (2005) *The archaeology of liberty in an American capital: excavations in Annapolis,* Berkeley: University of California Press.

Leone, M.P. and Silberman, N.A. (1995) *Invisible America: unearthing our hidden history,* 1st ed., New York: H. Holt.

Lough, J. (1985) *France observed in the seventeenth century by British travelers,* Stocksfield, Eng.; Boston: Oriel Press.

Machiavelli, N. and Donno, D. (1966) *The Prince,* New York: Bantam.

Marin, L. (1981) *Le portrait du roi,* Paris: Editions de Minuit.

Mitchell, W.J.T. (2005) *What do pictures want?: The lives and loves of images,* Chicago: University of Chicago Press.

Mousnier, R. (1979) *The institutions of France under the absolute monarchy, 1598–1789: society and the state,* Chicago: University of Chicago Press.

Mousnier, R. (1985) *Un nouveau colbert: Actes du colloque pour le tricentenaire de la mort de colbert,* Paris: Sedes Réunis.

Mukerji, C. (1994) The Political Mobilization of Nature in French Formal Gardens, *Theory and Society,* 23, 651–677.

Mukerji, C. (1997) *Territorial ambitions and the gardens of Versailles,* Cambridge; New York: Cambridge University Press.

Mukerji, C. (2007) The Great Forest Survey of 1669–1671, *Social Studies of Science,* 37, 227–253.

Mukerji, C. (2008) Women Engineers and the Culture of the Pyrenees, in P.S.A.B. Schmidt (ed.) *Knowledge and its making in Europe, 1500–1800,* Chicago: University of Chicago Press.

Mukerji, C. (2009a) *Impossible engineering: technology and territoriality on the Canal du Midi,* Princeton, NJ: Princeton University Press.

Mukerji, C. (2009b) The Mindful Hands of Peasants: The Eight-Lock Staircase at Fonseranes 1678–1679, *History of Technology,* 29, 141–160.

Mukerji, C. (2009c) The New Rome: Infrastructure and National Identity on the Canal du Midi, in C.E. Harrison and A. Johnson (eds) *National identity: the role of science and technology,* Chicago: University of Chicago Press, 15–32.

Mukerji, C. (2010) The Territorial State as a Figured World of Power: Strategics, Logistics and Impersonal Rule, *Sociological Theory,* 28, 402–425.

Mukerji, C. (2011) Jurisdiction, Inscription, and State Formation: Administrative Modernism and Knowledge Regimes, *Theory and Society,* 40, 223–245.

Murat, I. (1980) *Colbert,* Paris: Fayard.

Nietzsche, F.W. (1990) *The birth of tragedy: and, the genealogy of morals,* 1st Anchor Books ed., New York: Anchor Books.

Rolt, L.T.C. (1973) *From sea to sea: the Canal du Midi,* London: Allen Lane.

Schnapper, A., Mouquin, S. and Szanto, M. (2005) *Curieux du grand siècle,* 2. éd. rev. et mise à jour / ed., Paris: Flammarion.

Scott, J.C. (1985) *Weapons of the weak: everyday forms of peasant resistance,* New Haven: Yale University Press.

Scott, J.C. (1998) *Seeing Like a State,* New Haven: Yale University Press.

Soll, J. (2009) *The information master: Jean-Baptiste Colbert's secret state intelligence system,* Ann Arbor: University of Michigan Press.

Stein, P. (1999) *Roman law in European history,* Cambridge, New York: Cambridge University Press.

Stern, L. (1999) *The smoking book,* Chicago: University of Chicago Press.

Tilley, C., Keane, W., Küchler, S., Rowlands, M. and Spyer, P., (2006) *Handbook of material culture,* Los Angeles: Sage.

Turner, F. (2012) The Family of Man and the Politics of Attention in Cold War America, *Public Culture,* 24, 55–84.

Verlet, P. (1985) *Le château de Versaille,* Paris: Fayard.

Watenpaugh, H.Z. (2004) *The image of an Ottoman city: imperial architecture and urban experience in Aleppo in the 16th and 17th centuries,* Leiden; Boston, Mass: Brill.

Weber, M., Roth, G. and Wittich, C. (1978) *Economy and society: an outline of interpretive sociology,* Berkeley: University of California Press.

Zanker, P. (1988) *The power of images in the Age of Augustus,* Ann Arbor: University of Michigan Press.

5

The material politics of solid waste
Decentralization and integrated systems

Penny Harvey

In a village high up above Urubamba just off the road to Cusco, I talked with Miguel and Susana about their recycling business. Standing in a wide *cancha* filled with all manner of plastic bottles and containers, sorted by size, colour and function, they told me how their business had got started. Miguel's older brothers had moved to Lima to look for work and had learnt about the recycling trade there. Miguel's daughter had subsequently followed her uncles to the coast and had worked with them for seven years learning how to classify discarded plastics (learning what sells and where it sells) and learning where the risks lie and where the most secure profits can be made. She had then come back to Cusco and encouraged Miguel and Susana to move away from what had become an uncertain and vulnerable trade in cattle, to this new promising business venture. Miguel and Susana admitted that the recycling business had its own pitfalls, which they had learnt by trial and error. Some plastics are more dependable that others. The thick coloured plastics of washing basins and buckets always fetch good prices and are rarely rejected by their Lima buyers. Plastic drinking bottles are also good and easier to come by, but these have to be carefully sorted. Miguel and Susana had learned the hard way to separate out vinegar and soy sauce bottles after several tons of shredded plastics had been rejected for the traces of contamination that were detected, unfortunately only after Miguel and Susana had paid the processing and transport costs. As we talked, two of their employees sat on the ground nearby, surrounded by mountains of bottles, scraping off the labels and checking that the plastics were good. These men were trained to carefully sort the bottles and to watch for those bottles that no longer have life ('*ya no tienen vida*'), bottles that had contained soy sauce, vinegar, or certain energy drinks. Once they have accumulated enough of the plastics that do still have life, the plastics are shredded, and when Miguel has a full load to send on to his brothers, he hires a lorry and drives it down to the coast. At the coast, the plastics are again sampled, tested, washed, reshredded and then sold on. Miguel and his colleagues have been trying to get the municipality of Urubamba to give them a licence, to acknowledge their formal status as buyers of waste, and they are constantly on the look-out for new and regular sources of materials to recycle. I wondered where these chains of recycling ended up and Miguel said that he thought that they were bought by Japanese factories that use the plastics to make high-end, high-tech clothing (and he cast an eye over my jacket).

Solid waste management has grown in importance in recent years as the challenge of waste disposal is met by new technological possibilities for the conversion of rubbish into resource.[1] Where rubbish can be turned into money, waste matter does indeed have life, and the scaling up of this potential for life produces commercial possibilities for manufacturers, traders, industrial engineers and for public authorities charged by law to ensure the safe disposal of the waste matter generated within their jurisdiction.[2] The global recycling industry moves waste matter around the planet in a complex negotiation of fluctuating markets and regulatory regimes, which determine where the highest profits can be realized. The industry also seems to offer a redemptive possibility to the problematic consequences of rising levels of consumption, which are taken to indicate improved living standards, which in turn sustain the notion of economic growth as an absolute social good. Sustainable consumption is all about recycling, reconfiguring materials, finding new uses for things, reusing and remaking rather than starting afresh each time.

However, as Susana and Miguel had learned, and as all who begin to look more closely at recycling practices know, whether in one's own kitchen or on the global stage, the materials themselves play an important part in these procedures. Their liveliness is not encompassed by their capacity to turn a profit or their ability to regenerate or take on new forms and functions. Governments legislate with respect to waste matter because this matter continues to move, to transform, and at times to threaten other life forms. Waste has a toxic vitality that is integral to any serious consideration of what it is that is being managed in processes of solid waste management.

The vitality of matter has been a long-standing interest of scholars of science and technology, and in particular of those thinkers who have followed the development of modern chemistry from the secret experimental laboratories of the sixteenth-century alchemists to the high-tech procedures and preoccupations of those invested in creating new synthetics, materials that are responsive to environmental conditions, which can both carry and generate information in and through their relational engagements.[3] It has also, more recently, become the central concern of scholars in political philosophy, who have begun to elaborate ways of allowing materials into political theory by attending to the vitality of matter.[4] Anthropologists, of course, have attended to the lively materials and material forms that populate the pages of ethnographic accounts from all parts of the world. Thus, we have extensive literatures on the many ways in which things appear, or act, as persons.[5] Scholars of the Andean region have documented the importance of local understandings of the powerful energetic forces of the mountains and of the earth,[6] perspectives that recent ethnographies have shown to be alive and well in urban settings as well as in rural villages.[7] In a different vein, anthropology has also produced many accounts that attend to people's mundane material engagements, the skilled craft practices through which the work of farmers, hunters, healers, shamans, cooks, traders and all manner of ritual specialists and expert practitioners who become the subjects of our ethnographic accounts involve an attentive engagement with the intrinsic movement of matter.[8]

In this article, my focus on material politics signals an intention to draw together these diverse approaches to materiality by focusing on how technical experts approach the business of devising systems that attempt to release the lucrative potential of waste materials and contain their potentially toxic effects. The balance is hard to achieve. My argument suggests that the capacity of materials to 'leak' beyond the technologies of containment that engineers devise renders all solutions problematic. The transformative potential of waste materials entangles material and social worlds in ways that are never fully under the control of the technical expert.

The Vilcanota Project and the problem of solid waste

The ethnography on which I draw to make this argument was carried out in 2010 in the Vilcanota Valley, Peru.[9] This valley is a key Peruvian tourist destination, because it channels visitors from the Inka city of Cusco to the site of Machu Picchu. Prompted by threats from UNESCO that this lucrative site could be stripped of its world heritage status, the Peruvian state took out a World Bank loan of approximately $4.8 million to develop the tourist infrastructures required for the appropriate management of the site and its environs. We came across this project as part of an ethnographic study in decentralized government in which we were exploring the tensions between central, regional and local instances of the state, focusing in particular on the experimental deployment of technical knowledges and regulatory procedures in the working out of these political relations. The Vilcanota Project, as it was known, was in general terms a response to the uncontrolled and the largely unregulated growth of Cusco's tourist industry. The problem of waste management had become visible in the valley, with small towns struggling to adequately dispose of household rubbish. However, in the city of Cusco, the problem was acute. The main garbage dumps were no longer viable; they were collapsing, and an alternative solution was needed. The linking of the urban problem to the issue of improving tourism infrastructures in the valley seemed to offer the possibility of what all agreed was necessary: an integrated solution. Under the close supervision of World Bank officials, the Regional Government of Cusco was given administrative responsibility for the study, which in practice was assumed by Copesco, a tourism engineering entity housed within the Regional Government.[10] Following World Bank procedures (which involved direct approval not simply of the technical consultants but also of the procedures by which they would be chosen and contracted), the Spanish/Peruvian consortium Getinsa/Geoconsult were appointed. Their brief was to decide where the rubbish dumps should be located. From the perspective of Getinsa/Geoconsult, the problem was largely logistical. They gathered data on how much waste was generated by each district and looked at the transport issues implied by the possible sites available to them. They inspected these sites along with another company contracted to complete the environmental aspect of the overall study. The also began to draw up plans for recycling at scale. They were aware that the existing rubbish dumps, which were built in the 1990s and projected to last for 40 years, had barely lasted half that time. Central to their plans, then, was the need to reduce the bulk through extensive recycling. A modern highly technologized recycling plant lay at the heart of their technical proposal. This plant would of course not only reduce the bulk of waste matter; it would convert the waste to cash. A modern recyling plant offered the way forward to funding waste disposal in the city.

There are several aspects of Getinsa's work to which I wish to draw attention. The first concerns the determination of the company to provide an 'integrated solution' to Cusco's rubbish problems. This capacity to deliver integrated solutions to the problems of modern life is a commonplace in contemporary engineering practice. But the concept of integration elides two different understandings of what such integration might entail. On the one hand, an integrated solution refers to the importance of thinking of waste disposal in systemic terms. In this framing, waste disposal is imagined as a process that begins at a particular point (which might be the point of disposal but could even extend to the point of production, with packaging decisions and regulations concerning the kinds of materials available to consumers). From the point of disposal, the waste materials are moved through a further series of points: through processes of collection, transport, storage, treatment, monitoring, recirculation and final disposal. This notion of integration can be thought of as a set of technical and material relations: an infrastructure, conceived of as a regulated movement of matter through a procedural matrix. This kind of technical response to the problem of waste disposal was seen as straightforward by the engineers. The problems that they confronted emerged from an altogether different notion of integration, that is the integration between such technical systems and the unpredictable force of social relations. In Peru, we often heard people discuss the limitations of purely technical solutions. Politicians and engineers alike would emphasize their commitment to solutions that went beyond old-fashioned notions of infrastructure, generally referred to as solutions 'of cement and iron'. However, the challenge of delivering a technical solution that materialized a social agreement was highly problematic. The difficulties experienced in the design and delivery of the integrated solution mirrored the political challenge that faced the regional government across all its fields of activity: how to achieve a balance between the mode of centralization that a regional perspective (or solution) implies and stay true to the commitment to decentralization that was required if each municipality, indeed each citizen/consumer, were to buy into the solution, taking responsibility for such solutions and carrying them forward in such a way that they become sustainable into the future.

The World Bank, as we have seen, kept a watchful eye on the process. Their primary aim was for the development of robust procedures, systems of management that would ensure this complex notion of social integration. All were agreed that the classical engineering solution of iron and cement was no longer appropriate. Such technologies imply the top-down imposition of specific material configurations on populations that have shown themselves to be reluctant to use or maintain such systems. What is needed are systems that people feel comfortable with, that they are prepared to care for and maintain. Consultant engineering companies were thus required, as specified in their contractual terms of reference, to work alongside local people, keeping them informed of how they were working, seeking collaboration in the gathering of data, and ensuring that potential solutions were discussed in open fora with affected communities. To this end, the company set out to engage citizens and local governments through a series of workshops. In the following section, I present an account of two such workshops, hosted in the town hall of the city of Cusco. My interest is to track the ways in which the requirement to communicate with local people amplified the tensions posed by a discontinuous, decentralizing state structure. The multiplicity of local voices and understandings unsettled attempts to provide a centralized response to Cusco's solid waste problems, which emerged as inappropriately 'technical' despite the stated aims.

Defining a problem and finding a solution

The first workshop opened with the Director of Getinsa explaining the methodology by which their technical study had been developed. He told us that all the municipalities in the study area had been visited to collect detailed information on the quality and quantities of solid waste. Their aim had been to build up a picture of the waste materials that each district was generating. Their figures were then presented so that everybody could see at a glance both the scale of the problem and the specific contribution of the area where they lived. Having presented these statistics, the Director went on to talk about the need to identify adequate sites for new dumps and for recycling plants and the diverse technical details required to ensure that such sites were suitable. However, the job for this particular workshop was to address the social dimensions of the study. We, the workshop participants, had been invited as interested parties, local residents, a group of students, and representatives of public institutions. The idea was that together we would engage a common problem, own that problem and work with Getinsa to produce a solution. But before we got to work in small groups, we were invited to move away from the abstract presentation of the problem in terms of facts and figures and to engage a more visceral sense of how the rubbish currently appeared in the streets and public spaces of Cusco and the Sacred Valley. We were shown a short film. The camera followed the familiar tourist route, out of the city of Cusco, following the course of the highly polluted Huatanay river to the point where it joined the Vilcanota and from there down into the Sacred Valley. The focus was on the rubbish, piled up by the side of the road, overflowing on to the pavements, floating in the rivers and streams, plastics strewn along the river banks, caught in trees and undergrowth. We were shown how the rubbish was contaminating soils and water and degrading the aspect of public squares and monumental sites. The sound track was potent. It evoked a sense of desolation and abandonment. The mournful classical music accompanied the images of Cusco, presented as an ugly, dirty place, not somewhere you would want to live, and certainly not an attractive tourist proposition. The film seemed to have the desired effect, because subsequent comments from the floor referred to the need for everyone to take responsibility, to work together, to secure a better future for younger generations. Sensitized and suitably primed for the task ahead, we began to work in neighbourhood discussion groups.

The first thing we were asked to do was to elaborate the list of actors who might help solve the problem in our district. We had been given a list of those whom the company had invited to the workshop, and we were also encouraged to amplify and extend these lists. The idea was to widen participation and ensure that key actors were drawn into future conversations. My group enthusiastically got on with the job and began to talk about government ministries, private companies, professional associations, university faculties, neighbourhood associations and peasant communities. We also had things to say about the big hotels, the Church (owners of most of the large buildings in the centre of Cusco), and the families (or mafias as they called them) who control local tourism. The focus subtly shifted away from the sense of personal responsibility that the film had elicited. The rubbish was becoming less anonymous, and pre-existing understandings of lines of responsibility were back on the table. At the same time, we began to extend the category of solid waste. People suggested that the most urgent problems lay with hospital waste, with the waste from factories, and with sewage and liquid wastes that were the principal contaminants of the rivers and for which government (at some level) had to take responsibility. The Director of Getinsa, who was circulating, caught us heading off message and cut in. We had to focus our discussions on domestic solid waste: this was their brief, and therefore ours too.

Our discussions interrupted, we moved to the next task and got involved in drawing up lists of the 'causes' and 'effects' of the problem that Getinsa/Geoconsult had defined for us as 'the inadequate handling of solid waste'. Nothing surprising emerged from our conversations. The causes boiled down to a series of 'lacks': lack of public awareness, lack of education, lack of organization, lack of environmental policies. The effects were basically deemed to be ill health, contamination, and a bad image for their city linked to the threat posed to their primary source of income: the international tourists. By the time the various groups fed ideas back into the closing plenary session, the issue of personal responsibility had disappeared from the collective agenda; what people were calling for was a stronger state presence: better and safer dumps, incentives to get recyling going, environmental taxes on the private sector, and a stronger, more integrated civil society. Only in this latter sense did the 'social' appear as something that might involve individuals, and here primarily it referred to the education of other people: those who were not in the room. There was no discussion in this first workshop of Getinsa/Geoconsult's actual plans, nothing on where the new dumps would be, on who would run them, on the costs or the benefits. I wondered whether such discussions were avoided, because they might have undermined the conceit that we were there to solve this problem together. Nor was there any further discussion of the wider political issues, such as the role of the big hotels, the Church, the factories and the so-called tourist mafias. The general message seemed to be a call for a stronger state presence.

The second workshop, which was held a few days later, turned out to be the meeting in which these more technical issues were discussed. I was surprised to find that many of the people attending this second meeting had, like me, been at the previous event. Here, however, we were gathered not as residents or representatives of those working within a particular district but as people deemed to have a technical interest or specific expertise in the solid waste management. The meeting started in much the same way as the previous one, with the formal presentations of data, the film, and details of the Vilcanota Project. However, this time we were presented with a detailed account of Getinsa's proposed solution: three large dumps that would serve all the municipalities of Cusco and of the valley. Great emphasis was placed on the central importance of a large recycling plant. The key conclusion that underpinned this specific, high-tech solution was the impressive overall reduction in waste matter. We were told that with this plant in operation, over 75 per cent of the rubbish currently generated could and would be recycled.

The scale of the enterprise was central to the business model, because money can be made out of recycling only if there is sufficient rubbish to keep the plant working continuously. Centralized systems were needed, and if rubbish is to be turned to profit, it has to be accumulated at a scale beyond that generated by any single municipality. There is, of course, a certain irony here. Far from encouraging a reduction in the generation of waste, the markets for certain kinds of waste turn the rubbish into a new resource. People such as Miguel and Susana (the owners of the artisanal recycling plant that I described earlier) are already in competition for access to waste, and municipal actors were also aware of the possibility that they might have to pay others to collect materials that they themselves might be able to turn to profit.

The reactions to Getinsa's presentation were critical. One after the other, people stood up to challenge the solution. Had they thought about whether local governments were going to buy into this plan? Had they considered existing strategic initiatives that were being developed at the local level, particularly those that had a certain reputation in the region as 'model' responses? The discussions seemed to challenge the model of the integrated system that Getinsa/Geoconsult was proposing. People were not explicitly rejecting the solution, and several people acknowledged that it doubtless had its merits, but they also wanted to point out that the problem of solid waste is not a new problem. The organizations that this 'technical' audience represented had their own plans and strategies already in play. They were not passively waiting for a plan to come from an external agency. In the light of this response, Getinsa's integrated solution began to look rather problematic. If their solution had not achieved a folding together of the social and the technical, it would not be sustainable. There would be trouble down the line.

As I listened and subsequently analysed these engagements, I began to think that the trouble lay as much with how the problem had been formulated as with how it might be solved. At no point had the formulation of the problem been discussed. This formulation was already stipulated within the terms of the World Bank contract as the 'inadequate management of solid waste', and yet, as the first workshop made abundantly clear, bad management was an abstract formulation for what people generally understood the main problem to be: a lack of state presence. People were looking to state agencies to take on the problem as a matter of public interest, to properly regulate non-domestic waste, and to take responsibility for the organization of domestic waste disposal.

Between specifics and generics: decentralization and integrated system

Thus far, I have explored how technical experts set out to engineer a 'solution' to the problem of solid waste management within the terms of the Vilcanota Project. The solution that was proposed adhered to a general neoliberal commitment to opening up new markets, and to looking for ways to ensure that public works are not simply handed down from an external state apparatus, but appear as self-sustaining enterprises; hence, the attempt to imagine the solution in terms that assume the possibility of the financialization of waste. However, as I have also shown, such solutions bring new problems in their wake. Collier describes neoliberalism 'as a form of problem making that defines a style of reasoning about infrastructures and economic regulation'. He points out that 'the tools of the new economics of regulation were invented precisely as a new form of critical visibility through which intransigent things, embedded norms and patterns of social provisioning could be brought into view, down to minute technical details, as the product of prior governmentality that had to be rationalized' (Collier 2011: 242).

As the city has grown, Cusco's rubbish has become increasingly evident as a space of material and political intransigence and existing patterns of social provisioning in the form of refuse management services are certainly in question. The reconfiguration of infrastructural systems emerges as a highly politicized space of action as new relations between state responsibility, economic potential and social welfare are devised in what are often overtly experimental and open-ended ways (Graham and Marvin 2001). One of the key components of this configuration is, of course, the materials themselves and their double transformational capacities, their potential to turn into money, and their tendency to toxic decomposition. The example of the Getinsa study shows that confronting the problem of waste management in Cusco is not simply a question of finding a way to configure problems and formulate solutions; it is also about trying to bridge this gap between the value and the problem of decomposing matter. The engineers can try to create a sense of continuity or equivalence between these divergent fields of material relations, through the mobilization of metrics that render all rubbish equivalent in terms of weight and volume, or allows a categorization in terms of future use. The numbers can also be deployed to rescale the problem of local waste via an accumulation across districts and provinces to produce figures that render the technical treatments proposed commercially viable. But the limits of these metrics become evident when people are asked to relate to the problem of waste through the figures rather than through their own experience. When asked to join the 'experts' in configuring solutions, local responses immediately turned to the incommensurables in the system, the discontinuities that the metrics concealed. In both the workshops, a glaring lack of equivalence is found between a notion of waste as productive resource and waste as a relation of decomposition that smells, attracts rats, generates residues and run-offs, killing plants and diminishing property values. The recycling plant, when viewed from the perspective of the community where it might be located, begins to look like an uncertain speculation, creating a clear divide between the rising value of land purchased to locate the plant, and the falling value of land that can no longer be used to live on or to grow food. The technical solution has produced new incompatibilities and concerns. Should a community member be allowed to sell their land if it adversely affects the living conditions of neighbours? Should a neighbour be allowed to prevent the commercial transactions of another when 'community' no longer defines the inalienability of land, and community members are legally able to buy and sell as they will? Should the provincial government compensate a community or an individual? What are the legal implications of the uneven distribution of benefit? These dilemmas surfaced and made explicit the tensions between a commitment on both sides of the argument to a sense of moral economy, whereby neighbours should live harmoniously, attentive to each other's needs. And yet the sense of moral community is also revealed as a space of uncertainty. The man who wishes to sell his land accuses his neighbour of disrupting community harmony through the voicing of illegitimate objections; the neighbour in turn understands the disruption as stemming from one member seeking financial advantage at the cost of another. From the perspective of the provincial government, the community is meeting a wider public need in the provisioning of this land, a gesture that overrides the objection to the personal gain of the vendor. And yet they recognize that the purchase affects the whole community, but they struggled to find a mode of compensation that might treat all citizens equally.

Getinsa's solution was still under review when we left Peru. The Regional Government and the World Bank doubted its viability. It had failed to sufficiently address local capacities to sustain its technological complexity. It had begun to look self-interested. Getinsa had proposed a system that no local people would be able to either install or maintain. It was thus too technical, insufficiently social. In addition, when looked at from another angle, the 'solution' was also challenged by local alternatives. Municipalities rejected the idea that urban waste (as toxic matter) might be dumped on their doorsteps; and yet they also wanted to protect their access to the lucrative potential of their own waste. Aware of the value of the solid waste, local governments were actively exploring alternative possibilities that would allow them to maintain control of their recyclables. In this respect, it is clear that discontinuities within the state itself (i.e., between central, regional and local government), worked against any easy acceptance of an integrated system.

At the end of our ethnographic study of Regional Government in Peru, we convened a seminar to discuss our findings with several of our key informants, drawn from the institutions that had kindly allowed us to shadow their work and to understand how technical and legal norms offered possibilities as well as limitations, for configuring a space of potential action. We had asked several of them to comment on our findings. Our mention of solid waste management sparked the most conflictual moment of the afternoon. One of our invited local government officials picked up on arguments that we were making about the ways in which distinctions between political and technical fields of practice are drawn and began to broadly denounce the technical study that had been drawn up with respect to the management of solid waste in the valley. He argued that there were many slippages in the way it was formulated. Was it a technical or an economic solution? Was the supposedly political agreement in fact a decision taken to favour particular economic interests, interests that had more to do with urban elites than valley people? As the discussion opened out, some suggested that it was not simply a tension between technical and political responses to the solid waste issue but there were also tensions between technical solutions. Which solution was preferable? Who would take that decision? Whose opinions would count? Somebody commented that the technical study on which the decision would be based was paid for by the municipalities. The Vilcanota Project was funded from public funds, it involves public debt, and yet somehow these studies seem to be produced with no guarantee. Can the consultants simply propose what works best for them?

This issue of how projects are owned, shared and discussed was a theme that had recurred throughout our previous months of fieldwork. There is a sense that technical knowledge is imposed from above, despite the parameters of public works projects, particularly those subject to the norms of the World Bank, which require a degree of public engagement. How should this engagement best be managed? A representative of Copesco, the body of the Regional Government responsible in this instance for the subcontracting of the technical study, agreed that these studies can appear authoritarian and imposed. He agreed that engineering companies still have limited understanding of how to manage diversity. An ex-mayor from the region agreed: 'In Peru, people are still waiting to be citizens', he said.

A few days later, in the offices of the Regional Government, another conversation unfolded. The officials with whom we were talking were disturbed by the accusations that had surfaced at our seminar. After all, they were working to produce a viable technical solution. Why did the local authorities insist on pointing the finger at them, when the political difficulties are most acute in the municipalities themselves? They thought that the real difficulty comes in finding a way to work together across the levels of the state. Everybody wants to take the credit for public works. Centralized projects are not welcome because local governments want to be able to say 'We did that'. Politics gets in the way. The problem of the rubbish began to morph into a more diffuse set of problems that no recycling plant was going to be able to address. These problems ranged from a sense of general lack of civic responsibility to the problem of widespread informality. How should the state act when 80 per cent of businesses in the construction sector have no formal licence? From the Regional Government's point of view the municipalities are at fault, because the mayors do not take the lead in ensuring that existing norms are adhered to.

The neoliberal form of problem making that Collier alerts us to distributes both the problems and the responsibility for finding a solution. But there is no social agreement as to how the discontinuities of the state itself should be addressed. It is thus not surprising to find that when consulted, people begin by voicing their desire for a stronger state presence. The ways in which waste disposal is configured as a problem thus rests on a critique of current state practice. But the differentiated governance regimes (Graham and Marvin 2001) involved in the regulation of issues such as the treatment and disposal of waste from large cities do not easily 'add up' to any coherent sense of state presence. State presence emerges in the regulatory practices that are negotiated across and between competing sectors and levels, in relation to transnational technologies and markets, and via the enactments of the international regulatory standards of multilateral lenders who require evidence of public participation in the formulation of public policy.

In the face of such distributed authority, the 'experts' who win the contracts and have the authority to suggest solutions to government are necessarily offering integrated technical solutions: solutions that appear to aggregate existing skills, interests and competencies, producing a version of what others have called 'joined-up government'. The technical capacity to integrate carries authority and weight in its own terms, precisely because it can stand outside the minutiae of local political conflicts. However, as we have seen, the experts also have to show that they are committed to providing social solutions; that is, they have to assume that a viable technical solution is useless if it is not 'owned' or at least accepted and embraced by those most closely identified with the problem. Defining the problem in such a way that it is both recognized and 'owned' is thus a crucial aspect of the exercise of technical expertise. Integral solutions that are devised to work at the scale of a large city offer economies of scale. Indeed, the integration itself requires a 'scaling up' of infrastructural capacity, and also a 'scaling up' of local difficulties such that the 'problem' is no longer amenable to local solutions, and the complex technical solution becomes the only viable social solution.

It is in this process that we can observe some of what gets reassembled in the engineering of future change at scale. For rubbish to be reassembled as matter with life, with productive potential and a commensurate market value, it has to be detached from all kinds of previous relations. Only certain materials can be recycled, and only in certain combinations. Organic/inorganic distinctions are a starting point, but there are finer distinctions to be drawn and that must be drawn to give the waste life. The less productive materials have to be sorted from the more productive, the corrosive from the non-corrosive, the toxic from the nutritive. And once operating at scale, it all has to be fine-tuned to 'fit' other technological possibilities elsewhere, other markets, other desires for the things that can be fashioned from today's leftovers. And these processes generate their own leftovers, not just all that is most toxic or corrosive but also other ways of defining the problem that open the way to solutions at a different scale. In combination, these material and social residues play out a material politics, their disruptive vitality shaping both the viability and the limits of infrastructural systems.

Notes

1 The Waste of the World research programme has investigated this topic in terms of global circulations. See http://www.esrc.ac.uk/my-esrc/grants/res-060-23-007/read.
2 I refer in particular here to Peruvian municipal law (*la Ley Orgánica de Municipalidades*) discussed in detail by Tupayachi (2012).
3 See for example: Bensaude-Vincent and Stengers 1996; Bensaude-Vincent and Newman 2007; Hicks and Beaudry 2010; Küchler 2008.
4 For example, Bennett 2010; Coole and Frost 2010.
5 The literatures here are wide-ranging. Key examples might include Descola 2005; Gell 1998; Ingold 2011; Miller 2005; Pels 1998; Willerslev 2007.
6 See Allen 1997, Degregori 2000, de la Cadena and Starn 2010, Harris 1999.
7 Stensrud 2011 is a recent example.
8 For further critical reflection on the relationship between anthropological studies of animism and material culture studies more generally see Harvey 2013.
9 This collaborative research project was carried out with Deborah Poole, Annabel Pinker, Jimena Lynch Cisneros and Teresa Tupayachi Mar, with funding from the Wenner Gren Foundation, the ACLS, the NSF, and the AHRC.
10 Copesco was created in 1969 as a special project charged with overseeing a national integrated tourism development plan, particularly with respect to the construction of tourism infrastructures. The organization combines expertise in civil engineering and reconstructive archaeology, and their public works portfolio integrates the restoration of Inka sites and colonial building, and the design and implementation of tourism circuits, which involves the provision of footpaths, tourism services and basic transport infrastructures such as roads and terminals. The tension between the expertise of the civil engineer and that of the archaeologist constantly emerges in public debate as a tension between the preservation of cultural patrimony and the reconstruction for tourist consumption. The organization, which began its life over 40 years ago as a national body, has now been subsumed to the Regional Government of Cusco. It is interesting to note how the problem of solid waste was allocated to this organization. In part, this was because of their established expertise and successful track record in the administration of large-scale public works. However, it also shows how solid waste management was linked, via this project, to tourism infrastructure and thus removed, in many ways, from the direct control of local municipalities. This tension remained unresolved in the elaboration of the engineering designs that I describe, and resurfaced as problematic in terms of the possibilities for the acceptance and adoption of the proposed solution. My argument is that the problem was never defined in such as way as to ensure the possibility of a more inclusive outcome.

Bibliography

Allen, Catherine (1997) "When Pebbles Move Mountains: Iconicity and Symbolism in Quechua Ritual". In: R. Howard-Malverde (ed.) *Creating Context in Andean Cultures*, Oxford: Oxford University Press. pp. 73–84.

Bennett, Jane (2010) *Vibrant Matter: a political economy of things*, Durham: Duke University Press.

Bensaude-Vincent, Bernadette and William Newman (2007) *The Artificial and the Natural: an evolving polarity*, Cambridge, MA: MIT Press.

Bensaude-Vincent, Bernadette and Isabelle Stengers (1996) *A History of Chemistry*, Cambridge, MA: Harvard University Press.

Brown, Bill (2001) "Thing Theory", *Critical Inquiry*, 28 (1), 1–22.

Collier, Stephen (2011) *Post-Soviet Social: neoliberalism, social modernity, biopolitics*, Princeton, NJ: Princeton University Press.

Coole, Diana and Samantha Frost (eds) (2010) *New Materialisms: ontology, agency, and politics*, Durham, NC: Duke University Press.

Degregori, Carlos (ed.) (2000) *No Hay País Más Diverso: compendio de antropología peruana*, Lima: Instituto de Estudios Peruanos.

De la Cadena, Marisol and Orin Starn (2010) *Indigeneidades Contemporáneas: culturas, politica y globalizacion*, Lima: Instituto de Estudios Peruanos.

Descola, Philippe (2005) *Par-delà nature et culture*, Paris: Gallimard.

Gell, Alfred (1998) *Art and Agency: an anthropological theory*, Oxford: Clarendon.

Graham, Stephen and Simon Marvin (2001) *Splintering Urbanism: networked infrastructures, technological mobilities and the urban condition*, London: Routledge.

Harris, Olivia (1999) *To Make the Earth Bear Fruit: fertility, work and gender in highland Bolivia*, University of London: Institute of Latin American Studies.

Harvey, P. (2012) "Políticas de la materia y residuos sólidos: descentralización y sistemas integrados", *Antropologica*, 20, 133–150.

Harvey, Penelope (2013) "Anthropological Approaches to Contemporary Material Worlds". In: Rodney Harrison, Paul Graves-Brown and Angela Piccini (eds) *Oxford Handbook of the Archaeology of the Contemporary World*, Oxford: Oxford University Press.

Hicks, Dan and Mary Beaudry (eds.) (2010) *The Oxford Handbook of Material Culture Studies*, Oxford: Oxford University Press.

Ingold, Timothy (2011) *Being Alive: essays on movement, knowledge and description*, London: Routledge.

Küchler, S. (2008) "Technological Materiality: Beyond the Dualist Paradigm", *Theory, Culture and Society*, 25 (1), 101–120.

Miller, Daniel (ed.) (2005) *Materiality (Politics, History and Culture)*, Durham, NC: Duke University Press.

Pels, Peter (1998) "The Spirit of Matter: On Fetish, Rarity, Fact, and Fancy". In: P. Spyer (ed.) *Border Fetishisms: material objects in unstable spaces*, London: Routledge, pp. 92–121.

Pinker, A. (2012) "Papeles de doble cara: la política de la documentación en un proyecto de ingeniería pública", *Antropologica*, 30, 101–122.

Stensrud, Astrid (2011) '*Todo en la vida se paga': Negotiating life in Cusco, Peru*, PhD dissertation, University of Oslo.

Tupayachi, T. (2012) "Encuentros y desencuentros del estado local y regional en la gestión integrada de los residuos sólidos. Una tarea pendiente en el Valle Sagrado", *Antropologica*, 20, 123–132.

Willerslev, Rane (2007) *Soul Hunters: hunting, animism and personhood among the Siberian Yukahirs*, Berkeley: University of California Press.

6

From stone to god and back again
Why we need both materials and materiality

Soumhya Venkatesan

Introduction

This chapter focuses on embodied gods (*murthi*)[1] of the Sanskritic Hindu tradition. I describe briefly the techniques by which specially produced stone statues (mainly anthropomorphic, but also aniconic) are transformed into named deities and worshipped and the techniques by which an embodied god is separated into two distinct ontological entities (god-power and 'just a stone statue') and explore the dilemmas raised by this kind of separation. By means of these descriptions, I achieve two goals. First, I implement Tim Ingold's (2007) eloquent appeal for a renewed focus on materials (the constituents of objects/things). Second, I question his antipathy to the concept of materiality and his attempt to replace a focus on materiality with a focus on materials. Ingold himself does not define the term materiality,[2] but by materiality, I mean the state or quality of being material.[3] A focus on materiality means being attentive to the ways in which the state of being material is achieved or caused.

I show that if we are to understand people's relations with material things, particularly in instances in which they seek to materialize the non-material, enliven a hitherto inert object or remove spirit from matter, it is important to pay heed both to materials and to materiality. Attention to the former cannot replace that towards the latter.

The research on which this chapter is based was conducted over a period of several months between 2006 and 2011 in the small town of Mamallapuram, on the coast around 45 kilometres south of Tamilnadu's capital city of Chennai in southeast India. Mamallapuram is renowned both for its historic rock carvings and structures and for the large number of expert stone sculptors and temple architects (*stapathi*) who live and work in the town and its environs. Commissions from Hindu temples all over the world come to the various *stapathis* in Mamallapuram, many of whom have been trained in the nearby Government College of Architecture and Sculpture. I worked mainly with one *stapathi*, whom I call Mani, spending time in his sculpture yard and travelling with him when he went to temples to deliver and install commissioned images.

The stone sculptor's yard

Mani's sculpture yard is set in a part of Mamallapuram that is a short distance from the areas of town frequented by tourists, who arrive in large numbers from within and beyond India to view the Pancha Ratha (a group of five rock–cut monolithic structures), the Shore Temple and other structures dating from the seventh century AD. The yard is usually noisy and dusty. Large, roughly rectangular blocks of granite are stacked in dusty piles. These have been bought from a quarry near Kanchipuram (around 65 kilometres away) and delivered by Mani's regular supplier.

Mani's five employees are usually busy working on smaller blocks of granite that have been cut from these large blocks, whereas Mani supervises them or does his accounts in the room at the end of the yard. The men crouch over the stones and use hand chisels and electric rotary cutters to shape the stone into the desired forms. The sound is deafening: the bell-like striking sound of iron chisels overlaid with the whining grind of small rotary cutters slicing into the stone. Sparks, stone splinters and dust fly around in equal measure.

A few adventurous tourists who want to move off the beaten track wander past now and again and peer in curiously, but most people who walk past the yard are locals or people with commissions from temples who come specifically looking for Mani. Mani graduated from the Government College of Architecture and Sculpture over 30 years ago, and set up his own sculp-ture yard around 25 years ago. He is well known and liked and receives several commissions every year, most of them because a satisfied customer tells others who might want to build, restore or renovate temples about his work.

There are thousands of temples in Tamilnadu; some are small, mainly catering to worshippers in a particular locale, whereas others are large, with hundreds of stone–embodied and bronze–embodied gods, visited by worshippers who travel large distances to pray to the main deity or associated deities. Some temples are in a bad state of disrepair and are taken up as projects by local people or others who seek to renovate or rejuvenate the temple. In some cases, a temple committee might decide to replace a damaged *murthi* or to expand a temple by adding more *murthis* in accordance with scriptural rules. People also build new temples in neighbourhoods, within hospital, factory or company grounds. Commissions for new statues of gods (*vigraham*)[4] are, therefore, frequent.

Representatives of temples who come to Mani with commissions for him to execute tell him the names of the gods of whom they want images. They also give him information on the heights of the *murthis* that are already present and that they want to retain. The commission is sealed with the payment of an advance (usually 25 per cent of the total cost) and a date is agreed for collection. Mani and his workers then proceed over the course of a few weeks to make stone sculptures that are iconographically complete and iconometrically appropriate for each deity that is going to be invited into the temple.

In most cases, Mani knows, from the name of the god, the appropriate appearance (clothing, jewellery, body type, etc.), disposition (smiling, angry, etc.), gestures, attributes and accessories that each *vigraham* must bear. In some rare cases, he may be unfamiliar with a particular deity and have to consult a manual (of which he has a few) with line drawings of the various deities of the Hindu pantheon.

Mani's workers identify suitably sized stones in the yard or, at his directions, cut one of the larger blocks of stone into appropriately sized cuboids. Mani crouches over each cuboid and, using a ruler, marks out the dimensions and form of the deity with a stick of charcoal, on top of which one of his workers adds a stronger outline with a stick dipped into red paint. This serves as the guiding template for the carving of the stone: a job that will is undertaken by any one of Mani's workers, or, if necessary, by Mani himself.

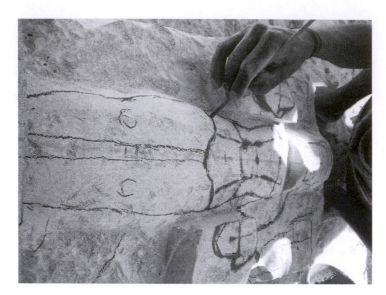

Figure 6.1   A two-dimensional picture of a deity being drawn on a stone block to guide the sculpting of the three-dimensional image. Image © Soumhya Venkatesan

A chisel and hammer are first used to break off larger chunks of stone from the block. Once this is achieved, a rotary cutter is used to cut into the stone following the outline. Chisels are then redeployed for details as the extraneous bits of stone break away and the outline becomes three dimensional. Finer detailing such as ornamentation, draperies, hair-dresses, jewellery, etc. is achieved using a lathe or a chisel and hammer. These, like the proportions, disposition and iconography, as has already been mentioned, follow closely the rules laid down in manuals for the depictions of each deity.

In a discussion piece entitled 'Materials against materiality', Tim Ingold takes issue with the widespread suggestion that 'the artisan … begins work with an image or design already in mind of the thing he plans to make, and ends when the image is realized in the material' (2007: 5). The problem with this way of thinking, according to Ingold, is that 'the surface of the artefact … is not just of the particular material from which it is made, but of materiality itself as it confronts the creative human imagination' (ibid.). In short, rather than paying attention to materials, we wrongly pay attention to materiality. Likewise, instead of paying attention to matter, we misguidedly pay attention to mind. Although I am sympathetic to Ingold's plea that we do not ignore materials, on the basis of my ethnographic fieldwork among stone sculptors, I take issue with his suggestion that the stonemason's knowledge is purely 'born of sensory perception and practical engagement, not of the mind with the material world' (ibid.: 14).

Of course, Mani and his workers have knowledge, born of experience and supported by simple tests, of whether a stone is fit to be subjected to the force of the chisel or the rotary cutter. At the stone merchant's before placing an order, the sculptor carves a small circle on a representative stone block. If this carving is successful, the stone from that particular quarry is deemed suitable for sculpting and an order placed. When the stones arrive, Mani taps each large block with a chisel to discern internal cracks or flaws. A ringing tone means the stone can be used for carving statues. Blocks that do not ring when tapped but produce a more thudding sound are deemed suitable for plinths, which require less carving, but not for statues. Once this basic test is carried out, the general procedure, as I observed it, is measured force applied precisely in order

Figure 6.2 Working on a *vigraham* of the god Ganesha. Image © Soumhya Venkatesan

to achieve a form that has been conceptualized beforehand and drawn out on the surface of the stone. There is, naturally, improvisation, but this is consonant with the intention to produce the desired form.

My description serves as an ethnographically informed corrective to the extreme position that Ingold adopts in his polemical piece, wherein he rejects outright the value in acknowledging that there can be a prior conceptualization of form and its imposition on matter. As must be clear from the description of Mani drawing the two-dimensional form of the deity on a block of stone to serve as a template for the three-dimensional sculpture that must be then produced, this viewpoint does not convince.

Neither does an approach that focuses on, for instance, 'stoniness' rather than the properties of a particular kind of stone. Humans select particular materials for particular projects. Within the constraints of availability, cost and other such considerations, they make judgements and choices between several kinds of what might naively be described as the same thing. This is not to suggest that humans have complete control over the objects that they have fashioned from particular materials. As Ingold points out, materials decay, change over time, are subject to the vicissitudes of weather, use, and so on. Nevertheless, it is important to note that people interact with materials instrumentally and selectively in order to fashion artefacts that, even if only for a time, are purposefully fixed.

Tilley, in his response to Ingold's discussion piece, argues that 'the concept of materiality is required because it tries to embrace subject–object relations going beyond the brute materiality of stones and considering why certain kinds of stone and their properties become important to people' (2007: 17). Mani and other sculptors with whom I have spoken insist that a certain grade of granite is most suitable for carving *vigrahams*. This grade of granite has to be soft enough to work and yet, once transformed into an embodied god, strong enough to withstand the many ministrations over many years of priests and worshippers. These include the daily bathing of the *murthi* with water, milk, honey, oil and other substances, dressing and bejewelling it, decorating it with flowers, and waving oil-lamps and camphor over it. The gradual softening of features due to erosion is an ever-present threat, as are, to a lesser extent, chipping or breakages. Shops catering to tourists in Mamallapuram stock small statues made from soapstone, but buyers are warned that these are not fit for temples; not because they have not been made according to scriptures, but because soapstone is soft enough to be carved into very small objects in the round with fine tools but too soft to be subjected to the rigours of ritual temple worship. Stoniness is important, but so are the properties of particular kinds of stone.

From stone to god

Hindu deities are conceptualized as simultaneously transcendant and immanent. In their transcendant aspect, the deities are beyond human conception: products of the imagination that are nevertheless very real entities to believers. In their immanent aspect, they are both immaterial and material, or rather permitting themselves to be made material or materializing themselves for the benefit of worshippers. It is this process of making material that I am concerned with.

When Mani and his employees finish work on the order for the temple, Mani informs the temple committee. Representatives of the temple get together the remainder of the money due, select an auspicious day (by consulting the Hindu lunar calender) and hire a suitable vehicle to transport the *vigraham*. On the day, Mani lines up all the *vigrahams* that are due to be collected. His workers oil the stone so that it is glistening. When the representatives from the temple arrive, Mani and his workers place flowers and vermilion and sandalwood marks on the *vigrahams*. The temple representatives place the money that they have brought on a plate and hand it over to Mani, who, having accepted it, asks one of his workers to bring a box of sweets. One sweet is circled in the air around the *vigrahams* and then broken on the ground as an offering. The other sweets are distributed to everyone present. The *vigrahams* are then carefully loaded into the waiting vehicle and driven away.

I now describe what happens to the *vigrahams* in the temples where they are to be installed as *murthis*, focusing in particular on rituals of preparation and transformation. Because the procedures followed are canonical, my description is abstracted from a number of consecrations that I observed.

On the day fixed for the installation, the statues are brought into the temple forecourt and each one is placed facing the direction appropriate for the deity that will enter it. At an auspicious moment, the sculptor who has come to the temple specifically for this purpose opens their eyes, thereby making them able to see and meet the gazes of others. The image is now alive and able to house the active presence of the deity (for a fuller account, see Harvey and Venkatesan, 2010). The sculptor and his attendants as well as a few priests then lift the stone images and place them on the pedestals that have been prepared for them in the shrines. There is a small space in the pedestal. A metal piece inscribed with a geometric diagram which is another embodiment of the deity (*yantra*), some gold and silver, the nine auspicious gems (*navaratna*) and some grain are placed within this space. The images are then placed on the pedestal over this now filled space and are fixed with a special paste (*marundhu*), which the sculptor has prepared. From this point onwards, only the priests may come into physical contact with the images.

In the meantime, specialist consecration priests, hired for the occasion, have already arrived at the temple. These consecration priests construct a series of sacrificial fires outside the temple under a specially built temporary structure. Around the sacrificial fires are placed a number of pots of water. Each set of pots corresponds to a deity, who will be invited into each *vigraham* and into the temple. Some of these pots are earthenware, others brass. Each pot is wrapped all around its surface with a white thread. The thread, according to one of the priests who was engaged in wrapping a pot, is identified as the nerves (*narambu*) of the deity. The pot itself is identified as the skin of the deity; the water within, which is enriched with turmeric and other auspicious substances, as the blood of the god. A coconut placed on top of the pot corresponds to the head and the three indentations on the coconut, the eyes of the god. The prepared pot as a whole then, acts as the body of the deity who is to enter it; it is the first embodiment.

A twisted strand of *darbha* grass (sacred and beloved of the gods) is placed within each pot of water in such a way that one end of the strand is in contact with the water and the other end with the air outside. The entire structure that houses the sacrifical fires is connected by means of threads made of *darbha*, silk and metal (ideally gold or silver) to the pinnacle of the temple. Priests sit around the various sacrificial fires and chant the names and attributes of the deities whom they are inviting. As they chant, they feed the fires with clarified butter, a number of dried herbs, seeds, fruit and other auspicious substances.

The chanting, as well as the feeding of the fire, are said to excite the simultaneously transcendent and immanent deities of the Brahmanical Hindu pantheon, who are present everywhere. It causes them to enter the pots of water by means of the twists of *darbha* grass that connect the air outside to the water inside. The deities also move, by means of the threads, into the temple, albeit as less material or embodied entities. Once the programme of chanting and other ritual tasks is completed and all the deities to be invited into the temple and the *vigrahams* are deemed to have become present in the water pots, the priests carry the pots in a ceremonious procession into the temple and pour the water from each of the set of pots containing the power, attributes and, indeed, the deity itself, onto the respective *vigrahams*. The *vigrahams* now become *murthis*: the statues become embodied gods. It is important to note that the *murthis are* gods and not merely representations of gods.

Before I turn to the implications of this, I want to dwell a little on the materials and substances used in the rituals of invitation and installation described above. In particular, I concentrate on water, because of the contrast that it provides with stone. Both the prepared pot of water and the stone *vigraham* are conceptualized as bodies into which the non-material deity is invited by ritual experts; thus embodied, the deity becomes actively present and is thence treated as an honoured guest, ministered to and worshipped. The difference between the two kinds of bodies is that the stone body is more enduring than the water-filled pot, which is conceptualized as a temporary body. However, water has a number of properties that make it eminently suitable for certain purposes. Water is a versatile substance: poured into a container, it fills it without crevices or gaps; in such a container, it is portable; it can be enriched by means of the addition of other substances; poured over an object, such as a stone *vigraham*, water flows downward easily and visibly, leaving surfaces wet and glistening. Equally, it dries without leaving a trace. Of course, other liquids possess most of these properties. But, compared with other important liquids like milk or honey, water is plentifully available. Also, water has cosmological import for Hindus. As one of the five main elements (*panchabhuta*), water, like fire, earth and air, is one of the key constituents of the material world. Its value is greater than the sum of its material properties and capabilities.

Once the charged water from the pots is poured over the stone *vigrahams*, they become, as I said, embodied gods.[5] The deities that were hitherto present everywhere permit themselves to be supplicated into the water and then to become actively present as *murthis* or embodied gods.

Once this ritual process is complete, the identification between deity and stone artefact is complete and stringent rules of conduct towards, and in the presence of, the *murthi* are imposed and observed. From this point onwards, only the temple priests are permitted to touch these statues, not even the sculptors who made them.

A consecration of an image is a movement from the non-material to the material. A variety of substances and things are deployed in this transformation. Each serves its purpose and then becomes irrelevant, except for the stone artefact in which the presence of the deity is concentrated in a way that unifies the material and the immaterial. But, and this is important, the power of the *murthi* is a product of ritual practices and expert knowledge. It is the priests who animate the stone *vigraham*. I reproduce the words of a priest below:

> The *shilpi* (sculptor) beats out the statue according to the Shilpa sastra [texts pertaining to the work of sculptors]. After that, with *mantrams* (*mandropttama*) according to each part of the body we give power – the power of the face (*mugam*) to the face, that of the heart (*hridayam*) to the heart. Like that one by one it is we who produce (*urpathi pannaradhu*) the power. Only after that does *prakasham* (light) develop (*yerpadaratrhu*). What we call the *murthi*, its power is created (*uruvaakka padarathu*) only by what we do. The statue does not have any of its own.
>
> *('Arya', interview, July 2009)*

The priest's description corresponds to what Peter Pels (1998) terms methodological animism. According to Pels, the use of the term animism is a way of saying that things are alive because they are animated by something foreign to them, a soul or a spiritual being. A spirit is made to reside in matter. Animism, as applied to things, transcends their materiality by suggesting that the perception of life in matter is possible only through an attribution of a derivative agency. In contrast, the use of the term fetishism indicates that things can be seen to communicate their own messages. To the fetishist, the thing's materiality itself is supposed to speak and act. Its spirit is *of* matter as opposed to the animist view that spirit is brought *into* matter (1998: 94).

Water and stone are important in and of themselves, both because of their material properties and because of the potent symbolism of water and suitably carved stone. This makes them suitable as dwellings, temporary or more enduring, for divine energy. However, the divine energy must be brought into them in an active form. This is the task of ritual experts. Indeed, the sculptors and, to a greater extent, the priests with whom I work may be described as methodological animists: they make sure that the materials and things that they use are fit for purpose but are quick to claim responsibility for the actual transformation of a stone statue into a god or water in a pot into divinely charged liquid. However, the agency or the capacity of the ritual experts to act effectively is tempered by the agency of the deities themselves. Thus, although every priest I met claimed that the rituals of consecration are efficacious (that is, they have their desired outcome), sometimes worries are expressed. At one consecration, a priest said 'The power is everywhere but you need the right technology and equipment to tap into it and make it come to you.' 'When we chant the texts and use the right materials, the power has no choice but to come,' added another. 'But,' said a third priest as a sort of postscript, 'we call and call. *If* he [a particular god] comes he will stay.' No one refuted this.

There is, then, simultaneously certainty and uncertainty even on the part of experts. Agency and intentionality are variously attributed even within the same conversation. The gods *must* come when called in particular ways; but then again, they may not. Likewise, the gods must vacate embodiments when requested to do so through the performance of appropriate rituals, but one can never be certain.

From god to stone

Just as images are charged with the power of the deities that they represent in bodily form, power can be removed from them for various purposes. This process works, logically enough, in the same way, but the sequence is reversed. Priests connect the embodied deity/inhabited image to specially prepared pots of water by means of strings. The priests chant from the specified texts and as they do so, the power moves from the image to the water, leaving the image inert: an empty container. The process as well as the temporary image are known as *balalayam*, which is simply translated as child's or small house.

Balalayam may be performed for a number of reasons. A particular image may need replacing with a new one and the power needs to be transferred. Or, the plinth on which an embodied deity image stands may need repair or its height raised. Or, an entire temple may go through a process of expansion and recharging with power. Or, there might be maintenance work that needs to be undertaken in the shrine in which the deity is installed. In all these cases, people other than priests need to enter highly purified and restricted spaces. They also need to touch the image (something that is normally prohibited).

The thing to remember as far as we are concerned here is that priests, sculptors and others are insistent that when the *balalayam* ritual is performed, the image is inert and empty. This is in theory. However, relationships with *balalayam* images are more complex than that in practice. Certainly, several people whom I encountered, although experts in, and committed to, the rituals, nevertheless remained doubtful that the image was truly empty of power.

An example serves to illustrate this point. A number of seventh-century frescoes that were behind the *murthi* of the main image in a small temple in a Tamil town were being restored in 2008 to 2009. Because restorers needed to go into the shrine, where only priests are normally allowed, *balalayam* had to be performed in order to temporarily separate the power of the deity from the stone statue. This was duly performed and the power transferred to a fig-wood plank on which was made a drawing of the deity. The stone sculpture in the shrine reverted to being, in the words of the temple priest, Kannan, 'just a statue' [he used the English word]. However, every morning, when Kannan went in to perform ritual worship in front of the *balalayam murthi*, he would nonetheless pay obeisance to the *vigraham* in the main shrine. When I asked him about it, he said: '... it has housed the deity for so long. It still has some power. You can't take it all away even with the rituals.'

Here, animistic thinking seems to be replaced by fetishistic thinking. The physical object that has been emptied of the deity does not vanish once the deity has gone from it. It remains physically present and that poses a problem: what to do with it? What is its nature? Can people, however adept, truly control ontological transformations: stone to god to stone again?

At least in the case described above, the power would have transferred back to the stone statue in the main shrine once the restoration work was complete. Uncertainty and affective ties are even more poignantly felt when the body of an embodied god is replaced. This is supposed to happen if there is any damage to a *murthi*, or if a temple is undergoing expansion, necessitating a change in size of various *murthis*. When a stone sculpture has been worshipped as god every day, often for years on end, people, especially priests, say they believe that the embodied god is like their child. After all, they put it to sleep, wake it up, wash it, dress it, adorn it with flowers. They know its contours intimately. Replacing an image is a grand event, and one in which priests take part. The new *vigraham* which becomes god will, in turn, become as much part of the priest's routine and affections as the old. But, detachment is difficult. Decommissioned statues are meant to be disposed of as soon as the power is removed from them. They are supposed to be cast away into a water body (the sea, a river or a well) and thus physically and mentally removed.

However, priests can rarely bring themselves to do this. One said to me when I asked about a decommissioned image that I spotted in a temple, 'I know it should be disposed of, but it did hold the god for a while and it does not seem right.' Often, old stone statues can be seen in forgotten corners of temples.

The dilemmas that surround the correct treatment of emptied images open up some interesting questions about the nature of things, the unpredictability of gods and the abilities of people. These questions arise precisely because of the thingness of things and differences between different materials/substances.

The same properties that make granite a suitable material for a statue that serves as an embodied god (i.e. durability and hardness) render it a source of unease and discomfort when the statue is no longer required as an embodied god. The continued physical presence of the once-animate embodied god confronts and confounds. Lingering in a forgotten corner, the stone statue serves as a testament to the weakness of humans who once shaped the stone for their own purposes. The same dilemma does not obtain for the water in the pot, which also serves as the temporary body of a god. Once this water has been poured over the stone statue, it disappears relatively quickly by a combination of evaporation and absorption. Unlike the stone statue, no worries attend its displacement as a dwelling for divine energy; its task is done and it can be forgotten.

Conclusion

Although I do not find convincing Ingold's rejection of materiality as a useful concept, I do find useful the distinction that he makes, following Heidegger, between a thing and an object. Heidegger, Ingold says in a paper he gave in Manchester in 2008 (which was published in 2010), 'was at pains to figure out precisely what makes a thing different from an object. The object stands before us as a *fait accompli*, presenting its congealed, outer surfaces to our inspection. It is defined by its very "over-againstness" in relation to the setting in which it is placed' (Heidegger 1971: 167 cited in Ingold 2010: 4). 'The thing, by contrast, is a "going on", or better, a place where several goings on become entwined. To observe a thing is not to be locked out but to be invited in to the gathering. Thus conceived, the thing has the character not of an externally bounded entity, set over and against the world, but of a knot the constituent thread of which, far from being contained within it, trail beyond, only to become caught with other threads in other knots' (2010: 4). The embodied god is, in this sense, a thing: part of a wide-ranging set of goings-on that set it up as a god and maintain its godness. When a *murthi* returns to being 'just a statue', the problem with its continued presence in a temple is precisely that it is unsatisfactorily cut off from the various goings-on. Its complete removal offers the only satisfactory solution. But, as we have seen, that is not emotionally easy to accomplish and it becomes an uneasy combination of a thing and an object. This, it seems to me, is what sets up the conditions for its fetishization in this kind of situation.

Materials (the constituent stuff of objects, artefacts and things) and materiality (a concept that I use to describe the state or quality of being material) make both materialization and dematerialization fraught activities, certainly with regards to stone, with the latter transformation seemingly presenting more problems than the former. Granite is desired for durable projects of materialization because it is durable in itself and capable of being sculpted into a three-dimensional object that has been conceptualized in a human mind as a suitable representation of a particular god and therefore as a suitable body. But once an immaterial power or the power of a deity has been rendered material, given a specially made stone body and persuaded to accept it, the very durability of the stone causes doubts when that particular body is no longer required for the separated-out divine energy. Methodological animism, or the claim that spirit in matter is a product of human intention and action, gives way to methodological fetishism; tangible, visible things challenge human capabilities and control. If a material such as granite can be said to haunt, here is where it seems to do so.

Notes

1 Among the meanings of this word, commonly used by my informants, are embodiment, manifestation, incarnation, personification (*A Sanskrit–English dictionary*, Monier-Williams, M., 2005: 824).
2 Interestingly, his opposition to the term seems to preclude a desire to pin it down: 'It seemed to me that the concept of materiality, *whatever it might mean*, has become a real obstacle to sensible enquiry into materials, their transformations and affordances' (2007: 3; my emphasis).
3 Other definitions of materiality in different disciplines or contexts are revealing. For instance, when referring to digital text and documents, the term materiality refers to the physical medium used to store and convey the text, as apart from the text itself. In architecture, materiality is the concept of, or applied use of, various materials or substances in the medium of building. Thus, materiality in architecture may refer to the materiality of specific projects, where one would need to consider the full range of materials used.
4 Among the meanings of this word, normally used by my informants, are individual form or shape, form, figure, the body (*A Sanskrit–English dictionary*, Monier-Williams, M., 2005: 957).
5 See Chris Fuller (1992), who insists that there can be no absolute distinction between a Hindu deity and its corresponding image. The image is a container or house for the deity and the image is the deity. It is inhabitation and embodiment.

Bibliography

Fuller, C. J. (1992) *The camphor flame: popular Hinduism and society in India*, Princeton, NJ: Princeton University Press.
Harvey, P. and S. Venkatesan (2010) Faith, desire and the ethics of craftsmanship. In M. Candea (ed.) *The social after Gabriel Tarde: debates and assessments*, London: Routledge: pp. 129–142.
Ingold, T. (2007) Materials against materiality. *Archaeological Dialogues* 14 (1): 1–16.
Ingold, T. (2010) Bringing things to life: creative entanglements in a world of materials. http://www.socialsciences.manchester.ac.uk/realities/publications/workingpapers/15-2010-07-realities-bringing-things-to-life.pdf (retrieved on 13 January 2012).
Pels, P. (1998) The spirit of matter: on fetish, rarity, fact and fancy. In P. Spyer (ed.) *Border fetishism: material objects in unstable spaces*, London: Routledge.
Tilley, C. (2007) Materiality in materials. *Archaeological Dialogues* 14 (1): 16–20.

7

New materials and their impact on the material world

Susanne Küchler and Peter Oakley

Introduction

This chapter focuses on an important yet neglected aspect of material culture: the appearance of new, made-to-measure materials that have begun to colonize the physical world. Within the social and historical sciences, we have barely begun to theorize materiality beyond the fetish, an approach that ignores the full import of the material composition of objects. Everything that we hold and everything that we see takes shape thanks to materials, but it is the social identities we construct for materials that lead to their selection or rejection in manufacturing and influences the adoption or refusal by consumers of the resulting products. Through an exploration of the development and social reception of the first synthetic materials, material classification, and the relevance of the prototype to design practice, together with a consideration of how fully made-to-measure materials relate to these phenomena, we present the reader with an outline of crucial changes that are reshaping the way we conceive of and interact with the material world.

Synthetic materials and the rise of design

Many current theoretical perspectives on materials remain heavily indebted to nineteenth-century notions. Nineteenth-century manufacturing regarded the form of an object to be coterminous with specific materials on account of the material requirement for selected tools and manufacturing processes. During the early industrial revolution, the prototype of an object was not thought to be independent from its realization in a specific material, a notion that was captured by the mid-nineteenth-century German architect Gottfried Semper, whose writing on style in the technical arts expounded on the 'truth to materials' (Semper [1854] 2004).

Semper asserted this interdependency of form and material in the face of new approaches that were developing after the discovery of new mouldable materials such as kautschuk (Wagner *et al.* 2005). Kautschuk, or natural rubber, could take on many different forms and be made to look like other materials. It could be kept flexible or vulcanized to make it hard and strong like stone. It was thought at the time that it could serve any conceivable purpose, as shown by Thomas Hancock's 1854 illustration of possible uses, which implied the creation of new object categories such as hosepipes, wetsuits, balls and tyres (Semper [1854] 2004).

Although there had always been an element of property selection through processing in the use of long-established materials, there were restrictions to the extent to which metal alloys, ceramic bodies or fibres could be compositionally manipulated. In addition, concentrations of material knowledge were discrete and sequestered within production communities, with the trade guild structure and apprenticeship system engaging in material knowledge protectionism. Artisans concentrated on developing their understanding of the properties of socially defined groups of materials, an education that then defined their social identities (e.g., blacksmith, goldsmith, potter, carpenter, stonemason or cloth dyer). The designing of an object and the process of its manufacture were so intimately entwined, they were not conceptually separated (Pye 1968). The specialization of material understanding and the conflation of intention and final realization still feature heavily in production practice in what are termed 'preindustrial' communities (Kentley 1999; Mahais 1993).

After the advent of rubber, design as a process began to lose its inherent materiality, increasingly being considered an abstract activity that could be imposed on materials in the same way as specific materials could be made to assume different textures, colours and functions simply by alterations at the molecular level made with barely any physical effort, for example by adding a small pinch of sulphur. The discovery in 1843 of vulcanized rubber and its commercial success began the rise of synthesized materials, spurred on by an increasingly economically significant chemical industry, which harnessed the botanical exploration of the world for the discovery of novel material properties (Schiebinger and Swan 2005).

In the 1920s and 1930s, chemists created the first synthetic polymers, enabling the production of synthetic stretchable materials (Ball 1997: 345). The plasticity of synthetic polymers has given rise to a million-dollar industry, because its products are relatively cheap, lightweight and durable. These ubiquitous plastics have become a symbol of the modern age (Meikle 1995). Their enthusiastic reception by consumers was linked to a more general optimism towards science and technological progress in the mid-twentieth century.

The challenge to the integrity of materials that plastics entailed was brilliantly captured by Roland Barthes in his now classic description of watching the manufacture of plastic objects in *Mythologies* (1972). For Barthes, plastic epitomized the dissolution of the material in that it 'hardly exists as substance', but is sublimated as movement and infinite transformation at the same time as it appears to replace all other substances (Barthes 1972: 97). The rise of plastic, and its colonization of more prosaic object types, meant that the luxury of design could become part of the mundane household and the everyday. The invention of new object forms, such as the 'bendable chair', resulted in new social forms of engagement and living arrangement, all of which were determined by this artificial, technologically constructed material (Rübel and Hackenschmidt 2008).

What is 'new' at the onset of the twenty-first century is that the functional and aesthetic properties of materials can now be more comprehensively tailored for production, leading to materials that exist as objects in their own right. Design itself now includes a phase in which materials are 'informed' with calculated purpose (Barry 2005; Ashby and Johnson 2002). Intentionality now informs objects at an earlier stage in the process of production, in the seclusion of the research laboratory rather than on the factory floor (Strathern 2001). The range of material properties available for use has now eclipsed formal restrictions as the determining factor in cutting-edge design practice.

At the same time, this new wealth of opportunity undermines the distinctiveness of any specific material classification, because its determining properties can be increasingly closely copied by a range of substitutes. What these 'new' materials and allied technologies impress upon us is a new kind of object ontology, which replaces the management of diverse preexisting physical tendencies with limitless physical transformation.

The social importance of materials

To appreciate the magnitude of this shift, it is necessary to recognize the full extent and social relevance of material classification. Historically, the whole spectrum of the spiritual, the cultural, the political and the economic informed material identities and the processes of selection by producers and reception by consumers.

This spectrum is shown in Michael Baxandall's (1980) research on the rise of German lime-wood sculpture in Renaissance Germany. He describes how the rising mercantile class in the newly established towns of southern Germany took over the commissioning of sculptures for altars from the clergy and chose limewood, the specific properties of which provoked a new technique of carving and created a new expressive style, which in turn resonated with a new sensibility toward individuation that came to form the basis of both reformation and industrialization. Limewood was not only the hardest and most expensive material, but it also was taken from trees that since medieval times had possessed ritual and cosmological significance, associated with fertility and prosperity. Its selection propelled merchants into the centre of cosmologies in the making, which informed norms and behaviours in the rapidly transforming markets and media of the time. The selection of limewood was not just a socially mediated process, but also presupposed knowledge and expertise in the distinctive properties of different types of wood and related materials (Klein and Spary 2009). Shrouded in secrecy and coveted as artisan knowledge, materials and ideas associated with materials tell us more about a culture and society than has generally been given credit (Gell 1992: 52–53).

More recently introduced materials have had to find their place in relation to these long-standing material identities. Once a material starts to circulate, its applications themselves generate additional meanings, helping to construct a more stable categorization. In the case of aluminium, shortly after its isolation in the mid-nineteenth century, the metal was so scarce that it was used only for jewellery, medals and small precision mechanical parts. After the development of electrolytic extraction, it became commercially viable to refine large amounts, but aluminium was still put to use only to create object forms more usually made using other metals. Aluminium developed a truly coherent social identity only at the start of the twentieth century. This was a result of the development of new classes of object: the airship and aircraft. These required light, malleable materials for their construction, requirements that gave aluminium alloys a unique niche and led to the perception of aluminium as a futuristic material. By mid-century, it was the material of choice for many overtly styled products that appropriated the visual vocabulary of speed, including the iconic Airstream caravan (Nichols 2000).

Such material histories show the extent to which conceptions of materials are context dependent, although at any point in time they are treated by subjects as fixed, an insight related to Appadurai's proposal of the temporary nature of the commodity state, and further theoretical extensions of this approach (Appadurai 1986; Godelier 2004; Weiner 1992). But although any object exists socially within a vast socially constructed matrix consisting of a moral economy and a value hierarchy of object forms, it is also situated in a conceptually separate moral economy and value hierarchy of materials. Because each of these sets of relationships is incommensurate with the others, all physical objects inevitably show complexity (Mol and Law 2002). Although we generally perceive these relationships to be static, changing social pressures are continually redefining relationships across the entire matrix, usually imperceptibly, but occasionally catastrophically.

An example of an obvious and dramatic shift is seen in the history of radium, which was propelled from scientific curiosity into diverse social roles during the early decades of the twentieth century. After its ability to kill cancerous cells was discovered, radium became considered a desirable and expensive medicine (Rentetzi 2009). After an increase in supplies and a concomitant drop in price, it was promoted as a beneficial addition to toothpastes, mineral water and even underwear to promote health. The luminosity of radium led to entirely different application in self-illuminating instrument displays and watch dials (meeting newly arisen needs in military aircraft and trench warfare technologies). Enthusiastic adoption changed to rejection after the infamous 'radium girls' US lawsuit of 1928, which publicized the damage radium caused to any living tissue, quickly destroying the panacea status of the material (Clark 1997).

The radical shift of radium from miracle material to health risk is echoed in the histories of many other materials, including asbestos, DDT and lead-based paint compounds. In each of these cases, it was not the inherent physical properties of the material that changed. What altered were the networks of intangible societal expectations, beliefs, needs and concerns, after extended engagement with the materials in question, which led to a recognition of their positive and negative potentials in different contexts.

Skeuomorphs and luxury materials

Although the examples presented above show how the types of input that inform the categorization of a material are informed by social context, they do not necessarily challenge the primacy of its functional properties in the selection process: limewood is hard; aluminium is light and ductile; radium glows. But the existence of alternative relational schema (skeuomorphs and luxury materials) fundamentally challenge the notion that 'truth to materials' was ever a viable axiom.

A skeuomorph is an object that has a duplicate form but that diverges in its constituent material from a prototype. The intention of the producer of a skeuomorph can be direct imitation, the creation of an ersatz version, or object differentiation (Knappet 2002). As Judy Attfield identified, the unselfconscious skeuomorph has proved problematic for design theoreticians; reproduction furniture is worthy only of pariah status (Attfield 2000). In design circles, any appropriation of moribund stylistic conventions has to be accompanied by a heavy dose of intentional visual irony in order to receive critical acclaim. But although imitation is essential to skeuomorphism, it does not follow that this inevitably leads to diminution or impoverishment. In many instances, a skeuomorph does something differently, or even does more, than its prototype.

Because of its workability and cultural resonances, gold has frequently been used in the production of skeuomorphs when the intention is to emphasize differentiation. Fabergé's famous Easter eggs, manufactured from gold, precious and semiprecious stones and technically demanding enamels, were specifically intended to construct a relationship of distance from their prototype, the painted hen's egg, a traditional Easter gift (Museum Bellerive 1989). The formal associations of each Fabergé egg enabled the Russian royal family to practise Easter gift-giving rituals in a similar way to other European Christian families, although the material composition of each egg acknowledged and actively supported the elevated social status of the Romanov dynasty.

The relationality of materials is a fundamental factor in the social construction of all luxury goods. To be considered a luxury item, any specific object must be partially but not wholly interchangeable with something else; it is not possible for anything to exist as a luxury good unless there is a more prosaic alternative (Berry 1994). The creation of a luxury item results in a hierarchy of refinement, which not only constructs the status of the luxury object but also redefines its prototype as the more basic non-luxury option, a classification it cannot escape.

The existence of luxury goods undermines the primacy of material functionality and the notion of truth to materials. Although possibly less workable, robust or durable, or more difficult to source, the symbolic associations of luxury materials make them essential for the creation of objects that will assume a particular cultural status (Bourdieu 1984; Helms 1993). But although luxury materials are an extreme example, the same relationality exists between every material. Hierarchies are continually being constructed, maintained, challenged and defended. The more social sedimentation of meaning any material acquires, the more it becomes anchored, but cumulative changes can still erode or build individual positions.

The appearance of any new object has an effect on the overall semiotic matrix. In most cases this is local and minute, but can be immensely magnified when objects have a wide social reach. During 2011, publicity surrounding a single object, Kate Middleton's engagement ring, had a noticeable impact on jewellery purchases across the UK and the USA; it not only directly stimulated the demand for blue sapphires with diamonds but also generated demand for similar ring designs using less expensive blue and white combinations of stones, such as cubic zirconia and tanzanite. Through its positively viewed associations, this one object elevated all others that were considered in some way to be related.

Artificial versus natural materials

One major opposition that has developed in the lexicon of material description is artificial versus natural, a notion that derives from the assumption that the manufactured can and should be contrasted to the harvested. But beyond the easily identified extremes of the untouched and the entirely synthesized, in use, this duality is highly inconsistent. Most materials described as natural have been processed to some degree, with the express intention of changing their composition in order to alter their physical properties. 'Naturalness' is constructed through ongoing comparisons with other materials; comparisons in which familiarity, traditions of use and a range of subjective values feature heavily. Lime mortar, despite being fundamentally restructured at a molecular level during processing, is described as a more natural building material than concrete. Walnut veneer is generally termed natural, even though it undergoes controlled stabilization and impregnation with manufactured polishing compounds (Pye 1968).

With regard to materials, the artificial has come to be defined by the use of scientifically derived technologies in processing. After such scientific interventions, materials are considered reborn, accordingly being given new names. This convention is supported by the behaviour of scientists, who assume the role of progenitor (Latour 1987). Although science as a philosophical approach and as a practice examines and manipulates the laws of nature, the material results of its activities are contrasted with the natural.

The laboratory, as the place in which science is performed, has assumed distinctive conceptual functions, which intertwine with its role in practice (Latour 1987; Knorr-Cetina 1992; Johansson 2009). Materials that enter this sphere undergo transformation. Minerals and parts and secretions of plants and animals become isolated and renamed according to chemical or biochemical nomenclatures, languages that privilege elemental composition but ignore provenance. Through this linguistic process and encapsulation in labelled drums, vials, jars and bottles, the materials are decontextualized, effectively denatured, becoming subservient neutral tools in the creative acts of scientists. The exception to this is the sample that undergoes analysis, which, because of its role as subject of scrutiny, has to retain its original identity.

In contrast to the distinct break with origins evident in the construction of artificiality, with natural materials, provenance is essential. This comes with its own issues. Natural materials are constantly under threat of contamination by the artificial. Such anxieties over pollution remind us that the natural has come to assume the status of the sacred, opposed by the profane artificial. The man-made contaminant is very much 'matter out of place' (Douglas 1966).

This need to protect the natural can reach the extreme of a harvesting process coming under scrutiny, followed by opprobrium. The rise of ecology and environmental concerns has led to international bans on the use of a whole range of animal and plant materials. Ivory was, until the late twentieth century, considered a desirable and eminently workable material. But concerns over the survival of the large mammals that produce it (elephant, walrus and whale) have led to widespread prohibitions of use. Similar restrictions have been extended to coral, tortoiseshell, rhinoceros horn, a range of animal furs, reptile and fish skins, and tropical hardwoods. Campaigns supporting such prohibitions emphasize the extent to which these materials are best left in their place of origin, as opposed to being subjected to human appropriation.

Emergent properties and smart materials

One of the reasons many now-taboo natural materials were widely valued for manufacturing was their subtle surface patterns and remarkable durability and strength. These are a result of microstructures rather than just molecular composition; they are emergent material properties. Such microstructures form the hatched grain in ivory that gives it such outstanding mechanical resilience and visual appeal. In the 1960s, there was a distinct difference between the physical complexity of such natural materials and the structural simplicity of synthetic plastics (Pye 1968). Today, the situation is radically different.

Recent technological developments have led to the ability to create 'smart' or 'meta' materials, synthetically engineered materials that have unusual properties not available in nature but gained through artificially created internal structures (Ball 1994). They can change shape, texture, colour or chemical composition in response to their environment. These qualities have been put to use in innovations such as photochromic glass, which darkens on exposure to ultraviolet light, or biomimetic smart valves, which contain no moving parts and can repeatedly expand and contract in response to changes in environmental conditions such as pH or calcium concentration.

Within electromagnetics, the term metamaterials specifically refers to nanofabricated materials that show 'negative refraction' (bending light the 'wrong' way). Such metamaterials have been proposed as a mechanism for building a sort of 'invisibility cloak' by surrounding an object with a metamaterial shell that affects the passage of light near it. This new wave of smart materials has the capacity to radically change the way we inhabit and perceive the material world (Meikle 1995; Antonelli 1995; Haynes 1953).

Research into the emergent properties of natural materials has been one of the cornerstones of the growing discipline of material science; this research has informed the development of many of the new smart materials. Although created in laboratories and with no direct counterpart in nature, smart materials such as aerogel, heat memory alloys and carbon nanotubes are more closely related to animal-derived and plant-derived materials in their microcomposition and resultant behaviour than any of the 'dumb' materials synthesized by the chemical industry during the last two centuries.

The results of this classificatory deadlock are evident in the little-known but thriving materials libraries, mostly situated in art, design and architecture studios. These repositories are attempting to organize an avalanche of designed materials (estimated at between 40,000 and 70,000), the complex, multiple and occasionally transformative properties of which resist previously satisfactory taxonomies dependent on groupings such as provenance or simple molecular composition (plastics, ceramics, metals and glasses). The growing need for consultants who can navigate this terra incognita and advise clients on making a selection from the tsunami of materials has led to the appearance of materials brokers, independent material archives and handbooks directed at a specialist audience in design and industry (Ashby and Johnson 2002; Beylerian and Dent 2005; Stattmann 2003).

The prototype, rapid prototyping and devolved design

The growth of the range of materials available is not the only issue that designers have to face. Recent developments are also beginning to threaten one of the core elements of design practice, the production of prototypes as distinct identifiable entities.

The arithmetic that defines a recognizable artefact form is known as the prototype, a concept of crucial importance to the mass production of objects since the industrial revolution. The prototypicality of a design is a fundamental part of its take-up and transmission in society, yet it is questionable whether the measure of a material made by design can be understood in the same terms.

The prototype is both original and model in so far as artefacts are related to it by virtue of formal likeness that results from emulating in the copy technical or material qualities. Yet such similarity is deceiving, because the prototype is capable of exerting a kind of compulsive self-replication on account of a translation of form that should be recognized as a change in scale, a technical invention that brought with it the emergence of a notion of design. The prototype is not usually of the same material as the mass-produced object created in its image; its materiality of wax, plaster or clay or marks on paper embraces the notion of transformation and movement that has become the hallmark of its rendering.

The first class of prototype the invention of which fashioned the world of design as we know it today was championed by John Flaxman (1755–1826), the famous English neoclassical sculptor. Flaxman created clay and plaster models for monumental marble sculpture (leaving the marble carving to hired hands) and wax models that were used to make the plaster models and moulds for ceramic relief decoration, but he also sketched designs for marble sculpture, pottery and silver (Bindman 1979; Bury 1979; Tattersall 1979). His sketches are important for their influence on the emerging practice of design in the early nineteenth century; the translation of two-dimensional into three-dimensional forms of representation became a conventional method of prototypical design.

The second early prototype is the Jacquard loom, invented in 1804–1805. Jacquard recognized that although an intricate and delicate task, weaving was highly repetitive. He developed a mechanical system that automatically created complex woven patterns. At each throw of the weaving shuttle, a stiff, pasteboard card was placed in the path of the rods. A pattern of holes in the card determined which rods could pass through and thus acted as a program for the loom (Essinger 2004).

Artefacts that result from the translation of two-dimensional images into three-dimensional forms are measurably alike each other; the scaled form is an essential element of mass manufacture. The scaled material world engendered a new way of thinking, in which sameness became a virtue in its own right (Hacking 1990; Adler 1998). By the end of the nineteenth century, variation was not just deeply unpopular as an unsettling reminder of a world that could not be predicted or controlled but had also become synonymous with the strange and exotic.

Although the prototype with its allusion of a measurable, repetitive world continued to hold popular imagination, fuelled by institutions and disciplines set up in its image, during the course of the twentieth century, science, art and technology began to recognize plurality as a viable alternative for thinking about the material world. An emphasis on the mechanics of scaling was increasingly replaced by dimensional and additive transformations of a fractal kind. This led to a reappraisal of the interactions between different levels of material composition, leading to discoveries about the features of microstructures and their role in the macroproperties of materials.

This new approach is exemplified in recent innovations in antenna construction that incorporate fractal approaches. Because of the repetition of the same arrangements at different scales, fractal antennae are capable of operating with good-to-excellent performance at many different frequencies simultaneously and, unlike a simple antenna, the physical length of a fractal antenna is unrelated to its performance. The development of length-independent fractal antennae helped make palm-size mobile phones a reality (Falconer 2003). Fractal geometry also underlies the creation of new composite, informed materials that can deform or stretch around any surface by virtue of their internal fractal self-replication. They enable the manufacture of conductive fibres woven into fabrics or engineered chemically into responsive surfaces, creating an alternative topological materiality (Quinn 2010).

The necessity of the prototype to production has also been inadvertently challenged by rapid prototyping (RP), a technology involving the automated construction of physical artefacts using digitized instructions. RP technology uses an additive mode of fabrication, bonding materials layer by layer to form objects, in contrast to previous mechanical processes of fabrication such as milling or lathing, where objects are created through a repetitive action that removes material to reveal an intended final form (Hopkinson *et al.* 2005).

RP was initially developed to make physically manifest the outputs of computer-aided design (CAD); the objects produced being conceived as three-dimensional manifestations of the two-dimensional imagery created by technical drawing programs. Although the earliest CAD programs were created to digitally reproduce reductive actions like milling or lathing, the flexibility of the RP additive process enabled material realizations of entirely different types of digitally envisioned structures.

Beneath the seemingly innocuous and familiar phrasing (of making the production of proto-typical objects more rapidly) lies a profound difference of effect: every material product of RP can be conceived as a singular, made-to-measure, finished artefact, because of the collapse of the stages of manifesting intention and manufacturing into a single process. Unlike Jacquard's punched cards, the digital code that is used to control the RP printer is inherently and infinitely mutable, consisting of assemblages of potentially independent moieties of data. The material transformation, which defines the technique, gives each artefact that is being produced its intrinsic properties. By changing the composition of the powder to be bonded, a different product can be created using exactly the same digital file.

In combination, RP and microlevel design are making rapid inroads into the automated knowledge-based generation of design, producing seamless garments or fabrics from powdered compounds that can be manufactured both fully assembled and with variable weave anywhere in the world that has access to a printer. RP offers visions of an entirely decentralized production of individuated things.

Conclusion

Current theoretical perspectives and practical approaches to production are being increasingly compromised by an avalanche of new materials that defy established classifications and conventions that are reliant on distinctions in provenance and processing history or comparisons informed by distinct physical differences in the molecular composition of materials. These taxonomic approaches cannot encompass the physical complexity, mutability and potentially infinite gradation that characterize new made-to-measure materials *en masse*.

Because of the increasing availability and variability of entirely made-to-measure materials, the way that society imposes its character on the world of things is now no longer solely through objects, but by the processes informing the marketing, distribution and selection of materials for design. Although these materials are increasingly colonizing the objects that make up the material culture of contemporary societies, their social reception is confused and an understanding of their properties and potential lacking. How these new materials will eventually be integrated into cultural cosmologies remains an open question, but one with direct significance to social development and stability.

With the advent of synthetically engineered materials and allied material technologies, the centre of gravity of design is shifting from abstract formal concerns towards the technical process that informs the designing of material. Calculation, and with it intentionality and social agency, are increasingly carried by the painstaking technical process of material invention. Our attention needs to be redirected from the glamour of discovery and revelation, to the geographically and temporally dispersed work that cumulatively develops made-to-measure properties. This process, inaccessible by conventional methodologies of observation, is more difficult to uncover, categorize and frame.

In the wake of these developments, the convention of the prototype as the preeminent physical manifestation of intention and the determining feature of design practice is now under threat. The role of the prototype as condensed intentionality in the sequence of production activity is now in danger of eclipse by the appearance of an alternative locus at the point of material creation and dispersal through the advent of new production processes that collapse the acts of form design and manufacture into a single act.

The pressing question for social science is how it should engage with materials and associated technologies that have become commodities and potential targets of cosmologies in their own right and are beginning to command attention in a way that makes the fetish pale in comparison.

Bibliography

Adler, K. (1998) Making Things the Same: Representation, Tolerance and the End of the Ancien Régime in France. *Social Studies of Science* 28 (4), pp.499–545.

Antonelli, P. (1995) *Mutant Materials in Contemporary Design,* New York: Museum of Modern Art.

Appadurai, A. (1986) 'Introduction: commodities and the politics of value', in A. Appadurai ed. *The Social Life of Things: Commodities in Cultural Perspective,* Cambridge: Cambridge University Press.

Ashby, M. and Johnson, K. (2002) *Materials and Design: The Art and Science of Material Selection in Product Design,* Oxford: Butterworth-Heinemann.

Attfield, J. (2000) *Wild Things: The Material Culture of Everyday Life,* Oxford and New York: Berg.

Ball, P. (1994) *Designing the Molecular World: Chemistry at the Frontier,* Princeton, NJ: Princeton University Press.

Ball, P. (1997) *Made to Measure: New Materials for the 21st Century,* Princeton, NJ: Princeton University Press.

Barthes, R. (1972) *Mythologies.* Translated by Annette Lavers. New York: Jonathan Cape.

Barry, A. (2005) Pharmaceutical Matters: The Invention of Informed Materials. *Theory, Culture and Society,* 22 (1), pp.51–69.

Baxandall, M. (1980) *The Limewood Sculptors of Renaissance Germany,* New Haven and London: Yale University Press.

Berry, C.J. (1994) *The Idea of Luxury: A Conceptual and Historical Investigation,* Cambridge, UK: Cambridge University Press.

Beylerian, G. and Dent, A. (2005) *Material Connexion: The Global Resource of New and Innovative Materials for Architects, Artists and Designers,* New York: Wiley and Sons.

Bindman, D. (1979) 'Designs Connected with Sculpture', in D. Bindman ed. *John Flaxman,* London: Thames and Hudson, pp.112–119.

Bourdieu, P. (1984) *Distinction.* Translated by Richard Nice. London: Routledge and Kegan and Paul.

Bury, S. (1979) 'Flaxman as a Designer of Silverwork', in D. Bindman ed. *John Flaxman,* London: Thames and Hudson, pp.140–148.

Clark, C. (1997) *Radium Girls: Women and Industrial Health Reform, 1910–1935,* Chapel Hill, NC: University of North Carolina Press.

Douglas, M. (1966) *Purity and Danger,* Abingdon, UK: Routledge and Kegan Paul.

Essinger, J. (2004) *Jacquard's Web: How a Hand-loom Led to the Birth of the Information Age,* Oxford: Oxford University Press.

Falconer, K. (2003) *Fractal Geometry: Mathematical Foundations and Applications,* Hoboken, NJ: Wiley.

Gell, A. (1992) 'Technology of Enchantment and Enchantment of Technology', in T. Sheldon and J. Coote eds. *Anthropology, Art and Aesthetics,* Oxford: Oxford University Press.

Godelier, M. (2004) 'What Mauss Did Not Say: things you give, things you sell, and things that must be kept', in C. Werner and D. Bell eds. *Values and Valuables: From the Sacred to the Symbolic,* Walnut Creek, CA: Alta Mira Press.

Hacking, I. (1990) *The Taming of Chance,* Cambridge, UK: Cambridge University Press.

Haynes, W. (1953) *Cellulose: The Chemical that Grows,* New York: Doubleday.

Helms, M.W. (1993) *Craft and the Kingly Ideal: Art, Trade and Power,* Austin, TX: University of Texas Press.

Hopkinson, N., Hague, R. and Dickens, P. (2005) *Rapid-Manufacturing: An Industrial Revolution in the Digital Age,* Cambridge, UK: Cambridge University Press.

Johansson, M. (2009) *Next to Nothing: A Study of Nanoscientists and Their Cosmology at a Swedish Research Laboratory,* University of Gothenburg.

Kentley, E. (1999) 'Design without Designers: boat building in the Palk Bay', in J. Peto ed. *Design Process Progress Practice,* London: Design Museum.

Klein, U. and Spary, E.C. (2009) *Materials and Expertise in Early Modern Europe: Between Market and Laboratory,* Chicago, IL: University of Chicago Press.

Knappet, C. (2002) Photographs, Skeuomorphs and Marionettes. *Journal of Material Culture* 7 (1), pp. 97–111.

Knorr-Cetina, K. (1992) 'The Couch, the Cathedral, and the Laboratory: on the relationship between experiment and laboratory in science', in A. Pickering ed. *Science as Practice and Culture,* Chicago, IL: Chicago University Press.

Latour, B. (1987) *Science in Action,* Cambridge MA: Harvard University Press.

Mahais, M. (1993) 'Pottery Techniques in India: technical variants and social choice', in P. Lemmonier ed. *Technological Choices: Transformation in Material Cultures since the Neolithic,* London and New York: Routledge.

Meikle, J.L. (1995) *American Plastic: A Cultural History,* New Brunswick: Rutgers University Press.

Mol, A. and Law, J. (2002) 'Complexities: an introduction', in J. Law and A. Mol. eds. *Complexities,* Durham, NC: Duke University Press.

Museum Bellerive (1989) *Carl Fabergé: Kostbarkeiten Russischer Goldschmiedekunst der Jahrhundertwende,* Zürich: Museum Bellerive.

Nichols, S. (2000) *Aluminium by Design,* Pittsburgh: Carnegie Museum of Art.

Pye, P. (1968) *The Nature and Art of Workmanship,* Cambridge: Cambridge University Press.

Quinn, B. (2010) *Textile Futures: Fashion, Design and Technology,* Oxford and New York: Berg.

Rentetzi, M. (2009) *Trafficking Materials and Gendered Experimental Practices: Radium Research in Early 20th Century Vienna,* New York: Columbia University Press.

Rübel, D. and Hackenschmidt, S. (2008) *Formless Furniture,* Frankfurt: Hatje Cantz.

Schiebinger, L. and Swan, C. (2005) *Colonial Botany, Science, Commerce and Politics in Early Modern Europe,* Philadelphia, PA: University of Pennsylvania Press.

Semper, G. ([1854] 2004) *Style in the Technical and Tectonic Arts; or, Practical Aesthetics.* Translation by Harry Francis Mallgrave and Michael Robinson. Los Angeles, CA: Getty Research Institute.

Stattmann, N. (2003) *Ultra Light–Super Strong: A New Generation of Design Materials,* Basel: Birkhäuser.

Strathern, M. (2001) The Patent and the Malangan. *Theory, Culture and Society* 18 (4), pp. 1–26.

Tattersall, B. (1979) 'Flaxman and Wedgwood', in D. Bindman ed. *John Flaxman,* London: Thames and Hudson, pp. 47–65.

Wagner, M., Rübel, D. and Wolf, V. eds. (2005) *Materialästhetik,* Berlin: Reimer.

Wagner, R. (1981) *The Invention of Culture,* Chicago, IL: Chicago University Press.

Weiner, A. (1992) *Inalienable Possessions: The Paradox of Keeping-While-Giving,* Berkley and Los Angeles: University of California Press.

8

Decay, temporality and the politics of conservation

An archaeological approach to material studies

Eleanor Conlin Casella and Karina Croucher

Temporality and biographical materiality

As a scholarly exploration of the residues of human cultures, archaeology has long been concerned with the specialist study of the material qualities of objects associated with the distant through contemporary past. Much of this literature has examined how a diverse range of 'raw' (or unmodified) materials (stone, clay, plant fibres, metals, minerals or bone) has become reworked, transformed and shaped into meaningful cultural objects. At the heart of these classic 'artefact studies,' we find a deep curiosity and detailed scientific appreciation of the intrinsic qualities of these material fabrics (Hurcombe 2007a). Such work draws from a multidisciplinary array of scientific research, with techniques adapted from: plant biology, zoology, biochemistry, genetics and haematology to help define organic components; mineralogy, geology and chemistry to identify inorganic elements and material processes of transformation; and physics, engineering and tribology (the science of 'wear') to characterize how objects are physically made, used and demolished over time.

Thus, as a discipline uniquely dedicated to the exploration of materiality, archaeology typically adopts the concept of *material* to describe the constituent fabric or physical qualities of 'things,' including specific affordances, malleability and processes of decay (Hurcombe 2007b). In contrast, the *object* may be loosely understood as those 'things' made, shaped or transformed through human or animal intervention, and the *artefact* as a distinctive subcategory of object that has been 'made' through archaeological intervention, and thus has specialist qualities traditionally defined as 'form', 'function' and 'style', which in turn enable a diverse array of comparative analyses and subsequent interpretations (Hurcombe 2007a).

Nevertheless, as much as all objects hold specific material qualities, they retain specific temporal qualities; indeed, these two ontological dimensions are inextricable, mutually constitutive and inevitable (Lucas 2005). Like places and people, objects are always enmeshed within a moment of change, flux, transition, rather than a fixed, essential or somehow 'permanent' state of being. The archaeological concept of a *use-life* was developed in the 1970s to explore the biography of these perpetual material transitions: to record, in other words, the many cyclical and sequential ways that objects are made, used, reused, modified, broken, repaired and eventually abandoned or discarded (Schiffer 1972). Through the study of *taphonomy*, archaeologists explore the various cultural and natural influences (including chemical decomposition, animal interference, manual crushing, agricultural ploughing, weathering, etc.) that continue to modify objects in their post-depositional context, ultimately forming the specific material nature of the archaeological site (Schiffer 1987; Schiffer and Miller 1999). Of course, the use-life of an object may be subsequently extended through its 'recovery' by later people for additional purposes (archaeological analysis, museum display, commemoration, public education, exchange, valuation, commodification) with the material qualities of the artefact again transformed through the social, political and economic meanings of these new biographical events.

Ultimately, as archaeologists, we work with temporal materials (with portable artefacts and architectural features that are partial, discarded and remnant objects) in order to interpret, reconstruct and fantasize about past lifeways, past social worlds. To imagine, in other words, *what might have been* before. Thus, the basic enterprise of archaeology is inherently nostalgic: a yearning to understand another temporal period, one that can never be fully captured, but only partially visualized through the material qualities of those transient artefacts that we encounter in a different physical state (a decaying state) from previous chapters of their use-life biography.

Of course, archaeologists are not limited to a study of objects. Artefacts of past human activities may frequently include the remains of built environments (clusters of associated remnant or decayed building materials [brick, stone, packed earth, mortar, wood, etc.]) that must be imagined backwards into a preexisting architectural state, or temporal sequence of states, to 'reconstruct' the taphonomy of the archaeological site over the course of its use-life. For example, excavations at the Ross Female Factory site in Tasmania, Australia revealed the subsurface remains of the Nursery Ward dormitory (Figure 8.1). When carefully integrated with data from soil stratigraphy, historic archival sources, and local oral histories, close material analysis of these heavily decayed site features suggested a complicated sequence of activities that could be temporally sequenced in order to interpret (or imagine) four distinctive built phases for the use-life of these architectural remains (Casella 2011):

Origins of the quadrangle (1842)

Originally established as a British colonial penal station for accommodation of approximately 220 male exiles, the original eastern and western rooms (materially indicated by the incomplete presence of remnant sandstone wall foundations) first served as a dormitory for male convicts. According to historic documents conserved by the Tasmanian Archives Office (Casella 2002), interiors of this original Ross compound were floored with sandstone flags. A drain system was constructed along the exterior southern wall, with the ditch feature exposed during excavations showing its original location and orientation (the absence of the feature itself providing a significant material property). A sandstone perimeter boundary wall enclosed the southern rear of the quadrangle compound, its subsurface remnant foundations of large irregular blocks similarly revealed in January 2007.

Establishment of the female factory (1847)

When recommissioned for exiled female convicts in 1847, the original sandstone flags were removed and replaced with wooden floorboards (see Casella 2002 for detailed history and stratigraphy). Archaeological evidence of this reflooring event appeared in two material forms: the absence of the original sandstone flagged floors (with enlarged depressions within the underfloor

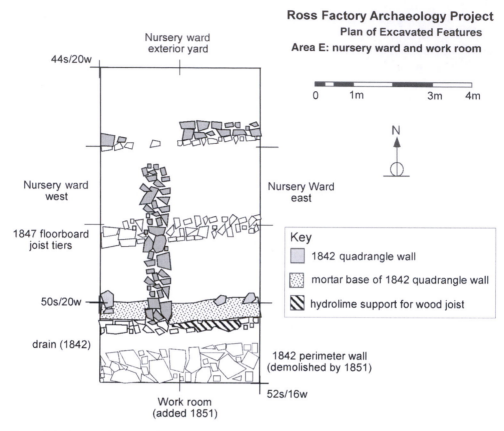

Figure 8.1 Excavation trench Area E, with temporal sequence of architectural features, Ross Factory Archaeology Project 2007. Image by permission of Eleanor Conlin Casella

space suggesting the removal of these rectangular stone blocks) and the addition of sandstone joist support piers abutting original wall foundations to provide suspension for newly introduced timber floorboards. Crucially, this interior modification created a discrete underfloor space where artefacts were able to gradually accumulate during the Female Factory use-life of the historic site, as a material signature of human activities within the dormitory. With the arrival of female inmates in January 1848, the eastern and western rooms became reclassified as nursery wards. Internally divided, this structure accommodated a maximum of 50 infants and toddlers, in addition to their adult female caretakers.

Reinforcing the factory regime (1851)

After a series of management scandals, a new Factory Superintendent was appointed in July 1850. Dr Edward Swarbeck Hall immediately requisitioned imperial funds for institutional modifications, including a dedicated work room (a structure that abutted the southern façade of the nursery ward in historic plans of the colonial prison) (Casella 2002). As a result of Hall's institutional redesign, the 1842 sandstone drain system and perimeter wall were demolished to ground level and covered by the new structure (see Figure 8.1). A single course of highly decayed handmade bricks and fragile lime mortar located against the original 1842 sandstone dormitory wall provided ephemeral physical evidence of this newly introduced structure within our excavation trench.

Transitions to heritage (1853–present)

The most dramatic stages of material transformation related to the post-depositional use-life of the excavated structure. After the cessation of British penal transportation in 1853, the compound was gradually demolished, with component materials of timber roofing, brick and sandstone walls, interior fittings and timber flooring subsequently recycled into new building projects, or abandoned to decay *in situ*. By the early twentieth century, the site was leased to local farmers (the Knowles), with the remaining and highly eroded building elements soon flattened and covered with alluvial silts. During the mid-1980s, the Ross Factory was inscribed as a Tasmanian heritage site. Abandonment led to increased animal intrusion, with snake and rabbit warrens further shifting and scattering the subsurface artefacts and architectural features. Thus, by 2007, our excavations revealed a partial jigsaw puzzle, an accretion of remnants and bits that required active (yet evidence-based) imagination to reconstruct the material biography of this heritage place.

On the inevitability of decay

Drawing from this temporal perspective, archaeologists appreciate how all materials (both portable objects and architectural features) exist within a perpetual state of decay. And yet, this inevitable process can be mediated against, with human actions and interventions producing a suspension of decay, if only temporarily.

Decay is not only essential, but an inevitable process. For organic (carbon-based) 'living' entities, death is inevitably followed by an unfolding decomposition. Even those elements traditionally seen as permanent or stable (stone, plastic, monuments, landscapes) are constantly, as previously shown, enmeshed within a transitional state. Thus, whether material is inorganic or organic, the processes of erosion, decay, transformation await all things. And yet, despite this inevitability of decay, the material process may frequently provoke feelings of unease, curiosity, discomfort, mortality or even revulsion.

Cultural measures enacted to prescribe against decay are multifaceted. For architecture, processes of maintenance provide a stabilizing effect, whether through plastering, repainting, cleaning or dusting. Similarly with bodies, one may strive to delay aging, whether through exercise and diet, cosmetic surgery, or simply cleanliness and hygiene. Indeed, the mundane acts of combing hair or brushing teeth offer a means for enfleshed personal conservation.

Although immortality can be sought, bodies die. Physical remains eventually decay. Decomposition not only unfolds throughout life but dramatically accelerates immediately after death, moving through several material stages before complete skeletization occurs. Depending on environmental factors (including temperature, weather exposure, microclimate and presence of insects), material decomposition can take anything from a few days to thousands of years (Clark *et al.* 1997). The head, that area with the least soft tissue, is usually the first part of the body to reduce to skeletal form (Pinheiro 2006: 108). From the position of the bones, it is possible to derive information about the burial, including whether the deceased was placed in a coffin, in a tomb, or covered with soil (Duday *et al.* 1991), all of which influence the speed of decomposition, as does the duration of exposure before initial burial (Gallowry 1997).

In the contemporary West, after death, we rarely encounter the deceased body. Specialists 'deal' with the mortal remains, and through embalming or cremation, create a material artifice of suspended serenity for the grave. Throughout (pre)history, attempts have been made to preserve the dead body, both human or animal (Casella and Croucher 2011), with intentional preservation of the dead traditionally rendered as the mummies from Ancient Egypt. In addition to these familiar dried and desiccated Egyptian bodies, there are cognate South American mummies of the pre-Hispanic Andes, and bodies preserved within frozen conditions, including human remains excavated from the Siberian Plains. Dating from *c.*700 to 200 BC, the Pazyryk preserved their dead by extracting organs and packing dead bodies with combinations of earth, pine needles and other plants and grasses, horse hair, bark and peat (Rudenko 1970). Facilitated by freezing conditions, decay was inhibited for thousands of years.

Alternatively, Iron Age 'bog bodies' of northern Europe (*c.* 400 BC–250 AD) are human remains preserved by the acidic, stable conditions of water-logged peat marshes. Whether this suspension of decay was intentional, or an unintended by-product of actions surrounding these deaths, remains disputed by scholars. Regardless, the preservative material qualities of the peat are unlikely to have been unknown and preservation may have been intended (Taylor 2002; Giles 2009).

Even in a modern context, the controversial work of Gunther von Hagens, a medical-cum-aesthetic anatomist, shows a contemporary yearning for preservation of the human and animal corpse (von Hagens 1982). Through his pioneering process of *plastination*, donated remains are treated to materially transform the dead body into an 'object' used for medical education and ghoulish entertainment (von Hagens and Whalley 2006).

Of course, numerous ethnographic and archaeological examples exist for intentional collection of dry bones, with human remains frequently reused within commemorative arrangements and architectural installations, including the Sedle Ossuary in Kutna Hora, Czech Republic, and the Chapel of Bones of Evora, Portugal. These displays incorporate the bones of the human dead into built features, such as archways and chandeliers, and also cement them into surrounding walls. Significantly, these infamous displays use skeletal remains whose flesh has already decomposed; the removal of decay renders them easier to view than decomposing flesh. Where the dead body is considered in an objectified way (engaged with more as object than person), the corpse has been described as 'abject' (Nilsson Stutz 2003), neither wholly object nor subject. Simultaneously, the decomposing body evokes strong physical reactions in the living. The smell and sight of decomposition (the temporal and material transformations of the body) assail the viewer. Reactions to decay may involve nausea, shock and revulsion, creating sensory experiences that are mnemonic, frequently unforgettable (Hertz 1960).

And yet, the decaying human corpse can be imagined with an 'agency' of its own. It shifts and omits sounds, fluids and gases, and thereby appears temporarily animated. Prominently, for instance, during cremation, the corpse may physically move as it transforms, oxidizes, and reduces under the flames (Williams 2004). Although the notion of objects retaining some form of 'agency' has provoked strong debate within archaeology (e.g. Robb 2004; Russell 2006/2007), artefacts may definitely be understood as affective – having an impact and affordance, 'acting back' on those who encounter them (Ingold 2007). This affective quality of the inanimate exists most acutely with decomposing objects – they evoke emotions, reactions, memories and physiological experiences.

Although our aversion to decay is most accentuated when encountering the human corpse, a yearning to avert decay is also applied to objects, with various field and laboratory techniques developed for preserving, conserving and retaining the recovered materials. But for archaeologists, the concept of decay offers a paradox, in that although our physical evidence is perpetually eroding, that same material process of decomposition itself provides valuable data. Radiocarbon (C^{14}) dating, a cornerstone of the modern practice of archaeology, is based on the regular decay cycle of the unstable carbon isotope, as are additional methods of radiometric age determination such as uranium and potassium–argon dating. These age determination methods are not without their flaws: a reliable uncontaminated sample is essential, age ranges may vary from centuries to millennia, and for some geographic regions, the accuracy of dates necessitates statistical calibration (Bronk Ramsey 2010). Despite these limitations, dating techniques based upon material decay provide vital data for archaeological research.

A more profound archaeological paradox is that our iconic research technique (site excavation) is itself an essentially destructive practice that actively hastens the decay of our study subject. Not only do we slice apart the site, extricating (or excavating) artefactual materials from their depositional contexts but those very objects we expose are subjected to immediate transformations of their environmental surroundings. These changing conditions lead to a rapid breakdown of the stable environment that enabled material preservation, causing, for example, an oxidization (rusting) of iron; a deterioration of bone, shell and glass; a decomposition of leather, wood and textile artefacts. Storage of artefacts may only exacerbate decay, with problems including destruction by rodents and insects within museum stores, and mould growth on organic matter within display cases. Our research therefore expedites the material transformations of decay. Yet without excavation, we lose a vital component of our material insight into past human lives, as powerfully debated in a recent edition of the leading journal *Archaeological Dialogues* (2011). And so the paradox of archaeology, with knowledge weighed against destruction, becomes mediated by concepts of preservation and conservation of our archaeological sites and transient materials.

The politics of intervention

As an expensive and time-consuming intrusion into the inevitable material process of decay, conservation cannot be applied to a universal sample of artefacts recovered from an archaeological excavation. Some, if not most, artefacts are sacrificed to material decomposition over time, with their potential interpretive (and nostalgic) values lost as they disappear from the physical record. Others are chosen for intervention in the form of cleaning, stabilization and restoration. As a highly artificial suspension of inevitable decay, archaeological conservation involves actions performed both on-site during excavations (Leigh *et al.* 1998) and subsequently as specialist techniques performed under laboratory conditions (Sanford 1975; Cronyn 1990; Rodgers 2004). Interventions include treatments for archaeologically recovered metals such as iron (Fe), copper-alloys (Cu+), gold, silver, lead, nickel and aluminium, organics (wood, leather, shell, textiles), in addition to materials typically considered 'stable' (possessing qualities less susceptible to rapid decomposition), yet always in a state of gradual transient decay (glass, ceramic, stone, plastic and rubber). Composites, or mixed-fabric artefacts, require particular conservatorial attention, because the material properties of one constituent element may actually hasten the decay of another, as in the case of metal lids on glass bottles, or metal buttons on textile clothing.

Interventions may include investigative cleaning, microscopic and chemical analysis of the constitutive material fabric, chemical alteration, filling of gaps to limit oxidization, and removal of obvious agents of deteriorization. Longer-term stabilization frequently involves storage conditions that manage exposure to humidity, temperature fluctuations, dust and gaseous pollutions, light, fingerprints/human oils, and organisms (such as mould spores and insects). In specific cases, organic elements can be slowly replaced by inorganic components to provide support for internal cell structures (in the case of organic wood or leather artefacts). Chemical reactions can be artificially introduced to remove corrosive layers and detain further oxidization (in the case of ferrous and lead objects).

For archaeological collections, the selection process immediately begs difficult questions on the underlying politics of conservation. What objects are considered 'worthy' of intervention? Whereas metal artefacts recovered from an early Anglo-Saxon period site in north-west England may inform us of technological change and local economic adaptation after the collapse of the Roman Empire, ferrous iron nails recovered from a Post-Medieval period site of the same region hold less individual interpretive significance, and would therefore be unlikely submissions for extensive conservation. To what degree does this process of human, chemical or environmental material interference alienate the artefact from both its current material associations and original social context? Once conserved, the archaeological object typically becomes a 'museum piece': a heritage artefact stored within environmentally controlled conditions, handled with acid-free cloth gloves under supervised access within a laboratory or storage facility. But through continuous human and environmental interaction, the object inevitably decays into non-existence. How do we best respect the material qualities of these artefacts?

For whom are these objects conserved? Do indigenous, local or associated communities desire these interventions? Are these artefacts deemed unique, and subsequently isolated for artificial suspension of material decay in order to satisfy archaeologists and heritage authorities? Should artefacts be conserved today because of currently perceived values for future populations? Or is this an ultimate act of material hubris? Perhaps there are objects that should be encouraged to materially decay, regardless of (or indeed, because of) their cultural significance. When existing as socially relational entities, objects may be specifically designed and intended for decomposition, as in the case of contemporary Irish holy well icons and votive offerings (Rackard *et al.* 2001; Rattue 2001), traditional Tiwi decorative wooden burial poles and fibre, hair and feather funerary baskets of Melville and Bathurst Islands, Northern Australia (Morphy 2007), and *malangan* wooden, hair and fibre masks of New Ireland, in the Bismarck Archipelago of Papua New Guinea (Küchler 1987). Within certain contexts, conservation interrupts the intergenerational transmission of cultural traditions, with material transformation through living practices embraced as far more important than 'fossilization' of some idealized past, as in the controversial example of indigenous community efforts to repaint a sample of historic rock-art sites in the Kimberley region of north-west Australia (Bowdler 1988). Given the temporal and material changes generated through the process of conservation, we must ask how such 'objects-out-of-time' gather alternative meanings through such artificial and transient efforts of suspension.

Archaeologists are confronted by these material questions with every excavation. After fieldwork in 2007 at the Ross Female Factory (described above), over two thousand individual artefacts were excavated, and yet only three were evaluated as worthy of laboratory conservation – a set of lead seals recovered from the underfloor deposits below the nursery ward. Highly unusual within this Australian context, the artefacts were deemed significant because of their association with powerful narratives of globalized female labour, maternal affect, colonial imprisonment and colonial distribution of manufactured commodities (Casella 2011). Further, although the best preserved of the set displayed the stamp of the Royal Army Ordnance Corps (that branch of His Majesty's Army charged with provisioning the imperial establishments of the Australian penal colonies), the lead fabric of all three items was in a rapid state of decay after their removal from the damp acidic soils of the excavation site. Subcontracted through the Museum of London laboratories during 2011, conservation works involved: delicate mechanical hand-cleaning with brush and scalpel, treatment with a 5 per cent solution of sodium hydroxide, immersion in a sequence of tap water, sulphuric acid, deionized water, and acetone, and finally three hand-brushed applications of a reversible clear non-reactive coating. Costing approximately GBP£100 (US$165) per item, these material interventions stabilized existing lead decay, cleaned objects of

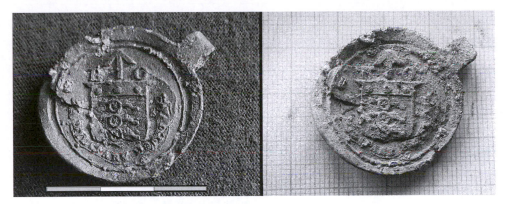

Figure 8.2   Detail of excavated lead bale seal artefact, Ross Factory Archaeology Project 2007. Left: special find artefact 20 after conservation treatment. Right: special find artefact 20 before interventions. Image by permission of Eleanor Conlin Casella

decomposed material, and chemically sealed the objects from further oxidization. Now holding new value as museum display items, the excavated objects are materially suspended from both temporal and material transformation (Figure 8.2).

But efforts at material conservation are not merely contemporary practices. Acts of preservation served as motivations behind treatment of the dead in various periods of (pre)history. Although ancient embalming has been discussed earlier and elsewhere within this volume (see Exell), pre-modern conservation of body parts also includes the phenomena of plastered skulls within the Neolithic Middle East. Dating from around 8500 BC in Ancient Levant and Anatolia, treatment of the dead involved, at least for some community members, the posthumous excavation of skulls or crania of dead kin, which were then covered with plaster of mud, lime or gypsum to sculpt a new 'face' over the skull (Figure 8.3), and thereby re-render human features onto the dead. In some cases, the 'face' may be enhanced, with inlaid shells used as eyes (e.g. from Levantine 'Ain Ghazal [Griffin *et al.* 2001], or charcoal simulating the eyelashes on plastered skulls from Tell Ramad [Stordeur and Khawam 2007]). Washes of colour were applied to many plastered skulls, producing a lifelike hue to the otherwise pale surface of the plaster. Several layers of plaster and paint were applied to some remains, indicating longevity of use before final burial.

Although only a small proportion of this population were adorned with plaster, material evidence for removal of plaster suggests that the practice was more common than intact remains suggest. Wear-marks previously assigned to facial defleshing activities are now reinterpreted as plaster removal, found on positions of the skull away from muscle attachments (Bonogofsky 2001). Furthermore, three plaster 'masks' recovered from 'Ain Ghazal were discovered to be remnants of such plaster faces, originally modelled over a skull before they were removed, and subsequently preserved with exceptional material care (Rollefson 2000: 171). Survival of these extremely delicate faces offers a testament to the careful handling afforded these objects before eventual burial.

Such enigmatic examples of pre-modern mortuary practices, despite being carried out on children as well as adults (Bonogofsky 2004), usually inspire archaeological interpretations of ancestor worship or ritual hierarchies that imagine these plastered skulls as ritual leaders or elders (Kuijt 2008: 177; Rollefson 2000). An alternative motivation may lie in the desire to retain the dead close to the living, thereby prolonging a departure of the dead, and also temporarily delaying decay and decomposition (Croucher 2012). Recovery of the human skull or cranium (well into the process of decomposition) was followed by active cleaning (or defleshing) of the human

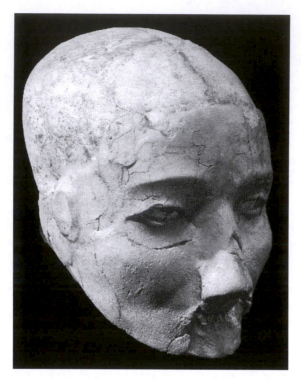

Figure 8.3   Conserved plastered skull, Jericho (Kenyon Jericho Archive held at University College London). Image by permission of the Kenyon Jericho Archive

face, and subsequent 'refleshing' as a material encounter through the plaster render. But this very process of reconstruction also remained non-permanent. Archaeological examples of artificial repair and conservation exist, including a skull from Tell Aswad, in which the nose was reconstructed after breakage (Stordeur and Khawam 2007), or the repeated episodes of painting and plastering found on the plastered skull from Çatalhöyük, which suggested a longevity of use-life (Hodder and Farid 2004).

Nevertheless, after an artificially extended period of display, handling and curation, deterioration inevitably commenced, with the rendered face itself experiencing deterioration. The crumbling plastered skull would then be reburied, either individually, or in caches with other plastered and unplastered crania.

Perhaps the processes of material intervention are not so distant from those practised by contemporary museum conservators and curators. The plastered skulls now receive their own episodes of replastering and restoration. In an echo of their original purpose, they are frequently found on public display within museums and laboratories, in specialist photographs and publications. One account of a skull from 'Ain Ghazal describes the cranium's fall from its display on a laboratory shelf (Griffin *et al.* 2001); the process of accidental breakage allowed further analysis, intervention and reconstruction of the face, with a fresh life span generated through contemporary conservation and intervention. Thus, decay remains an issue of intervention for both objects and bodies within both contemporary and ancient contexts, ultimately generating an enduring desire to retain our materiality through an artificial suspension of the inevitable processes of erosion and decomposition.

Conclusions

The archaeological study of objects uses a range of scientific techniques for analysis of the physical, biological and chemical qualities of materials. In addition, such scientific analyses have helped inform a second avenue of scholarship, focused more explicitly on the social roles, cultural meanings and temporal biographies of the material world. Furthermore, objects are affected by time, as (some) artefacts enter various stages of use, reuse, discard, discovery, conservation and display, ultimately existing in a perpetual state of deterioration. Archaeologists continually have to manage the nexus of temporality with the object/body, as time and decomposition act on the material remains that inform of past lives and societies.

Excavation itself creates a paradoxical relationship with the material qualities of objects, because it simultaneously generates an invaluable source of knowledge and a cause of expedited physical deterioration. Thus, the specific material qualities of objects, combined with concepts of social or economic worth, determine how archaeological artefacts may be systematically collected, recorded, manually and chemically conserved, preserved in a suspended state, and ultimately displayed. Through the diverse case studies of a historic prison site in Tasmania, Australia, and prehistoric plastered human skulls from the Middle East, we can see the influence of alternative approaches to conservation within both antiquarian and contemporary contexts. The prevention of decay serves not only as a modern cause for intervention but as a socially relevant activity for past communities. Archaeologists therefore inhabit a long and diverse trajectory of motivations behind the materiality of decay and temporality, erosion and conservation.

Acknowledgements

Many thanks to Melanie Giles and Amy Gray Jones for discussions of decay and access to unpublished material, and Gillian Evans and Penny Harvey for their insightful editorial feedback. Thank you to Stuart Laidlaw at the Kenyon Jericho Archive, University College London for kind permission to reproduce the photograph of a plastered skull from the Jericho excavations. Additional thanks are due to the Conservation Laboratory team at the Museum of London. The British Academy provided essential funding for both the Ross Factory Archaeology Project and a Post-Doctoral Fellowship held by Karina Croucher. Any errors of fact or representation are obviously those of the authors.

Bibliography

Archaeological Dialogues (2011) Thematic edition "The Role of Archaeological Excavation in the 21st Century," 18(1): 1–86.

Bonogofsky, M. (2001) Cranial modeling and Neolithic bone modification at 'Ain Ghazal: New interpretations. *Paléorient* 27 (2): 141–146.

—— (2004) Including women and children: Neolithic modeled skulls from Jordan, Israel, Syria and Turkey. *Near Eastern Archaeology* 67 (2): 118–119.

Bowdler, S. (1988) Repainting Australian rock art. *Antiquity* 62: 517–523.

Bronk Ramsey, C. (2010) *OxCal 4.1*. https://c14.arch.ox.ac.uk/oxcal/ocp_left.html (accessed March 2011).

Casella, E.C. (2002) *Archaeology of the Ross Female Factory: Female Incarceration in Van Diemen's Land, Australia*. Records of the Queen Victoria Museum, No. 108. Launceston (Australia): QVMAG Publications.

—— (2011) Little bastard felons: Childhood, affect, and labour in the penal colonies of nineteenth-century Australia. In Voss, B. and Casella, E.C. (eds), *The Archaeology of Colonialism*, Cambridge: Cambridge University Press.

Casella, E.C. and K. Croucher (2011) Beyond human: The materiality of personhood. *Feminist Theory* 12 (2): 209–217.

Clark, M.A., M.B. Worrell and J.E. Pless (1997) Postmortem changes in soft tissues. In Haglund, W.D. and Sorg, M.H. (eds.), *Forensic Taphonomy*, Boca Raton, Florida: CRC Press, pp. 151–164.

Cronyn, J. (1990) *The Elements of Archaeological Conservation*, London: Routledge.

Croucher, K. (2012) *Death and Dying in the Neolithic Near East*, Oxford: Oxford University Press.

Duday, H., P. Courtuad, E. Crubèzy, P. Sellier and A.-M. Tillier (1991) Anthropologie de terrain–identification and interpretation of mortuary practices. *Bulletin et Mémoires de la Societé d'Anthropologie de Paris, n.s.* 2 (3): 29–50.

Gallowry, A. (1997) The process of decomposition. In Haglund, W.D. and Sorg, M.H. (eds.), *Forensic Taphonomy*, Boca Raton, Florida: CRC Press, pp.139–150.

Giles, M. (2009) Iron Age bog bodies of north-western Europe. Representing the dead. *Archaeological Dialogues* 16 (01): 75–101.

Griffin, P.S., C. Grissom and G.O. Rollefson (2001) From behind the mask: Plastered skulls from 'Ain Ghazal. In Schmandt-Besserat, D. (ed.), *Symbols at 'Ain Ghazal Volume I*, Texas: University of Texas Press.

Hertz, R. (1960) [1907] *Death and the Right Hand*, Needham, R. and Needham, C., translator, Aberdeen: Cohen and West.

Hodder, I. and S. Farid. (2004) Season Review, Çatal News 11. http://www.catalhoyuk.com/newsletters/11/index.html (accessed August 2010).

Hurcombe, L. (2007a) *Archaeological Artefacts as Material Culture*, London: Routledge.

—— (2007b) A sense of materials and sensory perception in concepts of materiality. *World Archaeology* 39(4): 532–545.

Ingold, T. (2007) Materials against materiality. *Archaeological Dialogues* 14: 1–16.

Küchler, S. (1987) Malagan: Art and memory in Melanesian Society. *Man* 22(2): 238–255.

Kuijt, I. (2008) The regeneration of life: Neolithic structures of symbolic remembering and forgetting. *Current Anthropology* 49 (2): 171–197.

Leigh, D., D. Watkinson and V. Neal (1998) *First Aid for Finds*, London: Institute for Conservation of Historic and Artistic Works.

Lucas, G. (2005) *The Archaeology of Time*, London: Routledge.

Morphy, H. (2007) *Becoming Art*, Oxford: Berg.

Nilsson Stutz, L. (2003) *Embodied Rituals and Ritualized Bodies*, Stockholm: Almqvist and Wiksell Int.

Pinheiro, J. (2006) Decay process of a cadaver. In Schmitt, A., Cunha, E. and Pinheiro, J. (eds.), *Forensic Anthropology and Medicine*, Totowa, NJ: Humana Press, pp. 85–116.

Rackard, A., L. O'Callaghan, and D. Joyce (2001) *Fish Stone Water: Holy Wells of Ireland*, Cork: Cork University Press.

Rattue, J. (2001) *The Living Stream*, Woodbridge (UK): Boydell Press.

Robb, J. (2004) The extended artefact and the monumental economy: A methodology for material agency. In DeMarrais, E., Gosden, C. and Renfrew, C. (eds.), *Rethinking Materiality*, Cambridge: McDonald Institute Monographs, pp.131–140.

Rodgers, B. (2004) *The Archaeologist's Manual for Conservation*, New York: Kluwer Academic/Plenum Publishers.

Rollefson, G.O. (2000) Ritual and social structure at neolithic 'Ain Ghazal. In Ian Kuijt (ed.), *Life in Neolithic Farming Communities*, New York: Kluwer Academic/Plenum Publishers, pp. 163–190.

Rudenko, S. (1970) *Frozen Tombs of Siberia. The Pazyrk Burials of Iron Age Horsemen*, London: J.M. Dent and Sons.

Russell, Ian (2006/2007) Objects and agency. *Journal of Iberian Archaeology* 9/10: 71–88.

Sanford, E. (1975) Conservation of artifacts: A question of survival. *Historical Archaeology* 9: 55–64.

Schiffer, M. (1972) Archaeological context and systemic context. *American Antiquity* 37: 156–165.

—— (1987) *Formation Processes of the Archaeological Record*, Albuquerque: University of New Mexico Press.

Schiffer, M. and A. Miller (1999) *The Material Life of Human Beings*, London: Routledge.

Stordeur, D. and R. Khawam (2007) Les Crânes surmodelés de Tell Aswad (PPNB, Syrie). Premier regard sur l'ensemble, premières réflexions. *Syria* 84: 5–32.

Taylor, T. (2002) *The Buried Soul*, London: Fourth Estate.

von Hagens, G. (1982) *Verfahren zur verbesserten Ausnutzung von Kunststoffen bei der Konservierung biologischer Präparate.* Specification DE 32 32 756 A1, Munich: German Patent Office.

von Hagens, G. and Whalley, A. (2006) *Body Worlds: The Anatomical Exhibition of Real Human Bodies. Exhibition Catalogue*, Heidelberg: Art and Sciences Publishers.

Williams, H. (2004) Death warmed up. *Journal of Material Culture* 9 (3): 263–291.

Part II
Affective objects
Introduction

Eleanor Conlin Casella and Kath Woodward

Mrs Edna Younger regularly visited our project site over the 2003 field season. Funded by English Heritage to examine the archaeology of two post-medieval cottages in northern Cheshire, the Alderley Sandhills Project was in the process of excavating the material remains of her interwar period childhood home (Casella and Croucher 2010). When shown this fragmentary artefact, Mrs Younger shared a detailed and sweet memory of the dollhouse that her father, a skilled local tradesman, had made for one of her early birthdays. The fact that this artefact had been recovered from soils that overlay the foundations of the neighbouring house was irrelevant. She proudly told us her story on numerous site visits, and to the news and television reporters whose appearance inevitably followed our English Heritage press release. The artefact had

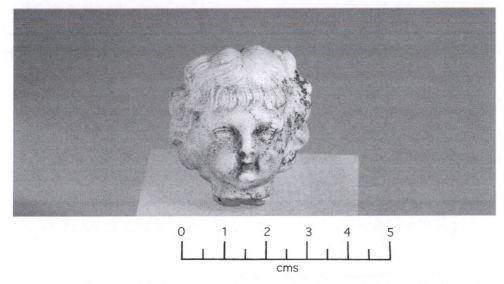

Figure II.1   Porcelain doll figurine, early twentieth century, Hagg Cottages, northern Cheshire. Alderley Sandhills Project, 2004. Photograph courtesy of Eleanor Conlin Casella

become hers: a recovered fragment of *her* past; an object of yearning for a nostalgic childhood half remembered, half created.

Towards the affective object

Personal, familial and community encounters with the object world may be deeply emotive, and a growing body of scholarship has begun to explicitly confront the materiality of emotional practices and affective experiences. The chapters within this part of the book shift beyond initial questions of metaphor and meaning (see Buchli 2007; Tarlow 1999, 2000) by exploring the mutually constitutive relationships between the material and affective worlds. They consider forms of linkage, resonance, sedimentation, recollection and commemoration that fold and unfold emotional relationships through the object world.

Certain themes can be seen to thread the chapters into loose clusters and overlapped conversations. Some contributions can be approached as 'affective objects' in themselves, in the sense that they have been authored to explicitly invoke (or provoke) an emotive reaction from the reader. But whether exploring the visceral dimensions of affect, crystallizations of the spectacular and sedimentations of the ordinary, the diffuse boundaries between the human and material worlds, or the complex temporalities generated by affective objects, the chapters of this section illuminate how the making and breaking of emotive relationships hold a profound materiality.

How sensational! On virtual and visceral forms of affect

For some authors, affective linkages and relationships are materially generated through the experience of 'being there.' For others, it is the process of remembering, reenacting and role-playing that shapes their emotive experiences through the material world. Thus, by way of a first theme, chapters in this part consider how affective experience may be both visceral and virtual in its materiality. The enfleshed encounter forms a significant, if not essential, aspect of 'being there' in Woodward's exploration of boxing as a masculine drama. Although horrific examples of mortal trauma can be found on the internet, far more common bodily injuries involve damage to the hands, ribs, jaw and nose of a boxer. More importantly, Woodward locates the 'sensation' of a fight through the simultaneously emotive and emotional relationships between muscle, sweat, sound, gloves, ropes and the ring itself. Anticipatory excitement over a Big Fight becomes intensified through the highly charged affect links from the boxers to their families, trainers and promoters, to their opponent, and to the audience of punters. 'Being there' thus requires a visceral connection to the spectacular live event as an explosive culmination of these emotive encounters. Similarly, McDonald describes how medical students undergo a deeply sensory experience when learning human anatomy. Through their courses, the students labour over their medical cadaver to see, hear, feel (and thereby comprehend) the tactile characteristics of a vein, artery and nerve, or the acoustic distinctions between the intestines and liver.

And yet, such moments of heightened viscerality blend into far more virtual experiences. Woodward traces the rise of boxing films as a cinematic tradition, finding that their deployment of familiar narratives of heroic masculinity offers a virtual space of viewing, a 'drama' of boxing, which extends the sense of corporeal spectacle for the live fight. McDonald's medical students also work seamlessly across multiple media (illustrated atlases, whiteboards, magnetic resonance imaging scans, tutorial instruction, live models and dissected human cadavers) to acquire an understanding of 'human anatomy' (or the medicalized body as conceptualized by surgeons) within their own minds. In her chapter on heritage debates over the Egyptian Collections at Manchester Museum, Exell explains how the visceral encounter not only supports but produces the virtual affective connection. According to Exell's feedback reports, museum visitors are keen to see the displayed mummified female body in order to imagine her daily life within this ancient social world.

The processes of remembering, reenacting and role-playing do offer a sublime example of virtual experience, with the museum or archaeological excavation offering material pleasures of time travel to spaces both exotic and nostalgic. But as Clough powerfully shows, the visceral experience of trauma and abuse may also be affectively invoked as a means of commemoration: a testimony of a hidden painful past reexperienced within the relative safety of a virtual world. Pollock introduces the 'fetish' to explore the object as a 'relic of a lost or dead person,' observing that 'things stand in for, disavow and, at the same time, monumentalize the very lack that is being disavowed, marking its site.' The sensory presence of the object, its demand for visceral encounter, thereby intensifies our awareness of the virtual (the affective links to the one no longer there).

Brown, Reavey and Brookfield also find the materiality of absence emotionally disconcerting in their chapter on the complicated negotiations of meaning and significance that surround the personal possessions of foster children on temporary domestic placement. In seeking to simultaneously protect the material possibility of future commemoration or self-narrative and protect the child from material reminders of their recent damaged pasts, the foster parents of Brown and colleagues' study show a deep awareness and discomfort with the role of deciding what is allowed to be remembered through objects, even when undertaken in a caregiving context. The burnt Snoopy Dog soft toy becomes both visceral and virtual testimony of the injured foster child, the painful childhood and triumphant survival, the absent parent, and their own role as temporary caretakers within the child's unfolding life. As they observe, '[to] get rid of the toy is to break that link.'

Moments both spectacular and mundane

Specialists in oral history have differentiated at least five types of memory (Abrams 2010: 83). Of particular interest are episodic (or autobiographical) memory, which enables the narrative recall of an event from the perspective of one's place within the scene, and vivid (or flash–bulb) memory, in which recollection is captured in sensory quality and is typically generated from a particularly poignant event of emotional significance. Affective objects appear to operate similarly, with materials gaining their emotive qualities through participation within either the unusual, spectacular, dramatic event, or conversely, the ordinary, routinized, habitual activities of everyday life. It seems to be the enmeshing of these two associative elements (the spectacular and the mundane) that sediments affect into the object world.

Thus, whereas Stewart explores how seasonal patterns of collective activities accrete over the passing years to cultivate a sense of 'place' in the swimming hole and coastal beaches of her chapter, Woodward describes how episodic routines of physical training and preparatory arrangements of boxing paraphernalia yield to the spectacular and singular moment of the Big Fight. The shock of a vivid affective encounter will live alongside the more habitual experience, as Clough articulates in her flash memories of explosive personal violation embedded within the more mundane alienation of child abuse, as materialized through the ordinary 'attendant objects' of her memoryscape. In certain instances, the shift from spectacular to mundane affective moments is not only intentional but essential. For McDonald's student medics, dissections must become a mundane learning experience. Cadavers must transform from objects of shock and revulsion to objects of routinized learning practice in order for the students to gain the necessary professional detachment required for a surgical career.

And yet, it is through their subtle evocative qualities that objects hold their greatest affective power. The material world actively choreographs our movements, renders our social selves, grasps our emotive responses because of its non-discursive existence. Unlike the written text, unlike the spoken word, the object works through its silent presence, not only offering a dense focal site for emotional overlay but also quietly shaping, attuning and framing our basic affective experiences. Returning to the concept of the 'fetish,' Stewart considers mundane 'things' that transport one to unspoken emotive spaces, places 'barely there,' worlds of 'force, virtuality, continuity, connectivity' that cannot be encapsulated within words or thereby reduced to the frozen still-life of a diorama. Brown, Reavey and Brookfield similarly describe the 'purloined trousers' as a petty domestic object that actively unfolds deeper feelings of guilt, shame and inadequacy when discovered by the recently single parent. Through this evocative affective power, objects quietly beckon us towards bodily practices; the fountain pen of Pollock's chapter 'constrains' Sarah Kofman to write, to give words to her absent father. Thus, objects hold tremendous emotive force in both spectacular moments and routinized patterns. But given this active influence upon humans, how may we better conceptualize the underlying relationships between subjects and objects?

Diffusions and boundaries

Boundaries between 'the human' and 'the object' are fluid, diffuse, mutable. Humans obviously hold emotive and affective relationships with objects. But objects respond to actions and intentions. Can these two aspects be separated into a human/object binary? Or perhaps the affective links between these two phenomena generate more complex ontological relationships? Various contributions within this part of the book echo earlier chapters by invoking Britain's *Human Tissue Act* (2004) and Gunther von Hagens' *Body Worlds* exhibitions of 'plastinated' anatomical remains to consider ambiguous legal, medical and aesthetic diffusions of the conceptual boundary between people and things. Like Casella and Croucher (Part I), both Exell and McDonald here consider the shadowy edges of personhood, exploring not only how, when and why certain dead bodies become actively transformed, or objectified, into non-humans but also how persistent affective links hinder a complete transubstantiation of these artificially preserved remains. Thus, human anatomy is rendered as a 'world of topography, of sections, planes, and landmarks,' with cadavers 'sculpted' to mimic the anatomical images from published training manuals. Of course, the embalmers of Ancient Egypt similarly 'sculpted' the dead through enchanted specialist technologies of surgical and chemical intervention. As Exell observes, the mummified body was granted the same linguistic determinative used in the word for statue or body-double. The ancient body is thus transformed from a human person into a tangible representation of the deceased: a process of affective resonance that proves circular as visitors to the contemporary museum express emotive responses to the (perceived) humanity of the embalmed remains on exhibition.

In both cases, the profound ontological instability of the cadaver or 'mummy' appears to produce a yearning for emotional resolution, a desire to reanimate (and thereby 'respect') the deceased person who once was the body. Or as one visitor wrote on *Egyptblog*, expressing outrage at the Museum's controversial decision to cover the displayed human remains, 'I could look into the face of a man 4,000 years old, and see that, like myself, he was a person … not just a stuffy old thing in a box in a museum.' After producing the cadaver body as a necessary element of their learning process, McDonald's medical students also resolve the ontological dissonance by reforming their study object as a person with an end-of-course 'thanksgiving ceremony,' attended by their instructors, fellow students and, in some cases, relatives of the deceased.

For Brown, Reavey and Brookfield, objects can be understood as 'participants' in the creation of affective links, in that they help make an assembly of relations in which the qualities and capacities of each entity are relationally determined. This approach shifts the underlying questions from that of a subject/object binary, to a richer exploration of how specific affordances or propensities (dis)allow both humans and objects to shape the nature, effect and significance of emotional relationships. Expanding the scope of these affective participants, Stewart's emotive scenes cohere through fluid interdependencies shared amongst humans, non-human beings (turtles, flies, dogs) and transitional recreation spaces where water meets land (beaches, waterholes, river springs). Stewart shows how this relational dynamic must be understood as mutually constitutive, with the 'ricochet' between humans and objects producing a moment of composition as 'some kind of real, a world.'

On durations

Stewart's approach begs an appreciation of multiple temporalities. The composition of her world 'settles for a minute on matter already configured,' thereby rendering affective objects as simultaneously transient and preexistent. The emotive qualities of materials therefore appear to require multiple temporal dimensions. Contributions within this part of the book variously explore affective objects as generational, as present, as momentary, as enduring, as repetitive, as frozen or as anticipated. For Stewart, the 'scenes becoming worlds are singularities of rhythm and attachment,' and yet the affective material practices of her tableaux become sedimented as repetitive seasonal events into an enduring (yet highly contested) sense of place. This confusion between transience and permanence is echoed by Brown, Reavey and Brookfield, with the foster child emotionally struggling to differentiate between 'stuff' that cycles through temporary ownership (the bed in a temporary placement) and personal possessions that travel with her to a new family home (soft toys or clothes). During one interview, the foster parent explains the difficult curatorial responsibilities raised by these poignant objects: anticipating that the foster child may want to encounter a material testimony of her painful past, the new parent saves a damaged toy to enable a possible future moment, although also protecting the present young child from this unsettling object by keeping it 'hidden at the back of the pile.' Similar 'foldings' of anticipatory and nostalgic time infuse Exell's chapter, with museum specialists preserving embalmed human remains as artefacts or heritage relics of an ancient society, while debating over what future punters will desire in their visitor experiences.

For Pollock, belongings may operate across generational time by 'transporting' trauma, rending the affective object itself as a deadly vector. The matrilineal spoon, a survival of a family history 'erased' by the Holocaust, works as both memorial and marker of absence, but also plays a 'real and symbolic part in the attempts to create a future.' Sarah Kofman's inherited fountain pen temporally indexes not only a previous technology of literacy (before the advent of the ballpoint pen, the computer, the ephemeral blog) but also her father's hideous alienation from his treasured obligations of faith and family and her own unspeakable shame at the process of her own survival. Perhaps McDonald's concept of the cadaver as a materiality of 'frozen time' recognizes a necessary affective relationship, rather than a rejection of temporality? As she observes, the artificial suspension of embodied decay enables 'an isolation and holding still of an object for inspection.' It also creates a suspension of time as a way of coping (materially and emotionally) with the messy, revolting dynamics of the decaying corpse. How do these various trajectories of time create different affective relationships with and through the material world?

Connections/disruptions and the affective object

Brown, Reavey and Brookfield powerfully illuminate how the everyday object becomes affective through an intermeshing of blood, love and memory. Through these phenomena, emotive relations are produced as an enclosed sphere of intimacy and belonging (a 'bubble'), which may expand or dissipate. To illuminate how these aspects work together in making and breaking connections with the emotive world, the contributions of this part offer new approaches to the mundane and spectacular moments, the visceral and virtual experiences of our material worlds. How do these affective objects open possibilities for future affective experiences? How do they acknowledge existing sedimentations and shape living practices? How do they 'respect' or 'reject' connections with distant points of transmission into memory, testimony or heritage?

For Woodward, the process is necessarily sensational; events invoke a relationship of 'vicarious causality,' in which objects (the equipment, ropes, gloves, gum shields) articulate with subjects (boxers, trainers, media, family, fans, punters) to create a moment of affect both visceral and virtual. Conversely, Pollock envisions the affective object as a vibrational string, connecting 'distant points in time and space, across generations and even death' not to bind them but to allow a transmission of emotions so that the 'shared vibration will resonate, will be different for each partner-point.' If we take materiality as our starting point in this complex relationship, does the object somehow direct or route these affective links, generating (as Clough writes) a causality 'where the sensual lures objects to each other'? How do we equally acknowledge a causality that disrupts, that unsettles, that violates these affective relations? Adopting the concept of the 'spectral object,' Brown, Reavey and Brookfield describe the material object as an ephemeral entity, an 'unfinished business,' that points towards a difficult emotive space of both memory and experience, of relations connected and broken: a rendered moment 'that cannot be simply erased without considerable cost.' The (un)folding qualities of affective objects haunt us, insisting that we acknowledge, commemorate and anticipate that the past 'is on our heels, following us like shadows' (Augé 1995: 26).

Bibliography

Abrams, L. (2010) *Oral History Theory*, London: Routledge.

Augé, M. (1995) *Non-Places: Introduction to an Anthropology of Supermodernity*, London: Verso.

Buchli, V. (2007) Afterword: Towards an Archaeology of the Contemporary Past. In McAtackney, L., M. Palus and A. Piccini (eds) *Contemporary and Historical Archaeology in Theory*, pp. 115–118. BAR International Series 1677, Oxford: Archaeopress.

Casella, E. C. and Croucher, S. (2010) *The Alderley Sandhills Project: An Archaeology of Community Life in (post-)Industrial England*, Manchester: Manchester University Press.

Tarlow, S. (1999) *Bereavement and Commemoration: An Archaeology of Mortality*, Oxford: Blackwell.

Tarlow, S. (2000) Emotion in Archaeology. *Current Anthropology* 41(5): 713–746.

9

Boxing films
Sensation and affect

Kath Woodward

Introduction

The writer Joyce Carol Oates argues that boxing is not drama; it is real (1987). Implicit in this argument is that what is authentic about boxing is flesh and the embodied material practices of the sport in the ring, which are real in a way that cinema or, in the case of Oates's argument, television cannot be; boxing is corporeally accessible only by 'being there' as a sentient being. The claims to authenticity of 'being there' have powerful resonance in sport and especially in boxing. The virtual authentic experience of big-screen football has had less impact on the culture of boxing, in which pay-for-view and collective viewing, for example in bars and pubs, have not created affects of the virtual real. Boxing offers particular relationships between people and things, words and flesh, images and practices, which are caught up in the dynamics of an event. The event may be the public spectacle of a big fight at a prestigious site embedded in the annals of the sport, like Madison Square Garden, or the routine of everyday practices in the local gym, and the art forms that represent boxing, such as literature, film, theatre or photography.

The Rumble in the Jungle, the name given to the heavyweight title fight between Muhammad Ali and Joe Frazier in Kinshasa, Zaire in 1974, has inspired great creative as well as social commentary. This epoch was the golden age of heavyweights, popularly described as *When We Were Kings*, which is the title of Leon Gast's 1996 film of the fight. Gast's film also shows a strand of the relationship between diverse components of what is authentic or real. For example, the real is constituted as documentary in the *Rumble in the Jungle* film and in journalists' accounts at the time and then reproduced in the creative narratives of writers like Norman Mailer in his account, *The Fight* (1975). In this book, Mailer engages with the intensities of being there bizarrely, by describing himself in the third person first as Norman, then Norm and occasionally as Norman Mailer. Great moments such as the Rumble in Zaire, which become classified as legendary, are made in the spaces between the real and the representational, here shown in that interface between documentary and drama.

Boxing lends itself well to the insights of the affective turn (Hardt, 2007). Boxing is both ordinary and spectacular; it is a back-and-forth dialectic of naturalism of affect and of iconography: the raw and the cooked. Boxing is an artificial creation that culture cannot resolve (Boddy, 2008: 391), but it is itself cultural and constitutive of culture and one beset by contradictions and ambivalences, which is also why boxing inspires imaging through art, cinema and photography. Boxing may always be raw because it always involves a one-on-one combat with one person trying to knock the other unconscious, but there are other ways of interrogating boxing, through the arrangement of people, things and places that make up boxing culture, which are considered in this chapter. Boxing has endurances and persistences, but it is not a linear narrative; although so many boxing films tell a story, especially one configured around the heroic legend, most crudely in the *Rocky* series.

The great iconic moments of boxing are never entirely absent from the affects that play out in the routine practices of the sport. These stories are part of the delivery systems that make up boxing and intersect with the enfleshed practices of the sport (Woodward, 2012) and the ways in which flesh is implicated at different sites: in the gym, in the ring, on film and in sentient spectatorship. This chapter explores the drama of boxing by working through the ways in which the relationship between the routine and spectacular affects of the sport play out within the genre of film, focusing on a particular example of a film that sought to embrace documentary coverage of the everyday experiences of boxing and of art: *A Bloody Canvas* (RTÉ 2010). I am writing about this film because I was part of the team that made it as an advisor on and participant in the film. The film was an eclectic mix of disparate strands, although underpinned by some of the enduring boxing relationships and connections, notably those forged through the discursive regimes of hegemonic masculinity. This regime was disrupted by my presence and by some of the questions raised by the disconnections as well as the synergies in putting together a film that included the materialities of histories, social, spatial and temporal axes of power, art forms and enfleshed practices. The processes through which *A Bloody Canvas* was made present a particularly good example of how the affects of boxing as a cultural event and set of practices are generative of and are themselves generated by the diverse strands that encompass the disparate elements of enfleshed routine practice, spectacle, and social and cultural inequalities that make up the world of boxing. The mix of the film recreates some of the spaces in between by highlighting some of the elements of boxing that affect and are affected by the sport and its perceptions.

Ordinary affects

After his defence of his World Boxing Association (WBA) heavyweight title on 3 April 2010, the erstwhile, occasionally charming and engaging (at least in media interviews, if not at weigh-ins, where his inappropriate pugilism is legend), David Haye was interviewed on BBC Radio 4. He responded to the interviewer's comment about looking good the day after a fight that went the full 12 rounds against an opponent who has been described as more fighter than boxer. Almost inaudibly, he slipped in that John Ruiz (his opponent) had come off worse, with a broken jaw, broken nose and broken rib. It is par for the course in boxing. Such injuries are not dramatic; you pick yourself up unless you are unconscious, and most boxers come back. These injuries are ordinary affects of boxing; as Kathleen Stewart writes of the everyday, material intensities of life (2007). Boxing has all sorts of capacities that affect and are affected by different social systems, including and perhaps especially the military and definitely masculinity (Woodward, 2007). Boxing embraces routine disciplines and mechanisms of control and the aggression and violent embodied practices that are powerfully linked to hegemonic masculinity.

In what I say, I move between the raw and the cooked, the spectacle and the routine, the heroic and the mediated, and the sensation, the dramatic and the real. Oates claims that you have to 'be there' to experience real boxing; drama is not real, for example, on TV (even pay-for-view) although the two are inextricably interconnected in myriad ways in sensation that is also unmediated and ordinary as well as sensational.

Although boxing is a sport associated with violence, it is not, however, the sport that tops the league table of injuries (Woodward, 2007). Nonetheless, violence is one of the ordinary affects of boxing. Boxers routinely damage their hands in training. Perhaps surprisingly, the most likely injury in boxing is damage to the hands. There are, of course, more dramatic injuries and even deaths in the ring, Becky Zerlantes was the first woman to die in the ring in modern times in 2005, and it is estimated that over a thousand boxers have died in the ring in the last 120 years. The horrors of the spectacle are manifest in the fact that some of the more recent tragedies can even be viewed on YouTube (YouTube, 2012). Boxing is also the dark continent (Woodward, 2007).

However, in the everyday, the most common damage is to the hands. These injuries and the broken jaw, rib or nose that might result from a competitive bout are ordinary affects of boxing; as Stewart describes the everyday, material intensities of life (2007), which, in the case of boxing, involve routine practice in the downtown gyms as well as by aspiring boxers on the support card at public venues. Boxing has all sorts of capacities that are swept up into the new consistency of the event: the aspirations of the dispossessed in the traditional route out of poverty and social exclusion, the spectacle of competition and the enfleshed materiality of a sport the main purpose of which is to render the opponent unconscious for the entertainment of those who watch and the profit of those who organise fights (Sugden, 1996, McRae, 1996, Lemert, 2003).

Boxing affects include the past, which generates consistencies in the making of heroic masculinities in particular in the sport. Sensation is implicated in these intensities in that the boxing event is drama, representation and enfleshed. What is spectacular, for example, through boxing legends and the display of boxing in public arenas, whether live, in film, on television or in other cultural forms, mixes up with what is ordinary and routine. Boxers in the gym routinely attribute their interest in the sport to some heroic figure, whether a family member or more public legend (Woodward, 2007), which then becomes swept up in the event of the fight (McRae, 1996). Boxers even claim to be thinking about their heroes when competing, and these thoughts are conventionally retold as stories. However, the hero is also created through the relationship with the different elements that make up the event, including how the hero is perceived.

Events, like a fight or a film, encompass a wide range of materials, and how they are arranged. The arrangement of people, places and things and the affects they generate are understood through sensation, which is central to explanations of affect. A focus on events invokes the relationship between objects, the equipment, the ropes, the gloves, the gum shields, the boots, the shorts and paraphernalia of the spectacle, perception in the to and fro between subjects, boxers, trainers, cut men, promoters, commentators and spectators. Affects are generated through encounters with and between both objects and subjects. The object vectors are not just the tools of the subject vectors; all are implicated and interrelated in the events of boxing.

Different and diverse materials include their pasts, which generate consistencies and duration and raise questions about representation and memory in relation to objects. Although some aspects of the event may seem static, framed in film or photograph, they incorporate movement; even objects can be arranged so that they develop their own consistencies and intensities and thus sensation. Sensation is thus both affective and material and is generated simultaneously through emotive and emotional encounters, which are enfleshed in the relationship between flesh, muscle, sweat, sound, gloves, ropes and the ring itself. The generation of sensation includes these object vectors and the subject vectors of trainers, promoters, referees, boxers and spectators. Flesh is implicated in sensation, as material, having its own affects and being affected, but also as having specific capacities and properties that contribute to sensory processes. Flesh and sentience are also implicated in the processes of constructing and regulating authenticity in the reality of being there. Movement takes place within sensation, which includes the embodiment and enactment of thought through sensory media. The whole event of the film, as of the fight, is sensory through the organisation of light, movement and matter (Deleuze, 2005), as in art and expressive systems, which boxing is as drama, as an enfleshed event.

Boxing films

The sport of boxing has a special place in film history, and boxing films represent a long tradition. Boxing has produced more high-class films than any other sport (Berlins, 2008). Some 150 films have been made, starting with some early recordings of fights, including 8 minutes of Gentleman Jim Corbett against Peter Courtney in East Orange, New Jersey in 1894 (Mitchell, 2005). Boxing was seen to have enormous potential as a spectator sport as early as the late nineteenth century, which transforming technologies could make more widely available and which could benefit the development of those technologies. Performance and display are integral to boxing. A Gentleman Jim Corbett fight (the 1897 Fitzsimmons–Corbett fight, in the Nevada desert in the USA, which was the site of technological experiment in a wooden amphitheatre, with peepholes for cameras) was crucial in shaping future links between film, spectacle and fighting. 'Filming of the fight was always integral to its planning' (McKernan, 1998), as was the choice of the location in the Nevada desert, of course. The links of boxing to illegality, the occupation by the sport of the interstices between legal and criminal activities make such sites particularly attractive for big fights, or any fights. The legacy of Nevada Territory shows the liminal spaces occupied by boxing in relation to illegal, quasilegal and semilegal, immoral practices, as well as the specificities of place in the North American landscape.

One of the most positive celebratory points at which boxing has the capacity to move centre stage is through the spectacle of film. Film offers possibilities for the enfleshed and the emotive dimensions of sensation through cinematic technologies that integrate heroic narratives with a visual and audible close-up focus on flesh and corporeal movement. However, although boxing films have a long history, the cinematic depiction of combat in the ring generates a set of aesthetic and ethical relationships that might be antithetical to commercial movie making. Films are part of the wider social and cultural terrain in which these tensions are played out through the points of connection and disconnection between the axes of power of social cultural and economic factors.

Boxing films are either only tangentially associated with boxing or, even if they do purport to be 'about boxing' 'are always about so much more, especially, they are about social commentary more or less bound up with issues of masculinity' (Buscombe, 2005: 67). Boxing, and particularly the archetypical boxer in film, have traditionally generated a singular heroic figure of troubled masculinity. This figure is 'a romantic-modernist representation of existential man in all his bleak grandeur, [who] attained definition in Hollywood post World War II, but also in other visual and textual arts' (Mellor, 1996: 81). In the twenty-first century, the trope of the heroic triumph over adversity and especially economic disadvantage, persists, for example, with *Cinderella Man* in 2005 and in a slightly less romanticised form in *The Fighter* in 2010. Familiar matters of honour, desire for respect and self-esteem combine to reiterate a story of honour.

Boxing films are frequently implicated in the representation of violence in the cinematic context. This representation invokes associations of violence within boxing, which Kevin Mitchell (2005) calls the 'glamour of violence'. One of the most highly rated boxing films ever made, Martin Scorsese's *Raging Bull*, has scenes of violence that are resonant of the experience of witnessing a fight and of 'being there'. Scorsese's hallmark themes of violent men in crisis and his 'signature directorial style with flashy, imaginative visual flourishes, long and complex takes and pervasive pop music in the background' (French, 2004: 125) lend themselves well to a powerfully intense portrayal of boxing and the elision of anger, corporeal contact and aggression that are in the material of boxing, its spectatorship and its films. The intensity of the spectacle invokes anxieties about voyeuristic spectatorship, which are integral to the practice as well as the representation of boxing.

Boxing films range from those films that explicitly tell a boxing story, for example, in the 1940s, such as Robert Rosen's *Body and Soul* (1947), Robert Wise's *The Set-up* (1949) and Mark Robson's *Champion* (1949), to films like David Fincher's *Fight Club* (1999), which are more tangentially concerned with the sport of boxing. Other films like Quentin Tarantino's *Pulp Fiction* (1994) have a boxing/fight element and can be cited illustratively, but could not be said to be 'about boxing'; even bare-knuckle fighting, although boxing films are never *just* about boxing. The internal conflicts of *Fight Club*, like the novel by Chuck Palahniuk on which it is based, are concerned with dislocation and alienation played out in scenes of violent pugilism. *Fight Club* assembles psychic conflict and brings together the discursive regimes of pugilism, especially as enacted outside the law and those of the internal, psychic drama of its main protagonist. The films that might be more narrowly categorised as 'boxing films' have often been biopics, some of the most notable being the Ali movies. Boxing biographies regenerate heroes, largely through chronological life stories, like Michael Mann's *Ali* (2001) and Robert Wise's *Somebody Up There Likes Me* (1956), about Rocky Graciano. These films also focus on pivotal moments in boxing history, such as the *Rumble in the Jungle* (1974), classified as a documentary film, and its reincarnation in 1996 in Leon Gast's *When We Were Kings* and, in 2000, *One Nation Divisible*, on the Frazier–Ali rivalry, again arising from key boxing events.

Boxing occupies the relational space between flesh, conflict and social forces of economic deprivation, racism and the insecurities of migration and mobility that become concentrated on a particular version of masculinity. Thus boxing and boxing films provide a useful context in which to explore and question the ubiquity and hegemony of existential angst, especially in relation to masculinity, at a time of change, as both 'true' and authentic, but which it has been difficult to regain (Mellor, 1996), especially since the 1940s and 1950s, in what has been called the heyday of boxing films (Telotte, 1989).

Boxing films may also appear to represent hyperbole and excess. Mitchell, following the claims of the boxing writer Richard Hoffer about the properties of melodrama and hyperbole of boxing, argues that such films are not required to exaggerate; characters such as Don King, Mike Tyson and Jake LaMotta are already personalities writ large (Mitchell, 2005). Hyperbole occupies the in-between relational spaces. This characteristic raises further questions about the relationship between what is real and what is artifice and between the pugilist and the actor who plays him, or more rarely her. Boxing films and boxing itself exaggerate in some respects, and it is boxing that aspires to magnification.

The hyperbole that may be demanded by boxing films can also lead to assumptions about what boxing per se can deliver and can produce bad films too. Sensation can be interrupted; films can show alienated sensation too. A bad boxing film can be particularly disappointing, because boxing promises so much in relation to expressivity, intensity and emotive narrative, such as was shown in Ron Howard's 1992 film *Far and Away*, in which the storyline of the migrant who seeks redemption through boxing produced a lame version of the traditional boxing story, which might be more the outcome of a lack of chemistry between the actors Nicole Kidman and Tom Cruise than the tiredness of the storyline.

Actors are expected to become caricatures of themselves, just as some boxers enact an excessive version of masculinity. Boxing and boxing films especially affect and are affected by the manifestations of excess and the complex relationship between authenticity and deception and between fantasy, aspirations and reality. Being there within the caricature is mobilised through the charged affect of emotive links that start long before the fight with the taunts and insults that so often mark the weigh-in.

Hyperbole also serves to reinstate gender binaries implicated in the reinstatement of the heterosexual matrix (Butler, 1990). The overstatement of masculinity reconstitutes the exclusion of femininity and the necessary avowal that boxing is for 'real men', who are made through the capacities of the sport to reproduce these corporeal practices and enfleshed dimensions as well as being embedded in the heroic narratives of boxing films. Women boxers, like Ann Wolfe, have engaged in what Judith Butler calls 'the performativity of doing masculinity' (1990, 1993) in a masquerade of performing masculinity (Woodward, 2007). Boxing masculinity is also constituted in relation to femininity through the inclusion of women in the narrative or of recognisably feminine traits and attributes and the status of femininity within the fight film genre. This situation raises questions about the spaces occupied by femininity in these stories of heroic masculinity. Boxing does have the capacity to create alternatives; for example, Leila Ali was made through the associations with her heroic father, the legendary Muhammad Ali, as well as through her sporting success; kinship ties are widely enmeshed in the generation of consistencies and endurances of boxing. Leila Ali is imbricated in the kinship/family group, caught up in the legend that is her father, but she is also part of a sport in which she has shown a high degree of competence; it is troubling in some ways but also celebratory of a strong black woman who has been part of the endurance of the power of boxing and is part of its transformations. The acceptance of women's boxing as an amateur sport in the Olympics in 2012 means that there are more young hopefuls across the world, even in the powerfully patriarchal Afghanistan, where boxing might be a site of some cultural change. However, these are largely private spaces, and the public arena of film offers more possibilities for change

Boxers become part of the popular imagination through their place in the movies, whether they are actual fighters or fictional ones like Rocky Balboa, a film character, albeit reputedly based on the boxer Chuck Wepner. Some boxers might have passed into cultural oblivion, apart from the memories of the boxing cognoscenti, if it had not been for cinematic representation. Were it not for Robert de Niro's Academy Award-winning performance and Martin Scorsese's direction of *Raging Bull*, Jake LaMotta might not be still remembered (Tosches, 1997). Cinema plays an important role in the reconfiguration of heroes and boxing heroes and villains are always implicated in the social and cultural processes through which they are constituted. It is difficult to disentangle the affects of the mechanisms of cinematic reproduction from the materials and objects here that make up boxing, which are reproduced. What is real is implicated in both.

A Bloody Canvas

A Bloody Canvas, directed by Alan Gilsenan and produced by Martin Mahon, presents an idiosyncratic journey into the world of the ring by the internationally renowned abstract painter Sean Scully, who has been fascinated by boxing and boxers since his childhood in post-war East London and has himself practised both boxing and martial arts. Although the film is primarily concerned with the points of connection between art and boxing, it aims to capture the specificities of boxing, its particular capacities and its enduring appeal. This is effected through conversations, often reinstating the conventional patriarchal networks of older men who reconstruct memories of boxing histories, but these forces are disrupted by different interventions, for example through abstract art, less predictable voices and even eccentric practices. The most notable of these eccentricities is probably the Irish trainer Brendan Ingle's Chaplin-like dance at the end of the film, which transforms into a parody of the British comic duo, Eric Morecombe and Ernie Wise, who always concluded their television comedy show by they turning their backs to camera and moving away, each kicking their legs sideways in an absurd parodic dance. The composition of the film was eclectic and aimed to present an off-centre take on boxing, which probably accounts in part for my role too.

My presence was disruptive in a number of ways, as a woman in a largely male assemblage of practitioners. Being a woman was more important than whether I had ever boxed or not; if I had boxed, I would have been as a woman and not as part of the networks of hegemonic masculinity that dominate the field. Even the artist Sean Scully had boxed; as is so often the claim of those who occupy the peripheries of boxing and whose central identity is not categorised as being that of a boxer. I was temporarily part of the network as a fan and as a sympathetic commentator. I was interviewed in the gym where I have carried out some of my work, and most of this material was included in the film, although my discussion of the homoerotic dimensions of boxing did not make it into the film; maybe because they were more interested in the synergies between art and boxing and sensation than erotic sentience.

The film uses the iconography of the ring as a framed space. As David Chandler argues, 'each boxing match is a picture' (1996: 13), with the ring as frame. However, this frame carries the movement of the picture image. The frame of the ring is a relatively closed composition, like the frame of the film, which shows movement image and not a series of separate still shots (Deleuze, 2005). Even a film can produce the new, and the event of the fight is always uncertain. Scully also visits the world-famous Petronelli Gym in south Boston, where Scully talks to Kevin McBride, the Irishman who beat Tyson in the last fight of his career. The ring is acknowledged as the frame of the event as an iconic frame embodying the endurance of boxing legends.

Art offers the transcendental possibilities of going beyond discourse (Massumi, 2002). Art plays an important part in the film, at some points with direct links to boxing. The notion of representational art underpins another conversation, this time in New York, where Scully talks to LeRoy Neiman, whose reputation as a boxing painter has had considerable weight through the second half of the twentieth century and into the twenty-first century. Scully is filmed in his own studio in Ireland and then in Rome, where the artist Caravaggio, himself a pugilist and street fighter, whose work is used in the film more for its use of planes of light and dark, although Caravaggio's life story of street fighting lends another strand to the mix of fine art and the art of boxing: the noble arts that are imbricated in the film. Scully draws analogies between the artist and the fighter and argues that the fighter, like the warrior, is always ready to fight (RTÉ, 2010); for example, in his paintings of David and Goliath (Caravaggio, 2010). Caravaggio's own violence on the street is used to situate some of the different materialities that intersect; the regulatory mechanisms of boxing and the brutalities inside and outside that framework. Caravaggio's preoccupation with the depiction of enfleshed sensation and the celebration of erotic masculinity, on occasion through cutting and damaging male flesh, invokes the stark contrasts of boxing: the black background, visceral simplicity and flat sculptural moments in which miracular moments are made permanent. This observation resonates with Deleuze's argument about Francis Bacon's paintings, in which he suggests that the essence of painting is experienced as rhythm. 'Rhythms and rhythms alone become characters, become objects. Rhythms are the only characters, the only Figures' (Deleuze 2005: xxxii). Thus, Bacon's accomplishment, according to Deleuze, is to show that painting offers a virtual surface for the expression of a logic of sensation that may be the most conducive surface for doing so, at least at the time Bacon was painting. Rhythm is also affect, in that affect needs a virtual surface for the expression of a logic of sensation.

The crew also visited a Robert Mapplethorpe exhibition in the UK, and images of Mapplethorpe's work are presented in contrast to other material but also as unmediated sensation, which generates instabilities in much the same ways as boxing can. These images are underpinned by the connections to homoeroticism that are not really critiqued, and in the film, there is some tension about sensualities that are more accepted in the art gallery than the gym. The film moves to and fro between boxing myths and iconography through a visit to the grave of Gene Tunney, the world heavyweight legend and champion from 1926 to 1928, who twice defeated Jack Dempsey. The direct engagements with artistic practices are interspersed with frames that include conversations with boxers and trainers, such as with the legendary Irish boxing trainer Brendan Ingle in Sheffield in the UK, who provides a discursive mix of the practicalities of the gym and training and claims to the spiritual transcendent qualities of boxing in a surreal display of enthusiasm. Conversations often focus on reflection and the ways in which memory affects and is affected by boxing. For example, Scully is filmed in his apartment and studio in Barcelona, where former World Champion Barry McGuigan joins him to 'look back at the mutual fascination between art and boxing, between what they call the men of art and the men of action' (RTÉ, 2010). The moments of reconstituting memory and the conversations between older men are resonant of the strong boxing tradition of making heroes through the framework of the dialogue between the present and the past, which so powerfully generates the endurances of hegemonic masculinity.

Even when a boxing film is overtly about a woman, it is hegemonic masculinity that is largely what dominates the discursive field. For example, *Million Dollar Baby* (Buscombe, 2005), directly the story of a white woman who attempts to follow the more traditionally masculine path of achieving a route out of the trailer park into financial success through the boxing ring in order to support her wayward and dependent family. Clint Eastwood, the director of the film, also stars in the film alongside Hilary Swank as Maggie the boxer, as her trainer Frankie; Morgan Freeman plays Eastwood's former sparring partner and friend, Eddie 'Scrap iron' Dupris. Maggie is the vehicle through which the film explores Eastwood's character, Frankie, and the problems and the dilemmas of contemporary masculinity (Woodward, 2007). Frankie's relationship with Scrap, which is deeply imbricated in hegemonic masculinity, takes precedence over Maggie's role as a boxing hero.

The presence of women in the gym is relatively new, especially in joining in at open sessions, rather than being permitted to attend only on particular occasions or being totally excluded. This invisibility of women is also part of their absence from the histories and legends that are the delivery systems of boxing culture. Spectacle and iconography are part of the gym. The real of boxing is not entirely separate from its dramas, but part of the assemblage, and boxing traditions are made through the capacities of boxing to recreate ordinary affects of masculinity in kinship ties and routine practices as well as through its cultural representations. My own part in the process shows the to and fro between inside and outside and the diverse components that make up sensation in relation to the affects of and upon boxing. Dramas in the ring, and on film, in the above example, are inseparable and are also core to boxing.

Conclusion

Boxing, in all its myriad forms, has particular capacities to generate affects, which range from the spectacular to the routine, and has a powerful presence in the field of artistic representation.

Boxing shows the flows of visceral forces that go beyond discourse and even beyond emotion and beyond conscious knowing.

Pain, flesh and nerves mixed up with agency and vulnerability are central to boxing; it is as much about defeat as success and damage as well as the noble art. Destruction is as much an ordinary affect of what happens in the ring as the routine damage to the hands in the gym.

Whatever binaries may still have some purchase in regimes of truth in boxing such as sex gender differences, winning and losing, the real versus drama is not one that is worth holding on to. Boxing is both and this is why it has the capacity to generate such affects. These capacities operate through assemblages of power, economic, social, enfleshed, embodied practices, psychic investment to draw in and to exclude and to invoke sensations that are sensate and not always sensational, although boxing can certainly be spectacular and always offers that possibility.

One of the major affects of boxing is its capacity to generate a particular version of hegemonic masculinity that has considerable purchase among the networks of men, in particular those who are implicated in its peripheries as well as its core enfleshed engagements, whose participation also affects boxing.

Enfleshed presence (being there) is bound up with the sensate person who can locate their own presence, an experience that may be described as transcendent and so real that it might be beyond discourse. Sensation is most powerfully expressed in the distinction between the reality of the enfleshed presence of boxing and the occupancy of virtual space of viewing at a distance, which Oates characterised as 'drama'. However, boxing has the capacities to generate affects and sensation that operate in diverse spaces through display and through representation, for example cinematically and in different art forms. Experiences are constituted through the event in which they take place through the processes and intensities in which people are implicated, and that intentionality too is constituted through these processes rather than agency being the starting point of action. In boxing, events include the routine enactments and the mega events and spectacles that create sensation in those caught up in the event and are themselves sensational in the mixture of materialities. *A Bloody Canvas* was implicated in these processes, reflected and refracted those materialities and offers a good example of some of the disparate capacities of boxing in a set of systems and processes that are more complex and unidirectional than conventional narratives of existential heroes or of economic determinism in explaining the endurance of boxing.

Bibliography

Ali (2001) Directed by Michael Mann, Columbia Pictures.
Berlins, M. (2008) 'Boxing has produced more top class fiction and films', *The Guardian*, 13 August, p.9.
Boddy, K. (2009) *The Culture of Boxing*, London: Reaktion Books.
Body and Soul (1947) Directed by Robert Rossen, Enterprise Productions.
Buscombe, E. (2005) *Million Dollar Baby*, London, British Film Institute (BFI), pp. 67–8.
Butler, J. (1990) *Gender Trouble: Feminism and the Subversion of Identity*, New York: Routledge.
Butler, J. (1993) *Bodies that Matter*, New York: Routledge.
Cinderella Man (2005) Directed by Ron Howard, Universal Pictures, Miramax Films.
Caravaggio (2010) http://abcnews.go.com/print?id=9886412 (last accessed 25 May 2012).
Champion (1949) Directed by Mark Robson, United Artists.
Deleuze, Gilles (1986) *Cinema I: The Movement Image*, trans. Hugh Tomlinson and Barbara Habberjam. London: The Athlone Press.
Deleuze, Gilles (2005) *Francis Bacon: The Logic of Sensation*, trans. Daniel Smith. Minneapolis, MN: University of Minnesota Press.
Far and Away (1992) Directed by Ron Howard, Universal Pictures.
Fight Club (1999) Directed by David Fincher, Twentieth Century Fox.
French, K. (2004) 'Art by Directors', *Granta*, 86, Summer, pp. 95–128.

Gregg, M. and Seigworth, G.J. (2010) *The Affect Theory Reader*, Durham NC, Duke University Press.

Hardt, Michael (2007) 'Foreword: what affects are good for', in Patricia Tinceto Clough with Jean Halley (eds) *The Affect Turn: Theorizing the Social*, Durham, NC, Duke University Press: pp. ix–xiii.

Lemert, C. (2003) *Muhammad Ali: Trickster in the Culture of Irony*, Cambridge, Polity.

McRae, D. (1996) *Dark Trade: Lost in Boxing*, Edinburgh, Mainstream.

McKernan, L. (1998) 'Sport and the silent screen', *Griffithiana*, no 64, October, pp. 80–141.

Mailer, V. (1975) *The Fight*, Harmondsworth, Penguin.

Massumi, B. (2002) *Parables for the Virtual: Movement, Affect, Sensation*, Durham NC, Duke University Press.

Mellor, D. (1996) 'The ring of impossibility, or, the failure to recover authenticity in the recent cinema of boxing', in D. Chandler (ed.) *Boxer: An Anthology of Writing*, London, Institute of International Film Arts: pp. 13–26.

Mitchell, K. (2005) 'Fights, Camera, Action', *Observer Sport Monthly*, July, no. 65, London pp. 36–41.

Oates, J.C. (1987) *On Boxing*, London: Bloomsbury.

One Nation Divisible (2000) Directed by Dave Anderson, HBO Sports.

Pulp Fiction (1994) Directed by Quentin Tarantino, Jersey Films.

Raging Bull (1980) Directed by Martin Scorsese, United Artists.

Rumble in the Jungle (1974) produced by John Daly, Don King Productions with Hemdale Film Co.

RTÉ (2010) ARTS LIVES: The Bloody Canvas RTÉ One (13 April) http://richardkendrick.ie/index.php?/ongoing/the-bloody-canvas (last accessed 7 June 2013).

Somebody Up There Likes Me (1956) Directed by Robert Wise, Metro-Goldwyn-Mayer.

Stewart, K. (2007) *Ordinary Affects*, Durham, NC: Duke University Press.

Sugden, J. (1996) *Boxing and Society: An International Analysis*, Manchester: Manchester University Press.

Telotte, J.P. (1989) *Voices in the Dark: The Narrative Patterns of Film Noir*, Champaign, IL: University of Illinois Press.

The Fighter (2010) Directed by David O Russell, Closer to the Hole Productions, Mandeville Films.

The Set-up (1949) Directed by Robert Wise, Enterprise Productions.

Tosches, N. (1997) 'Introduction', in J. LaMotta with C. Carter and P. Savage (eds.) *Raging Bull: My Story*, 1st edition, New York: de Capo Press, pp. vii–xii.

When We Were Kings (1996) Directed by Leon Gast, Das Films.

Woodward, K. (2007) *Boxing Masculinity Identity: The "I" of the Tiger*, London: Routledge.

Woodward, K. (2008) 'Hanging Out and Hanging About Insider and Outsider Research in Boxing', *Ethnography*, 9 (4) pp. 36–60.

Woodward, K. (2009) *Embodied Sporting Practices: Regulating and Regulatory Bodies*, Basingstoke: Palgrave MacMillan.

Woodward, K. (2012) *Sex Power and the Games*, Basingstoke, Palgrave.

YouTube (2012) http://www.youtube.com/watch?v=ymL5wmuM5C8 (last accessed 25 May 2012).

10

Tactile compositions

Kathleen Stewart

Opening things

This chapter is an opening onto compositional theory. Here, compositional theory takes the form of a sharply impassive attunement to the ways in which an assemblage of elements comes to hang together as a thing that has qualities, sensory aesthetics and lines of force and how such things come into sense already composed and generative and pulling matter and mind into a making: a worlding.

Something reaches a point of expressivity. A line, a refrain, a tendency, an icon, a colour, a groove of habit or hope, or a rhythm or chaos of living take on qualities, a density, an aesthetic, become somehow legible, recognizable. Rather than rush to incorporate the thing coming into form into a representational order of political or moral significance, compositional theory tries to register the tactility and significance of the process of coming into form itself. Some assemblage of affects, effects, conditions, sensibilities and practices throws itself together into something recognizable as a thing. Disparate and incommensurate elements (human and non-human, given and composed) cohere and take on force as some kind of real, a world.

Scenes becoming worlds are singularities of rhythm and attachment. They require and initiate the kind of attention that both thinks through matter and accords it a life of its own. The tactile composition of things is about the meeting point between interiority and world (Thrift 2009).

In his essay *The Thing* Martin Heidegger (1971) asks what it might mean to meet the world not as representation, interpretation or raw material for exploitation but as a nearing, a gathering of the ringing between subjects and objects into something that feels like something. To thing is to world. An object that has become a thing is not flat and inert before a voraciously dominant subject but an enigma, a provocation. It is matter already configured (Grosz 2001). Bill Brown theorizes the thing as the amorphous characterization of concrete yet ambiguous things so pervasive in, and basic to, the everyday. We say 'There's a thing' about that person, scene, phenomenon that we recognize but cannot quite name. The very naming of the something as a thing acts as a placeholder for some future specifying. The thing marks an excess in things that remains physically and metaphysically irreducible to an object and can take the form of a fetish, a still life, or a scene of some potential (Brown 2001).

Elizabeth Grosz describes a thing as a point of temporal narrowing and spatial localization that constitutes a singularity out of the sensations, vibrations, movements and intensities that comprise experience. We recognize a thing coming into form through a kind of empirical attunement: a leaning into the scene of something throwing together (2001). Thought becomes a responding, a recalling, a gathering together, a becoming vigilantly protective of the gathering of a world in the presence of a thing (Heidegger 1971). This is a basis of the animacy of things.

Tim Ingold outlines the qualities of what he calls the open world in which 'persons and things relate not as closed forms but by virtue of their common immersion in the generative fluxes of the medium – in wind and weather' (2007: S19). Such attunements are pervasive and ordinary. An atmospheric world or thing is mobile and generative; it produces multiple potentialities for coherence and shift. An emergent world, always almost there, is itself always leaning into a mobilization.

Thrift historicizes the question of emergent force and coherence in terms of sensory shifts in ways of being in the world prompted by emergent forms of capitalism, digitalization and built environments. Capitalism now aims to directly incite and capture the semiconscious flows of affect that constitute sensations and sensibilities. The minutely calibrated digitalization and mapping of objects in everyday use prompts the kinds of perceptual labor and expertise that can read the animacy of objects or the framing up of thin slices of life into worlds (Thrift 2004). New forms of intuition become capable of rapidly reading gatherings of elements as things. Sensory contact zones breed alterations in the sense of being in the world. Lived atmospheres are continuously generating suggestible forms of coherence. We live in a paradigm of suggestion, looking for ways to use built life within us (Thrift 2009, 2011).

Derek McCormack adds that an attunement to things coming into form is an ethics. Tactile compositions animate both objects and the attachments and attunements that constitute selves. They are 'felt as ways of going on in the world' (McCormack 2003: 495), as 'increases and decreases, brightenings and darkenings' (Deleuze 1998: 145). Approaching the generativity of an emergent world requires attention to the way that subjects and objects emerge from a connective multiplicity of human and non-human forces, the power of which traverses people and matter in extensive, intensive, temporal and ontogenetic ways (McCormack 2009).

River thing, Barton Springs

Newcomers to Austin first see Barton Springs from an elevation. You look down steep, green grassy banks shaded by century-old pecan trees to a river-pool thing a thousand feet long. Preternaturally long and river wide. The water swells against concrete sides built by the Civilian Conservation Corps in the 1930s, its colours almost bruised with force and density. In places it has a brilliant green and turquoise hue. In other places it goes turgid brown and even, where the plants grow thick and rise to the surface, a true black. The spring that fills the river-pool is a tear in the limestone bedrock eighteen feet below the diving board in the dead center of the pool. This tear in the rock pumps out twenty seven million gallons of water a day. Bodies twist and flip over it, cutting the surface of the water with a belly flop or the expertise of ten thousand dives. It is a thing to plunge deep enough to catch a watery glimpse of the spring-tear pulsing like a steady heartbeat: the literal 'heart of Austin.'

The water on the surface above the tear churns in a cold, dense vortex, like a wine cooler. At a year-round temperature of 68 degrees, it pulls body temperatures down fast on a triple-digit day.

At the shallow end of the river-pool thing, families, young lovers and rowdy groups of friends slip over the irregular rock bottom, slick with algae. Performing the shock of the unbelievable cold, they try to avoid full immersion, or they jump in, or flat out refuse to take a second step in.

People-watching here is a tactile, visual submersion experience. There are hairdos, tattoos, swim-wear of all kinds, dares, refusals, splashing, 'Oh, *come on.*' People explore the cliffs that line one side, looking for the crawfish that peak out from under the rock ledges.

The far end is for floats. On a hot summer day, it is an acre of bumper-to-bumper plastic beds in bright colors. Oiled bodies lie in the sun, wrists and ankles hanging in the dark water. Young women strut around topless on the sidewalks.

The high grassy banks on either side are a sea of gazes, reading and lazy talk. There are drum circles, Frisbee throwing, dope smoking, yoga, Tai Chi.

Lifeguards perch on high stands down the length of the pool, leaning over the water like the great blue herons that lurch over the concrete sides in the early morning, piles of crawfish car-casses and fish bones at their feet. In the winter, an early-morning fog rises from the water. Die-hard lap swimmers troll up and down in wet suits like sleek black river creatures. At night, lights sparkle across the water and there is only the sound of the quiet strokes or a giggle. There may be an element of fear.

The pool is in the channel of Barton Creek. A chain-link fence over the dam at the deep end divides the pool from the downstream creek that flows out into Town Lake. Here, the water rages out of the dam and then goes shallow across treacherous rocks. This area is called the dog pool. There are dogs, boom boxes, homeless people, kids, more dope smoking, kayaks, ducks, runners, babies in strollers. The rocks shape-shift as people fashion them into bridges across the creek or circles of Zen rock sculptures.

All of these scenes, moments and habits are 'things' at Barton Springs: the toplessness, the families with small children hunting out crawfish on the ledges below the cliffs, the practice of jumping into the freeze or slowly immersing, the people watching, what goes on at the diving board, the swimmer devotees, the music-making, the dog pool.

The compositional tactility of Barton Springs incites framed thing-events. I have seen a wed-ding (bride and groom taking the plunge off the diving board), modeling sessions with long-legged waifs in black leather and lace, a contact dance performance, a *Keep Austin Breastfeeding* flashmob, and an aqua dance troop performance in which fifty dancer-swimmers invented water figures and movements as they swam the length of the pool as a single wave, a seal, a brood of mermaids.

It also incites political movements and citizen action volunteer projects, infusing them with its compositionality. The *Save Our Springs* (SOS) alliance, created to fight upstream develop-ment on Barton Creek, became a force in Austin municipal politics beginning with an all-night performance of three-minute speeches before the state legislature and leading to many green initiatives in the city. Friends of Barton Springs Pool enlists city council members to work on their *Clean the Pool* days, when 100 volunteers, fed by Texas Coffee Traders, Torchy's Tacos, Maudie's Tex-Mex and Alamo Drafthouse, sweep up and down the drained pool in a Zen push-brooming conga line.

The tactile compositionality of a thing might be heavily marked, even iconic. Or it might be in a state of potentiality, or perhaps slowly accreting more or less unnoticed. It might be intimate or coldly calculating, eventful or a dullness, a drag. It might be densely consequential, the smell of a sea change. Or more mechanical, like revving an engine.

Compositional theory, then, might skid over the surface of a thing throwing itself together or take pains at a slow description that pauses on each element. It might spread itself across a scene, sampling everything, or hone in on a single strand to follow it as it moves, maybe docu-ment how it pulls into alignment with other strands or falls out of sync, becoming an anomaly or a problem. It might hone in on the cold of the water. Or tell the ironic story of unintended consequences of how the Barton Springs salamander became a protected species and forced the closure of the springs in a battle between the SOS alliance and developers. Or it might linger in the dressing rooms and showers, built without roofs so that the air is fresh and the sun warms wet bodies.

Beach thing, Holden Beach

Visceral attachments incite and animate identifications, responsibilities and connections (Connolly 1999: 21). Singularities of water, sand, sun, cold, shells, breasts, mold, blue herons, lifeguards, turtles, sharks, swimmers in suits, or a fleet of Portuguese men of war blown into contact with human skin throw worlds into form. This is why 'the beach,' for instance, is so compelling as a thing. And why surprise encounters across species carry the charge of an opening.

Coming in to Holden Beach, North Carolina, you drive through flatlands past country churches, farm stands, crab shacks, dollar stores, a bookstore. At the end of the road, there is a steep climb up the bridge that crosses the intracoastal waterway. It is only when you reach the top of the bridge and hit the sharp curve to the right that you see over the rooftops of oceanfront cottages built high on pilings to the blue green ocean stretching across a vast horizon. The sun is bright, the colours, saturated. A row of pelicans flies close to the surface of the gentle ocean.

At the centre of the beach thing here is the Turtle Watch Program. Volunteers patrol the beaches on all-terrain vehicles in the predawn. They are looking for crawls. Giant sea turtles, mostly loggerheads, use the island as their hatching grounds, returning to the same shore where they were hatched twenty or twenty-five years before. The intervening years of a long youth are spent travelling around the world on the great sea currents. Only the females return to ground, only to hatch. They are an endangered species. Their moon–crawls can be thrown off course by the lights of oceanfront property or the flashlights of night beachcombers. Every rental property is equipped with instructions on how to limit human interference, little squares of red cloth to cover flashlights, and a red turtle refrigerator magnet with the Turtle Patrol's 24-hour pager number to report mother turtles laying nests, injured or stranded turtles, unattended hatchlings, disturbed nests or the harassment of a sea turtle. Calls are returned in less than five minutes. A fine of up to $100,000 and/or a year in prison is the penalty for harassing a sea turtle or disturbing its nest. All unattended beach equipment must be removed from the beach each day between 6 p.m. and 7 a.m. to ensure a clear path for crawls. People are asked to pick up any rubbish, especially plastic, from the beach.

> Do not release balloons on the beach. These items look like jellyfish to sea turtles. Fill in any large sand hole you dig before nightfall, they could trap a turtle, cause a night or early morning beach walker to fall and possibly break a leg, or cause an accident to Turtle Patrol ATV riders in the early morning.
>
> Every Wednesday night, Turtle Patrol hosts an educational turtle programme at the Town Hall. The official Holden Beach t-shirts sport turtle designs. There are also, of course, turtle earrings, necklaces, flipflops, puzzles, boogie boards and beach towels.

The very air of Holden Beach rings sea turtle in a kind of ecstatic naturalism. Under the sign of the sea turtle, a responsive attunement, or at least the possibility of it, lodges on the surface of beachness here and becomes resonant in encounters with objects, creatures and scenes. It is as if the proliferating phenomena of sea turtleness here mobilizes a vague, worlding space between forms of reality, knowledge and practice (Thrift 2011). A pressing crowd of incipiencies and tendencies are thrown into a realm of potential (Stewart 2007). The virtual has an existence

(McCormack 2009). The subject, in searching out the contours of a world, attaches to the moving, striking, and sometimes strange or weird intensities that pull attention into alignment with phenomena.

Sea turtles are older than dinosaurs. They eat jellyfish, sponges, algae, sea grasses and crustaceans. They live to be over one hundred years old. Loggerheads can weigh up to four hundred pounds, but leatherbacks, now 'returning' to the island to nest, are much bigger. It is bizarre, beyond belief really, how sea turtles find their way back to the island where they were hatched twenty years earlier. Only females ever come ashore. A mature female turtle (twenty to thirty years of age) returns to her natal beach every two to three years to lay nests. Each season an egg-bearing female lays one to seven nests, with an average of four nests.

Once a sea turtle crawl is found, a team assembles to find the eggs. If the nest is in an unsafe location, as many of them are, each of the over one hundred eggs is painstakingly mapped in its place in relation to the other eggs as it is removed. Each is carefully carried to a new nest hole dug to exactly the same depth (i.e. the length of the mother turtle's fin) and precisely resituated. The site is staked off. A sign is put in place warning that this is a 'Sea Turtle Nest Protected By The Endangered Species Act.' For sixty days, the nest is monitored. Toward the end of the incubation period, shallow trenches are dug for the hatchlings' first crawl to the sea. The first sign of a hatching is a boiling of the sand. Turtle Patrol members hold vigil throughout the hatching and crawl, recording each hatchling and its progress to the sea, each non-fertile egg, each strangeness. The temperature of the sand determines the sex of the hatchlings. Only one in ten thousand hatchlings reaches maturity. There are freaks of nature: five-inch, elongated eggs with five yolks each, eggs whose shells are black and hard as nails. There are situations to become attuned to: tides, hatchling confusion, formations in the sand. There are natural predators to know: ghost crabs, foxes, raccoons, birds, dogs and large fish. The sharpening attunement to the turtle world comes with the deepening recognition that the real problem here is the very presence of humans: boat propellers, fishing gear, debris and trash, construction on nesting beaches, artificial lights and pollution are the bottom lines of sea turtle endangerment.

Turtle Patrol is the slow rhythm of watching for a hatching, sharp eyes looking out for a crawl, emergencies and dramas of good and ill, metrics and science factoids, and tones of voice. It is a thing made out of the existence of retirement and retirees and the concept of the vacation. Families with children are closely aligned with it, as is, I suspect, the very feeling for children for those who have it. Metrics and machines are also central to it, all the measuring of nests and eggs, the coolers used to transport the eggs, the all-terrain vehicles, the turtle sea rescues by kayak. In 2010, there were twenty-nine nests with 2897 eggs. The first nest of the season is usually late to hatch. There are stories of turtles being guided in from the sea. Returning turtles are often identified by their shell markings and scars; they are named. There is a Turtle Rescue and Rehabilitation Centre for those turtles that need medical care or a place to heal.

On Holden Beach, the sea turtle is a major scene of the beach thing coming into form. There are also things forming up around sharks, pools, yoga, heat, afternoon thunderstorms, hurricane season, boats, shrimp, beach music, peaches, Crazy Mary's folk art, class, race, ice cream, beach access, bicycles, the stuff that memories are made of, salt water taffy, specific forms or tempos of function and dysfunction, collective ownership of places, and spoiled and damaging utopic dreams of the getaway or the perfectly settled life.

Things within things

When the beach becomes a thing, it becomes a new medium through repetitive automatisms: forms, conventions, genres (Cavell 1980). It circumscribes limitless potentiality into a collection of somethings and so attests to the force of singular improvisations. The beach is a tactile composition that feels 'full' and so confirms its own worlding status (Thrift 2011). It is an emergent field on call, on the ready, in which there are always singularities in the process of actualizing (McCormack 2008). It is a field saturated with expressivity, a field in which form stretches from the physical to the virtual, in which form *is* at once material and potential (Deleuze and Guattari 1987).

Forms activate force, virtuality, continuity, connectivity. Producing examples as singularities is a way of activating worlds. The details of a thing matter not because of their truth value or what they symbolize but because they are the movements of a field forming up. They matter not because of a logic or a hierarchy of what matters but, first, because they have come to matter. And in that instant they pull attention into the form of a tactile perception in which 'the intensity of such attention can be as important as depth of insight gained, and ... what one folds into an encounter ... can be as important as what one finds out' (McCormack 2009: 493).

> The cracked crab that I recall having for lunch the day my father came home from Detroit in 1945 must certainly be embroidery, worked into the day's pattern to lend verisimilitude; I was ten years old and would not now remember the cracked crab. The day's events did not turn on cracked crab. And yet it is precisely that fictitious crab that makes me see the afternoon all over again.
>
> *(Didion 2006: 103)*

In the singularities of a beach thing, recursivity is a force of nature and thought is almost solid, or experienced. The tides, the waves, the shells, rocks, seaweed, boats on the horizon, bodies sunbathing, swimming, riptides and undertows that threaten, the possibility of sharks, the images that circulate, the stories, the habits of walking and looking, what happens to a mind sitting on a beach immersed in the sound of the waves and the unrelenting wind. In a form-become-thing, matter and circuits of reaction touch.

This does not mean that all beaches are the same. On the contrary, it means that the beach thing is a generative emergence of form composed out of the singularities of what happens.

The beach thing 2: Plum Island, Massachusetts

Plum Island, or 'PI' as it is called on the bumper stickers, is an eleven-mile long barrier island off the far northern tip of Massachusetts. Two-thirds of the island is dedicated to the Parker River National Wildlife Refuge, which supports over three hundred species of birds as well as a broad variety of other wildlife. It is the designated habitat of the federally endangered piping plover and the state-threatened least tern. Its miles of beaches, accessible only by a partially paved road or in some places only by foot, are closed from April 1st to mid-August to protect plover and tern nests. Volunteers are stationed on the beach at the boundary of the refuge to turn pedestrians back. The refuge is a major national research site for undisturbed beach and marsh habitats and the effects of mercury and other pollutants on them. Invasive plant species are pulled up, one plant at a time, to conserve landscape biodiversity: perennial pepperweed, purple loosestrife, brush honeysuckle, phragmites, oriental bittersweet. Three man-made freshwater marshes, or impoundments, are managed to provide optimal habitats for migratory birds and river otters. Water levels are lowered to exposed mud flat for feeding and resting areas during shorebird migration, and raised again during waterfowl migration. The ordinary habits of the saltmarsh sharp-tailed sparrow and the tree swallow are followed throughout the year across the microclimates of the salt pannes, shrublands, and extensive boardwalks nestled into the dunes.

The beach itself has been well known since the seventeenth century as a wild and dangerous place. The swift tidal currents make boating and swimming hazardous. The arctic Labrador current flows from north to south along the shore, migrating sand into the mouth of the Merrimack river and chilling the coastal waters to a deep navy blue, near-black, hue. The shallow beach shelf extending some distance out to sea produces deadly undertows and riptides, constant shipwrecks and drownings. During severe storms, the beach is inundated and the breakers strike the dune line.

The intensity of the place is long-figured in literature.

> Plum Island, a wild and fantastical sand beach, is thrown up by the joint power of winds and waves into the thousand wanton figures of a snow drift.
>
> (*Joshua Coffin, 1845, p. vii*)

> ... the roaring of the breakers, and the ceaseless flux and reflux of the waves, did not for a moment cease to dash and roar, with such a tumult that, if you had been there, you could scarcely have heard my voice the while; and they are dashing and roaring this very moment ... for there the sea never rests. We were wholly absorbed by this spectacle and tumult, and ... we walked silent along the shore of the resounding sea.
>
> *(Henry David Thoreau 1985: 46)*

Residents are divided between the rich and the poor; both ocean side and marsh side are eclectic mixes of housing but there is also a sense of class divide between the two sides, connected only in one place by a single road. There are vacation mega-mansions and shacks occupied by people who dig clams for a living. Local businesses are eclectic and show attitude or style: The BeachComa, Plum Crazy, Mad Martha's Beach Café, Bob Lobster, Blue – The Inn on the Beach. The winter is harsh. People do what they do. The year-round residents watch out for each other, or they just watch each other. There is a vigilance. There is a movement to secede from the two municipalities, Newbury and Newburyport, which are said to overtax the island for the benefit of the mainland. The tidal marshes are spectacular, especially at sunset, with a continually changing population of birds, ranging from plovers, redwing blackbirds and killdeer to egrets, gulls, marsh hawks, great blue herons, snowy owls and osprey.

And then there are the greenhead flies. They bite hard and persistently, attacking the soft wet flesh on the beach or the exposed areas of limbs in the nature preserve. Unlike mosquitoes, which insert a delicate, needle-like proboscis through the skin to draw blood, greenhead flies bite a chunk of flesh with their jaws and lap at the blood. Peak greenhead season is the month of July and the flies are pervasive on Plum Island because the island is ringed with robust marshland. Adult flies mate in the open marsh. The female lays her first egg mass, containing hundreds of eggs, within a few days. To lay additional masses she needs a blood meal. The larvae are also predacious, foraging through wet thatch, surface muck and marsh vegetation on other insect larvae or small animals. The larvae overwinter, form a pupa, and emerge as adults in late spring. Adult flies have long lives (three to four weeks), and can fly at fifty miles an hour in a range as far as thirty miles.

During greenhead fly season, the island sports hand-painted signs of human skeletons covered in flies to warn off visitors. The painted signs are even used at the entrance gate to the nature preserve.

But in the last two years something magical has happened. You may slowly begin to notice the large black boxes in the marsh. They look like a modernist art installation. These are traps developed originally by Rutgers researchers to measure the greenhead fly population. Box trap design is circulated on the web. It is very precise, although each trap costs only a few dollars to build. A four-sided box with a screen top and open bottom. Fifteen by thirty-two inches on each side. Forty-inch legs attached to stakes in the ground. The legs buried so that the top sits exactly twenty-four inches above the ground surfaces. This is important because the greenhead usually flies at about this altitude. It is important that the trap be painted a glossy black to contrast with its surroundings and to absorb heat from the sun. Flies enter the trap from below and move into secondary traps on the top of the box. The top of the trap is made of a metal insect screen. Inside there are the cones and collectors. (Cut holes two to three inches from the sides of the trap and two and a half inches in diameter; make cones of insect screen of precise dimensions; cement the cones around the holes; make two collectors out of clear plastic containers such as a shoe box or cake box; fit these over the cones …) A decoy can be added beneath the trap. A beach ball fourteen to sixteen inches in diameter and painted shiny black helps attract flies when suspended beneath the trap. The decoy should clear the ground by four to six inches so it moves with the breeze. Clusters of two or three traps in a fly path capture exponentially more flies than isolated traps. Vegetation beneath and around the trap should be kept low (four to six inches high) for about a six-foot radius. Traps have collected over one thousand greenhead flies per hour.

Last year on Plum Island, there were no flies at all, they say. This year there were some. But then one day when we decided to go into the preserve there was the hand-painted sign; we turned around.

Conclusion

A thing throws a worlding together out of objects and attunements, practices and incipient tendencies. The ricocheting between subjects and objects settles for a minute on matter already configured. An attunement to a thing not quite named, and yet singular and precise, produces an opening. A field of potentiality, a virtuality, takes on an existence and pulls itself into motions whether as a set of threats or possibilities, as a shining little something or the dull contours of what is too well known brought into cruel relief. There can be drama, beauty, horror, annoyance in this. The root process of things taking form is ordinary and pervasive: a process of making things matter (like it or not), a leaning in, a vigilance, a way of going on in the world (McCormack 2009).

Bibliography

Brown, W. (2001) Thing theory. *Critical Inquiry.* 28:1 pp. 1–22.

Cavell, S. (1980) *The World Viewed: Reflections on the Ontology of Film*, Cambridge, MA: Harvard University Press.

Coffin, Joshua (1845) *A Sketch of the History of Newbury, Newburyport, and West Newbury from 1635 to 1845*, Boston: Samuel Drake.

Connolly, W. (1999) Brain Waves, transcendental fields, and techniques of thought. *Radical Philosophy.* 94: pp.19–28.

Deleuze, G. (1998) *Essays Critical and Clinical*, London: Verso.

Deleuze, G. and Guattari, F. (1987) *A Thousand Plateaus*, Minneapolis, MN: University of Minnesota Press.

Didion, J. (2006) *We Tell Ourselves Stories in Order to Live: Collected Nonfiction*, NY: Alfred A. Knopf.

Grosz, E. (2001) The Thing. In *Architecture from the Outside: Essays on Virtual and Real Space*, Cambridge, MA: MIT Press. pp. 167–84.

Heidegger, M. (1971) The Thing. In *Poetry, Language, Thought*, NY: Harper and Row. pp. 163–86.

Ingold, T. (2007) Earth, sky, wind, weather. *Journal of the Royal Anthropological Institute.* S19–S38.

McCormack, D. (2003) An event of geographical ethics in spaces of affect. *Transactions of the Institute of British Geographers*. 28: pp. 488–507.

_____ (2008) Engineering affective atmospheres: on the moving geographies of the 1897 André expedition. *Cultural Geographies*. 15: pp. 413–30.

_____ (2009) Aerostatic spacing: on things becoming lighter than air. *Transactions of the Institute of British Geographers*. 35: pp. 25–41.

Sloterdijk, P. (1998) *Spharen: Blasen*, Frankfurt: Suhrkamp.

Stewart, K. (2007) *Ordinary Affects*, Durham, NC: Duke University Press.

Thoreau, H. (1985) *Thoreau*, NY: Penguin Putnam.

Thrift, N. (2004) Movement-space: the changing domain of thinking resulting from the development of new kinds of spatial awareness. *Economy and Society*. 33:4, pp. 582–603.

_____ (2007) *Nonrepresentational Theory: Space, Politics, Affect*, New Jersey: Routledge.

_____ (2009) Different atmospheres: of Sloterdijk, China and site. *Environment and Planning D: Society and Space*. 27: pp. 119–38.

_____ (2011) Lifeworld, Inc. – and what to do about it. *Environment and Planning D: Society and Space*. 29: pp. 5–26.

11

Bodies and cadavers

Maryon McDonald

Introduction

This chapter is about the practice of learning anatomy in medical education classes. The following paragraphs are about the UK particularly, although much of what I say also applies to anatomy classes elsewhere. The dissection of cadaveric material to learn about the human body became a part of medical education in Europe from the seventeenth and especially eighteenth centuries onwards, spreading from Italy and then Paris.[1] For generations of medical students in Europe, the USA and elsewhere, anatomy has conjured up dissection, a term that helped to distinguish the practice from the mundane, from the vernacular of its etymological 'cutting'. The working objects of medical gross anatomy are human cadavers. The making and remaking of these cadavers as anatomical objects is an important theme in this chapter, and other points take shape around it.

Histories of anatomy have generally cited Vesalius as the exemplary instigator, in the sixteenth century, of the dissection of human bodies (performing the dissections himself) to advance surgical knowledge (Cunningham 1997). Dissections were often public in Europe and had strong theatrical and ceremonial aspects, but private anatomical research was practised, too. Over the eighteenth and nineteenth centuries in the UK, anatomical dissection was progressively moved out of the public gaze into laboratories or dedicated dissection rooms. From the seventeenth century onwards, autopsies or post-mortem investigations had developed and the results of these, often performed on well-known figures, helped to give some public credibility to a practice otherwise regarded with fear and scorn (Chaplin 2007). With the body becoming the site of disease, the 'signs' seen in living bodies could be confirmed in the organs after death. The development of clinics or hospitals, with so many bodies together, facilitated and encouraged this (Maulitz 1987; Bynum 2008: Chapter 3). By the twentieth and twenty-first centuries, we have firmly moved into a world of the hospital or clinic, with all the attendant changes in understandings of bodies outlined by Foucault (1973). We live in a world in which anatomy has reconfigured what is visible, where commonalities across bodies have been discovered, depicted and published, with technologies constructed and used accordingly; a human body has been coordinated from the many dissections, and standardized through the practices and circumstances of medicine. There is a circularity embedded here: we can talk of the dissection of the human body, but it was partly through dissection that 'the human body' as a universalizable entity was invented. For better or for worse, the 'human body' has been imagined to be interchangeable across the globe, such that anthropologists have talked of 'local biologies', as if departing from the norm (Lock and Nguyen 2010). We can also imagine and experience a human body in the interiority of which disease can be detected, and detected through a range of standardized external tests, screenings and imaging (Edwards, Harvey and Wade 2010). In this medicine, anatomy played a foundational role.

Learning human gross anatomy now means acquiring the skills to see organs and tissues, to name them and to understand, above all, the relations between them. A focus on organs in the early eighteenth century expanded, with the work of men such as Bichat, to include tissues and their distinctions (Bynum 2008; Lawrence 2009). Dense tissue becomes, in anatomy, elements of site and connection, of structure and function. Anatomy is a classification or taxonomy which is itself a model; learning anatomy means grasping a three-dimensional structure and naming its parts. Examinations in anatomy involve recognizing and naming inherently relational parts.

Bodies

Medical bodies involve a collocation of bodies analytically bounded or unbounded in ways that are not always obvious. The work I present here draws on ethnographic research I have carried out in the fields of anatomy, surgery and organ transplants. Each of these areas deals with troubled body boundaries, and deals with different bodies. Anatomy has been seen as the historical master discipline for the investigation of life (Cunningham 2010:19), but in the modern medical curriculum, it has increasingly been jostled by cellular bodies and the molecular universe of genetics and genomics. Anatomy itself has been changing, with some of the fragility of its current disciplinary status summarized for me in its description as a 'slow physiology'. I concentrate in this chapter on anatomical dissection in dedicated dissection rooms in medical schools where cadaveric dissection is practised.[2] Some of the issues involved here are different in important ways from the issues that other medical bodies might present (e.g., Varela 2001; Mol 2002; Napier 2003). For example, we see that anatomical bodies still tend to implicate a previous and persistent self rather than later cellular socialities.

One anthropological issue that arises immediately is that of the language of my own analysis. What kind of corporeality can I take for granted? One analytical language I could use for medical students learning anatomy (students acquiring skills) might be 'embodiment'. However, this has several problems, not least of which is that it can appear to assume what should in this context be held up for inspection. Embodiment theory can appear to assume a stable substrate or sometimes a self congruent with the boundaries of an individuated body, a subject that is the seat of cognition and a will: an *a priori* body-subject or body-self that is at the centre of relations and anterior to them (Vilaça 2009; Lambert and McDonald 2009). Such a body-self is the object of ethnography here rather than the language of my analysis. A more helpful analytical approach therefore might be to think instead of the bodies that are *acquired* by the students. This can only be done in general terms here, but the approach I am taking is one in which the inherence of human bodies in an environing world is assumed to involve ever-active processes of microarticulation. Rephrasing this through a simple analogy, we might say that everything and every person in the dissection room (all the 'circumstances', literally) can be likened to Latour's example of the odour kit in the training of 'a nose' in the perfume industry (Latour 2004).[3] The kit becomes coextensive with bodies, bodies are dynamic trajectories, and the kit produces a transformation in the body of the person and in the universe of which they are a part, one element articulating another, one affecting the other. It is not a question of an anterior subject (is my nose accurate?) representing an object (is it an accurate representation of odours already existing in the world?), but it is instead a question of a mutual articulation process.[4] Using an odour kit (itself already set up through the publications, conferences, documentation, training, conventional materials and practices of the chemists and engineers who made it), the trainees in the perfume industry learn to be affected by ever more subtle distinctions. In a similar way, the medical students studying anatomy learn to be affected in the mutual articulations of bodies and cadavers, but with all the inevitable entanglements of matter and meaning.

Anatomical bodies

The anatomical bodies of medical education may be jostled by cellular and molecular bodies now, but anatomical bodies themselves have also changed over time. This can be seen in changes in the depictions found historically in anatomical atlases: in the shift from Figure 11.1 to Figure 11.2 or to Figure 11.3, for example; or from Figure 11.4 to Figure 11.5, below.

Figures 11.1 and 11.4 date from the beginning of the nineteenth century; they are posed and have personal content. The very different diagrammatic images of Figures 11.2, 11.3 and 11.5 date from the second half of the twentieth century.[5] The later images are the outcome of various forms of 'objectivity' that developed during the nineteenth century, themselves part of the many strategies of impersonality and impartiality that followed on the universalist ambitions of what we like still to call 'the Enlightenment'. This was a period in which knowledge became divided

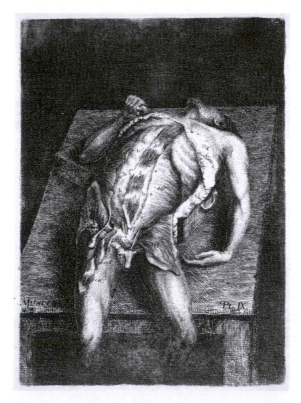

Figure 11.1 Engraving by John Bell from *Engravings, Explaining the Anatomy of the Bones, Muscles and Joints,* Longman and Rees (Plate III), 1794

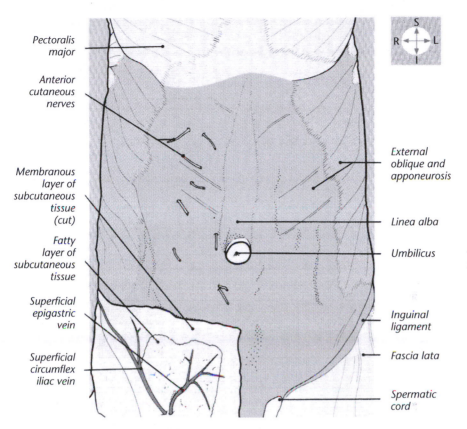

Pectoralis
major

Anterior
cutaneous
nerves

Membranous
layer of
subcutaneous
tissue
(cut)

Fatty
layer of
subcutaneous
tissue

Superficial
epigastric
vein

Superficial
circumflex
iliac vein

External
oblique and
apponeurosis

Linea alba

Umbilicus

Inguinal
ligament

Fascia lata

Spermatic
cord

Figure 11.2 This diagram was published in *Human Anatomy Color Atlas and Text* (4th edition), John Gosling, Peter Willan, Ian Whitmore and Philip Harris, p. 124, by permission of Elsevier (2002)

into subjective and objective and when science and the arts developed distinct identities. Important in the practice of objectivity was an epistemic virtue of self-discipline and restraint (Daston and Galison 2007) (approximating for some to the ideal of a factory machine) through which the dispassion, civility and discipline of earlier periods were reshaped. Ideally, a self-denying, interchangeable observer could offer direct representations of nature, of the body as it really is. Until von Hagens' *Body World* exhibitions in the 1990s, which appealed or appalled precisely because they transgressed these boundaries, anatomical bodies had been progressively sequestered, and ideally drained of the artistic, personal and social.

Within the learning environment of an anatomy class, anatomical bodies are also multiple now. Some of them (for example, atlases or X-rays) are flat, two-dimensional and mobile. Many bodies are brought together within one space, within centimetres of each other. In any one class, we might see atlases, diagrams, manuals, posters, radiology (including X-rays, computed tomography [CT] scans and magnetic resonance imaging [MRI] scans), cadavers for dissection, skeletons, prosections, black or whiteboards, colleagues and teachers. Each of these media, these bodies, whether two-dimensional or three-dimensional and whether human or otherwise, could be said to condense its own battery of cognition, rather like both the metaphorical nose and the odour kit. Simplification is often important; mathematicization, triangulation, purification and filtration (Lynch 1985) summarize some of the processes involved to produce, for example, the

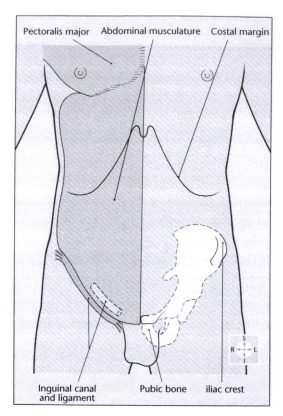

Figure 11.3 This diagram was published in *Human Anatomy Color Atlas and Text* (4th edition), John Gosling, Peter Willan, Ian Whitmore and Philip Harris, p. 127, by permission of Elsevier (2002)

body-objects seen in anatomical atlases. Atlases show the strong influence of cartography and of geology, which helped to supply the three-dimensional visual language of anatomy in the nineteenth century and have since provided a structural language to other areas of medicine too (Rudwick 1976; Varela 2001; Daston and Galison 2007). Anatomy often seems to be a world of topography, of sections, planes and landmarks. The result is an important three-dimensional topographical map that ideally enables the students as medical professionals empirically to engage with a body and its parts, and to locate lesions.

Throughout the classes, we heard regularly about the various landmarks and about planes. There are general orientating planes and also specific ones, such as the transpyloric plane. Diagrams simplify further, a common process in the production of scientific working objects. Diagrams have no shadows, suggesting a view from nowhere. There are also noticeably few words in most of the texts we consulted in anatomy classes. These are often non-linguistic, non-narrative objects. In the nineteenth century, language increasingly became the province of romanticism, the underbelly of 'positive' thought.

In a modern dissection room in the UK, students perform their own dissection, a practice described as having originated in Paris but already carried out in London in the eighteenth century (Cunningham 2010:135ff). By the nineteenth century, an older three-person system in which a professor read a book and a 'demonstrator' pointed, whilst a lowly barber-surgeon did

Figure 11.4   Engraving by John Bell from *Engravings, Explaining the Anatomy of the Bones, Muscles and Joints*, Longman and Rees (Plate IX), 1794

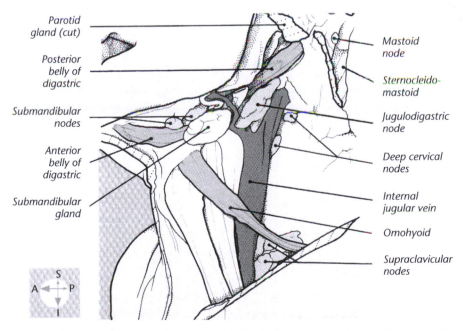

Parotid gland (cut)

Posterior belly of digastric

Submandibular nodes

Anterior belly of digastric

Submandibular gland

Mastoid node

Sternocleido-mastoid

Jugulodigastric node

Deep cervical nodes

Internal jugular vein

Omohyoid

Supraclavicular nodes

Figure 11.5   This diagram was published in *Human Anatomy Color Atlas and Text* (4th edition), John Gosling, Peter Willan, Ian Whitmore and Philip Harris, p. 294, by permission of Elsevier (2002)

the actual dissection, was giving way to teachers of anatomy ideally monitoring medical students performing the dissection themselves. The order of anatomical dissection once followed roughly that of putrefaction, then drew attention to 'systems' (given impetus by the work of men such as Harvey as well as by the French Revolution), but returned to regions of the body again by the late nineteenth century under the influence of a surgery that had gained new confidence with the development of anaesthetics (Tobias 1992; Sawchuk 2012). This consolidation of surgery and anatomy brought landmarks to the fore, a standardized orientating body-language was instituted in the early twentieth century, and an orderly sequential manner for travelling into a body demarcated through a series of planes and landmarks became common convention in anatomy, pathology and surgery (Sawchuk 2012:146). Systems or parts of them are still shown to be inter-connected within regions, following three-dimensional innervations and perfusion 'routes', for example, seeing where nerves, veins and arteries 'run', or what they 'serve'. Modern anatomy also uses sliced cadaveric cross-sections that seem to respect neither region nor system but are influenced by MRIs and CTs, and the slices of the Visible Human Project (Waldby 2000; Prentice 2005). The teachers, now generally anatomists or retired surgeons, are still sometimes called 'demonstrators'. In the dissection room where I worked most often, the teachers met before classes and decided on inclusion and exclusion, what to 'see' and not to see, for the dissection to follow, and they would remind each other to 'keep it simple'. In the classes, the students move from one medium to another: atlas, manual, skeleton, teacher, a drawing on the board, a diagram in a textbook, a colleague and the cadaver. It is not a case of a simple reality in all this ('the human body') of which students as subjects make a representation in their heads. The circumstances are rather more complicated. The students themselves acquire the medical body of an anatomist or surgeon, and they do so relationally both with other students and in an environment in which the boundary of 'cognition' or cognitive agency is not simply in the head but around the room and beyond. It is there not only in their own bodies, but in other persons, instruments, images and other artefacts, the cadavers included.

Armchair anatomy

Cadavers, where present, loom large. These are persons discreetly transformed into important anatomical working objects of structures and functions. This transformation has many aspects, some of which we return to shortly. Standardization of a kind occurs, and not just through publications. If we take the case of a cadaver and an atlas or manual: first, there is a selection of the body (avoiding gross pathology and obesity, for example, or the very young). The body then becomes, in this context, 'a cadaver' and the cadaver is dissected to approximate to the manual or atlas: drawings are made from dissections or prosections and these in turn guide dissection. Dissection performed by technicians produces prosections (already dissected parts of the cadaver) for classes or tests on specific regions or on regions that might be considered too complicated or time-consuming for the students themselves to dissect. The process can move from diagrams to dissection to diagrams. It is a process of 'sculpting', as some technicians and teachers describe it (cf. Hirschauer 1991 on surgery). Such circularity is not uncommon in the production of working objects.

The cadavers become depictions, some say, of the manual. This can cause concern. 'Corrections' do occur. When teachers are preparing a class, and looking at drawings in an atlas or the local manual of the dissecting room, I have heard some of them 'tut' disapprovingly and say that they must check with a cadaver and, if necessary, correct the atlases or the manual – instances that are, I am told, 'too rare'. Some copying of atlases from one to another inevitably goes on. In the assemblages of academia, its conferences, publishing and audit, atlases have undoubtedly copied each other, with one atlas having another as its baseline. Such transmission, without passing via a cadaver, has generated perceived dangers of what was described to me on several occasions as 'armchair anatomy'. That there is a perceived danger here of 'armchair anatomy' and the very fact of 'correction' suggest that the cadaver holds authority as a referent. The cadaver is still believed to be necessary to confer authority on what are seen as 'representations'. This seems to be so within any one dissection room as well as between institutions, with medical students coming from elsewhere to take vacation courses in those institutions that still have cadaveric material. It seems to be so even if the cadaveric referent gets 'corrected' in turn by what a 'living body would look like'. What is sometimes known as 'living anatomy' or 'surface anatomy', using peers or models in classes, often goes on side by side with or after dissection classes. This is believed to be important and increasingly so. Anatomical study through cadavers, or the time spent on this, has been diminishing for several reasons, notably pedagogical. Less memorizing of parts and more clinical problem solving was advocated in the 1990s, with reforms in medical education seeking to bring the personal and the social back in (General Medical Council 1993, 1997; British Medical Association 1995). The best-known dissection rooms have continued, with both dissection of cadavers and living anatomy taught, and sometimes 'applied anatomy', too, in which cadavers become objects in problem-based learning. Despite controversies and concerns, bodies as cadavers remain an important component of learning and can still carry moral weight in the distribution of what is to count as real. In the dissection room, time has been stopped. A cadaver involves an isolation and holding still of an object for inspection, from which students then depart in 'variations', in dynamics (in cellular and in living bodies), but to which they may well return. The medical images to which they increasingly have recourse present similar issues (Cohn 2010; Edwards *et al.* 2010).

'Get off!'

The students acquire new bodies in these classes in a dynamic way. It is a sensuous and progressive enterprise, producing at once a sensory medium and a sensitive world. The cadavers here are part and parcel of what it is to have a body, a particular body. Students are learning to be affected.

First, they acquire particular eyes; in an oculocentric world, they learn to see. Seeing 'what there is' always requires a practised vision, but vision is never solely vision. The students look at a picture of the femoral triangle (an anatomical region of the upper inner thigh). They dissect and examine the relevant part of the cadaver. They recite a mnemonic many times, tapping three fingers in the air: 'V–A–N … vein–artery–nerve'. It is important to know these distinctions. They feel the distinctions in the cadaver. Diagrams, manuals, atlases are consulted. The students reproduce the images, with the important distinctions drawn in their own colouring atlas, or actively coloured in by them in the manuals provided. The primary value of the colours is in their distinction. They do not 'represent' what is real but shape what is real. The students return to the cadaver: 'What are we looking at?' they ask each other. They consult the diagram again, then their own coloured notebooks and the atlases; then others' notes and pictures. They look at other dissections, other cadavers on neighbouring trolley-tables in the dissection room, then back to their own dissection and again at their own images, arrayed around the table now, and held up by colleagues to help.

The students may well, in their own terms, be matching up 'representations' with a reality here. However, the anthropologist might want to say that they are reconciling different objects (an image, an atlas picture or model with another image, model or cadaver) with both images and cadaver already 'landmarked' by the very same processes of 'representation'.

About six students, dressed in white coats and wearing gloves, are grouped around each cadaver, with each cadaver on a trolley-table. Students take it in turns in their group to dissect. One student cuts carefully with a scalpel, then pulls and tears with her fingers in what is known as 'blunt dissection'. They are through the skin, and then tackle the fascia and fat. One holds an atlas, another is asked to hold her hair back 'so I can see'. 'Show me my manual.' 'Where are my notes?' 'No, the coloured picture.' 'What has he drawn on the board over there?' Discussion with colleagues helps in the adjudication of 'what there is'. All the media are reconciled, some with more difficulty than others, through discussion and landmarks. The fingers are in the air and one of the ever-present mnemonics rings out again: 'V–A–N.'

Students are simultaneously seeing, touching and verbally defining, going back and forth. In the haptics of difference, they feel the distinctions in the cadaver and talk about them. The artery is large and springs back. The nerve is thinner. While one is just starting to articulate this verbally, a male student practices the triangle of 'V–A–N' in both singsong and fingers on a female colleague. She pulls away: 'Get off me!' This is a living person, a self in a body, a 'me'. Gendered and sexual bodies are not easily divested but there is something else at work here. 'You should ask,' she says. 'OK. May I?' 'No,' comes the swift reply. In that touch is a definitional or ontological resolution of persons and of person and object. Important boundaries are effected in this way and the person is reconstituted in such microarticulations as an individuated embodied self, autonomous with a will and choice.

We know from careful historical scholarship[6] that this body-self came into being historically over a long period in which (with considerable help from early anatomy) divisibility and indivisibility emerged together alongside, and then at the expense of, previously common ideas and practices of permeability. From roughly the sixteenth and seventeenth centuries onwards, the bounded and individuated body took shape in so many tiny instances of everyday life in articulation with the changing circumstances of religious reformation (and Protestant interiority), land enclosure, new conventions of landscape painting (separating person and the world), new architectures of privacy, machines and reflection on them, the publications of theologians and philosophers and new forms of knowledge, new institutions of work and education, ideas of improvement and progress, and new policings of body boundaries making leakage and spillage in both life and death abhorrent. And so on. There was no switch in all this from ideas of permeable bodies to a boundedness of bodies because it was discovered that they were not permeable; rather, there was an increasing idealization and regulation of new comportments and bodily control that began to speak of an autonomous 'self' within the individuated boundaries of the skin.

This autonomous, bounded body-self is part of what students may already have acquired in relational everyday instances of their lives, but which they have to learn here in a new way. It is not a natural given: 'Get off!' This is a boundary formally marked in the medical arena by 'informed consent'. Informed consent relies on some of the assumptions that have tended to make up understandings of embodiment, but more especially, it relies on an autonomy of self inhabiting a body, a self that reflects and chooses, an anterior subject that has a will and forms relationships. Informed consent is the foundation of modern bioethical governance, and, as so many scholars have pointed out (e.g., Manson and O'Neill 2007), it carries all manner of problems as well as being an assemblage of technologies that students will have to learn (from polite requests to, most commonly, consent forms). It can bring forth the very subjects it assumes, subjects that are required to reflect and decide (Reubi 2010, 2012; McDonald 2012), but it is in many respects a formal regulatory rendering of a subjectivity already taken for granted in the UK and beyond: 'Get off!'

Students acquire particular hearing in anatomy classes, through palpation and auscultation. They learn resonance over the intestines, for example, and dullness over the liver. However, this is acquired only through the study of 'living anatomy' or 'surface anatomy', in which permission is given to examine colleagues. Certain ontological qualities of the cadavers are distinguished at such moments, suggesting limits to what they can afford the students, and can become worrying: these objects are dead and resistant (cf. Leder 1992). For many young students, this is the first time that they have encountered dead bodies, and moments of awe, empathy and respect are elicited. However, bodies are social (Lambert and McDonald 2009). These are not bodies but 'cadavers', and so they can remain much of the time. Nevertheless, an ontology of a cadaver and then a 'soul', 'mind', 'life' or 'something else' is part of what some learn, confirm or reject here, discussed in hushed tones.

Long gone are the days when to study an element of God's creation or of some 'natural' world meant tasting or smelling it (see Roberts 1995; Daston and Galison 2007). The sensory regime of modern anatomical learning may not require smell and taste as part of its corporeal technology of learning, but it does involve learning that there are five senses plus proprioception, and the experience of the dissection room tends to get resolved into these senses. Smell figures strongly. Indeed, the boundary of the sequestered world where dissection takes place is commonly marked by a pungent smell. It is often described by students as 'formaldehyde', although teachers insisted to me that there was very little formaldehyde in the preservation fluid used in the cadavers (and it was mixed with chemicals such as glycerine, liquid phenol and methylated spirits). Not being able to bear the smell was one reason given by students who felt they could not face dissection. That smell marked the boundary between the dissection room and a social world outside, and between bodies and cadavers.

In the students' acquisition of bodily properties and proprieties, complex relationalities get resolved into categorical distinctions of sight and touch and smell, for example, with particular student-bodies brought forth. These are bodies very much aware of their boundaries and, as we shall see again, of a necessary control; they are bodies acquired through being affected by an anatomical working object in which distinctions are articulated. The more skilled the bodies become, the more the cadavers can seem to afford distinctions (including their limits) and seeing and understanding the relational distinctions increases the students' skill in turn; and so on. The cadavers have themselves been constructed by others in turn, constructed in mutual articulation with the dynamic trajectories that we might think of as other experienced bodies (anatomists and technicians) and their skills or technologies.

'Get a grip!'

The upkeep of a dissection room in medical education relies on the donation of bodies. The rhetoric of the gift distinguishes willing persons from objects, with market buying and selling excluded and both altruism and society seemingly materialized. Science and society offer two mutually defining moral languages, of detachment and attachment, which frame the production of cadavers. Once a body has been accepted, it has to be transformed into an anatomical model. This is a difficult process. The separation of the self, the person, from the body is difficult here as in other areas of life and death (e.g., Kaufman 2000; McDonald 2011). It may be that a person seems constantly to be re-evoked, but the anatomical objectification is important. The process is not the disfigurement of a body as some might see it but is the creation of a body, of a particular anatomical body or cadaver.

Many aspects of the initial transformation process for anatomy, the transformation of person to cadaver, are deliberately occluded. They have been so since the nineteenth century but have become even more so in the UK with the post-Alder Hey Human Tissue Acts of 2004 and 2006. This occlusion is built into the architecture of the university buildings up and down the country where dissection takes place. There are discrete entrances where bodies can be brought, often hidden entrances where vans or lorries can be backed in.

The preservation process is then effected largely by technicians in back rooms. It is important work and is hidden from the eyes of the students and from most of the teachers. The buildings housing dissection rooms have high or opaque windows, if any at all. This social sequestration of anatomical dissection was, some scholars have argued, part of the salvation of anatomy in the eighteenth and nineteenth centuries, rescuing it from associations with execution, taking it out of the realm of not only public spectacle but also of public and punitary dissections (Chaplin 2007).

The preservation arrests the process of death in preventing putrefaction; it fixes a moment in which the timing and registration of death have already colluded. Further practices then emphasize the sequestration process at work. Bodies that are inherently social become cadavers here and are anonymized: anonymity severs relations. The outside social world is kept at bay. Cloths are sometimes placed over faces, or students or teachers cover up parts not being dissected.

When students first encounter the cadavers they have to dissect (when they encounter them with the bodies the students have themselves acquired up to that point), it is not uncommon for some to faint, feel sick or in some instances to give up medicine altogether. Common excuses emerge from those so affected: they have recognized the dead man; they are menstruating; or they have simply drunk too much the night before and need to sit on the floor, cling to the trolley, leave the room to be sick. There are difficult boundaries to cross, boundaries at once conceptual and practical, and particular technologies of self are required. New bodies have to be acquired. 'When you start the dissection, it's science,' said one demonstrator. 'Just bear that in mind and it becomes easier.' 'Be objective.' 'Distance yourself.' Students commonly warned each other to do this and described their own epistemological proprieties in these terms. 'You have to distance yourself.'

We see at work here a particular heritage of largely eighteenth-century and nineteenth-century creations of the self in Europe, a period when knowledge became parsed in terms of objectivity and subjectivity. Objectivity and subjectivity constituted a duality of 'perspectives' on a world (or 'nature') deemed to exist independently. They were often congruent with other dualities of the time: male and female, reason and emotions, and so on. The subject of largely eighteenth-century and nineteenth-century creation has to learn discipline, to learn or relearn that they are a body-self composed internally of reason and emotions, a self that has to hold itself in check by acts of 'will' manifest in comportment.[7] If they do not hold it in check, the self or subjectivity dominates the objectivity of the representation or activity, getting in the way. The self, as in the nineteenth century, often appears now in dissection classes as the site of emotions, of the person and partiality. Students fear that they will cry, will faint, will get silly or simply not be able to learn. 'Just detach yourself from it,' one student warned another who was finding the process difficult. 'Distance yourself …' 'You've just got to get a grip!'

I have suggested that in the nineteenth century, anatomical representations (for so they were often seen to be) such as atlases similarly went through the transformations of different objectivities in which the self was believed to be dangerous intrusion. We have seen the images that resulted. New ontologies were wrought by a clear-eyed and disciplined scientific vision (Daston and Galison 2007). This was and is a moral position: sobriety and self-discipline for the common good. Often what was once a prized, 'hands-off' objectivity is now deemed to be a matter of embodied clinical judgement. But the clinician's body that is capable of such judgement has to be acquired and it takes discipline.

Transformations of the epistemological virtue that claimed objectivity in the representations of bodies in the nineteenth century can now seem to present themselves in practical conceptions of the capacity to get through, and learn from, dissection classes. 'Distancing yourself' is part of the technology of learning and it is also part of what is learnt. A demeanour of seriousness and equanimity results much of the time and is believed to be important. It is a demeanour gradually attained as the imbrications and articulations of cadavers, students and surrounding colleagues and technologies become routine. This is an epistemological propriety with which respect for the dead can and does collude. But it is not appropriate to cry in the dissection room 'Get a grip'.

Both horror and amusement are common in these circumstances. There is some deliberate teasing of those unable to 'get a grip' and there are jokes and pranks which it is feared that a new bioethical governance of medical and dissection room comportment, with respect and human dignity emphasized, will exclude. We live in a world accustomed to ontological multiplicities but the instability of the cadaver is important and can be worrying; it is also a source of amusement. Dissection classes are known for the jokes they provoke (e.g., Hafferty 1988). A boundary is breached and definitional rectitude regained in incongruence and laughter. Usually, the cadaver is 'he' or 'she' at first and then occasionally 'it' (or 'our cadaver' or 'yours'), locating agency elsewhere; or sometimes a nickname is used that is often not a name close to the students in everyday life ('Bruce', in one instance). The person reemerges at various points in other ways: when a tattoo is noticed, or nail varnish or a catheter or pacemaker, or the colour of the lungs (suggesting smoking) or when blood is seen ('Yuk') or when it is announced that the arms have gone or other parts have been removed for prosections: 'Oh my God … gruesome … I can't take this.' Such claims (or a 'yuk') increasingly elicit a 'Don't be silly' or 'Get a grip' from colleagues. This is ideally a world of reason not emotions, of sobriety not silliness. Often a 'yuk', or a similar concern, is heard when the person seems to reemerge in the cadaver during the dissection classes. When violated, that individuated body-self properly bounded by its skin elicits exclamations of 'gruesome'. Both horror and laughter can result when the reflexive selves of the students bring the outside world into the dissection room in this way. Humour is generated when students notionally reflect on their activity and the cadaveric objects as if it were all viewed by an outsider, by someone who has not acquired the bodies that they are themselves acquiring: 'If my mother could see me now …'. Or, in a deliberately mundane accent when washing hands at the basins afterwards: 'How time flies when you're cutting up dead bodies!' Both the humour and the chivvying to 'get a grip' are engagements that play on the ontological instability of the cadaver but they also, through the team around it, support the detachment acquired, a necessary detachment lived as a calmness and equanimity in the face of death, nakedness, leaking and spillages, and a scalpel into the skin, bowels on the surface, or an arm missing, and so on.

The cadavers are deliberately moved back to bodies (to social bodies) again at the end of the year. Memorial, thanksgiving services are generally held everywhere at the end of the course annually or biannually once the dissection is over. Donation and the gift are emphasized in speeches and poems from students, who express gratitude and respect for the donor and the help that they have given. This becomes a world of social connection again, but it is one that has moved away from Bentham's pioneering if eccentric donation in the nineteenth century (a donation that hoped to move the procurement of anatomical objects away from body-snatching) through a newer national rhetoric of 'society' and post-World War II welfare and on to a bio-ethical governance of which the object now is the *will* of donors (with their willing choice monitored in documentation) and for which, in these services, thanks are given.[8] These are services attended by both students and teachers, constituted as grateful recipients. Over the preceding year, everything from each individual cadaver (all the bits, all the fascia and fat, etc.) had gone into single, individuated receptacles under the tables throughout the dissection process. Now every part goes back together into individuated coffins. The coffins may be lined up in the services and sometimes relatives of the deceased also attend. In such services, the social person is reinstantiated: a subject again at the centre of relations.

Conclusion

We can see that learning anatomy is not a matter of individuated minds representing a world 'out there' and it is not a world analytically of either subjects or objects anterior to the relations that produce them. Rather, both students and students, and students and teachers, and students and teachers and all the working objects, are all articulated the one with the other. Students sometimes take on anatomical bodies themselves, understanding their own structure and functioning and injury through them. They also learn that other bodies intrude and that their divestment, or the conversion of a person into an object of examination, requires self-conscious attention to a subject with a will and choice: consent.

The use of technologies and objects (and of one another) to extend human capacities is not new, although it has been given some novel formulations in studies of scientific practice.[9] In the case of anatomical dissection, bodies become very much a part of the technology of learning and are necessarily changed by it. In an occulocentric conclusion, we might say that learning anatomy is a distributed process relying on connections between landmarks that are marks only to the knowing eye, and to eyes that are only knowing in the right body.[10] That body is one that has learnt to be affected by circumstances which have shaped an ethnographically interesting being: an individual composed of reason and emotions in a context valuing self-containment. The detachment that students acquire is not an inherent 'lack', a lack of sensitivity or empathy, for example (cf. Hildebrandt 2010), but a newly sensitized and sensitive body that has demanded its own engagement.

Acknowledgements

I owe special thanks to the Leverhulme Trust, which financed the research on which this chapter is based; to all those who tolerated me in their anatomy classes; to Bob Whitaker, Jo Wilton and Ian Parkin for their generous help and comments; and to Andrew Cunningham, Nick Hopwood and Ludmilla Jordanova for their scholarship and their help in sourcing the earlier images.

Notes

1 On the historiography of 'anatomy', see especially A. Cunningham 1997, 2010; also J. Sawday 1995; K. Park 2006; H. Cook 2006; S. Lawrence 2009; J. Robb and O. Harris (forthcoming).
2 See Turney 2007 for some of the changes in anatomy teaching; and Ganguly and Chan 2008 for a more general discussion. Plastic models, digital models (e.g., the Visible Human) and body painting are not uncommon in anatomy classes in the UK; plastinated prosections are also used, in one instance bought directly from von Hagens. Histology (or the microscopic anatomy of cellular structures) is everywhere taught alongside, but is not part of, gross anatomy. One new medical school in the UK famously declined to have cadaveric material for gross anatomy, whether for dissection or as prosections: see Mclachlan and Regan de Bere 2004.
3 Cf. C. Goodwin 1994 and 2000 on the acquisition in social interaction of a professional capacity to distinguish colours, using colleagues and a Munsell chart. In the circumstances (human and non-human) of the dissection room, a broad range of technologies takes the place of the odour kit or Munsell colour chart here. Some of this work on odour kits and colour charts is evocative of (but ignores) the earlier work on classification and definitional realities in 'semantic anthropology' (see the chapters by E. Ardener and M. Chapman in D. Parkin (ed) *Semantic Anthropology*. London: Academic Press, 1982). Anthropological readers will recognize that my general approach has also benefited from (although it does not necessarily follow) work such as Toren (e.g. 2012), Grasseni (2004) and Ingold's 'education of attention' (2001).

4 'Mutual articulation' is an expression found in anatomy, too (in the mutual articulation of joints, for example) and in related work, e.g. Prentice 2005.

5 Figures 11.1 and 11.4 were engraved by John Bell in Edinburgh and published in 1794 in his *Engravings, Explaining the Anatomy of the Bones, Muscles and Joints*, Longman and Rees (Plates III and IX); Figures 11.2, 11.3, and 11.5 were published in Gosling *et al.* 2002 on, respectively, p.124 (figure 4.1), p. 127 (fig. 4.10) and p. 294 (fig. 7.16). In these later images, an 'orientation guide' is included. For more details of developments in anatomical images, see Crawford 1996; Cartwright 1998; Daston and Galison 2007; Sawchuk 2012.

6 See Tarlow 2011; Robb and Harris (forthcoming).

7 There were several diseases of the will in the nineteenth century, including addiction.

8 On some related aspects of procurement and donation in the UK, see Titmuss (1970) 1997; Richardson 1987; McDonald 2009; Reubi 2012. For the USA, see Young, 1997; Sappol 2002; Goodwin, M. 2006.

9 See McDonald 2012 for a summary.

10 Cf. Candea 2008:209 on 'knowing' a place.

Bibliography

British Medical Association (1995) *Report of the Working Party on Medical Education*, London: BMA.

Bynum, W. (2008) *The History of Medicine. A Very Short Introduction*, Oxford: Oxford University Press.

Candea, M. (2008) 'Fire and Identity as Matters of Concern in Corsica'. *Anthropological Theory* 8(2): 201–216.

Cartwright, L. (1998) 'A Cultural Anatomy of the Visible Human project' in P. Treichler, L. Cartwright and C. Penley (eds) *The Visible Woman: Imaging Technologies, Gender and Science*, NY: New York University Press.

Chaplin, S. (2007) 'Exemplary Bodies: Public and Private Dissections in Georgian London'. Paper presented at *Representations of Early Modern Anatomy and the Human Body* Workshop, Centre for the History of Disease, Durham University.

Cohn, S. (2010) 'Picturing the Brain Inside, Revealing the Illness Outside' in J. Edwards, P. Harvey and P. Wade (eds) *Technologized Images, Technologized Bodies*, Oxford and New York: Berghahn.

Cook, H. (2006) 'Medicine' in K. Park and L. Daston (eds) *Early Modern Science (Cambridge History of Science*, vol. 3), Chapter 18: 407–434, Cambridge: Cambridge University Press.

Crawford, T. (1996) 'Imaging the Human Body: Quasi Objects, Quasi Texts, and the Theater of Proof'. *PMLA* 111(1): 66–79.

Cunningham, A. (1997) *The Anatomical Renaissance: The Resurrection of the Anatomical projects of the Ancients*, Aldershot: Scolar.

Cunningham, A. (2010) *The Anatomist Anatomis'd. An Experimental Discipline in Enlightenment Europe*, Farnham: Ashgate (The History of Medicine in Context Series).

Daston, L. and Galison, P. (2007) *Objectivity*, New York: Zone Books.

Edwards, J., Harvey, P., and Wade, P. (eds) (2010) *Technologized Images, Technologized Bodies*, Oxford and New York: Berghahn.

Foucault, M. (1973) *The Birth of the Clinic: An Archaeology of Medical Perception* (Translated by A.M. Sheridan Smith), London: Tavistock.

Ganguly, P.K. and Chan, L.K. (2008) 'Living Anatomy in the 21st Century: How Far Can We Go?' *South East Asian Journal of Medical Education* 2(2): 52–57.

General Medical Council (1993) *Tomorrow's Doctors*, London: GMC.

General Medical Council (1997) *The New Doctors*, London: GMC.

Goodwin, C. (1994) 'Professional Vision'. *American Anthropologist* 96(3): 606–633.

Goodwin, C. (2000) 'Practices of Color Classification'. *Mind, Culture, and Activity* 7(1 and 2): 19–36.

Goodwin, M. (2006) *Black Markets: The Supply and Demand of Body Parts*, New York: Cambridge University Press.

Gosling, J. A., Harris, P., Whitmore, I. and Willan, P.L.T. (2002) *Human Anatomy: Color Atlas and Text*. (4th edition), Oxford and Philadelphia: Elsevier.

Grasseni, C. (2004) 'Skilled Vision: An Apprenticeship in Breeding Aesthetics'. *Social Anthropology* 12(1): 41–55.

Grasseni, C. (2007) 'Introduction' in C. Grasseni (ed.) *Skilled Visions: Between Apprenticeship and Standards*, New York: Berghahn Books. pp. 1–19.

Hafferty, F. (1988) 'Cadaver Stories and the Emotional Socialization of Medical Students'. *Journal of Health and Social Behaviour* 29(December): 344–356.

Hildebrandt, S. (2010) 'Developing Empathy and Clinical Detachment During the Dissection Course in Gross Anatomy'. *Anatomical Sciences Education* 3(4): 216.

Hirschauer, S. (1991) 'The Manufacture of Bodies in Surgery'. *Social Studies of Science* 21: 279–319.

Ingold, T. (2001) 'From the Transmission of Representation to the Education of Attention' in H. Whitehouse (ed.) *The Debated Mind: Evolutionary Psychology versus Ethnography*, Oxford and New York: Berg. pp. 113–153.

Kaufman, S. (2000) 'In the Shadow of "Death with Dignity": Medicine and Cultural Quandaries of the Vegetative State'. *American Anthropologist* 102(1): 69–83.

Lambert, H. and McDonald, M. (2009) 'Introduction' in H. Lambert and M. McDonald (eds) *Social Bodies*, NY and Oxford: Berghahn.

Latour, B. (2004) 'How to Talk About the Body: The Normative Dimension of Science Studies'. *Body and Society* 10(2–3): 205–229.

Lawrence, S. (2009) 'Anatomy, Histology and Cytology' in P. Bowler and J. Pickstone (eds) *The Modern Biological and Earth Sciences (The Cambridge History of Science*, volume 6) Chapter 15: 265–284, Cambridge: Cambridge University Press.

Leder, D. (1992) 'A Tale of Two Bodies: The Cartesian Corpse and the Lived Body' in D. Leder (ed.) *The Body in Medical Thought and Practice*, Kluwer Academic Publishers. pp. 17–35.

Lock, M. and Nguyen, V.-K. (2010) *The Anthropology of Biomedicine*, Chichester: Wiley-Blackwell.

Lynch, M. (1985) 'Discipline and the Material Forms of Images: An Analysis of Scientific Visibility'. *Social Studies of Science* 15(1): 37–66.

Lynch, M. and Woolgar, S. (eds) (1990) *Representation in Scientific Practice*, Cambridge, MA: MIT Press.

McDonald, M. (2009) 'Organ Transplants' in A. Herle, M. Elliott and R. Empson (eds) *Assembling Bodies*, Cambridge: Museum of Archaeology and Anthropology.

McDonald, M. (2011) 'Deceased Organ Donation, Culture and the Objectivity of Death' in W. Weimar (ed.) *Organ Transplantation: Ethical, Legal and Psycho-Social Aspects*, Eichengrund: Pabst Science Publishers.

McDonald, M. (2012) 'Medical Anthropology and Anthropological Studies of Science' in U. Kockel, M. Nic Craith and J. Frykman (eds) *Companion to the Anthropology of Europe*, Oxford: Wiley-Blackwell.

Mclachlan, J.C. and Regan de Bere, S. (2004) 'How We Teach Anatomy Without Cadavers'. *The Clinical Teacher* 1(2): 49–52.

McMenamin, P.G. (2008) 'Body Painting as a Tool in Clinical Anatomy Teaching'. *Anatomical Sciences Education* 1(4): 139–144.

Manson, N. and O'Neill, O. (2007) *Rethinking Informed Consent in Bioethics*, Cambridge: Cambridge University Press.

Maulitz, R. (1987) *Morbid Appearances: The Anatomy of Pathology in the Early Nineteenth Century*, Cambridge: Cambridge University Press.

Mol, A. (2002) *The Body Multiple. Ontology in Medical Practice*, Duke University Press.

Napier, D. (2003) *The Age of Immunology: Conceiving a Future in an Alienating World*, Chicago: University of Chicago Press.

Park, K. (2006) *Secrets of Women, Gender, Generation and the Origins of Human Dissection*, New York: Zone Books.

Prentice, R. (2005) 'The Anatomy of a Surgical Simulation: The Mutual Articulation of Bodies in and through the Machine'. *Social Studies of Science* 35(6): 837–866.

Prentice, R. (2007) 'Drilling Surgeons: The Social Lessons of Embodied Surgical Learning'. *Science, Technology, and Human Values* 32(5): 534–553.

Reiser, S.J. (1993) 'Technology and the Use of the Senses in Twentieth-Century Medicine' in W. H. Bynum and Roy Porter (eds) *Medicine and the Five Senses*, Cambridge: Cambridge University Press. pp. 262–273.

Reubi, D. (2010) 'The Will to Modernize: A Genealogy of Biomedical Research Ethics in Singapore'. *International Political Sociology* 4(2): 142–158.

Reubi, D. (2012) 'The Human Capacity to Reflect and Decide'. *Social Studies of Science* 2012:1–21. Doi: 10.1177/0306312712439457

Richardson, R. (1987) *Death, Dissection, and the Destitute*, London: Routledge and Kegan Paul. (2nd edition Chicago: University of Chicago Press, 2000).

Richardson, R. (2000) 'A Necessary Inhumanity'. *Journal of Medical Ethics: Medical Humanities* 26: 104–106.

Robb, J. and Harris, O. (forthcoming) *The Body in History*, Cambridge: Cambridge University Press.

Roberts, L. (1995) 'The Death of the Sensuous Chemist: The "New" Chemistry and the Transformation of Sensuous Technology'. *Studies in the History and Philosophy of Science* 26(4): 503–529.

Rudwick, M. (1976) 'The Emergence of a Visual Language for Geological Science 1760–1840'. *History of Science* 14: 149–195.

Sappol, M. (2002) *A Traffic in Dead Bodies: Anatomy and Embodied Social Identity in Nineteenth-Century America*, Princeton, NJ: Princeton University Press.

Sawchuk, K. (2012) 'Animating the Anatomical Specimen: Regional Dissection and the Incorporation of Photography in J.C.B. Grant's *An Atlas of Anatomy*'. *Body and Society* 18(1): 120–150.

Sawday, J. (1995) *The Body Emblazoned. Dissection and the Human Body in Renaissance Culture*, London and New York: Routledge.

Tarlow, S. (2011) *Ritual, Belief and the Dead in Early Modern Britain and Ireland*, Cambridge: Cambridge University Press.

Titmuss, R. (1970) (1997) *The Gift Relationship: From Blood to Social Policy*. (Edited by Ann Oakley and John Ashton), London: London School of Economics.

Tobias, P. (1992) 'The Contributions of J.C. Boileau Grant to the Teaching of Anatomy'. *South African Journal of Medicine* 83: 352–353.

Toren, C. (2012) 'Anthropology and Psychology' in R. Fardon (ed.) *The Sage Handbook of Social Anthropology*, New York: Sage. pp. 42–78.

Turney, B. (2007) 'Anatomy in a Modern Medical Curriculum'. *Annals of the Royal College of Surgeons of England* 89(2): 104–107.

Varela, F. (2001) 'Intimate Distances'. *Journal of Consciousness Studies* 8(5–7): 259–271.

Vilaça, A. (2009) 'Bodies in Perspective: A Critique of the Embodiment Paradigm from the Point of View of Amazonian Ethnography', in H. Lambert and M. McDonald (eds) *Social Bodies*, New York and Oxford: Berghahn.

Waldby, C. (2000) *The Visible Human Project: Informatic Bodies and Posthuman Medicine*, London and New York: Routledge.

Young, K. (1997) *Presence in the Flesh: The Body in Medicine*, Cambridge, MA: Harvard University Press.

12

Domination and desire

The paradox of Egyptian human remains in museums

Karen Exell

There is no dialogue with the dead – or even a meeting – merely a monologue. Our own. Such explicit domination over an individual should evoke horror and disdain.

If nothing else, we should display the mummies to help us to fulfil our narcissistic urge to understand the fragility of our own lives.

Extracts from responses discussing the covering of the mummies at
The Manchester Museum in 2008: http://egyptmanchester.
wordpress.com/2008/05/06/covering-the-mummies/

Over the last ten years, ancient Egyptian human remains have been actively drawn into the debate over the ethical treatment of human remains in museums, a deliberate problematizing of the display of embalmed bodies that has been culturally and socially accepted in the West for over two hundred years (see Kilminster 2003; Jenkins 2011). The recent debate has centred on the argument that the bodies were once living people and therefore their public display is unethical and disrespectful, and can be contextualized within the wider debate over the retention of human remains in museum collections, in particular their display and interpretation, and broader issues of repatriation. (See Jenkins [2011] for a recent summary of the extensive literature detailing the emergence of repatriation claims over the last thirty years and the resulting guidelines and conventions aimed at archaeologists and museums.) In the literature assessing public reaction in the UK to the treatment of human remains, the Alder Hey children's organ scandal that came to light as a result of a public enquiry in 1999 and two exhibitions, *London Bodies: The Changing Shape of Londoners from Prehistoric Times to the Present Day* (The Museum of London, 1998–9) and *Body Worlds: The Anatomical Exhibition of Real Human Bodies* (London, 2002–3) are frequently cited (Brooks and Rumsey 2007, 2009; see also Jenkins 2011: 28–32, 112–3, 137–9), with the discussion focusing on issues of consent and the nature of the public reaction to viewing different types of human remains (ancient or recent, fleshed or skeletal).

In the human remains debate, there has been little discussion of the curation and display of ancient Egyptian human remains (Brookes and Rumsey 2007: 260). In 2000, the Petrie Museum of Egyptian Archaeology, University College London and the Egyptologist Dominic Montserrat curated *Ancient Egypt: Digging for Dreams* (Montserrat 2000; Brooks and Rumsey 2007: 282), which explored contemporary perceptions of ancient Egypt, including the display of Egyptian human remains, giving visitors the option to view, or not, an Egyptian 'mummy'. Research by Kilminster (2003) and Day (2006), based primarily on visitor questionnaires with a focus on UK museums, concluded that, although the majority of people were happy to view the bodies, it was still the duty of the museum to present the bodies 'respectfully', if at all (Kilminster 2003: 65; Day 2006: 168, 173–7). From the limited research carried out to date, it is clear that there is no general public desire to remove Egyptian human remains from display; indeed, quite the opposite, as the case study from the Manchester Museum, University of Manchester discussed later in this chapter shows.

One of the results of the ethical debate over the retention of human remains by museums has been the problematization of their categorization as 'objects'. In a museum context, 'object' is a term that refers to any and all items in a museum's collection. In the wider context of rationalist Enlightenment thinking, Western conceptions have configured the world as a dichotomy between subject and object, with the former controlling the latter (Gosden 2004: 34; Knappett 2005: 25; Thomas 2007: 212). It is in this latter context that there is a resistance to categorizing the human body or parts thereof as the perceived lesser status of 'object'. More broadly, it can be argued that archaeological bodies are both subjects and objects (Brooks and Rumsey 2007: 261): objects because they are material and subjects because their materiality is the 'materiality of process', i.e. the lived experiences and social worlds of the bodies are 'sedimented' in their bodies, making them 'quasi-objects' and 'quasi-subjects' (Sofaer 2006: 76, 84; Meskell 2005; see also Lazzari 2005: 128). In a predominantly humanist and liberal Western world, where the importance of the human reigns supreme (Gray 2003), archaeological bodies as the remains of people (and, by implication, people like us) have come to be regarded as deserving of privileged treatment (Sofaer 2006: 64; Thomas 2007: 211–13). The museum guidelines that have been developed in response to the human remains debate outline a framework of activities that articulate this privileged difference, from methods of storage and labelling to display and interpretation (see, for example, the Museums Association *Code of Ethics for Museums* [2002] and the Department for Culture, Media and Sport's (DCMS's) *Guidance for the Care of Human Remains in Museums* [2005]). In relation to Egyptian human remains, there is a central paradox: the nature of the embalmed body as object/artefact as well as object/subject (Meskell 2004a: 125–6; Wieczorkiewicz 2005: 61). Embalmed bodies have been altered through human intervention and the application of technology, and can therefore arguably be legitimately classed as 'artefacts'.

This chapter outlines the meaning and function of the embalmed body in ancient Egypt, and the contemporary West, discussing the differing concepts of personhood that underpin and illuminate the perception of the body in both cultures. The discussion explores why in general the majority of museum visitors are enthusiastic about viewing Egyptian human remains, when they might react differently to other kinds of bodies. In the latter part of this discussion, I draw on two primary sources for visitor reactions to embalmed bodies on display: the unpublished report of a focus group consisting of adults and families with children carried out by the consultancy firm Morris Hargreaves McIntyre at the Manchester Museum, University of Manchester, UK, in April 2008 in relation to the redevelopment of the ancient Egypt and archaeology galleries (Morris Hargreaves McIntyre 2008a, 2008b), and the discussion on the *Egyptmanchester* blog (http://egyptmanchester.wordpress.com) in response to the covering of three of the mummies in the Egyptian Afterlife Gallery at the Manchester Museum in the same month. The decision by senior staff at the Manchester Museum, University of Manchester, in late April 2008 to completely cover three of the twelve embalmed ancient Egyptian bodies on display is the most high-profile intervention yet in relation to the ethical debate surrounding the care and display of Egyptian human remains (Jenkins 2011: 127–9). Senior staff at the Manchester Museum had led the debate surrounding the ethical treatment of human remains in museums over the previous few years, repatriating the skeletal remains of six indigenous Australian people in 2004

(Besterman 2004; Brooks and Rumsey 2007: 266), hosting a conference on the treatment of British human remains in 2006 (*Respect for Ancient British Human Remains* conference, 17 November 2006), and constructing a much-critiqued human remains policy that goes beyond the 2005 DCMS *Guidance* in terms of what is regarded as human remains and giving consideration to all claims for repatriation regardless of the genealogy or cultural descent of the claimants (see DCMS 2005: 6; for a critique of the policy see, for example, Mays 2008).[1]

The meaning and function of the mummified body in ancient Egypt

The basic framework of beliefs and practices surrounding death in dynastic Egypt (*c.* 3100–30 BCE) consisted of a belief in an afterlife that necessitated the burial of the body with personal possessions and provisions. However, the forms of the burial and the preparation of the body varied at any given time in relation to social and economic status, gender and ethnicity, choice and taste, and regional traditions. Contemporary popular discussions and representations of the Egyptian way of death tend to conflate royal and non-royal practices, as well as glossing social, cultural and temporal variables into a coherent descriptive narrative of death and burial. Often written by established academics, these narrative accounts are market driven (Rice and MacDonald 2009: 15–16), responding to a constant demand for further accounts of one of the best-known aspects of ancient Egyptian culture: death, and, in particular, embalming (see Ikram and Dodson 1998, 2008; Taylor 2010; Teeter 2011: 119–49). Even if dates and other variables are inserted into such accounts, the fact that ancient Egypt is generally perceived as culturally monolithic and unchanging undermines any attempt at articulating the diversity evident in Egyptian burial practices (but see Szpakowska 2007: 179–207).

Ancient Egyptian texts such as the well-known *Book of the Dead* (Taylor 2010) and tomb representations of non-royal funerals present information on the role of the embalmed body in the identity of the deceased in elite concepts of life, death and the afterlife in ancient Egypt. The ancient Egyptian person consisted of a number of tangible and intangible aspects, some of which came into play only after death. In life, a person consisted of their physical body, their name (central to their identity), their shadow, their *Ka*, which can be defined as the life-force, and their *Ba*, depicted as a human-headed bird. The *Ka* was active in the burial chamber and tomb chapel, and required sustenance after death; it could use the embalmed body as well as two-dimensional and three-dimensional representations of the deceased (relief depictions and statues) as vehicles to gain nourishment through real or model food offerings donated by relatives and passers-by. Beyond the body and the intangible aspects of the self, Egyptian personhood overcame contemporary boundaries of the mind–body–world (Kjølby 2009: 34) and extended into a wide variety of representations, such as statues and stelae, status and wealth permitting. After the burial, the *Ba* returned to the body, its physical anchor, in order that the deceased could be reanimated and benefit from the offerings. The *Akh*, or transfigured spirit, came into being after death as manifestation of the dead person's personality, and, although inhabiting the world of the gods and the dead, was able to communicate with the living (Teeter 2011: 148–9; see Gee 2009 for an alternative interpretation of some of these entities).

The ancient Egyptian language has a number of words for the physical body, the writing of which articulates the changing role of the body as it transitioned from life to death (Meskell 2004a: 130). The pictorial script (hieroglyphs) makes good use of determinatives, signs that come at the end of a word to indicate the sphere of meaning to which a word belongs, to define the nature of the body in its different states. Figure 12.1 gives some of the common words for the body in Egyptian hieroglyphs, transliteration and translation.

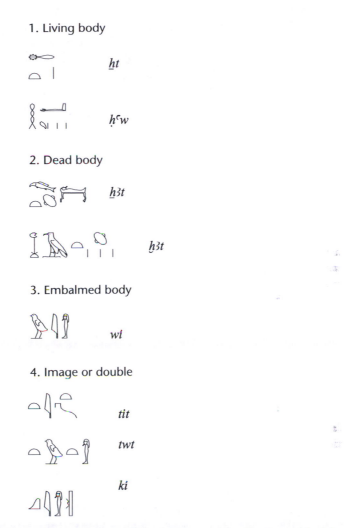

1. Living body

ḫt

ḥʿw

2. Dead body

ẖȝt

ẖȝt

3. Embalmed body

wi

4. Image or double

tit

twt

ki

Figure 12.1 Egyptian words for body, corpse, embalmed body and bodily image/double. Reproduced by permission of © Karen Exell

The words for the living body incorporate signs that represent fleshly parts of physical bodies: the animal belly with tail attached (the horizontal sign) in *ḫt* and the piece of flesh (the small teardrop-shaped sign) in *ḥʿw*. The words for the dead body include either signs indicating that the body is inert on a bier and/or the state of decomposition of the flesh after death (the egg-shaped 'pustule' hieroglyph). The word for embalmed body, *wi*, has the sign depicting a statue as its determinative, indicating that the body is now a representation of the physical form of the deceased; it is the same determinative used in the word for statue or double. In more elaborate funerals, statues of the deceased would undergo similar rituals to the embalmed body to (re)gain lifelike abilities and therefore be able to receive offerings (Teeter 2011: 141–3): the embalmed body and the statue occupy the same sphere of meaning, as tangible representations of the deceased (Meskell 2004a: 126; see also Kjølby 2009: 39). The word *tit*, image/double, has as its determinative the tool used in the 'Opening of the Mouth' ceremony, performed on the statue(s) and the embalmed body of the deceased at the funeral to restore their faculties, once again indicating the shared role of the statue and the embalmed body.

In the elite Egyptian conception of death, after death, the body became a thing deprived of capabilities. The body underwent the transformative process of embalming, which included physical interventions (evisceration, drying of the flesh, bandaging and so on) and the recitation of spells, including the 'Opening of the Mouth', resulting in an artefact similar to its living counterpart and able to function (Meskell 2004a: 126–7). Both the embalming of bodies and the sculpting of representations were processes carried out by specialists trained in both the physical techniques and the necessary rituals of enchantment: both the technical and the ritual practices were necessary to effect successful transformations. The ritual knowledge that animated the representations, and to a lesser extent the practical skills necessary for their creation, belonged to the domain of restricted knowledge (Baines 1990, 2007; Baines and Yoffee 1998); only the king was all-knowing. The sculptors, like the embalmers, were more than mere technicians; the ancient Egyptian word for sculptor is 'one who makes live', and the verb used for to sculpt is 'to give birth' (Kjølby 2009: 36). These embalmers and sculptors can be regarded as Gell's 'occult technicians' (2009: 217), creating prestige objects through an enchanted technology that resulted in artefacts imbued with power in and of themselves as well as over their audience (Gell 2009: 211–12). The mundane activities of commissioning and paying for statues and embalming did not diminish the magical efficacy of the finished artefacts once they had been animated (Meskell 2004b: 255; Kjølby 2009: 34). Whereas popular interest today focuses on the techniques and physical results of embalming (see below), it was the power in death of the perfected, transformed and enchanted body that mattered in antiquity. As for statues and other representation, these were never regarded as passive representations of their subjects but as active social agents, housing, extending and distributing aspects of an individual's personhood through space and time, and able to interact with the living (Meskell 2004b: 253; Kjølby 2009: 31).

The precise affect of these powerful agentic artefacts on any one individual in ancient Egypt is impossible to recover. We have few records of personal perceptions or individual experience, with the exception of a close reading of some of the laconic texts in the archive of the New Kingdom royal tomb-builders' settlement of Deir el Medina (see, for example, McDowell 2001; Meskell 1999, 2002), a community with an unusually high level of literacy (Baines 1983; Baines and Eyre 1983). The limited literacy of the majority of the population, and the role of writing as a restricted religious or administrative activity rather than a mode of personal reflection, allows, as with prehistoric archaeologies, only theoretical reconstructions of the personal and emotional context for the creation and use of the thousands of objects in museum collections. One literary text from ancient Egypt suggests that attempts at preserving the self for eternity did not go unquestioned: in the pessimistic philosophical text, *Dialogue of a Man with his Ba*, an elite man expresses his scepticism towards the survival of monuments and therefore of one's self (Parkinson 1997: 57 cited in Meskell 2004a: 144).

The changing meanings of the mummified body

In the twenty-first century, mummies are no big shocker any more due to the popular Hollywood movies such as *The Mummy* and *The Mummy Return*[s]. Besides, the visitors do expect to catch a glimpse of the mysterious mummies when [they] visit a museum that housed [sic] the ancient Egyptian collection.

Posting on the Egyptmanchester *blog in response to the covering of the mummies in April 2008*

The word 'mummy' comes from the Arabic word for bitumen, *mūmiyeh*, referring to the blackened state of many embalmed bodies through the darkening of the oils used in the embalming process; the use of this term has linguistically concealed the meaning and function of the Egyptian embalmed body in antiquity. The bursts of Egyptomania (Curl 1994; Moser 2006; Whitehouse 1997) triggered by the Napoleonic campaign to Egypt in 1798 (Bednarski 2005; Cole 2007; Rice and MacDonald 2009: 5–6) and the discovery of the tomb of Tutankhamun in 1922 (Frayling 1992) also triggered a fascination with the embalmed bodies discovered in the tombs and brought back to Europe and the USA by travellers and collectors throughout the nineteenth and early twentieth centuries. The meaning of these bodies evolved as they came to represent Western interests and ideas about Egypt in the context of what Edward Said called 'orientalism' (1991), in which the East was systematically stereotyped through the lens of Western colonialism (Day 2006: 19–63). The twentieth-century mummy films with their depiction of mummies as ambulatory, dirty and vengeful, and the development of the curse legend given impetus by the death of Howard Carter's patron, Lord Carnarvon on 5 April 1923, shortly after the opening of the tomb of Tutankhamun, allowed the development of a dominant popular reading of the embalmed bodies as things that were 'loathsome' (Day 2006: 9; see also Lupton 2009). Eighteenth-century and nineteenth-century displays at the British Museum presented Egyptian artefacts with little or no interpretation because of a lack of institutional expertise, allowing free engagement with the objects unhampered by a perceived need for a classical education; the embalmed bodies were the most popular antiquities in the museum, part of the 'sideshow or street spectacle' of the Egyptian galleries (Moser 2006: 204). Day (2006: 24) suggests that the very ubiquity of 'mummies' and 'mummy' parts in museums and private collections from the nineteenth century led to their perception as collectible objects, macabre souvenirs of a subjugated culture, rather than as the remains of once-living people. Nineteenth-century and early twentieth-century pseudoscientific investigations of mummies with invited audiences elided the experience with theatre-going, even as recently as 1908 and the public 'scientific' unwrapping of the two embalmed bodies known as the 'Two Brothers' at the University of Manchester by a team led by Margaret Murray (Wieczorkiewicz 2005: 59; Alberti 2009: 68–9). At the end of the 'performance' sections of linen were offered as souvenirs (David 2007: 103).

The establishment of Egyptology as an academic discipline from the mid-nineteenth century restricted direct access to the remains of the ancient culture to trained specialists (Exell 2012), prompting the parallel development of a more accessible 'popular' version of ancient Egypt, which now dominates public understanding (Rice and MacDonald 2009: 20). 'Mummification' is one of the most popular topics, and the process of embalming in ancient Egypt well known. What is less well known and rarely acknowledged is that the sources used are limited and unrepresentative. For embalming, the key source text is that of the Greek scholar, Herodotus, writing in the fifth century BC, in which he describes in detail embalming at its most expensive, the full 70 days (*Histories*, 2.86–9), with no mention of the belief systems that underpin the practice. The widely available discussions referencing Herodotus have led to the assumption that embalming was the norm in ancient Egypt rather than an exclusive and elite way of death. In addition, the extensive mortuary data extant as a result of biased preservation (cemeteries were located in the dry desert, whereas settlements were in the wet river valley, where little material evidence has survived), twentieth-century archaeological agendas, and the emphasis placed by popular literature on death and burial have actively produced the widespread and fallacious belief that the ancient Egyptians were 'obsessed with death', dedicating their life to their embalming and burial. As a result, for many people, the embalmed bodies are regarded as entirely representative of the ancient culture.

The contemporary perception of ancient Egyptian embalmed bodies: a person, an object, a loathsome thing of horror?

In April 2008, senior staff at the Manchester Museum decided to cover three of the fully or partially unwrapped embalmed bodies on display. At the time, I was the curator of the Egypt collection, having come into post late in the decision-making process to cover the bodies. I ran the blog called *Egyptmanchester* (www.wordpress.egyptmanchester.com) and posted a short description of the covering of the mummies with an image of the covered body of the Late Period temple singer, Asru (Figure 12.2). A total of 170 people responded, with over 85 per cent arguing in favour of uncovering the mummies. Criticism of the Museum's decision (see, for example, BBC News 2008, Harris 2008, Partridge 2008) centred on the fact that the term 'respect', used to explain and defend the decision by Museum spokespeople in the media, had not been defined and is culturally contingent (see Brooks and Rumsey 2007: 267; Jenkins 2011: 129–33), and that no consultation had been carried out before the decision was made and implemented.[2] The media attention and negative feedback led to the Museum reversing its decision in mid-2008: the body of Asru was partially uncovered, the body known erroneously as 'Khary' fully uncovered, and the loaned child's body taken off display for return to its home institution, Stonyhurst College.

Figure 12.2   The covered body of the Late Period temple singer, Asru, on display in the Afterlife Gallery of the Manchester Museum, University of Manchester, May 2008. Reproduced by permission of The Manchester Museum

The reaction to the covering of the embalmed bodies at Manchester is a useful barometer to assess the sensory and emotional impact of the bodies, as well as the affect of ancient Egypt in general, on museum visitors and the wider public. This section draws on both the blog postings arguing for or against the covering of the embalmed bodies, and the Morris Hargreaves McIntyre focus group work carried out at the same time, which also addressed the issue of displaying the bodies.

One of the most frequently repeated and emphatic arguments on the blog against the covering of the bodies was that it denied the visitors' 'rights', justified by stating that seeing the embalmed bodies was educational, informing the visitor about life in ancient Egypt, although the result of the embalming process was the only example cited of something that could be learnt. Respondents attempted to give weight to this argument by referring to scientists needing to study the bodies to learn about health and disease in ancient Egypt, thus associating the desire to see the bodies with the rational and objective world of contemporary scientific enquiry, with the implication that such scientific values were superior to those of ancient Egypt (Wieczorkiewicz 2005: 51, 55). Another of the 'scientific' justifications was the repeated statement that the dead Egyptians would have wanted their bodies to be viewed. This argument allowed respondents to display their knowledge of Egyptian afterlife beliefs, which, if inaccurate, is clearly self-sustaining and widely supported: the version of the Egyptian afterlife on the blog-postings understood that the continued existence of the deceased would be achieved through public viewing and repetition of the anglicized form of their names, if known, rather than that the body must remain in the tomb to perform its proper function as the tangible locus for the intangible aspects of the self (Meskell 2004a: 130). One respondent gave a teleological argument that covering the bodies was disrespectful to the excavators and funders, implying that the embalmed bodies were deliberately excavated in order to be publicly displayed, i.e. that the contemporary public fascination with the bodies was the impetus rather than the result of their exhumation and display.

Another line of argument stated that 'mummies' were the sole inspiration behind many people's interest in ancient Egypt: for many people, a gallery on Egypt without 'mummies' was regarded as unrepresentative; one respondent said that he would not visit an Egyptian display without a 'mummy'. Such beliefs reveal the impact of popular and media interpretations of Egypt on the public understanding of the ancient culture: 'mummies' = Egypt in the public imagination (Wieczorkiewicz 2005: 52; Lupton 2009: 23–4):

> If you went out onto the street now and asked about 100 people Egypt, mention the word Egypt to them and they'd come back with mummies and pyramids and that would be all.
> *Adult, Morris Hargreaves McIntyre edited transcripts, April 2008, p. 13*

Many of the respondents on the *Egyptmanchester* blog gave emphatically subjective reasons for wishing to view the bodies, stressing that the embalmed bodies elicited an emotional connection and generated a personal relationship with the visitor:

> I have found the uncovered body of Asru extremely moving as it helped me to imagine her life and what life was like in her lifetime and to realize the similarities and differences between her time and my own and between her and me.

> Asru uncovered communicated directly with me in a way no other medium can.

In addition, many of the respondents stressed the humanity of the embalmed bodies, and the requirement that we therefore treat them as people like us:

> I could look into the face of a man 4,000 years old, and see that, like myself, he was a person.

That it was a person. It is not just a stuffy old thing in a box in a museum. That did have a life and that was its life you know.

Family, Morris Hargreaves McIntyre edited transcripts, April 2008, p. 11

Finally, a clear distinction was made between fleshed and unfleshed bodies, where human skeletons or individual bones were not regarded as retaining the same level of humanity as embalmed bodies, i.e. they lack the necessary corporeality to allow recognition and attribution of social activity and role (Sofaer 2006: 10). Recognition and affiliation clearly shape reactions to bodies and can be generated by the bodies themselves through their state of preservation, or by the method of display and the use of humanizing tactics such as giving a name to bodies whose identity has been lost (Day 2006: 167–8; Brooks and Rumsey 2009: 346). As one respondent observed:

If you see a skeleton [it's] just some bones and people are usually happy with human bones and you can find them anywhere almost in cases, but when you see a mummy with a name then it sort of becomes different, because we know the names through the descriptions and it is suddenly a person and that is very different.

Adult, Morris Hargreaves McIntyre edited transcripts, April 2008, p. 15

The embalmed bodies were regarded by the respondents as people like us: the body is the person. Fowler argues (2004: 83) that in the West, the individual has become the most important social phenomenon, with an emphasis on the preservation of the youthful body in life. The living body is 'closed', bounded by skin (Knappett 2005: 17; Thomas 2007: 215), and from the moment of death the body is concealed, removing death from the sphere of daily existence, and the corruption after death, the disintegration of the perfect boundary, from view. An individual's afterlife consists of the preservation through images and words of memories of that person alive; the memory of the intact body in which Western personhood resides is central (Fowler 2004: 96). The body and the choices that we make in relation to it in terms of physical shape, adornment, dress, expressions of sexuality and gender, etc. have become one of the central ways of expressing our individuality and have contributed to the increasing importance of the body in contemporary Western conceptions of personhood and identity (see Rose 1999). Contemporary reactions to Egyptian embalmed bodies can be located within this philosophy.

Conclusion

Egyptian embalmed bodies exist today in an entirely altered and multivalent conceptual state, each an example of Ray's 'pure vehicle of meaning … invested with a new sense' (2001: 128). During the eighteenth and nineteenth centuries, Western culture regarded self-control and control of the material world as signifiers of civilization: the embalmed bodies represented uncivilized antiquity, whose pre-Greek cultures were categorized as 'emotional' rather than 'intellectual', whereas, as objects, the bodies were part of the material world over which cultured individuals had control (Gosden 2004: 34). The embalmed body is simultaneously familiar and shocking, attractive and repulsive: the embalming process preserves the materiality of the body, the individual facial features, hair, and finger and toenails, as well as the flesh, maintaining the humanity of the body in the eyes of the contemporary museum visitor whilst reifying the contemporary Western death taboo in which direct experience of the dead body is limited (Brooks and Rumsey 2007: 279; 2009: 344–5). Above all, the popular recognition of the embalmed body as a bounded person, preserved whole and intact, carries an enormous emotional weight for the museum visitor. As Sofaer has noted, through their physicality 'bodies intrigue', they act as the 'past personified … they are essentially *us*' (2006: 1) through an uncritical contemporary lens. By contrast, other forms of the ancient Egyptian distributed person go almost unnoticed: the statues and stelae, which, in antiquity, were animated with an individual's life-force endure today in museums and collections and are of interest for other reasons: the hieroglyphs, the text (traditionally studied without context; Exell 2009), the aesthetic form, the material. It is here that the distinction between the contemporary Western conceptions of personhood as bounded within the body and that of the ancient Egyptians is at its most emphatic. For the ancient Egyptians, these representations each held agentic force of great power; as Kjølby, after Gell, states 'individuals are not just where their bodies are' (2009: 35). Today, as a result of the contemporary Western conception of personhood, these forms of the self are dimmed and muted to the point of invisibility and silence.

The display of Egyptian human remains has been problematized by individuals and institutions with specific agendas (Exell 2013) that embrace all human remains in a liberal humanist interpretation, in which the human remains are regarded as having privileged value and comparable meaning regardless of their cultural origin. The culturally contingent nature of this agenda is illuminated by its failure to recognize or acknowledge other forms of a person, or the original function of the embalmed body. Audience research and consultation in relation to Egyptian human remains has revealed a large majority in favour of the continued display of the bodies because of their affective power, linked to and articulating the wider phenomenon of a dominant fascination with a culturally constructed 'other', the Egypt of our own invention, shaped by social, historical, political and philosophical events and developments of the last two hundred years (Wieczorkiewicz 2005: 66; see Smith 2007: 178–9). In the museum environment, which traditionally demands controlled behaviour and an intellectual rather than an emotional response (Ray 2001: 123, 131), Egyptian embalmed bodies are deeply affective, moving and disturbing, us and not us; their affect on us is extremely informative about our own culture and society, if not about their own.

Notes

1 The Manchester Museum Human Remains policy: http://www.museum.manchester.ac.uk/aboutus/reportspolicies/fileuploadmax10mb,120796,en.pdf
2 The original posting on the *Egyptmanchester* blog with the 170 responses: http://egyptmanchester.wordpress.com/2008/05/06/covering-the-mummies/ The summary of the responses with the Museum's own responses: http://egyptmanchester.wordpress.com/2008/07/29/covering-the-mummies-summary-of-discussion-and-museum-response/

Bibliography

Alberti, J.M.M. (2009) *Nature and Culture: Objects, Disciplines and the Manchester Museum*, Manchester: Manchester University Press.

Baines, J. (1983) 'Literacy and Ancient Egyptian Society', *Man*, New Series, 18: 572–99.

—— (1989) 'Communication and Display: The Integration of Early Egyptian Art and Writing', *Antiquity*, 63(240): 471–82.

—— (1990) 'Restricted Knowledge, Hierarchy, and Decorum: Modern Perceptions and Ancient Institutions', *Journal of the American Research Center in Egypt*, 27: 1–23.

—— (2007) 'Visual, Written, Decorum', in J. Baines, *Visual and Written Culture in Ancient Egypt*, Oxford: Oxford University Press, pp. 3–30.

Baines, J. and Eyre, C. (1983) 'Four Notes on Literacy', *Göttinger Miszellen*, 61: 65–96.

Baines, J. and Yoffee, N. (1998) 'Order, Legitimacy, and Wealth in Ancient Egypt and Mesopotamia', in G. M. Feinman and J. Marcus (eds), *Archaic States*, School of American Research Advanced Seminar Series, Santa Fe, NM: School of American Research Press, pp. 135–72.

BBC News (2008) 'Egyptian Mummies Are Covered' 21 May. Online article. http://news.bbc.co.uk/2/hi/uk_news/england/manchester/7413654.stm (accessed 18 November 2011).

Bednarski, A. (2005) *Holding Egypt: Tracing the Reception of the Déscription de l'Égypte in Nineteenth-Century Britain*, London: Golden House Publications.

Besterman, T. (2004) 'Returning the Ancestors'. Online article. http://www.museum.manchester.ac.uk/collection/humanremains/fileuploadmax10mb,120894,en.pdf (accessed 17 November 2011).

Brier, B. (1992) *Egyptomania*, Brookville, NY: Hillwood Art Museum.

Brooks, M.M. and Rumsey, C. (2007) 'The Body in the Museum', in V. Cassman, N. Odegard and J. Powell (eds), *Human Remains: Guide for Museums and Academic Institutions*, Lanham MD: AltaMira Press, pp. 261–89.

—— (2009) '"Who Knows the Fate of His Bones?"' in S.J. Knell, S. MacLeod and S. Watson (eds), *Museum Revolutions: How Museums Change and are Changed*, London and New York: Routledge, pp. 343–54.

Cole, J. (2007) *Napoleon's Egypt: Invading the Middle East*, New York: Palgrave Macmillan.

Cooney, K.M. (2007) *The Cost of Death: The Social and Economic Value of Funerary Art in the Ramesside Period*, Leiden: Nederlands Instituut voor het Nabija Oosten.

Curl, J.S. (1994) *Egyptomania: The Egyptian Revival, a Recurring Theme in the History of Taste*, Manchester: Manchester University Press.

David, R. (2007) *The Two Brothers: Death and Afterlife in Middle Kingdom Egypt*, Bolton: Rutherford Press.

Day, J. (2006) *The Mummy's Curse: Mummymania in the English-Speaking World*, London: Routledge.

Department of Culture, Media and Sport (2005) *Guidance for the Care of Human Remains in Museums*. Online report. http://webarchive.nationalarchives.gov.uk/+/http://www.culture.gov.uk/images/publications/GuidanceHumanRemains11Oct.pdf (accessed 16 November 2011).

Douglas, M. (1966, 2nd edn 1984) *Purity and Danger: An Analysis of the Concepts of Pollution and Taboo*, London: Ark Paperbacks.

Exell, K. (2009) *Soldiers, Sailors and Sandalmakers: A Social Reading of Ramesside Period Votive Stelae*, Oxford: Archaeopress.

—— (2012) 'Egyptology', in Neil Asher Silberman (editor-in-chief), *The Oxford Companion to Archaeology*, New York: Oxford University Press.

—— (2013) 'Covering the Mummies at the Manchester Museum: A Discussion of Individual Agendas within the Human Remains Debate', in H. Williams and M. Giles (eds), *Dealing with the Dead: Mortuary Archaeology and Contemporary Society*, Oxford: Oxford University Press.

Fowler, C. (2004) *The Archaeology of Personhood: An Anthropological Approach*, London: Routledge.

Frayling, C. (1992) *The Face of Tutankhamun*, London: Faber and Faber.

Gee, J. (2009) 'A New Look at the Conception of the Human Being in Ancient Egypt', in R. Nyord and A. Kjølby (eds), *Being in Ancient Egypt: Thoughts on Agency, Materiality and Cognition. Proceedings of the seminar held in Copenhagen, September 29–30, 2006*, Oxford: Archaeopress, pp. 1–14.

Gell, A. (2009) 'The Technology of Enchantment and the Enchantment of Technology', in F. Candlin and R. Guins (eds), *The Object Reader*, London and New York: Routledge, pp. 208–28.

Gosden, C. (2004) 'Aesthetics, Intelligence and Emotion: Implications for Archaeology', in E. Demarrais *et al.* (eds), *Rethinking Materiality: The Engagement of Mind with the Material World*, Oxford: McDonald Institute Monographs, pp. 33–40.

Gray, J. (2003) *Straw Dogs: Thoughts on Humans and Other Animals*, London: Granta Books.

Harris, S. (2008) 'Hide Your Mummies! Museum Displays of Human Remains are Covered up for Fear of Offending Pagans', *Daily Mail*. Online article. http://www.dailymail.co.uk/news/article-1323443/Museum-displays-human-remains-covered-fear-offending-pagans.html#ixzz1Vk703Idi (accessed 18 November 2011).

Ikram, S. and Dodson, A. (1998) *The Mummy in Ancient Egypt: Equipping the Dead for Eternity*, London: Thames and Hudson.

—— (2008) *The Tomb in Ancient Egypt*, London: Thames and Hudson.

Jenkins, T. (2011) *Contesting Human Remains in Museums: The Crisis of Cultural Authority*, London: Routledge.

Kilminster, H. (2003) 'Visitor Perceptions of Ancient Egyptian Human Remains in Three United Kingdom Museums', *PIA: Papers from the Institute of Archaeology*, 14, 57–69. http://pia-journal.co.uk/article/view/235 (accessed 17 November 2011).

Kjølby, A. (2009) 'Material Agency, Attribution and Experience of Agency in Ancient Egypt: The Case of New Kingdom Private Statues', in R. Nyord and A. Kjølby (eds), *Being in Ancient Egypt: Thoughts on Agency, Materiality and Cognition. Proceedings of the seminar held in Copenhagen, September 29–30, 2006*, Oxford: Archaeopress, pp. 31–46.

Knappett, C. (2005) *Thinking through Material Culture: An Interdisciplinary Perspective*, Philadelphia: University of Pennsylvania Press.

Lazzari, M. (2005) 'The Texture of Things: Objects, People and Social Spaces in NW Argentina (First Millennium AD)', in L. Meskell (ed.), *Archaeologies of Materiality*, Oxford: Wiley-Blackwell, pp. 126–61.

Lupton, C. (2009) '"Mummymania" for the Masses – Is Egyptology Cursed by the Mummy's Curse?' in M. Rice and S. MacDonald (eds), *Consuming Ancient Egypt*, London: University College Press, pp. 23–46.

McDowell, A.G. (2001) *Village Life in Ancient Egypt: Laundry Lists and Love Songs*, Oxford: Clarendon Press.

Mays, S. (2008) 'Remains of the Dead', *British Archaeology*, March/April. Online article. http://www.britarch.ac.uk/ba/ba99/letters.shtml (accessed 16 November 2011).

Meskell, L. (1994) 'Deir el Medina in Hyperreality: Seeking the People of Pharaonic Egypt', *Journal of Mediterranean Archaeology*, 7: 193–216.

—— (1999) *Archaeologies of Social Life: Age, Sex, Class Et Cetera in Ancient Egypt*, Oxford: Wiley-Blackwell.

—— (2002) *Private Life in New Kingdom Egypt*, Princeton and Oxford: Princeton University Press.

—— (2004a) *Object Worlds in Ancient Egypt*, Oxford: Berg.

—— (2004b) 'Divine Things', in E. Demarrais *et al.* (eds), *Rethinking Materiality: The Engagement of Mind with the Material World*, Oxford: McDonald Institute Monographs, pp. 249–59.

—— (ed.) (2005). 'Introduction: Object Orientations', in *Archaeologies of Materiality*, Oxford: Wiley-Blackwell, pp. 1–17.

Montserrat, D. (2000) *Digging for Dreams: Treasures from the Petrie Museum of Egyptian Archaeology*, Glasgow: Glasgow City Council.

Morris Hargreaves McIntyre (2008a) 'Manchester Museum Redevelopment of the Egypt and Archaeology Galleries Audience Consultation Paper, April 2008', unpublished report.

—— (2008b) 'Manchester Museum Redevelopment of the Egypt and Archaeology Galleries Audience Consultation Paper, April 2008: Edited Transcripts', unpublished report.

Moser, S. (2006) *Wondrous Curiosities: Ancient Egypt at the British Museum*, Chicago, IL: Chicago University Press.

Museums Association (2008) *Code of Ethics for Museums*. London: Museums Association, http://www.museumassociation.org/download?id=944515 (accessed 4 June 2013).

Parkinson, R.B. (1997) *The Tale of Sinuhe and other Ancient Egyptian Poems*, Oxford: Oxford University Press.

Partridge, B. (2008). 'Uncover the Mummies', *BBC Science and Technology*, May. Online article. http://www.bbc.co.uk/manchester/content/articles/2008/05/22/220508_mummies_egypt_feature.shtml (accessed 18 November 2011).

Ray, W. (2001) *The Logic of Culture: Authority and Identity in the Modern Era*. Oxford and Malden, MA: Blackwell Publishers.

Rice, M. and MacDonald, S. (2009) 'Introduction – Tea with the Mummy: The Consumer's View of Egypt's Immemorial Appeal', in M. Rice and S. MacDonald (eds), *Consuming Ancient Egypt*, London: University College Press, pp. 1–22.

Rose, N. (1999) (1996) 'Authority and Genealogy of Subjectivity', in P. Heelas, S. Lash and P. Morris (eds), *Detraditionalization: Critical Reflections on Authority and Identity*, Oxford and Malden. MA: Blackwell Publishers, pp. 294–327.

Said, E. (1991) *Orientalism: Western Conceptions of the Orient*, Harmondsworth: Penguin.

Smith, R. (2007) *Being Human: Historical Knowledge and the Creation of Human Nature*, Manchester: Manchester University Press.

Sofaer, J.R. (2006) *The Body as Material Culture: A Theoretical Osteoarchaeology*, Cambridge and New York: Cambridge University Press.

Szpakowska, K. (2007) *Daily Life in Ancient Egypt: Reconstructing Lahun*, Oxford: Wiley-Blackwell.

Thomas, J. (2007) 'Archaeology's Humanism and the Materiality of the Body', in T. Insoll (ed.), *The Archaeology of Identity: A Reader*, London and New York: Routledge, pp. 211–24.

Taylor, J.H. (ed.) (2010) *Journey through the Afterlife: Ancient Egyptian Book of the Dead*, Cambridge, MA: Harvard University Press.

Teeter, E. (2011) *Religion and Ritual in Ancient Egypt*, Cambridge: Cambridge University Press.

Whitehouse, H. (1997) 'Review Article: "Egyptomanias"', *American Journal of Archaeology*, 101(1): 158–61.

Wieczorkiewicz, A. (2005) 'Unwrapping Mummies and Telling their Stories: Egyptian Mummies in Museum Rhetoric', in M. Bouquet and N. Porto (eds), *Science, Magic and Religion: The Ritual Process of Museum Magic*, New York and Oxford: Berghahn Books, pp. 51–71.

13

A dream of falling
Philosophy and family violence[1]

Patricia Ticineto Clough

The violence of her touch
The crudeness of her gestures
The distain of her address
transform her beauty.
Like the iridescence of some horrid bug's wing
Beautiful, bright
in the flicker of sunlight,
but then, light gone
and in shadow's fall,
again ugly,
or even uglier
if it can be believed.

Do you? Do you believe me?
That the hurt repeats,
repeats its passage into eternity,
in the iridescent blue, purple and red
of her hand print on my face
and the banging in my head,
I cannot cry out.
The words can barely form in my mouth.
'What are you doing to me,
Mommy?'

Falling back into an ecstasy of fear,
young, and at the edge of despair,
abstraction will become in me
a call to philosophy.
Bold thoughts to suspend her hand in mid-air
so that it can not bear
down on me.

And then,
oh lovely philosophy,
the possibility
of comforting thoughts,
quieting thoughts
for a cessation in the realm of sensation.
To sleep, perchance to dream,
to dream in place of waking
amidst the night's violent scenes.

We are told that we do not fall asleep but that sleep falls upon us. Or, it is not an 'I' that falls into sleep, not an 'I' that can distinguish itself from anything else, 'from anything more than its own indistinctness.' 'I fall asleep' that is to say, '"I" fall …' 'In my own eyes, which no longer look at anything, which are turned toward themselves and toward the black spot inside them …', I am 'isolated from all manifestation, from all phenomenality, the sleeping thing … not measured, not measurable.'[2]

But there is measure and measuring for those who cannot fall into sleep. So many of them now: women, abused by those whom they know or who know them. And, like women, children, too, are badly mistreated by mothers, fathers, sisters, brothers, uncles, cousins, doctors, teachers, therapists, ministers, priests.

Three in ten girls. Three in twenty boys

A silent epidemic, they say,
and with that,
and the making of a statistical population,
I fear no one will hear
each woman or child crying,
sleeplessly not dreaming,
those who cannot let sleep fall,
who cannot let consciousness fall into that unconscious
that never simply was theirs: the world's unconsciousness,
the unthought that obsesses in ghostly figures walking
the endless day of sleepless night. The dark nights of the soul.

Is it that philosophy now is failing us? What bold thoughts for this overwhelming abuse? What comforting thoughts in the shameful shades of family violence? In our biopolitical state of governance, has a necropolitics brought philosophy to an end? Or must it come undone and begin again? From 'the dust of this planet', a start?[3]

Start again, the philosophers are saying, with objects withdrawn from all relations.

Start again with no presumed correlations between human and world, reason and life. Start again on a groundless ground, in a negation of negation.

And I?

I try to hide. I go inside myself
where some few objects are put away:
A rubber doll with washed-out eyes,
a stuffed yellow dog nearly life-sized,
so dirty from being dragged along the street,
outside the window

where no one sits.
And the clock and the metronome:
time machines, mysterious to me,
and the books of fairy tales and poetry.

All beloved
the objects more to me
than any of the humans can be
The objects still
awaiting me
there always
therefore, me.
Attending objects
truly being,
only being,
glistening in the shine
of the bright lights of a dissociation.

We who have damaged insight might perhaps have the foresight to see objects otherwise before we see with only human eyes, seeking an ontograph and discompose of hurt in the objects of a childhood faith.

But what of childhood faith? Can it withstand the profound perversion of what the psychoanalysts have told us: that 'the infant's first subjective experience of the object' is 'less as a significant and an identifiable object than as a process of accumulating internal and external transformations' and that the first transformational object is the mother, 'as a recurrent experience of being, as the rhythms of processes that inform the nature of the object-relation rather than the qualities of the object as object.'[4]

And alongside the perversities, there is the history of the relationship of politics and philosophy that inserts itself between process and object, between object and the name of mother. Most recently, the history has found itself again in yet another unsettling turn. From a generative ontology, or 'an ontology of generosity', of given-ness and giving, of being and becoming, there has been a turn to the speculative realism of an object-oriented ontology.[5] Will this philosophical turn call forth a more speculative psychology for our biopolitical state of governance?

After all, the genealogists tell us that there has been a shift from the family as model of governance, from the sovereign as a good father, who will provide, to the family as instrument in the biopolitical governing of populations. As the family becomes the privileged instrument for obtaining data pertaining to the life and death capacities of populations, the population becomes *the* medium of interests and aspirations. Family violence, if not violence in general, is made a normal matter, a matter of statistical populations. It is in terms of this socionormalization through populations that governance resets the limits of perversion, such that along with the hyperfamilialism of our times, family is abandoned to sadness, pain and fear.[6]

All subjects, objects and environs are here
to stand not before lack but before estimation and valuation.
No longer in relationship to desire,
our bodily wounds go to number and accounting.

Freed in a way,
although by some other hand than we might have imagined.

Freed of family ties
long after the reader of dreams revealed
a mix of desire in the story of abuse,
incest put in the shadowy grip of fantasy
and turned from the real: the becoming of the impossibly real.

But alas, philosophy begins again; it returns as a speculative realism to validate the realness of experience and the experience of the real, including that which is beyond human knowing. Speculative realism refuses the presumption of a primordial rapport between human and world. Its object-oriented ontology claims that objects are real in that they are forever withdrawn from us and from each other. They can come to us and to each other only through sensuality or each object's sensual profile: colour, texture, tone, taste, height, weight. It is by proxy of the sensual that a real object touches a real object in the interior of some other entity or surround that has been called 'an intentional whole'. But by no means is this only about human intentionality. The relations between objects are a matter of a vicarious causality, a causality where the sensual lures objects to each other. Causality is alluring: 'a lure to feeling', to a knowing beyond human consciousness, perception and cognition.[7]

A new metaphysics is called forth as philosophy returns to the real, while freeing thought
from being bound to human consciousness, even human unconsciousness.
And along with this freeing, the family shifts from model to instrument
to us being bits and pieces of populations, numbered,
with only some small part left for poetry. And incest slips
from fantasy's hold
to the rhythm of the counter's bidding,
a lullaby of probabilities,
a rocking back and forth of a statistical cradling.
Are you dreaming yet? Are we dreaming together?

And there is no human hand on the cradle.
The mother's hand nowhere near,
I dream of falling.
I feel my body shake
and pivot down to a groundless ground.
Falling, falling,
into ecstasy wide awake.

As everything is drawn to the count of endless measuring, counting like causality becomes alluring and it is no surprise that measure becomes a matter of aesthetic judgment. Against a surfeit of measures, each measure is designed to be singular or subjective, able to change its metric or perspective with each measuring so that with each measure, there also is a probe for the incalculable excess of calculation. However, this is not a matter of the sublime but of the beautiful, not about truth or falsehood but about delight and repulsion: measure becomes a speculative grasp of futurity or potentiality. An intense passion, repeatedly repeating.

I crawl to a spot on the floor,
damp with pee and tears.
Small bits of grey condense

into a hazy halo around my vision
like a child's dirty glasses
no one cared to polish clean.
I cannot see.

But there was a moment, I remember,
when we sat, my father and me, on the floor.
There was a tunnel of light
that blocked my peripheral sight
of her standing there.
My vision instead was directed straight ahead
to the shelf of books he read to me.
Leather bound with golden letters,
poetry and fairy tales inside
and fancy illustrations
in iridescent colours of purple, blue and red.
But the moment does not hold.
His fingers on my leg,
bent at the knee,
my thighs go clammy
and there is a much too intense sense
of a volcanic trembling in my stomach's pit
Blinded by the light,
ruined in her sight,
no one now will sit
with me.

Neither about truth nor falseness, measure is made to reach for the beautiful in assemblaging objects that otherwise are indifferent and disinterested. If one object lures indifferently or without caring which object it lures, the object that has been indifferently lured nonetheless finds the alluring object beautiful. For the lured object, the alluring object is beyond interest, use or need; it rather is an object of a disinterested but intense passion. It is this reach for the beautiful that makes measure alluring and gives it the capacity to probe for potentiality or the incalculable excess of calculation. But when need is not met or when there only is the drive of sheer interest or utility, the allure of measure may offer no potential but instead incite an avaricious repetition; the beautiful freezes the lured object in a repetitive reductive response to the alluring object's superfluous self-exhibition.[8]

And ought we not allow the psychoanalysts another word about the infant who they claim not only takes in the contents of the mother's communications but also their form. 'The mother's aesthetic', as they call it, is a facilitative environs that ought to make thinking irrelevant to the infant's survival. Sensual survival and the survival of the sensual: even the dream has its dramaturgical form thanks to this. That is, the mother's touching-hold gives form to the way the ego will hold instinctual needs. The dream holds as the ego does as the mother did.[9]

Beautiful Mother, alluring Mother
there, ice cold in the mirror,
combing your lead black hair.
Lips painted red

your blue, purple dress thrown across the bed.
Repulsive Mother,
mouth twisted
in a bottomless howl,
a hissing growl.
Hands raised like claws
too near
ready to tear.
Destructive Mother,
imploding the space of dreams
my bodily intensities unable to cohere.

A critical aesthetic is, perhaps, our only hope. At least this is what the philosophers tell us; it is a way, they say, to bring on the shock of love and with that activate potential once again.[10]

Notes

1 What follows is a response to the academic interest in the philosophical turn to objects, touching on the particular social, political and affective environment in which this interest has arisen. It is as well an articulation of an old and ever-new personal agitation provoked by movement in philosophical thought: a tension seeking a poetic writing. I owe Bruce Reis my deep gratitude for the conversations that inform this writing.

2 These thoughts and words are from Jean-Luc Nancy, *The Fall of Sleep*, Trans. by Charlotte Mandell, New York: University Press, 2009, pp. 7, 13–14.

3 I take this expression from Eugene Thacker, *In the Dust of This Plane, The Horror of Philosophy, Vol. 1*, Washington: Zero Books, 2010.

4 I take these thoughts and words from Christopher Bollas, *The Shadow of the Objects, Psychoanalysis of the Unthought Known*, New York: Columbia University Press, 1987, p. 14.

5 I take these thoughts and expressions from Eugene Thacker's work, especially *After Life*, Chicago: University of Chicago Press, 2010.

6 I am drawing on Michel Foucault, *Birth of Biopolitics: Lectures at the Collège De France 1978–1979*, Trans. by Graham Burchell, Palgrave Macmillan: New York, 2008. Michel Foucault, *Security, Territory, Population: Lectures at the Collège de France, 1977–78*, New York: Picador, 2007. Tiziana Terranova, 'Another life: the Limits of Sovereignty and the Nature of Political Economy in Foucault's Genealogy of Biopolitics,' *Theory, Culture and Society* 26(2009): 234–262.

7 I take these thoughts and expressions from Graham Harman, *Prince of Networks*, Melbourne: re.press, 2009. Here, in his treatment of allure, Harman is drawing on the work of Alfred North Whitehead on allure and the aesthetic.

8 Here I am drawing on the thoughts and expressions of Steven Shaviro, *Without Criteria*, Cambridge: MIT Press, 2009, pp. 5–6.

9 Bollas, op. cit., pp. 34–35, 64–81.

10 I am drawing here on the thought of Gilles Deleuze, *Proust and Signs*, Trans. by Richard Howard, Minneapolis: University of Minnesota Press, 2004.

14

Sarah Kofman's father's pen and Bracha Ettinger's mother's spoon

Trauma, transmission and the strings of virtuality

Griselda Pollock

In the twentieth century, objects found a place in modern art. Marcel Duchamp (1887–1968) transformed modern art by choosing manufactured objects from the everyday world, which he altered only slightly and exhibited as art: the idea was to liberate art from representation, from media and convention, and insist upon the conceptual plane of the artistic gesture, not on reproduction of the world. The most infamous 'ready-made'(the term that was coined after 1914 to define his gesture) was a commercial urinal, signed R Mutt and titled *Fountain* (1917), in which the recipient of male urination was inverted so as to reveal its unexpectedly vulval and hence feminine genital form, which sported, none the less, hermaphroditically, a prominent phallic extension. Commenting playfully on ambiguities of sexual morphologies while also acknowledging the erotics of manufactured commodities, Duchamp participated with his contemporaries in allowing objects from the world to take their place in art and not merely to become art, dumbly, but to become eloquent in themselves by being removed from daily use. Between breaching the borderline between art and commodity production, and between material things and their potentially psychic significance, the object is now ensconced as a multidimensional resource in contemporary, post-conceptual and post-medium forms of art such as performance and notably installation.

In twenty-first century installation art, objects have come to function as signs carrying cultural as well as personal memories, as well as being bearers of traumatic histories. This trend places the object in an intensely affective register.

Instances abound in contemporary art of a staging of a freighted or indexical object in the aftermath of traumatic and catastrophic loss. This chapter draws on psychoanalytical understandings of the processes of symbolic investment in actual objects in relation to the formation of psychic objects in order to understand how the relation to this material/metaphoric other can become a means of transformation of pasts and the creation of futures, or how it can fail thus to perform. Objects positioned aesthetically can thus become part of what the artist Bracha Ettinger has named 'transport stations of trauma'.

> The place of art is for me a transport-station of trauma: a transport station that, more than a place, is rather a space that allows for certain occasions of occurrence and of encounter, which will become the realization of what I call *border-linking and border-spacing in a matrixial trans-subjective space* by way of experiencing with an object or with a process of creation.
>
> *(Ettinger 2000: 91)*

In contrast to the notion of the object as memento or index of a lost person, time or world, Ettinger's post-Lacanian feminist theory of the object, psychoanalytically speaking, suggests an additional dimension of the object that can function as *link-not-quite-lost*. Identifying with an object or a process of creation, we remain suspended between loss and retrieval, solaced and affected in the contemplation of a loss, which is not absolute because a means of partial linking can be sustained by what we will have to name psychic strings of virtuality, which can transport trauma by means of the affectively invested object, but with unpredictable consequences.

In her book, *The Uncommon Life of Common Objects: Essays on Design and the Everyday*, design theorist Akiko Busch has argued that our current social, cultural and intellectual investment in objects may be in part a reaction to the virtual age in which we increasingly live. She writes:

> With our cell-phones, email, assorted forms of wireless communication, the elusive corridors of cyberspace have whetted our appetite for what we can touch, hold, taste, see. In the virtual age, the sorcery of the physical has intensified. We become attached to objects out of sentiment, perhaps, or for their symbolic value – a wedding ring, a grandmother's quilt, an old fountain pen, all of which may commemorate personal history.
>
> *(Busch 2004: 15–16)*

As an explanation for what is clearly a phenomenon that stretches across a range of disciplines (the focus on the object), this has an elegant simplicity, which sets the material, substantial, tactile, visible, haptic world of things against a dematerialized virtuality of wireless communication and technological gadgetry, which enables us to travel in ubiquitous cyberspace. Although it would be a foolish cultural analyst who did not take seriously the immense cultural, economic, social and phenomenological impact of digital technologies, the internet and the web with its communicational and social networking systems, it would also be a historically uncritical one who did not insist upon a much longer history of technological extensions to human sensory and intellectual capacity, starting with opposable thumbs, through the use of tools of all kinds, on to the crafting of useful as well as aesthetic artefacts, the mastery of inscription and written language, the use of brushes, pens and paper, and the invention of the printing press, the typewriter and so forth (Hirst and Woolley 1982). Technological determinism coupled with a kind of utopian belief in the recentness of the radically new oversimplifies the profound, intimate and almost defining entwining of humanness with objects over humanity's long history. From a Marxist perspective, objects as products of the interaction of human labour and skill with materials are already virtual anyway, because they represent congealed human labour even when their effects seem to distance us almost completely from any real sense of the *producedness* of the object and the often abject conditions of the lives of their producers.

The editors of the innovative collection of cultural studies on the contemporary object, *The Object Reader* (itself a monument to the complexity of contemporary thought about the object), Fiona Candlin and Raiford Guins, contest Akiko Busch's simplified opposition of new technical virtuality to a nostalgic materiality, quite rightly, on the grounds that such an opposition depends upon reading digital technologies as 'less material or less significantly material than other objects', which they are not (Candlin and Guins 2009: 5).

But Akiko Busch's statement must detain us a bit longer. Busch simply suggests that objects function as vehicles for sentiment. Existentially linked with someone loved or cherished, the object stands for the person metonymically, and as part to the whole. Relating to the object relates us, in mediated fashion, to a person. Objects are also metaphors. Are objects, therefore, to be understood as historical or as memorial; when and how? We might be tempted to place such objects closer to memory and even argue that they are formative of it in so far as the object is not merely what, Proust-like, ignites a spontaneous flood of involuntary memory, which is itself virtual – the object carries or transports meaning, *metaphorein* in Greek refers to travel – of another order.

Thus, the object that once belonged to another when I did not yet exist, which was once indexical of the other's existence or some aspect of that other's life and purposes, opens up a gap between the subject for whom the object carries its past forward, and the past social, cultural or personal context in which that object was, itself, for another, a meaningful adjunct. Objects hide trauma within their own capacity to mediate time, and this trauma can be 'transported' and detoxified or it may not, allowing the object itself to become deadly.

Thus refusing the opposition between a virtual world and a renewed investment in things material, my exploration of the object through the psychoanalytically inflected aesthetics of contemporary art practice seems to propose the object as itself virtual. It is always operating on the level not only of a signifier but also as a kind of string. The string idea avoids the oppositions set up earlier based on a phallic opposition of presence/absence. Strings may connect distant points in time and space, across generations and even death, not to bind them, but to allow a resonance and a transmission of an affect or sense of connection that, however, maintains differ-ence. For, although the string connects two points and may vibrate as a medium of shared dis-persion, leaving a trace of that vibration at each of its points, the two points of its anchorage retain their difference and the manner in which that shared vibration resonates is different for each partner-point. Thus the virtual string of memory for which the object may be the medium of transmission operates, in Ettinger's non-phallic theorization as *matrixial*: trans-subjective rather than intersubjective, allowing coemergence and coaffection in difference (Ettinger 2004 and 2005).

I want now to explore the different ways in which the traumatic object can function because its potency, psychically, in such an aestheticosubjective space depends upon the psychic economy into which it is drawn: towards life or towards death.

Case Study

A beautiful north London suburban house, 20 Maresfield Gardens, NW7, has become a museum not only memorializing the work of two exiled psychoanalysts who lived there after arriving in Britain in 1939, namely father Sigmund and daughter Anna Freud. The museum–house also dis-plays the objects collected and used by both Freuds. In the summer of 2009, I curated an exhibi-tion at the Freud Museum of the work of the artist Bracha Ettinger, who is also a practising analyst. Creating an installation, Ettinger introduced her own, resonating objects to interweave with those collected and created by Freud himself (De Zegher and Pollock 2011; Pollock 2013).

In the reconstructed consulting room is Freud's art-laden desk. On it also lies a facsimile of the diary Freud kept between 1929 and 1939. Not a sentimental record or a confiding com-mentary on his life, the bare one-line entries are laconic references to the constant menace of death. Each line merely registers that he had defeated his potentially lethal cancer by living another day. Beside Freud's diary, the artist Bracha Ettinger placed a diary written by Uziel Lichtenberg, the artist's father, between 1942 and 1945 as he struggled to survive in the Lodz ghetto, escaped, fought, was caught in Hungary, imprisoned, escaped, got to the British Mandate in Palestine and watched his recovered love, now his wife, mourn her way through pregnancy, both having lost almost all their families in the Shoah. The juxtaposition of two death-shadowed diaries links two Jewish men of pre-war Europe: they also create a father-space of writing.

On a simple wooden table behind Freud's desk, unseen if one is seated at it, an array of his collected ceramic bowls and rounded forms counter flat arrowheads or spearheads of heavy metal. Amidst this sundry collection of the homely and life-sustaining and the lethal, the artist tenderly placed a silver spoon. A little bent and misshapen with its semi-flattened point, it might look like a preserved family heirloom shining amidst the ancient flints, arrowheads and objects of violence. Evoking both a middle-class world of pre-war modernizing Jewish Europeans, after Auschwitz, such a spoon speaks of the radical dispossession of all such possessions and of life itself in a racist genocide. For those who were reduced to bare life in camps, the possession of a single utensil with which to eat became a precious and life-saving necessity.

The spoon belonged to the family that Uziel Lichtenberg and his wife Bluma Frieda created after the Shoah. Tracing a matrilineal and feminine line of succession, Uziel's grandmother's spoon was passed to his mother and then his sister, who donated it to his fledgling survivor family when, leaving the kibbutz in Israel where they had initially settled, the now four-person family needed at least one implement with which to feed themselves. This spoon, all that remains of an erased family history, is both its memorial and the marker of absence, but also played a real and symbolic part in the attempts to create a future. For the child, Bracha Lichtenberg (later Ettinger), named for Uziel's murdered mother, born into a world without grandparents (Bluma Fried had already lost her mother aged 12 and both her father and one sister were murdered in Auschwitz), the spoon 'is' mother. In her diaries, Bracha Ettinger, tells us that: 'When I was little I didn't eat anything. They called that infantile anorexia. In shared and silent despair, my mother cruelly saved my life in daily, sadistic gestures: food' (Ettinger 1993: 85). Flattening the point of the spoon, Bluma Fried Lichtenberg attempted to slip the slim silver implement past the closed lips of her starving child who had learnt her identification with death in prolonged prenatal coemergence with her bereaved becoming-mother.

The Lichtenberg spoon is also a very Freudian spoon. Bracha Ettinger notes that for children born to the generation of survivors of the Shoah, thus to parents without parents, parents already bearing their own parental bereavements too painful to articulate, the mystery of life is not 'Where do children come from?' It is rather 'Where do parents come from?' The absence of the previous generation within which to place the parent, surrounded by their unspoken fate, disrupts the Freudian narratives, patterning inverted time logics that have been increasingly studied by psychoanalysts and witnessed by those called 'the second generation' (Wardi 1992). Ettinger's placed spoon, the eloquent, yet enigma-sharing material object, becomes a sculptural presence in Freudian space that anchors a series of invisible threads, which now traverse it to insert the maternal within the Freudian father-space.

This is but a tantalizing fragment of a thick description of Ettinger's installation that I have written elsewhere (De Zegher and Pollock 2011; Pollock 2013). Ettinger's matrixial practice prevents the fetishizing function of objects, allowing each with its singular histories and resonances to function as a means of transmission that forges links across the gap created by loss. Ettinger invites us to recognize a dimension within subjectivity that she names the Matrix. With its mathematical associations of a constitutive, generative model rather than an organ, Matrix is theorized by Ettinger as a stratum of subjectivity that inherits postnatally, a prenatally generated capacity for feeling with a coemerging other which *severality* she theorizes as the legacy of the humanizing nature of our prolonged prenatal becoming that took place *with* an unknown humanizing and feminine other.[1] Without in any way positing a physiological,

165

biological or anatomical 'cause', and thus falling prey to reductive essentialism, as an analyst, she nonetheless, believes that the prenatal-prematernal *severality, psychologically,* and retrospectively once we have the means to fashion it into fantasy and thought, creates a capacity for sharing in the events and passions of the other. She names this gift of the maternal-feminine to human subjectivity com-passion. Thus Ettinger's installation, marking historical ruptures and dreadful losses (if Uziel Lichtenberg lost his family, so too would Freud, had he lived, have had to bear the knowledge of the murder of his sisters in Auschwitz), is neither melancholic nor fetishistic. It created solace and com-passion along its virtual threads that opened the past to a future willing to share it.

We can contrast Ettinger's artworking with a written text at the heart of which is an object whose traumatic freight, once acknowledged, appears to have been deadly in its effects rather than life-sustaining. The opening chapter of French philosopher Sarah Kofman's memoir of a childhood in hiding in Paris during the Second World War, *Rue Ordener, Rue Labat* (1994) opens thus:

> *De lui, il me reste seulement le stylo.*
>
> (Kofman 1994:9)

> Of him, all that remains [for me] is the pen. I took it one day from my mother's handbag where she had kept it with other souvenirs of my father. It is the kind of pen that is no longer made, the kind one has to fill with ink. I used it through my school days and studies. It 'failed' me before I was ready to let it go. Yet I have it with me still, patched up with scotch tape, it lies before me on my desk and it constrains me to write, to write.
>
> My numerous books have perhaps been the necessary detours [*voies de traverse obligées*] to bring me to write about 'that'.
>
> (Kofman 1996: 3)[2]

The passage has its own materiality as printed words on paper in a physical object, a book. A French book, it has a plain cover, is printed on slightly textured cream paper, using black, white and rarely red print (title and publisher Galilée). The opening paragraph is printed on the back paper jacket of the paperback book. Inside this, one single paragraph forms the first chapter, occupying the page under the large Roman numeral I.

De lui: 'of him' and 'from him' are both possible interpretations; 'of him' involves possession or attribution, whereas 'from him' suggests inheritance. 'Him' designates an unnamed, masculine other; he stands for the masculine other relative to which this writer is situated as a yet ungendered, but bereaved persona.

All that remains is *le stylo*, a manufactured object, what in English is named a fountain pen, which was an important development in the history of writing. Initially created by a tenth-century Egyptian caliph, a Romanian designer first created a cartridge fountain pen in 1827. Commercial mass-produced fountain pens date from the 1880s, with the American manufacturer Waterman dominating the field. By the later twentieth century, fountain pens became redundant not only because of the ballpoint pen and the typewriter but because of the computer.

However, *le stylo* of this passage is irreplaceable as both a token 'of him', *de lui*, and as an index of a historical moment associated with the fact that all that remains 'of him' is *le stylo*. Under what conditions could so little remain of an entire life, and a person who has a wife and a child to remember? That a single object remains with a few other souvenirs that can be kept in a handbag makes *le stylo* not only the metonymic trace of a past age of writing embodied by a specific hand that once held and used the pen, but it becomes now, in this moment, created by another writing of it, a silent/silenced witness of a traumatic loss, an irrecoverable void that once was a life.

In its specificity as a fountain pen, *le stylo* is the signifier of a literate man, a writer, but it is a sign that has become an anachronism at the moment at which it becomes the term/object/sign that opens this writing, this book. The writer of this passage took *le stylo* over, used it as a schoolchild and student in an era when writing neatly in fountain pen was one of the necessary and developed skills that marked educated literacy before the ballpoint pen. It also indexes a particular generation of education.

But this object has failed; it broke down before the writer desired to give it up. Thus it has become an object in a secondary psychodrama of abandonment and rejection, performing both, in its guise as stand-in for *lui* and in relation to the childhood and early adulthood in which its use functioned as both link and fetish, disavowing a loss being now confronted once again in its failure to survive. Yet, even now, the prematurely disabled *stylo* exercises the power to incite, even in its wounded, patched up and unusable form. It constrains the writer to write: constrains, from the Latin meaning to constrict, usually means to confine, compress, or hold back. In the case of a constrained smile, it means to force to produce in an unnatural or strained manner. Constrained writing is painful, obligatory, not spontaneous.

The constraining to write does not refer to the technological form, writing with an old pen by hand, but to write as a professional activity, that is both constant work, and a constant detour away. Yet it is also a required journey towards what needs ultimately to be written. Writing as a schoolchild gives way to a professional life of scholar, an intellectual and a life of writing as in the endless lines of words might cover over the absence or, as the final sentence, suggests, lead finally to a particular *telling* (note not writing, but a telling: *raconter*) of *ça*: it, this, that. Somehow, the word has to be found to speak 'it'. Matching the anonymity of the opening, *de lui*, the concluding demonstrative pronoun, *ça,* quarantined in italics in original, is as ambiguous and imprecise as it is enigmatic, menacing, secretive and awful.

The role of the object as relic of a lost or dead person is ancient, but in modern time, it has become secularized and domesticated. Like the fetish, things stand in for, disavow and, at the same time, monumentalize the very lack that is being disavowed, marking its site (Freud 1927). Perhaps nothing is as uncanny as the material thing that persists in the face of time that has, however, been touched by or in the possession of, invested in by the fragile human being who is subject to mortality, a topic that is utterly baffling and psychologically unthinkable. Freud wrote an essay on our attitude towards death in which he asserted that, although we know that death is the inevitable outcome of life, and that we owe nature a death, we behave otherwise. 'No one believes in his own death … or in the unconscious everyone of us is convinced of his own immortality' (Freud 1915: 77). Thus while mourning a loss, the attachment to an object that stands in for, virtualizes, the missing other, serves a deeper psychic compulsion to provide evidence of persistence in the face of the unacceptable and traumatic knowledge of the other's dying, which brings the living face to face with death, making the survivor the unwilling 'subject', that is the one who must bear the knowledge of death, the one who must carry this traumatizing knowledge that is ultimately the disavowed acknowledgement of one's own inevitable mortality.

The second chapter of the book that opens *de lui* confirms my initial reading that this pen is the presager of trauma. Chapter II opens with a date in italics 'On *16 July 1942*, my father knew he was going to be picked up.' 16 July 1942, known for the *Vél d'Hiv Rafle*, is a historic and troubling date in French cultural memory. On that day, the greatest mass arrest of Jews on French soil took place, involving 13,000 people, that is nearly one-third of the 42,000 French Jewish population sent to death camps during the German Occupation that began in June 1940.

They were kept in a bicycle-racing track: *Vélodrome d'Hiver*. The historical record of this appall-ing day suggests that the mass arrests were distinguished for the fact that women and children were arrested also. In fact, more children were arrested that day than either men or women. An at once invisible, undocumented event of personal extremity and a premeditated act of racist historical violence is registered in the bare prose that sets a scene, just one scene of what the word 'picked up' translates. Our text tells us that the father went to warn others in his com-munity of the impending round up, and then returned home to wait. Trapped by his position as a Rabbi, he could not consider saving himself if in doing so, it might bring worse to his own family or to his community. When the police come, the mother tells them her husband is not there. Afraid that they will take her and the children instead, the father comes forward. The mother lies about her youngest child's age; she pretends she is pregnant (a rumour is circulating they are not arresting pregnant women at this time). Thus she bargains for their lives. The writer, a watching, witnessing child, is shamed at her mother's mendacity, and at the public declaration of the delicate issue: the prospect of another sibling and hence her parents' sexuality. She tries to make sense of her father's sacrifice that can be experienced only as wilful abandon-ment. The police take both mother and father. The chapter ends with an image, a searing and seared memory, an emblem: the six children standing abandoned in the street, sobbing breath-lessly for a father whom they know (how?) they will never see again.

Was 'that' the 'it' that the pen incited its final, vicarious owner to travel back and yet always towards? Chapter III is written in retrospect: 'As it turned out, we never did see my father again.' The chapter recounts the one piece of news that they received, a postcard from the transit camp at Drancy, the working-class housing project in the outskirts of Paris that became a holding camp for deportees to Auschwitz. There was a postcard, bearing the portrait of Marshal Pétain. Written in French, in someone else's hand, because the prisoner was not allowed to write in Yiddish or Polish (languages not understood by their French guards), the postcard asked for cigarettes. 'That last sign of life we had from him' had been reread many times and the author wanted to save it. But after the mother's death, it was missing: 'It was as if I had lost my father a second time. From then on nothing was left, not even that lone card that he had not even written.' However, his death was certified in Auschwitz. So we confront two pieces of writing: the last sign of life and the official inscription in a register that confirmed two things: he was selected for slave labour, not immediate gassing, but he was killed. This is the bookend writing of his death. But later there came a story from an Auschwitz survivor who apparently witnessed how he died: the family were told that their father had been beaten and was then buried alive by a Jewish Kapo enraged at the rabbi praying on a Sabbath even in Auschwitz. Is this *ça*?

In part, but not all. I am not sure. For Sarah Kofman had already written a text in 1987 titled *Paroles Suffoqués: Smothered Words*, which indirectly bears to reference such a terrible death. Framed philosophically with a paraphrase of Theodor Adorno's final meditations on metaphys-ics 'After Auschwitz' (Adorno 1975), the passage makes this brutal statement:

> Because he was a Jew, my father died in Auschwitz: How can it not be said? And how can it be said? How can one speak of that before which all possibility of speech ceases? Of this event, my absolute, which communicates with the absolute of history, and which is of inter-est only for this reason. To speak: it is necessary – *without (the) power*: without allowing language, too powerful, sovereign to master the most aporetic situation, absolute powerless-ness and very distress, to enclose it in clarity and happiness of daylight. And how can one not speak of it, when the wish of all who returned – and he did not return – has been to tell, to tell endlessly, as if only an infinite conversation could match the infinite privation.
>
> *(Kofman 1998: 9–10)*

Endlessly to tell, because such endless telling alone matches the infinite privation recalls the *telling (raconter)* to which the author was eventually constrained by the pen itself in the opening chapter of *Rue Ordener, Rue Labat*, all that remained because he did not return, and he did not return because he died 'because he was a Jew'. This has to be spoken, voiced and enunciated by a language that threatens to betray the unspeakable death by its own illuminating power to master every experience. If the words to say this are themselves suffocated by the event that does not yet name the manner of his death (just that he died for being a Jew), is there, nonetheless, an indirect, oblique, veiled reference to a smothering of his words, Jewish words, words uttered to affirm that being a Jew meant more than being the lowest of the low in the horror of horrors that was Auschwitz?

Berek Kofman, born 10 October 1910, in Sobin, Poland, did not die in the industrially manufactured killing machinery of that place, Auschwitz–Birkenau. Nor did he did as a forty-two-year-old Jewish prisoner, selected because he was fit for being worked to a slower death, starved, exhausted and eventually gassed or worse, left to die the death of internal disintegration that the inmates of Auschwitz named a *Muselmann*, the living corpse (Levi 1987: 94). No, Sarah Kofman had to live with the knowledge of the fact that he was buried alive after suffering a brutal beating by a Jewish Kapo for daring to carry on an act of religious fidelity in a place where all such human aspiration and ambition for grace or hope had been systemically abolished in what David Rousset, a French political prisoner, defined as *l'univers concentrationnaire* (the concentrationary universe) (Rousset 1947).

It is of this man, suffocated to death in one of the horrors that we might all dread, that all that remains, to the writer, is a patched-up, unusable fountain pen. So of what is that object the material index, the emblematic icon and the intellectual symbol as well as the link in an affective chain between a now adult child and a missing father, a chain severed by what Blanchot named an absolute, both personal and historical, while being maintained precisely by the power of the object still to 'speak' a command: write, write. Do not cease from thought. Yet, all the books the author did write are to come to tell 'that'. 'That' might be naming the nature of her father's death, which she displaced in the earlier text in her study of others' writings by Blanchot and Antelme. I want to speculate that the *ça* that had to be told concerns *her severance from the act from which her father died*: the break in her relation to him, the Rabbi who died as a Jew, self-defining in the face of those who defined being Jewish as being vermin worthy only of extermination. They smothered his uttered words that signify a relation to a non-relational, radical alterity that sustains the humanity of the utterer. In *Smothered Words*, Kofman writes:

> In this unnameable 'place', he continued to observe Jewish monotheism, if by this, with Blanchot, we understand the revelation of the word as the place in which men maintain a relation to that which excludes all relation: the infinitely Distant, the absolutely Foreign. A relation with the infinite, which no form of power, including that of the executioners of the camps, had been able to master, other than by denying it, burying it in a pit with a shovel, without ever having encountered it.
>
> *(Kofman 1998: 34–35)*

Published on 24 May 1994, *Rue Ordener, Rue Labat* is for the most part the writing of the story of what happened to Sarah Kofman herself after the deportation of her father and the break-up of the family forced into disguise and hiding. Attempting to protect her six children as the Nazis and French police hunted them down, Madame Kofman hid the children in various places in France. Little Sarah, not even the youngest, traumatized by one sudden parental disappearance and the radical loss of ordinary life and security, could not tolerate any separation from her mother.

She constantly had to be fetched from many hiding places for herself refusing to relinquish Jewish food laws, until a Parisian neighbour who lived in Rue Labat (pronounced the same as the phrase *là-bas*, the oblique synonym for 'over there': Poland/Auschwitz) took in her and her mother. Named *mémé* in the text, this kind-hearted Christian woman began a systematic process of alienating the young child from her Jewish mother, heritage, food customs and beliefs. Renamed Suzanne, almost christened, forced to eat red meat and even pork, and encouraged to disown Judaism as archaic and irrational, Suzanne/Sarah was bribed by a form of love and attention, petting and favouritizing that a bereaved, traumatized Jewish mother of six living under daily risk of being caught and murdered could not offer. At the end of the war, another war broke out between the two women, contesting for custody of the child. Sarah was divided in her loyalties and eventually returned to live, in constant war, with her mother, because she relentlessly chose to study rather than to go out to work. The pen was already constraining.

The pen was the Rabbi's pen, the sign of all the writing, speaking and practices in faithful observance of which he was murdered in the most ghastly way imaginable, not as part of the process of annihilation of the Jewish population under racial laws: he was killed in a confrontation over that very religious identity that Sarah Kofman had been seduced into abjuring as a vulnerable child in an extreme historical situation.

Thus I am suggesting that Kofman's father's pen links writing to daring to speak, daring to confess the apostasy and its psychological/emotional complexity. In an article on Kofman's complex relation to philosophical fathers, Freud and Nietzsche, Diane Morgan reads *Rue Ordener, Rue Labat* as

> a disarmingly blatant account of the rejection of a mother, the bios, in search for a freer cultural identification with another. The Jewish mother in Rue Ordener is bad, restrictive, suffocating. The French mother in Rue Labat provides access to a higher, less backward looking cultural realm. That which is 'made in France' is modern, European; by contrast, the Jewish *bios* is archaic, hampered by strange and frightening customs that belong to some dark and unenlightened world. Her separation from her family and her adoption by her French Mémé, which the war permitted, allowed the young Sarah to liberate herself from this biological drag on her development.
>
> *(Morgan 1999: 233)*

I could not disagree more. Unintentionally, this argument seems to replicate the passively anti-Semitic and Christian point of view of the woman named *mémé* in which Judaism is seen as archaic, strange and unenlightened (Kofman 1996: 41–42 and Chapter XIV). Morgan is not alone in tending to read Kofman's little book in terms of a struggle between her mother and the adoptive rescuer, straddling Jewish and French Christian worlds, the old and the new. By staying close to the opening passage that installs the father's pen, on her desk, constraining her even while it has repeated the original abandonment, I want, however, to see the drama of the text otherwise. Instead, I read it as stretched between the absent father and the contesting maternal spheres. Sarah Kofman never made peace with her mother, but she returned to live with her and was sent to Jewish boarding schools to recover her alignment with Orthodox practices and ways of life. She did not remain faithful to them. Morgan is right that *mémé* had severed Kofman from her roots, viscerally by breaching food rules. Yet she had also regendered her (in Jewish terms) by introducing her to both secular literatures and alternative and equivocal Jewish philosophical fathers: Spinoza and Bergson.

How to be a scholar and a writer involved breaking the conventions of her Orthodox Jewish home in more than no longer eating Kosher meat. It involved an identification with the masculine, the scholar, the rabbi, the philosopher: with the pen, and of this Sarah Kofman made a creative and productive life, writing over twenty books. But there is something else in that pen: *ça*.

About Auschwitz, and after Auschwitz no story she declares (*récit*) is possible, if by a story one means to tell a story of events that makes sense. So the pen incites a memoir that is not a story that makes sense. It is the writing of its senselessness contained in the presence of the *pen*, and not the father, and the senselessness (the unnegotiable, irrecoverable trauma) of the daughter, who having broken the covenant in fidelity to which he outrageously suffered an exceptional death, and in her having loved and been loved for it, writes her way back through not only the still unbearable grief over the nature of her father's death, but also an unspeakable shame at the process of her survival (seduction into apostasy) and her compensatory but transgressive identification with the masculine scholar. Both grief and shame cannot be disentangled. On 15 October 1994, a year after completing the book that begins, *Of him all that remains is the pen*, six months after its publication, Sarah Kofman took her own life.

Along with the increasing number of scholars fascinated and enthralled by Kofman's final book, I cannot but wonder what is the relation between the book and her own death. Without personal knowledge of the author and in no position to speculate on another's private agony, it seems clear that the writing of this text, the final utterance of words that pointed to if never directly spoke of *ça*, functioned catastrophically. Rather than being a transport station of trauma, the pen of the father called for a writing of a trauma that found no relief. Her friends report that after completing the book, Kofman could find no joy in words, in writing, in painting, in music, in cinema: all that has sustained her life. Her writing smothered her as if the surrogate identification fractured to leave a gap and breach between father and daughter that could not find a link or a string to transport the trauma.

Thus my brief encounter with two cases of objects in the staging of trauma concludes that the power of the object depends, in a truly life-and-death way, on the psychic economy in which it is called upon to play its part.

Notes

1 For a series of introduction to papers relating to the concept of Matrix see Ettinger 2006.
2 Translator Ann Smock chose 'detours'. *Voies de traverse* is a technical term in Lacanian analytical vocabulary akin to the Freudian *Durcharbeiten* (working through) and also has resonance with the term independently created by Ettinger: transport–stations.

Bibliography

Adorno, T. (1973) 'After Auschwitz', in *Negative Dialectics* (1966), trans. E. B. Ashton, New York: Seabury Press.

Blanchot, M. (1985) 'After the Fact', afterword to *Vicious Circles*, trans. Paul Auster, Barrytown, NY: Station Hill Press.

Busch, A. (2004) *The Uncommon Life of Common Objects: Essays on Design and the Everyday*, New York: Metropolis.

Candlin, F. and Guins, R. (2009) *The Object Reader*, London and New York: Routledge.

De Zegher, C. and Pollock, G. (2011) *Bracha L. Ettinger: Act as Compass(ion)*, Brussels: ASA.

Ettinger, B. (1993) *Matrix Halal(a)-Lapsus: Notes on Painting*, Oxford: Museum of Modern Art.

Ettinger, B. (1999) 'Traumatic Wit(h)ness-Thing and Matrixial Co/in-habit(u)ating.' *Parallax* Vol. 5/No. 1.

Ettinger, B. (2000) 'Art as a Transport-station of Trauma,' in *Bracha Ettinger: Artworking 1985–1999*, Brussels: Palais des Beaux Arts and Gent: Ludion, pp. 91–115.

Ettinger, B. (2004) 'Weaving a Woman Artist With-in the Matrixial Encounter-Event.' *Theory, Culture and Society* Vol. 21, pp. 69–94.

Ettinger, B. (2005) 'Matrixial Co-poiesis: Trans-subjective Connecting Strings.' *Poiesis* Vol 7.

Ettinger, B. (2006) *The Matrixial Borderspace*, edited Brian Massumi, Preface by Judith Butler, Minneapolis: University of Minnesota Press.

Freud, S. (1915) Zeitgemässes über Krieg und Tod. *Imago*, 4: 1–21; Thoughts for the times on war and death. *SE*, 14: 273–300.

Freud, S. (1927) 'On Fetishism,' in Penguin Freud Library Vol. 7. *Sexuality*, London: Penguin Books, 347–357.

Hirst, P. and Woolley, P. (1982) *Social Relations and Human Attributes*, London: Tavistock.

Kofman, S. (1987) *Paroles Suffoqués*, Paris: Galilée.

Kofman, S. (1994) *Rue Ordener, Rue Labat*, Paris: Galilée (trans. Ann Smock, Lincoln and London: University of Nebraska Press, 1996).

Kofman, S. (1998) *Smothered Words*, trans. Madeleine Doby, Evanston: Northwestern University Press.

Levi, P. (1987) *If this a Man* [1958], trans Stuart Woolf, London: Abacus Books.

Morgan, D. (1999) '"Made in Germany": Judging National Identity Negatively,' in *Enigmas: Essays on Sarah Kofman*, edited by Penelope Deutscher and Kelly Oliver, Ithaca: Cornell University Press, pp. 219–232.

Pollock, G. (2006) *Psychoanalysis and the Image*, Boston and Oxford: Blackwell.

Pollock, G. (2013) *Act in the Time-Space of Memory and Migration: Bracha L. Ettinger and the Freudian Museum*, Leeds: Centre CATH.

Rousset D. (1946) *L'univers concentrationnaire*, Paris: Editions de Pavois (*The Other Kingdom* trans. Ramon Guthrie, New York: Reynal and Hitchcock, 1947).

Turkle, S. (2007) *Evocative Objects: Things We Think With*, Cambridge, MA: MIT Press.

Wardi, D. (1992) *Memorial Candles: Children of the Holocaust*, London and New York: Routledge.

15

Spectral objects

Material links to difficult pasts for adoptive families

Steven D. Brown, Paula Reavey and Helen Brookfield

Introduction

Whilst analysing the data from a study of adoptive parents engaged in the practice of maintaining a 'life story' book for the children in their care, we were struck by the repeated references made by parents to objects that had accompanied children from their former care placements: photographs, shoes, hats, a Pooh bear, a battered Snoopy dog, plastic toys. Our analysis concentrated on the first of these objects (photographs), because these are particularly potent artefacts, around which the work of remembering former carers and biological parents is done, and are central to the creation and maintenance of life story books (see Brookfield *et al.* 2008). We described how these images presented dilemmas to adoptive parents. Some photographs depicted former carers, to whom, parents feared, adopted children might still be overly attached. Other photographs showed children in states all too easily readable as neglect, or worse. In both cases, adoptive parents were torn between the need to preserve for the child the past that was legible in the photographs and the corresponding need to manage and 'tame' that past within a narrative and practice of building a 'new home'. More difficult still were cases in which photographs simply did not exist, leading some parents to specially construct new images, sometimes at the behest of the child, to assist in filling out the gaps.

But we continued to be fascinated by these other objects: the clothes, the toys. Clearly, these objects have considerable significance for the relationship between adoptive parents and their children, yet they also appear to be ambiguous, difficult. Parents described some objects in disparaging terms, detailing their efforts at hiding them whilst feeling unable to actually get rid. How best to understand this complex sets of meanings? What is the power that these objects have over parents? We found an echo of this in a recent newspaper article. 'Diary of a separation' is a weekly account of a relationship breakdown that provides forensic descriptions of the practical and emotional problems involved in separation and shared childcare. In an article entitled 'Where have the all the trousers gone?' (*The Guardian*, Saturday 11 June 2011), the author describes a frantic search for clothes for the children before school:

> 'Why are there no trousers?' I mutter. I kick aside an abandoned bag of swimming gear, damp and mildewed. 'Why are there no *trousers*?' I shout this time. The children ignore me.

They are watching TV. The eldest looks up, momentarily, confused. 'What?' 'Why can't I find any trousers? How is it even possible that you have no trousers?' … X must have them all, I think, irritably. Of course, that isn't possible, really. The eldest can't be stockpiling trousers at his father's house. Common sense dictates that he must leave here, and return, with one pair. I frown. I suspect what's really happening is that he leaves here with what I consider a decent pair of trousers and comes back with something I don't: shorts, tracksuit bottoms with holes in the knees, trousers that only reach his shins. Nothing he can decently wear to school. I call X, trying to keep the note of complaint out of my voice. 'I haven't got any trousers for the eldest,' I say. 'Have you got them?' 'But … surely I can't have them all?' he reasons, correctly. 'That makes no sense.' 'No, I know, but …' I trail off. 'But somehow I don't have any decent ones. And last weekend he came back in his karate trousers.' Wow, I sound amazingly petty. 'Fine,' he says. 'You can come and get some if you need to.' He sounds appropriately bored by the discussion, which is, indeed, very boring. No one cares except me.

(Reproduced by permission of The Guardian*)*

The author consciously reflects upon why exactly she is so upset with such apparently trivial matters. Surely, if one has been through the process of agreeing the separation of the 'big stuff' such as finances, housing and child custody, a missing pair of trousers ought to count for very little? And yet they do. They provoke anger and suspicion about the inferred actions of the ex-partner ('X'). They lead the author to behave in ways that she herself sees as unreasonable and 'petty'. Lurking behind it all is a sense of lacking control in one's own daily affairs, and of sneaking, rising guilt at the shortcomings of one's newly single parenting. All of this arises from a missing pair of trousers.

We might be tempted to view both the possibly purloined trousers described above and the sorts of objects discussed by the adoptive parents in our study as *symbols*, around which psychic processes of desire, investment and displacement are being played out. The notion that soft toys function as transitional objects for children during times when there is a shift in family relationships is particularly apt when that change involves either parental separation, or, in the case of adoption, the movement from one set of adult carers to another. A psychoanalytic reading of the 'holding power' of objects then seems appropriate (Bollas 2008). However, in this chapter, we deliberately resist such an approach for a number of reasons. First of all, as part of a wider general cultural saturation of post-Freudian and neo-Freudian ideas (see Parker 1997), this kind of psychoanalytic thinking is already a part of the practice of adoption itself (at least in the UK). Adoptive parents already recognize the psychological and emotional significance of the objects that travel with adoptive children between care settings; a further layering of psychoanalytic description does little to clarify how this sensitivity is practically managed. Second, attending to psychic process rather than physical engagement with objects, or, perhaps more precisely, reducing the complexities of the space in which parents and children interact with these objects into a purely mental/psychic space, seems at best to be foreclosing on the range of possible understandings and at worst to be downright reductive. Finally, in line with many of the contributions to this volume, we want to suspend automatic recourse to the kind of established subject (i.e., agent)/object (i.e., acted upon) binary prevalent in neo-Freudian thinking as the starting point for our analysis.

In previous work, we have followed the analytic move popularized by Michel Serres and Bruno Latour of treating objects as 'participants' in the work of forging relations, including those that are commonly taken to define family relationships. Rather than divide up the empirical field under the headings of subjects and objects, this approach posits an assembly of relations where the qualities and capacities of each 'actor' (i.e., what is taken to be an entity within the given empirical field) are relationally determined. Such an assembly can be 'summed up' or 'condensed' in ways that distribute agency and its lack. For example, in accounts given by survivors of child sexual abuse of the spaces in which abuse happened, we have treated some of the objects described (such as locked doors, wardrobes, roads that were crossed) as lending a shaping force to how survivors are able to articulate their own agency both at the time and in subsequent recollections (see Reavey and Brown 2009). Objects do not just mediate human actions, they are critical to efforts to establish the nature, effects and significance of those actions (e.g., the locking of a door has implications for attributions of intentionality and forethought). We can then speak of the affordances (Costall and Dreier 2006) or propensities (Jullien 1999) of objects as emerging from the assembly of relations to form potential trajectories or tendencies along which action can unfold (and which can be rearticulated in the work of remembering). For example, crossing a road and going towards a house where abuse will occur may be retrospectively constructed as a conscious decision because of the spatial organization of the activity (see Reavey and Brown 2006).

If we use this analytic tack to understand the current problem, then we begin from the position that the adoptive family constitutes an assembly of relations that is in flux. One of its 'tendencies' is to condense itself around an enclosed space of belonging, where adoptive children are constructed as having legitimate participation in the family, all of whom share in a notion of a joint future. But there are other tendencies, which may be actualized, in which this enclosure is widened or dilated to incorporate other relations, such as with former carers, biological parents or perhaps entire cultural or ethnic lineages, either real or imagined. Blood, love and memory intertwine in opening out the family to other forces and relations. Sometimes, this can prove unsustainable altogether and the enclosure dissipates; relations come apart. These tendencies might be characterized using Sloterdijk's (2011) image of 'bubbles'. The tendency towards producing the family as an enclosed sphere of intimacy and belonging is opposed by the tendencies towards overexpansion and dissipation.

Our question then becomes that of the role that these mundane objects play in condensing relations into the 'bubble' of the family. What propensities do they contribute to this process? How do they assist in enclosing the family? And how at the same time do they act to threaten or dissipate the bubble?

Spectral objects

Over the course of a life, each of us typically accumulates a sizeable number of possessions. Some objects 'travel with us', becoming important markers of identity: a much-loved and resoled pair of shoes, a mask bought on a trip to Africa, an ornament that used to stand on a grandparent's fireplace. These objects may be tied to particular periods of our life and can thus serve as the means through which the past can be recalled and put to work in the present. Radley (1990), for instance, describes how the act of rediscovering some forgotten and misplaced object can surface contrasts between past and present: 'a silver lighter from one's smoking days, a cribbage board from times when the family came round to play cards' (Radley 1990: 51). This is particularly acute in circumstances in which the contrast is between a desired past that is irrevocably foreclosed and a present that is dissatisfactory or found wanting, such as in Said's (1989) description of the importance of objects as markers of a lost homeland in Palestinian homes. The value of such objects lies in their ability to make that past present. Hence, when elderly people faced with the move from independent to sheltered accommodation are asked to give up or 'clear' a significant number of their possessions, this is experienced as a threat to memory, to the ability to narrate one's past (Marcoux 2001).

It is not really sufficient to describe such possessions as merely cues to memory, because both the process and the content of what can be remembered appear to depend on the propensities of the objects themselves. Elena Bendien's study of a 'reminiscence museum' located in an elderly care home, for example, shows that the kinds of recollections that elderly visitors produce are thoroughly interdependent with and shaped by the particular objects (e.g., old washing machines, bathtubs) with which they interact (see Bendien 2009; Bendien *et al.* 2010). Remembering is a practice that is collective not simply in that it involves people supporting one another's efforts at recall, but also in that objects lend their forces and propensities as constitutive of the practice itself. For example, Bendien *et al.* (2010) describe an episode in which the exposed working parts of a washing machine give rise to a recollection by an elderly woman of an incident from forty years ago, when her son risked injury by playing with a similar machine in the kitchen of the family home. The son had recently died, an event that is woven into the recollection as it is discussed by the woman with her adult daughter and a volunteer in the museum.

To argue that objects such as the washing machine above are integral to remembering pushes at the boundaries of how we typically define the psychological. In Sherry Turkle's (2007) collection of autobiographical sketches drawn around 'everyday things', for instance, the contributors follow in the long-standing anthropological tradition of 'thinking with things'. Here 'thinking' is undoubtedly conditioned by the individual artefacts that are described in each chapter, but there is no doubt that it is the 'investigations' and personal journeys of each author that are central, rendering the objects as literary ciphers for *Bildungsromans* in miniature. Similarly, Steven Connor's (2011) essays on objects opens with the image of an infant's 'researches' with an object dangling over its head. In both cases the properties and qualities of artefacts are certainly important, but what is really at issue is the drama of the thoughts, feelings and activities that arise when a lone subject explores a given object and finds a place for it in their life.

Although we might reject the 'subject-centred' approach taken by Turkle and Connor, they are equally insightful in their delineation of the particular sorts of objects that are of concern. Turkle speaks of 'evocative objects' that have the power to give rise to powerful attachments and emotional experiences. Connor similarly points to objects that appear to have a life of their own, one that exceeds their mundane material appearance. These 'magical objects' enable an exchange of qualities with the subjects who engage with them[1]. We want to follow this analytic suggestion by proposing a definition of our own that gives us a purchase on the objects that prove troubling for adoptive parents: 'spectral objects'. These objects make possible memorial practices that inflate particular versions of the past in such a way as to both unsettle the present and to render projected visions of the future as uncertain. Their qualities project a sense of 'unfinished business', which can be experienced as threatening and requiring ongoing management. Spectral objects point the way to a difficult past, but do so in a way that renders that past as something that cannot be simply erased without considerable cost.

Our choice of the word 'spectral' arises directly the way this term sometimes appeared in the talk of adoptive parents:

> B. … there was a great deal of fear about the father within social services and that permeated through all of the file and through all of the, um all of the discussions we had with social workers throughout there was this great spectre um and, and he remained a spectre didn't he I think until we got a letter from him…

Biological parents and former carers are clearly important figures in any account of the life of an adopted child. Yet they can also give rise to tremendous anxieties about how this early life can reappear in the present. This is particularly so when these figures are not directly present, but are experienced at a remove, such as through case file details in the example above and in the traces of them that appear to be woven into the objects that we discuss. Spectral objects are then not objects in the usual sense of the term in that they appear to have a kind of agency of their own, which arises in part because of the residue of absent or phantom subjectivity left on them by the actions or choices of former carers or biological parents. There are parallels here with the pun that Miller (2001) makes on 'estate agency' to refer to the ways that houses seem to be 'haunted' by the subjectivity of former occupants who have left their mark through the aesthetic and practical decisions they have written into the property. However, in Miller's example, the spectrality is made present through the relative solidity and longevity of the property into which new occupants move. The spectral objects that we discuss (toys and clothes) travel with the adoptive child. It is their displacement from a past life and the precarious way in which they have survived to accompany the child that gives them their unsettling holding power. To dispose of such an object is to choose to break that fragile link to the child's past, however difficult it might have been.

Memorial boundaries

In one of the earliest discussions of collective memory, Maurice Halbwachs (1950) clearly articulated the role of objects as markers of the shifting boundary between past and present within a community of rememberers. If we consider the family as a particular instance of such a community, then our attention rapidly falls to the diverse range of memorabilia that adorns a typical family home, from treasured objects that have passed between generations to souvenirs of travel or important events and 'prized possessions'. The generic term 'stuff' seems best to capture the heterogeneity of these objects and the way in which they seem to point out constitutive relationships of ownership and experience: 'this is our stuff', 'she still has a lot of her stuff here', 'going through all that old stuff really reminded me of how things used to be'.

Adopted children move into a space that is already populated with objects that speak to a particular past. Entering this space means both a break with the past and the incorporation into a new present. The delicacy of this transition can be handled in part by exchanging the properties of the child with the 'stuff' with which they are travelling. In the following example, C describes how contact with former carers during this transitional period was assisted by the movement of objects:

> C. And that was really helpful. Um, because they were fostering other children and she went there and the bed that <u>had</u> been her bed was now somebody else's bed, somebody else's posters were on the wall and it, it really clicked with her that all <u>her</u> stuff was now at <u>ours</u> and, and that was it, you know, that, that, that was completed and the reason that she'd been there was as they had said, that she was waiting for a permanent family and um, that had happened.

Visiting her former home, the child sees that the space that defined relations of care has now been reshaped. What was her bed now belongs to someone else. Or more properly speaking, the bed that she had thought was hers is now revealed as belonging to no one in particular, as a marker of a transitional space that is temporarily occupied by a string of fostered children in turn. What is permanent is 'her stuff', the objects that she has accrued in her life to date and that travel with her. They are now in place in the new family home. The sense of this home having stood there waiting to receive the adoptive child is communicated by the physical organization of the home space as being receptive to the depositing of the child's 'stuff'.

This sense of the 'destining' of the child to be with the adopting family (the 'completion' of the transition to the 'permanent family') is not straightforward. Permanent placements can break down through the rejection of the arrangement by the child, adoptive parents or other parties. Here again, 'stuff' can be referred to as the material token in which this complex affective atmosphere is registered. In the following extract below, C describes another adoptive child who oriented to the placement process in a different way:

> C. Um, and he, he was then told the judge has <u>ordered</u> him (laughs) to be, placed with us and he, he again got this image you know, that sort of out of the blue, um, he was picked up and carried off and he always sold his stuff and, and he, he stayed overnight with people on the streets without clothes, staying out all night. He always felt he needed to break free from us, because he feels we took him and imprisoned him.

The child here treats the boundaries between past and present as one reflecting the subordination of his own agency into the formal will of the law: a judge legally bound him to a future that was not of his choosing and he was transported, much like a commodity, to a new home, where he was 'imprisoned'. His rebellion against this supposed commodification takes the form of divesting himself of all the things that travelled with him and that he subsequently accrued in the new family setting: 'he always sold his stuff' and 'stayed overnight with people on the streets without clothes'. It is as though it is the stuff itself that holds him to the adoptive family, and conversely, from the perspective of the adoptive parent, that it is stuff that expresses the relations of care that the child has rejected.

In the previous two examples, 'stuff' was comparatively undefined, referring to the heterogeneous array of materials that travel with the child. Whereas stuff is invested with a kind of spectrality (a residue of the past in the present that makes this boundary an ongoing concern) the particular things that we would characterize as spectral objects have more ambiguous and complex qualities. In the following example, two adoptive parents discuss an episode in which a particular soft toy (Pooh bear) is mislaid:

> W.   F has got a Pooh bear
> B.   That she got from the foster parents
> W.   That she got from the foster parents, that is a true transitional object, that we nearly lost in the woods once.
> B.   And we both nearly killed ourselves when we crossed the road searching for him.
> W.   Pooh's jumper…
> B.   She's asleep in the buggy
> W.   *Oh it's Pooh Bear, my god!* Ohhh
> B.   We found him, on the side of the road, just, life would not have been worth living…

It is worth pointing out that the parents here use the psychoanalytic language of 'transitional object' to refer to the toy. But this does not entirely capture the emotion that is generated around the possible loss of Pooh bear. The child mentioned is an infant, one small enough to still need to be pushed in a buggy, and therefore one who might presumably have very little by way of memories of her life before adoption. Although it might be unfortunate to lose Pooh bear, over time it might be replaced with other objects that become more important as durable markers of caring relations. However, this particular toy is not simply transitional. It is a link to a past (to the former foster parents) which is constitutive of the present. Although this may now be the permanent home for the child, it cannot be formed on the basis of a rejection of everything that came before without risking at some point in the future that this child may place importance on this early period. The past must then be accessible; it must be given a place within the adoptive family such that the family does not seal itself off in a way that would make a desire to connect with the past impossible to address. Pooh bear is not a symbol of the past; it is that past made manifest in the material form of the toy, the safekeeping of which is simultaneously the preservation of a conduit to an early past in the ongoing work of making the present of the permanent family.

The stakes involved in such safekeeping become considerably heightened when the past that is marked out by the spectral object are problematic. In the next extract, the parent F talks of a toy whose material state threatens to make a particular version of the past inescapable:

> F. R, at three, she came with a tiny little white, like Snoopy dog and that was from, that was from birth mother era and that has a cigarette burn on it, the same as she has a cigarette burn, she has, um, and then she paid no attention to it whatsoever. You know, they accumulate so many toys and things. I've always kept that in her room but it's hidden at the back of the pile.

The Snoopy dog described here has been burned with a cigarette, which F compares directly with a similar injury inflicted on the child during the 'birth mother era'. In memorial terms, the past is unfolded from the burn mark. To examine the damaged toy is to be drawn immediately to the scalding hot tip of the cigarette that inflicted the mark, the hands that held that cigarette, the action itself (intentional? incidental? a moment of fury? regretted? or enjoyed?). A whole set of deeply troubling worlds seem to spring from or grow out of the burn mark, in a way akin to the unfolding origami image that Proust offers in the famous madeleine example, or the worlding of the peasant's labour that Heidegger articulates in his analysis of Van Gogh's *A Pair of Shoes* (see Middleton and Brown 2005). And if F can do this work, what is implied here is that the child might themselves also do the same work at some point in the future. So why not simply throw away Snoopy dog? Because like Pooh bear it is a surviving link to the past, one that almost triumphantly survived the precarious transition from a problematic early life to the projected settlement of the present. To get rid of the toy is to break that link. If Snoopy dog has survived the horrors that led to the cigarette burning, then so too will the child. That narrative needs to be preserved. But Snoopy dog must nevertheless stand waiting to do that (for now at least) from the relative solitude of being 'hidden at the back of the pile'.

Trajectories

Spectral objects point a way to versions of the past that make manifest a range of figures and actions that are either already significant for the child or may yet come to matter. This work of attending to the boundary between past and present in which adoptive parents engage has its corollary in the concern to anticipate the future needs of the child. In our data, adoptive parents routinely describe their anxieties about how adopted children make sense of their past in relation to anticipated futures as they grow. For example, a child might see himself or herself as having inherited 'bad blood', which they imagine to destine them to a life of criminality. Other children may report having witnessed acts of violence, which they come to believe will inevitably recur in their adult life. Whether these memories are 'actual' in the strict sense or not matters less than the power of these images to indicate to the child and to adoptive parents the possible life trajectories that the child lives out.

In the following long example, we see how a particular piece of clothing is fraught with significance for these anticipated trajectories. Beginning with a mention of a play costume owned by her daughter, C articulates how the costume poses the risk of opening up a discussion of a particularly dramatic episode from her daughter's early life, when her birth mother accidentally started a fire in her home:

C.   My daughter's obsessed with fire and um, we don't talk, we don't um, she's actually got a fireman's costume, a firefighter's costume, a firefighter's kit you know, age-appropriate children's things but I don't talk about fires and there was, you now the New Town fire.[2] Of course, we haven't mentioned it, haven't shown her pictures but, um, today she was out visiting a friend who has a younger child and doesn't realize how big ears she's got and talking about, you know, those explosions there and the sky so she's heard about it and we … and then um M had promised to show her a newspaper picture because she's obsessed with it. She just…

B.   Amazing what they take in, isn't it you know?

A.   It's amazing … when she's three

C.   Yeah

W.   It's quite unsettling

C.   Oh, but also you sort of think it's alright because there's this huge picture of like, like a mushroom and there's three um firefighters in the picture and the main interest was one didn't have his hat on! (Laughter) You have to think, you know

A.   You're building this up, yeah

C.   Well, it's like, well it's like, you know what do I do when she's, you know, talking to her about this, this sort of thing about what her mum did you know, I suppose it's quite hard to talk to her without having an example apart from the drugs, having pictures and things like that, you know that sort of thing, other sorts of scenarios but um, she will hear about that because siblings, you know will, will tell her. Anytime really, but anytime and it is so, and I know that I'm doing it myself, I'm sort of visualizing it and I know I have to talk it down, the fact that she wasn't an arsonist she had started a fire by mistake, you know, um it was the fact that she went much longer into distress, you know but the flat got burned down and the fact was she went to prison because of it and had a long sentence, so that's unfortunate but you have to sort of try to work out

The firefighter's costume is a thoroughly ambiguous object. C reports that her daughter is 'obsessed with fire'. The costume is then, on the one hand, an 'age-appropriate' way of entertaining the child's interests. It is, we might say, a way of normalizing these interests, of framing them as innocent childish concerns with the dangers of the adult world, in the same way that other children might be bought doctors or soldiers play outfits. But what C is aware of is that this obsession has roots in an actual episode from her daughter's early years of which the child is apparently unaware. There is a secret (her birth mother's role in a fire) that will be revealed at some point, most likely by siblings. C has apparently spent some considerable time imagining or 'visualizing' how this story will be framed, the kinds of images and resources that she will need to draw upon to do so. The firefighter costume then stands as the centre of a future effort to recapitulate a past that is continuously reiterated by the child's current obsession with fire.

It is the future revelation of this shared secret that is written into the costume. To refuse to allow her daughter to engage with her obsession would be for C to stand accountable at some later date of having misdirected her daughter, of having deliberately steered her away from having gotten onto the path that would eventually lead her to a confrontation with this particular aspect of her past and her relationship to her birth mother. Allowing her to have the costume gives C the resource of being able to present herself as having merely delayed rather than dismissed the possibility of this confrontation. And indeed this choice appears to have worked to the extent that the daughter's interest in images of fire seems to be age-appropriately skewed (e.g., whether hats are being worn properly by firefighters rather than on the consequences). The costume is then something akin to Poe's famous 'purloined letter' discussed by both Lacan and Derrida. It is a secret or mystery, the quality of which is both intensified and managed on account of its being hidden in plain sight. To stretch a metaphor, we might say that this future confrontation with the past is hidden in the folds of the costume, waiting to be unfolded and opened up at any point.

As spectral objects, what is afforded by both the firefighter costume and soft toys that we have described is a means for adoptive parents to anticipate a range of future life trajectories for their child. Some trajectories are the desired outcomes that follow from the child's integration in the new family. Other less desirable trajectories are those in which the child seems fated to return to the circumstances and kinds of life experience that dominated their early years. Spectral objects play an ambiguous role. On the one hand, they are a visible link to a difficult past, a material means by which that past continues to exert an influence over the present, which threatens the effort to sustain a stable life trajectory for the child. But on the other hand, they represent one of the few means through which an emotional link to the past can be sustained for the child, and through which they might, at some future date, be able to reflect upon and place that past in the context of their subsequent life. The spectral object is a threat and a promise, an affectively charged medium through which the past continues to act, and the means by which it might be tamed.

Summary

Objects do not offer a simple gateway to the past. Their power to link past and present comes from the contingent and situated manner in which they are encountered in acts of remembering. It is this complex work of handling the past in adoptive families that is our focus in this chapter. Although the toys and clothes (the 'stuff') discussed here are affectively highly charged and certainly rich interpretatively, we have deliberately chosen not to treat them as symbols or as psychoanalytic 'objects'. We believe that such an approach would overlook the material affordances of the objects that enable them to become participants in the ongoing dilemmas of managing the past. For example, the choices made in the burying of Snoopy dog in the pile of toys, or the work around the 'open secret' contained in the firefighter costume, is what concerns us, rather than any psychic drama.

Ownership and agency are at the very centre of the problem. For the bubble of adoptive family to survive, it is necessary for the difficult past of the child to be tamed, despite its ongoing manifestation in the present, by way of the stuff that has come with the child. In a mundane sense, the child 'owns' the objects, and the choice to dispose of them is therefore not properly speaking that of the parents to make. But more importantly, that ownership is simultaneously an owning of the past that is affectively mediated through the spectral object. If the object survives, then so too does the possibility of the child being able to assert some sense of agency in relation to the past at some later point and find a place for early difficult experience in their ongoing life trajectory. Curiously then, the adoptive parents here need to attribute quasi-subjective status to spectral objects (to let them live, so to speak) in order to avoid the risk of reducing the child to the status of a commodity who has been traded between adult carers. This complex exchange of properties adds to the semi-magical patina that accrues on the object, or as we have called it, using the terms of our participants, 'spectrality'. It is this property that adoptive parents fear (as seen in the desperate search for Pooh bear) and on which their ongoing efforts to maintain the bubble of adoptive family ultimately come to depend.

Notes

1 Connor (2011) draws here upon Michel Serres' notions of the quasi-object, which reappear in the work of Latour and actor–network-theory (see Brown 2002).
2 Actual name replaced with pseudonym.

Bibliography

Bendien, E., Brown, S.D. and Reavey, P. (2010) Social remembering as an art of living: Analysis of a 'reminiscence museum', in M. Domenech and M. Schillmeier (eds) *New technologies and emerging spaces of care*, Farnham: Ashgate.

Bollas, C. (2008) *The evocative object world*, London: Routledge.

Brookfield, H., Brown, S.D. and Reavey, P. (2008) Vicarious and postmemory practices in adopting families: The construction of the past in photography and narrative, *Journal of Community and Applied Social Psychology* 18 (5): 474–491.

Brown, S.D. (2002) Michel Serres: Science, translation and the logic of the parasite, *Theory, Culture and Society* 19 (3): 1–27.

Connor, S. (2011) *Paraphernalia: The curious lives of magical things*, London: Profile.

Costall, A. and Dreier, O. (eds) (2006) *Doing things with things: The design and use of ordinary objects*, Aldershot: Ashgate.

Halbwachs, M. (1950; 1980) *The collective memory*, New York: Harper and Row.

Jullien, F. (1999) *The propensity of things: Towards a history of efficacy in China*, New York: Zone.

Marcoux, J.S. (2001) The refurbishment of memory, in D. Miller (ed.) *Home possessions*, Oxford: Berg.

Middleton, D. and Brown, S.D. (2005) *The social psychology of experience: Studies in remembering and forgetting*, London: Sage.

Miller, D. (2001) Possessions, in D. Miller (ed.) *Home possessions*, Oxford: Berg.

Parker, I. (1997) *Psychoanalytic culture: Psychoanalytic discourse in Western society*, London: Sage.

Radley, A. (1990) Artefacts, memory and a sense of the past, in D. Middleton and D. Edwards (eds) *Collective remembering*, pp. 46–59, London: Sage.

Reavey, P. and Brown, S.D. (2006) Transforming past agency and action in the present: Time, social remembering and child sexual abuse, *Theory and Psychology* 16 (2): 179–202.

Reavey, P. and Brown, S.D. (2009) The mediating role of objects in recollections of adult women survivors of child sexual abuse, *Culture and Psychology* 15 (4): 463–484.

Said, E. (1989) *After the last sky: Palestinian lives*, London: Verso.

Sloterdijk, P. (2011) *Bubble: Spheres 1*, Cambridge, MA: MIT Press.

Turkle, S. (ed.) (2007) *Evocative objects: Things we think with*, Cambridge, MA: MIT Press.

Part III

Unsettling objects
Introduction

Elizabeth B. Silva

Sitting at my desk to write this chapter, I look at the René Magritte postcards I have pinned on the board in my office. 'These are not Magritte's', I think, as I read '*Ceci n'est pas une pipe*' and '*Ceci n'est pas une pomme*'. Indeed, they are (regrettably!) just postcards of paintings that Magritte made about objects. The shapes and colours of the painted figures are recognizable. Yet, a picture of a painted apple is not an apple; the flower painted in the place of the face of a woman is not a face, and it is not a flower either. Magritte's pictures are factual statements. Like other works of modern art, these paintings explicitly seek to unsettle habitual perceptions and understandings. But why are these paintings unsettling? Is it because they are explicitly factual? Do they unsettle our functional fictions? Although the experience of unsettling by and with objects is something that I want to reflect upon in this short introduction, answering these questions of Magritte's paintings is not my concern. Here, my interest lies in how objects themselves can unsettle, and in the processes by which they do so.

How do objects unsettle? Or how are objects deployed to unsettle? Is such unsettling a quality or an effect? These questions are central to the six chapters in this section of the book. In this introduction, I outline some key methodological orientations presented in the studies here assembled and discuss the key relations each chapter brings to processes and matters of unsettling.

Perceiving the unsettling

There are many conflicting views about how to approach objects, a number of which are discussed in this section. A common assumption that I retain in setting out this discussion is that the qualities or effects of objects are felt or assessed through human ways of seeing and making sense. This does not mean that objects can be only what humans make of them. Objects routinely exceed the horizon of human sociality, and can indeed be unavailable to human perception even when their effects are tangibly present. Sometimes their presence is acknowledged by paying attention to the haunting of their ghostly presence, listening to the 'noises' that they make in our surroundings and in our person (Gordon 1997), other times by the movements that they cause in other objects (Harman 2005). Objects are accessible to humans only as part of regimes of vision, practice, touch, taste, smell and knowledge. It is in relation to this limited access to object worlds that we approach the unsettling object. There is something in the presence of an unsettling object that disturbs, renders unstable, agitates or decomposes the knowledge, perspectives and emotions of those who encounter it. Such unsettling can be terribly disconcerting, of course, but it can also be socially productive and individually enlightening, as we can see in the cases investigated by contributors to this part of the book, in which individuals, materials and objects are drawn together in ways that are perceived as unsettling. This can happen by revealing intrinsic connections between disparate entities in a field, noting what links and what sets them apart.

In the chapters assembled in Part III, a diverse range of objects are considered in terms of their unsettling effects: book, table, lemon, computer, software program, powder and collection of things all feature as unsettling objects. But how does one go about researching unsettling objects, how does one attend to that which is by definition resistant to conventional frames of understanding? The methodological orientations to unsettling objects that are present in these chapters reveal four basic orientations, which appear in isolation or as interconnected. One orientation indicates that a new point of view emerges from looking at the simple (ordinary) labour of doing what one must. A mundane material process, not usually attended to as significant, can unsettle, emerge as something special, arousing curiosity and interest. Another orientation indicates that the significant connections are those between personal or human matters and objects of interest to the person (an unsettling interest, in this case) through which new ways of seeing appear. A subjective interest invests things with significance. A third orientation shows that knowledge and interest develop over time and across sites, such that knowledge and perspectives are amplified or extended through the relational dynamics that form collective understandings. Often in this process, the unsettling triggering of the process is settled. A fourth orientation points to relations between transformation and conservation in the processes through which objects are renewed, as they settle and unsettle.

An important point raised by these methodological orientations is that objects are matters of fact and have particular qualities that can be unsettling within a specific field. The delineation of the field is essential because objects can have an unsettling character (quality) only in and through their relations with other beings or objects positioned in a particular space (concrete or abstract). Unsettling objects thus emerge in relation to particular domains; they are not independent from environment, purpose, politics and so on. Objects never work alone, yet they can produce intangible effects. This is the central character of unsettling objects. The materiality of objects produces immaterial effects and the immaterial effects are read back into the materiality of objects. These ideas are elaborated in the specific cases provided by the chapters in this section.

Perspectives on the unsettling object

Elizabeth Silva's central argument concerns the ways in which obscure social relations can be revealed through the haunting of objects. These are echoes of past occurrences and future desires that come about in the narratives about possessions and uses of things. The field of this particular exploration is ordinary home life. Objects mediate the everyday relationships between people and become part of the way that people exist, their practices, identities and ways of relating to others (people and materials). Objects also mediate the research interaction and generate knowledge beyond their deliberate and explicit use in 'talk with a purpose'. Biographical material weaves with everyday domestic practices, revealing haunting presences, marked in the body, in the home and in ways of relating with other individuals and with household technologies and mundane objects. The investigation is concerned with processes of making visible, with discoveries that, although not sought, emerged because they were (unexpectedly) present in the research relationship. The chapter addresses centrally both the transformational work of everyday objects and the haunting or traces of the immaterial, pointing out connections between impersonal forces and personal life.

However, relations involve connection and disconnection, and Morten Pedersen disputes the claim that connections are always good by considering what happens when people use things in order not to think, or in order to develop a process of engaged separation. He claims that according to the thesis of 'extended mind', which has become increasingly influential within some branches of philosophy, psychology and anthropology, certain human mental processes involve an embodied or distributed mode of cognition in which the mind-brain is augmented by diverse 'cognitive scaffolds', such as notebooks, mnemonic tools and religious paraphernalia. From this perspective, connections are almost by definition good things: the more the human mind can distribute itself into its material and social surroundings, the better (the more efficient) is the resulting cognitive process. What happens then if people do not want to extend their minds? What happens if people use certain objects in order not to think certain things? Based on ethnographic fieldwork in Northern Mongolia, Pedersen argues that the extended mind theory is based on a fetish of connectivity, and that, by exploring the labour of division and the 'creative cuttings' performed by shamans and their clients, a different analytical space may be forged, which accounts for a different relationality in the cutting of relations. The focus of the chapter brings a particularly important reflection to the discussion of the unsettling of objects as it asks about separation, viewed here as the deliberate destruction of connection.

Like separation, another unsettling concern is that the importance of objects may be found not in their use but in their uselessness. That a politics of objects must focus on the uselessness of objects is the concern of Nicholas Thoburn's chapter. An affinity with a process of defamiliarization is found in Thoburn's argument, by which only when the familiar becomes strange can its diverse invisible connections with microstructures and macrostructures become apparent. He develops a politics of the 'useless object' through Marx's critique of commodity fetishism and Walter Benjamin's account of the collector. This he brings into relation with the Surrealist trope of the 'found object', the classical formulation of which is considerably less unsettling than it at first seems. In its place, Thoburn pursues the useless object through the fringes of Surrealism, in Ghérasim Luca's 'objectively offered object' and Georges Bataille's 'document'. Of course, the Magritte postcards discussed above are also an illustration of the unsettling powers of Surrealist objects.

The power of the object and the production of effects are also addressed by Matthew Fuller and Andrew Goffey, but on the basis of a different field of practices. They engage with the practice of programming to enquire about the powers of computational objects: what power the programs have, the effects they generate and how effects are produced. These programs model relations, processes and practices in abstract material spaces, which, through processes of stabilization are also, paradoxically, territories. As a cognitive process, computation appears, presumably, outside the material textures of culture and of 'things'. From this perspective, objects are concepts, i.e., they are materially represented in a logical calculus. Yet, while representing something else, a computational object is also an entity in its own right, with a specific material form. Fuller and Goffey adopt a relational approach to claim that computational objects model behaviour with objects (not of objects). This approach is here put to use to understand the 'sociotechnical quality of contemporary relations of power'. The entities produced are obscure and the relations that they create can exceed the design of the programmes that engender them; what is created has a degree of autonomy that may unsettle its creators.

If the object appears as taking over the sets of relations it is implicated in, as seems to be the case of the computational programmes, in Martin Holbraad's chapter, an analytical perspective is developed to allow heuristically identified 'things' to set the terms for their own analysis.

He builds on the posthumanism of the recent literature on 'the rise of the thing'. Such an approach places the focus on things' conceptual affordances, defined as the difference that the material characteristics of things make to attempts by analysts to think them. The agency of things is here taken to an extreme position. The focus is on concepts, whereby things act as originators of analytical conceptualization. Critically reexamining his earlier anthropological fieldwork, the argument is developed with reference to the example of *aché*, a concept-cum-substance associated with Afro–Cuban divination. Deemed by diviners as both a form of power and, more prosaically, as a kind of powder, *aché* is able to exert an influence over the manner in which it might be conceived anthropologically, by virtue of its own material properties.

The various ways in which objects are integral to social relations, as discussed in the empirical cases presented in this part of the book, are reflected upon in the broad philosophical discussion of Graham Harman's chapter. Harman presents a summary of various antiobject positions and outlines why these positions 'undermine' or 'overmine' objects. This undermining or overmining occurs because objects are not either simply expressions of their physical microcomponents or of their relations to other things or humans. Objects are the basic ingredients of reality, says Harman. To accept this implies a recognition that there is an objective reality outside the mind, in which objects are palpable physical facts, each one an autonomous unit of ghostly presence in every layer of the universe.

The chapters in this part show us why we need to acknowledge the presence and influence of such ghosts. Their presence may be manifest in the domesticity of homes or in the research encounter, as for Silva; in the thought about a thing to prevent connection, as for Pedersen; fetishized in intangible commodities, as for Thoburn; in the modelling of behaviour via computer programmes, as for Fuller and Goffey; in the power of powder as a conceptual tool of relationality, as for Holbraad; and in the intrinsic 'reality' of objects and materials, as for Harman.

These chapters share a concern with the making visible of the object that unsettles. They also suggest that unsettling objects require their presence to be acknowledged and that light be shed on them such that new relations come into view, enlightening our theoretical understanding of unsettling objects and manners – or methods – through which we set about capturing their qualities and effects.

Bibliography

Bendien, E. (2009) 'From the art of remembering to the craft of ageing', PhD thesis, Universiteit voor Humanistiek, the Netherlands.

Gordon, S. (1997) *Ghostly Matters: Haunting and the Sociological Imagination*, Minneapolis: University of Minnesota Press.

Harman, G. (2005) *Guerrilla Metaphysics: Phenomenology and the Carpentry of Things*, Chicago: Open Court.

16

Haunting in the material of everyday life

Elizabeth B. Silva

Introduction

In an article in *The Guardian* 'Review' section (18 February 2012), Colm Tóibín writes that '[p]erhaps a book is a weapon; perhaps an unwritten book is an even more powerful weapon. It has a way of filling the air with its menace, or its promise.' Tóibín's mother made a book sound like a weapon, he claims. For it mattered to her that she could have been a writer, like him, perhaps an even better writer, but life opportunities had failed her. There was a great deal of silence in the house in which he grew up, where some deaths were significant enough not to be mentioned, absences were too palpable, what you thought about and did not speak were only the important matters and silence was inspiration. This was a case of haunting taking one to places of imagination and to a literary position in the world. The book, as a weapon of social mobility, failed Tóibín's mother and gave him success, while centrally being mediator of their relationship.

My premise in this chapter is that social life involves a prominent link with materiality that is often unnoticed. Yet, it is possible for one to know oneself and one's relations through things and one can be known through things. Although histories of things in the social world of a person conjure up a life trajectory, and objects can mediate a person, devices are never innocent, acting as props, story-telling devices, mnemonics for certain experiences, messy and entangled components of a way of living and crucial life-changing instruments. Here, the setting of my engagement with these issues is everyday life, in which materials conform and inform relationships physically manifesting culture, acting on identity formation and performance and intervening in practices patterned by the resources that these same materials are themselves responsible for generating. Social divisions of class, gender and sexuality are some of the diverse configurations with which material resources appear entangled and that concern me in this chapter.

The relationship between things and people has been central to my work for some time. The 'things' that have conspicuously moved my investigation into the sociocultural explorations of everyday life have been technologies in the home. What sorts of things are wanted by people and why, how they deal with these things, how things make people do certain things. Questions of these sorts have been explored by a vast array of academic literature.[1] Themes of agency, determinism, interaction, the power of materiality and the makings of subjectivity have from various angles emerged in these explorations. Often, these themes have appeared to welcomingly address increasing complexity without, however, putting the finger where it matters: on those interstices between what is revealed and what is hidden, what is clearly important and what seems not to matter, on the objects that are evidently significant and those that unsettle without any apparent reason, on the things that are done with things that appear incongruous with what the thing calls for to be done, and so on.

The exploration of everyday life in homes offered me a significantly ordinary site to reflect about the interactions of lives and objects, as well as the process of knowing about these interactions. In an ethnographic study of home life centred on the uses of machines, I immersed myself in individual biographies, family dynamics and the myriad ways in which individual lives connect with the social. In this chapter, I consider two of these domestic cases to discuss how events occur as related to objects. In one case, objects enable continuity; they settle. In the other case, they trigger life-change events; they unsettle. What objects do, the events that they generate, are thus not a property of the object, but their property is a part of the action involved in the event, of the circumstances. How can we know about events? How does the object carry the story? Can the ability to know be in itself unsettling?

The two cases are linked to different experiences of sexuality, a theme that I neither explicitly sought in the investigation nor that was obvious from the mundane encounter with the objects that occasioned the narratives shown by them. Because of the manner in which sexuality matters emerged, I deal with the cases guided by an epistemology of haunting informed by the work of Avery Gordon (1997). The ghostly aspect of sexuality is confronted as it moves out of the shadow in the narratives of lives within the acknowledgement of the complexity of individual and social life. In the next section, I present each of these cases, followed by a reflection about the engagement with haunting in the process of knowing, to then develop a conversation between mainstream social science frameworks aiming to turn what is invisible visible and to contribute to developing the idea of haunting as a social phenomenon. I conclude with a discussion about the productive engagements of social research with haunting and the unsettling of objects to enhance an agenda for further development of this concern.

Encountering the ghosts

Presence and absence, the holes in the stories and the traces of something else in lived experience are serious matters in Gordon's (1997) challenge to sociology to take up the material reality, the matter, of ghosts. Life is understood as being more complicated than those who study it usually take for granted. To capture the ghosts empirically, I simply followed matters as they emerged and connected in my ethnographically informed research practice. I describe the two cases broadly following Gordon's approach. I detail her discussion about 'ghost matters' in sociological theory after the presentation of the cases. I am aware that I could have not seen the ghosts. Once acknowledged they seemed such an obvious presence.

Rena

Rena (44 years old) lived in a village in the east of England with her family, near her parents' home. She worked a couple of days a week in the summer cleaning boats. She had married John at the age of 24. She was 'never one for babies', but mothered three sons (aged 12, 14 and 17), whom she never breastfed because she 'could not bear that sort of relationship with babies'. Every one of her sons was born underweight, by Caesarean section, the first with a cleft palate, which 'freaked her out', after which she 'cried for days'. She was clinically depressed during the second pregnancy, and depressed again during the third. She had difficult menstrual cycles, feeling well just for a week every month, until she had a hysterectomy, when she began to feel 'lovely'. After this operation, she enrolled on a month's return-to-work course, which included computer skills. When I first saw Rena, it had been four weeks since the course had ended.

In the house, the use and care of the technologies for housework were identified with the use and care of Rena's body. All the machines for housework (in particular, the dishwasher, washing machine, fridge and freezer) were overused, running many times a day, or, filled up to the brim; they did not always work properly, or were left not functioning for periods of time without maintenance. The activities that the main machines performed were then accomplished with lower-quality substitutes, and the home had an accumulation of useless things ('I don't know what's in there', said Rena, commenting about the contents of the freezer. Bath towels were said not to have been seen for months, lost in the bedrooms around the house). Rena felt overwhelmed by piles of laundry waiting to be ironed, while demanding of herself that she ironed everything.

The industriousness of everyone in the household was apparent to me from my first entrance to the home. The noise of machines running was incessant. The biographies of the objects, both present (like the current washing machine, the freezer out of order) and absent (all the washing machines that preceded the existing one, the dishwasher that had just been replaced, the very first microwave oven bought when the first son was born) related to life events and connected to ways of living marking personal and family trajectory and change. Yet, permanence prevailed in the constant disorganization of everyday domestic life, in the never catching up, the sentiment of being overloaded, forever just out of control.

A conservative gendered feminine culture pervaded Rena's story. She formally embraced the prescribed feminine roles of housewife and mother, but she lived these as adversarial. Her trajectory appeared straightforwardly scripted: to be a wife and a mother. She married someone whose job required the support structure traditionally dependent on a wife. Rena was not able to do that on her own but the kin network, particularly her mother, supported family life during Rena's frequent illnesses. Her mother visited daily and dealt with Rena's kitchen with great familiarity. This pervaded the whole dynamics of the household, the very history of adoption of the various machines and indeed of their operation. Because Rena could not cope with housework, machines were brought in to help. Because housework was excessive, machines were overloaded and collapsed, making housework accumulate. The pressure Rena felt was overwhelming.

A masculine culture that benefited her husband John, making him a self-reliant individual, countered and complemented Rena's ways. This was also reflected in the independence of the sons, who appeared to cope generally well with their mother's withdrawals. The three of them knew 'how to cook', often sorting themselves out with microwave foods. They knew how to operate the washing machine, the oldest did his own laundry, and not one of them mentioned the mother's health as a problem. This was a problem significant enough to be mentioned, yet, it created silence, echoing Tóibín's story about his home life that I mentioned in opening this chapter. Rena's low level of support appeared to have been enough for them to get by with.

Rena suffered from the definition of women in terms of sex and reproduction with motherhood placed at the centre of what it is to be female. Rena lacked proper work qualifications, hated exams and had a low educational grade and low self-esteem. With low cultural capital, she felt actually 'out of place' in life. Her story shows great conflict with the culturally assigned traditional feminine roles of wife and mother. She had had babies whom she did not particularly want, suffered huge health problems related to pregnancies and had lived with depression and a lack of energy. She had some hope for a happier life after her hysterectomy. It appears that Rena suffered from the symbolic violence attached to the prevailing gender order and what she took as being assigned to her as a wife and mother, which narrowed her options in life. Her conflicts in face of her assigned attributions indicate her feelings of ambivalence in relation to the determinations of her habitus, which directed her to pursue the roles of wife and mother in a taken-for-granted manner. Although in practice she undertook these roles, she did so with unease, which was evident in her suffering body and in the emotions of anxiety and revulsion that she had displayed towards her motherhood and the mothering of her sons.

Henry

Henry (53 years old) was an orthopaedic consultant living in the north of England with a wife and a 14-year-old son. Before becoming parents, they had travelled a lot and had had jobs abroad. Lucey, Henry's wife, was foreign and worked as a solicitor. They had all sorts of home technologies, including cable television, one computer and three laptops, and in 2002, as early users, they also had broadband and a wireless internet connection.

My ethnographic study involved various visits to most of the 24 households included in the investigation. Some of the visits happened over an extended period of time of nearly two years. About one year after I first contacted this family to become part of my study, and after having spent time in their home and interviewed both adults, what Lucey called a 'tragedy' occurred. I was surprised by their sharing of this story with me. It came about because of their need to talk (or Lucey's need), to come to terms with things, and I was perceived as a safe ear with a non-judgemental stance. I understood this openness also in the context of our previous talks about home life and of sharing a similar habitus and intellectual concerns. This ghost appeared to me very much because of the rapport revealed in the method of my investigation, in the very attitude of 'following connections' (cf. Latour 2005). As I encountered stories (some stories haunting like ghosts and informing, sometimes unconsciously, the whole sets of practices talked about), I went along with them.

On an entirely casual occurrence, picking up dirty mugs to put into the dishwasher, Lucey had found on Henry's printer, in his study, a page describing a sadomasochist (SM) session. Confronting Henry, she learned that he had been, in his words, 'an active masochist' since as far as he could remember. He told me that as a boy he would hurt himself in unimaginable ways. He said: 'Of course, I didn't know what to call this until my twenties. I simply thought I was weird gay. I discovered I liked women in my early twenties and then began to have SM sessions with dominatrices.' As a public school boy, he had suffered beatings by teachers on a number of occasions, and with friends had had endurance competitions in classrooms.

At the time that Henry's secret masochist practices came out of the closet of their home life, Lucey and he had been together for over 20 years. His job had often taken him away to meetings and conferences. He had timed his SM sessions so that his body would be 'healed' by the time he came back home. He had always been so careful, that he was utterly surprised at Lucey's discovery. 'I love Lucey and wouldn't know what to do without her. She was never meant to know about this', he said. Lucey saw the printout of the description of an SM session, Polaroid photographs of 'scenes of pleasure-in-torture', a web film of a session that the printout related to, and various pornographic websites listed under Henry's 'favourites' on his internet browser. These sites, said Lucey, were 'racist, sexist, offensive, grotesque, un-imaginable'.

The ghost took form as the first object, the forgotten printout description of an SM session that Henry had planned to stage that was found by Lucey, who then followed her search to discover other objects that were part of the same story: the photos, film, list of websites. Added to these objects was a confrontation with Henry for an account of the story. Like the book that can be a weapon, a printed page too can destroy a life story, create a new one.

Lucey asked herself how she could not have seen this for so long and she reflected: 'He pays a strange woman semi-dressed in a kinky outfit to bondage, whip and torture him in a weird candle lit cave-like room. It's awful to know he gets pleasure from this! I know he has a very particular childhood story that could explain that but I cannot understand how an intelligent and sensitive man could get hooked into something like this.' On the other hand, Henry asked: 'How could she have discovered this so well-kept secret of a lifetime now?' Their world became entirely different, bewildering and tragic for both of them. He had never trusted Lucey enough to share with her any of his 'other' sexual activities.

Writing about secrets and lies, Carol Smart (2007) says that secrets and the creation of 'fiction' may be felt to be necessary for the preservation of relationships. In these cases, secrets matter more than truths. Of course, this echoes Tóibín's household, in which some deaths were significant enough not to be mentioned. How is it possible for a haunted life to exist without the ghosts? Well, it doesn't. The revelation of Henry's secret came about as an act of everyday forgetfulness of a piece of paper with written information on it. A Freudian slip? It was banal and yet life-changing. The secret was connected to a closeted sexual practice and to a specific contemporary development in information technology. The sexual practices engaged in by Henry were 'out of place' within the ethos of the marriage he had with Lucey. Yet, it was Lucey's choice about how to deal with the discovery of the object (the printout and the objects and events associated to it) that unsettled a way of living.

The haunting in the stories

In these two case studies, individual lives show events of wide social significance in relation to family, marriage, gender, motherhood and also prescriptive, alternative and resisted sexuality. What are the connections between these matters?

The confrontation of ghosts (the things that haunt personal and social life) requires a particular way of knowing and of making the known knowable. Gordon's (1997) proposition is to look at haunting as a generalizable social phenomenon. Haunting accounts not only for memory but also for the ways in which we interact and understand each other and ourselves. In her work, Gordon shows entire countries experiencing states of haunting: Argentina and the state terror that created the 'disappeared' and the United States' lingering inheritance of racial slavery. The materials that she uses include literary novels, photography, records and psychoanalytic and sociological theory. Ghosts (an apparition, a form, of something lost or barely visible that makes itself known or apparent to us [p.8]) disturb those bits of the past that haunt us, that undercut the narratives of the present.

Ghostly matters, argues Gordon (1997), are made marginal through the violence of modernity. The prevailing gender order and its attached prescribed sexuality are such matters. The impact of sexual prescriptions may be felt as the haunting of ghosts, both for what they 'tell' must be done and for what must not be done. What matters then is not the sexuality per se in these stories, but how the sexual comes to matter. How do things move out of the shadows and become visible? How can haunting show the ghost and how can this be perceived?

To address these questions another question matters. How do researchers and ghosts mediate? The researcher is part of the story. How am I haunted by the stories generated in/by my research encounters? Speaking to the ghosts, not for them, recognizes that the narrative passes through the mediation of the investigator. One way of speaking to this is by finding the ghost in the presence of its absence, measuring the silences (Spivak 1988; Van Wagenen 2004), taking account of the matters that are significant enough not to be mentioned, that are quietened by what is said, muted by the noise of other matters, and also tuning in with the noises.

The conventions of a sociological ethnographic investigation vary, and it is relevant to indicate here that my approach was based on relatively long-term involvement with both of these case studies. The relationship that I developed led to knowledge about the circumstances of the personal lives of those involved in the stories, gathered through a variety of methods, ranging from observations to individual interviews focused on life histories following a narrative-of-lives approach (Josselson and Lieblich 1993), attentive to psychosocial dimensions of the research relationship (Hollway and Jefferson 2000). At different times, I focused on different themes in my conversations with individuals. I also observed everyday life and domestic practices such as cooking, cleaning, childcare and leisure, biographies of particular household technologies (cookers, washing machines, dishwashers, computers, etc.) and invited people's descriptions of their relationships with these (Silva 2010, Appendix 1). Through this dense involvement with biographical and home lives of these people and the reading of notes, interview transcripts, reflections and analysis, things not anticipated emerged. What is there that was never there, never expected to appear? What was lost that seemed never to have existed? Gordon (1997) refers to the encounter with the unsought for as 'distractions'. Signs of these are repetitions that trouble. They appear like fiction, like making up social facts. In terms of method, it includes consideration of the paths that were disavowed, left behind, covered over and unseen. Above all, it includes a question about the fields in which fieldwork occurs.

When I saw that sexuality was revealed as relevant to my investigation, what could I do about it? Narrative themes of masculinity, femininity and motherhood were interwoven across individual accounts. Masculinity entered via many areas of life like the experiences of work, family roles, power in institutions and discourses, all of which acted as a frame for constructing sexuality and gender identity. Narratives related to femininity also included work, family matters, power, but frequently also motherhood, although not as an explicit concern. Motherhood was often unthought about, although in some cases, it strongly established women's credentials, providing them with an occupational identity, which was particularly relevant in the absence of realistic and satisfying alternatives of social roles, as shown by Rena's case. These themes seemed to emerge slowly to me in the various narratives. Rena's case was the tenth of the families in my study. When I heard her stories, they resonated with stories I had heard in other families, and I began to pay attention to sexual stories. Henry's family was the last case, the twenty-fourth in my study. It is a blown-out sexual story. Here the ghost had already been revealed to Henry and Lucey before being presented to me. Would I have been given knowledge of its existence had I not been sensitized to the theme? Would it have come my way had I not been prepared to engage with sexuality from ordinary links with technologies in the home? I can certainly say that I was not consciously seeking this story, or Rena's problematic engagements with motherhood. Surely, these were 'distractions'. But then, how could I interpret these stories and my encountering them? How can I know that my interpretation is 'right'?

With these questions, I make salient the theme of making humans talk. In the research process, I was producing answers through the framework of engagement with objects for housework, with machines in the everyday living of the person. Although diverse, the stories interwove personal biography and episodes of life together. Yet, the diversity of the stories that I found shows that accounts were not produced solely by my frameworks. The individual stories had similarities and complexities because people elaborated similar issues in different ways. The haunting of themes brought about in a salient individual narrative or the singularity of a personal story is nevertheless interactive and social.

The revelation of ghosts depends on a process of reception of what is, or was, repressed, hidden and invisible. As a container for these two stories, I had diverse interactive rapport. Although in the case of Rena the ghost pervaded the narrative, making its presence clear to me, it remained not fully known or named by her or those in her household. Troubled sexuality involved in her motherhood and mothering was addressed via complex bodily problems and the overuse and lack of care of machines. If in this case I saw the ghost haunting the story but did not reveal it as such, except for in my writing about it, in the case of Henry, the presence of the ghost was acknowledged and revealed to me while their conscious dealings with the haunting was in process.

A narrative of a story manufactures something that does not as yet exist, as, in the narrative, the real is fictionalized. The 'real story,' alleges Gordon (1997:44), is always a 'negotiated interruption ... with often times barely visible presence of several parties or things moving in and out ... of a kind of haunting'. To consider the ways in which sociology grapples with what personal and social life represses (haunting), to trace matters of relating with invisibilities in things, some other considerations about objects are needed.

Knowing matters with things: haunting as social

Rena's kitchen machines are objects with their intrinsic qualities (beyond projections) but also charged with emotion. The text of Henry's SM session is a piece of paper with ink, yet also of high psychic value. These emotions and value are articulated via the processes by which the objects/things are manifested in personal and social life.

The frameworks of Pierre Bourdieu and Bruno Latour can shed some light on this process of social manifestation. They deal with the idea of the thing/object in very different ways. Their approaches share the desire to make visible what is hard to pin down: those relationships that concern complex, messy, hidden and heterogeneous realities. They also share a concern with how particular practices of social scientists shape the social as part of their explorations of the ways in which 'intellectual technologies' (documents, writings, charts, files, paper clips, maps and organizational devices) are used. They work predominantly in different 'fields': Bourdieu on the production and appreciation of aesthetics (the consumption of art, literature and taste as marks of social distinction) and Latour on the production of science and technology (engineering and the laboratory). However, the field of my investigation here is home life. This is part of everyday social life and is full of objects.

As Bourdieu and Latour grapple with ways of discussing the relationship between things and people, the concern about how things and humans 'talk' is revealed as important. Humans speak. But the disjuncture between certain kinds of lives and language, or the fit of experience with certain contexts of talk or vocabulary, often requires translation. Linguistic incongruence is found in matters of gender, class, ethnicity, nationality and in the very process of listening to talk (DeVault 1990). Humans speak in ways limited to hierarchies of social position, by loud and muted sounds, through bodily gestures and emotions. The complexity of human communication also means that talking plus listening does not directly result in understanding. The problem is increased for researchers because the invisible structures that organize talk in research situations often derive from different social spaces, the hierarchical marks of the academic space being notably present in the capturing of talk (Silva and Wright 2005). Objects actively engage with humans and social worlds, and we could say that they 'speak' when they are created, that their 'talk' is often disclosed in studies of design and innovations, and that they also 'speak' when not taken for granted and brought out of the 'seamless web' of which they often become a part, in particular when they unsettle.

I am intrigued by the haunting of Rena's body in the stories of acquisition, use and mainte- nance of her household technologies, how becoming a mother made her incapable of dealing with housework and childcare demands, requiring more and more machines to aid with the work, machines that, overused and not looked after, participated in the disorganization of daily life and the senses of burdening always present in her narrative. I am equally intrigued by Henry's forgotten printout which opened the closet of his long and well-guarded secret, which was to change his personal life and the family arrangements he had invested in all his life. Whereas I see in the first case, strong continuity of a way of living, guaranteed by the presence and the workings (or not working) of the objects, in the second one, I see objects (printed sheet, photos, film, internet sites) inexorably transforming a life trajectory as they are inserted in life-changing events.

Bourdieu (1988) claims that theory, and therefore also research, is performative, because classifications make effective the perspective of the classifier, or of the researcher who classifies to bring about intelligible patterns and relationships. I am classifying as 'stable' the objects that sustain Rena's everyday live and as 'changing' the ones associated to Henry's story. For Latour, the apprehension of reality is made by 'following the actor' and thus drawing networks of connections. My practice of following the ghosts is mirrored here. Yet, a basic difference in Bourdieu's and Labour's approaches derived from choices of classification becomes evident.

Latour, expounding the actor-network-theory (ANT) approach, seeks to describe the operations of technologies and individuals and the ways in which they connect. The tendency is to put everything on the same plane level and notice the way that they work. What counts is what is said, as a fact, and the way of saying it. Bourdieu engages with a different empirical project, seeking to analyse how things work. What is said is not taken at face value. He searches for deep underlying meanings, uses, functions and origins of what is said and done, seeking to unravel how the vision of the social relates to the division of the social world. Whereas for Latour, echoing Foucault, all relations, including those between humans and objects, are relations of power (expressed in capacity and effectiveness) and reality is a social construction (a textual creation with no objective life), Bourdieu contends that power (expressed in hierarchy and domination) is specific to context, where realities of structures and dispositions prevail.

Both Latour and Bourdieu recognize that a series of interlocking microcosms exist, which, speaking in Bourdieusian language, have relational positions and associated effects of positioning. Latour's proposition is helpful in seeking to associate these by tracing connections through descriptions. In my view, this is complemented by Bourdieu's notion of hierarchical power, which counters the flatness of ANT's view of social relations, allowing the associations between humans, and between humans and objects, to be traced in a more stratified and differentiated view of social reality, restoring human primacy. After all, even though things make humans do things, and also stand for humans,[2] humans act with things in a world of things/objects that is made by humans.

How can we discover the ways in which the social and the material are entangled together and speak to each other? Even if we emphasize the agency of matter, or the social life of things (Appadurai 1986), it is the storyline that counts. There is no opposition between the factual presence of an object in a story and the account of its felt presence. Objects become active only as they become embedded in a narrative (Harre 2002). It follows that for Latour, objects that do not move or are 'mute' do not count. In the same way, for Bourdieu, things that are not classified are 'out of place'. For both, agents become part of a story through movement. However, movements are in themselves a product of selection. In this dense formulation, where is the ghost to be found? Drawing from Gordon's account, is the ghost in the 'mute' or 'out of place' state, haunting because it is undisclosed?

Researching the haunting: unsettling objects

Stability and permanence are both viewed through the prism of movement. My purpose to investigate the haunting in the material of homes has been to move things out of the shadow to let light shine on them.

The whole process of investigation reflected about in this chapter is centred on generating knowledge through an exploration of objects: relations between people and between people and objects. In Rena's story, objects are entangled in a way of living: they are potently 'mute', yet they are agentic, enabling, performing the needed disorganization that marks her life. Although the machines are brought in with an explicit purpose to assist with an ordered life in which utensils are cleaned, clothes are washed, the physical demands on the body are saved and so on, these same machines enable, through their particular insertion in the ordering of the home practices, the event of a known 'disorganized' lifestyle. Ultimately, these objects change nothing. However, in Henry's story, objects are a crucial life-changing instrument, crying out because of their out-of-placeness in the home lifestyle built around a partnership that made the practices revealed strange and intolerable.

In the two stories, objects were devices in everyday life events and in the narratives of lives. For Rena, the materiality of the 'muted' objects haunted the continuing noise of a theme of sexual role discomfort: housewifery and motherhood lived as burden. The objects acted to settle her way of living. For Henry, objects transformed everything, unsettling a narrative pattern with the creation of life-changing events.

In both movement and stability, the knowledge invested in by the researcher emerged only through a relationship with the unsettling: the ghosts have to move in order to be seen, although movement is not a guarantee of visibility. The ghosts appear to have remained invisible to Rena, still haunting her household, although they were manifest to me. However, the social ghost shown by her case was, like in the case of Henry, fully illuminated as a sociological matter. Frameworks to shed light on ghosts need further development for haunting to be tackled as a socially significant matter with an important place in methodological practice and social theory.

Acknowledgements

I'd like to thank my colleagues editing this volume for engaged comments to earlier versions of this chapter and, in particular, Nick Thoburn.

Notes

1 For an account of these main debates see Silva 2010, Chapter 1.
2 Prominent view of this is found in the British Object Relations School of Psychoanalysis.

Bibliography

Appadurai, A. (1986) 'Introduction: Commodities and the Politics of Value' in Appadurai, A. (ed.) *The Social Life of Things*, Cambridge: Cambridge University Press.
Bourdieu, P. (1988) *Homo Academicus*, Cambridge: Polity.
Bourdieu, P. (1992) *The Logic of Practice*, Cambridge: Polity.
Bourdieu, P. (2004) *Science of Science and Reflexivity*, Cambridge: Polity.
DeVault, M.L. (1990) 'Talking and Listening from Women's Standpoint: Feminist Strategies for Interviewing and Analysis', *Social Problems*, 37: 96–116.
Gordon, A.F. (1997) *Ghostly Matters. Haunting and the Sociological Imagination*, Minneapolis: University of Minnesota Press.
Harre, R. (2002) 'Material Objects in Social Worlds', *Theory, Culture and Society*, 19(5/6): 23–33.
Hollway, W. and Jefferson, T. (2000) *Doing Qualitative Research Differently*, London: Sage.
Josselson, R. and Lieblich, A. (eds) (1993) *The Narrative Study of Lives*, London: Sage.
Latour, B. (2005) *Reassembling the Social. An Introduction to Actor-Network Theory*, Oxford: Oxford University Press.
Silva, E.B. (2010) *Technology, Culture, Family: Influences on Home Life*, Basingstoke: Palgrave.

Silva, E.B. and Wright, D. (2005) 'The judgement of taste and social position in focus group research', *Sociologia e Ricerca Sociale*, Special double issue, 76/77: 241–253. Milan: Angeli. Also on: http://www.open. ac.uk/socialsciences/includes/__cms/download.php?file=w4lkl1zo6ef8h2c0b0.pdf&name=judgement_ of_taste_and_social_position_in_focus_group_research.pdf (accessed 19 August 2009).

Smart, C. (2007) *Personal Life*, Cambridge: Polity.

Spivak, G. (1988) 'Can the Subaltern speak?' in Nelson, C. and Grossberg, L. (eds) *Marxism and the Interpretation of Culture*, Urbana: University of Illinois Press.

Tóibín, C. (2012) 'Ghosts in the room', *The Guardian*, Review, 18 February: 2–4.

Van Wagenen, A. (2004) 'An Epistemology of Haunting: A Review Essay', *Critical Sociology*, 30(2): 287–298.

17

The fetish of connectivity

Morten Axel Pedersen

Introduction

When a person uses pen and paper to give form to his ideas, this 'can be understood as quite literally extending the machinery of mind out into the world ... that are themselves minimal material bases for important aspects of human thought and reason' (Clark 2008: xxvi). This is what Andy Clark writes in *Supersizing the Mind*, his recent work on the 'extended mind' thesis, which he formulated with fellow philosopher David Chalmers more than a decade ago (1998). For Clark and Chalmers and other proponents of an 'externalist' model of human cognition, much thinking amounts to an 'embodied' or 'distributed' mental process in which the human mind-brain is 'augmented' by material artefacts or 'cognitive scaffolds', like notebooks, mnemonic tools and religious talismans (see Clark and Chalmers 1998; Clark 2008; Hutchins 1995; Mithen 1996; Day 2004).

Some years ago, this model of human cognition inspired me to write a paper on 'Shamanist Ontologies and Extended Cognition in Northern Mongolia' for the volume *Thinking Through Things* (2007). My aims were interdisciplinary: I wanted to explore what seemed like an obvious theoretical connection between, on the one hand, the aforementioned writings on distributed cognition and, on the other, the anthropological literature on 'distributed person' in Melanesia and beyond (Strathern 1988; Wagner 1991; Gell 1998). After all, as Clark (2008: xiv) notes in a recent paper, it 'is natural to ask whether the extended mind thesis might itself be extended. What about extended desires, extended reasoning, extended perception, extended imagination, and extended emotions?' 'Talismans of Thought', as my article is called, was an attempt to argue in support of such a double extension of what might count as a 'distributed mind' in a given cultural context. Apart from showing how certain Mongolian shamanic artefacts provide crucial 'external cognitive scaffolding' that renders 'religious cognition computationally [p]ossible' (Day 2004: 113), I also wanted to show how these talismans allow for people to be constituted as specific kinds of persons through these things. People, I thus concluded, 'are not only thinking through things. They also come to be through them' (Pedersen 2007: 162).

However, this begs a question or indeed set of questions (of the sort that tend to come up with a few years of hindsight). For what happens in those situations in which people do *not* want to think through things? Surely, there are people out there in the world who do not want their thoughts extended to things, and who spend a lot of energy avoiding their minds becoming distributed into the world. Further, even when artefacts are being used in religious practices, as is the case in many animist or shamanic contexts around the world, this is not always done simply with a view to enhancing peoples' obligations towards, or enhancing their beliefs in, spiritual phenomena, but also in order to reduce their attachment to them.

The fact that these kinds of questions are not high on the agenda of extended mind scholars suggests that they, like many social scientists, have fallen victim to what might be called the 'fetish of connectivity'. The title of Clark's latest book is telling in this respect. For if the use of certain artefacts is posited to be all about 'supersizing the mind' and therein 'give human cognition its distinctive power, character, and charm' (Clark 2008: 108), then it appears to be given beforehand that connections must be inherently Good Things: that the more the mind can extend itself into the world (without losing its integrated nature, including basic trust in its various tools of thinking), the better it is. My aim in this chapter is to 'challenge the interpretive possibility of limitlessness' (Strathern 1996: 531) that underwrites this fetish of connectivity. While many phenomenologists focus on practices that bring the cosmos into closer proximity with itself by facilitating ever less distance between subjects and objects, and ever more closeness between subjects, my aim in this chapter is to explore creative cuts that expose dormant cracks in the fabric of worlds by triggering capacities within persons and things for self-differentiation. Could it be that, by critically examining the fondness for connections and closeness that seem to be shared by so many phenomenologists, externalists and other students of relatedness, a new 'post-relational' theoretical space could be laid bare? (Pedersen 2012).

Based on a revisit to my ethnography on Northern Mongolian shamanism, I begin by showing that the magical gown worn by shamans while possessed by their spirit performs a 'labour of division' that curtails the same spirit's capacity for influencing both shamans and their clients outside ritual contexts. I then turn to the more specific question of 'creative cutting' by showing how, in practices of wood chopping and other seemingly violent acts of material detachment, the world becomes relationally reorchestrated in particular ways. In doing so, I critically examine the relational ontology upon which 'the fetish of connectivity' rests and, in the same process, also sketch the contours of a theoretical alternative.

Shamanism without shamans

The Darhads, who numbered 21,558 individuals according to the 2010 national survey, are a Mongolian-speaking group of pastoralists, hunters and village dwellers who inhabit the far northwestern corner of Mongolia's Hövsgöl Province, in what is a highly remote, mountainous and forested region situated 1,000 km away from the national capital of Ulaanbaatar and 200 km away from the provincial capital, Mörön. The Darhads originate from a mixture of clan groupings, only some of whom were Mongolian in cultural and linguistic terms, whereas the rest were Tuvinian, Turkic and Tungus of origin (Badamhatan 1986: 24–25, 41–63; Sandschejew 1930). Today, these clans (*ovog*, *yas*) are largely defunct in sociological and economical terms, although people still make reference to them, particularly in the context of possession rites and other shamanic contexts, as I describe below.

It is no coincidence that Shishged Valley is the only region in Mongolia where Darhads are in a majority. For a period of nearly two hundred years, and possibly longer, the Shishged region constituted the main territory of the Darhad Ih Shav', a Buddhist ecclesiastical estate belonging to the office of the Jebtsundamba Khutuktu, the leading reincarnation (or 'Living Buddha') of prerevolutionary Mongolia's Lamaist church (Badamhatan 1986: 24–26; Bawden 1986: 68–80). It was the workings of this estate that rendered the Darhads into an ethnic group of ecclesiastical subjects (*shabinar*) corresponding to a specific territory of land, and it was this ecclesiastical estate that served to firmly establish the Buddhist religion in the Shishged region (Pedersen 2011: 115–147). Thus, in addition to the 'submission of the shamanic institution to clan law' (Hamayon 1994: 83), Darhad shamans were also made subject to the 'Buddhist laws' of an ecclesiastical estate. This did not happen without a fight. Darhad lore is full of narratives about the conflicts between Buddhist lamas and local shamans (*böö*). Although the Buddhist church never succeeded in annihilating shamanism from Darhad traditions (as in many places elsewhere in Mongolia [Heissig 1980; Humphrey 1994]), the presence of pre-socialist Mongolia's biggest Buddhist ecclesiastical estate in the Shishged did have the effect of 'pushing' the shamans and their objects of worship further towards and into the *taiga*. Thus, the genius loci of most Darhad shamanic spirits (*ongod*) are today found in or around the edge of the *taiga*, whereas, on the other hand, its flat steppe zone is dominated by Buddhist (or Buddhist-influenced) spiritual entities, such as mountain spirits (*gazryn ezed*).

After Mongolia's communist-led revolution in 1921, and the death of the eighth and last Jebtsundamba Khutuktu in 1924, the Shishged region was made subject to a series of socialist reforms that steadily undermined the position of the Buddhist church. In 1938, as part of the communists' final showdown with the Buddhist church, the Shishged region's monasteries were demolished, and the monks (*lamas*) were killed, imprisoned or otherwise immobilized. Darhad shamanism fared marginally better during socialism. Of course, like the other occult specialists who were active in those years, the shamans were forced to practise outside official contexts to avoid political repercussions from the authorities, repercussions that could range from public denouncement over the loss of social rights (like access to high school or university for one's

Figure 17.1 Shaman Tree (*böögiin mod*), site of *ongod* worship. Photograph by Morten Axel Pedersen

children) to, in the more extreme instances, imprisonment or even (in the 1930s) execution. Still, shamanic ceremonies were performed 'in secret' (*nuutgai*) throughout the period, just as shamans were consulted for divinatory and other purposes that did not require full-blown rituals in which the shaman is possessed by shamanic spirits (Pedersen 2011: 108–112).

From 1956 and onwards, the Shishged's population was offered 'voluntary' membership of two newly established collective farms (*negdel*) (and, from 1985, a state farm as well), and these socialist institutions eventually came to organize practically all aspects of political and economical life. In 1989–90, with the collapse of state socialism, and with the subsequent introduction of a market economy and various democratic reforms, the institutional framework of Mongolia's planned economy was wiped away (Bruun and Odgaard 1996; Rossabi 2005). During the early 1990s, most livestock and other collective assets from the former *negdels* were privatized and, faced with a nationwide economic crisis and a rapidly deteriorating infrastructure, most Darhad households reverted to a substance economy based on nomadic pastoralism as well as a variety of supplementary economic activities, such as hunting and berry foraging (Pedersen 2011: 20–29).

Darhad shamanism has been a topic of significant scholarship since the early twentieth century (Badamhatan 1986: 157–94; Dulam 1992; Diószegi 1961, 1963; Pürev 1999; Sandschejew 1930: 41–65). I was therefore more than a little disappointed, when I first began fieldwork in Northern Mongolia in the late 1990s, to hear people telling me that there were hardly any 'genuine Darhad shamans' (*jinhene Darhad böö*) left. Instead, as I was eventually to learn, the seminomadic community in which I conducted my fieldwork was full of 'half shamans' (*hagas böö*): a distinctly post-socialist cohort of men and women in their thirties, who, because of a shortage of shaman teachers (*böö bagch*) caused by several generations of repressive state socialism, were stuck in the process of becoming shamans for lack of the necessary esoteric knowledge and sacred objects to complete their metamorphosis.

The problem about these potential shamans, as one might refer to them, was that their presence was perceived to signal a more general occult awakening in the community, whereby shamanic spirits, which had largely left people alone during the state socialist era, had increasingly begun interfering in peoples' lives with the advent of liberal democracy and the 'age of the market' (*zah zeeliin üye*). Thus, people found themselves in the paradoxical situation in which, at the same time as the shamans had largely disappeared, the spirits had come back. Above all, it was the annoying and dangerous abundance of potential shamans in the community that sparked the fear that too many shamanic spirits were on the loose, and that too little knowledge and skill were available to rein in this occult excess.

In fact, as I describe in more detail in my recent monograph *Not Quite Shamans* (Pedersen 2011), if there was one common thing that was on peoples' minds all over Northern Mongolia in the late 1990s, it was how to establish a safe distance between themselves and the omnipresent spirits. With the advent of transition, people found themselves exposed to a violent intrusion of invisible spirit souls, energies and forces, which, for seventy years of socialism, had hovered only in the shadowy margins of self, household, community and nation (2011: 47–53). As one Darhad man told me, it was as if all sorts of uninvited guests crashed the gates of the household's *hashaa* (compound), forcing him and his family to engage with all sorts of spiritual entities that he had never quite believed (*itgeh*) in, let alone shown any real interest in knowing (*medeh*) about.

Far from trying to establish more connections with the shamanic spirits, my Darhad Mongolian interlocutors seemed more concerned about how to best avoid them. For it was only by identifying ways of cutting, curtailing and severing a perceived overabundance of spiritual connections (as opposed to celebrating an imagined treasure of spiritual relatedness) that the relentless flow of spirit metamorphoses and shamanic affects (including worries about the presence of spirits) could be slowed down and, perhaps, managed. Yet, the paradox was that the people who alone were considered to be able to fulfil this role (namely the shamans) were not present in the community any more.

The labour of division

All this begs a question: how do the 'genuine shamans' (a handful of whom could be found in a neighbouring community 100 km to the north of my main field site) go about managing the spirits? What methods of spiritual detachment did they master that the not-so-genuine shamans lacked? As I also argued in my 2007 paper, the shamanic costume (*böö huvtsas*, also known as *huyag*, meaning 'armour') and the associated sacred paraphernalia are of crucial importance here.

In fact, possession of a shamanic costume always seems to have served as a key marker of authenticity and efficacy for Darhad shamans. During the heyday of Darhad shamanism around the late nineteenth and early twentieth centuries, the shamanic costume apparently represented a material proof of clans' acceptance of their shamans. The consecration rite of new shamans was considered vital for the continual well-being of the clan; the cost of the initiation (as well as the costume) was also incurred collectively by the clan members (Sandschejew 1930: 35, 50–57; Badamhatan 1986: 185–86; Pegg 2001: 130–37). Although the clans have stopped playing a central role in the social reproduction of Darhad communities, as also reflected in the composition of audiences at séances (who tend to come from all areas and segments of Mongolian society), it is still the norm that shamans receive their gowns and other sacra from members of local ritual communities, whether bilateral kin networks or non-cognate shaman teachers (Pedersen 2011: 150–156).

However, possession of a gown is not only a material sign of the ritual's community's acceptance of the shaman. It is also what enables the shaman to fully master the spirits by curtailing the shaman's relationship with them to a restricted set of ritual sequences. As her indispensable 'armour,' the gown protects the shaman by 'absorbing' (*shingeh*) the 'souls' (*süns*) of both people and spirits into its many bundles and 'layers' (*salbagar*), so that they do not 'pierce' (*tsoolnoh*) her body too deeply. At the same time, donning the gown also exposes the shaman to the potentially lethal risk of becoming lost in the world of the sprits and never returning to the world of humans. Unlike the ordinary gown (*deel*), which protectively encloses its wearer with a minimum of openings (Lacaze 2000), the gown (which is not worn with the otherwise ubiquitous sash [*büs*], and from whose baggy exterior multiple cotton knots, strings and flaps point in all directions) is a sort of hypersurface, which, far from patrolling the boundaries of the shaman, invites maximum intervention on her body.

In that sense, the attire donned by the Darhad shaman during possession rituals simultaneously invites and exorcises spiritual attention. For although it is true that the shaman is made able to enter the realm of the spirits by donning the gown (which is what the literature on shamanism usually focuses on), it is also true that she, ipso facto, also becomes able *not to see* the spirits (and not to be seen by them) by taking it off. This ability opposes to that of the 'half-shamans' who, for lack of ways of blocking the paths (*güidel*) of the spirits, are exposed to them all the time, without being able to see them, let alone control them (Pedersen 2011: 176–180).

Yet, make no mistake: this does not make the spirits less important in Darhad lives. In fact, the spirits seem to be made stronger, more durable and more distinctive because of the attempts by

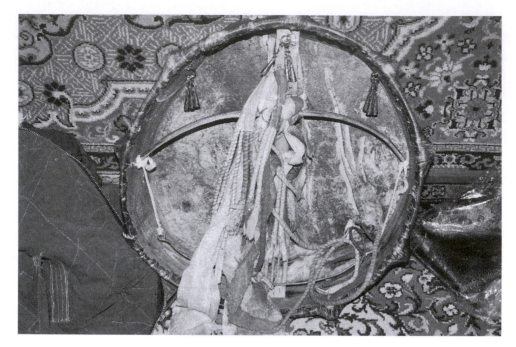

Figure 17.2 Shamanic drum with characteristic 'bundle' of ceremonial silk scarfs (*hadag*) attached. Photograph by Morten Axel Pedersen

shamans and others to detach them. After all, were the shamanic cosmos not to be continually bounded off, the spirits might become half-spirits like the wannabe shamans without costumes, who are doomed to remain in a permanent state of metamorphosis. Instead of constituting durable entities with known origins and distinct names and personalities, like proper spirits are supposed to (Humphrey 1996), for lack of magical calibration tools to apportion optimal distances between human and nonhuman worlds, the spirits might turn into ghosts (*üheer*): ephemeral quasibeings too amorphous to even deserve a name. That is to say, the spirits *need to be* detached from the shamans to remain intact.

On this analysis, connections (and more generally, relations) are not always considered good things (as in most work on distributed cognition, my own included), but are also annoying, bad or even downright dangerous. Indeed, in many places across the world, ranging from Melanesia over Mongolia to the Amazon, relations are conceived of an immanent feature of the world, as the stuff that everything is made of (Wagner 1981, 1986; Strathern 1988, 2004; Viveiros de Castro 1998; Pedersen 2011; Empson 2011; Holbraad 2012). Whereas many anthropological studies of 'relatedness' have focused on practices that, so to speak, bring the world into ever more proximity with itself by collapsing ever more distances between persons, or between persons and things, these studies have instead highlighted practices that trigger latent potentials in persons and things for self-differentiation. Here, the cutting of connections is understood, not as a way of doing away with relations, but as a technique of doing something with relations by turning persons, things and worlds into something different from what they were before. In this sense, the recent focus on 'relations that separate' (Strathern 1988) within anthropology amounts to a *widening* of the concept of the relation to encompass also engagements (like antagonisms and conflicts), which cannot meaningfully be described as connections, and certainly not in the fetishized sense criticized in the introduction to this article (see also Pedersen 2012).

Once again, it should be emphasized that I do not mean to say that this cutting of connections is 'less relational' than the seemingly more peaceful art of making connections. What it does mean is that we as ethnographers need to take seriously that the world is full of people who are making a 'social quality of engaged separation' (Stasch 2003: 325; see also Candea 2010), and who, for this reason, invest a considerable amount of energy into what might, to coin a term, be called the labour of division. Thus understood, the costume worn by the Darhad shamans does not reduce the world into a less complex place. Rather, such artefacts are fine-grained relational tools applied to the cosmos to redistribute its complexities and its uncertainties along specific trajectories of change and transformation, which ideally serve the interest of the shaman as well as her clients.

Creative cutting

Let us now try to theorize further 'what the "labour of division" does'. To begin with, it may be noted that in Mongolian shamanism (as indeed in many Amerindian shamanic traditions [Turner 2009; Viveiros de Castro 2007]), the forms of things are considered to be alive, to *be* rather than to *have* force; namely, the occult capacity to compel the cosmos to orchestrate itself in a particular manner. Thus, shamanic forms are not mental schema through which some structure of order or meaning is imposed on an empty container of social and material content, but immanent features of the cosmos itself, which must be continually reapportioned for it to assume its right shape, and for human and nonhuman lives to unfold at a suitable pace (Willerslev and Pedersen 2010; Pedersen 2011).

But, if forms are not about the imposition of shape on shapeless matter, what then is the nature of creativity: how are new things brought about? It is here relevant to consider Tim Ingold's (2007) work on lines and associated practices like drawing and writing, in which he offers an alternative to recent theories of networks. The problem with the network imaginaries of scholars like Latour, Ingold suggests, is that the nature of lines is presented as a 'join[ing of] dots. They are connectors. However, the lines [I study] form a meshwork of interwoven trails rather than a network of intersecting routes ... *along* which life is lived' (2007: 81). For the same reason, Ingold (2010: 92) convincingly argues, creativity is not about imposing 'preconceived forms on inert matter [but about] intervening in the fields of force and currents of material wherein forms are generated'. Ingold himself offers an illustrative example of what such a cocreation of new forms out of other forms might involve, namely the skill of the seasoned woodsman, who,

> ... brings down the axe so that its blade enters the grain and follows a line already incorporated into the timber through its previous history of growth, when it was part of a living tree. The carpenter is 'one who fashions' (Sanskrit, *taksati*) ... not [through the] imposi[tion] of form on pliant substance but the slicing and binding of fibrous material.
>
> *(Ingold 2010: 92)*

This is a compelling phenomenology of the creativity of (wood)cutting. Indeed, when reading Ingold, one is left with the impression of a seasoned woodsman; of someone who is himself very familiar with the skilled material practice of 'reading creativity forwards' in a 'generative movement that is at once itinerant, improvisatory and rhythmic' (Ingold 2010). But what about those people of whom the world has more than its share: people like myself and a few (mostly female) of my informants who know how to prepare firewood without chopping their fingers off, but who have little or no capacity for carpentry proper? Presumably, what such persons do also amounts to a certain kind of skilled woodsmanship, namely the creation of new forms through acts of chopping and splitting.

Figure 17.3   Preparing firewood for the winter. Yaks and *sarlag* (cow and yak crossbreed) are being used to transport logs from the forest to the village. Photograph by Morten Axel Pedersen

Not surprisingly, people spend a lot of time preparing firewood in Northern Mongolia, and they are very good at it. Yet, the many cold afternoons that I spent with the male members of my host household splitting wood at their winter residence was never about 'slicing and binding of fibrous material' into new shapes, like the recognized woodsmen (*modchin*) were recognized to do. Rather, the skill of splitting firewood involved using our hands and our eyes to locate the best cracks in the surface and gaps in the texture of the wood at which we could apply our skill of chopping. The same can be said for many other Darhads. They are undoubtedly skilled woodsmen; yet, for most of them, this skill does not involve connecting wood together to bind it into new forms, but in revealing hidden fissures buried within the firewood itself. In that sense, the skill of creative cutting may be said to involve the ability 'to go through the crack' (Deleuze 1990) to expose otherwise hidden fault lines within the texture of things by eliciting, exposing and expanding gaps and voids that are, so to speak, part of the world as such.

In many ways, this point is already anticipated in Ingold's theory about creativity as the elicitation of forms and lines of flight that are already immanent to the world's ongoing autocreation. The one thing that my focus on creative cutting as a distinct variety of what I have called the labour of division might add to Ingold's argument is my idea that 'crude' and 'violent' practices of cutting amount to a distinct mode of creativity, also without any accompanying 'binding'. There is, I suggest, an entire dimension of forgotten form-making waiting to be explored by anthropologists: the dark side of creativity. This largely ignored 'kind of creativity' (Leach 2004) comprises those skilled practices that involve detaching connections through different forms of cutting, as opposed to affirming connections through different forms of binding. Thus, creative cutting – no matter whether it involves the esoteric art of cutting the shamanic spirits down to size (but without for that reason severing all relation to them) or the rather mundane skill of chopping tree logs into manageable lumps of firewood – may be defined as the fundamentally transformational and creative process of cracking open hidden fissures buried deep inside the interiority of things, which are, so to speak, patiently waiting to be brought out in the open by the gifted relational cutter.

Returning now to the dual role performed by the Darhad shamanic gown by simultaneously inviting and exorcising spiritual attention, I suggest that this ongoing calibration of spiritual relatedness may be conceptualized as a form of creative cutting: essentially, the shaman's gown works like an occult axe that chops, cuts and slices the shamanic cosmos into a 'pile' or 'heap' of ontologically distinct 'logs' of spirits. To substantiate this point, it is relevant to consider the work of the feminist posthumanist philosopher Karen Barad, notably her concept of 'intra-action':

> The notion of intra-action (in contrast to the usual 'interaction,' which presumes the prior existence of independent entities/relata) represents a profound conceptual shift. … A specific intra-action (involving a specific material configuration …) enacts an agential cut (in contrast to the Cartesian cut — an inherent distinction — between subject and object) effecting a separation between 'subject' and 'object.' … In other words, relata do not preexist relations; rather, relata-within-phenomena emerge through specific intra-actions. Crucially then, intra-actions enact agential separability — the local condition of exteriority-within-phenomena.
>
> *(Barad 2003: 815; emphases omitted)*

With Barad's concept of 'intra-action' in mind, we may think of Darhad Mongolian shamanic artefacts as 'intrafaces'. Unlike the more well-known *inter*faces, which serve to bring things into closer contact with one another by establishing a bridge between realms that would otherwise be less connected (or perhaps not be connected at all), *intra*faces like the shamanic gown work by outstretching things and realms that might otherwise become too close (if not collapse into one). In that sense, the shamanic gown emerges as a technology of optimal (dis)connection, which helps to maintain a necessary and strategic distance between people and otherwise omnipresent but invisible spirit entities (cf. Willerslev and Pedersen 2010). Because the spirits are always already (virtually) 'related' to people before they even meet them in the form of an immanent potential for misfortune and luck, my Darhad interlocutors (and the shamans in particular) were constantly striving to identify procedures for keeping this otherwise infinite totality of potential spiritual relatedness at bay. Thus, in Northern Mongolia, shamans' talismans are used, not only as magical interfaces that serve to expand the power and the reach of the shamanic spirits, but also as magical 'intrafaces' that serve to cut the spirits down to a manageable size and reach.

Conclusion

What I have argued in this chapter flies in the face of the fetish of connectivity and its insistence on the moral, epistemological and ontological superiority of closeness and connections in human and nonhuman lives. Still, in making my case against the fetish of connectivity, I have not meant to say that relational complexity is in any sense being reduced in processes of cutting connections. Far from being a way of making the world a simpler, less relational place, the cutting of connections is, or can be, a subtle art, which makes the world complex in new and sometimes surprising ways. Thus, as we have seen, there are many different kinds of relations to be found, and still more ways of doing and accomplishing things by means of them and their transformation, one of which is the material practice that I have referred to as creative cutting. Clearly, in order to study ethnographically such practices of intra-active cutting or engaged detachment, anthropology needs to engage in what might be called a phenomenology of distance: a return to the *other* side of things as they are.

Although it is undeniably the case that Mongolia's shamanic talismans are sort of 'cognitive scaffolds' that help people to entertain religious ideas that they would otherwise not be able to think (or at least find it highly difficult to think [cf. Day 2004; Pedersen 2007]), it is also true that these artefacts are imbued with the obverse capacity of aiding people *not* to think about the spirits all the time. As well as 'supersizing the mind' (Clark 2008), by extending peoples' cognitive apparatus, one could argue that the shamanic gown curtails the reach of shamanic thoughts by 'downsizing' peoples' minds. In fact, might this be the role, or one of the roles, of many religious talismans across the world? Rather than being instruments for connecting with occult realms that are otherwise too distant, magical objects might in many situations serve as cutting tools by which optimal distances are calibrated between humans and nonhuman intrafaces. This certainly is the case with the magical paraphernalia used by Darhad shamans, which, in addition to being talismans of thought (as I argued in my 2007 paper), are also talismans by which the spirits cannot be thought. Unthinking things, as it were.

Acknowledgements

I thank the organizers of and the participants in the Centre for Research on Socio-Cultural Change workshop 'Materialising the Subject: phenomenological and post-ANT objects in the social sciences' held at the Manchester Museum, 26–27 February 2009. In particular, I am grateful to my two co-panellists, Tim Ingold and Christina Toren, as well as the editors of this volume, especially Elizabeth Silva, for their challenging comments and questions about my chapter.

Bibliography

Badamhatan, S. (1986) Les chamanistes du Bouddha vivant. *Études Mongoles … et sibériennes* 17.

Barad, K. (2003) Posthumanist Performativity: Toward an Understanding of How Matter Comes to Matter. *Signs* 28(3): 801–823.

Bawden, C. R. (1986) *The Modern History of Mongolia*, London: Kegan Paul International.

Bruun, O. and Odgaard, O. (eds) (1996) *Mongolia in Transition – Old Patterns, New Challenges*, Surrey: Curzon.

Candea, M. (2010) 'I fell in love with Carlos the meerkat': Engagement and Detachment in Human–Animal Relations. *American Ethnologist* 37(2): 241–258.

Clark, A. (2008) *Supersizing the Mind. Embodiment, Action, and Cognitive Extension*, Oxford: Oxford University Press.

Clark, A. and Chalmers, D. J. (1998) The Extended Mind. *Analysis* 58, pp. 10–23.

Day, M. (2004) Religion, Off-line Cognition and the Extended Mind. *Journal of Cognition and Culture* 4(1): 101–121.

Deleuze, G. (1990) *The Logic of Sense*, London: Continuum.

Deleuze, G. (1994) *Difference and Repetition*, London: Athlone.

Diószegi, L. (1961) Problems of Mongolian Shamanism. *Acta Ethnographica* 10(1–2): 195–206.

—— (1963) Ethnogenic Aspects of Darkhat Shamanism. *Acta Orientalia Hungaria* 16: 55–81.

Dulam, S. (1992) *Darhad böögiin ulamjlal*, Ulaanbaatar: MUIS-iin Hevlel.

Empson, R. (2011) *Harnessing Fortune: Personhood, Memory, and Place in Northeast Mongolia*, Oxford: Oxford University Press.

Gell, A. (1998) *Art and Agency. An Anthropological Theory*, Oxford: Clarendon Press.

Hamayon, R. (1994) Shamanism in Siberia: From Partnership in Supernature to Counter-power in Society. In *Shamanism, History, and the State*, edited by N. Thomas and C. Humphrey, 76–89, Ann Arbor: The University of Michigan Press.

Heissig, W. (1980) *The Religions of Mongolia*, London: Routledge and Kegan Paul.

Holbraad, M. (2012) *Truth in Motion: The Recursive Anthropology of Cuban Divination*, Chicago: University of Chicago Press.

Humphrey, C. (1994) Shamanic Practices and the State in Northern Asia: Views from the centre and periphery. In *Shamanism, History and the State*, edited by N. Thomas and C. Humphrey, 191–228, Ann Arbor: University of Michigan Press.

Humphrey, C. with Onon, U. (1996) *Shamans and Elders. Experience, Knowledge, and Power among the Daur Mongols*, Oxford: Clarendon Press.

Hutchins, E. (1995) *Cognition in the Wild*, Cambridge MA: MIT Press.

Ingold, T. (2007) *Lines. A Brief History*, London: Routledge.

Ingold, T. (2010) The Textility of Making. *Cambridge Journal of Economics* 34: 91–102.

Lacaze, G. (2000) *Représentations et Techniques du Corps chez les Peuples Mongols*. PhD Thesis, Université de Paris-X.

Leach, J. (2004) Two Kinds of Creativity. In E. Hirsch and M. Strathern, eds. *Transactions and Creations. Property Debates and the Stimulus of Melanesia*, Berghahn Books: New York.

Mithen, S. (1996) *The Prehistory of the Mind: A Search for the Origins of Art, Religion and Science*, London: Thames and Hudson.

Pedersen, M. A. (2007) Talismans of Thought. Shamanic Ontology and Extended Cognition in Northern Mongolia. In *Thinking Through Things. Theorizing Artefacts Ethnographically*, edited by A. Henare, M. Holbraad and S. Wastell, 141–166, London: University College London Press.

Pedersen, M. A. (2011) *Not Quite Shamans. Spirit Worlds and Political Lives in Northern Mongolia*, Ithaca, NY: Cornell University Press.

Pedersen, M. A. (2012) The Task of Anthropology is to Invent Relations: For the Motion. *Critique of Anthropology* 32(1).

Pegg, C. (2001) *Mongolian Music, Dance, and Oral Narrative*, Seattle: University of Washington Press.

Pürev, O. (1999) *Mongol Böögiin Shashin*, Ulaanbaatar: The Mongolian Academy of Science.

Pürev, O. (2004) *Mongolian Shamanism*, Ulaanbaatar: Admon.

Rossabi, M. (2005) *Modern Mongolia: From Khans to Commissars to Capitalists*, Berkeley: University of California Press.

Sandschejew, G. D. (1930) *Darkhaty*, Leningrad: Akademiia nauk.

Stasch, R. (2003) Separateness as a Relation: The Iconicity, Univocality and Creativity of Korowai Mother-in-law Avoidance. *Journal of the Royal Anthropological Institute* 9: 317–337.

Stasch, R. (2009) *Society of Others. Kinship and Mourning in a West Papuan Place*, Berkeley: University of California Press.

Strathern, M. (1988) *The Gender of the Gift. Problems with Women and Problems with Society in Melanesia*, Berkeley: University of California Press.

Strathern, M. (1996) Cutting the Network. *Journal of the Royal Anthropological Institute (N.S.)* 2: 517–535.

Strathern, M. (2004) *Partial Connections* (Updated Edition), Walnut Creek, CA: AltaMira

Turner, T. (2009) The Crisis of Late Structuralism. Perspectivism and Animism: Rethinking Culture, Nature, Spirit, and Bodiliness. *Tipití: Journal of the Society for the Anthropology of Lowland South America* 7 (1): 3–40.

Viveiros de Castro, E. (1998) Cosmological Deixis and Amerindian Perspectivism. *Journal of the Royal Anthropological Institute* 4: 469–488.

Viveiros de Castro, E. (2007) The Crystal Forest. *Inner Asia* 10: 153–172.

Wagner, R. (1977) Analogic Kinship: A Daribi example. *American Ethnologist* 4(4): 623–642.

Wagner, Roy (1981) *The Invention of Culture*, Chicago: University of Chicago Press.

Wagner, R. (1986) *Symbols that Stand for Themselves*, Chicago: University of Chicago Press.

Wagner, R. (1991) The Fractal Person. In *Big Men and Great Men: Personifications of Power in Melanesia*, edited by M. Godelier and M. Strathern, 159–173, Cambridge: Cambridge University Press.

Willerslev, R. and Pedersen, M. A. (2010) Proportional Holism: Joking the Cosmos into the Right Shape in North Asia. In *Experiments with Holism. Theory and Practice in Contemporary Anthropology*, edited by N. Bubandt and T. Otto, 262–278, London: Blackwell.

18

Useless objects

Commodities, collections and fetishes in the politics of objects

Nicholas Thoburn

Introduction

Our everyday experience of objects is ordered by clichés, routine patterns of perception and action, in which objects are at once constrained and constraining. That at least is Deleuze's assessment, as he elaborates in this comment on Bergson:

> [W]e do not perceive the thing or the image in its entirety, we always perceive less of it, we perceive only what we are interested in perceiving, or rather what it is in our interest to perceive, by virtue of our economic interests, ideological beliefs and psychological demands. We therefore normally perceive only clichés.
>
> *(Deleuze 1989: 20)*

If this is a problem to be overcome, how might we conceive of a *politics* of the object? Well, for Deleuze (1989: 18–20), such a politics must breach clichéd patterns of perception and action to allow 'the thing in itself' to come forth, in all its 'inexhaustible', 'unbearable' and 'intolerable' excess. It is a politics not of the routine economic, ideological or psychological functionality of the object, its *use*, but of its *uselessness*. To access the object in itself, 'we must have the power to value the useless' (Bergson 1991: 83).

One could be forgiven for thinking this an overly arcane pursuit to warrant designation as 'politics'. Yet there is a strong resonance here with Marx, and it is in this direction that I take my argument, for it allows me to posit a politics of the 'useless object' in relation to the commodity form. My principal interlocutor is Walter Benjamin, who not incidentally has probably done most to develop a politics from a weave of Marxian and Bergsonian philosophies. I start with discussion of 'commodity fetishism' as the social form of the clichéd object, the social subjection to amaterial value, before setting out the contours of the useless object in Benjamin's account of the 'collection'. I then show how the useless object can critically engage with the Surrealist 'found object'; a helpful point of contrast and development, given the significance of Surrealism for political aesthetics and the relative paucity of political engagement with the qualities of objects.[1] I consider André Breton's canonical account, Ghérasim Luca's 'objectively offered object' and Georges Bataille's 'document'. The latter pulls the argument out of Surrealism and back into the domain of the 'fetish', although now no longer designating the structure of the commodity but rather a cross-cultural entity at the juncture of heterogeneous value systems, a means of thinking the material valences of the useless object in the midst of the commodity form.

Commodity fetishism: the amaterial form of the object

As Benjamin elaborates through a series of notes and essays on the subject of 'collecting', the proper materialist approach to objects 'entails the liberation of things from the drudgery of being useful' (Benjamin 2002: 209). This will already sound familiar, although it is not from Bergson that he draws direct support, but from Marx. Benjamin's flight from utility is deduced from this passage in the *1844 Manuscripts*:

> Private property has made us so stupid and one-sided that an object is only *ours* when we have it, when it exists for us as capital or when we directly possess, eat, drink, wear, inhabit it, etc., in short, when we *use* it.
>
> *(Marx 1975: 351)*

I will make two observations on this passage, in order to better understand the environment within and against which the useless object operates. First, Marx's suggestion here is that our clichéd (or 'stupid and one-sided') patterns of perception and action are not a product of human physiology in general, as they largely are for Bergson, but are a structural effect of specifically capitalist social relations. Put another way, the clichéd object is the object of *commodity fetishism*. In a dozen or so dazzling pages of *Capital*, Marx famously argues that the capitalist commodity has a strange kind of agency, a mystical power that appears to emanate, fetish-like, from the object itself. However, Marx is explicit that this mystical agency is not a product of the *material qualities* of the object (it has 'absolutely no connection with the physical nature of the commodity and the material [*dinglich*] relations arising out of this' [Marx 1976: 165]) but of its specific existence in capitalism, its *commodity form*.

To précis Marx's account of commodity fetishism, the source of value in capitalism is social or 'abstract' labour, labour that is expended in general by the social whole. Social labour is a product of the myriad different forms of 'concrete labour' undertaken by the multiplicity of producers. However, the fully social aspect of labour is not manifest in the labour process itself, in which concrete labour is undertaken in relative isolation, but in the circulation of commodities after they have been produced. For it is only through the myriad practices of exchange that the uniform quality of labour in general (abstract labour) can emerge from all the different kinds of private, concrete labour. Because this all occurs in the sphere of commodity circulation, apart from and outside the sphere of their fabrication, the social character of capitalist *labour* appears to be a characteristic of *commodities*, with the circulation of the latter in a very real sense determining the structure or form of the former:

> Since the producers do not come into social contact until they exchange the products of their labour, the specific social characteristics of their private labours appear only within this exchange. In other words, the labour of the private individual manifests itself as an element of the total labour of society only through the relations which the act of exchange establishes between the products, and, through their mediation, between the producers. To the producers, therefore, the social relations between their private labours appear as what they are, i.e. they do not appear as direct social relations between persons in their work, but rather as material [*dinglich*] relations between persons and social relations between things.
>
> *(Marx 1976: 165–6)*

One should not draw the conclusion from this theory of commodity fetishism that humanity is overly enamoured with objects, as Peter Stallybrass (1998) has rightly insisted. Marx's point, rather, is that the production and circulation of commodities *structure the form of labour*, isolating producers from a fully social relation with other people *and* with objects. Insofar as commodity fetishism is an experience of the object, it is a 'stupid and one-sided' experience. For objects-as-commodities have a social agency from which producers are excluded and that acts to enforce the subjection of work and its identities. To be clear, this is not the fault of the object; the perverse aspect of the commodity form, the fetish-like inversion, is that it is the very characteristics of social labour that performs and entrenches its asocial subjection.

Commodity fetishism, then, is a structural feature of labour in capitalism, 'it is inseparable from the production of commodities' (Marx 1976: 165). But if we move from this form of labour to consider the more affective relations to the commodity that are described by this concept, the *adoration* of the commodity, it is adoration not of material objects, but of abstract wealth, money that begets more money. As such:

> To fetishize commodities is, in one of Marx's least understood jokes, to inverse the whole history of fetishism. For it is to fetishize the invisible, the immaterial, the suprasensible. The fetishism of the commodity inscribes *im*materiality as the defining feature of capitalism.
>
> *(Stallybrass 1998: 184)*

This generalized social subjection to the amaterial or suprasensible takes particular *subjective* forms. Marx (1975: 352) identifies it in the desire for *ownership* of objects: 'all the physical and intellectual senses have been replaced by the simple estrangement of *all* these senses – the sense of *having*'. And it can be seen in more specificity in his account of the affect of 'greed', as manifest in its two capitalist modalities of 'miserliness' and 'hedonism' (here I follow Cesare Casarino's [2008] compelling analysis of 'pleasure' in Marx). In order to satisfy the greed for money, the miser must *forgo the object* and its pleasures, she 'must sacrifice all relationship to the objects of particular needs, must abstain, in order to satisfy the need of greed for money as such' (Marx, cited in Casarino 2008: 238). However, it is a doomed endeavour, because by withdrawing money from circulation in this way, the miser forgoes precisely that which attracts them to money in the first place, namely its capacity to beget more of itself, its self-expanding power. The hedonist, by contrast, is *greedy for objects* and their pleasures. This initially sounds like a more promising mode of engagement with the object. However, again, it is a product of the peculiar dynamics of abstract wealth, for hedonism is not greed for a material particular, but for wealth in general, for 'an object which possesses all pleasures in potentiality' (Marx, cited in Casarino 2008: 239). Because this is a capacity only of money in circulation, it cannot be realized in particular consumption, and so hedonism is an equally doomed pursuit, with a result not unfamiliar to modern cultures of consumption:

> If money as capital 'possesses all pleasures in potentiality', each actual pleasure can then be realized only in the next pleasure, each present pleasure is always already waiting for the coming pleasure – and hence pleasure is achieved only by not having any pleasure at all.
>
> *(Casarino 2008: 239)*

This leads to my second observation on Benjamin's favoured passage from the *1844 Manuscripts*, although on this I can be brief. It is the point that most attracts Benjamin's attention. Faced with this situation of commodity fetishism, it is not uncommon for critics (including Marxists) to reach for 'use value' as the reassuring ground for a politics of the object, use value grasped as an extracapitalist relation to the object that is only secondarily caught up in commodity relations and from which it can hence be disinterred. But this is a position that Marx here refutes; the clichéd relation to the object is not only a product and experience of 'property' and 'capital', but also of '*use*'. Not an exteriority to the commodity form, 'use' is born of it. It is the metabolic relation to the object that is formed within and functional to the atomized, everyday life of capital: the uses of objects are a '*means of life*; and the life they serve is the *life of private property*, labour and capitalization' (Marx 1975: 352). As I show below, it is credit to Benjamin's great originality that he takes this elusive and unsettling critique of 'use' as the basis for his politics of the object.

The collection: suffering the object

If objects (in the form of commodities) are fundamental, then, to the structures of capitalism, they are no less important to its overcoming. Against the clichéd, amaterial relation to objects accorded by property and use, Marx in these pages counters with a politics of exuberant relations between humans and objects, relations that are devoid of the constraining '*egoistic* nature' of the property relation, and where inorganic nature 'has lost its mere *utility*': a world of '*social* organs' in mutual and transformative exchange with '*social* object[s]' (Marx 1975: 352). Here, communism, in Marx's ecstatic formulation, is the 'complete *emancipation* of all human senses and attributes' as enabled precisely by an experience of the object:

> To be *sensuous*, i.e. to be real, is to be an object of sense, a *sensuous* object, and thus to have sensuous objects outside oneself, objects of one's sense perception. To be sensuous is to *suffer* (to be subjected to the actions of another).
>
> *(Marx 1975: 352, 390)*

It is in this context of a vertiginous, sensory materialism that we should understand Benjamin's move into the politics of collecting, for him a mode of experiment in the 'Sisyphean task of divesting things of their commodity character' (Benjamin 2002: 9). Benjamin's collector has a 'tactile instinct', an immersive relation to the object that complements the optical sense with touch, handling, smell, contemplation, love and imagination, experiencing the object as an affective 'strike' on the sensorium (Benjamin 2002: 205, 206). Marx's sense of 'suffering' the object becomes clearer. As Esther Leslie (2001: 80) argues, this is 'an intensified perception, bound up with shock, impact and curiosity', one that at the level of everyday material culture complements the enhanced technological perception that Benjamin famously detects in photography and cinema: 'everything – even the seemingly most neutral – comes to strike us' (Benjamin 2002: 206). It is not the functional, useful properties of objects that are experienced in this way. These 'physiognomists of the world of objects' value everything *except* the object's usefulness: 'The period, the region, the craftsmanship, the former ownership – for a true collector the whole background of an item adds up to a magic encyclopedia whose quintessence is the fate of his object' (Benjamin 1992: 62).

Benjamin's object requires an environment that allows this 'useless' experience to endure, if only momentarily. He finds this in the unstable and temporary arrangement of objects that is the 'collection'. A collection is an arrangement of objects in a relation that is the 'diametric opposite of any utility, and falls into the peculiar category of completeness' (Benjamin 2002: 204). We can think of a collection as holding utility at bay, warding off use to allow for an undetermined set of attributes and affects to emerge. It is a 'circumscribed area' within which a sensory field is opened that overtakes the collector: 'for a … real collector … ownership is the most intimate relationship that one can have to objects. Not that they come alive in him; *it is he who lives in them*' (Benjamin 1992: 62, 69; emphasis added).

It is perhaps difficult to appreciate the collection as a *dynamic* mode of association until one recognizes that for Benjamin (1992: 62), it is a 'balancing act of extreme precariousness' and psychological intensity, created of chance encounters, protracted searches, perhaps even criminal activity. It is hence maintained at the edge of disorder. Moreover, the tactile appreciation of the object contains a destructive aspect that aligns the collector with Benjamin's formulation of the 'destructive character' and the non-continuous mode of historical perception he conjures in the 'Theses on the Philosophy of History' (Abbas 1989: 232). For in the appreciation of the singular 'fate' of the object (its orbits, its streams of past and future), the collector is attuned to the dissipative properties of matter. Against the delimiting temporal patterns of commodity circulation, the collector's mode of relation thus opens to the many and singular durations of things, so displaying an 'anarchistic, destructive' passion, a 'wilfully subversive protest against the typical, classifiable' (Benjamin, cited in Wizisla 2007: 5).

Given Marx's critique of property as the amaterial experience of the object, it is a little disconcerting that Benjamin makes acquisition and ownership constituent elements of the collected object. But the collection has 'a very mysterious relationship to ownership' (Benjamin 1992: 62), one that has little to do with capitalist modes of wealth and property. Collecting certainly has an association with speculation and accumulation, but this correlation is broken in Benjamin's 'real collector', whose 'passion' is not principally found in objects of commercial value, but in the anomalous, kitsch, mysterious, and discarded items of mass production: in the margins or pores of commodity culture. It is as if Benjamin is trying to find a mode of everyday relation to objects that is situated in the field of property and consumption, but that strains against the concomitant structures of value and use, and so property here becomes the starting point for its undoing.

The Surrealist object found too soon

The contours of the useless object can be augmented through consideration of the Surrealist 'found object'. Benjamin (1986: 181, 182) places great stress on the revolutionary transformation of things ('enslaved and enslaving objects') in Surrealism, a movement that 'bring[s] the immense forces of "atmosphere" concealed in … things to the point of explosion'. These are objects that slip out of and rise up against the circuits of commodity exchange; indeed, Breton (1988: 126) characterizes such objects of 'prolonged sensual contact' as precisely 'useless'. Yet Breton's found object does not fully escape the cliché, for it is ordered by chains of psychic and sexual association that impose a second-order use upon that which had initially escaped into uselessness. This is no more apparent than in Breton's account in *Mad Love* of flea market finds with Alberto Giacometti, where the narrative moves from an initial flux of undetermined objects ('between the lassitude of some and the desire of others', as Breton describes the object constituted in a field of chance encounter) to the imposition of a most determined psychoanalytic pattern of meaning, as the secret of the wooden spoon that attracts Breton's attention is found to be 'a symbolic figuration of the male sexual apparatus' (Breton 1988: 28, 36).

When pushed, the Surrealist formulation of the found object may reveal further compromised patterns of association. In bracketing off the avant-garde pedigree of the Surrealist approach to objects and mapping instead its emergence in relation to its sociohistorical milieu, Romy Golan (1994) detects a strong correspondence between the structure of the Surrealist object and the colonial fantasies, art markets, and commodity tastes of 1930s France. This adds a socioeconomic dimension to Deleuze and Guattari's (1995: 135) polemical assertion that 'Surrealism was a vast enterprise of oedipalization'. But instead of pursuing further these constraining patterns of association, I prefer to look for more resources for thinking the useless object, turning now to the margins of Parisian Surrealism.

The objectively offered object

Things do indeed get more interesting with the mutation of the found object in Ghérasim Luca's (2008) formulations of the 'objectively offered object', or 'O.O.O.'. These objects can exist as found, but they more often involve a degree of fabrication by Luca, as the photographs of seventeen examples attest in his 1945 book, *The Passive Vampire*. Luca shares Breton's understanding of the found object as constituted in an eroticized field of 'objective chance', the revelation and fulfilment of desire achieved through apparently coincidental encounters. But Luca 'forces the membrane between subject and object' to the limits of what the clichéd patterns of psychoanalytic association can bear (Fijalkowski 1993: 625). The object here is not the essentially beneficent entity it is for Breton, for it can have *malevolent* effects on libidinal relations. And so I start discussion of Luca's O.O.O. on the understanding that objective chance is a *wild* terrain, considerably less subject to pregiven patterns of meaning and association, the better to allow the object to 'blossom in all its dynamic and multiple complexity' (Luca 2008: 26).

Luca's object has considerably more *social* orientation than it does for Breton. Against Breton's rather individualized relation to the found object, the O.O.O. is constituted as a gift, something *offered*, and in this way it more immediately helps 'establish between individuals relationships founded on an active *collective* unconscious' (Luca 2008: 27; emphasis added). For the same reason, the essential rarity of the found object, dependent as it is on an individual chance encounter, is overcome in Luca's object, giving a mass or everyday character to the field of objective chance, the potential to be 'endlessly accessible' (Luca 2008: 32). And this collective extension of the unconscious field of objective chance is matched with an opening to a certain *inorganic* desire. The libidinal field is not limited to erotic relations between individuals, for Luca raises the possibility of an 'object offered objectively *to an object*', or 'O.O.O.O.' (Luca 2008: 76; emphasis added). Although the examples seventy years on are a little hackneyed (champagne poured into a lover's dancing shoes and so forth), the formulation is most intriguing, because here the object transcends the circuits of human congress to come forward in its own right:

> [F]or a given moment the object is divested of its nature as a mediating symbol in erotic practices (like poems, dreams, daydreams, games of exquisite corpse, or collages), putting us in the delirious state of fetish worshippers in which the symbol supersedes the thing it symbolizes.
>
> *(Luca 2008: 76)*[2]

It is at this point that Luca's approach to the object comes closest to Benjamin, providing me with an occasion to summarize the features of the 'useless object' encountered so far. Benjamin's formulation is the richer of the two in resources for thinking the useless object, along the lines set out above, of the critique of use value, sensory complexity and shock, agential capacity, polytemporality, and atypicality. But from Luca one can add additional possible features, as I have shown: a mode of association that weaves a more *collective* set of relations through the modality of the gift; and a *fashioned* or *assembled* quality to what in Benjamin is experienced as already constituted (albeit that the collected object is always worked by time and relation).

It is not a point that I can pursue here in any depth, but this latter feature suggests possible association with useless objects in the realms of art and labour, such as Jean Tinguely's kinetic artworks like 'Homage to New York' (1960) (a machine that functions in a useless manner by destroying all functionality) or, more in keeping with the themes of this chapter, the 'homers' produced illicitly by industrial workers while on the job, objects created through the immersive and wilfully useless diversion of materials and labour time. In his study of capitalist labour practices in socialist Hungary, Miklós Haraszti (1977: 9) defines the homer as 'an object made for his own purpose or pleasure by a worker using his factory's machines and materials'. As with Benjamin, Haraszti (1977: 144) considers the politics of such objects to reside in the momentary breach that they enact with both exchange value *and* use: 'these two steps toward the senseless – producing *useless* things and *renouncing* payment – in fact turn out to be two steps in the direction of freedom, even though they are swiftly blocked by the wall of wage labour'. Rancière (1989: 8) observes a not unrelated production of 'useless things' among the workers of nineteenth-century France, 'hieroglyphs of the anticommodity' that express workers' momentary flight not only from wage labour, but also from the labour movement's pernicious image of the dignity of work.

The useless object, then, has a potential *zerowork* quality. On this point Benjamin (always hostile to the vulgar Marxist glorification of labour) would be in accord with Haraszti and Rancière, but it is important to stress that this feature of creative fabrication does not indicate an *improvement* on Benjamin's collected object. To value productive activity over consumption in that way would be to risk confirming the capitalist partition of these two modalities of social activity, when the useless object points toward the *overcoming* of the distinction, and the social fixation on production that it sustains.

Returning to Luca's object, there is one more feature to consider, a peculiar *geological-political* aspect, for this too adds to the possible features of the useless object, its power of *fabulation*. In one of Luca's accounts, three O.O.O.s serve as premonitions of a major Bucharest earthquake, a catastrophic event that invokes and channels at the level of individual desire Luca's impulse for social revolutionary change (albeit, as he recognizes, in a somewhat desperate mode):

> The panic-desire to satisfy all my desires through panic, substituted for my perpetual desire to change the world through revolution, met the external causality of the earthquake at the heart of the mountains, and the objects I had irrationally created several hours beforehand took their place in my consciousness in the form of a prediction of a catastrophe, which I had wished for and participated in.
>
> *(Luca 2008: 62)*

It might be tempting to dismiss this as megalomania. But I would prefer to see in it something of the 'fabulation' function that Deleuze draws from Bergson, a concept that Bergson (1935: 153–60) himself develops in part through discussion of the psychological effects of an earthquake. For Deleuze, fabulation or myth-making occurs when the shock of an event (be it an earthquake or a literary construction) produces visions or hallucinatory images that substitute for routine patterns of perception, supernatural agential powers that appear to guide the event (Bogue 2006). In Deleuze and Guattari's (1994: 171) reading, such fabulation is a weapon of the weak, a means of fabricating 'giants' (often from the most inauspicious resources) as germinal agents with real-world effects in the service of political change. In Luca's case, the most feeble of objects become yoked with the geological movements of the Earth as material expressions of the impulse for revolutionary change. The conjunction floods his sense impressions as a real or effectuating hallucination that, for a moment, mistakes the catastrophe of the earthquake for the chaotic joy of a revolutionary transformation of the world, a joy manifest or handled (and perhaps preserved) in the O.O.O.

Materialism of the fetish

In this structure of fabulation, one can see how Benjamin's shock-value of the object might be extended into volitional images with explicit political goals. However, this points to a broader set of sociopolitical issues, whereas my intention in this short essay has been to stay close to the use-less object in sketching a kind of degree zero of its politics. So my final point returns to the core features of the useless object, as I indicate its relation to a figure that appeared momentarily above in Luca's O.O.O.O., the 'fetish', now designating something rather different to the alienating power of the commodity. I draw again from the Surrealist fringe, this time from Bataille's dissident journal *Documents*.

The title displays the journal's obsessions, its pages filled with 'documents': Hollywood film stills, images of abattoirs, prayer scrolls, coins, flies, flowers and works by Giacometti, Pablo Picasso, André Masson. There is an ethnographic levelling here that breaches divisions between artefact and art, while heightening appreciation of the heterogeneity and material specificity of each documented entity. As Hollier (1992: 20) describes it, the journal's formulation of the 'document' signifies less a *sur*-real experience, than a realist 'condemnation of the imagination': the document in its alien heterogeneity presents a material and antimetaphorical 'shock-value'. Marx and Benjamin clearly find echoes here. But Hollier (1992: 22) adds an additional aspect, irreverently positing the *fetish* as the true material valence or promise of the document or object, a valence he seeks to convey with this quotation from Bataille: 'I challenge ... any art lover to love a canvas as much as a fetishist loves a shoe'.

If one keeps in mind that it is not the psychoanalytic modality of the fetish being developed by Hollier (despite the classical example from Bataille), then his formulation is most interesting.[3] As Peter Pels (1998: 99) elucidates in his reckoning with 'the spirit of matter', the fetish is a destabilizing object, an anomalous singularity 'whose lack of everyday use and exchange values makes its materiality stand out' and 'threatens to overpower its subject'. In this sense the fetish is close to Benjamin's collected artefact, an excessive and unsettling materiality. But there is an aspect of the fetish that sheds light on a feature of the useless object that is less clear in Benjamin: its persistent interaction with capitalist forms of value. As William Pietz (1985: 5, 7) shows, the fetish as 'object' and 'idea' is a cross-cultural entity, one 'arisen in the encounter of radically heterogeneous social systems' and having no proper existence in a prior discrete society. The modern meaning of the concept lies in the efforts of seventeenth-century European merchants to account for what they perceived to be the irrational attribution of value in west Africa to arbitrary objects. That which was valued was not the universally exchangeable object of political economy, but 'any "trifle" that "took" an African's "fancy"' (Pels 1998: 98).

The fetish existed, then, only in the encounter of non-capitalist and capitalist value systems. And if we can use the fetish today (giving a positive valence to this category born of colonial misrepresentation and plunder, and no longer using it to name a relation in need of demystification), then it is this feature that lends itself especially well to thinking the useless object. For the category of the fetish helps highlight how the untrammelled materiality of the useless object exists not only in the object and its encounters, but always also in relation to capitalist regimes of value. To characterize the useless object as a fetish is to hold together both its excessive materiality and its disruptive interaction with the commodity form, a compound apparent in this description from Peter Pels:

> The fetish is an object that has the quality to singularize itself and disrupt the circulation and commensurability of a system of values. ... [I]ts singularity is not the result of sentimental, historical or otherwise personalized value: The fetish presents a *generic* singularity, a unique

or anomalous quality that sets it apart from *both* the everyday use and exchange *and* the individualization or personalization of objects.

(Pels 1998: 98)

With the fetish I have come full circle: from the 'commodity fetishism' that Marx rightly challenged and unmasked as a delimiting social subjection to the object as amaterial value, to a fetishism of unbound and disruptive materiality in the object proper, in and against the commodity form. Uselessness, here, is not the demise of the object, but the degree zero of its politics, the immanent anticommodity potential of materials. As my discussion of Benjamin and Luca suggests, the useless object is never given as such. Rather, it is constituted in particular sets of relations or procedures, and partakes of the 'inexhaustible' quality of matter. So long as these situated and emergent features are kept in mind, then Deleuze's observation on the object in Werner Herzog's *Stroszeck* is a fitting opening with which to close:

When Bruno asks the question: 'Where do objects go when they no longer have any use?' we might reply that they normally go in the dustbin, but that reply would be inadequate, since the question is metaphysical. Bergson asked the same question and replied metaphysically: that which has ceased to be useful simply begins to *be*.

(Deleuze 1986: 185)

Notes

1 In Thoburn (2010), I explore this theme of 'uselessness' in relation to a different tradition in political art, that of Russian Constructivism, where I develop a more extensive concept of the 'communist object'.
2 The end of this sentence is a little confusing, but by 'symbol' I take Luca to be referring to the object, which now comes into its own *qua* object, and by 'thing', to the *human relation* that the object-as-symbol hitherto mediated.
3 Hollier is interested, as I am here, in a certain *useless* quality to the fetish, although he formulates this in terms of an alternative 'use value': '[T]he shoe is in effect a useful object, an object that works (it is used for walking, etc.). But it is not for walking that the fetishist 'uses' the shoe. For him it has a use-value that begins, paradoxically (this is what Bataille will later call the 'paradox of absolute usefulness'), at the very moment it stops working, when it no longer serves to walk. It is the use-value of a shoe out of service' (Hollier 1992: 13).

Bibliography

Abbas, A. (1989) 'Walter Benjamin's Collector: The Fate of Modern Experience', in A. Huyssen and D. Bathrick eds *Modernity and the Text: Revisions of German Modernism*, New York: Columbia University Press.
Benjamin, W. (1986) *Reflections: Essays, Aphorisms, Autobiographical Writings*, trans. E. Jephcott, New York: Schocken Books.
Benjamin, W. (1992) *Illuminations*, ed. H. Arendt, trans. H. Zohn, Harmondsworth: Fontana Press.
Benjamin, W. (2002) *The Arcades Project*, trans. H. Eiland and K. McLaughlin, Cambridge, MA and London: Harvard University Press.
Bergson, H. (1935) *The Two Sources of Morality and Religion*, trans. R. A. Audra and C. Brereton, Garden City, NY: Doubleday and Company.
Bergson, H. (1991) *Matter and Memory*, trans. N. M. Paul and W. S. Palmer, New York: Zone Books.
Bogue, R. (2006) 'Fabulation, Narration and the People to Come', in C. V. Boundas ed. *Deleuze and Philosophy*, Edinburgh: Edinburgh University Press.
Breton, A. (1988) *Mad Love*, trans. M. A. Caws, Lincoln and London: University of Nebraska Press.
Casarino, C. (2008) 'Time Matters: Marx, Negri, Agamben, and the Corporeal', in C. Casarino and A. Negri, *In Praise of the Common: A Conversation on Philosophy and Politics*, London and Minneapolis: University of Minnesota Press.

Deleuze G. (1986) *Cinema 1: The Movement-Image*, trans. H. Tomlinson and B. Habberjam, London: Athlone Press.

Deleuze, G. (1989) *Cinema 2: The Time-Image*, trans. H. Tomlinson and R. Galeta, London: Athlone Press.

Deleuze, G. and Guattari, F. (1994) *What Is Philosophy?* Trans. G. Burchell and H. Tomlinson, London: Verso Books.

Deleuze, G. and Guattari, F. (1995) 'Balance-Sheet Program for Desiring Machines', in F. Guattari, *Chaosophy*, ed. S. Lotringer, New York: Semiotext(e).

Fijalkowski, K. (1993) 'From Sorcery to Silence: The Objects of Gherasim Luca', *Modern Language Review* 88(3): 625–38.

Golan, R. (1994) 'Triangulating the Surrealist Fetish', *Visual Anthropology Review* 10(1): 50–65.

Haraszti, M. (1977) *A Worker in a Worker's State: Piece-Rates in Hungary*, trans. M. Wright, Harmondsworth: Penguin.

Hollier, D. (1992) 'The Use-Value of the Impossible', trans. L. Ollman, *October* 60: 3–24.

Leslie, E. (2001) 'Telescoping the Microscopic Object: Benjamin the Collector', in A. Coles ed. *The Optic of Walter Benjamin*, London: Black Dog Publishing.

Luca, G. (2008) *The Passive Vampire*, trans. K. Fijalkowski, Prague: Twisted Spoon Press.

Marx, K. (1975) *Early Writings*, trans. R. Livingstone and G. Benton, Harmondsworth: Penguin Books.

Marx, K. (1976) *Capital: A Critique of Political Economy*, Volume 1, trans. B. Fowkes, Harmondsworth: Penguin Books.

Pels, P. (1998) 'The Spirit of Matter: On Fetish, Rarity, Fact and Fancy', in P. Spyer ed. *Border Fetishisms: Material Objects in Unstable Spaces*, New York and London: Routledge.

Pietz, W. (1985) 'The Problem of the Fetish, I', *RES: Anthropology and Aesthetics* 9: 5–17.

Rancière, J. (1989) The Nights of Labor: The Workers' Dream in the Nineteenth Century, trans. J. Drury, Philadelphia: Philadelphia Univeristy Press.

Stallybrass, P. (1998) 'Marx's Coat', in P. Spyer ed. *Border Fetishisms: Material Objects in Unstable Spaces*, New York and London: Routledge.

Thoburn, N. (2010) 'Communist Objects and the Values of Printed Matter', *Social Text* 28(2): 1–30.

Wizisla, E. (2007) 'Preface', in U. Marx, G. Schwarz, M. Schwarz and E. Wizisla eds *Walter Benjamin's Archive: Images, Texts, Signs*, trans. E. Leslie, London: Verso.

19

The unknown objects of object-orientation

Matthew Fuller and Andrew Goffey

Introduction

Object–orientation names an approach to computing that views programs in terms of the interactions between programmatically defined objects (computational objects) rather than as an organized sequence of tasks incorporated in a strictly defined ordering of routines and subroutines. Objects, in object-orientation, are groupings of data and the methods that can be executed on that data, or *stateful abstractions*. In the calculus of object-oriented programming, anything can be a computational object, and anything to be computed must be a computational object, or must be a property of a computational object. Object-oriented programming is typically distinguished from earlier procedural (such as C) and functional (such as Lisp) programming, declarative programming (Prolog) and, currently, component-based programming. Some of today's most widely used programming languages (Java, C#) have a decidedly object-oriented flavour, and object-orientation is deeply sedimented in both the thinking of many computer scientists and software engineers and in the multiple, digital-material strata of contemporary social relations.

This chapter explores some aspects of the turn towards objects in the world of computer programming (a generic term that incorporates elements of both computer science and software engineering). Developing a consideration of computational objects that goes beyond their technoscientific enframing in representational terms (the idea that computational objects are models of real-world entities) the chapter asks more broadly what powers computational objects have, what effects they produce and, more importantly perhaps, how they produce them. Our aim is to make perceptible the territorializing powers of computational objects, as they work to model and remodel relations, processes and practices in a paradoxically abstract material space. Such powers might be best understood in terms of a process of *ontological modelling*. Computational objects are susceptible of a notation that frames them as *epistemic operators*, the technoscientific incarnation of concepts in a formal-logical calculus. However, framing them in these terms by no means exhausts their pragmatic virtues, their material efficacy, which bears more enduringly and obscurely on the new forms of existence that they bring into play, shaping and reshaping users, their dispositions and habits.

Whereas in its broad and varied service as a metaphor for cognitive processes (witness the ongoing search for artificial intelligence), on the one hand, and as a synecdoche of a mechanized, dehumanized and alienated industrial society on the other, the formal qualities of computation might appear divorced from the rich material textures of culture and a concern with the ontological dimension of 'things', computation also has very efficacious and productive traction 'in the real'. The formal calculus of signs that permits the effective resolution of a problem of computation is at the same time a matter of the successful creation, through programming, of a more or less stable set of material processes, within, but also without, the casing of the machine. We refer to calculus of signs as 'abstract materiality', because computational objects are not really immaterial; their operations unfold on a material plane, a plane of relative 'consistency' composed of specific forms of agency that are abstracted from other kinds of material processes and composed in a sometimes fragile ecology of relations. At the same time, computational objects remain in contact with the material processes from which they are abstracted but only through 'redefining' or pacifying them, making them invisible and/or problematic.

To take up the question of the production of this abstract materiality and its unsettling qualities, we briefly consider object-oriented programming and its transformative effects, addressing object-orientation as a sociotechnical practice. The argument develops in a number of stages. A first section considers several key features of object-oriented programming through a consideration of its earliest avatars, and highlights an ambiguity in understandings of programming as a kind of modelling, the implications of which we then start to unpack in the second section. Here, we seek to address such computational objects in non-representational terms as a set of processes capturing agency, allowing us to reframe programming in sociotechnical terms that do not fall into the trap of representation. We then turn our attention to a more direct consideration of the efficacy of programming as a constructive process of modelling with objects. Of particular importance is the question of how typical programming constructs, such as design patterns, operate to stabilize patterns of relations between objects and their environments. In a final section, we explore in more detail some of the ways in which the programming practices that develop out of the use of computational objects are generative of obscurity, unknowability and ignorance. Two main arguments are developed: (1) computational objects have historically been understood in technoscientific terms as a set of formal-material 'concepts', and yet (2) in the sociotechnical qualities of their development and deployment they concomitantly operate as a limit *to* and as limiting *of* knowledge. In this respect, computational objects form a critical relay in the generation of relations of power, which thus become something that is exercised in the supple fabric of materiality that they generate.

Modelling objects

Object-oriented programming comes into the world through the development of new forms of programming language. Such languages are intermediating grammars for writing sets of statements (the algorithms and data structures) that get translated or compiled into machine-coded instructions that can then be executed on a computer. Every programming language forms a carefully and precisely constructed set of protocols established in view of historically, technically and organizationally specific problems. This is as true in the case of object-oriented languages as it is with other kinds of programming language. For instance, the SIMULA language, developed in Norway in the 1960s, aimed at providing a means to both describe (that is, program) a flow of work, and to simulate it, with the aim of bringing the capacity to design work systems (despite their relative technical complexity) into the purview of those who made up a workplace. In this respect, the project had much in common with other contemporaneous developments in higher-level computing languages and database management systems, which aimed to bring technical processes closer to non-specialist understanding, and developed out of a tradition that would become known as 'participatory design' (Bødker *et al.* 2004). The first version of SIMULA, SIMULA I, was not developed with a view to establishing object-orientation as a new format for programming languages per se but rather as a way of modelling the operation of complex systems. Although it was not greatly popular as a general programming language, SIMULA's technical innovation of providing for structured blocks of code (called classes), which would eventually be instantiated as objects, was taken up fifteen years later in the development of C++, a language developed in part to deal with running UNIX-based computational processes across networks (Stroustrop n.d.), which later became a driver in the development of another object-oriented programming language, Java.

The crucial feature of object-oriented programming as a way of modelling entities in software becomes more obvious in another precursor of today's programming languages. In the language Smalltalk, developed under the leadership of Alan Kay at Xerox PARC, in the 1970s and 1980s, it is the relations *between* things that become central (Kay 1998). Objects are generated as instances of ideal types or classes, but their actual behaviour is something that arises from the messages passed to them from other objects, and it is the messages (or events; the distinction is relatively unimportant from the computational point of view) that are actually of most importance. This is important because although the effective order in which computational messages/events are executed is essentially linear, the order itself is not rigidly prescribed and there is an overall sense of polyphony of events and entities in dynamic relation. This represents a significant shift in relation to the extreme rigidity and inflexibility of the user interfaces that were available on the mainframe computers of the time. An approach organized around computational objects allows for a flexible relationship between the user and the machine.

These early developments in object-oriented programming languages both point towards and beyond the epistemic framing of computational objects and the ambivalence that computer programming as a kind of modelling incarnates. Kay (1998), for example, argues that '… object-oriented design is a successful attempt to qualitatively improve the efficiency of modelling the ever more complex dynamic systems and user relationships made possible by the silicon explosion'. However, if that were the case, modelling could not be understood as a simple representation. This is because when the complex dynamic systems and user relationships that object-oriented design models are those that are made possible by technology, it is no longer a matter of representing the world through artefacts but of creating models of non-preexistent things. Yet, the framing of computational objects in epistemological terms as representative concepts is widespread. Kay (1993) himself suggests: 'everything we can describe can be represented by the recursive composition of a single kind of behavioural building block that hides its combination of state and process inside itself and can be dealt with only through the exchange of messages'. On this count, a computer program written in an object-oriented programming language develops a kind of intensional logic, in the sense that the objects that the program comprises each have an internal conceptual structure that determines its relationship to what it 'refers' to. Computational objects are, in this sense, concepts that offer a mechanistic materialized representation of objects generated through a kind of logical calculus. In this respect, we can consider that computational objects have an 'analytic' function, embodying an understanding of the entities that they model. However, given that the 'silicon explosion' makes possible new kinds of system and new kinds of relations, a computational object must be seen as having a 'synthetic' function that adds to and is in excess of the reality it might otherwise be thought to model. It is, we would suggest, this second, synthetic aspect of computational objects (in which modelling is not so much modelling *of* objects, but modelling *with* objects) that needs to be understood more precisely.

Abstraction, errors and the capture of agency

It is often argued that with the development of object-oriented programming, a new era of *interaction* between humans and machines was made possible. There is some truth in this, not least because of the way that the architecture of relations between objects obviates having a program structure in which the order of actions is rigidly prescribed. However, the notion of interaction, as descriptive of a *reciprocal* relation between two independent entities, is sometimes insufficient when trying to understand the historical genesis and the peculiar entanglement of computers and humans. Indeed, given what we have said about modelling, it would be more appropriate to consider these relations in terms of a series of forms of the abstractive creation, *capture* and codification of agency: a click of the mouse, a tap of the key, data input, affective investments and so on. By referring to the creation and capture of agency we seek to underline two things: (1) computational objects do not simply or straightforwardly build on preformed capacities or abilities, they generate new kinds of agency, which may be similar to what went before but are nevertheless different (for example, a typewriter, a keyboard and a keypad capture the agency of fingers in subtly different ways); (2) the agency that is created is part of an asymmetric relation between human and computer, a kind of cultivation or inculcation of a *mechanic habitus*, a set of dispositions that is inseparable from the technologies that codify it and give it expression (Pickering 1995). It would be too long a diversion to examine in detail how and why this asymmetry exists, but such asymmetry is crucial to developing an appropriately concrete understanding of the sociotechnical quality of contemporary relations of power.

Part of the rhetoric of interactive computing insists on the 'intelligent', 'responsive' nature of computational devices, but this obscures the dynamics of software development and the partial, additive quality of the development of interactive possibilities. Computers are not very good at *repairing* interactions. They tend, in use, to be considerably more intransigent than their users, bluntly refusing to save a file, open a web page or even closing down altogether. The everyday experience of the development of human–computer interactions has been one in which humans have been obliged to spend considerable amounts of time learning to think more like computers, developing workarounds, negotiating with and adapting to computational prescription. In this sense, 'bugs' have played an important role in setting up the asymmetric relations between humans and machines. Relatively speaking, humans adapt to (or at least learn not to notice) the stupidities of the computer more quickly than the computer adapts to humans, in part simply because the time between software releases (with bug fixes) is greater than that between individual interactions with an application. This asymmetry suggests that there is something of a strategic value to the stupidity of machines, a stupidity that gives machines a crucial role and a dual meaning in *modelling* the user with which they interact.

In any case, and *pace* Kay, a computational object is a *partial* object: the properties and methods that define it are a necessarily selective and creative abstraction of particular capacities from the thing it models and which specify the ways with which it can be interacted. For example, the objects (text boxes, lists, hyperlinks and so on) that populate a web page define more or less exactly what a user can do. This is a function not just of how the site has been designed and built but, importantly, of a range of previously defined sets of coded functionality. (A website is dependent on a browser, which is in turn dependent on the operating system of the machine on which it operates). There is a history to each of these objects and their development, which means that the parameters for interaction are determined by a series of more or less successful *abstractions* of a peculiarly composite, multilayered and stratified kind.

However, it is important to note here that abstraction is a contingent, *real*, process. The taken-for-granted ways in which humans now interact with machines are the product of material arrangements that do not always apply. More pointedly, these real abstractions are concretely and endlessly reactualized by the interactions between and with the computational. Such processes of abstraction might be better understood as forms of *deterritorialization*, in Deleuze and Guattari's (1987) sense. Considered in these terms, the capture of agency links the formal structuring of computational objects to the broader processes of which they are a part, allowing us in turn: (1) to specify more precisely that the formal structuring and composition of objects has a vector-like quality; and (2) to attend more directly to the correlative feature of reterritorialization. Abstracting *from*, in this sense of a real process, is equally an abstracting *to*: an abstraction is only effective on condition that it forms part of another broader set of relations, in which and by which it can be stabilized and fortified.

We now turn to a more direct consideration of these issues.

Stabilizing the environment

In theory, anything that can be computed in one programming language can also be computed in another: this is one of the lessons of Turing's conception of the universal machine. What that means more prosaically for the case in hand is that an object-oriented programming language provides a set of *design* constraints on the engineers working with it, favouring specific kinds of programmatic constructs, particular ways of addressing technical problems, over others. The existence of such design constraints is particularly important when trying to consider the dynamics governing the material texture of software culture. The question then becomes this: given the way in which the asymmetries in human–machine relations enable the capture of agency, is there a way in which the propagation and extension of those relations can be accounted for? Can something in the practices of working with computational objects be uncovered that might help us understand this dynamic?

One feature that is associated in particular with object-oriented programming is the way that it is argued to facilitate the *reuse* of code. Rather than writing the same or similar sets of code over and over again for different programs, it saves time and effort to be able to write the code once and reuse it in different programs. Reusability is not unique to object-oriented programming; the routinization and automation of computational tasks implies it as a basic operating feature of software per se. But object-oriented programming favours the reusability of code for computationally abstract kinds of entity and operation; in other words, for entities and operations that are more directly referent to the interfacing of the computer to the world outside. *Class libraries* are typical of this. Although not unique to object-oriented programming languages, they provide sets of objects, with predefined sets of methods, properties and so on, that find broad use in programming situations: in the Java programming language, for example, the *Java.io* library contains a '*File*' object, which a programmer uses when a program needs to carry out standard operations on a file external to the program (reading data from it, writing to it and so on). Code reuse in general suggests that the contexts in which it is situated, the purposes to which it is put, the interactions to which it gives rise, and the behaviours it calls forth, are relatively regularized and stable. In other words, it suggests that typical forms of software have found their ecological *niches*.

The possibility of reusability must thus be understood from two angles simultaneously: (1) as something given specific affordance within the structure of an object-oriented language; and (2) as something that finds in its context the opportunity to take root, to gain stability, to acquire a territory. The simple dynamics of adaptation or habituation, we have just suggested, might account for the latter. The former can be located directly in the technical features of object-oriented programming languages. We address reusability first before moving on to a broader consideration of stabilizing practices.

One of the main features of object-oriented programming, distinguishing it from others, is the use of *inheritance*. A computational object in the object-oriented sense is an instantiation of a *class*, a programmatically defined construct endowed with specific properties and methods enabling it to accomplish specific tasks. These properties and methods are creative abstractions. Inheritance is a feature that is often (albeit erroneously) characterized semantically as denoting a relationship: a Persian or a Siamese *is a* cat, a savings account *is an* account. The relation of inheritance defines a hierarchy of objects, often referred to in terms of classes and subclasses. How that hierarchy should be understood is itself a complex question but crucially the relation of inheritance allows programmers to build on existing computational objects with relatively well-known behaviour by extending that behaviour with the addition of new methods and properties.

The relation of inheritance implies a situation in which objects extend and expand their territory through small variations, incremental additions that confirm rather than disrupt expectations about how objects should behave. To put it crudely, it is easier to inherit and extend (to *assume* that small differences are deviations from a broadly accepted norm) than it is to consider that such variations might be indices of a different situation, a different world. Modelling behaviour through the technical constraint of inheritance offers a discrete way of capturing practices and relations in software through a logic of imitation (cf. Tarde in Deleuze and Guattari 1987).

Design patterns extend this logic of code reusability to the situation of a more complex set of algorithms designed to address a broader problem. A design pattern in software provides a reusable solution to the problem posed by a computational context, and although such a pattern is obviously a technical entity, it is also a partial translation of a problem that will not originally be computational in nature (Gamma *et al.* 1994; Shalloway and Trott 2005). This is what makes it interesting, because its very existence is evidence of the increasing complexity and shifting social relations that computational abstractions are required to address. A business information system that is designed to keep track of stock, for example, based on a 'just-in-time' model of stock control creates design problems entailing a different set of object-relations than in a system based on more traditional models of stock control (such as amassing large amounts of uniform items at lower unit cost) because the system needs to do different things. Design patterns imply varied sets of relations between software and users, perhaps entailing an automated set of links between one company and companies further up the supply chain. The latter might thus reasonably be expected to entail online 'business-to-business' communication on a 'multitier' model, whereas the former might adopt a more traditional 'client–server' relationship. Although a user might experience these as similar, the relations between the objects that make them up are considerably different.

In one respect, such patterns respond to the core difficulty of object-oriented software development: the analytic decomposition of what a program has to do into a set of objects with well-defined properties. Indeed, that is traditionally how design patterns are understood by software engineers. Their very existence is interesting not just because they provide evidence of the growing complexity of the computational environment, but also of its stability and regularity, qualities that such patterns in turn produce. Such material presuppositions are not normally considered in discussions of object-oriented programming (or indeed any programming at all), where the self-evident value and thinking in object-oriented terms is generally shored up in textbooks by means of analogy with more commonsensically object-like objects: tables, chairs, papers, books, and so on (Goldsack and Kent 1996). Yet, the stability of an environment is absolutely critical in enabling computational objects to exert their powers effectively (Stengers 2011). However, the pedagogical emphasis on the relatively simple does not do justice to the processes at work in the historical development of software culture. Perhaps, it would be more appropriate to view the stable, simple and self-evidently given quality of computational objects as the outcome of a complex sociotechnical genesis.

Encapsulation, exceptions and unknowability

Thus far we have sought to address material aspects of the complex processes of abstraction that are at work in object-oriented programming. We need nevertheless to insist that computational objects do have a cognitive role. This role is fulfilled primarily through the, often blind and groping, ways in which such objects give shape to non-computational processes.

The world in which computational objects operate is one to which they relate through precisely defined contractual interfaces that specify the interplay between their private inner workings and public façades. One does not interact with a machine any old how but with a latitude for freedom that is precisely, programmatically, specified. Along with the *exception* construct, *encapsulation* is often held to be one of the primary features that object-oriented programming enforces, a strict demarcation of inside and outside that is only bridged through the careful design of interfaces, making 'not-knowing' into a key design principle. The term 'encapsulation' refers to the way in which object-oriented programming languages facilitate the hiding of both the data that describe the state of the objects that make up a program, and the details of the operations that the object performs.[1] In order to access or modify the data descriptive of the state of an object, one typically uses a 'get' or a 'set' 'method', rendering the nature of the interaction being accomplished explicitly visible. Encapsulation offers a variant (at the level of the formal constructs of a programming language) of a more general principle observed by programmers, which is that when writing an interface to some element of a program, one should always hide the 'implementation details', so that users do not know about and are not tempted to manipulate data critical to its functioning.

In addition to promoting code reuse, encapsulation minimizes the risk of errors that might be created by incompetent programmers getting access to and manipulating data that might lead the object to behave in unexpected ways. A key maxim for programmers is that one should always code 'defensively', always write 'secure' code, and even accept that input (at whatever scale one wishes to define this) is always 'evil' (Howard and LeBlanc 2003). A highly regulated interplay between the inner workings and the outer functioning of objects makes it possible to ensure the stable operations of software. Arguably, this is part of a historical tendency and proprietary trend to distance users from the inner workings of machines, effecting a complex sociotechnical knot of intellectual property, risk management and the division of labour, the outcome of which is to restrict the programmer's ability to gain access to lower levels of operation (whilst theoretically making it easier to write code).

As a principle and as a technical constraint, encapsulation and the hiding of data at the very least give shape to a technicoeconomic hierarchy in which the producers of programming languages can control the direction of innovation and change by promoting 'lock-in' and structuring a division of work that encourages programmers to use proprietary class libraries rather than take the time to develop their own. By facilitating a particular (and now global) division of labour, the development of new forms of knowing through machines is in turn inhibited through the promotion of technically constrained, normative assumptions about what programming should be. Indeed, a more finely grained division of the work of software development is made possible when the system or application to be built can be divided into discrete 'chunks'. Each class or class library (from which objects are derived) may be produced by a different programmer or group of programmers with the details of the operations of the classes safely ignored by other teams working on the project.[2]

Finally, let us look briefly at *exception handling*. Where encapsulation works to create stabilized abstractions by closely regulating the interplay between the inside and the outside of computational objects, defining what objects can know of one another, exception handling shapes the way in which computational objects respond to anything that exceeds their expectations. A program and the objects that make it up are only ever operative within a specified set of parameters, defining the relations it can have with its environment and embodying assumptions that are made about what the program should expect to encounter within it. If those assumptions are not met (your browser is missing a plug-in, say, or you deleted a vital.dll file when removing an unwanted application), the program does not operate as expected. Exception handling provides a way to ensure that the flow of control through a program can be maintained despite the failure to fulfil expectations, ensuring that an application or system need not crash simply because some unforeseen problem has occurred. And in object-oriented programming, an exception is an object like any other (one can create subtypes of it, extend its functionality and so on[3]), suggesting it too facilitates the logic of imitation.

Technically, the rationale for exceptions is well understood and their treatment as objects, with everything that entails, facilitates their programmatic handling. What is less well understood, however, is the way that practices of exception handling give material shape to the kinds of relations that computational objects have with their outside. From the point of view of computational objects, the world in general is a vast and largely unknown ensemble of events, *to* which such objects can only have access under highly restricted conditions, but also *in* which those objects only have a limited range of interest, the role of the programmer being to specify this range of pertinences as precisely as possible. This is something that can be achieved in many ways: the practice of 'validating' user input, for example (by checking that the structure of that input conforms to some previously specified 'regular expression', say), ensures that the computational objects processing that input do not encounter any surprises (such as a date entered in the wrong format).

Because the use of exception handling in a program makes it possible for computational objects to go about their work without too much disruption, and because their status as computational objects in their own right allows them to be programmatically worked with in the same way as other objects, the need to pay closer attention to what causes the problems giving rise to the exceptions in the first place (systems analysis and design decisions, the framing of the specification of the software and so on) is minimized. The common practice of programmatically 'writing' information about the problems that give rise to exceptions to a log file (because this enables software developers to identify difficulties in program design, the routine causes of problems and so on) mitigates such ignorance, to a point. However, it must be understood that the information thus derived presumes the terms in which the software defined the problem in the first place. As a result, one can only ever make conjectures about the underlying causes of that problem (a log file on a web application that repeatedly logs information indicating that a database server at another location is not responding cannot tell us if the server has been switched off or broken down, for example), leaving the commonplace of the information technology helpdesk (for users having problems with software, 'read the fucking manual') as evidence of the structure of judgement this situation yields.

The point is that because exception handling facilitates the smooth running of software, it not only helps to stabilize the software itself but also the programming practices that gave rise to it. Exceptions work to preserve the framing of technical problems *as* technical problems, allowing errors to be typically defined as problems that the user creates through not understanding the software (rather than the other way round). In this way, exception handling obviates developing a closer consideration of the relationship between computational objects and their environment or problematizing the framing of programming practices. Although this can allow software to gain a certain routinized unobtrusiveness (Kitchin and Dodge 2011), this 'grey' quality makes it difficult to obtain a better sense of the differences (Stengers 2006) that its abstract materiality produces.

Conclusion: ontological modelling and the matter of the unknown

In the course of this chapter, we have endeavoured to sketch out some reasons for developing an account of object-oriented programming that considers computation not from an epistemic but from an ontological point of view. It is true that there is historically well-sedimented association between computation and discourses about knowledge, that computer programming seeks to model reality, that there are links between programming languages and formal logic, and so on. But this is not enough to make understanding computer programming as a science in the way that say physics, chemistry, or even the social sciences (sometimes) are, a legitimate move. On the contrary, we have tried to suggest that the abstractive capture and manipulation of agency through software in the calculus of computational objects is better understood as an ensemble of techniques engaged in a practice of *ontological modelling*. In other words, computer programming involves a creative working with the properties, capacities and tendencies offered to it by its environment that is obscurely productive of new kinds of entities, about which it may know very little. Such entities make up the fabric of 'abstract materiality', a term that gestures towards the consistency and autonomy of the zones or territories in which computational objects interface with other kinds of entity.

Object-orientation might be approached from many points of view: the angle taken here is one that insists, in a manner analogous to Michel Foucault discussing power, that the problem is not that the sociotechnical practice of programming does not know what it is doing. Rather the techniques and technologies of object-orientation produce a situation in which one does not know what one does does.

Notes

1 Not all computer scientists or software engineers agree that encapsulation is the same thing as information or data hiding. The details of the disagreement need not concern us here.
2 The contemporary trend towards the globalization of software development, with its delocalizing metrics for productivity, would not have acquired its present levels of intensity without the chunking of work that encapsulation facilitates. The global division of programming labour is discussed in Mockus and Weiss 2001 and Greenspan 2005.
3 One might, for example, refer to Microsoft's documentation of the *System.Exception* class for details of the complex structure of inheritance relations, the properties and methods of exception objects in the C# language, its subclasses and so on.

Bibliography

Bødker K., Kensing F. and Simonsen, J. (2004) *Participatory IT Design, Designing for Business and Workplace Realities*, Cambridge, MA: MIT Press.

Deleuze G. and Guattari F. (1987) *A Thousand Plateaus*, trans. Brian Massumi, Minneapolis: University of Minnesota Press, p. 193.

Gamma E., Helm R., Johnson R. and Vlissides J. (1994) *Design Patterns. Elements of Reusable Object-Oriented Software*, Indianapolis: Addison-Wesley.

Goldsack S. and Kent S. (eds) (1996) *Formal Methods and Object Technology*, New York: Springer-Verlag.

Greenspan A. (2005) *India and the IT Revolution, Networks of Global Culture*, London: Palgrave Macmillan.

Howard M. and LeBlanc D. (2003) *Writing Secure Code*, Redmond WA: Microsoft Press.

Kay A. (1993) *The Early History of Smalltalk*, http://www.smalltalk.org/smalltalk/TheEarlyHistoryOfSmalltalk_Abstract.html/

Kay A. (1998) 'Prototypes Versus Classes', *Squeak Developers' Mailing List*, 10 Oct, http://lists.squeakfoundation.org/pipermail/squeak-dev/1998-October/017019.html/

Kitchin R. and Dodge, M. (2011) *Code/Space. Software and Everyday Life*, Cambridge, MA: MIT Press.

Mockus A. and Weiss D.M. (2001) 'Globalization by Chunking, a Quantitative Approach', *IEEE Software*, March/April, pp. 30–37.

Pickering A. (1995) *The Mangle of Practice*, 2nd edition, Chicago: Chicago University Press.

Shalloway A. and Trott J.R. (2005) *Design Patterns Explained: A New Perspective on Object-Oriented Design* (2nd Edition), Boston: Addison-Wesley.

Stengers I. (2006) *La vierge et le neutrino*, Paris: Les empêcheurs de penser en rond.

Stengers I. (2011) *Thinking with Whitehead, a Free and Wild Creation of Concepts*, trans. Michael Chase, Cambridge, MA: Harvard University Press.

Stroustrop B. (2007) *A History of C++: 1979–1991*, www2.research.att.com/~bs/hopl2.pdf/

20

How things can unsettle

Martin Holbraad

Introduction

Much has been written about the possibility of a posthumanist critical social science that is able to emancipate 'things' (objects, artefacts, materiality, etc.) from the ensnaring epistemological and ontological bonds of 'humanism', 'logicentrism' and other modernist imaginaries (e.g., Strathern 1990, Gell 1998, Latour 2005, Miller 2005, for critical comment see Fowles 2008 and 2010). The aim of this chapter is to take this project further by exploring the possibilities for an anthropological analytics that is able to allow the 'things themselves' to generate their own terms of analytical engagement. Might the feted posthumanist emancipation of the thing be shown to consist in their capacity to unsettle whatever ontological assumptions we, as analysts, might make about it (including, perhaps, the ontological premises of a 'posthumanist turn' itself)? Might things decide for themselves what they are, and in so doing emancipate themselves from us who would presume to tell them? Might they, if you like, become their own thing-theorists, acting as the originators (rather than the objects) of our analytical conceptualizations (cf. Viveiros de Castro 2003)? What might come to count as a 'thing' through such analytical efforts? Following the suggestion of the present volume's editors,[1] I address these questions by returning with a critical eye to an edited volume with which I was involved some years ago, namely *Thinking Through Things: Theorizing Artefacts Ethnographically* (henceforth TTT for short) (Henare *et al.* 2007). Suitably reconsidered and improved, I suggest, TTT may provide some of the elements for developing an analytical methodology that would allow things to have just these kinds of unsettling effects, providing the conceptual wherewithal for their own analytical emancipation.

Rethinking through things

Plotted onto the trajectory of increasingly radical attempts to erase the human/thing divide, which have been characteristic of posthumanist arguments about the significance of 'things', TTT should probably be placed at the far posthumanist extreme. The argument is post-posthumanist, in that it takes on board Bruno Latour's (1993) landmark suggestion that the distinction between people and things is ontologically arbitrary but adds (contra Latour among others) that, this being so, the solution for emancipating the thing must not be to bind it to an alternative ontological order (e.g., that of the Latourian actor-network), but rather to free it from any ontological determination whatsoever.

As put forward in the Introduction of TTT, the argument in favour of such a position involved two key claims: one critical and one positive. The critical move went as follows. If in any given ethnographic instance things may be considered, somehow, also as non-things (e.g., ceremonial gifts in Oceania, which, as has been famously argued, are deemed to be both things and persons; see Mauss 1990, Strathern 1988), then, anthropologically speaking, the notion of a thing can at most have a heuristic, rather than an analytical, role. So attempts to analyse the things we call objects, artefacts, substances or materials in terms of their objectivity, substantiality or, as what has become most popular, their materiality, are locked in a kind of ethnographic prejudice: they skew the analysis of things with conceptualizations that may well be entirely alien to them. This goes also for theoretical attempts to emancipate things by attributing them with all sorts of qualities that earlier takes on material culture would take to belong only to humans, such as sociality, spirituality and, most popularly, agency. In other words, if what a thing may be is itself an ethnographic variable, then the initial analytical task must not be to 'add' to that term's theoretical purchase by proposing new ways to think of it, e.g., as a site of human beings' objectification (Miller 1987, 2005), an index of agency (Gell 1998), an ongoing event of assemblage (Latour 1993, 2005), or other. Rather, the task must be to detheorize the thing by emptying it out of its many analytical connotations, rendering it a pure ethnographic 'form' ready to be filled out contingently according only to its own ethnographic exigencies. To treat the notion of 'thing' as a mere heuristic (a tag for identifying it as an object of study) is offered as a way for allowing the things we habitually call 'things' to set their terms for their own analysis, terms that in principle may be as varied as there are things to analyse.

Indeed, if half of the way towards addressing this problem is to empty out the notion of 'thing' of its contingently a priori metaphysical contents (thing-as-heuristic as opposed to thing-as-analytic), the other half is to formulate a way of allowing it to be filled by (potentially) alternative contents in each ethnographic instance. This can be seen as the second, positive move of the TTT argument, which is captured by a complementary methodological injunction, namely 'concepts = things': instead of treating all the things that informants say of and do to or with things as modes of 'representing' the things in question (i.e., as manners of attaching various concepts to things by way of 'social construction' and so on), treat them as modes of defining what these things are. Tactically, the point of this move is to placate the abiding tendency in socially inclined theories of material culture to parse ethnographic alternatives to our metaphysic of things in terms of just that metaphysic; in fact, in terms of what well-nigh all recent thing-theories consider its crassest version: the idea of inert and mute things invested with varied meanings only by human fiats of representation. The strategic advantage of rather parsing the issue by treating 'representations' of things as definitions of what they might be is that it renders wide open precisely questions about what kinds of things 'things' might be. Instead of merely offering sundry ways of confirming the base metaphysic of mute things invested with varied meanings by humans, the things-as-concepts tack holds up that very ethnographic variety as a promise of so many ways of arriving at alternative metaphysical positions, whatever they might be. If every instance that anthropologists would deem a different representation of a thing is conceived as a potentially different way of defining what such a thing might be, then all the metaphysical questions about its character qua 'thing' (e.g. questions about what materiality might be, how to conceive of objectification, or indeed of agency, and so forth) are now up for grabs, as a matter of ethnographic contingency and the analytical work it forces upon us.

At the time this mode of analysis was presented in TTT, it appeared to me at any rate to have solved the problem of the thing's analytical emancipation; one that released things' powers of conceptual self-determination. Taken together, it seemed that the two key moves of this argument effectively opened up the space for things themselves, as one encounters them heuristically in any given ethnographic instance, to dictate their own metaphysics, unsettling analytical presuppositions about what a thing might be in the first place and replacing them with their own metaphysical coordinates in each case. This seemed like the posthumanist dream of thing-emancipation at its purest! Yet, to see why my self-satisfaction may have been hasty, one needs only to contemplate how the prospect of things' capacity to 'unsettle' analytically in this way measures up to an important caveat recently formulated by Tim Ingold (2007): that a proper anthropological engagement with things, whatever that may mean or involve, cannot afford to ignore those characteristics that one would ordinarily (i.e., on a purely heuristic basis and with no metaphysical prejudice!) call 'material'. Impatient with what he sees as perversely abstract and intractably abstruse debates about 'materiality' in recent years, Ingold urges anthropologists to 'take a step back, from the materiality of objects to the properties of materials [... —] a tangled web of meandrine complexity, in which — among myriad other things — oaken wasp galls get caught up with old iron, acacia sap, goose feathers and calf-skins, and the residue from heated limestone mixes with emissions from pigs, cattle, hens and bears' (Ingold 2007: 9). Although one may query the particular ontological presuppositions from which Ingold's plea for a renewed attention to materials might flow, his call to 'materials' can be heeded as a powerful reminder of a whole terrain of investigation that any attempt to take things seriously cannot afford to ignore.

The problem, if you like, is one of wanting to have one's cake and eat it. Eating the cake means to take fully on board the posthumanist point that allowing things to unsettle modernist analytical prejudices must involve eschewing any principled distinction between things and humans as a starting point. Having the cake is to find a way to credit the Ingoldian intuition that a full-hog emancipation of the thing must place those characteristics that are most thing-like or 'thingy' (again, speaking heuristically) at the top of the agenda. Asking whether the thing can unsettle is to ask for it to unsettle on its own terms. Any interesting answer to this question, I suggest, would have to start form the rather blatant observation that, prima facie at least, the terms that appear to be most peculiar to things must somehow relate to the characteristics that make them most obviously thing-like in the first place: their material qualities (heuristically construed, once again, with no metaphysical prejudice).

In the sometimes flamboyantly programmatic pronouncements of the TTT Introduction, nothing is made of material qualities, and their role in 'thinking through things' is left largely unspecified. It is indicative that this first dawned on me when faced with a searching question by an archaeologist in a conference at which my coeditors and I presented our argument (Holbraad 2009). Being himself consigned to working with things without the benefit of rich ethnographic information about them, he found himself at a loss as to how archaeologists might deploy our approach to any effect. Notwithstanding our claim to have found a way to let things speak for themselves, our argument seemed at most a method for allowing the ethnography of things to speak on their behalf; to set, indeed, the terms of their analytical engagement. If what motivates the whole approach is the fact that in varied instances people speak of or act with things in ways that contradict our assumptions about what a thing might be; and if, furthermore, it is just those ways of speaking and acting around things that are supposed to provide the 'content' of their potentially alternative metaphysics; then how might TTT be of use to archaeologists, for whom, what people might have said or done around the things archaeologists call 'finds' is so often *the primary question*? If anyone ever needed a way of letting things speak for themselves, that is the archaeologist, for whom things are so often all he has to go on. Our unproblematized reliance on, and unabashed love for, ethnography in our way of 'thinking through things' would be of little help.

These misgivings go to the heart of the problem of how things 'as things' might have the capacity to unsettle analytically. The TTT project was about putting 'things' at the centre of anthropological analyses by entangling them heuristically with all that the people concerned with them say and do around them, subsuming things and their ethnographic accounts under the terms of a broader concern with anthropological methodology in general. As far as TTT is concerned, things 'as things' are just what our ethnographic descriptions of them define them to be. Still, the Ingoldian bugbear remains: what of materials and their properties; what about the thingness of things? In what remains of this chapter, I argue that the force of this line of critique pertains more to the rhetoric of the TTT argument than to its substance. Suitably reconsidered, the methodological approach of TTT is indeed able to release the potential of material characteristics to have unsettling effects, making analytical virtue of them as material.

Taking things seriously, as things

How, then, might ethnographers allow things to speak, not as proxies for their informants, but for themselves? How might things unsettle by yielding their own concepts? I suggest that the clue as to why the argument of TTT might be suited to stage such a move lies in the pivotal role it accords to the heuristic continuity between concepts and things, as per the 'concept = thing' formula. All one needs to do is read the formula backwards (by symmetry of equality): 'thing = concept'. The thought here is in a pertinent sense the reverse (though not the opposite) of the one advocated explicitly in TTT. If the formula 'concept = thing' designated the possibility of treating what people say and do around things as ways of defining what those things are, its symmetrical rendition 'thing = concept' raises the prospect of treating things as ways of defining what we as analysts are able to say and do around *them*. At issue, to coin a term, are a thing's conceptual affordances.

Let us consider that one way of describing the analytics advocated for in TTT would be as a form of 'empirical ontology', where 'empirical' denotes the ethnographic grounding of the resulting anthropological concepts. We may ask: what would be the equivalently empirical grounding of the reverse procedure that we seek to articulate for things? Quite logically, the answer can be found only in the material characteristics of the thing itself. What was empirical about (ethnographically driven) concepts that defined things must now be empirical about (ethnographically given) things that define concepts. With what other 'stuff' (materials) can things feed their conceptualizations than the very stuff that masks them heuristically as 'things'? The materials that make a conceptual difference, in this case, are no longer what people (natives, informants, or what have you) say and do around things, but rather what we, as analysts, hear, see, smell, taste and touch of the thing as we (analysts engaged with things) find it or as it is presented to us.

Thinking of the present argument as a symmetrical reversal of the one made in TTT moves us in Ingold's direction, towards the question of materials and their properties. There is a difference from Ingold's argument, however. Overtly vitalist and inclined towards phenomenology, Ingold's analyses tend to dwell, as he might put it, in the material and sensuous level of things, exploring their mutual 'enmeshment' with people and other organisms, as well as their 'affordances' for people in the broader ecology of living (Ingold 2007). By contrast, in raising the question of the *conceptual* affordances of materials and their properties, my interest is not in the ecology of their material alterations but rather in the economy of their conceptual transformations: how their material characteristics can give rise to particular forms for their conceptualization. At issue is not the horizontal traffic of materials' enmeshment in human and nonhuman forms of life, but rather what one might imagine as a vertical axis of materials' transformation into forms of thought: what might be called the 'intensional vertizon' of things (to mark its orthogonal relationship to phenomenological notions of things' 'intentional horizon' in the Husserlian usage). Simply put, this vertizonal movement would be what 'abstraction' would look like were it to be divorced from the ontological distinction between concrete (things) and abstract (concepts). This is what the 'thing = concept' clause of the analytical method I propose would suggest. Where the ontology of things versus concepts would posit abstraction as the ability of a given concept to comprehend a particular thing, external to itself, in its extension, the heuristic continuity of 'thing = concept' casts this as a movement internal to 'the thing itself' (to echo Husserl again): the thing differentiates itself, no longer as an instantiation 'of' a concept, but a self-transformation *as* a concept.

With reference to Marilyn Strathern's (2004) notion of 'partial connections', Morten Pedersen and I have elsewhere tried to articulate in some detail the analytical implications of things' capacity for vertizonal transformation; we called this self-motion 'abstension', to indicate the intensive (as opposed to extensive) character that abstractions acquire when they are thought as self-differentiating transformations of things-into-concepts (Holbraad and Pedersen 2009). Rather than cover this ground again, let me now show what such an analytical move might look like by reconsidering in some detail the main ethnographic example with which the original argument of the Introduction to TTT was cast, focusing on the notion of *aché* in *Ifá*, a form of divination brought to Cuba in the nineteenth century by Yoruba-speaking slaves, which is still practised pervasively in Havana and elsewhere on the island (Holbraad 2007).

Powder and its conceptual affordances

Much like the notorious notion of *mana* in Oceania, *aché* is a term that *babalawos*, as men initiated into the prestigious Afro-Cuban diviner-cult of *Ifá* are called, use in a wide variety of contexts (cf. Lévi-Strauss 1987). Crucially, the term is used to refer both in the abstract to their 'power' (*poder*) or 'capacity' (*facultad*) to divine, for which they are most renowned ('to divine you must have *aché*', as they say), and, more concretely, to certain powders that they consider to be a prime ritual ingredient for making divinities appear and 'speak' during divination (Holbraad 2007, 2012). Among the many ways in which specially prepared powders are deemed necessary to *Ifá* ritual, perhaps the most striking is its role as a 'register' (*registro*) upon which the divinatory configurations through which Orula, the god of divination, is said to be able to 'speak' during the ritual. Spread on the surface of the consecrated divining-tray that *babalawos* use for the most ceremonious divinations they conduct for their clients (particularly during the initiation of neophytes), this powder becomes the medium through which Orula's words appear. They do this in the form of a series of 'signs' (*signos*, also referred to in the original Yoruba as *oddu*) that are marked (*marcar*) by the *babalawo* on the surface of the powder, following a complex divinatory procedure in which consecrated palm-nuts are used to generate distinct divinatory configurations, each corresponding to its own sign. Sometimes considered as guises of Orula himself (or as his 'paths' or 'representatives'), these figures, comprising eight single or double lines drawn by the *babalawo* with his middle and ring finger in the powder, are considered as potent divinities in their own right that 'come out' (*salen*) in the divination: crouching around the divining board as they 'mark the sign', the *babalawos* and their consultants are in the presence of a divine being, a symbol that stands for itself if ever there was one (*sensu* Wagner 1986).

Crucially, *babalawos* emphasize that the powder itself is an indispensable ingredient for effecting these elicitations of the divine personages. Properly prepared according to secret recipes that only *babalawos* know, *aché de Orula*, as the powder is referred to in this context, has the power to render divinities present, not only by providing the surface on which they can appear as 'signs' 'marked' on the divining-tray, but also because it constitutes a necessary ingredient in the consecration of each of the various objects used in the divination, including the divining-tray itself, the palm-nuts and various other items that *babalawos* must have consecrated for divinatory use during their own initiation. As *babalawos* explain, none of these items 'work' unless they are properly consecrated, and this must involve 'charging them with aché-powders' (*cargar con acheses*) according to secret procedures.

This brief description serves to show the kind of problem to which the TTT argument was addressed, as well as the kind of solution it sought to offer. Much as with classic anthropological controversies about so-called 'apparently irrational beliefs' (Sperber 1985; Holbraad 2010), we seem here to be confronted with a series of notions that are counterintuitive. After all, it appears that the terminological coincidence of *aché* as both power and powder corresponds to an ontological one, to the extent that, as *babalawos* affirm, a diviner's power to elicit divinities into presence is irreducibly a function of his capacity to use the consecrated powders at his disposal as an initiate. Power, in this sense, is powder. This seems to raise the classical anthropological question: why might Cuban diviners and their clients believe such a thing? Indeed, as long as our analysis of *aché* remains within the terms of an axiomatic distinction between things and concepts, we cannot but ask the question in these terms. We *know* that powder is just that dusty thing there on the diviner's tray, so the question is why Cubans might 'think' that it is also a form of power. How to explain this?

By contrast, treating the distinction between concepts and things merely as a heuristic device, as per TTT's first methodological step, allows us to ask questions about that powder that we would intuitively identify (again, only heuristically) as a 'thing', without prejudicing the question of what it might be, including questions of what its being a 'thing' might even mean. Answers to such questions may be culled from the ethnography of all the data we would ordinarily be tempted to call people's 'beliefs' about this powder, including the central puzzling notion that it may be a source of divinatory power. As per the second move of the TTT method (concept = thing), we may treat such data as elements of a conceptual definition of the thing in question. Thus, Cuban diviners do not 'believe' that powder is a form of power, but rather define it as such. To the extent that our own default assumption is that powder is not to be defined as power (it's just a dusty thing, we assume, a collection of particles even), the challenge now must be to reconceptualize those very notions and their many empirical and analytical corollaries (powder, power, deity, etc., but also thing, concept, divinity, etc.) in a way that would render the ethnographically given definition of powder as power reasonable rather than absurd.

It is just this kind of analytical work that I attempted to carry out in my chapter in TTT (Holbraad 2007). Rather than rehearse the whole argument here, I wish only to make explicit an aspect of the argument about which I was unclear at the time, namely the irreducible contribution that powder 'itself' (viz. heuristically identified) made to this work of conceptualization. One might say that whereas ethnographic information derived from *babalawos* serves to set up the anthropological conundrum in this instance, it is what one might call the 'pragmatographic' information culled from powder itself, in the form of vertizonal conceptual effects afforded by its heuristically identified material properties, that delivers the most crucial elements for its solution.

True, the very question as to what a powder that is also power might be is itself ethnographically driven: it is not powder that tells us it is power, but rather the diviners who use it. Certainly, a host of ethnographic data are required to frame and develop the problem itself, as well as parts of its analytical solution. For example, because what powder might be in this instance depends on the notion of power, part of an attempt to articulate the question involves developing the cosmological conundrum that lies at its core: if power refers to *babalawos*' ability to render divinities present as 'signs' during divination, then are we not in some pertinent sense dealing with a version of the age-old theo-ontological conundrum (familiar in the anthropology of religion, e.g. Keane 2007, see also Holbroad 2012: 109–14) of how entities that are imagined as transcendent might in divinatory ritual be rendered immanent? Conceptualizing powder as power requires us to understand how Afro-Cuban divination effectively solves this 'problem of presence', as Matthew Engelke (2007) denominates it in his book on a related conundrum. It is to this question that powder, finally, speaks. I cite the relevant passage from my original article at length in order to show how determining to the analysis the conceptual effects that powder engenders are:

> Considered prosaically, powder is able to [allow deities to 'come out' and 'speak' during divination] due to its pervious character, as a collection of unstructured particles – its pure multiplicity, so to speak. In marking the oddu on the board, the [diviner]'s fingers are able to draw the configuration just to the extent that the 'intensive' capacity of powder to be moved (to be displaced like Archimedean bathwater) allows them to do so. The extensive movement of the oddu as it appears on the board, then, presupposes the intensive mobility of powder as the medium upon which it is registered. [In this way] powder renders the motile premise of the oddu's revelation explicit, there for all to see by means of a simple figure-ground reversal: oddu figures are revealed as a temporary displacement of their ground, the powder. [...] This suggests a logical reversal that goes to the heart of the problem of transcendence. If we take seriously babalawos' contention that the oddu just are the marks they make on aché-powder [...], then the constitution of deities as displacements of powder tells us something pretty important about the premises of Ifá cosmology: that these deities are to be thought of [not as] entities, but rather as motions. [...] If the oddu [...] just are motions [...], then the apparent antinomy of giving logical priority to transcendence over relation or vice versa is resolved. In a logical universe where motion is primitive, what looks like transcendence becomes distance and what looks like relation becomes proximity. [So, qua motions, the deities have inherent within themselves the capacity to relate to humans, through the potential of directed movement that] aché-powder guarantees, as a solution to the genuine problem of the distance deities must traverse in order to be rendered present in divination.
>
> (Holbraad 2007: 208–9)

It in not an accident that the content of this analysis (i.e., the relationship between transcendence and immanence) is recursively related to its form (i.e., the relationship between analytical concepts and ethnographic things). Leaving this analogy to one side, however, in this chapter, I focus on the latter question of form to draw attention to the work powder does for the analysis, by virtue of its material characteristics. If ethnography carries the weight of the analytical problem in this argument, it is the material quality of powder that provides the most crucial elements for its solution. If deities are conceptualized as motions to solve the problem of presence, after all, that is only because their material manifestations are just that, motions. Those motions, in turn, only emerge as analytically significant because of the material constitution of the powder upon which they are physically marked: its pervious quality as a pure multiplicity of unstructured particles, amenable to intensive movement, like the displacement of water, in reaction to the extensive pressure of the diviner's fingers, and so on. Each of this series of material qualities inheres in powder itself, and it is by virtue of this material inherence that they can engender vertizonal effects, setting the conceptual parameters for the anthropological analysis that they 'afford' the argument. As an irreducible element of the analysis of *aché*, it is powder that brings the pivotal concepts of perviousness, multiplicity, motion, direction, potential and so on into the fray of analysis, as conceptual transformations of itself, as per the 'thing = concept' clause. In this way, it is powder that makes the most crucial conceptual contribution to its own analysis, providing its own answer to its own problem, displaying its power to unsettle the ways in which we may think of it.

Conclusion: anthropology and/or pragmatology

To conclude, I want to further clarify what the dividends of this kind of focus on things' conceptual affordances might be. It is important to be precise about the degree and manner in which this way of sourcing anthropological conceptualizations in things counts as a way of analytically emancipating them 'as such'. One might be tempted to object that, whatever the merits of the case I have sought to make for the power of things' to unsettle analytically, the role given to them in this way remains, nevertheless, unavoidably circumscribed by the human-oriented agendas to which these anthropological analyses are directed. Sure (the objection would go): powder may be operative in the analysis of my Cuban example, providing the material source for the conceptual abstentions, as we have called them, of such analytical ingredients as perviousness, multiplicity, intensive motion, and so on. Still, these ingredients are part of a longer list that includes not only things like powder, but also divinities, diviners, their clients, and so on. What this analytical strategy is meant to address is an argument about Cuban practitioners of divination (that is people, my informants) and how we may best conceive of their notion that powder, in a divinatory context, is a form of divine power. Although part of the answers to such questions might be driven by things 'as things' in the manner I have proposed, their anthropological significance is nevertheless a function of their association, in the economy of anthropological analysis, with people and the ethnographic conundrums they may pose. So the aforementioned archaeologist's bemused complaint, it seems, remains after all: could things really speak without their association to human (in this case ethnographically talkative) subjects?

The correct response, I suggest, is to bite the bullet. Anthropological examples such as the one on Afro-Cuban powder indeed do not show that things can speak of their own accord, and seem bound to continue to render them subservient to the analysis of the human projects into which they enter. Arguably, however, this line of scepticism is contingent squarely on the anthropological (by which I mean also human-centric) character of the example. Although admittedly staying within the economy of undeniably anthropological analyses, what I have ventured to argue is that such analyses may involve an irreducibly thing-driven or, as we may call it, 'pragmatological' component or phase (cf. Witmore 2012). Indeed, although the analytical difference things can make pragmatologically might in this instance be gauged with reference to the anthropological mileage they give, the very notion that things might make such a difference of their own accord, by virtue of their heuristically identified 'material properties', also raises the prospect of pragmatology as a sui generis mode of inquiry, one that may feature in a variety of disciplines, beyond sociocultural anthropology, to include not only archaeology, but also other fields in which things feature as an object of concern and in which the analytical extraction of concepts from them might be at issue.

This gives rise to an absurdly programmatic speculation. Might one imagine a thing-centric discipline called pragmatology in which things' material properties would form the basis of conceptual experimentations that would be unmediated by, and run unchecked from, any human projects whatsoever? I have to admit that my own conception of what such a discipline might look like is hazy to say the least … Certainly, notwithstanding my earlier comments, I do not think that archaeology would be enough to provide a model, if only because archaeology shares the anthropocentric slant of social anthropology, its problem being mainly that its otherwise thing-oriented methodology suffers from a deficit of human conformation. Theoretical physics may come considerably closer, because so much of it apparently takes the form of radical conceptual experimentations in the service of understanding the material forms of the universe. Still, this also has problems, partly because of physicists' encompassing demand for causal explanation (a demand that is certainly distinct, and possibly incompatible, with our pragmatological concern with conceptualization). At any rate, there is no reason to limit our putative pragmatology to physicists' takes on matter, to the exclusion of those of chemists, biologists, engineers, or, indeed, artists, sculptors or musicians. In fact, I suspect the closest one might get to the kind of inquiry pragmatology might involve would be an inverse form of conceptual art, construed, of course, very broadly. If the labour of the conceptual artist is supposed to issue in an object that congeals in concrete form a set of conceptual possibilities, the work of the pragmatologist would be one that issues concepts that abstend in abstract form a set of concrete realities. Pragmatology, then, as art backwards.

Acknowledgements

I am grateful to Gillian Evans for the original invitation to participate in this project and to Elizabeth Silva and Nick Thoburn for constructive criticism of an earlier draft of this chapter. Whatever I have to say about the argument of *Thinking Through Things* should not be taken to represent the views of my coeditors. I note that the substance of the present argument is elaborated in more detail in Holbraad (2011) and has benefited greatly from editorial interventions by Morten Pedersen.

Note

1 The material presented here (as in the detailed analysis in Holbraad 2007) is based on ethnographic fieldwork conducted in Havana in 1998–2000 and shorter visits since.

Bibliography

Engelke, M. (2007) *A Problem of Presence: Beyond Scripture in an African Church*, Berkeley: University of California Press.
Fowles, S. (2008) 'The perfect subject: Postcolonial object studies'. Paper at Annual Conference of Theoretical Archaeology Group, 24 May, Columbia University, New York.
—— (2010) 'People without things'. In *An Anthropology of Absence: Materializations of Transcendence and Loss*, M. Bille *et al.* (eds.), New York: Springer, 23–41.
Gell, A. (1998) *Art and Agency: An Anthropological Theory*, Oxford: Clarendon Press.
Henare, A., Holbraad, M. and Wastell, S. (2007) 'Introduction'. In *Thinking Through Things: Theorising Artefacts Ethnographically*, A. Henare *et al.* (eds.), London: Routledge, 1–31.
Holbraad, M. (2007) The power of powder: multiplicity and motion in the divinatory cosmology of Cuban Ifá (or mana again). In *Thinking Through Things: Theorising Artefacts Ethnographically*, A. Henare *et al.* (eds.), London: Routledge, 189–225.
—— (2009) 'Ontology, ethnography, archaeology: an afterword on the ontography of things'. *Cambridge Archaeological Journal* 19(3): 431–441.
—— (2010) 'Ontology is just another word for culture: against the motion.' (Debate and Discussion, from GDAT 2008, S. Venkatesan (ed.)). *Critique of Anthropology* 30(2): 179–185, 185–200 passim.
—— (2011) 'Can the thing speak?' OAP Press, Working Paper Series #7. Available online: http://openanthcoop.net/press/http:/openanthcoop.net/press/wp-content/uploads/2011/01/Holbraad-Can-the-Thing-Speak2.pdf.
—— (2012) *Truth in Motion: the Recursive Anthropology of Cuban Divination*, Chicago: University of Chicago Press.
Holbraad, M. and Pedersen, M.A. (2009) 'Planet M: the intense abstraction of Marilyn Strathern'. *Anthropological Theory* 9(4): 371–94.
Ingold, T. (2007) 'Materials against materiality'. *Archaeological Dialogues* 14(1): 1–16.

Keane, W. (2007) *Christian Moderns: Freedom and Fetish in the Mission Encounter*, Berkeley: University of California Press.

Latour, B. (1993) *We Have Never Been Modern* (trans. C. Porter), London: Prentice Hall.

—— (2005) *Reassembling the Social*, Oxford: Oxford University Press.

Lévi-Strauss, C. (1987) *Introduction to the Work of Marcel Mauss* (trans. F. Barker), London: Routledge and Kegan Paul.

Mauss, M. (1990) *The Gift: Forms and Functions of Exchange in Archaic Societies* (trans. W.D. Halls), London: Routledge.

Miller, D. (1987) *Material Culture and Mass Consumption*, Oxford: Basil Blackwell.

—— (2005) 'Materiality: an introduction'. In *Materiality*, D. Miller (ed.), Durham and London: Duke University Press, 1–50.

Sperber, D. (1985) *On Anthropological Knowledge*, Cambridge: Cambridge University Press.

Strathern, M. (1988) *The Gender of the Gift: Problems with Women and Problems with Society in Melanesia*, Berkeley: University of California Press.

—— (1990) 'Artefacts of history: events and the interpretation of images'. In *Culture and History in the Pacific*, J. Siikala (ed.), Helsinki: Transactions of the Finish Anthropological Society, 25–44.

—— (2004) *Partial Connections* (Updated edition), Walnut Creek: AltaMira Press.

Viveiros de Castro, E. (2003) *And*, Manchester: Manchester Papers in Social Anthropology.

Wagner, Roy (1986) *Symbols that Stand for Themselves*, Chicago: University of Chicago Press.

Witmore, C. (2012) 'The realities of the past: archaeology, objectorientations, pragmatology'. In *Modern Materials: Proceedings from the Contemporary and Historical Archaeology in Theory Conference 2009*, B.R. Fortenberry and L. McAtackney (eds), Oxford: Archaeopress, 25–36.

21

Objects are the root of all philosophy

Graham Harman

Introduction

Objects have been under assault in philosophy for several centuries. This chapter seeks to defend them. Of all the features that might be ascribed to objects, two stand out as especially crucial: unity and autonomy. *Unity*, because the object is one thing despite its numerous qualities and effects and the various roles it can play in different contexts. *Autonomy*, because objects have a private reality not generated by its interactions with humans or with other objects. If you hold as I do that objects are unified and autonomous, then philosophy must be object-oriented philosophy, because anything that is both one and independent must count as an object, whether or not it is physical. There are numerous additional features found in some philosophies of objects, but I hold these to be purely optional, much like power steering and cruise control for 1970s automobiles. An object does not need to be natural, as in Aristotle's theory of substance. It does not need to be indestructible, as are the Leibnizian monads. The object need not be made of purely physical stuff, as many scientific naturalists believe. Neither does it need to be a possible correlate of consciousness, as phenomenology holds. It does not need to be exhaustively present-able by accurate propositional statements, as in the so-called correspondence theories of truth. Despite important shared features, the object is not a classical substance. But neither is it merely a mental entity, because objects unleash forces against one another even when there are no humans or animals to witness them. An object-oriented philosophy need only maintain that there are many objects, that each of them is one thing, and that they are what they are apart from the various events in which they might participate.

However, even to defend this minimalist version of objects can be difficult in the circles in which most of us travel, where even unity and autonomy are under siege. My first thesis is that most recent philosophy has proceeded by denouncing the unity and autonomy of objects in one way or another. My second thesis is that these anti–object-oriented trends, which were valuable when directed against the vices of the old theories of substance, have now reached the end of their natural life span. The unified and autonomous object has been so thoroughly assaulted or debunked from all sides that criticism of these features has become an overheated medium with little room for further development. But a reversal is not only needed: it is already available, if only we choose to look for it. If we move away from plurality and interdependence toward unity and autonomy, we need not readopt the crusty old-fashioned model of substance with all its grievous drawbacks. In fact, I argue in this chapter that both of these extreme positions share the same vices. If we focus purely on the requirements of unity and autonomy, the model of objects that results turns out to be incommensurable with those traditional forms of realism the weaknesses of which are rightly shunned. Objects are not rock-hard reactionary bulks, foisted upon philosophy by grizzled and oppressive patriarchs: instead, they are *weird*, as described in my article on Lovecraft and Husserl (Harman 2008). The first part of my chapter cannot avoid covering a number of key points from the history of metaphysics. I will try to keep these discussions clear and interesting.

Objects and their foes

To repeat my initial point, the only features of objects that need to be defended are unity and autonomy. This already departs from Aristotle's theory of substance, which is often accused semi-wittily of being too devoted to 'mid-sized physical objects'. In fact, it is a bit worse than this, because for Aristotle and especially Leibniz it tends to be a question of *natural* mid-sized physical objects: including horses, trees, and flowers, but excluding mid-sized machines or mid-sized

Figure 21.1   Objects are not rock-hard reactionary bulks. 'The Outward Urge' by Isabel Nolan, 2009 (balsa, jesmonite, paint, MDF). Reproduced courtesy of Kerlin Gallery, Dublin and the artist

battalions of soldiers. There are no grounds for defending this traditional restriction, because in principle, there is no reason to deny objecthood to artificial entities such as computers, bicycles or gigantic international corporations. It is not obvious nonsense to think of Pizza Hut or Manchester United as unified things and as partly autonomous from their surroundings, even if they have many pieces and participate in many complicated events.

Furthermore, it should be noticed that Leibniz represents a backslide from Aristotle in one important respect. For Aristotle it is possible that *perishable* substances exist, unlike the earlier Greek thinkers, whose preferred substances were all eternal: numbers, being, fire, water, or perfect forms. Returning to the bias of these earlier Greeks and their Christian successors, Leibniz also holds that the ultimate substances (monads) will not be destroyed once they are created. But because we ourselves are only committed to the unity and autonomy of objects, we need not agree that objects must be permanent: mayflies, humans, animal species, and mountain ranges might qualify as objects even if all are doomed to destruction, and even if none turn out to have immortal souls.

Nor do we need to obey the presumed priority of physical objects, as scientific naturalism wishes us to do. If unity and autonomy are our only criteria for objects, then armies, dreams, and mythical creatures might deserve the status of objects even if they do have some sort of physical underpinning in the brain. On a related note, there is no need to privilege the *smallest* physical entities over intermediate ones. Atoms, or rather quarks and electrons, need not have more reality than the objects of geology, botany, carpentry, or music criticism. If unity and autonomy are our only standards, then there may well be real objects at every level of scale.

Finally, the object need not be accessible to human knowledge. It could turn out that the object in its reality is so inscrutably dark and deep that any attempt to know it always involves a translation or even a terrible distortion. In other words, if the autonomy of objects commits us to a form of realism, in no way does it commit us to a correspondence theory of truth. It could make perfect sense to uphold the maxim 'one reality, many truths', which is in fact my position. I mention all of this only to avoid any preconceptions about what a philosophy of objects might cover. As long as they are somehow unified and autonomous, objects might include such diverse things as atoms, molecules, stones, flames, societies, guitars, literary genres, people, horses, rave parties, basketball teams, comic book characters, and living and dead languages. Some of these might turn out to be nothing but pseudo-objects, but there is no basis for saying so at the outset: not as long as our only criteria for an object are that it be one thing and that it have some reality independently of its outward properties or relational effects.

Undermining and overmining

Now, if you want to dump this unruly mob of objects as the topic of philosophy, there are only two basic options. The first is to say that objects are *insufficiently* deep, a purely superficial crust atop something much more fundamental. The second option is to say that objects are *too* deep: that they have no genuine independence and are really nothing more than a convenient way of tying together diverse outward qualities or effects. We can call the first option an *undermining* of objects, and by analogy we can also coin a new term and call the second option an *overmining* of objects. The first says that objects are not deep enough to be the truth, whereas the second holds that they are too mysteriously deep to be of any value. My claim is that reality plays out between these two extremes. Objects are not reducible downward to a physical substratum that explains them, but neither are they reducible upward to a set of empirically detected properties or effects. If we reduce objects either to a scientific substratum or a humanized superstratum, their reality is lost.

Let us start with undermining, which is found most commonly in metaphysics, natural science, and sometimes religion. The most extreme form of undermining would be to chant that 'All is one'. The shifting multitude of entities is nothing but an illusion of the senses or a temporary cosmic injustice, and reason or mystical experience can lead us beyond this deception. This position is found not only in various Eastern religions, but also in a number of the pre-Socratic thinkers of ancient Greece. For example, Anaximander, Pythagoras, and Parmenides all held that the apparently vast number of entities was either an illusion of the senses or a cosmic accident, whereas either 'being' or the boundless *apeiron* is considered the true reality. In another variant of this position, the great Anaxagoras claims that all was one until it began to rotate very rapidly through the workings of *nous* (or mind) and only then broke into pieces, each of them containing bits of the others, so that tables, trees, and human arms would also contain minute fragments of sharks or moons. In modern times, Giordano Bruno (1998) defended a similar thesis.

A slightly less extreme version of this undermining position can be found today in more timely thinkers such as Gilbert Simondon (2005) or Manuel DeLanda (2002), who point to a 'pre-individual' realm in which things are somehow autonomous, but not quite fully formed into discrete actual objects. Their ancestor is clearly Henri Bergson, who speaks of our world as both heterogeneous *and* continuous. Here, individual objects are viewed as a superficial encrustation atop a deeper flux of pre-individual forces or topologies.

Finally, there is the most familiar form of undermining, the everyday view of most educated people today, found in all forms of scientific naturalism. Such relatively large phenomena as smoke rings, thunderstorms, earthquakes, and solar eclipses are fully explained in terms of deeper physical phenomena. In different ways, all of these theories contend that the familiar objects of everyday life are derivative or even illusory, that they emerge from a more primal zone of the world where genuine reality can be found. Now, many of them simply try to extend this program to human consciousness, which was previously the last bastion of the anti-naturalists before it came under siege by cognitive science.

But for most people working in philosophy and the human sciences today, at least in the circles in which I travel, none of these options seems entirely feasible. Here we find a greater attraction to the opposite strategy: the *overmining* of objects, which mounts a crusade against the apparently naive traditional view that there are objects over and above their manifestations. Let us consider two variants of this strategy.

The first variant tells us that there are no objects, only 'bundles of qualities'. This is the view of classical British Empiricism, and it remains greatly influential in our own time. Consider a supposed everyday object such as a lemon. This lemon is treated by empiricism as nothing more than a collective nickname for a set of properties habitually found together, such as yellow, sour, round, knobby, pulpy, slippery, and soft. The claim is that we do not experience a lemon, but only these qualities. Any claim that there might be a unity to this object over and above its assembly of traits merely points to some invisible substratum or *je ne sais quoi*, and this has no real status. A lemon may be just a word, and in any case it merely ties together qualities, the true reality in all experience. A similar view is often held even among those who are not empiricists. Namely, even hardcore realists who insist on a real world outside human experience often claim that their *real* objects are really nothing more than bundles of definite traits. Such people may become very aggressive about eliminating the *manifest image* in consciousness, but then they immediately replace it with a *scientific image* of the object. They see nothing in their real objects over and above their specific qualities, even when they concede that science might not yet be equipped to exhaust all of these qualities for any given object. This is the first way to overmine objects: saying that they are nothing more than a sum total of qualities, whether directly experienced in pre-reflective everyday life, or unlocked after a great deal of crafty scientific labor.

But there is at least one other way to overmine objects, dismissing them as the fictions of a false depth. Instead of calling them bundles of static qualities, we can say that they are bundles of dynamic *relations*. And here at last we have a theory enjoying widespread appeal in the humanities, and not just among empiricist philosophers and zealous scientistic eliminators. In philosophy, the dominant way of doing this, ever since Kant's Copernican Revolution in the 1780s, is to say that we can speak of the world only insofar as it is accessible to humans. We cannot speak of things in themselves outside human access, the argument goes, because to do so is already to *speak* of them, and this automatically turns them into objects of experience. The French philosopher Quentin Meillassoux has termed this closed loop 'the correlational circle' (Meillassoux 2008: 5). He uses the word 'correlationism' to describe the still-dominant philosophy that says we can think neither of world without humans nor of humans without world, but only of a primal correlation or rapport between the two. The status of the object in correlationist philosophy is obviously not very high. It is stripped of all autonomy from human consciousness, and either eliminated completely or reduced to a flickering real thing-in-itself that may or may not be hidden behind our awareness, depending on whether you prefer Kant, the German Idealists, or some other variant of their positions. The object is overmined, treated as nothing more than how it is manifested to us.

But let us imagine that we do not wish to place humans in the center of philosophy in this way. We wish instead to reverse the Kantian Revolution and place all animate and inanimate entities on exactly the same footing. Instead of requiring humans to be a full half of any interaction that occurs, we broaden our view. We might speak then of the causal relations between fire and cotton, raindrops and wood, or comets and distant planets without a human or animal observer needing to be on hand to witness these interactions. Instead, the reality of these objects would be their *effects* on all other objects, and not just on the human mind. In short, objects would be part of networks, events, relations, or dynamic negotiations. Because we are no longer trapped in the prison of the human–world correlate, this is no longer a form of correlationism. But it is still a form of *relationism*, because an object is not allowed to be more than whatever it 'modifies, transforms, perturbs, or creates', in the memorable formula of Bruno Latour (1999: 122). Or as described in Whitehead's similar theory, an object is not a vacuous actuality sealed away in some private, hermetic vacuum, but is analyzable into its *prehensions*: its relations with everything else that exists. Relationism is closely allied with pragmatism, because in both theories the object is nothing more than its effects, and cannot be called real if it makes no difference to anything else. There is no hidden essence, no surplus of reality in objects lying behind what they perform or enact, or beyond the events in which they participate. Here again, the unified and autonomous object is overmined and disappears as a true philosophical theme. It is portrayed as the very symptom of an obsolete philosophy.

But before criticizing all these anti-object standpoints, we should note that there is one philosophy that seems to be guilty of undermining *and* overmining simultaneously. That philosophy is materialism. For on the one hand, materialism obviously sees most objects as derivative, as the by-product of more fundamental and usually tinier pieces. Any object we might name is undermined by this theory, treated as merely the surface effect of some deeper layer of reality. But notice that once we undermine objects in favor of these ultimate tiny constituents, whatever they are supposed to be, we find no mysterious depth that is impossible to fathom. Instead, at the bottom of the world, we find nothing but our old overmining friend, the bundle of qualities. The atom or its smaller components can in principle be exhaustively known in terms of specific, tangible properties, whether these pertain to its own features or to its spatial position and velocity. And even if these positions are rendered unknowable by Heisenberg's complications, they can still be known statistically.

Here again the object is overmined, treated as a useless fiction: the ultimate constituents of reality are not unified and autonomous objects, but bundles of real qualities fully expressed in the world rather than hidden behind expression. In this sense, materialism posits a deepest ultimate layer of the world while *also* holding that this layer is purely relational, made up entirely of qualities that can be measured and investigated, or at least fully expressed in the world at any given moment. For materialism, the object is a two-time loser. This philosophy gives us an ultimate material substance, but a substance expressible through qualities. Objects receive a traumatic mixed message: 'You are too shallow! … No, you are too deep!' Now, it is often said that if someone or something receives a great deal of criticism, then it 'must be doing something right'. But this is clearly untrue, because we often criticize vandals, profiteers, and the congenitally rude not because they are doing something right, but because they are clearly doing something wrong. The more convincing form of the maxim is that if something or someone is criticized simultaneously *for opposite reasons*, then it must be doing something right, because in this case it is likely that the attacks from both sides are missing the point. It is my opinion that objects are criticized for being both too shallow and too deep because they are *doing something right*, and are therefore misunderstood from both sides.

Why the criticisms of objects fail

So far I have summarized the various anti-object-oriented positions without saying what might be wrong with them. We can start with the underminers. Three such positions were mentioned, each of a less radical character than the one preceding it. The most radical version was to say that all is one, that change and diversity are illusions. As nobly spiritual as this sounds, it leads to immediate difficulties. The most obvious of them is the lack of any reason why the primordial unity should ever break into individual pieces. If all is truly one, then all should *remain* one. The small number of recent philosophers who have toyed with such a position (namely, Emmanuel Levinas [1988] and Jean-Luc Nancy [1993]) are left with unconvincing theories of how the unified reality is carved up into the numerous districts we actually experience. For Levinas being is a rumbling whole, a pure *il y a* or 'there is' most easily visible in insomnia. Only human consciousness has the power to hypostatize the rumbling of being into numerous parts. It remains unclear both how humans are able to generate such a godlike event, and also why humans would be sufficiently separate from the whole to have such a unique power anyway. Nancy (1993) terms the primordial whole, in slang-like fashion, 'whatever'. It cannot be pre-divided into parts, since he fears that this would establish a Platonism of perfect objects copied by inferior sensual doubles. Therefore, the 'whatever' is more like a formless material, one that splits up into discrete parts only through the work of relation. But it is impossible to see how an inarticulate 'whatever' could ever generate relations of any kind, for there could never be anything distinct amidst its bubbling Lovecraftian cauldron of vague and shapeless entity.

There remains the more sophisticated variant of a 'heterogeneous yet continuous' reality as found in Simondon and DeLanda, but which stems originally from Bergson. The actual dogs and trees we encounter in everyday life are treated as derivative of a pre-individual dynamism laced with attractors, phase spaces or virtual genera of some sort. But these authors admit that this pre-actual realm cannot be one, because otherwise it would be vulnerable to the same criticisms that work against Levinas, Nancy, and Parmenides. Hence, the world before actual objects must have different zones that make different actualities possible. But if this pre-actual world is already riddled with various specific districts, then it is difficult to see how this is any better than simply accepting distinct objects from the outset, because the pre-individual trajectory embodied in dogs will have to differ from those that generate trees and aircraft.

That leaves us with the materialist way of undermining objects, in which objects are treated as naive everyday surfaces, explainable through the workings of physical micropieces. The main problem here is that the physical construction is conflated with ontological construction. Granted that a table is made of wooden pieces, these wooden pieces made of a molecular structure, the molecules made of quarks and electrons, and so forth, it does not follow that the table has no autonomous reality. Although it is surely true that the table would be destroyed if all its quarks and electrons were removed, this case is far too extreme to be enlightening. The more interesting point is that a large number of these particles can be replaced or removed without destroying the table, a phenomenon that DeLanda (2006: 37) calls 'redundant causation', in a sense different from that of analytic philosophy, by which he means that many different processes can yield the same result. We could say that the table is emergent, blocked by firewalls from many of the dramatic machinations of its tiny pieces. In other words, the dependence of objects on their components is not complete. The world is not made up of just two zones: the brute physical bedrock of ultimate particles and the accessible sensory surface of human praxis and consciousness. Instead, the cosmos is riddled with layers and levels, each of them having a certain autonomy from what lies below.

The question, of course, is whether these layers also have autonomy from what lies *above*, and this brings us to the two different ways that were cited of overmining objects. Consider the example of the table. When I said that a table remains the same even when some of its material microcomponents are shuffled around, the intelligent objection might have been made that it is only the same table insofar as other objects (namely *people*) use it as a table. This is sometimes called 'functionalism', the view that an object has reality only insofar as it is recognized or used by other objects in a certain invariant way. In other words, because people are too large to notice or care about changes in the electron state of various atoms in the wood of the table, only for this reason does it remain the same. No table-in-itself exists. There are only table-effects or table-events. This is one example of what I have called an overmining position, and it must be rejected for the same reason that all relationisms must be rejected. Namely, from the fact that only humans and a few mid-sized animals can use tables, it wrongly concludes that the table is first constituted through this use, through an event of table-use. But this is untrue.

First of all, consider the fact that multiple living objects can use the table simultaneously as a table, but all in slightly different ways. The fact that the table supports the arm of one person and the teacup of another, and the fact that it is seen from various different angles and distances or in slightly different moods by each person in the room, does not mean that it is a different table in each case. Just as the table can withstand certain variations in its subatomic particles without changing, so too it withstands countless small fluctuations of precise usage without changing into a different table each time. We might imagine other people not currently in the room, perhaps including those who are dead or not yet born. If they were to enter the room and join us, this would certainly generate new *events*, but there is no reason to say that it would generate new tables. The fact that we have access to tables only in concrete events does not mean that these events exhaust its reality; other minutely different table-uses are always found for it, unthinkable present or future rare objects might be placed on it, and all of these events would rely *on the table* as one constituent of these new events.

More generally, if the table were completely exhausted by its current uses, there is no reason why anything in the world would ever change. As I see it, this is the key flaw of both relationism and correlationism. If objects were nothing more than their effects on the human mind or other non-human objects, then everything in the world would already be exhaustively deployed. All objects would have achieved total expression of themselves through the sum total of events in which they are currently involved. And as Aristotle complains about his enemies the Megarians

(1999: 170–1), there would be no difference between a house builder who happens to be sleeping and someone who has no idea how to build a house. In short, objects are not fully expressed *either* in the features of their physical microcomponents *or* in their current relations to other things. Objects cannot be undermined or overmined at all, because they are the basic ingredients of reality. The physicist Eddington is famous for speaking of how the table lives a double life as *two* tables, the one perceived by the senses and the other as described by science (1981). But in fact *both* of Eddington's options are misfires. The table itself lies between those two extremes, although it might not bear much of a resemblance to the table as encountered in various events involving humans and cats.

Such points are often resisted, and sometimes with reasonable arguments, although there is a sense in which the arguments often seem beside the point. It seems to me that the real (and fully understandable) reason why so many of my friends resist these arguments is simply because they seem to be made in defense of a *boring* philosophy. Namely, it is *realism itself* that sounds boring to many people these days, as if it were nothing more than intellectual police work, forcing people to accept that there is an objective reality outside the mind, and forcing their minds to correspond to that reality by observing the rules and regulations of epistemology. This would indeed be a terrible bore, and I would certainly join in resisting such a philosophy. But if we consider the rather *weird* model of objects that results from the preceding discussion, it turns out not to be boring at all, but strange to a somewhat unnerving degree. Objects are built of pieces, yet they are something over and above those pieces. Objects enter into relations and events, and yet they always hold something in reserve behind those events. Any attempt to make contact with an object, whether through theory, praxis, or sheer causal interaction, will not be able to grasp its full reality.

But strangely enough, it is impossible even to make *partial* contact with an object, given the point that an object is a *unity*. We cannot claim to make contact with 70 per cent or 80 per cent of an object, because a unity cannot be divvied up in this way. But this makes it puzzling how anything could ever touch anything else at all. Instead of a dull realism of bulky atoms and billiard balls slapping each other around in physical space, we have a strange realism of ghostly objects inhabiting every layer of the universe, each autonomous from its own pieces and from its dealings with external objects. There is no reason to go into this problem here; I mention it only to assure the reader that the undermining and overmining methods are not being opposed in the name of a dull, table-pounding appeal to palpable physical fact.

Bibliography

Aristotle (1999) *Metaphysics*, trans. J. Sachs, Santa Fe: Green Lion Press.
Bruno, G. (1998) *Cause, Principle, and Unity*, trans. R. de Lucca, Cambridge: Cambridge University Press.
DeLanda, M. (2002) *Intensive Science and Virtual Philosophy*, London: Continuum.
DeLanda, M. (2006) *A New Philosophy of Society: Assemblage Theory and Social Complexity*, London: Continuum.
Eddington, A. (1981) *The Nature of the Physical World*, Ann Arbor: University of Michigan Press.
Harman, G. (2008) 'On the Horror of Phenomenology: Lovecraft and Husserl', *Collapse* IV, 333–4.
Latour, B. (1999) *Pandora's Hope: Essays on the Reality of Science Studies*, trans. C. Porter, Cambridge, MA: Harvard University Press.
Levinas, E. (1988) *Existence and Existents*, trans. A. Lingis, The Hague: Martinus Nijhoff.
Meillassoux, Q. (2008) *After Finitude: Essay on the Necessity of Contingency*, trans. R. Brassier, London: Continuum.
Nancy, J.-L. (1993) 'Corpus', trans. C. Sartiliot, in *The Birth to Presence*, trans. B. Holmes *et al.*, Stanford: Stanford University Press.
Simondon, G. (2005) *L'individuation à la lumière des notions de forme et d'information*, Grenoble: Millon.

Part IV

Interface objects
Introduction

Nicholas Thoburn

What kind of object is an *interface*? An initial answer might be that an interface is not an object at all, but a point of relation *between* objects, or between objects and subjects: a 'common boundary' or 'interconnection', as the dictionary has it. But this answer assumes that objects and subjects exist as discrete entities before their interface. As such, it downplays the significance of the interface as a process of *constituting* objects and subjects. It is this dynamic, generative quality of the interface that drives the chapters collected in this part.

If the interface plays a role in constituting objects and subjects, it is an aspect *of* these objects and subjects. To say this does not mean that we lose the specificity that the word interface identifies. It is a matter of where we place our attention; to be concerned with the interface is to focus on the dynamic and generative relations between and among objects and subjects, the specific ways that they are interfaced, and the particular effects of the interface. The chapters collected here approach these aspects of the interface through particular objects designated as 'interface objects', objects that are especially oriented toward constituting interfaces, toward having interface effects. These interface effects are at once qualities and propensities of the specific interface objects under consideration, relatively discrete and identifiable objects with particular characteristics. But interface effects are simultaneously features of the environments within which these objects operate.

Let us consider these object-specific and environmental features in two interface objects explored in this part: the 'driverless car' and the 'environmental teapot'. In the chapter 'True automobility', Tim Dant traces the development of the car to a stage at which we can speculate on the possibility of moving beyond the car–driver assemblage to a vehicle that is fully automobile, truly self-moving. The car is an interface object along two axes: it is a driver–vehicle interface, and a vehicle–road interface. Along the first axis, true automobility would see the driver diminished as a significant component of the interface, their agency lost to that of the vehicle. Indeed, a range of technological features like adaptive cruise control, artificial intelligence systems that anticipate collision, and automatic parking are reducing the agency of the driver to the extent that one can imagine the role becoming equivalent to that of passenger. But a modern-day Herbie is probably not what is in store for the future of the car. Dant here suggests that this is more likely to be played out along the second axis, where the driver again loses agency, but so does the *vehicle*, as something along the lines of a 'cooperative intelligent vehicle-highway system' takes over its management, operative through the object of traffic *flow*, where the car is only a component in an externally managed (or self-managing) system or environment. The consequences for this most privileged (and pathological) consumer object of individual autonomy and freedom are considerable.

In Noortje Marres's chapter, 'The environmental teapot and other loaded household objects: reconnecting the politics of technology, issues and things', our interface objects are the teapot and kettle. Again, there is a physical specificity and a certain autonomy or agency to the object. The 'eco-kettle' or Chris Adams's Arduino-equipped teapot, for instance, have particular affordances and technological enhancements (sensors, data feeds) that enable the object to express something of its ecological consequences. Marres is interested in these ecological enhancements and the normative capacities of such objects, but she sees these residing not in their 'scripted' *impact upon subjects* but, rather, in the capacity of the objects themselves to become 'charged' or 'loaded' with a *spectrum of issues*: climate change, peak oil, carbon economy, and so on. Importantly, Marres indicates the *methods* that can be used to map the 'issuefication' of objects, the ways they come to embody and express political problems and issues. The interface object here, then, is 'used to establish connections between disparate issues, settings and actors', it 'help[s] to connect the rhythms of everyday social life with the technological dynamics of energy provision'. It is significant that for Marres, the environmental issues that the object channels and bends are themselves material events, constituted across a social plane that is always also a 'plane of objects'.

In other interface objects explored in this part, the 'object' is less immediately identifiable as a distinct physical entity. In her chapter 'Interfaces: the mediation of things and the distribution of behaviours', Celia Lury takes the 'brand' as her interface object. A brand is not a 'unitary physical entity' but something 'open, incomplete, always changing, and defined in terms of relations rather than in terms of type or even function'. The physical object is, then, only one moment in a set of relations that form the object of the brand, an object 'that does not occupy a single time and space, but rather is to be found in many places, and is always in transformation'. The brand is a quintessential interface object, an interface (or 'frame' or 'surface') between producer and consumer, a two-way mechanism for communicating information in the 'dynamic and noisy' commercial environment. Not that this 'information' is in any way a closed loop; the interface of the brand seeks and enacts an open, processual and 'serial' set of relations that are continuously reestablished in affective and participatory connection across and between objects and subjects.

The objects of synthetic biology are similarly resistant to demarcation by the bounds of the physical object, as Adrian Mackenzie shows in his chapter 'Idempotent, pluripotent, biodigital: objects in the "biological century"'. Indeed, synthetic biologists 'very rarely speak of objects'; the object of their science is more often understood in terms of 'genes, pathways, devices, clocks, switches, networks, circuits, constructs, models and modules'. 'Interface' has an important role to play in these characterizations. In synthetic biology, the word interface has considerable *rhetorical* force, for it is part of a set of technical descriptors that convey the desire of synthetic biology to emulate the highly successful industries of microelectronics, software, and network media. Interface is here a problem of *engineering*, to interface life and computer code in the production of the stable platforms, compatible standards, and computer-assisted design processes that are seen as crucial to generating engineering principles for the production of biodigital objects. But interfacing between biological and digital processes with their different qualities is not so easy. It produces specific 'problems of interface', which Mackenzie explores through the BioBrick, synthetic biological modeling, and difficulties associated with transposing principles of 'idempotency' (when something changes without side effects) from computational environments to those that are living.

The interface object takes a more *diagrammatic* form in the chapter by Hannah Knox on digital modeling, 'Real-izing the virtual: digital simulation and the politics of future making'. Certainly, the architectural model is a concrete entity, but it is an entity that seeks to map features of the social and built environment while simultaneously projecting and realizing *future* possibilities and associations. With this understanding, Knox's chapter considers the digital model of the City of Manchester developed by design and consultancy firm ARUP Associates. Drawing together a multiplicity of data from various sources, the model is an interface object in a number of ways. By locating different knowledges in the same digital space, it interfaces between various disciplinary experts while serving also as an interface between experts and public, seeking to actualize (in urban development parlance) a 'participatory' city planning. It can mediate also with external pressures of governmental legislation, environmental targets, and unpredictable markets. It is key to Knox's account that, designed as at once a means of 'imparting information', 'winning hearts and minds', and 'giving people a vision', the model works by binding data and affect in an effort to actualize a virtual future. It is an interface, then, with emergent worlds, even as these worlds come into tension with the concerns, interests and visions of the tenants of Toxteth Street, planners in the city council, or sponsors of Sport City. The interface object here would be 'misinterpreted as a bounded tool that would mediate a prespecified set of relations', for it is most definitely a *generative* object.

As means of exchange, money is a quintessential interface object, and some of its many forms are considered in this part. In 'Money frontiers: the relative location of euros, Turkish lira, and gold', Sarah Green explores how people, place and power are differently interfaced through the movements, associations and forms of three currencies used in the Aegean region. The frontier (the national interface, if you will) has a significant place in Green's argument. These currencies represent different understandings of relations within, between and across frontiers: historically transnational (gold sovereigns); state-based (Turkish lira); and the ambiguous form of cross-border relation implied by the euro. Green considers how currencies both shape and are shaped by the border dynamics of any given region, both as material objects (cash) and as traces of wider political, social and historical relations. As such, the chapter provides a different vantage point from which to think about the eurozone, and explores how the value of all currencies, however value is defined, is always at least partially dependent upon their cross-border value. In that sense, all currencies have 'relative locations'.

Green's chapter draws attention to the physical forms and qualities of money, noting in the course of her argument the tendency of newer currencies to emulate the look of those that are more established, so as to borrow from confidence in their value. The money in Marc Lenglet's chapter, 'Algorithms and the manufacture of financial reality', is different, being abstracted from its physical form as currency in 'dematerialized' financial instruments and stock exchanges. This is not to suggest that financial transactions constitute an 'immaterial' world, for Lenglet's interest is in the specific materiality of contemporary financial markets. His focus in particular is the move to automation through trading algorithms. Moving well beyond easing the price-discovery mechanism and ordering the exchange structure, trading algorithms are increasingly reconfiguring the agencies that make markets themselves, able to 'decide' when and how to send orders without human intervention. For Lenglet, the interface nature of the trading algorithm takes the form of a 'boundary object', 'those scientific objects which both inhabit several intersecting worlds ... *and* satisfy the informational requirements of each of them', as he quotes Star and Griesemer. Boundary objects can break down, and Lenglet here uses such moments of disruption or anomaly in four case studies, his aim to investigate the role of trading algorithms in the co-construction of 'the market', an arena by no means devoid of ideology.

The interface object has emerged from this short introduction as a most dynamic entity, and that is its purpose, to order certain kinds of material processes in certain kinds of ways. We have seen that interface objects can take the form of particular physical entities (cars, kettles) but they can also be more abstract forms or patterns, such as brands. The interface is certainly not only a technical process; interface objects can embody and extend brand values or political issues, and the word itself has rhetorical force, assisting in conjoining entities (in Mackenzie's case, computational code and organic life) that in their specific materiality resist interfacing. Time can play a significant part in the dynamism of the interface object, as ARUP's architectural model shows, as it seeks to actualize virtual futures among multiple and conflicting parties. Spatially, the interface may extend across whole regions, where the movement of money in the form of metal and paper is associated with various and overlaid patterns of identity, economy and authority, the frontier being as much of a constitutive power as the national territory. Or the interface object might operate at the more microdynamics of computer code, not only interfacing commodities, markets, monetary flows and people but constituting their patterns of behaviour. In the trading algorithm, we see how interface objects order relations, but that this order also breaks down; the latter is no doubt also a quality of the interface.

22

True automobility

Tim Dant

The motorcar is also called an 'automobile' because it can move itself, unlike a carriage that needs the external motor power of a horse or an engine. The etymology of 'automobile' is a conjunction of the Ancient Greek word αὐτός (*autós*, 'self') and the Latin *mobilis* ('movable') but the motorcar as we know it is not properly a movable self; its mobility depends on the selfhood of a driver to motivate and control it. As Tallis elegantly puts it: 'The car largely runs itself and the steering is powered, but we are still required to grip the steering wheel and manipulate it directly in order that the car shall follow the route to our destination' (2003: 177). We could say that the human person is properly an 'automobile' because not only does it have motor power in its leg muscles, it also has the perception, intentionality and sense of direction that motivates movement; it has a self. If the human is an automobile, then so are all animals whose lives are characterized by mobility as well as other bodily capacities that motivate and coordinate movement. Looked at this way, it is only the assemblage of driver and car that is truly 'automobile', alongside other assemblages such as the carriage–horse–driver and the bicycle–rider (Furness 2010). I have previously argued that we should continue to think of the cars on the road as 'driver–car' assemblages of human and machine and boldly asserted that: 'The object of the car is likely to undergo a dramatic transformation within the next few decades, yet even if the weight, body shape, controls, engine and fuel are transformed, it seems likely that the driver–car will continue to include an object on wheels in which a human being can sit and, with simple adjustments of peripheral limbs, steer and direct to go faster or slower' (Dant 2004: 75).

But what if the motorcar itself were to become truly 'automobile'? What if it had its own integrated apparatuses for perception and direction and even a measure of intentionality? The driverless car promises a new possibility for enhancing the mobility of humans, in which the driver becomes just another passenger, trusting the car not only to move itself but also to go where it needs to. The driverless car is a technology that has been thoroughly demonstrated, albeit under special conditions, and is coming ever closer to the consumer market, but would this be a good thing or a bad thing? At the moment, the driverless car exercises a routine level of intentionality that does not amount to motivation, although once the car goes in search of its own fuel and seeks out its own replacement, it will have taken on an animal level of automobility. As this happens, the manual interface between driver and car will change, because the steering wheel, floor pedals and levers on gears and brakes will no longer be needed for control.

251

Instead, an electronic interface, probably at first a keypad-and-screen but in the not-too-distant future, spoken or gestural instructions will be all that is needed to tell the car where to go. Unlike the dog or horse, which responds only partially to spoken instructions, the car will not even need the haptic interface of reins or a leash. But the interface between the car and the road system will also change and a digital leash will most likely link the car to an external, socialized and electronic 'master', which can override on-board controls to manage speed and route in the interest of keeping the traffic flowing.

There are things to be lost as well as gained by following the sociotechnical logic that is leading towards the driverless car, and in this chapter, I want to explore what they might be. It is largely a speculative exercise that involves imagining what the world would be like if the technology was fully realized. As science fiction builds future scenarios that have utopian or dystopian elements, sociology also has a role in thinking about the future to forewarn us of what might happen. If the driver–car has already driven us towards a future in which the 'freedom of the road' is a fantasy of advertiser's myths, where might the driverless car drive us?

Utopias and dystopias of automobility

The first driverless car was probably Herbie, the Volkswagen Beetle in the 1968 Disney film *The Love Bug*, who is better at driving himself to win races than his owner-driver, Jim Douglas. As well as being fast, the car brings together his owner and a girlfriend, smashes up a car rival for his owner's affections and saves his owner from falling off the Golden Gate Bridge. Herbie is the archetypal 'machine that is adored [and] is no longer dead matter but becomes something like a human being' in the apparatus of a consumer society (Marcuse 1998: 47). If Herbie hints at the automobile utopia of benign intentionality subordinated to the will of a human, Christine, the 1958 Plymouth Fury in the Stephen King novel and eponymous film (1983), is a techno nightmare, because the car changes her owner's personality and destroys other humans. The self-restoring car kills, one by one, the members of a gang that had vandalized it. Both Herbie and Christine displayed human emotions and attachments, and had the abilities of self-repair and to drive themselves. These true automobiles owed more to the history of mythical beings with super powers than to the developing technology of the car. In contrast, the US television series *Knight Rider* (NBC, 1982–6) featured KITT, a modified Pontiac Trans Am, distinctive because of its artificial intelligence (AI). The virtually indestructible as well as 'intelligent' car is partnered with its driver Michael, a field agent in a public justice organization, to form a modern-day knight in shining armour, whose role is 'to champion the cause of the innocent, the helpless, the powerless'. Although the advertising puff refers to the values of traditional mythology, the machine is a product of modern industry, with its AI and super strong materials.

In the 1989 movie *Batman*, the Batmobile came to Batman's call, rather like the Lone Ranger's horse, but over the last couple of decades, other cars with more sophisticated AI have featured in a series of futuristic movies (*Total Recall* 1990; *Demolition Man* 1993; *Timecop* 1994; *6th Day* 2000; *Minority Report* 2002; *I Robot* 2004; *Cars* 2006). Autonomous machines have more usually appeared in media culture as 'automobile' robots of various sorts, sometimes with tracks (like Wall-E), sometimes with wheels (like R2D2), but often with legs (CP3P0, *I Robot*). However, as the technology of true automobility has become realized in fact, it has become less interesting as fiction.

The car takes over

True automobility has involved the vehicle taking over the capacity to control itself and reduce its dependence on the effort, strength, skill, attention and judgement of its driver.

The technology of the car has followed a trajectory of making driving easier, with automatic gears, servo brakes, power steering and powered windows, which began as indicators of high-status vehicles but are often now standard on cheap, small cars. The introduction of powered steering and brakes reduced the need for strength in the driver (nowadays, a small person can easily drive a large car or truck), but the introduction of cruise control in the 1950s also relieved the driver from the need to continually adjust the accelerator to maintain a steady speed. Since in the 1970s it became an electronic rather than mechanical device, adaptive cruise control (ACC) has been incorporated into the engine management system to enhance fuel saving, and, when linked to sensors and AI, has become part of a collision warning system with automatic braking and speed control to respond to the car in front. As ACC is installed in an increasing number of cars, it has the capability of changing collective traffic dynamics and may lead to a reduced number of accidents, fewer stop-go waves and improved fuel efficiency as well as maintaining traffic flow (Kesting *et al.* 2010).

On-board sensors with AI can already assist drivers with parking and even complete the task of parallel parking with the driver outside the vehicle. They are able to warn if the vehicle is leaving its road lane with visual, audible or haptic (vibration through the steering wheel) signals, and some systems actually keep the vehicle from leaving the lane if the driver does not. Over the last ten years, AI systems that anticipate a collision, tighten safety belts, close windows and sunroofs, emit warning bells and lights and even begin applying brakes have been introduced on some high-priced models. Other on-board systems that are currently available use sensors and servos to support the driver in a variety of ways. Some alter the suspension and steering characteristics to make it easier for the driver to control the vehicle when avoiding a collision. Others use sensitive radar to be able to identify potential collisions with animals and pedestrians and yet others use cameras to spot cars in blind spots and monitor the driver's wakefulness.

Three things are noticeable about how the interface between driver and the vehicle has been changed by these technological advances. First, they tend to be introduced on a manufacturer's luxury models; they are expensive and seen as added value rather than a necessity for ordinary safe driving (although the US National Highway Traffic Safety Administration [2011] is currently considering whether to require crash avoidance and vehicle-to-vehicle communication systems on new cars). Second, the systems are designed not to intrude on the autonomy of the driver and are oriented towards the 'intelligent' car warning and assisting the driver. Honda's Collision Mitigation Braking System (CMBS), for example, progresses through two stages of warnings, before beginning to brake forcefully: 'strong seatbelt retraction will automatically be applied to provide maximum protection for front seat occupants before applying brakes to reduce impact speed' (Honda 2010). The Audi 'Pre-sense' system will do much the same; full braking control is taken over only when the driver has failed to respond, but maximum braking can still reduce the collision speed 'by up to 40 kilometres an hour' (Audi 2011). Third, technology has, until now, been introduced as a consumer benefit rather than for any social purpose, and the manufacturers emphasize the benefits for the occupants of the car in terms of saving effort, saving fuel and avoiding a collision.

These in-car systems treat the assemblage of the 'driver–car' as a discrete entity within an environment of roads and traffic, but on-board AI can be arranged to communicate directly with other vehicles. One approach is to link vehicles together into a 'road train' or 'platoon', so that a lead vehicle takes control and the others are 'slaved' to it (SARTRE 2011). The technology takes over driving all but the lead vehicle so the drivers in the slave vehicles can work, read, sleep, eat and so on. When they wish to leave the train, separating and regaining control over their own vehicle will require particular skills and road space for the manoeuvre. The road train notion has much in common with that which was at the heart of the ill-fated Aramis project that Bruno Latour (1996) researched in the late 1980s.

The driverless car

The advances in technology that combine sensors, AI and motor power, assist drivers in ways that they may never be aware of. But the arrival of the driverless car in 2005 finally challenged the driver's autonomy; this technology, which is still experimental, promises to make the automobile truly 'automobile' and autonomous. What is interesting is how rapid the emergence of the driverless car was. In Europe in 1987, vehicle guidance by computer vision was demonstrated, and the Prometheus project in the early 1990s led to the AI and sensor technology that is used in contemporary visual assist systems on production vehicles. In 1995, one of the project's multicamera-equipped vehicles drove for 95 per cent of the time without the intervention of the safety driver on a demonstration run of 1600 kilometres along an autobahn from Munich to Odense (Dickmanns 2002: 275). Other teams around the world were also developing autonomous driving systems, but in 2004, when the Defense Advanced Projects Agency (DARPA) Grand Challenge involved only getting vehicles to negotiate a 200-mile route on and off road, no teams completed and many did not even manage to start. In 2005, 'Stanley' successfully completed the same off-road challenge in 6 hours 54 minutes and five other teams finished within ten hours. In November 2007, Carnegie Mellon University won the DARPA 'Grand Urban Challenge' with a Chevrolet Tahoe called 'Boss'. It is an ordinary sports utility vehicle that can be driven by a person but is also equipped with sensor equipment, computers running complex programs and motorized devices to control the steering, accelerator and brakes. In the DARPA challenge, the car drove itself through a simulated urban environment, including other cars negotiating the same streets.

There is of course a long way to go before the driverless car arrives in the showrooms. The challenge that Boss won was an artificially created simulation of an urban environment on George Air Force Base, with checkpoints and different types of roads. The autonomous vehicles had to interact with each other and cars driven by humans, although the average speed was slow compared with most urban environments, and even successful systems confused static and moving objects. As Campbell *et al.* say, the DARPA Urban Challenge '… despite its enormous success, demonstrated the brittleness of robotic intelligence, where small perception mistakes would propagate into planners, causing near misses, human-assisted restarts, and even a few small accidents' (2010: 4658). The AI systems have been improved and developed since then but it is likely that advances in intervehicle and vehicle-to-infrastructure (traffic management systems [TMS]) communication will be needed for successful driverless cars. What is more, until humans are banned from driving cars, driverless cars will have to cope with sharing the road with some bad and aggressive human drivers.

In a press release in October 2010, Google announced that Sebastian Thrun, an AI professor from the Stanford team that developed Boss, had been working with them on a driverless car with the aim of reducing road deaths, congestion and wasted time. The Google cars had already completed 140,000 miles across California through cities as well as autoroutes, night and day, autonomously, albeit with drivers at the ready.[1] The driverless car, a truly automobile machine, appears to be technically feasible, but motor vehicles do not operate independently and are always socially situated.

The road system

If the interface between the driver and the car has changed over the last century, so has that between the driver–car and the road. The developing technology of the road system has, while making the passage of cars much easier especially when there are large numbers of them, progressively eroded the autonomy of the driver in directing and controlling the motorcar. A road provides a route that the car is expected to travel on and the technology of the car is progressively modified to anticipate the engineered and surfaced road. The early Model T with large wheels and loose suspension was not as easily driven across the plains of America as a horse, but it was more capable of going 'off-road' than most modern cars. In many rural cultures today, the standard 'car' is a pickup truck, which as well as carrying a load in an open-top cargo area, has larger wheels, leaf-spring high suspension on a live rear axle, often with four-wheel drive, so that it can cope easily with moving from good-quality surfaced roads to uneven rutted tracks and paths. The Western fashion for 'recreation vehicles' and 4×4s, strong and powerful vehicles, not dependent on roads, is a symbolic response to the socially organized constraints on the driver that direct and control how a car can be used.

Material interfaces such as kerbs, roundabouts, traffic islands and chicanes control the possible path of the car, while white lines, road signs and traffic signals constitute a highway code of speed limits, rights to turn and mandatory stopping that specify how the car should be driven. By the middle of the twentieth century, the critical theorists pointed out how the road system was exemplary of modern society's instrumental control over the autonomy of the individual. For Max Horkheimer, the speed limits and white lines meant that the freedom brought by the car changed the very meaning of 'freedom': 'We must keep our eyes on the road and be ready at each instant to react with the right motion. Our spontaneity has been replaced by a frame of mind which compels us to discard every emotion or idea that might impair our alertness to the impersonal demands assailing us' (1947: 98). For Marcuse, the illusion of the freedom of the individual behind the wheel of their car summed up their vulnerability to a sociotechnical apparatus in which 'business, technics, human needs and nature are welded together into one rational and expedient mechanism' (1998: 46). The path of the driver–car has been mapped out, dotted with fuelling stations for vehicle and human body and corralled by a range of traffic control systems that include the police car with blue flashing lights. If the density of traffic does not effectively restrict the speed of the driver–car, speed-bumps, responsive electronic signs and ultimately the Gatso radar-triggered speed camera will.

The design of roads has, of course, been one of the success stories of modernity, reducing deaths and injuries while accommodating ever-larger volumes of traffic flow. The development of cameras feeding into AI systems that can identify blockages and control sequences of traffic lights and on-road displays now supplements the traditional radio broadcast of traffic information to the driver. Already the in-car 'sat-nav' has taken over from the driver the concern of 'how to get there' as the device issues oral instructions and a 'head-up display' of the route, but it can also warn of roadworks, heavy traffic and the location of speed cameras. As well as taking in information about traffic and road conditions through eyes and ears, drivers are now encouraged to drive 'gently' to consume fuel and avoid creating stop-go waves in the flow of traffic that slow everyone down when a motorway is near capacity (Sugiyama et al. 2008).

The road is becoming directly responsive to driver behaviour, with interactive warning signs telling drivers their current speed or warning of a hazard. Coloured lights in road studs give drivers warnings about hazards and incidents, and when sensors in the studs are linked to intelligent road systems, they will be able to count, classify and note the speed of vehicles as well as identifying fog or ice (Lam et al. 2005). TMS can draw on various road sensors, including automatic number plate recognition, to manage and control traffic. At the moment, they are able to control traffic lights and feed information to drivers, but once the TMS is able to communicate with AI in the car, gathering location and speed information directly, it will be able to influence traffic flow through instant road charges and regulations based on precise information about weather, traffic volume and incidents. Information from cameras and sensors, both in cars and along the road, will evolve into a TMS linked directly with AI in the car to produce a 'cooperative intelligent vehicle-highway system' that takes over the residual autonomy of the human commander (Miles and Walker n.d.). True automobility of the car is just a step on the way to an autonomous mobility system in which the car is only a component with not much more agency than its passengers. Instead of the interface being between the driver and the car, it will be between external systems controlling the traffic and internal systems controlling the car.

What is to be gained?

The driverless car does promise to be safer and more fuel-efficient than the average human driver and, as the number of vehicles on the road has increased, driving cars has become a dull and routine activity suitable for assigning to a machine for those of us who cannot afford a chauffeur. Reducing car accidents would save human death, injury and pain, but it would also save the resources of emergency services, hospitals and clear-up services. The true automobile could be programmed to be consistently polite and respectful of the law, including speed and parking restrictions. Driverless cars could drive closer together so using up less space and reducing congestion, and speed limits could be made variable according to weather and road conditions, in the sure knowledge that the true automobile would respond to them.

In aircraft, AI systems have now become standard kit and have clearly saved lives on many occasions, as well as making pilots' lives easier. Nonetheless, the safety mechanisms for true automobility would need to be thoroughly tested and put beyond the capacity of being manipulated by their human users, as happened with early fly-by-wire systems (Langewiesche 2009). If electronic systems malfunction, then the consequences can be more catastrophic than any individual human failing. The system does not need to go 'bad' after the fashion of Hal in Arthur C. Clarke's *Space Odyssey*; in 2009 and 2010, millions of Toyotas were recalled after faulty braking and accelerator systems had led to a number of collisions. It remains unclear whether all the problems were mechanical but some problems, including braking problems on the Toyota Prius (the car that Google have been using for its driverless trials), seem linked to electronic systems. Like the 'lane assist' and 'collision avoidance' systems in some cars, aircraft fly-by-wire systems 'assist' rather than threaten the autonomy of the pilot; they merely shift a measure of agency from person to machine. A truly automobile car would turn the driver into just another passenger so long car journeys could be made at night with everyone comfortably asleep and road freight could be moved continuously and more cheaply without a driver and at times when roads are quiet.

The social consequences

At first glance, society has much to gain, but the idea of the driverless car goes against the cultural role that the automobile has enjoyed over much of the twentieth century. The driver has always derived social status simply from having the power to control a large and dangerous machine and the sort of car one drives (such as a sports car, a luxury car or a 4×4) can still be a sign of wealth and identity. More importantly, there are cultural benefits from the social, emotional and embodied aspects of driving (see Redshaw 2008). The ability to realize one's own wishes for mobility and to be able to show one's control over the material world give the driver a sense of autonomy that is apparent to others. This is the freedom that cars have given to their drivers: to go where they want, when they want, much faster and more comfortably than with any other means of personal transport. The exercise of judgement and fine motor skills needed to realize one's desire for motility gives the driver pleasure, and mastery over such a complex object is rewarded with sensations of speed and precise control. Those who are unable to drive (teenagers, 'joyriders', those with insufficient money) are perhaps more aware of these benefits than those who drive regularly and take them for granted. In the films, popular music and advertisements of twentieth-century culture, the car symbolized freedom and social status and actually being able to drive promised to deliver them. New models were reported for showing design and sociotechnical progress. But by the turn of the twenty-first century, the car had become almost ubiquitous while its freedom was curtailed by the legal and practical constraints of speeding, parking and traffic congestion. There has been a decline in the consumption of the car in rich northern cultures such as the UK, where it is criticized as an instrument of death, pollution and global warming.[2] But still the car is a convenient mobility aid and there will be many who resist losing the autonomy, mastery and sense of freedom that driving gives them.

Beyond the individualist rewards of driving, the road system continues to be a distinctively modern space of sociality and morality in which those in control of cars recognize the other members of their society through social relations characterized by responsibility and tolerance. What is remarkable about drivers in traffic is their capacity for sustained and very close interaction that, through following rules, codes and norms of behaviour, respects the rights and interests of other road users. Driver–cars interact with one another as strangers through the limited communication devices they have; winking indicators to warn, flashing headlights to give way and a horn to express impatience, anger and alarm (see Juhlin 2010 for a fascinating empirical account of 'Traffic as situated interaction'). These crude signals are nuanced by drivers' more expressive use of engine revs, swerves, sudden turns of speed or excessive braking as well as facial and hand gestures. Some drivers even resort to opening a window or door to vocalize their feelings or ask for directions. Driving, especially in traffic, depends on a mutual social cooperation that expresses an unspoken solidarity, a 'conscience collective' that is taken for granted and only noticed when a transgression occurs. The road environment is a meaningful *umwelt* inhabited by different types of users (all sorts of vehicles, pedestrians and other animals), who must each be responsive to the signals that all the others give off.

Driving involves an emotional investment in the practice that includes reacting to the way others do it (Katz 1999). Sometimes 'normal' driver–car interaction breaks down and road rage, a burst of anger at the transgression of the other, can lead to out-of-car interactions and occasionally violent attacks. Even the sociability of in-car conversation has a special quality that is partly shaped by the driver's interaction with the world beyond the car (Laurier *et al.* 2008). Some difficult conversations are much easier to handle within the forward-seated and closed environment of the car, because driving tasks provide a diversionary topic or a way of managing pauses and cues. Driving has been a source of employment for chauffeurs and drivers of freight vehicles, delivery vans, taxis and a significant part of the work of police, ambulance, fire and other emergency workers, as well as those like sales staff, area managers, doctors and social workers. The state regulation of the right to drive means that the driving licence is a recognized document of identity and membership of one's society. Not only will the driverless car take away work, it will also remove the citizen status of licensed drivers who share interests and responsibilities in relation to the political authorities of government, police and highways.

The driverless car currently appears to be an extension of systems that 'assist' the commander of the vehicle, who retains ultimate autonomy. But if the right to determine speed, style of driving and choice of route is left with a person inside the car, the gains to be made will be threatened. They will only be fully realized by linking in-car AI with an external traffic system; true automobility would then be a dispersed function of a remote official source operating on behalf of all road users. The speed and precise route will be set not by the vehicle alone but by 'smart' road systems that direct traffic according to conditions and demand. The road system might be managed by the state or perhaps by a privatized multinational Google/News Corp institution with economic and technological power to circumvent the politically legitimated demands of states and regional authorities. But whoever manages the road system, the autonomy of drivers will disappear as they become just passengers who, even if they own a mobility pod, can do no more than request to be taken to a destination.

The driverless car seems to promise a true automobility that will supersede that of the driver–car assemblage. But what I argue here is that the driverless car will necessarily become part of an interconnected 'smart' environment over which individual humans have little control; a politically constituted authority will invest in and prescribe the principles by which the day-to-day management of traffic is operated by an artificially intelligent system. This will restrict direct individual human engagement with the social as well as material environment of traffic; the driverless car promises yet another retreat from sociality into a privatized world. Mobility, one of the defining qualities of the human species, would be even more shaped by a sociotechnical system responding to the needs of the social collective. But for those inside the driverless cars it would be experienced simply as a system: intransigent, insensitive and lifeless. Up to now, the technological advances of AI have been introduced on more expensive models, in which speed, lines and luxury are giving way to safety, comfort and space as the signs of high status. The increasingly autonomous car is a further opportunity for the owner to show their status through consumption, and the driverless car that enables more miles to be driven for less effort and less fuel offers a new opportunity for the 'consumption of excess' (Urry 2010). Just as the true automobility of the car seems about to arrive, it will be dispersed in a collectivized system that deprives not only the citizen but also the vehicle itself of autonomy over its mobility. That is until the oil runs out or a climate-change premium on mobility finally stops the car in its tracks.

Notes

1 At a TED (Technology Entertainment Design) lecture in March 2011, Thrun explained with video clips how the Google cars had been developed. See: <http://www.ted.com/talks/sebastian_thrun_google_s_driverless_car.html> (accessed 3 December 2011).

2 From a peak of 3.2 million in the mid-2000s, the number of new registrations dipped to 2.4 million in 2009, the lowest figure since 1995. In 2009–10, the number of practical driving tests taken fell to about 1.5 million from a peak of 1.8 million in 2005–6. Transport Statistics Great Britain Vehicles: 2010 DOT. <http://www2.dft.gov.uk/pgr/statistics/datatablespublications/tsgb/latest/tsgb2010vehicles.pdf> (accessed 5 October 2011).

Bibliography

Audi (2011) 'Integrated safety' <http://www.audi.co.uk/new-cars/a8/a8/safety.html> (accessed 16 April 2011).

Campbell, M., Egerstedt, M., How, J. and Murray, R. (2010) 'Autonomous driving in urban environments: approaches, lessons and challenges', *Philosophical Transactions of the Royal Society A*, 368, 4649–4672.

Dant, T. (2004) 'The driver-car', *Theory, Culture and Society*, special issue on automobility, 21(4): 61–79.

Dickmanns, E. D. (2002) 'The development of machine vision for road vehicles in the last decade'. In *Proc. IEEE Intelligent Vehicle Symp.* 268–281. New York, NY: IEEE.

Furness, Z. (2010) *One Less Car*, Philadelphia: Temple University Press.

Honda (2010) 'Accord Saloon and Tourer 2010' brochure, <http://www.honda.co.uk/cars/_assets/downloads/accordsaloon/Accord_Saloon.pdf> (accessed 16 April 2011).

Horkheimer, M. (1974 [1947]) *The Eclipse of Reason*, New York: Continuum Books.

Juhlin, O. (2010) *Social Media on the Road: The Future of Car Based Computing*, London: Springer Verlag.

Katz, J. (1999) *How Emotions Work*, Chicago: University of Chicago Press.

Kesting, A., Treiber, M. and Helbing, D. (2010) 'Enhanced intelligent driver model to assess the impact of driving strategies on traffic capacity', *Philosophical Transactions of the Royal Society A*, 368, 4585–4605.

Lam, J-K., Casey J. and Vogel L. (2005) 'Trial and evaluation of intelligent road studs', *European Transport Conference* <http://www.etcproceedings.org/paper/trial-and-evaluation-of-intelligent-road-studs> (accessed 16 April 2011).

Langewiesche, W. (2009) *Fly by Wire: The Geese, The Glide, The 'Miracle' on the Hudson*, London: Penguin Books.

Latour, Bruno (1996) *Aramis or the Love of Technology*, Cambridge, MA: Harvard University Press.

Laurier, E., Brown, B.A.T., Lorimer, H., *et al.* (2008) 'Driving and passengering: notes on the natural organization of ordinary car travel and talk', *Mobilities*, 3(1): 1–23.

Marcuse, H. (1998 [1941]) 'Some social implications of modern technology' in H. Marcuse, *Technology, War and Fascism: Collected Papers Volume One*, London: Routledge.

Miles, J. C. and Walker, J. A. (n.d.) 'Science review: the potential application of artificial intelligence in transport', *Foresight Intelligent Infrastructure Systems Project* <http://www.bis.gov.uk/assets/bispartners/foresight/docs/intelligent-infrastructure-systems/artificial-intelligence-transport.pdf> (accessed 16 April 2011).

NHTSA (2011) *National Highway Traffic Safety Administration Vehicle Safety and Fuel Economy Rulemaking and Research Priority Plan 2011–2013* <http://www.nhtsa.gov/staticfiles/rulemaking/pdf/2011-2013_Vehicle_Safety-Fuel_Economy_Rulemaking-Research_Priority_Plan.pdf> (accessed 16 April 2011).

Redshaw, S. (2008) *In the Company of Cars: Driving as a Social and Cultural Practice*, Aldershot, Hampshire: Ashgate.

SARTRE (2011) 'First Demonstration of SARTRE vehicle platooning', Safe Road Trains for the Environment, press release <http://www.sartre-project.eu/en/about/news/Sidor/Pressrelease20110117.aspx> (accessed 16 April 2011).

Sugiyama, Y., Fukui, M., Kikuchi, M., Hasebe, K., Nakayama, A., Nishinari, K., Tadaki, S. and Yukawa, S. (2008) 'Traffic jams without bottlenecks – experimental evidence for the physical mechanism of the formation of a jam', *New Journal of Physics*, 10.

Tallis, R. (2003) *The Hand: A Philosophical Inquiry into Human Being*, Edinburgh: Edinburgh University Press.

Urry, John (2010) 'Consuming the planet to excess', *Theory Culture and Society*, 27(2–3): 191–212.

23

The environmental teapot and other loaded household objects

Reconnecting the politics of technology, issues and things

Noortje Marres

Introduction

In Dutch, a 'teapot' refers to, among others things, a particular type of children's story. According to this formula, the story-teller uses the word *theepotje* to provide a cue to the listening children, prompting them to guess the word that should come next in the story. When the story-teller says: one bright Saturday morning, Lucy woke up early and went to the 'teapot', those listening are supposed to fill in the blank, and say: 'market' or 'toilet' or 'mountain'. If there is more than one listener, suggestions tend to multiply, because the answer to this type of cue is both easy to guess and by no means self-evident. I was reminded of this game of generative story-telling in recent years, because teapots were proliferating with special intensity in publicity media, in the context of a broader hype around sustainability and environmental living. In this period, teapots (and related household objects like kettles, cups and, in Britain, 'the cuppa') became a routine presence in environmental campaigns, advertising, news, brochures and infotainment online (see Figure 23.1 for an example). These teapots were usually accompanied by slogans advertising the special opportunities offered by kettles and teapots for saving money, energy and the environment: 'only boil what you need', 'keep your kettle in check', 'green your cuppa', or more plainly 'Drink a Cuppa Tea', 'find out the true cost of that cuppa', 'Help Protect the Environment' and so on.

Although teapots were pretty much a constant presence in environmental publicity in this period, there were some subtle and not so subtle shifts in their connotations. One could say that kettles and teapots came to serve as a kind of placeholder-object, because they were deployed to invoke a range of related but different issues: climate change, the smart grid, sustainable design, coal-fired power plants. Two examples can serve as an indication of the range of issues that teapots were used to conjure up. At one end, there is the teapot that featured in *Teatime Britain*, a film co-produced by the BBC and the energy company EDF in 2009, which seeks to show the basic idea behind the so-called 'smart grid'. This film places us in the control room of the UK national electricity grid control centre, showing us the grid controller at work, whose moment comes with the end of *Coronation Street*. The end of this TV show is followed by a surge in kettle boiling across Britain, with millions of kettles being switched on at more or less the same time, which in this case require the manager to make an impromptu intervention, bringing online a

Figure 23.1   Only boil what you need. DIY Planet Repairs, publicity campaign for the Mayor of London, Henley Centre Headlight Vision, now The Futures Company (2007)

French hydraulic dam at the last minute, highlighting the dynamic, real–time and 'social' nature of grid management.[1]

Around the same time, teapots also made an appearance in *A Time Comes*, a documentary about the occupation of the Kingsnorth power station by Greenpeace activists in the English county of Kent. During an interview, one of the activists, who famously scaled the tower of the power station, equally invoked teapots when she said: 'What we did that day is shut down a giant power station. Which was a pretty big deal. But lots of people doing little things makes just as much difference.'[2] Here, the teapot is used to invoke not smart but dirty, CO_2-emitting technology, with the coal-fired power plant as a case in point.

As in the generative game of telling a 'teapot', then, teapots were used to insert a range of different issues into the 'stories' told in publicity media in this period. In this chapter, I explore this capacity of teapots to invoke issues, by considering them as a particular type of 'interface' objects, to use the term proposed by the editors of this volume. As in the examples above, teapots can be used to establish connections between disparate issues, settings and actors: they help to connect the rhythms of everyday social life with the technological dynamics of energy provision. As such, I want to propose here, teapots provide an interesting site for a wider exploration of how objects may become 'charged' with issues, or what I call the 'issuefication' of things (Marres and Rogers 2005). I argue that the normative capacities of such issuefied objects can be usefully distinguished from other types of normative or 'political' objects, most notably the 'scripted object' (Akrich 1992). As I discuss below, the latter object has normative effects insofar as it projects a particular role onto subjects, but in the former case what matters is the 'resonance' of the object itself: the range of issues that it is able to invoke.

In distinguishing these two forms of object-politics, I concentrate on how to conceptualize them, but I touch as well on the empirical methods that we can use to analyse different types of normative objects. I also pay special attention to the role of technology, and in particular the role of digital technologies, in enabling the 'issuefication' of objects. The loading of issues into objects, I propose, depends heavily on the ways in which said objects are equipped. All this means that I approach teapots as 'interface objects' also in a second sense: this type of object can be used to investigate wider connections between the politics of things, technologies and issues, as they arise in the case of 'issuefied' objects.

The politics of augmented objects versus that of scripted objects

Perhaps especially in Britain, but by no means exclusively, it is difficult to think of a more 'social' object than a teapot. Generally speaking, teapots (and related household objects like kettles, stoves, and the aforementioned cuppa) are closely associated with sociability, as in the phrase 'I'll put the kettle on', which recurs in countless clips and moments of English life, and so obviously invokes a reassuring domesticity, the comfort of a welcoming host. The teapot may also be considered a 'political object', and this insofar as it is invoked to affirm political bonds, such as those of the nation-state. As the *Mail Online* stated in a recent article, 'Britain is a nation of tea and coffee drinkers' and '97% of Brits own a kettle'.[3] The very ordinariness of the teapot makes it possible to invoke a population: because it is both ubiquitous and supposedly culturally specific, an everyday practice like tea drinking can be taken to imply membership in a larger collective. Indeed, in recent decades sociologists, anthropologists, philosophers and historians have directed attention to precisely this capacity of material objects and practices for the organization of political collectives (Anderson 1983; Winner 1980; Latour 1993). (Tea and coffee seem to have special affordances in this respect: they figure prominently in historical accounts of the emergence of 'modern publics' as a distinctive moral and political form in the seventeenth century, in the coffeehouses of Vienna and Istanbul (Sennett 1977; Leezenberg 2007).)

The 'environmental' teapots under discussion here equally show these social and political features, but this type of object also complicates our understanding of them. In their case, the capacity of objects to help forge political or moral bonds does not just extend to people, but is also made to include other categories like nature or 'the future' (Braun and Whatmore 2010). Moreover, these teapots are made to serve a particular normative purpose: they are used to establish connections between everyday living and complex issues. To make sense of these particular normative capacities of objects, I propose, it may be useful to distinguish this type of normative object from another one, namely the scripted object.

The latter concept was put forward by sociologists of technology in the 1980s and 1990s to expose the ways in which seemingly 'neutral' technologies can be deployed to pursue political ends (Akrich 1992; Latour 1992; Oudshoorn and Pinch 2003; see Wilkie 2010 and Berker 2011 for recent elaborations). Most influentially, Madeleine Akrich (1992) proposed the idea of the 'script' to describe how technological objects could be used to turn people into national subjects, in a classic case study of electricity meters in Ivory Coast. Noting that the government of Ivory Coast had few resources at its disposal for involving people as citizens in the nation-state, she argued that the electricity grid became an important means for forging political bonds between the government and its subjects. The device of the electricity meter, she argued, was crucial to this project: by rendering electricity use measurable, the device enabled the ongoing registration of individuals, and thereby their enrolment as 'documented subjects' in an infrastructure that was national in scope. In Akrich's account, then, the installation of household electricity meters amounted to a nation-building exercise.

Inevitably, in proposing the concept of the 'script' to account for the normative capacities of this type of object, sociologists made a number of assumptions about the nature of their politics (Akrich 1992; see also Oudshoorn and Pinch 2003). First, scripted objects are called 'political' *insofar as they act upon subjects*: the electricity meter is here a political object insofar as it projects a particular role to be played by subjects, in this case, that of a documented individual subject who may be addressed by an administrative system. Second, and relatedly, in order to ascribe normativity to scripted objects, it was necessary to attribute *determinate effects* to these objects. That is, the Ivory Coast electricity meter counted as a political object for a precise reason: because it rendered electricity use measurable in a context in which strong bureaucratic institutions were absent, this device could fulfil the politically useful function of defining people as documented individuals implicated in a national arrangement. *This* (and no other feature) is what made the electricity meter a political object, in this case. Finally, it should be noted that a scripted object like Akrich's electricity meter is only *latently* political: the object's political intervention here happens below the radar of what is generally assumed to be going on, and this circumstance *adds* to its political efficacy. The fact that electricity meters are *not* widely recognized as capable of political intervention makes it easier to deploy them to such ends (see on this point also Marres 2010). And it then becomes the task of social studies of technology to *expose* these normative capacities of objects, to show that it is going on and analyse its workings.

The teapots under scrutiny here are suggestive of a different type of 'object-politics', which I will call, for now, the politics of 'augmented objects'. This type of object can be called 'political' insofar as it comes to resonate with issues. Here, what requires special attention are not, in first instance, the effects of objects on subjects, but rather the 'normative range' of the object itself: the spectrum of concerns that it 'carries' or may 'activate'. A useful example here are the technologically enhanced teapots that in recent years featured in publicity about sustainable innovation, especially blogs. These are teapots and kettles to which have been added some technical (often digital) component, like a display or a light that changes colour, in order to communicate an environmental message (see also Marres 2011). Augmented teapots come in different shapes and forms: from the eco-kettle that sells for £39.99 in the Ethical Superstore, which has a simple measuring strip and helps you 'boil the exact amount of water you need' to more sophisticated and experimental versions, such as Chris Adam's Arduino-equipped teapot (see Figure 23.2), which provides real-time cues about the 'environmental quality' of electricity, by drawing on a network feed from a website that monitors the 'carbon intensity' of the current electricity supply in the UK.

In contrast to scripted objects, such augmented teapots present us with *demonstrably* political objects: they wear their normative capacities on their sleeve, so to speak. These teapots are equipped with what Lisa Adkins and Celia Lury (2009) have called 'empirical technologies': they come with auxiliary devices attached to them, such as lights, informational 'feeds', and displays, which quite literally put on display the ability of these objects to act on environmental issues. The special capacities of these objects tend to be proclaimed in other ways too, through slogans and other forms of publicity. Thus, the blog on which Chris Adams (2009) presents his augmented teapot carefully explains how his augmented teapot makes it possible to insert environmental issues into everyday life: 'Placing the [teapot] in a relatively high traffic co-working space is a great opportunity to speak to people and see how best to communicate on issues related to climate change.'

Figure 23.2 'Yes, now is a good time to make tea'. 'Tea, Arduino and Dynamic Demand', Chris Adams and James Gardner, 24 April 2009

In this respect, Chris Adams's carbon teapot can clearly *not* be called a 'latently' normative object. To the contrary, his teapot can only be called political insofar as it is equipped with explicit visual, textual and technical cues indicating its capacity for action on the environment: a light, a measuring strip, a feed, a name: eco-kettle. Two further points follow from this.

First, the politics of augmented objects does not seem to derive exclusively, or even principally, from their ability to act *on subjects*. Their normativity is more open-ended than that: it hinges on the capacity of the object, not to project a definite role onto human actors, but to become 'charged' with issues. In this case, the focus rests very much on the explicit investment of objects themselves with political and moral capacities, such as the ability to make global issues relevant on the plane of everyday living. What is at stake here, normatively speaking, is the question of what *objects* are capable of: can a teapot really facilitate effective, significant, meaningful engagement with environmental issues? Here, then, it is the object that is being equipped for political or moral action, at least as much as the subject. Partly as a consequence of this, the politics of augmented objects seems much less 'determinate' than that of scripted objects. In this case, whether the object can be ascribed a politics hinges on the capacity of the object to resonate with a *spectrum* of issues: climate change, smart grid, peak oil, innovation, the carbon economy, and so on. What matters here is the normative range of the object, the spectrum of issues that may be 'loaded' into the object, or as the case may be, that it is not able to accommodate.

This account of augmented teapots has some wider implications for how we understand the connections between the politics of objects and technology in this case. These teapots provide a useful reminder of the auxiliary role played by technology in enabling the politics of objects. Of course, the ability of technology to extend and amplify the capacities of both subjects and objects has long been recognized in social and cultural theories of technology (McLuhan 2001 (1964)). However, augmented teapots invite a particular empirical question and a more general philosophical comment on this score. To begin with the question, augmented teapots invite us to probe further what exactly is the role of digital technologies in enabling the politics of objects, and 'issuefication' more in particular. Digital devices, it has also long been recognized, have special affordances when it comes to the 'animation' of things: sensors can be used to render things 'aware', chips can make them 'smart', and provide them with other actor-like qualities like feedback and control (Suchman 2011).[4] However, in the case of augmented teapots, we are dealing not so much with the investment of things with actor-like capacities (talking, thinking, speaking) but with the loading of issues into objects. This particular ability of digital devices I further explore in the last section of this chapter.[5]

As regards philosophy, to direct attention to the normative equipment of objects, as I do here, is to suggest a particular take on political ontology. This branch of political philosophy is classically concerned with the 'innate' normative capacities of different beings, but augmented teapots remind us that the normativity of objects also depends on how objects are decked out: they direct attention to the *artefactual* nature of the politics of things. In this case at least, it is only insofar as the object is technologically enhanced with features like feeds and sensors, and is 'plugged' into various networks, that it may seem capable of opening issues up for action. Augmented teapots, I argue, are suggestive of a different version of what the philosopher Graham Harman (2007) has called a 'non-exceptionalist' understanding of objects: just *like* other beings capable of normative action, i.e. humans and institutions, objects depend on auxiliary devices for their ability to exert political and/or moral force. In order to grasp the politics of objects, we must then pay attention not just to these objects themselves, but also to the particular devices with which they are equipped. In the case of augmented objects at least, the politics of objects includes the politics of technology.

Issuefication: a pragmatist politics of objects?

But there is also another relation to consider, that between the politics of objects and the politics of *issues*.[6] If we are right to say that teapots may be charged with issues, what relation between objects and issues does this imply? What does 'issuefication' actually mean? In the post-war period, the politics of issues has principally been understood, in the social and political sciences, as a *discursive* politics, one that involves the deployment of salient ideas, terms or 'issue frames' (and not so much things) to instigate and organize social movements, political processes and/or news cycles (Snow and Benford 1988). How does the more peculiar phenomenon of the issuefication of objects relate to, or differ from, these more familiar forms of issue politics? And how should we understand the relations between a particular object of issuefication, say a teapot, and broader societal and political processes of issue formation, i.e. those associated with the formulation of 'issue agendas' by political and other organizations and the 'issue cycles' that unfold in the news and other media?

Minimally speaking, 'issuefication' refers to a dynamic in which an object comes to 'resonate' with particular matters of concerns (Marres and Rogers 2005). However, such a definition raises as many questions as it answers, for what does it mean to speak of 'resonance' in this context, and what is it that issuefied objects resonate with? These questions can be approached conceptually and empirically, and in the remainder of this chapter, I touch on both. Conceptually, issuefication invokes a particular argument of American pragmatist political philosophy. Among others, it calls to mind the intellectual project of John Dewey, who proposed that many of the things we associate with politics and morality (like values, problems, desires, conflict and interests) are best regarded as 'aspects of objective situations' (see on this point also Marres 2010; Muniesa 2012). As Dewey (1998 (1908)) forcefully put it: 'such things as lack and need, conflict and clash, desire and effort, loss and satisfaction [must be] referred to reality'.

In making this claim, Dewey proposed to displace all sorts of normative phenomena that we have learned to associate with humans (conflict, interest, pain and values) onto the plane of objects. It turns conflict, pain, trouble into aspects of what Dewey insists on calling objective, problematic situations. Which is also to say, from a Deweyan perspective, if we are to account adequately for the 'politics of objects', we must pay careful attention to the *problematization* of things. To quote him one more time: 'valuation takes place only when there is something the matter; when there is some trouble to be done away with, some need, lack or privation to be made good, some conflict of tendencies to be resolved by means of changing existing conditions' (Dewey 1955 (1908)). To take our cue from John Dewey's pragmatism in the analysis of the politics of objects is then to insist that there is nothing resolved, or neat or fixed about a politics of objects. Instead, we must consider the ways things may become charged with a range of problems, issues and trouble.

Dewey's object-centred theory of normativity, then, suggests a particular account of how objects acquire their moral and political capacities. He invokes a very diffuse process in which 'trouble' ('conflicts of tendencies') emerge on the plane of objects. Normativity here is first and foremost something that 'happens' on the level of things. This approach can be contrasted to a 'legislative' or 'prescriptive' understanding of normativity, which can still be recognized in the notion of the 'script', and suggests that normativity resides in the 'blueprints for action' that are inscribed in objects and projected or forced onto subjects. Dewey proposes to understand normativity rather as a material event, as something that involves inevitably muddled forms of trouble emerging on the level of objects. He directs attention to problematization as something that plays itself out in things: it is of the order of the event, and not of intentional action or purposeful effects and the design of objectives into things.

However, of this troubling politics of objects we can still ask: how do entities succeed in 'piggybacking' on unfolding events of politicization? Just as we can ask of political actors how they succeed in taking advantage of existing political currents, and in making them serve their purposes, so we can ask of objects and devices: how, as part of a wider, unfolding dynamics of issuefication, do they succeed in 'bending' the currents of issuefication? How do objects come to accommodate wider issues and how do they contribute to the specification of these issues?

A pragmatistically informed approach to the politics of objects then opens up a number of questions that we may take up in the empirical analysis of the issuefication of things. First, if we understand issuefication as a wider ontological process that may be instrumentalized, i.e. made to serve specific ends, the question is how, exactly, this is done.[7] How does the equipment of objects, as in the case of the augmented teapot, provide a way to specify an issue-object, and to align it with particular moral and political purposes? To begin answering this question, it is useful to consider the particular devices that are deployed to do this work of the specification of issue-objects. On this point too, the augmented teapot may offer some useful examples: in the 'Only boil what you need' poster in Figure 23.1, for instance, the object (teapot) and issue ('environment') are associated by the graphic trick of *overlaying* issue and object (Marres 2012). By establishing a visual connection between a teapot and the planet, the suggestion is helped along that the former offers a point of access to the latter. In the case of Chris Adam's 'digitally enhanced' teapot (Figure 23.2), object (teapot) and issue (climate change) are associated through a real-time feed, which literally makes it possible to load live environmental data (about carbon emissions associated with the UK electricity supply) into objects. Here, the supposed 'liveness' of the environmental information feed may (or may not) help to dramatize the liveliness of the issuefied object.

Indeed, there seems to be a plethora of other devices available for channelling currents of issuefication, from the labelling of consumer products to the spatial tracing of waste with the aid of GPS (Global Positioning System) technologies. Empirical description of these techniques would surely help to clarify the mysterious phenomenon of the issuefication of things. However, I want to conclude this chapter by considering another, although related, empirical question: by what methods can we analyse the 'issue content' of a given object? This question brings us back to a point raised at the beginning of this section: that of the similarities and differences between the phenomenon of 'issuefication' and those processes of 'issue formation' that have been analysed in such great depth in post-war political and social science. Our brief excursion into pragmatist philosophy has made it clear that dynamics of issuefication do *not* principally operate on the level of ideas, as many political and social scientists have assumed about issue politics. But despite this obvious difference, social and political methods of 'issue analysis' may still prove useful for researching the issuefication of things.

Object variability as an index of politicization and how to analyse this

Issuefied objects, as mentioned, may host a variety of issues. In the examples above, teapots were variously associated with climate change, the smart grid, coal-fired power plants and geeky innovation cultures. In this regard, issuefied objects present highly variable or unresolved objects, and this resonates well with Dewey's insistence that the normativity of things is marked by trouble and conflicting tendencies. This 'variability' of issuefied objects also seems important for their empirical analysis, in a number of ways. First and foremost, the variation among the issues with which a given object becomes associated is something that we may well be able to measure. Of course, in some respects, fluctuations in the 'normative charge' of objects may be tricky to detect, but it is not so difficult in others. For a well-publicized object like the environmental teapot, it is easy to get at least an indication of the spectrum of issues with which this object is associated in different media and settings.

To get an indication of the 'normative range' of this household object, we must then consider its *distribution*: we must examine the different settings in which the object appears, and plot the different connotations with which it has become associated here. These varying associations may tell us something about the issue content of the object, or more precisely, its current state of issuefication. Here, textual methods of issue analysis may prove relevant for the study of the issuefication of things. Digital technologies of content analysis may prove especially useful. Turning to the Web, we can use basic tools of online textual and visual analysis to document the range of issues with which a given object has become associated in different media settings (Rogers 2009; see also Marres and Rogers 2005).[8] Using these instruments, we can make an indicative mapping of 'resonant' terms with which teapots are associated in relevant online spaces, or 'spheres'. Thus, Figure 23.3 presents an overview of keywords and phrases that appear with some frequency in proximity to 'teapot' and 'kettle' in different groups of websites: energy companies, a sustainable innovation network, and green blogs (the size of the respective teapots indicates the relative frequency of its mentioning in the sphere in question).

As it turns out, analysis of these sources indicates an issue range for the environmental teapot that is substantial in some ways, but limited in others. Although the connotations of the teapot here extend from 'peak oil' to 'health', and from 'thought bombs' to 'veg box recipes', they do *not* include some of the more challenging issues associated with 'environmentally aware' household objects, such as fuel poverty: the mounting evidence that the rising costs of domestic energy use are hurting relatively poor people disproportionately (Preston and White 2010).

This type of analysis could be further developed to capture variations not just across spheres and settings but also in time.[9] But in both cases, the variability of the object might be taken as an index of its state of politicization. Political theorists from Machiavelli to Habermas have

Figure 23.3 'Environmental' teapots in three spheres on the Web: energy companies, a sustainable innovation network, and green living blogs (March 2011). Figure designed by, and reproduced by permission of, Jeanne Giraud

insisted on the fact that the capacity to *change* one's mind or one's political alliances is a crucial asset in politics. Relatedly, it has been argued that political arguments made by seemingly non-political actors, such as scientists, are especially powerful (Barry 2001). Perhaps something similar may be said of everyday, 'non-political' objects taking on a normative charge. Their ability to adopt varying issue agendas may then serve as an index of its normativity.

These dynamics requires further exploration, but I would like to conclude this section by flagging that, in analysing dynamics of issuefication, we must take care *not* to assume that it is only connotations and not the objects that vary. That is, we should not think as a matter of course that variations occur exclusively on the level of issue-associations or objects attributes, whereas 'the thing itself' would somehow remain stable (see on this point Mol 2002). Teapots come in many different shapes and sizes, and this applies to environmental teapots just as well. Online textual and visual analysis can help out on this point too: Figure 23.4 gives an indication of the range of teapots that figure in environmental energy spaces on the web, based on Google Image Search. No doubt the issues invoked on these pages vary, but so do the teapots themselves. Just because a teapot is 'just a teapot', this is no reason to not take seriously the variability of the object 'itself'.

Conclusion

The investigation of environmental teapots, then, can help to bring into view some notable differences between the politics of 'issuefied' objects and those of scripted objects. The latter objects, we have seen, can only be called political insofar as *determinate* effects can be traced back to them, such as the constraints that they place on people's behaviour, and their influence on people's self-understanding. In this case, the more singular its effects, the stronger the scripted object's claim to politicality. In the case of issuefied objects, by contrast, it is the variability of forms, issues and associations that the object may accommodate, which signals that we are dealing with a 'normative' object. The higher the contrasts and tensions among the issues and associations

Figure 23.4 Teapots in three spheres on the Web: energy companies, a sustainable innovation network, and green living blogs (December 2011). Figure designed by, and reproduced by permission of, Jeanne Giraud

that are loaded into the object, the stronger it must be coded on the political spectrum (going from 'highly' normative to a 'not so' normative object). Normativity here is a matter of bandwidth. The variation of its normative charge is what makes an issuefied object a political object, and the 'range' or 'scope' of this variation can be treated as an index of its state of politicization.

It is a task for us as analysts to determine which dynamics (those of scripting or those of issuefication) are most relevant to understanding the politics of objects in particular cases. Teapots may be analysed for the scripts built into them, but also for the issues they are used to invoke, canalize and specify. The divergences and confluences between these two normative dynamics of objects no doubt require further examination. Perhaps the most important thing about analysing 'issuefication' is that it directs attention to political *contestation* as something that plays itself out through objects, rather than limiting this capacity to human actors (who refuse to follow scripts, for instance). To attend to this trouble also requires us to recognize the various ways in which the politics of issuefication may be untraceable. Jeanne Giraud, the graphic designer who designed Figures 23.3 and 23.4, put it well during a discussion of what such figures might possibly tell us. Pointing to the words that leave the teapot like smoke, Jeanne made a quick stroke with her arm in the air, saying 'into the atmosphere', thereby turning the teapot for a moment into a factory, a source of emissions.

Notes

1 BBC/EDF, *Teatime Britain*, http://www.bbc.co.uk/britainfromabove/stories/people/teatimebritain. shtml
2 *A Time Comes: The story of the Kingsnorth Six*, directed by Nick Broomfield, *The Observer*, 31 May 2009, http://www.guardian.co.uk/environment/video/2009/may/31/nick-broomfield-kingsnorth
3 Our Cuppa Habit is Heating Up, *Mail Online*, 25 Oct 2011.
4 This suggests a wider significance for the concept of the 'Internet of things', which is often taken to refer, in a more limited sense, to the technological possibility of assigning IP addresses to objects.
5 In taking up this question, we should not forget that many of these features have also been ascribed to other technologies in the past. Electricity, for instance, has long been thought to make possible communication among objects (Nye, 1999; see also Bennett, 2010).
6 I am grateful to David Oswell for insisting on the importance of this question.
7 There are then at least two parts to processes of issuefication: the emergence of ontological trouble as event and the specification of this trouble through the deployment of devices. It seems characteristic of issuefication that these two parts cannot be clearly distinguished, although this requires further discussion.
8 For an overview of tools developed by govcom.org and the Digital Methods Group at the University of Amsterdam, see https://wiki.digitalmethods.net/Dmi/
9 Erik Borra and Ingmar Weber have developed a more sophisticated version of this type of issue analysis, in their project Political Search. This application relies on online dynamics to determine the fluctuating 'political charges' of data-objects. Data-objects are visualized using a literal spectrum bar, which shows the political composition of the object at a given moment (does 'Obama' tend towards the red end of the spectrum or rather towards the blue? How about last week?). See http://politicalinsights.sandbox.yahoo. com/

Bibliography

Adams, C. (2009) 'Tea, Arduino and dynamic demand', blog post, 24 April, http://chrisadams.me. uk/2009/04/24/tea-arduino-and-dynamic-demand/ (accessed 28 March 2012).
Adkins, L. and Lury, C. (2009) Introduction to special issue 'What is the empirical?', *European Journal of Social Theory* 12: 5–20.
Akrich, M. (1992) 'The de-scription of technical objects', in W. E. Bijker and J. Law (eds.) *Shaping Technology/ Building Society: Studies in Sociotechnical Change*, Cambridge, MA: MIT Press: 205–224.
Anderson, B. (1983) *Imagined Communities: Reflections on the Origins and Spread of Nationalism*, London and New York: Verso.
Barry, A. (2001) 'Sights and sites', in *Political Machines: Governing the Technological Society*, London: Athlone Press.
Bennett, J. (2010) *Vibrant Matter: A Political Ecology of Things*, Durham: Duke University Press.
Berker, T. (2011) 'Domesticating spaces: sociotechnical studies and the built environment', *Space and Culture* 14: 259–268.
Braun, B. and Whatmore, S. (2010) 'The stuff of politics: an introduction', *Political Matter: Technoscience, Democracy and Public Life*, Minneapolis: University of Minnesota Press.
Dewey, J. (1998 (1908)) 'Does reality possess practical character?' Reprinted in L.A. Hickman and T. M. Alexander (eds.) *The Essential Dewey* Vol. 1, *Pragmatism, Education, Democracy*, Bloomington: Indiana University Press: 124–133.
Dewey, J. (1955 (1908)) 'Theory of valuation'. Reprinted in O. Neurath, R. Carnap, and C. Morris (eds.) *International Encyclopedia of Unified Science* Vol. 2, No. 4, Chicago: University of Chicago Press.
Harman, G. (2007) 'On vicarious causation', in R. Mackay (ed) *Collapse: Journal of Philosophical Research and Development*, Vol II, Special issue on speculative realism, Falmouth: Urbanomic: 187–220.
Latour, B. (1992) 'Where are the missing masses? The sociology of a few mundane artifacts', in W. Bijker and J. Law (eds.) *Shaping Technology/Building Society: Studies in Sociotechnical Change*, Cambridge: MIT Press: 225–258.
Latour, B. (1993) *We Have Never Been Modern*, trans. C. Porter, Cambridge: Harvard University Press.
Leezenberg, M. (2007) 'Comparatieve filosofie van het koffieleute', *Krisis* (2): 25–44.
McLuhan, M. (1964, 2nd edn 2001) *Understanding Media: The Extensions of Man*, London and New York: Routledge.

Marres, N. (2010) 'Frontstaging nonhumans: publicity as a constraint on the political activity of things', in B. Braun and S. Whatmore (eds.) *Political Matter, Technoscience, Democracy, and Public Life*, Minneapolis: Minnesota University Press: 177–210.

Marres, N. (2011) 'The cost of involvement: everyday carbon accounting and the materialization of participation', *Economy and Society* 40(4): 510–533.

Marres, N. (2012) *Material Participation: Technology, Environment and Everyday Publics*, Basingstoke: Palgrave.

Marres, N. and Rogers, R. (2005) 'Recipe for tracing the fate of issues and their publics on the Web', in B. Latour and P. Weibel (eds.) *Making Things Public: Atmospheres of Democracy*, Karlsruhe/Cambridge: ZKM/MIT Press.

Mol, A. (2002) *The Body Multiple: Ontology in Medical Practice*, Durham: Duke University Press.

Muniesa, F. (2012) 'A flank movement in the theory of valuation', *Journal of Cultural Economy* Special Issue on Value and Measure.

Nye, D. (1999) *Consuming Power: A Social History of American Energies*, Cambridge, MA: MIT Press.

Oudshoorn, N.E.J. and Pinch, T.J. (eds) (2003) *How Users Matter. The Co-construction of Users and Technology*, Cambridge, MA: MIT Press.

Preston, I. and White, V. (2010) 'The distributional impacts of UK climate change policies, final report to the Eaga Charitable Trust', Centre for Sustainable Energy and Association for the Conservation of Energy.

Rogers, R. (2009) *The End of the Virtual*, Amsterdam: Vossiuspers UvA.

Sennett, R. (1977) *The Fall of Public Man*, New York: Knopf.

Snow, David A. and Benford, R.D. (1988) 'Ideology, frame resonance, and participant mobilization', *International Social Movement Research* 1: 197–217.

Suchman, L. (2011) 'Subject objects', *Feminist Theory* 12(2): 119–145.

Wilkie, A. (2010). 'User assemblages in design: an ethnographic study', Goldsmiths, University of London.

Winner, L. (1980) 'Do artifacts have politics?' *Daedalus* 109: 121–136.

24

Interfaces

The mediation of things and the distribution of behaviours

Celia Lury

Introduction

A number of writers propose that we are currently experiencing not only an increase in the number of objects, but also a transformation in what an object is. Objects today, it is said, are incomplete, in the sense both of continually appearing in new versions, and also of being open or requiring participation by subjects to be completed. The sociologist Karin Knorr Cetina (1997, 2000) proposes that objects are no longer fixed, discrete things of a material nature but the obverse of this insofar as they are characterized by a changing, unfolding character. Sony, for instance, manufactured over 700 versions of the Walkman, aspirin is available in multiple formats, and mobile phones and computers are always being updated. As Knorr Cetina puts it, objects now lack objectivity: they are not fixed or static but are constantly in a condition of transition and transformation. She also argues that objects increasingly make relational demands on us; indeed, she suggests that non-human or object-based sociality pervades some of the important sites of power in contemporary society (for example, the stock exchange and government) as well as saturating mundane practices. She describes the relationality between subjects and objects in terms of an ongoing affinity between subjects conceived as structures of wanting and objects that are unfolding things. Similarly, the science fiction writer and cultural critic Bruce Sterling (2005) suggests that objects today can be understood as what he calls spime; that is, they are 'a set of relationships first and always, and an object now and then' (2005: 77). Spime are data in computational environments, which are designed, accessed, managed and recycled into objects. The important questions, he says, are 'not about the material object, but where it comes from, where it is, how long it stays there, when it goes away, and what comes next' (2005: 109). Like Knorr Cetina, he emphasizes the increasing significance of relating to objects: 'I don't worry much about having things. I worry plenty about relating to them' (2005: 79).

This chapter asks: what is an object today? How is an object to be recognized as such when it does not appear as a single or unitary physical entity, but is, rather, open, incomplete, always changing, and defined in terms of relations rather than in terms of type or even function? More precisely, how is it possible to think of an object as a set of relations that is actualized in multiple forms? The answer proposed here is that objects today may be described as artefacts, that is, as things that are brought into existence by way of the activity of an interface. In its organization by an interface, an object is always multiple, always being multiplied and divided from itself, disassembled and reassembled as an ongoing series of physical entities. The object as artefact does not occupy a single time and space, but rather is to be found in many places, and is always in transformation. In the words of N. Katherine Hayles (1999), objects today can be identified or located not in terms of presence or absence, but rather patterns and randomness. The artefact that is described to support these claims is the brand (Lury 2004; Lash and Lury 2007; Lury 2009).

The notion of artefact used here derives primarily from the work of the economist Herbert Simon (1981 [1969]), who developed an approach to the study of economics that drew on information theory in order to address issues of power in the economy. Simon suggests that an artefact can be thought of as emerging in the activities of an interface 'between an "inner" environment, the substance and organization of the artefact itself, and an "outer" environment, the surroundings in which it operates. If the inner environment is appropriate to the outer environment, or vice versa, the artefact will serve its intended purpose' (1981: 9). For Simon design is understood as the organization of an artificial entity in terms of an intended purpose, that is, it is the organization of an interface or surface of communication between inner and outer environments. In other words, it is the organization of an object as a set of relations. He says, the 'description of an artifice in terms of its organization and functioning – its interface between inner and outer environments – is a major objective of invention and design activity' (1981: 13). In relation to brands, the objective is the organization of an interface for the communication of information between 'producers' and 'consumers', and branded products or services are instances of the series of things that emerge from this organization. The first part of this chapter discusses the brand as artefact in terms of the mediation of things, whereas the second considers the consequences of the relationality of brands in terms of the distribution of behaviours.

The mediation of things

Let me begin the first part of the argument by outlining some ideas about the interface drawn from media theory. From this point of view, an interface may be seen as an example of a frame: a communicative surface or boundary that both connects and separates disunified or disparate spaces (Rodowick 1997). As a type of framing device, the interface of the brand is not located in a single place, at a single time; rather, it is distributed across a number of products and services, publicity and packaging, screens and sites. The interface connects and separates disparate spaces in particular ways: it informs how consumers relate to producers and how producers relate to consumers, but these exchanges, although they are two-way and dynamic, are not direct, symmetrical or reversible. The brand's interface thus has its own (recursive) logic or 'artificial depth'; as design theorist Ezio Manzini puts it,

> The idea of a mute and static border is ... replaced by an idea of the surface as an interface between two ambients, with a role involving an exchange of energy and information between the substances put into contact. The surface as semiotic membrane capable of promoting or inhibiting such an exchange thus becomes a component of the object ... capable of standing between the inside and outside of the object itself, or to provide a range of performances of its own.
>
> *(1989: 183)*

Moreover, because the activity of an interface is not defined in relation to a final goal, it inevitably leads to a continual reformulation of goals. In the case of the brand, the production process continuously feeds on itself, that is, it provides information for itself about itself. This is in part what explains how it is that brands contribute to a logic of flows (Lash and Urry 1994; Appadurai 1996; Castells 1996; Urry 2003), in which products and services are always part of a series, always connected to what has come before and what will come after. This is what is meant by the mediation of things (Lash and Lury 2007).

In his discussion of artefacts Simon identifies a number of distinguishing characteristics or 'advantages'[1] to do with the way in which the interface divides and connects an 'inner' environment from an 'outer' environment. In the case of the brand, these advantages are identified most clearly if they are explored first from the perspective of the outside-in, and then, second, from the perspective of inside-out.

Outside-in

One consequence for artefacts of dividing outer from inner environments is that knowledge of the goals of the system and its outer environment can be used as the basis for action, with only minimal assumptions being required for the inner environment. Two advantages follow from this for Simon. The first of these is that it is possible for those involved in design activity to identify and exploit different inner environments to accomplish identical or similar goals in relation to identical or similar outer environments. Consider the interfaces of the brands Swatch and Nike in this regard.

First, Swatch. A key component of the logo of the brand Swatch from 'outside-in' is a consistent self-identification in relation to Switzerland. Swatch watches display not only the name Swatch (itself a contraction of Swiss and watch) and the Swiss flag, but also the description 'Swiss' on their faces. In addition, much of the promotional literature accompanying products refers to the Swiss-ness of the Swatch ethos. Such references are held to have the effect of strengthening consumer perceptions of trust in the quality of Swatch products in a global commercial environment. This design activity enables Swatch products to sell by securing the trust of (certain) consumers, providing a guarantee of quality, by tying the brand to an origin. This is also one way of saying that Swatch may be seen (from the outside-in) as both a national and a corporate brand.

In contrast, the origin-ality of the Nike interface is less clearly tied to a single place of origin. To some extent, the physical location of the company itself (in Portland, Oregon), dedicated retail outlets such as Niketowns and sports events sponsored by the company may serve as such an origin. Certainly the perception of the flagship retail outlets, Niketowns, as origins is encouraged not only by the highly charged design of the stores, but also by the greater range of stock available. However, alongside such intense and exclusive sites, Nike presents itself as original in relation to the almost endless multiplicity of the sites of its products' uses through the brand's elevation (and ownership) of an ethos of competition, determination and individuality. *Just Do It*, is the brand injunction, and in this 'doing', multiple origins for the brand are brought into being. Of course, it is possible to argue that a culture of competition, determination and individuality is the national culture of the USA and in this sense there is a parallel between the interfaces of the Nike and Swatch brands. But what makes the interface of the Nike brand so distinctive is that it appears as if there is no need to locate this ethos within territorial boundaries in order to secure its ownership or claim its effects. The commercial advantage to be derived from this is that because the brand's origins are not visibly tied to specific places of production, the Nike company is able to exercise enormous spatial flexibility in relation to the place of manufacturing of its products. The Nike interface does not tie the brand to any specific inner environment; it is deterritorializing. Famously, or rather infamously, the Nike company has in fact continually shifted the sites of production from country to country within East Asia in such a way as to be able to take advantage of the cheap and poorly protected workforces in these countries.

A second advantage of the organization of an artefact by way of an interface according to Simon is that the face of an artefact may connote 'perceptual similarity but essential difference, resemblances from without rather than within' (Simon 1981: 17). This, like the first advantage described above, follows from the fact that it is possible for those involved in design activity to identify and choose to develop different inner environments accomplishing similar goals in relation to similar outer environments. This second advantage enables the brand to function as a mechanism of modelling, imitation or simulation. Thus, Simon argues that,

> … the artificial object imitates the real by turning the same face to the outer system, by adapting, relative to the same goals, to comparable ranges of external tasks. Imitation is possible because distinct physical systems can be organized to exhibit nearly identical behaviour.
>
> *(1981: 17)*

In the case of the brand the face presented to the outer environment is typically a logo: the Swatch name, the Nike swoosh. And in many cases the abstraction and generality of this face means that the brand is able to function as a locus for the simulation of product innovation. In other words, innovation need not derive from or be limited to innovation in the production process. Instead it may be produced in the practices of simulation or behaviour modelling, that is, through trials (market research and new product development) in which products are experimentally tested in relation to the goal or aim of reaching a target market.[2] What is being suggested here is that innovation is no longer tied to the production process, or indeed to the 'improvement' of specific products, but rather is understood in relation to meeting the needs of the market, understood in terms of information about consumers.

Let me illustrate the possibilities of the simulation or modelling of innovation with the example of Nike. The origins of Nike are in a company called Blue Ribbon Sports, which Phil Knight, a former runner at the University of Oregon and now Nike Chief Executive Officer, and Bill Bowerman, Knight's former track coach, created in 1962. The company initially did no more than distribute running shoes in the USA for a Japanese company; however, it soon shifted to designing its own shoes and outsourcing their production to East Asia. At this stage in its history, the company's market competitiveness was characterized by a series of functional product innovations linked to developments in the production process (most famously the 'waffle' method of aerating the rubber sole of shoes) and an early mastery of the spatial dynamics of outsourcing. But in the mid-1980s, there was a turning point in the company's fortunes. Nike's growth during this period was fuelled by the expansion of its market brought about by the rise of jogging as a national pastime in the USA, but in the mid-1980s the company suddenly lost its footing. It was overtaken in market share by Reebok, who had tapped into the growing (female) aerobics market, deploying a new understanding of the trainer as accessory or fashion good. As Knight comments,

> We made an aerobics shoe that was functionally superior to Reebok's, but we missed the styling. Reebok's shoe was sleek and attractive, while ours was sturdy and chunky. We also decided against using garment leather, as Reebok had done, because it wasn't durable. By the time we developed a leather that was both strong and soft, Reebok had established a brand, won a huge chunk of sales, and gained the momentum to go right by us.
>
> *(in Willigan 1993: 92)*

Nike was forced to accept a reframing of the market, in which the organizing principles of product innovation were not to do with product function, but rather with communication with consumers. The setback was a defining moment in company history:

> For years, we thought of ourselves as a production-oriented company, meaning we put all our emphasis on designing and manufacturing the product. But now we understand that the most important thing we do is market the product. We've come around to saying that Nike is a marketing company, and the product is our most important marketing tool.
>
> *(in Willigan 1993: 92)*

Inside-out

Simon goes on to identify a further characteristic of the division of a system into goals, inner environment and outer environment, this time from the standpoint of the inner environment. He points out that in very many cases whether a particular system achieves a particular goal or adaptation depends on only a few characteristics of the outer environment and not at all on the detail of that environment. As a consequence, it is possible that the inner system (the production process in this case) may be insulated from the environment, so that an invariant relation may be maintained between an inner system and its goal, independent of a wide range of parameters that characterize the outer environment. Various forms of adaptive insulation maintain such quasi-independence from the outer environment: the suggestion here is that the interface of the brand can be organized to the same effect.

Let me try to elaborate this claim by developing a comparison with price. In discussing the importance of the limits to market processes posed by the human capacity for information processing, Simon quotes from the Austrian neoclassical economist Friedrich von Hayek:

> We must look at the price system as such a mechanism for communicating information if we want to understand its real function. … The most significant fact about this system is the economy of knowledge with which it operates, or how little the individual participants need to know in order to be able to take the right action. In abbreviated form, by a kind of symbol, only the most essential information is passed on, and passed on only to those concerned. It is more than a metaphor to describe the price system as a kind of machinery for registering change.
>
> *(1945, quoted in Simon 1981: 42)*

From Simon's point of view, what is most striking about Hayek's formulation is that the price system is presented as a distributed cognitive device; it reduces and localizes informational and computational requirements. Within this model, 'markets may be seen as rich information networks – even as a kind of "conversation" between buyers and sellers' (Slater and Tonkiss 2001: 53). The brand, it is suggested here, is a (re-)framing of this conversation: it provides 'a communicative middle term – a meta-stability – affording exchanges and transmitting tension across many and varied systems of influence' (Kwinter 2001: 47).

Hayek was an exponent of the view that economics should concern itself not with static models, but with 'an explanation of the economic process as it proceeds through time' (quoted in Slater and Tonkiss 2001: 52). What might also be noted is Hayek's formulation of price as not simply a mechanism for communicating information but also as 'a kind of machinery for registering change'. Adapting these terms, the interface of the brand may be seen as a mechanism for communicating information in a market that is (performed or brought into being as) dynamic and noisy.

What is fundamental here, as Lev Manovich (2001) notes in his discussion of the new media object,[3] is the use of looping techniques as a way of registering change. Historical developments in the emergence of branding (the application of the marketing mix, the use of information about the consumer in the qualitative differentiation of products, and the use of the product as a marketing tool) are absolutely fundamental in this regard. In these developments, the brand as artefact emerges from attempts to address and manage precisely those aspects of relations between buyers and sellers that are not governed by price through the use of information about the consumer in product qualification trials (Callon *et al.* 2002). Such information is used, variously, to anticipate, stabilize or direct the spatiotemporality of the markets in which the brands participate. It is in this sense that the brand may be understood in terms of transductive relations, where transduction is 'a process whereby a disparity or difference is topologically and temporally restructured across some interface' (Mackenzie 2002: 25).

The distribution of behaviours

Simon suggests that it might be possible to combine the two sets of advantages described above, that is, those deriving from the outside-in and the inside-out. He says,

> We might hope to be able to characterize the main properties of the system and its behaviour without elaborating the detail of either the outer or inner environments. We might look toward a science of the artificial that would depend on the relative simplicity of the interface as its primary source of abstraction and generality.
>
> *(1981: 12)*

This is one way of describing the aims of the 'artificial science' of brand management. That this aspiration is even conceivable is a consequence of the increasing role of information in the coordination and conduct of the economy (Castells 1996; Lash 2002; Mackenzie 2002). But as the earlier reference to Manovich suggests, the role of information itself may usefully be situated in relation to the history of (old and new) media. Indeed, this second part of the chapter is going to suggest that the significance of the interface for making relations can usefully be explored by way of a discussion of developments in media. The argument will be that in relation to the artefact of the brand as it is brought into existence in media there is a redistribution of subjects (that is, of subjectivity, will and mind) in terms of behaviours.

To explore this claim, consider the art critic Rosalind Krauss's discussion of the medium of video (1976). In developing her argument, Krauss draws a contrast with the claim made by art critics in the 1960s that the strict application of symmetry in the space framed by the flat surface of the picture allowed a painter 'to point to the center of the canvas' and, in so doing, to invoke the internal structure of the picture-object. She asks, however: 'what does it mean to point to the center of a television screen?' To answer the question, she discusses a video work by the artist Vito Acconci, *Centers* (1971), in which he literalizes the critical notion of 'pointing' by filming himself pointing to the centre of a television monitor that shows him pointing to its centre, a gesture he sustains for the 20-minute running time of the work. The gesture, she argues, is intended to disrupt critical engagement with the formal properties of the genre of works known as 'video art'. She writes,

> The kind of criticism *Centers* attacks is obviously one that takes seriously the formal qualities of a work, or tries to assay the particular logic of a given medium. And yet, by its very mise-en-scène, *Centers* typifies the structural characteristics of the video medium. For *Centers* was

made by Acconci's using the video monitor as a mirror. As we look at the artist sighting along his outstretched arm and forefinger towards the center of the screen we are watching, what we see is a sustained tautology: a line of sight that begins at Acconci's plane of vision and ends at the eyes of his projected double. In that image of self-regard is configured a narcissism so endemic to works of video that I find myself wanting to generalize it as the condition of the entire genre. Yet, what would it mean to say, 'The medium of video is narcissism?'

(1976: 50)

Krauss answers her own question by saying that the medium of video is the situation of someone who has, in Freud's words, 'abandoned the investment of objects with libido and transformed object-libido into ego–libido'. She says that very often in the case of video, there is a tendency towards mirror-reflection and 'the vanquishing of separateness': 'the agency of reflection is a mode of appropriation, of illusionistically erasing the difference between subject and object'. She contrasts this with the asymmetry at work in some other artistic practice. So, she argues that Jasper Johns' *American Flag* deploys reflexivity (rather than reflection) to achieve a radical asymmetry from within:

> In his *American Flag*, Johns uses the synonym between an image (the flag) and its ground (the limits of the picture surface) to unbalance the relationship between the terms 'picture' and 'painting'. By forcing us to see the actual wall on which the canvas hangs as the background for the pictorial object as-a-whole, Johns drives a wedge between two types of figure/ground relationships: the one that is internal to the image; and the one that works from without to define this object as Painting.

(1976: 56)

For Kraus, reflexivity is 'the fracture of the work into two categorically different entities that can elucidate one another insofar as their separateness is maintained' (1976: 56). It is a *dédoublement* or doubling back in order to locate the object and thus the objective conditions of the viewing subject's experience. In contrast, the mirror-reflection of absolute feedback in video is a process of bracketing out the object.

I want to use this example to suggest that neither position (reflection or reflexivity) adequately captures the ways in which artefacts organized by interfaces engage subjects. This is because they rely either on the collapse of the object-subject distinction (reflection) or its reinstatement (reflexivity). There is perhaps an alternative that is a consequence of the way in which subjects are caught up in relations with an interface in (a)symmetrical relations with objects in ways that remain open, in which there is neither an erasure of the difference between subject or object that comes from absolute feedback nor its (critical) re-establishment. Rather, it is one in which, although the subject is indeed always in relation to an object, this is a relation that is never stabilized, is always being (and always requires to be) re-established. This is the work of the interface described above; it produces a surface that is organized so as to permit not only (a)symmetrical relations between an artefact and its environment, but also relations that need to be defined continuously. This is the relation of transitivity described by Brian Massumi (2002).

A transitive verb in linguistics is one that requires an object. So, for example, 'to buy' is a transitive verb; we do not just buy; we buy something, we buy (into) brands. We do not just do; we do 'it'. The artefact invites our participation and organizes that participation, and although it operates in terms of an injunction not that you must, but that you may (Zizek, 1999), the invitation to participate is one that is increasingly difficult to refuse. In this respect, to continue with the case of branding, brands as artefacts are not only so ubiquitous as to be obscene

(Baudrillard 1994) they are also obsequious (Bourdieu 1977). As Bourdieu notes, the term obsequium was used by Spinoza to denote the 'constant will' produced by the conditioning through which 'the State fashions us for its own use and which enables it to survive'. Bourdieu adopts the term to designate the public testimonies of recognition that are set up in every group between individuals and the group. Here, however, the term may be used to apply to the continual attenuation and renewal of attentiveness called into being by the taken-for-granted ubiquity and never-ending 'schismogenesis' (Bateson 1972) provided by the surface forms of the interface. As such, it relates to the behaviour of individuals in relation to each other rather than the will of autonomous subjects.

Schismogenesis[4] is the term used by Gregory Bateson, an anthropologist and theorist of information, to describe the continual reproduction, confirmation and intensification of difference in ways that lead to progressive differentiation between groups or individuals. One example that he gives is the way in which feedback loops can produce an antagonistic difference or opposition that spins out of control:

> If, for example, the patterns X, Y, Z include boasting, we shall see that there is a likelihood, if boasting is the reply to boasting, that each group will drive the other into excessive emphasis of the pattern, a process which if not restrained can only lead to more and more extreme rivalry and ultimately to hostility and breakdown of the whole system.
>
> *(1972: 68)*

To explore the implications of schismogenesis a little further for relations between subjects and objects, let me provide some contemporary examples of the measurement of consumer perceptions about brands (Moor and Lury 2011). The aim is to try to elucidate how some forms of schismogenesis (that is, the reactions of individuals to the reactions of other individuals) differ from both reflection and reflexivity.

In early attempts to measure consumer perceptions about brands (sometimes called brand equity), indices of 'customer satisfaction' were used, but such indices have recently been criticized as being too open to manipulation (because questions can be framed in ways that elicit a positive response) and (significantly) as too subjective, in the sense that they measure the gap between expectation and perception in ways that are open to reflexivity. In the place of such measures, two alternative approaches are being developed, both of which seek to bypass the phenomena of conscious, subjective experience or reflexivity. One is the use of neuroimaging to access the thought processes underlying decision-making by imaging the brain when subjects are exposed to stimuli such as advertising. This is the nascent field of neuromarketing (Ambler *et al.* 2003). The second involves techniques for the measurement of what might be called interindividual reactions or (one form of) relationality (Moor and Lury 2011).

So, for example, an increasingly common metric for accessing consumers' feelings about brands is the 'propensity to recommend' model. This is imagined to be a more robust measure because it is held to connect feelings with observable behaviour between individuals, and thus is an example of what I am calling a relational measure. 'propensity to recommend' measures are used in the UK by agencies such as YouGov, which conduct routine surveys of consumer perceptions of brands, asking respondents which brands they would recommend to friends or colleagues and which brands they would tell them to avoid. But 'Propensity to recommend' measures are also being adopted online. Here, in part because of the potential to track actual as well as stated behaviour, 'propensity to recommend' is elaborated as simultaneously a property of the brand (where its 'recommend-ability' is something internal to the brand as artefact) and as a capacity of consumers and their interindividual networks: some individuals are assumed to be more likely to recommend a product than others; some individuals are assumed to have bigger or better 'networks' than others; and technologies of various kinds are assumed to enable the activation of these networks. In these measurements it is (one form of) relational behaviour (the reactions of individuals to the reactions of other individuals) rather than intention or will that is of significance.

'Propensity to recommend' is not the only measure of brand equity that tries to capture the distribution and qualities of relational behaviour. Another measure used by YouGov asks respondents to consider which brands they would feel 'proud' to work for and which would make them 'embarrassed', measures that try to capture intensity of feeling about a brand through reference to its effect on people's appearance before others. A similar approach can be found in the 'Brand Asset Valuator' developed by Young and Rubicam. This proposes 'envy' as a key measure of the strength of brand equity. Like 'pride', 'embarrassment' and 'propensity to recommend', envy is seen as a robust measure of brand equity, because it asks consumers to imagine a brand in the context of behaviour, that is, interindividual relationships. It is important to note here that such measures of interindividual behaviour are by no means a complete account of everything that is happening in the environment of the brand; they do not, and are not intended to, encompass very much of everyday relations with brands but only those aspects of the environment that may be recognized by the organizing activities of the interface of the brand. As such interindividual behaviour is recognized as a measure of the environment rather than of the subjective depth, desire or will of individuals; indeed, this is its strength.

Moreover, as is also true of 'propensity to recommend' measures, 'envy' is not just a measure but also a target and an incentive for organizational change (Espeland and Sauder 2007). Although it is included by Young and Rubicam in the context of a valuation service, the service is offered partly as a means to enable brands to think about the future and to reimagine their position within a given market. The cultivation of the brand's capacity to inspire envy is proposed as a strategy for the restructuring of markets and the brand's place within them. Through a variety of techniques, including the restriction of access to a brand and the adoption of alternate pricing strategies, Young and Rubicam explicitly suggest that brands can harness the 'fundamental' human quality of envy to turn themselves into positional goods and invert traditional forms of price elasticity. However, what is being pointed to here is the way in which the activities of subjects are being reconstituted in relation to the organization of objects as artefacts by way of the activities of an interface in terms of intraindividual and interindividual or relational modes of behaviour. These activities are not to be understood in terms of either reflection or reflexivity, but transitivity. The overall argument has been that just as objects do not have a single mode of appearance, so subjects cannot be assumed to stay the same as the relations between them change.

Notes

1 Although Simon describes these characteristics as 'advantages', they are not necessarily advantageous (in the sense of beneficial) for anyone or everyone involved.
2 Although this mode of innovation does not derive from innovation in the production process, it may of course require it.
3 Manovich has made a compelling case for the use of categories from computer science as categories of new media theory.
4 Etymologically it means 'the creation of division'.

Bibliography

Ambler, T., Ioannides, A. and Rose, S. (2003) 'Brands on the brain: neuro-images of advertising', *Business Strategy Review*, 11(3): 17–30.

Appadurai, A. (1996) *Modernity at Large: Cultural Dimensions of Globalization*, Minneapolis and London: University of Minnesota Press.

Bateson, G. (1972) *Steps to an Ecology of Mind*, New Jersey: Jason Aronson.

Baudrillard, J. (1994) *Simulacra and Simulation*, Ann Arbor: University of Michigan Press.

Bourdieu, P. (1977) *Outline of a Theory of Practice*, Cambridge: Cambridge University Press.

Callon, M., Meadel, C. and Rabeharisoa, V. (2002) 'The economy of qualities', *Economy and Society*, 31(2): 194–217.

Castells, M. (1996) *The Rise of the Network Society*, Cambridge, MA and Oxford: Blackwell Publishers.

Espeland, W. and Sauder, M. (2007) 'Rankings and reactivity: how public measures recreate social worlds', *American Journal of Sociology*, 13(1): 1–40.

Hayles, N. K. (1999) *How We Became Posthuman: Virtual Bodies in Cybernetics, Literature and Informatics*, Chicago: University of Chicago Press.

Knorr Cetina, K. (1997) 'Sociality with objects: social relations in post-social knowledge societies', *Theory, Culture and Society*, 14(4): 1–30.

Knorr Cetina, K. (2000) 'Post-social theory', in G. Ritzer and B. Smart (eds) *Handbook of Social Theory*, London: Sage.

Krauss, R. (1976) 'Video: The aesthetics of narcissism', *October*, 1(Spring): 50–64.

Kwinter, S. (2001) *Architectures of Time: Toward a Theory of the Event in Modernist Culture*, Cambridge, MA and London: MIT Press.

Lash, S. (2002) *Critique of Information*, London and New York: Sage.

Lash, S. and Lury, C. (2007) *Global Culture Industry: The Mediation of Things*, Cambridge: Polity.

Lash, S. and Urry, J. (1994) *Economies of Signs and Spaces*, London: Sage.

Lury, C. (2004) *Brands: The Logos of the Global Economy*, London: Routledge.

Lury, C. (2009) 'Brands as assemblages: assembling culture', *Journal of Cultural Economy*, 2(1–2): 67–82.

Mackenzie, A. (2002) *Transductions: Bodies and Machines at Speed*, London: Continuum.

Manovich, L. (2001) *The Language of New Media*, Cambridge, MA: MIT Press.

Manzini, E. (1989) *The Material of Invention*, London: Design Council.

Massumi, B. (2002) *Parables for the Virtual: Movement, Affect, Sensation*, Durham and London: Duke University Press.

Moor, L. and Lury, C. (2011) 'Making and measuring value: comparison, singularity and agency in brand valuation practice', *Journal of Cultural Economy*, 4(4): 439–455.

Rodowick, D. N. (1997) *Gilles Deleuze's Time Machine*, Durham and London: Duke University Press.

Simon, H. A. (1981 [1969]) *The Sciences of the Artificial*, Cambridge, MA and London: MIT Press.

Slater, D. and Tonkiss, F. (2001) *Market Society: Markets and Modern Social Theory*, Cambridge, and Malden, MA. Polity.

Sterling, B. (2005) *Shaping Things*, Cambridge, MA: MIT Press.

Urry, J. (2003) *Global Complexity*, Cambridge: Polity.

Willigan, G. (1993) 'High-performance marketing: an interview with Nike's Phil Knight', *Harvard Business Review*, July–August: 90–101.

Zizek, S. (1999) 'You may!', *London Review of Books*, 21(6): 3–6.

25

Idempotent, pluripotent, biodigital

Objects in the 'biological century'

Adrian Mackenzie

In the so-called 'biological century' (Sunder Rajan 2006), objecthood is likely to undergo change. What kind of objects come to us from contemporary biology? Synthetic biology is one version, or projection of a biotechnological culture. Synthetic biology lies at the intersection of molecular biology, genomics, computer science, software programming, microelectronics and network cultures (see Carlson 2010 for a popular description). Synthetic biologists rarely speak of objects. They are more prone to speak of genes, pathways, devices, clocks, switches networks, circuits, constructs, models and modules. Little more than ten years into the life of the field, their investment in objects is in some ways strikingly unsurprising: synthetic biologists say they want to 'do for biology what Intel does for electronics' (Pollack 2006). This is unsurprising to the extent that synthetic biology is seen as another, more pragmatic version of that much discussed twentieth-century transformation of life into computer code. Synthetic biology endeavours to arrange things such that biology will reboot as BIOS, the code that sets the 'machine ... in a known state so that software stored on compatible media can be loaded, executed and given control' (Wikipedia Foundation 2010).

A quick glance at the past decade's scientific publications in synthetic biology suggest that the metaphor of the computational object has been worked up explicitly and in many closely related varieties. For example, 'we advocate the metaphor of the cell as an algorithmic machine, rather than a mechanical one, and the use of machine-orientated engineering language to implement synthetic biology' (de Lorenzo and Danchin 2008: 825). The commonness of terms such as 'logic', 'circuit', 'device', 'programming', 'interface' and the more interesting technical verb 'interfacing' in this literature indicates the rhetorical imprint of algorithms, digital devices and network media in this field (see Purnick and Weiss [2009] for a review, but almost any publication in the field says something similar).

What is at stake in this unsurprising desire to *interface* the eminently technological success of digital logic, algorithmic processes and 'machine-orientated engineering language' with living things? Emulating Intel, synthetic biology places great stock in stable platforms, modularity, combinational logic, compatible standards, controllable programming interfaces and computer-assisted design (CAD) processes. These are not just convenient tropes or metaphors. The borrowing of an engineering control discourse from computer science is seen as crucial to the initializing or bootstrapping of biodigital objects in synthetic biology: 'The defining question of synthetic biology research moving forward will not be whether biology can be engineered, but how to develop engineering principles for biological systems' (Boyle and Silver 2009: 543).

This is an interesting statement. The question of whether biology can be engineered seems to have a foregone conclusion: yes, it can be. The real question is: can be it engineered according to principles? In contrast to the many now familiar borrowings of notions of code, program, memory, etc. by molecular biology, synthetic biology thus regards various principles and practices (of computer science and software engineering, and particularly those associated with open source software) as the way to normalize the making of biodigital objects. The real stake here, it seems, is not just change in work on biological material that leads to technologies, but 'principles' that regenerate potential for change.

In this setting, objects themselves matter less than how they are made. How they are made depends on engineering principles. What are engineering principles? We see a plethora of models, standards, design processes, biological part repositories, prototypes and devices welling up around synthetic biology. Models, standards and parts are the engineering practices to which many synthetic biologists turn as they seek to develop biological objects of diverse technicity. In many different ways, synthetic biology is an organized belief in the idea that models, standards and design can yield biodigital objects of greater logical and material complexity in the twenty-first century because they have so manifestly produced objects of great logical and material complexity in the twentieth: computers. However, this belief in sophisticated algorithmic biological objects, iterated in countless accounts of synthetic biology, is prospective, and subject to many partial, hedged realizations. In explicitly bringing Intel-BIOS engineering design to biology, synthetic biologists find themselves faced with several different kinds of uncertainty that we might understand as problems of interface in several senses.

The first sense of interface concerns the boundary between different materials. In order to become biodigital, the materials, organisms, cultures, molecules, instruments, data and reagents of twentieth-century biology need to be worked on in new ways that are compatible with and familiar from the engineering of electronics and software where the materials are metal–mineral–logic mixtures. Aligning biological processes with digital ones is not easy, because they have such different qualities. (For instance, an oscillation in a gene network is a palpably different event to an oscillation in a crystal.) A second sense of interface, this time drawn from software engineering itself, is implicit in much of the synthetic biology research. This is the idea of the interface as a way of separating things off from each other so that they need only come into relation in a narrow range of ways. The epitome of this sense of interface is the human–computer interface that both affords and limits what people and computers can do in order to somewhat decouple their interactions. Similarly, in synthetic biology, the manipulation of biological processes must be normalized through coordinated biological work. Not only the notion of the biological thing, the subject of biology, but the notion of the subject who works in biology, the biologist, must be reconfigured, shifting her or him away from the figure of the research scientist and more towards the designing engineer. In both respects (the interface as boundary between different materials, the interface as what separates and hides), ideas, values, practices and problems borrowed from the highly economically and culturally leveraged economies of software and microelectronic industries, as well as various network culture tendencies at large pervade synthetic biology.

Parts of biological objects

Do any biodigital objects exist? We might say that there are *parts* of such objects. The globally publicized announcement in June 2010 'Venter boots up first synthetic cell' (Walter 2010) echoed the words 'boots up' of the *enfant terrible* of genomic science, Craig Venter, to headline the technical achievement of synthesizing a minimal whole genome in vitro and then persuading an organism to regard it as its own (Lartigue *et al.* 2009). The salience of the Venter team's achievement is distracting. Venter's whole genome work is an outlier in synthetic biology, and the scale of his team's achievements is not representative of the mainstream work in the field focused on *parts*, *components* and *devices*. In many respects, the titles of other scientific publications suggest a less ambitious enterprise: 'a synthetic oscillatory network' (Elowitz and Leibler 2000), 'reconstruction of genetic circuits' (Sprinzak and Elowitz 2005), 'combinational logic design' (Densmore and Anderson 2009). Rather than pointing to a self-contained object, each of these titles designates a part or component: an oscillatory network, a circuit, or some logic. More generally, they acknowledge that biological systems are difficult to control precisely because they are so thoroughly integrated and present too many shifting, fluid interfaces.

In trying to make biodigital objects (devices, systems, platforms) synthetic, biologists often talk about parts. Although there are various kinds of parts in synthetic biology, primarily these parts are pervasively conceived in terms of genetic elements:

> We define a biological part to be a natural nucleic acid sequence that encodes a definable biological function, and a standard biological part to be a biological part that has been refined in order to conform to one or more defined technical standards.
>
> *(Shetty et al. 2008: 5)*

As is well-known, molecular biology has for over a half-century attempted to describe genetic elements in cells in material-semiotic terms such as 'program', 'code' and 'machine' (Kay 2000). From the mid-1950s on, nucleic acid sequences (DNA), genes and, subsequently, genomes became the primary locus of biological attention. Four decades of recombinant DNA biology have yielded a wide variety of practical techniques for cutting, copying and pasting DNA, mainly using enzymes isolated from various bacteria (Watson 2007). Despite the sophisticated techniques for *in-vivo* and *in-vitro* manipulation of DNA, DNA comes nowhere near complying with the form–matter, or coding–coded distinctions that are layered into most industrial and engineering concepts of a *part*. Even the heavily invested promise of the genomic sciences starting in the 1990s (to unfold an exhaustive sequential specification of the DNA ground-plan of any organism) has inadvertently dismantled the important control concept of the gene as program, and proliferated ever more intensive and extensive attempts to sequence and resequence every genome in sight (epigenomics, metagenomics, etc.) in pursuit of elusive variations, subtle interactions and inordinately complicated regulatory mechanisms (Keller 2000).

For its part, synthetic biology responds by saying that this supersaturated diversity, generated by the fluxing, differentiating mass of reactions, signals and criss-crossing feedback paths, needs to be pared down to something more layered, hierarchical and ordered and that can be modelled in terms of parts in logical combination. Here, the model of digital integrated circuits comprising logical elements such as gates and switches closely interconnected on semiconductor wafers seems to be almost ineluctable. Almost without exception, synthetic biologists promote and indeed insist on engineering biology using parts, most quintessentially and reductively, in the form of BioBricks (BioBricks Foundation [BBF] 2010).

The descriptions, design and use of BioBricks explicitly predicates biodigital objects comprising parts tailored to a 'standardized interface technology' (Knight 2007). BioBricks are made from DNA sequences. These sequences conform to a standard proposed by the Massachusetts Institute of Technology computer scientist Tom Knight (Knight 2007). The BioBricks standard says nothing about the specific function of the biological parts. It really only addresses how parts can be assembled. The standardization concerns only those aspects of the part that pertain to assembly, or linking together. Obviously, parts that cannot be connected or interfaced easily are not engineerable. The BioBricks standards documents (BBF 2010), an RFC (Request for Comments) modelled on the grass-roots standardization of internet protocols undertaken by the Internet Engineering Task Force in the 1970s and 1980s (Abbate 2000), is brief. It lists the DNA sequences with which every BioBrick must begin and end, and lists the sequences that may not appear in the BioBrick. With the right start and end sequences, some well-known and widely used laboratory techniques of DNA assembly can be applied to bring BioBrick parts together in a given order. The connection of several parts together will perhaps make a device with a particular function (a logic switch, an oscillator, a sensor, an actuator, etc.). Once parts can be put together, something more recognizable as an object, with particular technical function, comes into view.

Importantly, putting several parts together makes something that is still a BioBrick. This is a key point, because it opens, in principle, the door to many further compositions:

> The key innovation of the BioBrick assembly standard is that a biological engineer can assemble any two BioBrick parts, and the resulting composite object is itself a BioBrick part that can be combined with any other BioBrick parts.
>
> *(Shetty et al. 2008: 2)*

For instance, the device might be concerned with vision. In the biochemistry of animal vision, molecules such as beta-carotene are broken down into retinal by an enzyme called beta-carotene monooxygenase. Retinal forms the chemical basis for vision. So a simple BioBrick device could couple a part that synthesizes beta-carotene with a part that produces retinal from beta-carotene. Such a device might be useful in building things that respond to light. In fact, such a device exists in the Registry of Standard Biological Parts (Registry of Standard Biological Parts 2010), along with several thousand others.

Synthetic biologists, influenced by computer science, say that the process of putting parts together must be, in principle, *idempotent* (Shetty et al. 2008: 5). *Idempotency* is a term borrowed from mathematics and computer science to describe operations that can be applied to something (a number, a data structure, etc.) multiple times without changing the kind of result that it yields. Idempotency has been shown in certain mathematical techniques and achieved in certain computational processes, especially in software architectures. It basically means: something changes without any side-effects. Searching a database for an address is said to be an idempotent operation on the data in the database because it does not change that data (although such a search might itself cascade into many other changes). Idempotency is a huge restriction in the context of things in general, let alone in the context of living things. Indeed it does turn out to be difficult in practice. In synthetic biology, no matter how many BioBricks are combined, the result is still a BioBrick. No matter how many parts make up the device, the device is still a part. This idempotency of BioBricks promises certain design and production potentials. From an engineering perspective, the process of design becomes a matter of logical composition, perhaps guided or automated by various rules; the process of fabrication becomes a matter of synthesis of DNA sequences; and above all, 'cultures of circulation' (Lee and LiPuma 2002) can begin to accrete and coalesce around the parts. Practically, in the engineering of devices, the opacity and convoluted interiority of living cells is replaced by lines of BioBricks, neatly concatenated in clear and distinct diagrams that can be manipulated and automated using engineering techniques of recomposition and 'abstraction hierarchies'.

Putting parts together: the problem of pluripotent composition

The engineering ideal of putting things together from parts, often described in the introductory chapters of software engineering textbooks as 'modularity' (Abelson 1996), is difficult to realize in practice. It relies on interfacing or constitutive 'regimes of engagement' (Thevenot 2009). Regimes of engagement allow abstractions, hierarchies, layers and logic to provisionally stabilize. Like all regulatory ideals, the attributes that engineering design principles ascribe to things can be guaranteed only through pluripotent engagements with things. The engagements constantly undermine the notion that objects have attributes or stable properties, including the attribute of idempotency. In other words, idempotency as an engineering principle of change risks running against the processes of change that would allow technical objects to mediate nature-cultures anew.

Various regimes of engagement already impinge on synthetic biology. Molecular biologists have for several decades routinely assembled DNA sequences using many different methods and materials. As Christine Smolke, a leading researcher in the field observes, 'many laboratories build up their own assembly methods and constructs and will have a laboratory-specific catalogue of parts that are incompatible with any proposed standard' (Smolke 2009: 1100). However, the BioBricks standards imply a standard way of putting parts together. As the realization dawned that parts need to be put together in different ways, various modifications of the BioBricks standard appeared, such as the BioFusion standard (Phillips and Silver 2006) and the BioScaffold standard (Norville *et al.* 2008).

Variations are nothing unusual in the evolution of technical objects. Standards often replace each other in quick succession, especially in the ferment of change associated with early technologies. The very process of putting parts together might well affect the nature of the parts in deep ways. The biological premise of all BioBricks and most of the other parts produced by synthetic biologists is the central dogma of molecular biology (Crick 1970): information flows from DNA-encoded genes to RNA and then to proteins, which direct cell metabolism through their activity as enzymes. Ideally, biodigital function is programmed in DNA, and via the transcription and translation processes of the cell assembled into proteins. Unlike the exhaustively designed materiality of microchips, themselves fabricated in a high-precision production process, BioBricks have to be not only assembled (increasingly by DNA synthesis services such as DNA2.0 or GeneArt), but introduced into laboratory microbes such as *Escherichia coli*. Although they grow quickly, and have relatively simple architectures compared to animal and plant cells, *E. coli* are not amenable to the 'digital discipline' of binary voltage levels and constant clocked repetition on which algorithmic processing implicitly depends and which most contemporary electronics design simply takes for granted. Despite a century of laboratory manipulations (see Landecker 2007), the temporal dynamics of cells are difficult to tune because the regulatory processes taking place there are interwoven on many different timescales ranging from microseconds to months. Whereas synthetic biology imagines life as a set of processes that can be disaggregated into useful functions (and this is almost the primary item of faith), the regulatory mechanisms operating in cells are sensitive to many different reactions and interactions. Through metabolic fluxes, DNA, RNA, proteins, carbohydrates, lipids and many other molecules come together and come apart in ways that blur the specificity of biodigital functions.

In order to skirt around this massively overinterfaced relationality, synthetic biologists have concentrated on making parts that stay close to the DNA-related processes of the cell, especially the transcriptional and translational mechanisms that control when and how DNA sequences become RNA and then proteins. Most of the work in synthetic biology to date has focused on the transcriptional machinery that synthesizes the RNA molecule from nuclear DNA.

The parts, modules and systems that have been made nearly all seek to use, modify or control cells via the transcriptional processes that synthesize RNA from DNA templates. Transcription is of such central importance that many descriptions and definitions of biological parts or modules take it as axiomatic. For instance, the definitions of parts or module is intrinsically transcriptional:

> We define a module as the simplest element of a gene regulatory network, consisting of a promoter, the gene(s) expressed from that promoter, and the regulatory proteins (and their cognate DNA binding sites) that affect the expression of that gene.
>
> *(Kaern* et al. *2003: 180)*

The promotor, the gene, the DNA binding sites: all of this refers to parts of the regulatory mechanisms for transcription of DNA into RNA. By making transcription into the foundation of biological parts, synthetic biology can combine DNA sequences according to a combinational logic, as typified in BioBricks. It has been productive and yielded, with varying degrees of viability, several hundred devices, for instance, made by teams in the iGEM competitions.

How to regulate biological parts: the problem of interfacing

Logical sophistication comes at a cost. The cellular milieu remains largely unthought. The design of idempotent parts largely treats the many interactions between environment, cell and genome as a platform for combinational logic. The timing and the fluxing variability of these processes is more difficult to deal with. In contrast to digital devices, in which increasingly rapid synchronized clocking has been a regulatory constant that allowed many different kinds of automated design to take root (computer-assisted circuit design, the many layers of software ranging from microcode to scripts), regulation in synthetic biology remains an ongoing problem in several senses.

First, transcription is relatively slow in relation to other biological processes. As authors of one review write, 'transcriptional and translational devices are easy to connect and are capable of great logical complexity, but such devices cannot be assembled into systems that respond in seconds' (Andrianantoandro *et al.* 2006). Transcription and translation take place over minutes through a process of successive elongating synthesis. As a result, synthetic biologists have been compelled to also begin to develop devices that are not reliant on the processes of DNA transcription into RNA, and RNA translation into proteins. There is no space here to describe how they have achieved this, but sometimes it involves engineering RNA, sometimes engineering proteins. In either case, these alternatives alter the part-based composition of biodigital objects.

Second, even if transcription is fast enough, transcription may produce many side-effects, and the products of transcription may themselves be inhibited or thwarted by other forms of metabolic interaction in the organism. An 'endogeneous protein network' (Boyle and Silver 2009: 539) affects almost everything that takes place in the cell. Hence some authors speak of the 'ultra-sensitivity of transcriptional cascades' (Hooshangi *et al.* 2005). Others discuss the inherent 'noisiness' or 'stochasticity' (tendency to behave as if the product of random processes) of synthetic gene networks (Kaern *et al.* 2003: 188). Still others speak of the need to design 'orthogonal constructs' (that is, biochemical constructs that do not rely on the cellular regulation of DNA transcription and that are independent of the endogenous protein networks (Dueber *et al.* 2009: 758). These other interactions need to be understood and taken into account somehow. Behind all of these difficulties, which are to be expected in the context of biology, lie broader issues of living milieus where heat, light, humidity, nutrients and stimuli all affect growth.

Acutely aware of these problems, problems that threaten the very ambition to make biodigital objects, synthetic biologists have responded by developing models and simulations (and also by using microfluidics to alter the settings in which biodigital objects are made). The dynamics of gene networks models cannot themselves be known, even if their logical function can be predicted. They need to be expressed in the mathematical form of rate-determined, spatially compartmentalized reactions and then verified through experiment. Because events in cells are so noisy, the models themselves need to be stochastic (that is, treating the cell as a domain of random events). Because many of the parameters in these models cannot be measured directly, sophisticated simulation techniques are often needed to estimate them (Yuting and Ganesh 2010). Many publications in the field actually focus more on developing models than devices. These models are motivated by regimes of engagement or interfacing concerns rather than practical technical functions. This investment in models accounts for the many synthetic biology articles on counters, oscillators, clocks, switches, logic gates and circuits that have been published in *Nature*, *Science*, *Nature Biotechnology* and other major scientific journals (Sprinzak and Elowitz 2005; Friedland *et al.* 2009; Drubin *et al.* 2007; Endy 2005). What appears in such articles are usually graphics that convey (1) a gene network diagram for the device (clock, oscillator, switch, etc.), (2) plots of the response signals produced by the device over time, and (3) images of fluorescence produced by cells over time (i.e., fluorescence is one of the most common ways of signalling that a designed function is performed by cells). Each of these visual forms displays patterns that can be treated as engineered regularities (see, for instance, Danino *et al.* 2010). Although the patterns shown in the plots and images suggest the presence of regularities, these regularities themselves are tuned by varying the parameters of mathematical models, and by conducting model analysis in support of design of synthetic circuits. The development of the models is perhaps more important than the things that are made, for only the models offer the possibility of predicting the behaviour of parts and collections of parts. These models owe more to chemical engineering than they do software or microelectronics. They are almost always expressed in terms of changes in the concentrations of metabolites, and they rely on the techniques developed by chemists and chemical engineers to describe the rates of chemical reactions.

Still, the models cannot supply a regime of engagement. The real stake here is not engineered biological objects, but ways of organizing change so as to give rise to a series of differentiated objects. Models become important as ways of capturing an artifice or a schema. They are developed at the confluence of the encyclopaedic drive of genomics and the design and engineering techniques of industrial innovation. In attending to the specificities of reactions, dynamics, networks and fluxes, models are sometimes said to deliver information about 'device physics' (Andrianantoandro *et al.* 2006). But this term, itself borrowed from semiconductor engineering, covers over the significant differences in underlying modelling practices. The development of semiconductors in the 1950s could draw on a century of statistical mechanics (and later quantum mechanics), electromagnetic field theory and a long history of electrical and electronic communication (telegraph, telephone, radio, radar, television) in order to bring together 'device' and 'physics'. The evolution of microelectronic devices (integrated circuits) was in some ways more linear. By contrast, the horizontal transfer of engineering principles from electronics to biology has to move greater distances. It does not have large technical systems such as electricity and electronic communication to connect to. There is no biological equivalent to the detailed mathematical models of statistical mechanics and electron transport that underlay the development of semiconductors. Although there are many industrial and biomedical settings in which biodigital devices of synthetic biology might be used, in hardly any of these settings are there existing devices or systems to which biodigital objects would easily interface.

Overflowing objects

Where does the combination of Intel-inspired idempotency and chemical engineering-inspired modelling of pluripotent reactions and metabolic fluxes leave biodigital objects? On the one hand, the ideal of idempotency is meant to guarantee that biological parts can be put together without the aggregate exhibiting unexpected or emergent properties. On the other hand, the painstaking development of quantitative models that simulate the behaviour of parts in order to interface with the metabolic fluxes of cells seeks to validate that guarantee. Yet the fixation on parts and models does not take into account the regimes of engagement that bring parts together.

The philosopher of technology and biology Gilbert Simondon contrasts the artificiality of technical objects with their concretization. He writes: 'the essential artificiality of an object resides in the fact that man [sic] must intervene in order to maintain the object in existence by protecting it against the natural world, and by giving it the status of a part of existence' (Simondon 1958: 47). In concretization, the object, originally artificial, becomes 'more and more like a natural object' (Simondon 1958: 47). The confluence of ideas, values, practices and problems of the digital with biology presents an interesting twist on the quasi-naturalizing process of concretization that Simondon describes. In its emphatic attempts to couple engineering design principles with biological techniques, synthetic biology perhaps cannot fully regulate what is copied, what is transferred or transcribed from one domain to the other. This problem of transcription or overflow might prompt us to rethink how things come to be more generally. It might occasion new ideas about how things exist synthetically at the interfaces between different scientific disciplines, economic, industrial, media and cultural settings.

Bibliography

Abbate, J. (2000) *Inventing the Internet*, Cambridge, MA: MIT Press.

Abelson, H. (1996) *Structure and Interpretation of Computer Programs* 2nd ed., Cambridge, MA: MIT Press.

Andrianantoandro, E., Basu, S., Karig, D.K. and Weiss, R. (2006) 'Synthetic biology: new engineering rules for an emerging discipline', *Molecular Systems Biology*, 2: 2006–2028.

BioBricks Foundation (BBF) (2010) *The BioBricks Foundation*, http://biobricks.org/ (accessed 8 March 2010).

Boyle, P. and Silver, P.A. (2009) 'Harnessing nature's toolbox: regulatory elements for synthetic biology', *Journal of the Royal Society Interface*, 6: 12–24.

Carlson, R.H. (2010) *Biology Is Technology*, Cambridge, MA: Harvard University Press.

Crick, F. (1970) 'Central dogma of molecular biology', *Nature*, 227(5258): 561–563.

Danino, T. *et al.* (2010) 'A synchronized quorum of genetic clocks', *Nature*, 463(7279): 326–330.

Densmore, D. and Anderson, J. (2009) 'Combinational Logic Design in Synthetic Biology', *ISCAS: 2009 IEEE International Symposium On Circuits And Systems*, 301–304.

Drubin, D.A., Way, J.C. and Silver, P.A. (2007) 'Designing biological systems', *Genes & Development*, 21(3): 242–254.

Dueber, J.E. *et al.* (2009) 'Synthetic protein scaffolds provide modular control over metabolic flux', *Nature Biotechnology*, 27(8): 753–759.

Elowitz, M.B. and Leibler, S. (2000) 'A synthetic oscillatory network of transcriptional regulators', *Nature*, 403(6767): 335–338.

Endy, D. (2005) 'Foundations for engineering biology', *Nature*, 438(7067): 449–453.

Friedland, A.E., Lu, T.K., Wang, X., Shi, D., Church, G. and Collins, J.J. (2009) 'Synthetic gene networks that count', *Science*, 324(5931) (29 May): 1199–1202.

Hooshangi, S., Thiberge, S. and Weiss, R. (2005) 'Ultrasensitivity and noise propagation in a synthetic transcriptional cascade', *Proceedings of the National Academy of Sciences of the United States of America*, 102(10): 3581.

Kaern, M., Blake, W.J. and Collins, J.J. (2003) 'The engineering of gene regulatory networks', *Annual Review of Biomedical Engineering*, 5(1): 179–206.

Kay, L.E. (2000) *Who Wrote the Book of Life? A History of the Genetic Code*, Stanford, CA: Stanford University Press.

Keller, E.F. (2000) *The Century of the Gene*, Cambridge, MA: Harvard University Press.

Knight, T. (2007) *RFC10: Draft Standard for BioBrick Biological Parts*, http://hdl.handle.net/1721.1/45138 (accessed 4 July 2011).

Landecker, H. (2007) *Culturing Life: How Cells Became Technologies*, Cambridge, MA: Harvard University Press.

Lartigue, C. *et al.* (2009) 'Creating bacterial strains from genomes that have been cloned and engineered in yeast', *Science*, 11737: 59.

Lee, B. and LiPuma, E. (2002). 'Cultures of circulation: the imaginations of modernity', *Public Culture*, 14(1): 191–213.

de Lorenzo, V. and Danchin, A. (2008) 'Synthetic biology: discovering new worlds and new words – the new and not so new aspects of this emerging research field', *Embo Reports*, 9(9): 822–827.

Norville, J., Belcher, A. and Knight, T. (2008) 'A new BioScaffold family of BioBrick(R) standard biological parts to enable manipulations such as protein fusions, library construction, and part domestication', http://openwetware.org/wiki/The_BioBricks_Foundation:BBFRFC15 (accessed 12 April 2011).

Phillips, I. and Silver, P. (2006) 'A new BioBrick assembly strategy designed for facile protein engineering', http://dspace.mit.edu/handle/1721.1/32535 (accessed 12 April 2011).

Pollack, A. (2006) 'Custom-made microbes, at your service', *The New York Times*, http://www.nytimes.com/2006/01/17/science/17synt.html?_r=1 (accessed 26 April 2010).

Purnick, P.E.M. and Weiss, R. (2009) 'The second wave of synthetic biology: from modules to systems', *Nature Review Molecular Cell Biology*, 10(6): 410–422.

Registry of Standard Biological Parts (2010) 'Part:BBa K343006', http://partsregistry.org/wiki/index.php?title=Part:BBa_K343006 (accessed 12 April 2011).

Shetty, R.P., Endy, D. and Knight, T.F. (2008) 'Engineering BioBrick vectors from BioBrick parts', *Journal of Biological Engineering*, 2(1): 5.

Simondon, G. (1958) *Du mode d'existence des objets techniques*, Paris: Aubier.

Smolke, C.D. (2009) 'Building outside of the box: iGEM and the BioBricks Foundation', *Nature Biotechnology*, 27(12): 1099–1102.

Sprinzak, D. and Elowitz, M.B. (2005) 'Reconstruction of genetic circuits', *Nature*, 438(7067): 443–448.

Sunder Rajan, K. (2006) *Biocapital: The Constitution of Postgenomic Life*, Durham: Duke University Press.

Thevenot, L. (2009) 'Postscript to the special issue: governing life by standards: a view from engagements', *Social Studies of Science*, 39(5): 793–813.

Walter, P. (2010) 'Synthetic biology Venter "boots up" first synthetic cell', *Chemistry and Industry*, (11): 5.

Watson, J.D. (2007) *Recombinant DNA: Genes and Genomes: A Short Course*, New York: W.H. Freeman/Cold Spring Harbor Laboratory Press.

Wikipedia Foundation (2010) BIOS – Wikipedia, the free encyclopedia, http://en.wikipedia.org/wiki/BIOS (accessed 25 March 2010).

Yuting, Z. and Ganesh, S. (2010) 'Mathematical modelling: bridging the gap between concept and realization in synthetic biology', *Journal of Biomedicine and Biotechnology*, Volume 2010, 541609, doi:10.1155/2012/541609: 1–16.

26

Real-izing the virtual

Digital simulation and the politics of future making

Hannah Knox

The plan to demolish Toxteth Street, a row of low-quality, dark, and cramped Victorian houses in the Openshaw area of East Manchester had been many years in the making. By 2009, the phased relocation of people, some of whom had lived on the street for 40 years, was already well under way. Planners had worked hard to make sure that residents were fully cognizant of the urban regeneration process that they were a part of: an ambitious plan to transform some of the most deprived parts of Manchester into safer, more healthy and more sustainable communities.

The process of public consultation had proceeded for the main part along familiar lines: public meetings, brochures, newsletters and bulletins updating residents on the planning process had been used, whilst maps of the relandscaped neighbourhood and documentation outlining the details of planning committees and public consultation events had been placed on notice boards screwed to the walls at the end of the street. In addition, the transformation of East Manchester had seen the introduction of a new tool into the consultation exercise. A digital model of the area had been brought in, which was to serve the purpose both of capturing a visual depiction of the street as it existed before demolition and of envisioning the neighbourhood as it would look after regeneration. In the course of various public consultation events, those being moved into new properties had had the opportunity to take a walk through a virtual rendering of their future neighbourhood and had looked inside the visualizations of the houses they were to move into (Figure 26.1).

They had been encouraged to think about the decoration that they would like, and where they would put their furniture in their new houses. Consultation with residents about the changes that they would be experiencing had been both a matter of imparting information, and of 'winning hearts and minds', of allaying fears about the future by 'giving people a vision' that they could hold on to when familiar landmarks were demolished. The digital model was seen to have played an important part in making this process a success.

The use of a digital model during the public participation exercise of the Toxteth Street redevelopment was part of a broader excitement about the possibilities that such a model of the city of Manchester could hold for the transformation of the city. It had been in 1996, after the bomb planted by the Irish Republican Army that destroyed much of Manchester city centre, that the idea of the model was first developed by a self-employed engineer. Funded by a small business loan, he had used various surveys and architectural drawings to build a digital model of

Figure 26.1   Visualization of interior of new housing © Arup

the devastated area, which was then being developed by the regeneration company, Manchester Millennium Ltd. The model was used to develop short animations, which were used by MML board in their planning for the area.

There was much enthusiasm for this developing tool. In 2000, it was installed in Manchester's visitor centre and during the early 2000s, the engineer who developed the model was commissioned by another urban development project, Ancoats Urban Village Company, to extend the model to the Ancoats area of the city. There were other groups within the city who were developing similar models, including a team at Salford University, but the strength of the city model being described here lay in the ambition to generate a common city model, which could be used 'as a collaborative platform which might help build relationships, professionals and citizens'.[1] By the time I began my research, the engineer had joined the international design engineering firm Arup, and was working to convince the firm of the power of just such a collaborative modelling tool.

In recent years, processes of planned social change have increasingly come to centre around the question of participation (cf. Barry 2001; Marres 2008). In development settings, participatory approaches have become a dominant mode of organizing knowledge and enacting transformation, with the aim that multiple points of view can be collected and incorporated into planning decisions (Green 2003). Government policy is made through processes of consultation with different parties in the hope that incorporation of a variety of views will lead to better interventions (Mosse 2004), meanwhile, scientists are being asked to make themselves accountable by improving communication with the general public in whose name they act (Wynne 2006). The method of participation has become the promised panacea to social problems, which in turn are reconceived as stemming from a lack of local knowledge and a failure to communicate.

It was in relation to the question of how to engage different people in development processes that the digital model was being developed in Manchester. Its supporters imagined that it would provide a new means of communicating more effectively between planning departments and citizens in projects like the Toxteth Street redevelopment. It was also hoped that it might be used to improve communication between disciplinary experts concerned with different aspects of urban transformation, and would be able to cross over the silos of disciplinary knowledge production by locating different knowledges in the same digital space. Moreover, it was seen that the model would provide a means by which cities could engage more effectively with external pressures, such as those posed from the environment, government legislation and unpredictable economic markets. Finally, as a tool in a broader project of social engineering, the model was imagined as a new, more effective and often uncontentious means of effecting 'behaviour change' amongst populations. In many respects, the model appeared to be yet another example of a more generalized attempt to incorporate publics into decision-making processes. At the same time, the anticipation, excitement and sometimes ambivalence shown towards this technological means of achieving these ends was noteworthy. There was deemed to be something about the digital model that differed from previous means of interfacing between experts and their publics in the ways described above.

The purpose of this chapter is to explore the ways in which the digital model was thus being mobilized as a novel means of interfacing between experts and publics. In what follows, I pay particular attention to the relational commitments of the digital model itself. Recent work on digital media has begun to suggest that new information collation and interrogation techniques are having the effect of reorganizing relations between subjects, objects and information (see Savage *et al.* 2010). As I follow the ways in which the digital model of Manchester draws upon and extends the possibilities afforded by emerging techniques of data organization and interrogation, I look at some of the intended and unintended effects of this work, and in doing so point to some of the political implications of the model as a contemporary means through which a certain form of participatory politics is being enacted.

The model as interface

During the course of my research on the digital model, its developers were in discussion with an astonishing range of potential users. Meetings were held with the principal of a new school who wished to generate a model to market the school to future pupils, with the developer of a new healthcare facility who needed to visualize the redesign of hospital wards, with the manager of the visitor centre at the Manchester City Football Stadium, with a radical artist based in London, another art group based in China, with property developers, architects and academics working in departments of engineering and urban regeneration. Indeed, my own involvement in the digital model came as part of an experimental collaborative exercise that aimed to explore the mutual benefits of a conversation between engineers and anthropologists for understanding the persuasive effects of digital models in public consultation exercises.

One of the key intended beneficiaries at the time of research was Manchester City Council. Much emphasis was placed by the engineers developing the model on the need to argue the case for why the digital model could be of use to the city council, not least because it was envisaged that at some point in the future, the core of the city model would be transferred over to the council who were its primary intended recipients. Arup Manchester, who were developing the model, saw it primarily as a research and development tool. No other cities were known to have successfully developed a complete digital model that mapped the urban environment using the engineering techniques that the Manchester model had used. In this sense, the project to model

Manchester was an experiment oriented towards the exploration of new technological possibilities and their imagined social effects.[2] The resulting model that would be the outcome of these experiments was both a potential blueprint that could be used for other city models, and a useful and functioning tool that could be used within Manchester to assist in its future development.

Given the experimental nature of the project, even the uses to which the model might be put within the council were not fixed. However, there were particular uses that were seen as more likely than others. For example, the engineers developing the model were excited at the potential that the model held for assisting the council in responding to external pressures associated with a need to reduce their carbon emissions in line with the UK target of an 80 per cent reduction by 2050. In a key meeting with the city council, the engineers showed how the model might become a key resource in collating and representing already existing data on the energy efficiency of council owned buildings. They showed how the data analysis and scenario modelling capabilities of the model could provide a series of suggested interventions and modifications to buildings, based on different calculations of relative cost versus relative reduction in carbon emissions.

The people working at the council who were at the meeting were not easily convinced. The convenor of the meeting, who was a champion of the model within the council, explained to me later that people working at the council had been through several recent changes to information systems and were sceptical of the benefits of introducing yet another new system into the workplace. They were concerned about the cost of transferring data into the model, and unsure of the benefits that they would get out of it.

In turn, the engineers who had designed the model were frustrated at this attitude. They saw in this response a misunderstanding among council employees that this was simply another information technology (IT) system. For the engineers, it was something radically different. Its difference lay in its capacity to draw together the disparate knowledges and data sources existing at the council and to put them together into a single system.[3] Although they acknowledged that work would need to be done to make these data compatible, the potential of the new relations that would be produced between previously siloed databases truly excited them.[4]

This work of translating the benefits of the model was an issue to a greater or lesser extent in each of the meetings that I attended. Another meeting, this time with the head of the visitor centre at the City of Manchester Stadium, revolved around a different use for the model: not of data analysis but of providing visitors to the stadium site with an affectively charged interaction with the stadium site. The City of Manchester Stadium sits at the heart of the regeneration area of East Manchester, and dominates the landscape. Located on the site of former Bradford Colliery and Brickworks, the space was cleared and the stadium built for the 2002 Commonwealth Games. As well as including the stadium, which is now home to Manchester City Football Club, the site also houses a velodrome, a training football pitch and acres of car-parking space. The whole area is known by developers as 'Sport City'.

Sport City has become something of a draw for visitors. As home to Manchester City Football Club, it is a mecca for the international fan base, and as a former site of the Commonwealth Games it attracts its fair share of delegates responsible for other large sporting events. As the heart of the regeneration area of East Manchester, it attracts people involved in projects of regeneration, and other visitors include potential users of the site, for example organizers of pop concerts, circuses and other large public events. Yet the head of the visitor centre explained that he faces a problem when people come to visit the site. Coming with an expectation that being at the site will confer the excitement of a football match, the value-creation effects of a sports legacy programme, or the social benefits of urban regeneration, what visitors are more usually faced with is a bleak expanse of empty car-parking space. Hanging baskets of flowers on the lampposts around the stadium attempt to inject some colour and life into the otherwise quiet and uninviting scene, but it is difficult to impart to visitors the potential effects that the stadium is able to produce. Here, the model of the city was discussed as a means of reconnecting visitors with the affective potential of the stadium. How could it help connect people with the aroma of hot-dog stands and the hubbub of pre-match anticipation? How might it capture the histories of the site and impart the stories of local people who had benefited from its construction to interested visitors? How might it transmit the lights and music of a rock concert, or the whoosh of racing bicycles?

How, indeed? Although the chief engineer was sure that this must be possible and was enthusiastic about the possibilities of trying to manipulate the model to these ends, talk of video clips and sound recordings, quotes from residents and photographs failed to produce the same kind of enthusiasm that we saw from the engineers in the city council meeting. Here, in contrast, the passion of the potential user of the model was met with the ambivalence of the engineer. Thinking on his feet, the engineer came up with an idea himself that he thought might be possible: perhaps they could use the model to provide a way of allowing people to see what seat they had chosen and to see the view from that seat?

In both the discussion at the city council, and in the discussion with the visitor centre manager, the assumed potential of the model as interface was questioned and reframed by the engineers who were building it. First, as we have seen, the city council employees were deemed to have misunderstood the model as merely another IT system. As an interface it had been misinterpreted as a bounded tool that would mediate a pre-specified set of relations: between the finance and the planning department, for example, or between people working within environmental services. In contrast, the engineers saw the model as an inherently flexible resource the power of which to transform came from its capacity to incorporate an as-yet-undefined multiplicity of data from a variety of sources, which could be put into relation in previously unanticipated ways. In the second instance, the model was imagined as a tool for conjuring an affective relationship with a particular space. The interfacing capacity of the model was assumed by the visitor centre manager to lie in its ability to generate a virtual visual world, which could draw people out of the mundanity of the everyday and into the spectacle of the event. Although the engineer designing the model certainly did not contest its capacity to persuade and enchant through techniques of visual representation, the suggestion of using video clips or interview quotes was superseded by the possibility of accurately locating one's place within the model.

These examples provided in this section suggest that there was something particular about the promise of the model as a new kind of digital technology that differentiated it from other previously available means of presenting and analysing information. The apparently infinitely extendable list of people who might find the model useful itself implied an unusual mutability to this interface object, which could turn its hand to any manner of interventionist projects. At the same time, the extendibility of the model revealed its limits in the misunderstandings and difficulties of mutual enthusiasm encountered in these meetings. To understand the basis of the promise of the model to provide a flexible and mutable new form of communication, and the politics of its limits, I turn my attention in the following section to the relations that were built into its design.

Building the model

The digital model of Manchester is based on data collected by LiDAR, an aerial laser scanning technology that has been used to generate a topographic map of the whole of the city of Manchester.

The LiDAR technique allows for a relief map to be constructed of all of the architectural and geographic features of the city landscape, which are translated into a block model. This block model is linked to map data provided by Ordnance Survey (see Harvey 2009 for a more detailed account of this process) in order to fix the coordinates of the LiDAR data in geographical space. This provides the basic structure for the city model onto which other data can be applied. Photographic data are linked into the block model through the technique of photogrammetry, which correlates points on a photograph with points on the model, allowing buildings to be provided with a basic level of photographic detail. Further to this, more detail can be added in at later stages into the model; recently, for example, the developers have been working on improving the modelling of vegetation and foliage.

Before the development of the city-wide model, digital models of architectural features within Manchester did already exist, but they were self-contained representations of particular buildings and spaces, which tended to be discarded after the building had been constructed. The vision of the city-wide digital model was to replace this *ad hoc* act of virtual construction with a technology that would incorporate all the single models built for individual projects, and would evolve with the changing city.

The dream of a continually evolving model of the city had a precursor in the form of a material model of the city, which now sits as a historical curiosity in the offices of Arup Manchester. During the period of its use, this physical model was updated regularly by craft-workers who would remove demolished buildings and add new structures as they appeared. Like the digital model, the physical model mapped landscape and space from a bird's-eye view of the city, providing an overview of the space from the privileged vantage point of an omniscient observer.[5] However, unlike the digital model, the scale at which the city was represented and the form of the representation were singular and fixed.

In contrast, the digital model of Manchester uses the geographical data provided by LiDAR and Ordnance Survey to organize sets of information at different levels of detail. This allows the user to move apparently seamlessly from a view of the whole city down to the level of the street and even inside some of the buildings. Although the experience of the user is one of greater and greater levels of magnification, the effect is in fact produced by a clever conjuring trick that substitutes different sets of data at different scales. Whereas with the physical model the act of moving closer to gain more knowledge actually reduces rather than improves our understanding of the object represented, drawing us into the object-like qualities of the representation itself (the grain of the wooden office blocks, the wire of the architectural trees and the brush strokes on the painted roads), the substitution of data in the digital model allows for infinitely finer levels of detail to be experienced by a single user from the vantage point of a single screen.

The effect of moving across different scales is just one example of the way in which the digital model promises to incorporate and connect up multiple data sources, capturing and encapsulating them into a geographic and analytic tool. Anything that can be numerically measured or spatially plotted is thus potentially available for incorporation into the Manchester model. The team building the model includes not only engineers and programmers but acousticians, geologists, transport planners and all manner of other expert producers of data, whose informational outputs are linked into the geographical data that lie at the heart of the model.

The flexibility of the model derives then, from its ambition to incorporate without limit all manner of informational data collated from any number of different sources. This ambition is intimately linked to the proliferation of data-producing technologies: from mobile phones that provide location data on users, to smart electricity meters to the transactional data produced by online purchases, store loyalty cards and credit cards. In this respect, the digital model of

Manchester can be seen as part of a broader development of technologies of data collation and analysis, which are committed to the analytic and communicative potential of 'total data'.

The politics of data

Recent developments in digital data collation have begun to be explored by a number of scholars who have become interested in the political claims made for these techniques and the social and cultural implications of their use (Thrift 2007; Amoore 2009; Knox *et al.* 2010; Savage *et al.* 2010; Ruppert 2011). Much has been made by developers and potential users of these technologies of the analytic potential of 'total data' to provide new ways of tackling long-running political and economic issues as diverse as international terrorism and consumer behaviour. According to these literatures, a key claim made on behalf of these techniques is that they offer a move away from prejudicial forms of data analysis based on an *a priori* categorization of social 'types', to an inductive mode of analysis where transactional data provide a benign basis out of which patterns of behaviour can be revealed (Dodge and Kitchin 2005).[6] Amoore (2009), for example, quotes US Secretary of Homeland Security Michael Chertoff to illustrate these claims as they appear in relation to border security practices,

> We use this data to focus on behaviour, not race and ethnicity. In fact, what it allows us to do is move beyond crude profiling based on prejudice and look at conduct and communication and actual behaviour as a way of determining who we need to take a closer look at.
>
> *(quoted in Amoore 2009: 17)*

Amoore warns against acceptance of the notion that calculated projections such as this are apolitical, arguing that in the context of border security, these techniques 'simply redraw the lines between those with entitlement (to visa, to cross a border, to be in a public place without disclosure of purpose) and those without' (Amoore 2009: 18). In this respect, these techniques do not erase the politics of classification but rather relegate it into an underspecified realm of action that lies outside the control of the data analysts.

Ruppert (2011) has also suggested that greater attention needs to be paid to the ways in which transactional data operate as tools as governance. Whereas initial concerns voiced about these technologies focused on questions of privacy and surveillance (e.g., Graham and Wood 2003; Andrejevic 2009), Ruppert argues that we need to be sensitive to the equally powerful role that they play in not only revealing, but constituting populations as subjects. Population metrics provide data that 'identify and categorize populations of "benefits thieves", tax dodgers, patients at risk of re-hospitalization, security risks or frequent migrants' (Ruppert 2011: 222). Moreover, through a focus on transactions rather than responses to survey questions, population metrics appear to be transforming the ways in which populations are enacted from an 'interactive' to what Ruppert calls 'interpassive' form of participation. In contrast to survey methods, which aim to elicit the thoughts, interpretations or opinions of populations, transactional data privileges the patterns that are detectable in daily practices of purchasing, form filling and communicating, producing an outcome that is more 'empirical and descriptive, rather than subjective and meaningful' (Ruppert 2011: 228). To what extent, then, were these informational dynamics at play in the Manchester model?

One idea being proposed during the period of my research was that the model of Manchester could be used to monitor the carbon consumption of different businesses. A suggestion was being mooted at the time of my research that energy use of particular companies could be displayed in real time on screens outside the building, with the intention that simply the display of relative consumption of power would create a competitive environment that would encourage people to turn off lights, switch computers off at night and turn down thermostats. Here, the question of how to intervene in the social was cast not as a project of social control or even discipline, but was being reconceived in line with other data collation techniques as a knowledge-based form of intervention. The question of how to intervene successfully focused on how to capture accurate information (empirics) and how to design appropriate techniques of display (description).

By acknowledging the political effects of the model to lie not in an underlying logic of control but rather in the functional project of capturing and displaying information, we can extend our understanding of the way in which the model operated as an interface object. It was in the process of data collection and the decisions over appropriate forms of display that the terms within which the city and its residents were expected to conceive of themselves and their concerns were reconceived. Far from operating as a simple form of translation or mediation between different political concerns, the processes through which the model was constantly brought into being was generative of questions and debate, in both predictable and unexpected ways.

As an interface object, we have seen how the model was envisaged firstly as a way of *displaying* all manner of information that had been collated from a range of different sources. Yet the practice of display itself was fraught with all kinds of interpretative difficulties that the engineers had not predicted. Despite its accuracy, the computer imagery was sometimes deemed unrealistic and much to the frustration of the modellers, consulted publics were more convinced by the 'reality' of an artist's drawing than by the digital representation of a future architectural feature. In contrast, during the Toxteth Street redevelopment the model appeared to exceed its role as descriptor of a possible future. It ending up being so convincing that the developers had to mitigate its effects by telling residents not to place too much hope that the actual redevelopment would look the same as the digital model.

The ambition of the model to provide an inductive method of *revealing* hitherto unknown connections, correlations and relationships derived from its interconnective and layering capacities. The hope was that the redescription of total data through patterns of association would produce generative forms of relationality. However, one unforeseen effect of the display of available data was the inadvertent revelation of gaps in the data. The model of East Manchester, for example, was striking for the unevenness in the depiction of space. Most of the area was described only through the basic block modelling produced by the LiDAR technology, which gave the effect of a uniform grey landscape. This was occasionally interspersed with areas of much more detail, such as Sport City and Toxteth Street. Inadvertently, the representational unevenness of the city model told a story of the geography of investment in urban regeneration and the politics through which the model had itself been produced. It also provided the basis for the future direction that the development of the model might take; the appearance of gaps in the model produced awareness of places where new uses for the model could be proposed or developed. As an interface object, the model therefore not only provided the means for data analysts to reveal new relationships between datasets, but through the revelation of gaps in the data, it generated a 'virtual' space out of which new social and political relations would necessarily be formed.

Finally, the emergent nature of the model meant that the changes in 'behaviour' induced by the model would necessarily be reincorporated into its calculations. This allowed it to constantly be reestablished as a *recursive* technology of public engagement (Kelty 2008). The model was not a static instrument of data display but a mutating technique through which residents of the city were expected to be reconstituted as they simultaneously remade the object of their subjectification. Unlike other methods of participatory planning (Green 2010), this technique did not so much rely on the incorporation of the opinions and culturally specific perspectives of stakeholders into the development process. Rather, the public appeared in the model on the one hand as inadvertent producers of data and on the other as navigators of the digital terrain with which they were confronted. Savage *et al.* (2010) have recently suggested that one of the effects of digital technologies is to displace the expertise that was previously associated with the governance of populations, 'Publics are now enacted and enabled to intervene actively by making up their own devices as well as by contributing to the dominance of particular devices through their mass take up' (Savage *et al.* 2010: 9). However, in the case of Manchester's digital model, I suggest that the recursivity of these data-driven techniques, far from displacing the role of expertise, is instead reorganizing it in new ways. The centrality of a data-driven model of intervention may disavow planning expertise based on the teachings of twentieth-century sociology (Savage and Burrows 2007), but in its place it appears to be valuing another kind of expertise oriented towards the capture and presentation of data. Finding themselves with a key role to play in this activity, it is perhaps unsurprising that engineers have begun to claim for themselves the new title of 'information masterbuilder' (Kolarevic 2003).

Conclusion

Some time after residents living on Toxteth Street had walked their way around a digital model of their new neighbourhood, been encouraged to virtually inhabit their new homes and to imagine what their future lives might be like, a compulsory purchase order was served on their homes. Materially, the model might thus appear to have been a cynical detour, a distraction from the 'real' politics that decides who lives where and for what purpose transformations in people's lives are deemed necessary. However I have suggested in this chapter that if we are to understand the politics of public participation, we need to distance ourselves from the assumption that we already know the relational basis upon which politics is conducted. To this end, I have focused on various ways in which the Manchester model produced its interfacing effects.

Although computer technologies are often labelled as 'interfaces', my interest in the digital model as interface has required moving away from the assumption that we already understand the relations that the interface implies. In computing terminology, the 'interface' is a term that is usually taken to mean the capacity of the screen to translate between the technology of circuit boards and electrical pulses as contained within the computer casing on the one hand, and the sociality of the human user, eyes glued, fingers poised, looking at and interpreting the images on the screen on the other (e.g., Turkle 1997). In contrast, I have approached the digital model by asking what relational commitments it entails and how these might help us understand the way in which it is being mobilized as an alternative means of participatory politics. Focusing on both the internal relations built into the model and its appearance within a broader project of social transformation, I have explored the multiple ways in which the model operates as an interface object. This has allowed us to observe a restructuring of the relationship between humans and machines, and between experts and publics, as digital data are made to stand in for the decision-making capacities of either planners or those who are asked to participate in processes of urban transformation. At the same time, the promise of total data produces unexpected effects for both the producers and users of the interface object. In this way, techniques of data organization and presentation like Manchester's digital model appear to be producing new objects of contestation and negotiation and revealing in new ways, the politics of urban transformation.

Notes

1 Personal communication.
2 See Marres (2009) for a discussion of experimentation as a contemporary mode of public participation.

3 Nonetheless, there are distinct similarities between the claims made for this model and those made for other business information technologies such as enterprise resource planning (ERP) systems, see for example Kallinikos (2004) and Pollock and Cornford (2004).
4 For a comparable example of the technological integration see Green *et al.* 2005).
5 Recall Michel De Certeau's reflections on the ecstatic pleasure of experiencing the city from the top of the World Trade Centre,

> It transforms the bewitching world by which one was 'possessed' into a text that lies before one's eyes. It allows one to read it, to be a solar Eye, looking down like a god. The exaltation of a scopic and gnostic drive: the fiction of knowledge is related to this lust to be a viewpoint and nothing more.
>
> *(de Certeau 1984:92)*

6 The interest in new forms of data collation and analysis has been paralleled by a reawakening of interest in the French sociologist Gabriel Tarde, and his alternative theory of the social, which appears to preempt the social logic of information systems based on a notion of 'total data' (see Barry and Thrift 2007 and Latour 2010).

Bibliography

Amoore, L. (2009) 'Lines of Sight: On the Visualization of Unknown Futures', *Citizenship Studies*, 13(1): 17–30.

Andrejevic, M. (2009) 'Control over Personal Information in the Database Era', *Surveillance and Society*, 6(3): 322–326.

Barry, A. (2001) *Political Machines: Governing a Technological Society,* London; New York, Athlone Press.

Barry, A. and Thrift, N. (2007) 'Gabriel Tarde: Imitation, Invention and Economy', *Economy and Society*, 36(4): 509–525.

de Certeau, M. (1984) *The Practice of Everyday Life,* Berkeley; London, University of California Press.

Dodge, M. and Kitchin, R. (2005) 'Codes of Life: Identification Codes and the Machine-Readable World', *Environment and Planning D,* 23: 851–882.

Graham, S. and Wood, D. (2003) 'Digitizing Surveillance: Categorization, Space, Inequality', *Critical Social Policy,* 23(2): 227–248.

Green, M. (2003) 'Globalising Development: Policy Franchising through Participatory Project Management in "Non-Places"', *Critique of Anthropology,* 23(2): 123–143.

Green, M. (2010) 'Making Development Agents: Participation as Boundary Object in International Development', *Journal of Development Studies,* 46(7): 1240–1263.

Green, S., Harvey, P. and Knox, H. (2005) 'Scales of Place and Networks: An Ethnography of the Imperative to Connect through Information and Communications Technologies', *Current Anthropology,* 46(5): 805–826.

Harvey, P. (2009) 'Between Narrative and Number: The Case of Arup's 3D Digital City Model', *Cultural Sociology,* 3(2): 257–276.

Kallinikos, J. (2004) 'Deconstructing Information Packages: Organizational and Behavioural Implications of ERP Systems', *Information Technology and People,* 17(1): 8–30.

Kelty, C. M. (2008) *Two Bits: The Cultural Significance of Free Software,* Durham, Duke University Press.

Knox, H., O'Doherty, D., Vurdubakis, T. and Westrup, C. (2010) 'The Devil and Customer Relationship Management', *Journal of Cultural Economy,* 3(3): 339–359.

Kolarevic, B. (2003) *Architecture in the Digital Age: Design and Manufacturing,* London, Spon.

Latour, B. (2010) 'Tarde's Idea of Quantification' in *The Social after Gabriel Tarde: Debates and Assessments,* M. Candea, Ed. London, Routledge: 145–162.

Marres, N. (2008) 'The Making of Climate Publics: Eco-Homes as Material Devices of Publicity', *Scandinavian Journal of Social Theory,* 16: 27–46.

Marres, N. (2009) 'Testing Powers of Engagement: Green Living Experiments, the Ontological Turn and the Undoability of Involvement', *European Journal of Social Theory,* 12: 117–134.

Mosse, D. (2004) *Cultivating Development: An Ethnography of Aid Policy and Practice,* London, Pluto.

Pollock, N. and Cornford, J. (2004) 'ERP Systems and the University as a "Unique" Organisation', *Information Technology and People,* 17(1): 31–52.

Ruppert, E. (2011) 'Population Objects: Interpassive Subjects', *Sociology,* 45(2).

Savage, M. and Burrows, R. (2007) 'The Coming Crisis of Empirical Sociology', *Sociology,* 41: 885–900.

Savage, M., Ruppert, E. and Law, J. (2010) 'Digital Devices: Nine Theses', *CRESC working paper series,* Manchester, University of Manchester.

Thrift, N. J. (2007) *Non-Representational Theory: Space, Politics, Affect,* London; New York, NY, Routledge.

Turkle, S. (1997) *Life on the Screen: Identity in the Age of the Internet,* London, Phoenix.

Wynne, B. (2006) 'Public Engagement as a Means of Restoring Public Trust in Science – Hitting the Notes, but Missing the Music?' *Community Genetics,* 9(3): 211–220.

27

Money frontiers

The relative location of euros, Turkish lira and gold sovereigns in the Aegean

Sarah Green

Introduction

On 28 February 2012, Standard and Poor's, one of those infamous rating agencies, downgraded Greek debt from junk status to being in 'selective default'. Few people knew that there was anything below junk status until that day. Some analysts and the Greek government announced that it did not matter, because they were expecting it and it is a 'technical' issue anyway.[1] The news reports outside Greece switch between saying that Greece should never have been let into the eurozone, and asserting that the euro was a currency experiment just waiting to go wrong, and it is now doing so spectacularly, if tortuously slowly.

Already in the 1990s and early 2000s, some had argued that the euro was an unorthodox currency because it does not belong exclusively to any one sovereign state (Dodd 2005a); others had predicted that the euro would not survive any severe economic shocks (Goodhart 2007). Geoffrey Ingham argued that the deep diversity of economic, social and political conditions in different eurozone countries, combined with a lack of sovereign authority to oversee the euro, had possibly doomed the currency from the start (Ingham 2004: 188–196). So whereas some are waiting for Greece to go under, others are waiting for the euro to go under. The distinction between the two is ambiguous: even though the eurozone is a monetary union of European Union (EU) member states, the media are still describing Greece as a separate economy that is imploding and that may pull other countries with it because of its links via the euro. Or not. Nobody really knows. In any event, it is clear that the euro has not smoothed out the economic and political differences between eurozone countries, but has instead highlighted them.

That ambiguity between the euro as a single currency and the diversity of the eurozone countries has intriguing implications for the wider relations between money and borders. It could be argued that the EU as a project has been nothing but an effort to rearrange borders, most particularly in economic and political terms: officially at least, to enable trade and to reduce the potential for war (Holmes 2000). The foundation of the eurozone, as well as initiatives such as the Schengen Agreement, the European Neighbourhood Policy, the Barcelona Process (which was supposed to reunify all parts of the Mediterranean in a new trading and cultural collaboration) and other initiatives, have been aimed at rearranging the meaning of European borders and how they become involved in different aspects of people's economic, social and political lives

(Del Sarto 2010, Liikanen and Virtanen 2006). The introduction of the euro is intended to play a key part in these border-reducing and border-rearranging policies (Shore 2000). What this might mean in practice in the Aegean region, an area that involves not only the euro, but also two other types of currency (the Turkish lira and gold sovereigns) is the focus of this chapter, as a means to explore the interface between currencies and borders.

This focus not only concerns the way cross-border relations help to generate the meaning and value of these currencies, it also concerns the different physical forms of the currencies and the question over the degree to which each of them is persuasive as money. This is related to a point that Bill Maurer makes about the 'adequation' of money: the extent to which it is possible to bring concepts and reality, mind and matter together sufficiently for money to 'work' (Maurer 2005: xiii). Maurer outlines a tension between commodity theories of money, which argue that there must be a material object that underlies the value of money (e.g. gold), and token theories of money, which suggest that all forms of money are symbolic, because there is no intrinsic value to any object, so any money object always stands for that which is valued: social relations, creative action, etc. (Maurer 2005: 129–130). Based on his study of gold coins minted for sale to people saving for Muslim pilgrimage (Haj) in Indonesia, Maurer argues that some forms of money combine these two approaches (Maurer 2005: 130–132). He also implies that theories of money are guiding the people who use the money as much as those who study it, echoing the work of Callon (2007), MacKenzie (2006) and others. My additional point is that the persuasiveness of money objects, whether as commodities or symbols, often involves cross-border relations of both people and currencies. I call this *relative location*, i.e., that the meaning and worth of people, places and things is generated in relation to, and compared with, other people, places and things; that this is inevitably political in the sense that the outcome of the comparison is not known in advance and is often negotiated or contested (Massey 2005: 11); and that it changes over time.[2]

Taking this approach involves paying close attention to the form of relations across borders over time, and not only the fact of them. The period during which empires dominated the Aegean region involved different kinds of relations between places and peoples than were introduced with the founding of Greek and Turkish states; and the more recent interventions of the EU, aiming to bring together the two sides of the Aegean, at least for the purposes of trade and ensuring political stability, if not as yet to allow Turkey to join the EU, has the effect of rearranging relations yet again. People in the region closely associated the three currencies with those different forms of border arrangements (empire, state and EU), and this is a brief exploration of the shifting interfaces between them.[3] The account begins with the violent events surrounding 1922, for much that people said about the region led into or away from these events, which are kept very much alive on both sides by Greek and Turkish national commemorations and in the teaching of history.

The 1922 events

The more official Greek accounts of the Aegean region's recent history, which are entirely bound up with the formation of the modern Greek and Turkish states, evoke a sense of loss and separation (Hirschon 2003, Koufopoulou 2003, Papataxiarchis 1999, Veremis 2003). The focus is on the violent conflicts between Greece and Turkey shortly after the break-up of the Ottoman empire, and especially the final battle, which occurred in Izmir (Smyrna in Greek), located on the Aegean coast and in the far western mainland of contemporary Turkey. The Greek military had occupied Izmir and the wider mainland region in 1919. Three years later, the Greek forces were violently driven out by the Turkish military under the leadership of Kemal Ataturk, in

September of 1922. The only escape for many residents was via the city's port; but there were few boats, and the Allied warships (British, French and American) stationed just outside the harbour had been instructed not to intervene, and most obeyed that order (Clogg 1992: 94–95, Milton 2009: 316–326).

Afterwards, a forcible exchange of populations between Greece and Turkey was organized by the League of Nations and agreed under the 1923 Treaty of Lausanne: Muslims from Greece were moved to Turkey and Orthodox Christians from Turkey were moved to Greece. Several million people (nobody knows exactly how many) were forcibly moved, despite the fact that most had lived their whole lives in the country that they were now leaving (Hirschon 2003). The exchange was explicitly intended to be irreversible. It marked the end of many decades of relative prosperity and, according to many reports, the end of a distinctive cosmopolitanism in the Aegean region based in the city of Izmir/Smyrna (Milton 2009). Izmir had been the foremost trading city of the Ottoman Empire, and had been noted for its social diversity. The fracturing of political and economic relations across the Aegean also radically changed the social landscape of this region. Before this period, the Aegean Sea had been a key trading route of the Ottoman Empire; it was now a hostile borderland between two new countries: an expanded Greece and the new Republic of Turkey.

National currencies: the era of the Turkish lira and the drachma

In the period after 1923 and until the euro was introduced, the two national currencies in the Aegean region were thoroughly associated with the separation between Greece and Turkey and their establishment as autonomous nations and states. The Greek drachma had replaced the Turkish lira after Greek independence of the southern part of its current territory in the 1820s, and the drachma was now introduced to the Aegean. The imagery on the drachma notes and coins drew heavily on the imagery of classical Greece, and combined with the naming of the currency after a classical Greek coinage, left no doubt about the associations being evoked: the contemporary Greek state was the continuation of an ancient polity that undoubtedly had the right to self-government over the territory that had been the land of the Greeks for centuries (Herzfeld 1986).

Meanwhile, in the new Republic of Turkey, established in 1923 under Kemal Ataturk after the end of the conflict with Greece, a new currency was designed, but its name, Turkish lira, subdivided into 100 kuruş, was the same as was used at the end of the Ottoman Empire. After 1923, the coins were reminted so that all sported images of Kemal Ataturk. In the few years after 1923, all Arabic script was removed from the coins and replaced by Latin script. In 1926, the first Turkish lira notes were introduced, all with images of Ataturk on them. 1926 was the last year that any Turkish currency contained Arabic script.

Thus the Turkish lira became thoroughly involved with Kemal Ataturk's aim of making Turkey into a secular, modern and transnationally accessible country. In addition to transforming the written Turkish language by replacing Arabic script with a slightly adjusted Latin alphabet, Ataturk banned the wearing of the fez, headscarves and veils; and he separated religion from the state. All of this was enshrined in the new Turkish constitution (Özyürek 2006: 13–15).[4] In short, although the first post-Ottoman Turkish lira was deliberately associated with the Ottoman empire in terms of its name, most political and some social aspects of that Ottoman heritage were explicitly rejected. In particular, the fact that the Ottoman state was based on a complex religious structure, and the strong association with the Arab world through the use of Arabic script, were removed by Ataturk. So the new republic in part turned its back on its Ottoman heritage, but the lira and its subdivision, the kuruş, remained.

Yet the lira and kuruş were only part of the Ottoman story about money. As Pamuk (2000) describes, there were many periods when the main currencies used by the Ottoman territories were minted by other empires (most notably the ducat of Venice and the florin of Florence, as well as the Hungarian coinage from the Austro-Hungarian empire, and the gold sovereign of the British Empire). And Ottoman-minted currencies were not always lira and kuruş. Most notable amongst the others was the silver *akçe*, which was replaced by the silver *kuruş* in the eighteenth century after a severe economic debasement of the *akçe*; and the gold *sultani*, which was later replaced by the gold lira for the same reason (Pamuk 2000: 20).

The period of the late nineteenth century and up to 1914 saw a particularly large-scale use of gold and silver coins minted by other regimes within Ottoman territories, particularly the British gold sovereign, which was used at times to peg the value of the Ottoman gold lira (Pamuk 2000: 219). So in the final decades of the Ottoman empire, the populations of the Aegean were entirely familiar with British gold sovereigns used as currency.

Returning to the story of the contemporary Turkish lira, Turkey has experienced a number of economic crises since 1923, and a couple of bouts of hyperinflation also radically affected the exchange value of the lira. In 2005, the currency was recalibrated and six zeros were removed, so that 1 million old lira became 1 new Turkish lira.[5] The kuruş, which had fallen out of use because of hyperinflation, was returned as a subdivision of the lira. And by coincidence or design, the 50 kuruş and the 1 Turkish new lira bimetallic coins looked remarkably like the 1 euro and 2 euro coins respectively, both in size and design.

That apparent mimicry of other territories' currencies is an old and common habit. The fact that many currencies are called 'lira' itself points to this: lira initially referred to a pound weight of silver (from the Latin *libra*), and many currencies subsequently used either lira or 'pound' to refer to the biggest denomination of their currency, whatever its metal content. In Turkey, the lira originally referred to a gold coin, and the kuruş (translated as *piastre* in many other languages) referred to the silver coin (Pamuk 2000: 20), but the point is the same: the words used to refer to different polities' currencies were often identical. Ducats, florins, *piastres* or pesetas were all also minted in diverse forms in different parts of the world. And the major and relatively stable currencies such as the ducat were regularly used as a means to set the value of other, newer or less familiar currencies. When the Ottoman gold *sultani* was introduced, it was deliberately designed to emulate the weight and metal quality of the more familiar Venetian ducat (Pamuk 2000: 61).

This habit of evoking similarities between diverse currencies, and in particular, emulating the characteristics of the most recognized currencies in form or name, often following trade routes and other paths of political and social relations between places, highlights the way currencies reflect their cross-border relations as much as their own territories. Many theorists of money suggest, borrowing from Keynes, that one of the most important things that money does is to act as a yardstick (money of account): money acts as a standard against which relative worth can be calculated (Ingham 2004: 70). That is not in itself a controversial idea; the critiques have concerned the way that the concept 'value' has been taken for granted by many commentators, as if value simply exists and money measures it. Chris Gregory, amongst others, suggested instead that as the concept of value is historically, politically and socially variable, the place to begin to understand money in any given context is to understand how value works in that context. As he suggests: 'to define money in one way or another is always to adopt a standard of value of some sort. But how many standards of value are there? How are they related?' (Gregory 1997: 6).[6] His point is that no definition of money exists independently of the system of values for which it provides a standard. Combined with the observation that the form currencies take often emulates those from elsewhere, even while asserting territorial specificity in other ways, implies that currencies have a *relative location*: their meaning and use is constituted as much from their location relative to other currencies as by the 'local' conditions that generated them. That relative location usually also involves convertibility, a relation to others through conversion/exchange systems (some more transnational than others). The most famous of these mechanisms was the gold standard, the collapse of which in the 1970s led to what Chris Gregory refers to as 'savage money', a kind of free for all in which there is no base yardstick against which all are calibrated (Gregory 1997: 2–4). In Maurer's terms described above, all money has become token money.

This brief account of the shifting use of currencies in the Aegean in the past has given some indication of the relative locations involved, the way different currencies became associated with particular political arrangements *and* the kinds of cross-border relations in which they engaged. Judging from my conversations with people in Mytilene (capital of the island of Lesvos) and Ayvalik (a Turkish coastal town on the other side of the Aegean from Mytilene), in 2007, 2008 and 2011, these associations became a part of the socially understood meaning and perceived worth of the currencies associated with those periods. What is more, those associations were not simply the result of the actions of political authorities who design the currencies and the accounting systems: people's everyday use of these currencies, combined with their travels from one place to another, contributed to their reputation as currencies. Even Pamuk repeatedly describes moments when a given political authority loses control over their currency's meaning and worth (Pamuk 2000: 226). And although researchers such as Zelizer and Cohen point to the complexity of the relationship between money objects and value (Cohen 2004, Zelizer 1997, 2011), my additional point is simply that the perceived worth of many currencies is at least partly based on their relative location, compared with the value of other currencies, and to the political and social reputation of their associated territories.

Gold sovereigns

One of the differences between currencies in terms of relative location is the degree to which they require conversion as they cross borders (i.e., the degree to which they themselves become the yardstick against which others are measured). Benjamin Cohen suggests that certain currencies (most famously the US dollar) break out of their own territorial boundaries and can be used in many other places as money (Cohen 2004). As already outlined, chief amongst those border-crossing currencies in the Aegean during the Ottoman period, but also later, were specific types of gold and silver coins. Immediately before the end of Ottoman rule, the main gold coins were the Turkish lira and British gold sovereigns. The gold sovereigns took precedence, for it was the British gold standard to which the Ottoman and later Turkish lira were initially pegged.

Here, Maurer's point about combining commodity and token theories of money comes into play. During my time in the Aegean in the late 2000s, the topic of gold sovereigns came up regularly. Mostly, the stories concerned the possibility that stashes of these coins might still be hidden somewhere in the fabric of the houses that were abandoned by the Greeks when they were forcibly removed from Turkey; or there were discussions about heirlooms passed on after births, marriages and deaths. Some mentioned that until as late as the 1970s, many Greeks bought large items (cars, houses) in gold sovereigns, and that some still do so. There was room for confusion about which coins people were referring to: in Greek, the phrase for gold sovereign is χρυσή λίρα, (*chrisi lira*), which literally means 'gold pound'; and the Greek word for the Turkish currency is also λίρα/*lira*, that being the Turkish name for both the Turkish currency and the Turkish gold coins. This (non-coincidental) name confusion meant that I regularly asked people to specify which coins they meant. Almost, but not quite, invariably, the answer was the British sovereign. One man, who used to live in the Aegean but had now moved to Athens and travelled regularly between Turkey and Greece to buy house linens in Turkey, which he sold on in Greece, said that most people preferred the gold sovereigns because they were 'guaranteed 24-carat gold' and you could trust them.

Over time, I began to understand the differences in people's understanding of these coins, and I briefly discuss the accounts of Julia, Dimitry and Sophia to show some sense of this diversity. Unusually, Sofia, a woman in her fifties with close past relations with Turkey, said that for her, *chrisi lira* explicitly meant the Ottoman coins. This was because, she said, her family were amongst those who had lived in Turkey and were part of the exchange of populations. Her grandmother spoke Turkish in the house and kept a bag of the coins tucked into her bosom, which she had brought with her from Turkey. She used to take them out from time to time and play with them with the children. When Sofia married, her mother gave Sofia two of these coins, and she has recently divided them between her two children. Sofia repeated what all others had also said, that the gold stashed away in the houses on the Turkish side were always in the fabric of the house.

In contrast, for Dimitry, a man in his forties who spoke fluent Turkish and had been married to a Turkish citizen, *chrisi lira* is a British gold sovereign and nothing else. He quoted the exact weight of the British gold sovereign coin (7.322381 grams in 24-carat gold) and said this is why people trusted it: the weight was always precise, whereas the Ottoman liras were much less accurate; you would get a heavy one sometimes and a light one the next time. For Dimitry, *flouri* (florin), often used to refer to the gold coin put into the new year's cake in Greece, is a synonym of *chrisi lira*. He said the word *flouri* came from Dutch florins, not Florentine ones (again evoking the confusion of similarities of names of currencies). He was certain of all these things; he had researched them, he said.

For Julia, a woman in her forties who had lived abroad for many years and whose family was also part of the exchange of populations but not from the Aegean region, the *chrisi lira* stashed in the fabric of Turkish houses is a 'myth', something parents tell their children like telling them about the tooth fairy. And it was just a piece of gold, not really a coin at all, because the ones that she inherited did not have any monetary value stamped on them. She was right about that: gold coins rarely have any value stamped on them, because the price that they fetch is based on their weight and varies according to the price of gold. She said most people in her family called these coins *flouri*. She was given one in her mother's will, but she could not recall where she put it. For her, the coins were part of the past, part of that mythological and nostalgic story of loss.

So there was no singular story; on the contrary, particular past and present relations across borders strongly informed how people understood the relative value and location of the gold coins. Nevertheless, in all, a key characteristic of the gold sovereign was that it is the kind of money that can travel across borders, hold its value and be recognized anywhere. In that sense, the gold sovereign was, for these people, iconic of crossing the Aegean, of a way of life that was built upon an order of things that had stopped in 1923. At the same time, the gold sovereign also often fixed people in their relationships and located them: whereas the sovereign was transnational, a coin that stood for another (British) empire, the particular gold sovereigns that people had were *theirs*; these sovereigns, both literally and metaphorically, part of their family and their house.[7] So the desire for gold sovereigns, to have them and to pass them on to relatives, was not individualistic; rather, it combined personal family histories with political and economic conditions before 1923. Much of the mythical gold, the gold hidden in the fabric of houses, was no longer circulating or growing into a family fortune; it was stuck in the abandoned houses in Ayvalik. And the coins themselves evoked a previous era of empires trading with each other and generating a particular way of life by doing so.

In sum, within the commodity theory of money, the gold coins were preferred to fiat money (notes and cheap metal coins) because they travelled well, both across time and space.

However, some gold coins were preferred over others, and that *did* relate to the perceived reliability of different political regimes: people believed that some regimes more reliably produced gold coins of a precise weight than others. Pamuk supports that belief, saying that towards the end of the Ottoman Empire, the Ottoman gold lira became less reliable: 'The instability of the Ottoman gold coins inevitably reduced their appeal in international payments and for purposes of hoarding' (2000: 167). So it is not simply the price that the metal could fetch as a commodity that mattered, but also the transnational reputation of the political authority that issued the coins. And although the British government today still issues new gold sovereigns every year, in the Aegean region the coins are associated with the period of British empire. And the 'order of things', to borrow from Foucault (1974) had a different logic to it then.

The euro: locations and dislocations

The commonly perceived time of the gold sovereign was a pre-1923 moment, during which life was rich, at least in terms of a repeated Greek nostalgic narrative of the inevitability of a subsequent 'fall' that Herzfeld has so evocatively described (Herzfeld 1997: 22 and Chapter 6). This rhetoric is strongly reflected in the title of Giles Milton's (2009) book about the 1923 events, *Paradise Lost: Smyrna 1922*. What was lost, according to one type of account (there are others), was a time and place when peoples from many different countries and backgrounds gathered together to trade; they developed, so the story goes, an enormously rich artistic, intellectual, cultural and social existence. All of that was founded on the trade, on the ability of peoples to travel and to bring goods to and from all the Ottoman regions and beyond. Gold coins of all types circulated with the goods, coins from all over the empire and beyond. In terms of that account, the 1923 Treaty of Lausanne, which divided the Aegean into two hostile sides, seriously disrupted a centuries-old order of things. Yet things may be changing once again, if the EU's policies are anything to go by, which appear to be implying the possibility of reconstituting that older order of things once again. Since 1995, there have been a range of transnational agreements made, brokered by the EU, that are aimed at bringing free trade back to the whole Mediterranean region, including the Aegean part of it. The first of these agreements was the Barcelona Process (Scott 2006), and the more recent variation, signed in the summer of 2008, is called the Euro–Mediterranean Partnership.[8] The whole aim is to 'restore' the former trading and political relations across this region. It is in that context that the euro has taken on its particular relative location in the Aegean, and I finally turn to that.

On the face of it, and taken as a token, the euro travels easily across borders, and has even been used, like the US dollar, in places where the local currency has lost its value (e.g. in Kosovo). As outlined earlier, the EU's purpose was to break down previously strongly guarded borders, to allow a free flow of people and trade within the EU's territories and, more recently, with the EU's neighbours. And the euro itself was supposed to draw the eurozone countries ever closer together, both in political and economic terms (Dodd 2005b). Yet people in Mytilene did not speak about the euro in any way even remotely similar to the border-crossing British gold sovereigns, as a currency that represented some clearly understood political regime, and which would hold its value on its travels. Well before the current financial crisis in Greece, many complained about the euro in predictable ways, especially about prices going up after it was introduced. More interestingly, many also said that the euro is insufficiently associated with an identifiable 'home' location: 'it is a nowhere kind of currency, belonging to an imaginary place called Europe', one retired civil servant commented. And he was not the only one to express the sense that some fiat currencies are more 'fiat' than others, in that some currencies seem less clearly linked to some place and peoples. The euro was not seen as a currency that travels well like gold sovereigns, but instead as one whose home is everywhere and therefore nowhere. Gold sovereigns located people in the geopolitical realities of empire, and those realities were drawn into the complex locating practices and social relations that people lived within in the Aegean region at the time. People associated that earlier period not only with nostalgic views of prosperity, but with a slow, socially collective habit of saving wealth for the future. In contrast, people in Mytilene spoke about the euro as a non-local currency that was dependent upon spending, borrowing and debt rather than saving, and on markets more than it was dependent upon a political authority or social location. In this perspective, the euro was invented by a political economy reflecting the era of 'savage money' in Chris Gregory's terms, money with no fixed measure against which its value can be judged, dependent only on what people will pay for it (Gregory 1997). From the Mytilene residents' perspective, this meant that the euro has no reliable value that can travel across time and space in the way the gold sovereign could.

Today, as the fiscal crisis in Greece is reaching its nadir, that attitude might seem prescient; but my point not only concerns the way that the euro, as a currency of the EU, both reflects and helps to create the wider political and economic context in which Greece is embedded: it also reflects something about the relative location of Greece in relation to the euro, which is where I began. I have suggested that in the past, cross-border currencies such as gold sovereigns acted as a yardstick to measure the worth of other gold currencies and the relations between places, people and things. Yet if the euro also acts as a yardstick, it is a strange one, in that it has no pretence at any fixed value, and its sovereign location is unclear; and in Greece, the place it is supposed to represent, Europe, is not a polity in the same way as the British empire or even Greece, as a country, are polities. Nevertheless, by being a currency, the euro is a yardstick, and what it measures (and simultaneously creates) is, unsurprisingly, a hierarchically ordered diversity within the eurozone, or what could be called the relative location of eurozone countries (north, south, west, and the 'former east'). The thing about yardsticks is that they standardize the means of measurement: in that sense, the euro did not, or did not only, bring every member state together into a bigger European entity; it made the differences between them measurable and comparable in a standardized way. Greeks in Mytilene understood that capacity for the euro to differentiate European regions (or to generate self-fulfilling prophecies) all too well. In this, it is the relation between the Aegean region and other places that is once again being redefined: the relative location defined according to the criteria of those who built the euro, rather than a place in itself.

This echoes Herzfeld's (2004) view of the 'global hierarchy of value', in which those who invent the classification system that defines what counts as cultural difference and authenticity have the power, as such a system acts as a standardized means of defining everyone as being different in a particular way. The euro appears to have some of that air about it, classifying and defining the diversity within the eurozone according to a set of criteria that reinforce preexisting hierarchies. Yet what I have described as relative location not only means relative in relation to a standard measure or yardstick; it also implies an inherent contingency, because the yardstick is never there on its own, but is surrounded by the traces of other ways of generating relative locations. This suggests that nothing is global in the sense of being a blanket that covers everything in the same way: the euro exists in the company of other, past and present, yardsticks: the gold sovereign, the various forms of the Turkish lira, even the Greek drachma and the mimetic effects of currencies with the same name and appearance. In Mytilene, the euro has been understood in terms of these other ways of linking and separating peoples and places in the past. In the comparison, what emerges is a currency that simultaneously hierarchically classifies those within its territories, but that is also strangely non-located, in that its value appears to be contingent and it does not stand for a particular place. Nor does it appear to be mimetic of any one thing, but instead invites diverse interpretations according to context. As a result its relative location is ambiguous in a way that the Turkish lira and gold sovereign were not, and that makes it an entity that is difficult to locate, or value, at all.

Notes

1 http://www.bbc.co.uk/news/business-17187068 (accessed 22 April 2012).
2 For some further discussions on this idea of relative location, see Green (2010).
3 The majority of this story is told from the Greek side, because of current language limitations on my part.
4 In recent years, Turkish politics has turned moderately towards Islam again, under the leadership of Recep Tayyip Erdoğan (Öktem 2011: Chapters 4 and 5).
5 Research has actually been done on the psychological effects of removing six zeros all at once (Amado et al. 2007).
6 See also Graeber (2001), Maurer (2005, 2006), Guyer (1995, 2004) and Hart (1986, 2000, 2009).
7 This point is related to one made by Zelizer about 'pin money' (Zelizer 1997), and Hutchinson's work on the Nuer (Hutchinson 1992).
8 http://www.eeas.europa.eu/euromed/index_en.htm (accessed 23 April 2012).

Bibliography

Amado, S., Tekozel, M., Topsever, Y., Ranyard, R., Del Missier, F. and Bonini, N. (2007) 'Does "000,000" matter? Psychological effects of Turkish monetary reform', *Journal of Economic Psychology*, 28: 154–169.

Callon, M. (2007) 'What Does it Mean to Say that Economics is Performative?', in D.A. MacKenzie, F. Muniesa and L. Siu (eds) *Do Economists make Markets? On the Performativity of Economics*, Princeton: Princeton University Press, 311–357.

Clogg, R. (1992) *A Concise History of Greece*, Cambridge: Cambridge University Press.

Cohen, B.J. (2004) *The Future of Money*, Princeton, NJ; Oxford: Princeton University Press.

Del Sarto, R.A. (2010) 'Borderlands: The Middle East and North African as the EU's Southern Buffer Zone', in D. Bechev and K. Nicolaidis, (eds), *Mediterranean Frontiers: Borders, Conflict and Memory in a Transnational World*, London: Tauris Academic Studies, 149–165.

Dodd, N. (2005a) 'Laundering "Money": On the Need for Conceptual Clarity within the Sociology of Money', *Archives Europeennes De Sociologie*, 46: 387–416.

Dodd, N. (2005b) 'Reinventing Monies in Europe', *Economy and Society*, 34: 558–583.

Foucault, M. (1974) *The Order of Things. An Archaeology of the Human Sciences*, London: Tavistock.

Goodhart, C.A. (2007) 'Currency Unions: Some Lessons from the Euro-Zone', *Atlantic Economic Journal*, 35: 1–21.

Graeber, D. (2001) *Toward an Anthropological Theory of Value: The False Coin of Our Own Dreams*, New York; Basingstoke: Palgrave.

Green, S. (2010) 'Performing Border in the Aegean', *Journal of Cultural Economy*, 3: 261–278.

Green, S. (2012) 'A Sense of Border', in T.M. Wilson and H. Donnan (eds) *A Companion to Border Studies*, Oxford: Wiley-Blackwell, 573–592.

Gregory, C. A. (1997) *Savage Money: The Anthropology and Politics of Commodity Exchange*, Amsterdam; London: Harwood Academic Publishers.

Guyer, J.I. (ed.) (1995) *Money Matters: Instability, Values and Social Payments in the Modern History of West African Communities*, Portsmouth, NH; London: Heinemann; James Currey.

Guyer, J.I. (2004) *Marginal Gains: Monetary Transactions in Atlantic Africa*, Chicago; London: University of Chicago Press.

Hart, K. (1986) 'Heads or Tails: Two Sides of the Coin', *Man*, 21: 637–656.

Hart, K. (2000) *The Memory Bank: Money in an Unequal World*, London: Profile Books.

Hart, K. (2009) 'The Persuasive Power of Money', in S. Gudeman (ed.) *Economic Persuasions*, Oxford: Berghahn Books.

Herzfeld, M. (1986) *Ours Once More: Folklore, Ideology, and the Making of Modern Greece*, New York: Pella Publishing.

Herzfeld, M. (1997) *Cultural Intimacy: Social Poetics in the Nation-State*, London: Routledge.

Herzfeld, M. (2004) *The Body Impolitic: Artisans and Artifice in the Global Hierarchy of Value*, Chicago; London: University of Chicago Press.

Hirschon, R. (ed.) (2003) *Crossing the Aegean: An Appraisal of the 1923 Compulsory Population Exchange between Greece and Turkey*, New York; Oxford: Berghahn Books.

Holmes, D. (2000) 'Surrogate Discourses of Power: The European Union and Discourses of Society', in I. Bellier and T. Wilson (eds) *An Anthropology of the European Union: Building, Imagining and Experiencing the New Europe*, Oxford: Berg, 93–115.

Hutchinson, S. (1992) 'The Cattle of Money and the Cattle of Girls among the Nuer, 1930–83', *American Ethnologist*, 19: 294–316.

Ingham, G.K. (2004) *The Nature of Money*, Cambridge: Polity.

Koufopoulou, S. (2003) 'Muslim Cretans in Turkey: the Reformulation of Ethnic Identity in an Aegean Community', in R. Hirschon (ed.) *Crossing the Aegean: An Appraisal of the 1923 Compulsory Population Exchange between Greece and Turkey*, New York; Oxford: Berghahn Books, 209–319.

Liikanen, I. and Virtanen, P. (2006) 'The New Neighbourhood: A 'Constitution' for Cross-Border Cooperation?', in J.W. Scott (ed.) *EU Enlargement, Region Building and Shifting Borders of Inclusion and Exclusion*, Aldershot, Burlington, VT: Ashgate, 113–130.

MacKenzie, D.A. (2006) *An Engine, not a Camera: How Financial Models Shape Markets*, Cambridge, MA: MIT Press.

Massey, D.B. (2005) *For Space*, London: Sage.

Maurer, B. (2005) *Mutual Life, Limited: Islamic Banking, Alternative Currencies, Lateral Reason*, Princeton NJ: Princeton University Press.

Maurer, B. (2006) 'The Anthropology of Money', *Annual Review of Anthropology*, 35: 15–36.

Milton, G. (2009) *Paradise Lost: Smyrna 1922 – The Destruction of Islam's City of Tolerance*, London: Sceptre.

Öktem, K. (2011) *Turkey since 1989: Angry Nation*, London: Zed.

Özyürek, E. (2006) *Nostalgia for the Modern: State Secularism and Everyday Politics in Turkey*, Durham, NC; London: Duke University Press.

Pamuk, S. (2000) *A Monetary History of the Ottoman Empire*, Cambridge: Cambridge University Press.

Papataxiarchis, E. (1999) 'A Contest with Money: Gambling and the Politics of Disinterested Sociality in Aegean Greece', in S. Day, E. Papataxiarchis and M. Stewart (eds) *Lilies of the Field: Marginal People who Live for the Moment*, Boulder, CO: Westview Press, 158–175.

Scott, J.W. (2006) 'Wider Europe: Geopolitics of Inclusion and Exclusion at the EU's New External Boundaries', in J.W. Scott (ed.) *EU Enlargement, Region Building and Shifting Borders of Inclusion and Exclusion*, Aldershot, Burlington, VT: Ashgate, 17–34.

Shore, C. (2000) *Building Europe: The Cultural Politics of European Integration*, London, New York: Routledge.

Veremis, T. (2003) '1922: Political Continuations and Realignments in the Greek State', in R. Hirschon (ed.) *Crossing the Aegean: An Appraisal of the 1923 Compulsory Population Exchange between Greece and Turkey*, New York, Oxford: Berghahn Books, 53–62.

Zelizer, V.A. (1997) *The Social Meaning of Money: Pin Money, Paychecks, Poor Relief and Other Currencies*, Princeton, NJ: Princeton University Press.

Zelizer, V.A. (2011) *Economic Lives: How Culture Shapes the Economy*, Princeton, NJ, Woodstock: Princeton University Press.

28

Algorithms and the manufacture of financial reality

Marc Lenglet

Rise of the machines

This chapter[1] deals with the production of materiality in contemporary financial markets. It addresses one of the major changes that markets have been witnessing for more than twenty years now, namely the general movement towards automation and the related 'dematerialization' of financial instruments and stock exchanges. Early signs of such a movement took place in the mid–1980s, when electronic systems began to substantially frame financial practices, performing simple tasks and easing the dissemination of information.[2] This evolution has recently been explored, thanks to a series of works in the history of markets (Lee 1998, Michie 2006), in the sociology of market automation (Muniesa 2003 and 2007, Pardo-Guerra 2010a and 2010b) and electronic trading (Preda 2009a), and through anthropological accounts of shifting practices (Zaloom 2006) or insider narrations (Leinweber 2009). But digitizing the market infrastructure was and still is the first step towards greater automation of financial transactions. The introduction of technologies such as the telegraph (Preda 2006), the pantelegraph (Preda 2009b) and later the telephone (Muniesa 2008) heralded the quest for integrated interfaces and devices being able to receive, store, record and stabilize flows and chunks of financial information: in fact, spreadsheets, charts and market mappings are just the visible tip of the iceberg (Knorr Cetina and Bruegger 2002a and 2002b, Pryke 2010).

Since the mid–2000s, a series of modifications in the design of automated markets, both related to technological innovation and regulatory homogenization has been reconfiguring the financial landscape: those initiatives led the automation of financial practices a step further. The initial shift from open-outcry markets to electronic markets accounts for a first phase of the automation movement, leading to the fragmentation of marketplaces, the rapid disappearing of pits and floors and their replacement by networked trading rooms, that is an apparently atopic, dislocated and less monolithic ensemble best expressed by electronic connections. But this was only the first step of the automation process and its resulting consequences: we are currently witnessing a second phase of this technical revolution, in which it is not the exchange structure that gets replaced by computerized systems, but rather the practices themselves, that is, the routines activated by human beings (market operators) in order to transact. This second phase is the result of the development, deployment and dissemination of trading algorithms designed with a view to make transactions more 'perfect', and maximally cleared of human components (literally 'dismembered').

This distinction between two phases is an important one for what follows. First-generation algorithms were mostly focused on facilitating the 'price-discovery' mechanism lying at the heart of financial exchanges (Domowitz and Wang 1994, Mirowski 2002). Moving from dislocated marketplaces to market participants, algorithms now reconfigure the nature of agencies making markets, and overflow the market frames. Not only are algorithms used in order to 'find' prices and match buy-and-sell orders but now they are also able to 'decide' when and how to send orders without direct human intervention. Hence the publication by the Federal Reserve Board of Washington, in October 2009, of a report entitled 'Rise of the Machines', addressing a set of issues relating to the fast-growing use of algorithmic trading in financial markets. Providing insights into the most recent improvements in technology, the report explains that

> In algorithmic trading (AT), computers directly interface with trading platforms, placing orders without immediate human intervention. The computers observe market data and possibly other information at very high frequency, and, based on a built-in algorithm, send back trading instructions, often within milliseconds. [...] Among the most recent developments in algorithmic trading, some algorithms now automatically read and interpret economic data releases, generating trading orders before economists have begun to read the first line.
>
> *(Chaboud et al. 2009: 1)*

Therefore, the question that needs to be raised is: how can we get a grip on the manufacture of financial reality, if a portion of traders' abilities and practices has been delegated to such tools? What is at stake here is our ability to understand the kind of agency now taking place in fragmented financial markets, where we have introduced objects that add further layers of mediation between market participants. More precisely, we need to ask what 'happens' and materializes within this interface, that is, the place between the tip of a trader's fingers and the 'meeting' of two algorithms within an electronic order-book, itself contained within a market server. To answer those questions, I look into execution algorithms contributing to the crafting of financial reality, with a view to describing and qualifying them, focusing on their plasticity, the processes they take in charge and the practices they represent and carry at the very heart of exchange mechanisms.

Algorithms, mediations and boundaries

There are still very few accounts of what financial algorithms are, and what they do, from an anthropological or sociological perspective.[3] The execution algorithm that I describe hereafter, as object, still needs conceptualization. In order to initiate this work and set a scene for further discussion, we are helped by two notions that developed at the intersection of symbolic interactionism, science and technology studies and actor-network-theory: namely that of 'intermediary object' on the one hand, and that of 'boundary object' on the other. Both notions have developed in parallel, and offer interesting means towards better qualification of technical objects.

'Intermediary objects' have been defined as physical entities linking human actors, entities with different ontological status (Vinck 1999 and 2003). Those objects are either 'fixed' in space and time (like a blackboard in a classroom) or they 'circulate' between actors (like a gift or a text). It is possible to describe and understand them from a temporal perspective, for they allow, as receptacles, the development of human/non-human interactions in time, and constitute a trace for such development. Moreover, intermediary objects can be viewed as 'intermediary results', as the materialization of a 'construction resulting from negotiations between actors and with matter' (Vinck 1999: 408). They have agentic power, for they make people do things while at the same time carrying choices inherited from the past (ibid.: 409); this ability being translated through the crystallization of choices and compromises.[4]

'Boundary objects', on the other hand, have been defined in a seminal article by Star and Griesemer as those 'objects which both inhabit several intersecting social worlds [...] *and* satisfy the informational requirements of each of them' (1989: 393). Those entities, whether abstract or concrete, they write,

> are both plastic enough to adapt to local needs and the constraints of the several parties employing them, yet robust enough to maintain a common identity across sites. They are weakly structured in common use, and become strongly structured in individual-site use.
>
> *(1989: 393)*

Developing their argument, the authors distinguish four different types of boundary objects: 'repositories' (databases), 'ideal types' (representations), 'coincident boundaries' (shared referents) and 'standardized forms' (methods and indexes) (ibid.: 411). All in all, boundary objects are 'one way that the tension between divergent viewpoints may be managed' (Bowker and Star 1999: 292), for they allow interests residing at the margins of their own areas of influence to converge.

From a theoretical perspective, this chapter intends to determine whether execution algorithms used in financial markets belong to one of those two categories ('intermediary object' or 'boundary object'), or else if they require a new category. In the rest of this chapter, I use a series of stylized vignettes to follow the dissemination of algorithms through the diverse foldings and unfoldings they incur, in the course of which I provide an answer to this question.

Investigating errors, mismatches and malfunction

Algorithms develop in some 'background dimension' (Thrift 2005) like many of the mundane objects that we routinely use, sometimes causing financial operators to forget about their existence. This is more than ever the case in the realm of contemporary markets, where information flows are exchanged between participants through the mediation of walls of screens, offering an interface for market operators to channel instructions through wires towards gatherings of servers. Parts of this ecology sometimes produce a feeling of autonomy, in that its complexity somehow evades our ability to represent what it is, if not impairing our ability to conceptualize portions of the whole system: algorithms tend to be forgotten even by their direct users, and on the contrary appear when they do not work well. The deficiency of the algorithmic tool reveals its presence through its dysfunction: it is usually because of mismatches, failures and the temporal spans that they open, that we can get a grip at algorithms. In the following section, I list a few cases that routinely happen in the course of a trading day within a brokerage house.

Case 1: submitting an algorithm to the market

It is a quiet afternoon on the trading floor of a financial institution located west of Paris.[5] But on the Corporate Brokerage trading desk, Tom is grumbling against one of his not so docile algorithms: 'Look at the bastard ... it blew up again'. While I am approaching his desk and before I can even notice something on his screen, he shuts the bugged window away and resumes clicking on the part of the 'algo box' allowing him to access the different strategies that have been made available on his trading station by the information technology (IT) department. All of these strategies refer to a different algorithm, with its own specificities, requirements, and path-dependent sequences. Almost instantly, a list drops down, displaying strange names such as 'Dagger', 'Guerrilla', 'Hunt', 'Iceberg', 'Implementation Shortfall', 'Stealth', 'VWAP', etc.[6]

Tom then chooses the 'Iceberg' algorithm and accesses a second window displaying the different criteria that are being used by the software to trade. Iceberg algorithms intervene in markets by replicating a pattern best expressing the metaphor they are identified with: they slice the initial order in smaller parts, and place the first chunk as a limit order in the order book, then automatically send another chunk once the first one has been filled, and again until the initial order is completed (or, metaphorically speaking, until the full 'melting' of the iceberg). The 'Iceberg submission window' is folded in two distinct areas: the upper part relates to the 'order description', and displays lists of names of financial instruments together with their references (the ISIN codes), a place to enter the quantity, and a drop-down list referring to the side ('buy' or 'sell'). The lower part offers an interface to the 'automaton parameters': the trading destination (the marketplace), the shown quantity (because the algorithm is an Iceberg and does not display the full order at once), the price and the end time.

Tom enters the required numerical parameters, and draws my attention to the order book appearing on a second screen on his left: 'Look ... it should appear here, at the first limit of the book'. The order becomes visible for a fraction of a second on Tom's screen, is almost immediately 'filled', and is then swiftly replaced by another segment; it then stops, while the market continues to move. 'You see, it should have executed 1,000 shares and then run over a third time and so on ten times ... Instead of this it chucked away half of the order ... how can I work with this?'

Here, the algorithm appears in motion: we see how it accounts for a technical prosthesis that sometimes meets its limits while failing to work as it should, thereby ruining its 'unobtrusive quality' (Harman, 2002: 45).[7] The punctual deficiency is important: when he grumbles, Tom shows the frustration experienced because of malfunction of his tool, a tool that somehow fails to deliver the kind of smoothness, swiftness and perfection it has been designed for. Through such punctual deficiencies, algorithms reveal how important they can be and how much they account for an essential cog of the financial machine. The boundaries they so materialize exemplify the ideas put forward by financial economics, translating into the promotion of an 'impersonal efficiency' (Beunza et al. 2011) designed to bring perfection at the heart of transaction mechanisms. Creating dimensions corresponding to what financial economics says, pushing representations beyond the limits, algorithms have in some respect made markets more efficient, at least theoretically. But in this movement, they also have expelled a portion of human practice and knowledge, for human traders are incapacitated when they want to access their tool, which evolves in categorical dimensions closed to human beings: infra-times (microseconds) and infra-spaces (servers, cables).

Case 2: monitoring failures leading to 'fails'

The interaction described in case 1 is simple and straightforward. And yet it may cause cascading consequences resulting in multiple market microfailures: algorithms create and span boundaries while at the same time interfacing dismembered practices. A bugged algorithm can make a simple trade go wild, incurring a risk position at the end of the day for the client, maybe resulting in its inability to deliver securities to a counterpart. And some markets, like the Austrian Wiener Börse, have stringent buy-in procedures (redemptions) and also heavily fine market participants that fail to deliver financial instruments in time. For this very reason, financial intermediaries may decide to prevent failing clients from trading until they manage to solve their 'settlement and delivery' issues.[8]

The following conversation translates such a situation; it takes place between a sales trader sitting in London and a middle-office desk located in Madrid. The Sales Trader [ST] receives a message from the Middle-Office [MO], listing clients who failed to deliver, and he reacts as follows:

> [ST]: The fail on BBVA for [Name of client] was our fault. Blocking them compounds the issue. Can we not block them ... I'll give you details of the issue that we had with our algos?
>
> ...
>
> [MO]: My back-office told me that the client at 3 pm did not have the stocks to deliver. Could they / you provide us with an explanation of the fail?
>
> ...
>
> [ST]: Yes, there was an issue with our algo which resulted in the client trading too many shares by about 33,000 shares. We spent some time trying to work out whose fault it was and then only confirmed the right amount of shares too late for them to deliver on time. The correct amount is 100,478 as you have stated. If they are late tomorrow then block them. Today my opinion is that it's a little harsh.

In this second routine case, it is the algorithm that is responsible for the failure of the client: binding operators located in different countries together with the systems they use to record the transactions, but also the regulations applicable in both countries. Furthermore, the use of algorithms also entails some controls involving other functions such as the permanent control, the compliance or the IT department. All of which might have not had a chance to work together on this specific issue, without the bug occurring in London: the algorithm qualifies as a reference indicating other references, a process itself embedded in a wider space made of social relations (should a client fail too often, then the broker and maybe even the market could decide that the client should be definitively banned).

Case 3: containing the algorithm (1)

Algorithms cannot, then, be let alone. Constant efforts to contain them are made within market institutions and market participants. Informational barriers taking the form of filters need to be put in place to frame the flow of orders initiated by algorithms. But those barriers, which automatically check that the trader or the client does not overflow its limits, add a further obstacle slowing down the speed of instructions and the transmission of information, through a new mediation that is often criticized by algorithmic traders, thereby resulting in them asking that such IT 'levees' be raised. This may cause other problems, because traders are usually not keen on turning down those barriers again afterwards, as is shown in the following discussion between the Head of Trading [HT] and his Compliance Officer [CO]:

> [HT]: With regard to the Target Close algo behaviour, which will slice the order in parts small enough to reduce market impact at the fixing, and possibly begin to work the order rather early to smooth the impact, what would you think about turning up the verifications on capital linked to the order submission?
>
> ...

[CO]: I agree … but we need to make a disclosure to those markets who require a prior statement (Frankfurt, Dublin and Vienna).

Here, the CO acknowledges that the nature of the algorithm (designed to trade small volumes) does not require a specific frame, and that any fuzzy trade resulting from a potential bug would be stopped by meta-filters (either on the broker's or the market's side). What we can infer from the previous conversation is that algorithms need to be accounted for, that is: identified, explained and disclosed to relevant market authorities. And some markets (like the Swiss Exchange) perform audits of market participants to make sure that they effectively disclose the use of algorithms, whereas others (like the London Stock Exchange [LSE]) do not focus on this disclosure and rather tend to consider that participants are responsible for what their systems send to the LSE trading platform.

We can therefore infer from these remarks that algorithms bind and are bound by infrastructures and their normative architectures. Algorithms can be controversial, because multiple participants refer to them, while at the same time they remain black boxes that seem difficult to access. They are the object of attention of traders, sales, IT quants, regulators and other surveillance functions spanning the complex systems that are called financial markets: being mediators and vectors of multiple intentions, they contribute to the binding of worlds.

Case 4: containing the algorithm (2)

When algorithms 'misbehave', then market surveillance asks for explanations: what went wrong? And how is the market participant intending to address the issue? What kinds of guarantees can the market obtain that algorithmic misbehaviour will stop?[9] Explanations about the reasons why something went wrong need to be provided swiftly and persons in charge (usually compliance officers) are always keen on being reasonably transparent with their surveillance counterparts. The following paragraph, drawn from a message sent to the Irish Stock Exchange, shows the kind of details that are required: in this case, an algorithm fired a series of orders for one share, with the trader in charge failing to notice the erroneous behaviour.

[CO]: After investigating the case, I can confirm the trade was made by one of our DMA clients. To monitor such orders, we have put filters in place that are designed to prevent price manipulations and errors (e.g. 'fat fingers'). The filters check that (a) prices are not abnormal with regard to the last price quoted on exchange, and (b) that volumes remain strictly beyond the risk threshold related to the client profile. Furthermore, the trading specifications of the ISE state that 'the minimum order size for all securities traded on ISE Xetra is a round lot of one share' (Release 8.1, 01/11/2007, p.8). Therefore, the very small orders entered by the client have not been stopped. Further to your call, we immediately reverted to the client, who was not able to stop his algorithm: we then decided to reject the client's remaining orders.

The DMA client (that is, a client who uses the broker as a direct entry-point into the market, but sending the orders himself) was not able to stop his machine, which resulted in the algorithm sending loads of ridiculously small orders to the market, not only impairing the 'price-discovery' mechanism but also making its trading counterparts pay excessive settlement and delivery fees (for orders sent and executed need to be settled and delivered). Then comes the answer by the market surveillance desk:

While we accept that you do not have controls built into your system to block orders for one share as they are within the trading specifications of ISE Xetra, we would still expect that orders entered through your DMA are monitored on an on-going basis by one of your traders as was agreed when your firm became member of the Exchange so that trading issues like this do not occur. Can you please advise whether the orders and trades dealt through your DMA were being monitored by someone when the issue arose? Also, please confirm that you can ensure that in the future there will always be a trader responsible for monitoring the DMA so that should a similar incident occur, it will be detected and resolved immediately.

Case 5: ascribing responsibility

Whereas some romantic views would probably take it for granted that algorithms have a life of their own (an idea that is sometimes used by traders to detach their acts from their mediators), one must on the contrary emphasize the fact that 'behind every algorithm lies a human' (Beunza 2012). Or at least, there should be, for when it is not the case, then errors do occur. Markets usually ask that algorithms be ascribed to a dedicated person, that is, not only a function or an institution, but a human being: depending on the specificities, it can be the Head of Trading or an individual trader ID. But such an identification of responsible persons can sometimes prove difficult, for algorithms can be stocked together at different points of the trading chain: either on the trader's computer, or in a shared basket that every trader can access through a dedicated interface. Articulating around the positioning of the algorithm, a dance may take place between the traders, the IT personnel and the compliance officers, for the compliance tries to get a precise view of who does what, and teams sometimes change rapidly, as do algorithms (which in some cases might not 'live' more than a few weeks).

Getting a view into the internal organization of an IT system is always tricky, especially when it involves several departments, specialized in connectivity issues, software development or systems migrations. Trying to delineate a clear path through shared representations and a common vocabulary is not an easy task, not to speak of the status of such an attempt, sometimes referred to as 'boring paperwork' by traders and IT personnel alike. But the paperwork serves as a tracking device articulating around the algorithm, thereby interfacing functions through mail threads, documents and informal discussions. Here, we get a grip on the controversial nature of algorithms, for they are vectors of multiple perspectives that underlie intentions, and are able to materialize those intentions in the 'substance' of the market. As such, algorithms express a form of market politics, through the representation of financial space (i.e., they run within this space and turn around it, delineating paths for transactions to happen), while accounting for the underlying intentions of different participants, thereby contributing to the crafting of financial reality.

Algorithmic handcrafting: discussing the manufacture of financial reality

Built as a result of conversations defining needs between users (clients and traders) and designers (engineers, markets and regulators), algorithms differentiate themselves from other processing devices in use in trading rooms (screens, keyboards or phones) in that they aggregate, concentrate and synthetize a multiplicity of elements replicating human practice. They do so not only as path-dependent descriptions of gestures leading from the acceptance of an instruction to its execution within the market, but also as expressions of a series of co-constructed processes that cannot be reduced to a static expression of facticity: enacting successive states of 'the market', execution algorithms are the new handcrafters of financial reality. As such, they configure and reconfigure essential categories such as time (acting within milliseconds) and space (creating their own 'state' between IT servers), and question our ability to get a grip on them, and to form a representation of the reality they produce.

But how do they qualify? Should they be understood as 'intermediary objects', or 'boundary objects'? Our small vignettes provide some indications here: algorithms are physical entities in their own right (case 1), allowing for the mediation of practices, while being located between market participants (case 3). They circulate between actors, but in order to act, they need to be fixed in a dedicated place (case 1). Also, they allow the deployment of human/non-human interactions in time, and make people do things (case 4). As such, algorithms may well fit with the description of 'intermediary objects' as proposed by Vinck (2009 and 2011): incorporating an invisible infrastructure, they carry practices from one community to another.[10] But yet they somehow exceed the limits of such definition: if we dig a bit further, we can also say that algorithms qualify as places where extensive financial practices are encapsulated (case 1): as coding, they amount to a specific kind of text describing and following the market's materiality (case 2). In so doing, they contribute to the very definition of financial space, making this arena different each time they are activated or deactivated (case 4). Moreover, they offer a space for the deployment of responsibilities, thereby taking part in the embodiment of accountability, while at the same time impairing the clear ascription of responsibility between market actors (case 5).

In this respect, algorithms seem to share some traits with 'boundary objects', for they literally materialize the intersection of different social worlds while satisfying the informational requirements of each of them (Star and Griesemer 1989). Being 'repositories' for financial action, they are also 'ideal types' (best expressing the idea of efficient markets), 'coincident' (as a shared referent) and 'standardized' (for they are sometimes sold as pre-packaged software suites), thereby encompassing the four types of boundary objects initially identified by the authors (ibid.: 411). Depending on the market context, however, they can constitute a controversial device, creating (and not diminishing) tensions between divergent viewpoints (case 4), which means algorithms show some 'interpretive flexibility' in contributing to 'the stuff of action' (Star, 2010: 602 and 603). But can we say that algorithms are 'a sort of arrangement that allows different groups to work together without consensus'? Probably not, unless we define what a *consensus* is in the specific case of algorithmic trading, and this exceeds the limits of the current chapter.

If they materialize some boundaries, algorithms also constitute, in themselves, some kind of a *limit* when it comes to the definition of practices. Because they take on so much of the practice they replicate, they oppose a limit to human beings: when we want access to what they precisely make in markets, we face a black box that we usually fail to understand thoroughly and open completely. To put it another way, algorithms can be described as technical membranes for the replication, dissemination and deployment of financial practices; but these membranes also represent, in the very movement of their deployment, the end point of our ability to access what they really produce, as a mechanism (cases 2, 3, 5). Accounting for an ontological shift in the making of markets, we can understand that algorithms add a mediation between people, that is both thick and difficult to access (case 1), while at the same time remaining unnoticed. Somehow, algorithms assume an ambivalent position: they seem to share traits that can be found in both 'intermediary' and 'boundary' objects while at the same time carrying much more. Being processes that interface market participants, they account for the backbone of financial transactions, as the material pivot of an ideology in place since the mid-1970s, for they intervene in a space framed with the ideology of 'impersonal efficiency' (Beunza *et al.* 2011). As artefacts expressing the spirit of efficient markets (places with less friction), they contribute to the 'invisible' market infrastructure through the standards and conventions they carry with them; and at the same time, they allow for the material aggregation of different worlds. Algorithms are a powerful expression of what financial markets have become: as calculating devices, they build agencies between market participants, while making the marketplaces 'hold'.

For all of these reasons, algorithms are the temporary but paradigmatic expression of the current manufacture of financial reality. Working towards the deployment of markets through new handcrafting techniques, the development of algorithms definitely signs an ontological shift in the machinery of finance.

Notes

1 This chapter extends arguments that I have published elsewhere (Lenglet 2011) and focuses on the 'interface' nature of algorithms used in contemporary financial markets.
2 A year after the 1987 market crash, a symposium was held at the joint initiative of the Center for Research on Information Systems and the Salomon Brothers Center for the Study of Financial Institutions in New York. In the proceedings later published, one reads: 'An important aspect of market design is the information technology used to disseminate floor information (transaction process, quotes, and trading volumes), to support decision making, to handle orders, and to translate orders into trades' (Lucas and Schwartz 1989: 3).
3 There are a few notable exceptions, like for instance MacKenzie (2011) and MacKenzie et al. (2012). For a summary of current issues raised by algorithms, see IOSCO (2011).
4 In this respect, 'intermediary objects', though not initially conceptualized as such, seem very close to Latourian mediators (Latour 1999, Chapter 6 and 2005).
5 Materials used here were gathered during a long-lasting participant-observation at a pan-European brokerage house based in Paris (October 2006–September 2009). Names have been changed for the sake of anonymity.
6 Every denomination refers to a dedicated strategy, so designated by a metaphorically significant name. VWAP is the only exception here, an acronym standing for 'Volume Weighted Average Price'.
7 The classical Heideggerian analysis of the 'broken tool' is the main underlying reference here, with the revelation of its un-usefulness ('*Unzuhandenheit*'), through the deployment of three different modalities: '*Auffälligkeit*', '*Aufdringlichkeit*' and '*Aufsässigkeit*'. See Heidegger (1993). It is through these three modalities that the tool is both indicated and lost, somehow revealing itself through its own lack.
8 'Settlement' and 'delivery' are technical terms referring to the process taking place once an agreement has been made between them (a certain price 'discovered' for a certain volume of financial instruments in the market, for instance). This process best expresses the legal obligation binding both parties as a consequence of the exchange materialized through the mediation of the order book. For more details, see Muniesa et al. (2011) and Norman (2007).
9 For a detailed example, see Lenglet (2011: 58–61).
10 Bowker and Star do not make any reference to Heidegger's views on the distinction between 'things' and 'objects' detailed in a 1949 conference held in Bremen, where Heidegger made a strong case to differentiate between things (*Dingen*) (elements allowing for the gathering or the holding of the world) and objects (*Objekten*) as understood from a metaphysical perspective (i.e., as opposed to a 'subject'). See Heidegger (1994).

Bibliography

Beunza, D. (2012) 'Behind every HFT algorithm there is a person, but it's more fun to think they have their own soul', Socializing finance: a blog on the social studies of finance. Available <http://socfinance. wordpress.com> (accessed 10 March 2012).

Beunza, D., MacKenzie, D., Millo, Y. and Pardo-Guerra, J.P. (2011) 'Impersonal efficiency and the dangers of a fully automated securities exchange'. Working paper DR11, Foresight Project on the Future of Computer Trading in Financial Markets, Foresight Driver Review, London, June.

Bowker, G.C. and Star, S.L. (1999) *Sorting Things Out: Classification and its Consequences*, Cambridge, MA: MIT Press.

Chaboud, A., Chiquoine, B., Hjalmarsson, E. and Vega, C. (2009) 'Rise of the machines: algorithmic trading in the foreign exchange market', International Finance Discussion Papers No. 980, Washington, Board of Governors of the Federal Reserve System, October.

Domowitz, I. and Wang, J. (1994) 'Auctions as algorithms: computerized trade execution and price discovery', Journal of Economic Dynamics and Control, 18(1): 29–60.

Harman, G. (2002) Tool-Being: Heidegger and the Metaphysics of Objects, Chicago, IL: Open Court.

Heidegger, M. (1993) [1927] Sein und Zeit, Tübingen: Max Niemeyer Verlag.

Heidegger, M. (1994) [1949] 'Einblick in das was ist', in Bremer und Freiburger Vorträge, Gesamtausgabe 79, Frankfurt am Main: Klostermann.

IOSCO (2011) Regulatory Issues Raised by the Impact of Technological Changes on Market Integrity and Efficiency, Consultation report CR02/11, Madrid, International Organization of Securities Commissions, July.

Knorr Cetina, K. and Bruegger, U. (2002a) 'Inhabiting technology: the global lifeform of financial markets', Current Sociology, 50(3): 389–405.

Knorr Cetina, K. and Bruegger, U. (2002b) 'Traders' engagement with markets: a postsocial relationship', Theory, Culture and Society, 19(5/6): 161–185.

Latour, B. (1999) Pandora's Hope: Essays on the Reality of Science Studies, Cambridge, MA: Harvard University Press.

Latour, B. (2005) Re-assembling the Social: An Introduction to Actor-Network Theory, Oxford: Oxford University Press.

Lee, R. (1998) What Is an Exchange? The Automation, Management, and Regulation of Financial Markets, Oxford: Oxford University Press.

Leinweber, D. (2009) Nerds on Wall Street: Math, Machines and Wired Markets, Hoboken, NJ: John Wiley and Sons.

Lenglet, M. (2011) 'Conflicting codes and codings: how algorithmic trading is reshaping financial regulation', Theory, Culture and Society, 28(6): 44–66.

Lucas, H.C. and Schwartz, R.A. (1989) 'Introduction', in Lucas, H.C. and Schwartz, R.A. (eds) The Challenge of Information Technology for the Securities Markets: Liquidity, Volatility, and Global Trading, Homewood, IL: Dow Jones-Irwin.

MacKenzie, D. (2011) 'How to make money in microseconds', London Review of Books, 33(10): 16–18.

MacKenzie, D., Beunza, D., Millo, Y. and Pardo-Guerra, J.P. (2012) 'Drilling through the Allegheny Mountains. Liquidity, materiality and high-frequency trading', Journal of Cultural Economy, 5(3): 279–296.

Michie, R.C. (2006) The Global Securities Market: A History, Oxford: Oxford University Press.

Mirowski, P. (2002) Machine Dreams: Economics Becomes a Cyborg Science, Cambridge: Cambridge University Press.

Muniesa, F. (2003) 'Des marchés comme algorithmes: sociologie de la cotation électronique à la Bourse de Paris', unpublished PhD thesis, Centre de Sociologie de l'Innovation, Ecole Nationale Supérieure des Mines de Paris.

Muniesa, F. (2007) 'Market technologies and the pragmatics of prices', Economy and Society, 36(3): 377–395.

Muniesa, F. (2008) 'Trading room telephones and the identification of counterparts', in Pinch, T. and Swedberg, R. (eds) Living In a Material World. Economic Sociology Meets Science and Technology Studies, Cambridge, MA: MIT Press.

Muniesa, F., Chabert, D., Ducrocq-Grondiny, M. and Scott, S.V. (2011) 'Back office intricacy: the description of financial objects in an investment bank', Industrial and Corporate Change, 20(4): 1189–1213.

Norman, P. (2007) Plumbers and Visionaries. Securities Settlement and Europe's Financial Market, Chichester: John Wiley and Sons.

Pardo-Guerra, J.P. (2010a) 'Computerizing gentlemen: the automation of the London Stock Exchange, c. 1945–1995', unpublished PhD thesis, University of Edinburgh.

Pardo-Guerra, J.P. (2010b) 'Creating flows of interpersonal bits: the automation of the London Stock Exchange, c. 1955–90', Economy and Society, 39(1): 84–109.

Preda, A. (2006) 'Socio-technical agency in financial markets: the case of the stock ticker', Social Studies of Science, 36(5): 753–782.

Preda, A. (2009a) 'Brief encounters: calculation and the interaction order of anonymous electronic markets', Accounting, Organizations and Society, 34(5): 675–693.

Preda, A. (2009b) Framing Finance. The Boundaries of Markets and Modern Capitalism, Chicago, IL: University of Chicago Press.

Pryke, M. (2010) 'Money's eyes: the visual preparation of financial markets', *Economy and Society*, 39(4): 427–459.

Star, S.L. (2010) 'This is not a boundary object: reflections on the origin of a concept', *Science, Technology, and Human Values*, 35(5): 601–617.

Star, S.L. and Griesemer, J.R. (1989) 'Institutional ecology, "translations" and boundary objects: amateurs and professionals in Berkeley's Museum of Vertebrate Zoology, 1907–39', *Social Studies of Science*, 19(3): 387–420.

Thrift, N. (2005) 'Beyond mediation: three new material registers and their consequences', in Miller, D. (ed.) *Materiality*, Durham: Duke University Press.

Vinck, D. (1999) 'Les objets intermédiaires dans les réseaux de coopération scientifique. Contribution à la prise en compte des objets dans les dynamiques sociales', *Revue Française de Sociologie*, 40(2): 385–414.

Vinck, D. (ed) (2003) *Everyday Engineering. An Ethnography of Design and Innovation*, Cambridge, MA: MIT Press.

Vinck, D. (2009) 'De l'objet intermédiaire à l'objet-frontière. Vers la prise en compte du travail d'équipement', *Revue d'anthropologie des connaissances*, 3(1): 51–72.

Vinck, D. (2011) 'Taking intermediary objects and equipping work into account in the study of engineering practices', *Engineering Studies*, 3(1): 25–44.

Zaloom, C. (2006) *Out of the Pits: Trading and Technology from Chicago to London*, Chicago, IL: Chicago University Press.

Part V

Becoming object
Introduction

Chris McLean and Gillian Evans

Our final part, *Becoming object*, explores a set of empirical cases consisting of objects and materials that are neither definitively enduring or stable, nor necessarily open to change and transformation. Our section title *Becoming object* is intended to evoke both the once stable object that is becoming otherwise, and the unstable relational entity that is becoming still or objectified. The focus is thus on this two-way process of becoming, in which heterogeneity, movement and change are aspects (rather than opposites) of homogeneity, stability and endurance. However, the specific ways in which the coexistence of change and continuity is analysed and understood varies, both with respect to the empirical cases discussed and the theoretical approaches that are brought to bear on the analysis. Thus the reader finds a focus on the relationship between time, space and action inflected in particular ways in different chapters, as are the approaches to the differentiations between entities. Thus a difference between humans and non-humans might be taken as the outcome of social processes, or as a starting point from which to examine the specific configurations of human worlds.

In their introduction to the edited collection, *Deleuzian Intersections: Science, Technology, Anthropology*, Jensen and Rödje refer to Deleuze's interest in the constant reconfiguration of realities. They argue: 'the basic elements in Deleuzian thought are not static but entities in becoming. Consequently, the question to be asked is not what something is, but rather what it is turning into, or might be capable of turning into' (Jensen and Rödje, 2010). This question of what something might be turning into highlights the processual character of things, rather than simply pointing to a linear narrative of transformation. In Deleuzian thinking the image of such movement is more akin to a pulse or a vibration, whereby specific happenings or materializations (the actual) and the virtual realm of possibilities or potentialities coexist in ongoing dynamics of emergence and erasure. Thus, although many of the objects and materials discussed in this volume may be considered multiple, ontologically unstable and in some cases quite literally on the move, this section seeks to focus more specifically on the coexistence of heterogeneity and singularity, stability and change, openings and containment. In this way we find that specific practices (such as the enactment of routines, standards, protocols, laws and plans) are not taken as definitive, but are rather apprehended as repeated acts of material and conceptual differentiation: between things and persons, humans and non-humans, heterogeneous relations and standardized metrics.

Indeed, the double meaning of the becoming object (an arrested movement, or a forward impulse) suggests a rhythmic sense of temporality; an orientation to the future and enfolding resonances from the past. The arguments and positions in each chapter address specific situations, or relational sites of action in which we find people and things in a process of becoming, taking form and transforming, through specific events, practices and processes of mutual engagement.

In the first chapter by Law and Lien, we can begin to see how this idea of 'continuity as an empirical achievement' plays out within their study of salmon farming as they explore how humans and human-reared salmon emerge as distinctive entities in and through the relations that constitute a salmon farm. Here, what it is to be human and what it is to be salmon are worked out, and performed in practice. Indeed, their research reveals how humans are constantly wrestling with the 'slippery' and transforming qualities of what it is to be salmon in relation to human beings-as-salmon farmers. Human-grown-salmon are thus not simply an effect of the sociotechnical relations that produce them. Humans become who and what they are in relation to the material and technical specificity of the practices in which they engage. In this sense, a salmon farmer is not a lion tamer, a sheepherd or a deep-sea fisherman. Law and Lien insist that human experience is the actualization of the particular qualities of the non-human entities and ordered technical arrangements that constitute the specific relations we know as 'salmon farming'. Their case study also draws our attention to a more general point about the fragile and highly particular configurations of human/non-human relations, even in a field such as theirs where we might assume, at first glance, that human beings are simply producing farmed salmon. By emphasizing the uncertainties of salmon farming, Law and Lien force us to reflect on the temporal dynamics of productive practices more generally. They propose we think in terms of architextures, the emerging relationships between the material qualities of technologies and the entities and relations that emerge as they are woven together to become the basis for the choreography of life.

Becoming in relation to animals, people and things is also explored by the social anthropologist, Candea. His study of the science of meerkat behaviour, at an observational field-site in South Africa, examines the role of technical devices in the production of what counts as 'behaviour'. Whereas Law and Lien allude to questions of 'control' concerning the relations between humans, animals and objects, Candea takes this further by considering how humans may be seen in some cases to be 'tamed' by the technologies they use. In this case, he looks specifically at how the hand-held Psion mediates the ways in which 'meerkat', 'scientist' and 'behaviour' become identifiable as distinctive and specific entities. The Psion device mediates the relationship between scientist and meerkat, requiring the scientist to work through the keyboard, the computer code and the coding sheets. The observations registered in this way are limited by the coding system, and 'meerkat behaviour' emerges as an abstract and standardized entity that not only produces meerkats as data, but also produces the observers as 'scientists' trained and oriented in how to see and record. Behaviour as an abstract, standardized entity is then, as much a 'generative fact-fiction' as the meerkats and the scientists themselves. Behavioural data also register a transformation from the qualitative to the quantitative as the flow of the meerkat's life-world is translated into numerical and digital form. This also raises questions of how other relations, including the highly affective interspecies relations between meerkats and scientists-as-lovers-of-meerkats/scientists-as-observers-of-meerkats, disappear from descriptive accounts. In Latour's terms (1993) this making of 'facts' (or factishes) concerning meerkat behaviour could be described as a process of purification and abstraction. However, Candea argues that although scientists could be described as engaging in a creative system of information production, their creativity also relies on a process of erasure that obfuscates the potential of all that is not allowed to count as knowledge.

Michael and Rosengarten are also concerned with issues of agency and control, and with processes of measurement and standardization. In particular, they explore how the multiplicity and complexity of qualitative practices and experiences become stabilized and delimited as standardized, medical objects. In the context of the human immunodeficiency virus (HIV) epidemic, their case study examines the trial of a supposedly preventative, preexposure prophylactic pill called PrEP. As in the work of Law and Lien, situatedness is seen to be key to understanding how people and things 'become together' through heterogonous relations. Thus, for example, they describe how the bioethical standards that are applied to the trialling of the pill fail to take account of the situationally specific attributes of the 'communities' that the pill gathers around itself as well as ignoring the specificity of the places where the trials take place (in terms of political economy, cultural logics and existing material practices such as associated forms of contraception). Situational specificity is ignored in favour of the generalized practices of bioethical standardization and, as a consequence, the problem of HIV prevention is not articulated in relation to other possible, and already existing solutions. In some cases, the trials even jeopardized the health and well-being of the people whom they were apparently seeking to help, because no attention was given to the effects of PrEP in relation to other forms of contraception. For Michael and Rosengarten, closer attention needs to be paid to the articulation of a 'relational good' in addition to how things 'become' in relation to each other. Furthermore, user communities need to be included in the formulation of both the problems and the potential solutions with respect to new technologies. They describe that although alternative approaches to 'posing the problem clearly' were more typical in the early response to HIV infection in the USA, thereafter the capacity for 'good problem articulation' has declined. Finally, by contrasting the desire for a non-relational and context-free medical object (a generalized version of abstraction and standardization locked into a historical and spatial amnesia) with an alternative process of 'becoming', the authors describe how different ethical and political concerns can be considered in relation to the specific materials and practices that comprise these complex assemblages.

McLean's chapter also shares an interest in material practices of recording, documentation, standardization and the situatedness of becoming. Her study of the shift towards 'community' mental health care in the UK shows how new forms of becoming emerge through different form-filling practices associated with the needs assessment process. Here we see the role of metrics, standards and information practices within complex relational settings. This includes exploring how particular medical events and interventions emerge in relation to this new administrative process and the role of specific practices in this process of forming and informing. The study examines diverse settings in which the needs assessment form and the ratings it produces involve protracted negotiations between mental health workers and patient/clients in relation to a standardized set of criteria about what can count as a need and the expression of need as a numerical term. On the one hand, McLean traces how the abstraction of the quantitative ranking of needs can be seen as working to obscure and sanitize what it is for a health worker to 'know' about his or her clients' needs as an expression of a long-standing, complex and affectively intense relationship between health worker and patient; and on the other, as a tool which is seen to help in allocating clinical staff to different levels of care. Inspired by a Deleuzian notion of the crystal image, McLean analyses the movement or the becoming together with the multiple potentials and possibilities of qualitative and quantitative apprehensions of need and the management of mental health care.

The chapter by Alexandra Hall and Jonathan Mendel explores the effects of another controversial digital object: a terrorist detection system. Risk scoring and rule-based assessments produce specific populations of risk, and related practices of border and security control. Their case study describes the relationship between digital footprints and the categorization of travellers who, at the point of potential boundary crossing, become classified as a risk to national security. Digital footprints (also known as slug trails) involve a process of tracing an individual's digital interactions. The trails left by such interactions appear as silent witnesses, connecting multiple previous trace-making activities (e.g., the use of specific routes, last-minute third-party ticket purchasing, short and frequent trips to specific locations, suspicious lack of luggage, etc.). These traces index a series of mundane actions and communications in new spaces of threat and intervention. Although these informational traces and associated modes of categorization can appear to provide objective and neutral data, they are the outcome of highly specific and continuous processes of abstraction and standardization. For instance, by assembling traces of behaviour and consumption habits, they classify and categorize people on the basis of some anticipated and predicted future behaviour. Most interesting about this chapter is the way that the digital footprint is being used in an oracular fashion, to anticipate and to categorize persons on the basis of their predicted future behaviour. In this sense, the digital footprint is perhaps the most controversial kind of becoming-object, an actor that could be seen as literally bringing the future into being, but that leaves little space for further reflection on the ethical implications of the effects of securitization processes in the present.

Also thinking about the implications of the move towards the production of abstract objects is Biagioli, whose chapter focuses on recent controversies surrounding patent applications. Through an innovative and historical journey that delves into various developments and transformations in patent law, Biagioli describes the role of specific practices, disputes and the intersections of different agencies in rethinking and redefining the emergence of categories such as materiality, objectivity and specificity. For instance, he outlines how the concept of materiality has called into question existing understandings of material features and effects, and set up a new distinction between natural discoveries and those deemed to be inventions (e.g. an artefact of human ingenuity and an 'inventive step'). Through a series of examples, the chapter describes how the boundaries between material and immaterial, tangible and intangible, and the general and specific have been redefined not only in terms of patent law, but also in the development of technologies and artefacts more generally. For example, he explains how in the case of information-based inventions the opposite of 'abstract' is no longer 'material' but 'specific'. Furthermore, in addition to raising questions concerning the role of patent law in redefining materiality, he also draws out connections to the development of future technologies, artefacts and innovations. In this way, Biagioli outlines how existing categories (such as materiality, specificity and novelty) and associated categorical distinctions (the definable attributes of things or defining aspects of human inventiveness) are continually in a state of becoming, and not as stable as they may first appear.

The final two chapters in this section, by Oppenheim and Evans, both ask, in different ways, about how things configure and reconfigure places. Evans focuses on the unique capacities of urban planning documents to act as technologies of persuasion and, to become, therefore, relational matrices for bringing about the necessary transformation of scale that proposals for projects (in this case, plans for the legacy of the Olympic Park in London) require if they are to gather the necessary momentum to move from fragile paper plan, to more durable contract and finally, realized outcomes in terms of built environment effects. Oppenheim focuses on the Korean city of Kyŏngju and combines an approach to place via phenomenological anthropology with the spatial theorization of post-ANT approaches. He is concerned to understand places in terms of 'lash-ups' or modes of connection/articulation among unlike elements that lead to the configuration of place as a mediator among heterogeneous things. Both chapters address issues, also raised by Law and Lien, about situation as a necessarily spatiotemporal phenomenon. It is action and the doing of things that bring together, gather, orientate and sustain the elements that at once create a relational set, a spatial order and a temporal framework as a force or movement towards future potential. The chapters by Evans and Oppenheim are both concerned with controversies generated by the reordering of urban space and they therefore incorporate into their analyses of the crafting of new urban realities, the oppositional politics of contestation. Those who would either prefer that the order of things were not changed or not changed in such a way that important presences are absented by the heavy-handed top-down character of state interventions in cities are given voice here and remind us that at the boundaries of situations that bring new realities into being are the hoards of actors (human and non-human) who arc displaced by processes of change.

In conclusion, although there are many possibilities and paths that this introduction could have taken with regards to becoming, we have focused on specific aspects that both link and set these chapters apart. Connections are apparent in the ways in which the chapters focus on the situated, material practices and heterogeneous relations of becoming. Moreover, in reconsidering ideas of movement and change, each of the studies within this section questions ideas of being, identity and stability. We can also see how potentialities and possibilities are explored within the chapters and how some studies have focused on specific practices of standardization, documentation and knowledge production (e.g., the making of facts and truths and what 'counts' as knowledge), as well as the different ethical and political implications underlying these processes of becoming. These questions could also be played back through other sections of this companion volume. Indeed, in general terms, it could be asked of any human collective: what are your becoming objects? What are the objects through which you are becoming human in your own collectively distinctive way? Equally, the question could be asked in different terms: how are human and non-human entities distinguished? How are the unstable boundaries between living and non-living beings defined and maintained?

Common to both sets of questions is a preoccupation not just with relational processes in the present or with the significance and the potential of past action and future configurations. For some the emphasis is placed on the ways in which past action is sedimented and stabilized through repeated practice over time. Others focus on the unexpected sensations that summon or actualize a specific sense of the past that emerges suddenly and without warning to destabilize the habitual and open new possibilities, whereas others focus on how the past and future coalesce through specific events of becoming in order to capture the oscillating coexistence of stability and change. In each case, becoming something or someone distinctive entails a temporal folding that disrupts any simple notion of linear progression from past to future. From an analytical perspective, such becoming points us towards how the enduring process of becoming object involves not only a fragile instability, but also a great deal of work and multiple acts of engagement.

Bibliography

Jensen, C.B. and Rödje, K. (2010) *Deleuzian Intersections: Science, Technology, Anthropology*, Oxford: Berghahn Books.
Latour, B. (1993) *We Have Never Been Modern*, New York: Harvester-Wheatsheaf.

29

Animal architextures[1]

John Law and Marianne Elisabeth Lien

Introduction

Surely animals are neither objects nor people?

Perhaps they are not endowed with reason, but they respond to their surroundings; they can feel pain; perhaps they have emotions; and sometimes they have cultures too. True, animals are often treated as if they were 'objects', especially if they are made useful for humans. Hence, theories of domestication tend to define animals through idioms of purposeful human mastery, and emphasize control as a characteristic feature of human–animal relations.[2] But the stories about the uses of animals that emphasize control have been paralleled by stories about care that recognize the sentience of animals. Indeed, biology runs the two together too, in one version telling us that happy farmed animals are productive animals and vice versa.[3] And then there are lay concerns with animal welfare, and the recent remarkable growth in animal studies, post-human and otherwise.[4] Animals have become actors with rights or propensities, and have become significant topics for social research. At the same time and as a part of this, human exceptionalism has been eroded: human beings are no longer unique.

In these stories people and animals go together. As many have noted, to learn about animals (for instance about dogs or farm animals) is also to learn about people. In this short chapter, we address human–animal relations by taking a less obvious case, that of salmon farming. Using resources from anthropology and STS (science, technology, and society), we explore how human beings and animals emerge in specific relations embedded in material practices. Our focus is on what a person or a salmon *is made to be*, relationally, in particular circumstances. Our counter-intuitive guiding assumption is that the character of objects (and animals) has no shape or form outside practices and their relations. In short, it is that practices are *performative*.[5] Second, and following from this, we explore how different practices generate different versions of what it is to be an animal or a person. Then, third, we consider what is animal about the 'animal object' in human–animal relations. In particular, we touch on the qualities or *textures* of those relations, and their choreography as they extend through and order relations in time and space, in what we refer to as *architextures*. Finally, we briefly note that agency is a relational matter, and that, notwithstanding the self-evidently restrictive and industrial character of agriculture, animals shape people just as much as people shape animals.

So what can salmon tell us about animals, or human–animal relations? Some differences are obvious. Unlike four-legged, furry mammals, farmed salmon occupy fluid spaces. The surface of the water marks a boundary between our habitat and theirs. They are mostly out of sight, their body language is difficult to 'read'. Some would even argue that they do not count as animals at all, because they are fish, and fish are not animals. Or perhaps they are, for cultural categories are dynamic. Recent animal welfare legislation in the European Union includes farmed fish, and recognizes their ability to feel pain.

Exploring animals from the vantage point of farmed salmon, we draw attention to the margins, to relations that are currently in the making. We enter a field in which few things are 'given', where practices are invented every day, and where new ways of being animal (and being human) are constantly performed. The textures of material practices that we describe here are indeed 'salmon-specific': animals are known only through situated practices. Hence, it is through their different textures and architextures that human–animal relations take their distinctive form. A study of pigs or cattle would necessarily involve different relations. However, we suggest that this study of an animal that is so visibly in the making is instructive, precisely because its very marginality raises the question of what it is to become animal.

First feeding: symmetry and performativity

STS 'material semiotics' explores *how* objects (or animals or people) get assembled in different practices. In order to do this, it adopts what Michel Callon calls '*generalized symmetry*'.[6] We need, he says, to try to put our assumptions about objects (or actors or animals or people) on one side, and treat all the elements in a practice in the same terms. Famously, he explored the relations between fishermen and scallops in this way, looking to see what form these took in practice. So what happens if we extend this approach to the salmon farm?

> In the hatchery the eggs hatch out to form alevins. The alevins are not-quite-fish that feed on their yolk-sacs. They live in shallow, water-filled trays lined with Astroturf. After a few weeks, they turn into tiny fish and are decanted into cylindrical tanks a metre and a half across, and a metre deep. At first, they mostly cower at the bottom, clustered together, heads facing into the flow of water.
>
> Irene is looking down at them. Then she presses a button to start the feeding system. This is a screw-thread that gently sprinkles tiny amounts of powdered feed onto the surface of the water. Irene looks into the tank intently. She's holding still: she doesn't want to frighten the tiny fish. She's not quite holding her breath, but she's just a little tense. For a few minutes she watches. Then, suddenly, she smiles and relaxes. 'They're *feeding*', she says. And indeed they are. Every ten or fifteen seconds one of the small fry is detaching itself from the dark shoal at the bottom of the tank. It darts up, gulps down a particle of feed, and then it darts down again. Now she is smiling broadly. It's a crucial moment. Sometimes they don't feed. There's something wrong. But there isn't going to be a problem with this tank.

Seen in this way, first feeding is a *performative* practice. Something important is being done in the web of relations that make up the practice. We can see this if we try, symmetrically, to avoid making assumptions about the attributes of fish and see what they are being made to be. This practice starts with fish that are passive, fish that do not feed, and it ends with active fish that do. The transformation is possible because the fish are lodged in a web of relations with other objects or actors including Irene, the feeding mechanism, the feed itself, and the water. *It is this web of relations that turns the fish into feeders* and people into carers worrying about those fish. However, to be sure, that web reaches further into fish propensities, or fish biology, and into other materials too. So, for instance, the feeding mechanism depends on electricity, whereas the feed is an industrial product that draws on a web that includes fishing fleets in Chile, feedstock fish, and a network of financial and logistical relations. All of these (or something like them) are webbed together to turn non-feeding fry into feeding fry. Fish (or feeding fish) – are *done* in practices. They are an *effect of relations*. This is our core argument. It is the core argument of material semiotics.

Vaccinating: heterogeneity and insecurity

Actors, objects, and animals are shaped in practices, and their relations, but those relations are *materially heterogeneous* and they are *never entirely secure*.

> A few months on, and the fish are around eleven centimetres long. They've been delivered by lorry from the hatchery to a second site, where they will grow until they move to the sea. And the first task is to vaccinate them.
>
> There's a complicated arrangement of pipes and pumps that delivers them to the vaccination cabin. Here, they slide down a stainless steel chute, flapping in protest, and fall into a wire basket in a trough. There's water in this, together with anaesthetic: the fish need to be anaesthetized before they are put in the vaccination machine.
>
> Kristin pulls a lever: the basket lifts out of the water–anaesthetic mix, and the fish slide onto a tray where she picks them up, two at a time with rough waterproof gloves. She makes sure they are pointing the right way, and drops them into the grooves on a tiny conveyer belt, which feeds them into the vaccination machine. It is all quite fast. And it is important that the fish are limp when this happens. If the anaesthetic gets too dilute the fish start flapping in protest. Then Kristin needs to stop everything, add anaesthetic to the water, and feed the fish back into it until they are docile.

This scene can also be understood as a web of relations that shapes the fish on the one hand and people on the other. But this time it is the other way round: the fish start out lively and they end up passive. The web of relations includes the fish themselves, Kristin, and her gloves. And then it includes water, pipes, some more or less high-tech machinery, anaesthetic, pumps, and an electricity supply. The vaccination machine includes vaccine itself, optical sensors, electric motors, and needles, so the web of relations leads quickly to the pharmaceutical industry. But let's make two other points.

First, the elements in the web of relations are materially and socially *heterogeneous*. As with the first feeding, humans, animals, technologies, institutions, and naturally occurring elements (such as water) are all being woven together. The character of the animal (the passive salmon) is being done in a particular socially and materially heterogeneous weave. And then, second, that weave is *precarious*. It does not go wrong most of the time, but the potential for failure is always there. If the anaesthetic gets too dilute then the fish are lively. If the electricity fails everything stops. (Indeed, the site has a back–up generator). How objects (or animals) are done in practices depends on the weave. Nothing is fixed or given. Everything is in process, everything is a matter of becoming. As it unfolds (and notwithstanding the industrial concern with order) a large part of what is happening looks more like tinkering than centralized planning or control.[7]

Feeding on the fjord: multiplicity

If objects (and animals) take the shape that they do in webs of practice, then this implies that they are likely to change their form between different practices. Salmon starting to feed are not, for instance, like those about to be vaccinated. But let us add another ethnographic layer to this tale of difference.

> We are another year on. The fish have moved to the sea. Nearly a metre long, they are now in large sea pens, 25 metres across, and 30 metres deep. If you look down into the water you can see some them, but most are invisible. The feed, now in the form of pea-sized pellets, rattles down air ducts and blows out onto the surface of the pen. But how much feed do they need? How much do they want? These are pressing questions: the cost of feed is around 60% of the cost of raising a salmon.
>
> Christoffer is up on the gantry above the water with a bucket of feed and a scoop. He is flinging pellets at the surface of the water, and he is trying to see what is going on. Do the fish rise greedily and gulp the pellets down? Does the surface of the water boil as they do this? That would be a good sign (though it may mean they are not getting enough to eat). Or, here is another possibility: do they eat but without very much enthusiasm? Perhaps, then, the level of feeding is just about right? And then, here is a third possibility: perhaps the salmon are ignoring some or all of the feed? If this is happening, then it is worrying. Perhaps they are being overfed. But why? There may even be disease in the tank.

In the first ethnographic snippet, passive salmon were rendered active. In the second, active salmon were rendered passive. And now, in this third ethnographic moment, the salmon are being done in the web of relations as hungry, not very hungry, or not hungry at all. Again this is a relational effect. It is tempting to say 'they *are* hungry', full stop, or 'they *are* not'. But in practice this is misleading, because the only direct way of determining this from a human point of view is by dropping feed on them, and looking to see what happens. So what we are saying is that although we tend to imagine that objects (or salmon) have more or less stable and context-independent attributes, in practice if we look at scenes in this way, then *they are done differently in different locations*. In this world of becoming, this has the following consequence: any kind of *continuity is an empirical matter*.[8] This means that if we talk of 'objects', 'animals', or 'salmon' as stable between practices, then this is itself some kind of achievement. It takes effort to link different practices together to arrive at continuity. So how is this done? STS answers this question in three ways.[9]

First, much of the time the issue simply does not arise because differences (and their practices) do not overlap. So, for instance, if salmon in relation to humans take one form in the hatchery and another different form out on the fjord, then usually this does not matter. The issue of difference does not arise; nobody knows, and nobody cares: there is social and geographical segregation.

Second, it is taken for granted that objects express themselves in different ways in different circumstances. Salmon get bigger, or they get ill and stop eating, or they need to move from fresh water to the sea, or they escape and are encountered in rivers as 'alien species'. These are cases in which they, the salmon, express themselves differently, so they need to be handled differently too.[10] This pragmatic and 'realist' assumption has a powerful grip on Western ways of thinking about the world.[11] The argument is that reality (including objects) is pretty determinate, but it has to be handled in different ways in different places. A similarly 'realist' strategy focuses more on knowledge, and says that *perspectives* vary. So, for instance, if you look at a textbook on salmon, it juxtaposes the anatomical, the endocrinological, the behavioural, the physiological and the environmental. Each chapter says something different, but the assumption is that the different approaches simply offer different perspectives on a single (kind of) entity.

The third approach, and the one adopted here, is different. This says that salmon (or objects) are shape-shifters: that in practice, they are not particularly stable because different practices do them in different ways; that they are therefore multiple in form; perhaps, indeed, that they are fluid, changing shape as they flow between practices. To put it succinctly, the assumption is that *objects have a variable geometry*. And then the argument is that if we want to understand the character of objects (or animals) in practice, in this way of thinking, the challenge is to find ways of tracing and talking about that variable geometry.[12]

Dead fish: texture

Objects are done in practices and their webs of relations: this is our argument, and it applies to people and to animals, including salmon. But at the same time it is clear that animals are not the same as objects, and indeed that different kinds of animals are not like one another. So what is it that distinguishes animals (or salmon, or farmed salmon) from objects? How is this to be understood from an STS or material-semiotic point of view? To answer these questions we need to talk about *choreographies* and *architextures* on the one hand, and *textures* on the other. Textures first.

> Out on the fjord with 50,000 fish in each of the pens, the farm as a whole may be holding over half a million fish. With a population that size, some die each day. It is important to separate out the dead from the living each day. There is a pipe that pumps up water and dead fish from the bottom of each pen and deposits them on the deck. Then you pick up the fish and put them in a wheelbarrow. They can be large (around five kilos) and picking them up is not easy for beginners. You put on rough gloves and you go to pick them up, but then you discover that even with those gloves they are very slippery. Sometimes you think you have got a grip of a fish, only to discover that you have not, and it slips from your hands. Those who know what they are doing grab the fish very firmly around the base of the tail. This is because the tail itself is rigid cartilage, and very slightly broader than the fleshy base of the tail. Then, if your grip is tight enough, you can lift the fish with one hand and toss it into the wheelbarrow.

Here is the argument: that the webs of relations in practice have specific relational *textures*. That is the importance of this ethnographic moment. For the people doing this work, salmon, even dead salmon, are *slippery*. Return, now, to Christoffer.

> He is flinging pellets at the surface of the water and then he is looking intently at how the salmon react. But this is not as easy as it sounds. If he is lucky the day is calm; it is overcast, but it is not raining. Then at least he can see a little way into the water. If he is unlucky, then wind, waves, or rain are breaking up the surface of the water, or sun is reflecting off it and he cannot see much at all. But even when conditions are ideal, he can see only two or three metres into the water. If there are 50,000 fish, he can see only a few dozen of them. He really cannot see what most of them are up to. And they are constantly on the move as well.

What can we say about the web of relations here? What do salmon become for people in this context? Here they are no longer slippery. Instead, and barely visible at best, they have become *elusive*. So here we have a second relational texture to set alongside the first. Slippery, elusive, and in other ethnographic contexts we could go on adding to the list; timid, perhaps, for Irene at the moment of first feeding; lively and resistant for Kristin when the anaesthetic gets too dilute in the course of vaccination. And so on.

So this is our argument: the *textures* of the relations that make up the webs of practice characterize whatever is caught up in them. They also differentiate animals from one another (the textures of dog–human relations are unlike those relevant to fish and people). The argument is relational. Salmon are slippery in relation to people in particular practices, and not, for instance, in relation to parasites such as sea-lice. which anchor themselves firmly to scales or fins. On the farm, they are slippery, and they are elusive, they are difficult to see, secretive, and sometimes mysterious. *For people.* What are they up to, down there in the pen? The answer is that even though they are confined, it is not very clear, at least to the humans on the farm.

The argument needs to be made with care. We are not necessarily (and perhaps even usually) talking about relations between salmon and people that are direct. In the heterogeneous webs of practice textures are more often *mediated*.

> At the end of their lives, the salmon end up in the slaughterhouse. Piped from a boat, they slide flapping down a chute. Carried by a small conveyer belt, they enter a long metal box, where they are stunned. At one moment, this is the theory, the salmon are conscious, they are sentient, and they are capable of suffering pain. And at the next moment, they are unconscious, still alive but unconscious. Emerging from the box they are carried to a place where they are killed, with a quick knife stroke to the major artery to the gills.
>
> This is another practice: the practice of humane slaughter, the way of minimizing pain for the fish. Contemporary veterinary science has condemned the alternatives. For instance, suffocating fish with carbon dioxide causes them distress. Electrical stunning is to be preferred in the moment before death.

Textures, then, are mediated. There are other materials and other relations at work in the textures that relate animals and humans, and these help to define animals for humans in those practices. If you need to pick up dead salmon, gloves are useful. Indeed, they are more or less necessary. They make the fish slightly less slippery. And Christoffer's attempts to see whether the salmon are eating (themselves mediated in relations that include pellets, scoops, and polarizing sunglasses) are assisted in a few of the pens by underwater television cameras.[13] And then, at the end of life in the slaughterhouse, the web of relations extends through machinery to welfare science, to the study of fish sentience, and to the official state regulations that follow from those studies. And here is the bottom line: the textures of fish–human relations have changed in the slaughterhouse. They are being done differently. Now fish can feel pain. Even fear.

Roofs and lights: choreography and architexture

Textures define and characterize the qualities of relations in practices, including the only relations we know about: those that bind and shape people and the worlds in which they are caught up. Some of these assemble animals and people. Read Donna Haraway on dogs, and you see those textures take a series of specific forms: eye contact; gesture; the importance of treats; the touch of hand and fur, or tongue and face.[14] Go to a fish farm and look at how people work with salmon, and those textures are entirely different: slippery, elusive, timid, and all the rest. So textures help to determine the character of the animal in relation to the human, but so too do *choreographies* or *architextures*.

> Go back to the moment of vaccination. The fish are washed along a pipe and dropped into a large tank in a building. There is no daylight here. Instead there are powerful lights. The young salmon are going to spend four, six or eight months here feeding and growing. And sometimes those lights will be on, and sometimes they will be off. So what is the pattern?

The answer is, it depends. Some salmon follow the cycles of the Nordic season, short days in December and more daylight towards June. Triggered by these changes they become smolt, ready to go to the sea, in spring. Others, destined to be autumn smolt, are speeded up. Given artificial light for twenty-four hours a day for six months in the Norwegian winter, they live through an artificial six-week winter in the Norwegian summer. Then the lights go back on to trigger smoltification in the autumn. The reason for this? The fish farmers do not want to send all their fish to the fjord at the same moment. The market for salmon is not seasonal.

Choreographies have to do with ordered arrangements. Partly these have to do with heterogeneous relations *within* particular practices; think of the process of vaccination. However, they also have to do with relations *between* practices. The latter extend across space: the processes of fish farming include hatcheries, freshwater farms, and sea farms. And they also extend across time: chronologies and successions and repetitions are ordered in a fish farm. More correctly, times are relations that are ordered or choreographed within and between practices. Times may be stretched out or contracted. This is what is happening as the farmers switch the lights on and off. And/or they are chained together, so that the fish indeed move from hatchery to the freshwater farm to the fjord, and then, at the end, to the slaughterhouse. Or they may come in the form of cycles; daily, weekly, or seasonal.

So what does this have to do with animals? The answer is that the timing, sequencing and choreographing of relations needs to be set alongside the textures of relations. Human–animal relations are defined by textures (slippery or furry, or lively or elusive, or susceptible to pain) but they are also defined by the ordering of sequences. And it is the quality of these orderings that we want to call architextures. The dog needs to be walked twice a day. The fish need to be fed eight hours a day, or vaccinated at certain times, or moved from fresh water to the sea. Our argument is that it is particular combinations of relational *textures* and *architextures* that characterize human–animal links and turn animals into objects or subjects with particular lively attributes.

Conclusion

We have argued that objects are an effect of heterogeneous and more or less precarious webs of performative practice that also enact humans. These webs take different forms in different practices, and those different forms are woven together to make more or less continuous objects. But we have also suggested, first, that the relations enacted in practices display particular qualities or textures, and second, that there are specific patterns or textures of choreography (or architextures) that order time and space and their qualities both within and between practices. And finally we have argued that it is in these textures and architextures that animals (or more precisely human–animal relations) take their distinctive form. Animals are not in and of themselves furry, scaly, elusive, prone to sickness, endowed with a life cycle, loyalty, and all the rest. They develop attributes such as these in relation to people who are also, and at the same time, being given form and endowed with relational qualities and attributes. In short, practices enact people and animals together.

This way of thinking about animals has a number of implications. First, it stands in tension with any version of human exceptionalism: both people and animals are taken to be relational effects. Second, it resists those versions of materialism that argue that it is possible to apprehend the material world outside, or apart from, situated practices.[15] It argues instead that although humans are not exceptional, it is only in practices that enact humans alongside animals that it is possible to know anything about the latter. Third, it makes no assumptions about agency, human or otherwise, outside the webs of practice that constitute these. In the first instance, people are not prime movers, but then again, neither are animals or objects. Rather, it is assumed that agency draws on and is distributed through webs of relations. It is only in particular practices (and for particular reasons) that it becomes possible to locate it in particular human (or animal) places. And then, finally, and as a part of this, it notes that it only makes sense to say that people control domesticated animals in very particular contexts and respects. Even at a highly ordered site such as a salmon farm, it is also plausible to argue that salmon, in fact, control people. If humankind is to consume salmon on an industrial scale, then people are put to immense effort to fit round the demands made of them and their (multispecies) surroundings *by* the salmon that they farm. The breeding, the feeding, the trawling to secure fish feed, and the journey from fresh to salt water: for even if people end up eating the salmon that thus sustain human lives, what the salmon have made people do along the way is scarcely trivial.

Notes

1 We are grateful to the anonymized 'Sjølaks AS' for their kind agreement to let us locate our study within the firm, and for its additional generous practical support. We would like to thank all those who work for Sjølaks (they too are anonymized) for their warm welcome, help, and willingness to let us watch them at work. In many cases their kindness vastly exceeded any reasonable expectation or need. We are grateful to Kristin Asdal, Annemarie Mol, Vicky Singleton, and Gro Ween for continuing discussion. The project, 'Newcomers to the Farm', was funded by Forskningsrådet, the Norwegian Research Council (project number 183352/S30), with additional research leave and financial support from Lancaster University, the Open University, and the University of Oslo, and we are grateful to all.
2 A definition which is often cited is provided by Juliet Clutton-Brock, who defines a domesticated animal as 'one that has been bred in captivity for purposes of economic profit to a human community that maintains complete mastery over its breeding, organization of territory, and food supply' Clutton-Brock (1989, 7). See also Leach (2003).
3 See, for instance, Fraser (1993).
4 For examples of a large genre see Wolfe (2003) and Despret (2007).
5 The approach comes in various forms, including feminist material semiotics (for an animal-relevant illustration, see Haraway (2007), and actor-network-theory and its derivatives, and recent work in anthropology. For animal-relevant illustrations see, for instance, Thompson (2002), Hinchliffe *et al.* (2005), Helmreich (2009), Singleton (2010), Abram and Lien (2011), and Law and Moser (2012) and (on salmon), Lien and Law (2011) and Law and Lien (2013).
6 Callon (1986).
7 For an exploration of the tinkering implied by care in the context of health care see Mol (2008).
8 The point is carefully explored in Mol (2002).
9 For survey and discussion of these strategies see Mol (2002) and Law (2004).
10 See Lien and Law (2011).
11 Realism is a family of philosophical positions which assume that reality has more or less determinate attributes, even if these are often unclear to human beings.
12 For discussion of fluid and other more complex objects see Mol and Law (1994) and Law and Singleton (2005).
13 The use of underwater cameras adds another texture to the relation. For more ethnographic details on feeding farmed fish, see Lien (2007).
14 Haraway (2003). On people and cows, see Law (2010).
15 This is a possible reading of, for instance, Bennett (2010).

Bibliography

Abram, S. and Lien, M.E. (2011) 'Performing Nature at World's Ends', *Ethnos*, 76: (1), 3–18.
Bennett, J. (2010) *Vibrant Matter: A Political Ecology of Things*, Durham and London: Duke University Press.
Callon, M. (1986) 'Some Elements of a Sociology of Translation: Domestication of the Scallops and the Fishermen of Saint Brieuc Bay', pages 196–233 in J. Law (ed.), *Power, Action and Belief: A New Sociology of Knowledge?* Sociological Review Monograph 32, London: Routledge and Kegan Paul.

Clutton-Brock, J. (1989) *The Walking Larder: Patterns of Domestication, Pastoralism, and Predation*, London: Unwin Hyman.

Despret, V. (2007) *Bêtes et Homes*, Paris: Gallimard.

Fraser, D. (1993) 'Assessing Animal Well-Being: Common Sense, Uncommon Science', pages 37–54 in B.R. Baumgardt and H. Glenn Gray (eds), *Food Animal Well-Being*, Indiana: USDA and Purdue University Office of Agricultural Research Programs, also available at http://www.ansc.purdue.edu/wellbeing/FAWB1993/Fraser.pdf.

Haraway, D.J. (2003) *The Companion Species Manifesto: Dogs, People, and Significant Otherness*, Chicago: Prickly Paradigm Press.

Haraway, D.J. (2007) *When Species Meet*, Minneapolis and London: University of Minnesota Press.

Helmreich, S. (2009) *Alien Ocean: Anthropological Voyages in Microbial Seas*, Berkeley: University of California Press.

Hinchliffe, S. *et al.* (2005) 'Urban Wild Things: A Cosmopolitical Experiment', *Society and Space*, 23: (5), 643–658.

Law, J. (2004) *After Method: Mess in Social Science Research*, London: Routledge.

Law, J. (2010) 'Care and Killing: Tensions in Veterinary Practice', pages 57–69 in A. Mol, I. Moser, and J. Pols (eds), *Care in Practice: On Tinkering in Clinics, Homes and Farms*, Bielefeld: Transcript Publishers.

Law, J. and Lien, M.E. (forthcoming) 'Slippery: Field Notes on Empirical Ontology', *Social Studies of Science*, published online September 2012.

Law, J. and Moser, I. (2012) 'Contexts and Culling', *Science, Technology and Human Values*, 37: (4), 332–354.

Law, J. and Singleton, V. (2005) 'Object Lessons', *Organization*, 12: (3), 331–355.

Leach, H.M. (2003) 'Human Domestication Reconsidered', *Current Anthropology*, 44: (3), 349–368.

Lien, M.E. (2007) 'Feeding Fish Efficiently. Mobilising Knowledge in Tasmanian Salmon Farming', *Social Anthropology*, 15: (2), 169–185.

Lien, M.E. and Law, J. (2011) '"Emergent Aliens": On Salmon, Nature and their Enactment', *Ethnos*, 76: (1), 65–87, also available at http://www.sv.uio.no/sai/english/research/projects/Newcomers/publications/working-papers-web/Emergent%20aliens%20Ethnos%20revised%20WP%20version.pdf.

Mol, A. (2002) *The Body Multiple: Ontology in Medical Practice*, Durham, NC and London: Duke University Press.

Mol, A. (2008) *The Logic of Care: Health and the Problem of Patient Choice*, London: Routledge.

Mol, A. and Law, J. (1994) 'Regions, Networks and Fluids: Anaemia and Social Topology', *Social Studies of Science*, 24, 641–671.

Singleton, V. (2010) 'Good Farming: Control or Care?', pages 235–256 in A. Mol, I. Moser, and J. Pols (eds), *Care in Practice: On Tinkering in Clinics, Homes and Farms*, Bielefeld: Transcript.

Thompson, C. (2002) 'When Elephants Stand for Competing Models of Nature', pages 166–190 in J. Law and A. Mol (eds), *Complexity in Science, Technology, and Medicine*, Durham, NC: Duke University Press.

Wolfe, C. (2003) *Animal Rites: American Culture, the Discourse of Species, and Posthuman Theory*, Chicago: Chicago University Press.

30

Objects made out of action

Matei Candea

Objects made out of action

Debates around 'the agency of objects' have occupied the humanities and social sciences for some time now. This chapter, by contrast, raises the symmetrical question of the objectivity of action. My focus will be on 'behaviour': action itself taken as an object. The concrete setting for this discussion is an ongoing ethnographic study of the world of behavioural ecology, and specifically of one research site in the South African desert called the Kalahari Meerkat Project. More specifically still, I examine one particular technical object (a hand-held computer), which is used in data collection at this site, and which, I argue, is centrally involved in the way behaviour emerges as a scientific object.

This talk of 'emerging' is intentionally ambiguous; I am attempting, for now, to leave open three different types of explanations of the 'object-like' qualities of behaviour that are currently in play in the literature. One of these is ideally exemplified in the arguments of sociologist of science Eileen Crist. Crist's detailed study of the changing discourses of the science of animal behaviour has described a process of 'epistemological objectification', in which a new technical language was forged that avoided treating animals as subjects with a meaningful world of their own (Crist 1999). For Crist, this shift emerges with particular starkness in the contrast between the observational techniques of traditional naturalists and those of post-1970 behavioural biologists informed by sociobiological theories. The former, Crist argues, operated in a personalized knowledge-economy premised on an intersubjective engagement with the meaningful lived world of the animal; they gave animal actions a 'face'. By contrast, the latter base objectivity on the identification of detached and generalizable units of behaviour, which multiple external observers can agree upon without any reference to the animal's perspective or subjective state (ibid.:146). Crist sees the prototype of the contemporary notion of behaviour in Descartes' concept of animal 'motion caused from pure corporeality', which the philosopher strove to distinguish from specifically human motion caused by the 'incorporeal mind' or 'thinking substance' (Descartes 1970 in Crist 1999:212–213). From this original distinction, Crist claims, derives the later elaboration of a split between (mere animal) behaviour and (human, intentional, meaningful) action, which has become a commonplace in much social and behavioural science.

The second type of explanation of the object-like qualities of behaviour is well exemplified by behavioural biologist Marian Stamp Dawkins' reflection on the problem of identifying units of behaviour:

> At first sight, behaviour appears to have no building blocks, no equivalent of the cells and organs that build up a physical body. Nor does it appear to have units that can be measured like units of heat or light or length. It appears to be ephemeral, elusive, and constantly shifting, a will-o'-the wisp that defies definition. But if you look for a while longer, you will see that not only does it have units of its own, those units can also be measured and quantified.
>
> *(Dawkins 2007:73)*

Dawkins' solution to the problem relies on a twofold regularity (see 2007:73–74). There is first of all a regularity in the animals' own activity: of all the physiologically possible combinations of animals' movements, a 'restricted subset' of patterns nevertheless emerges (animals chew before swallowing, build the foundations of their nests before they build the sides, etc.). However, far from giving such patterns a 'face', or seeing in them evidence of intentionality, Dawkins takes a different tack, in which the regularity of animals' patterned behaviour echoes directly with the regularity of the ways in which different observers can recognize the same patterns. This regularity of recognition (in the sense, now, of pattern-matching) in turn is the effect of an objective property of observers themselves: '"the computer in the head" (their own brain)' (ibid.:74). Dawkins' own exposition relies explicitly on intersubjectivity (between observers, and between author and reader) as evidence of a direct communication of objectivities: 'You know exactly what I mean by "pecking" or "flying" because your brain will have picked out these common and highly distinctive behaviour patterns itself' (ibid.). For Dawkins, (the unit of) behaviour's objective reality is thus sealed *both* 'out there' in the regularity with which animals behave, *and* 'in here' in the regularity with which different observers, or rather 'the computer in their heads', behave in picking out the same pattern.

In sum, Crist locates behaviour firmly in the realm of human language and epistemology: 'behaviour' is a conceptual object historically excised by philosophers and scientists from the flow of life. By contrast, Dawkins locates behaviour just as firmly in the realm of animal biology (including the biology of the animals that the observers themselves are).

To these two locations of the object-ness of behaviour (in human epistemology, in animal biology), an influential tradition in science studies urges us to add a third: the equipment and apparatuses with the help of which researchers frame and stabilize their encounters with the animals they study. Bruno Latour, for instance, describes the way in which the material equipment, as well as the concepts, deployed by human primatologists lend solidity to the fluid social practices of non-human primates (Latour 1996:np; Strum and Latour 1987:791). In a related vein, Donna Haraway points towards the mutual implication of 'people, organisms and apparatuses' that gives behaviour its object-like quality:

> A behavior is not something just out there in the world waiting for discovery; a behavior is an inventive construction, a generative fact-fiction, put together by an intra-acting crowd of players that include people, organisms, and apparatuses all coming together in the history of animal psychology. From the flow of bodies moving in time, bits are carved out and solicited to become more or less frequent as part of building other patterns of motion through time. A behaviour is a natural-technical entity that travels from the lab to the agility training session.
>
> *(Haraway 2008:211 see also 1989)*

The objectivity of behaviour, in this vein, is an outcome of a particular, successful, networking of humans and non-humans.

This chapter starts from this now canonical material-semiotic approach in science studies, in which attention is shifted away both from 'ideas' and from 'nature', towards the primacy of material arrangements in concrete research settings (Rheinberger 1997; Latour 1987). I focus on a particular piece of kit, a Psion hand-held computer that accompanies researchers at the Kalahari Meerkat Project as they collect observational data about meerkat behaviour. The Psion could be seen as a classic instance of what Rheinberger would term a 'technical object', one of the stable, predictable elements of the 'experimental system' that enables enquiry into, but simultaneously constrains and restricts, the 'scientific object' under investigation: animal behaviour itself (Rheinberger 1997:28–29).

However, the aim of this account is not merely to provide (yet) an(other) exemplification of this approach, but also to raise a few partial challenges to some of its implications. In particular, I suggest in the following that our concerns with what things can do may risk begging the question of what it means for doing itself to be thing-like.

Introducing the Psion

Set up in the early 1990s, the Kalahari Meerkat Project (KMP) is a meticulously organized assemblage of humans, technical objects, and animals, which have managed the following impressive feat: in its first 15 years of existence, the KMP had collected millions of lines of data each standing for an instance of a meerkat behaviour, commonly referred to locally either as 'a line' or simply as 'a behaviour'. Although the ostensible achievements of this project are more often measured in terms of high-profile articles in scientific journals, the sheer amount and detail of data collected is impressive in its own right. These behaviours, each precisely dated and timed, are each associated to one of hundreds of named individual meerkats, whose weight, parentage, life-history and present and past social position within its group is carefully and continuously documented by a rolling team of 15 or so volunteer observers, each of whom spends a year living in this remote field-site. If a field-site is a particular kind of 'scientific instrument' that answers questions about behaviour (Rees 2009), then the KMP is an extremely well-tuned and success-ful such instrument, or, in Rheinberger's terms 'experimental system' (1997), which has enabled scientists working there to publish a raft of high-profile articles.

But how does the system work? How is the numerical feat described above actually achieved, and crucially, maintained through time? The answer would require an exhaustive description of processes of research at the KMP, but also of the history of successful funding applications and other economic–epistemic alliances (with television producers, film-makers and the charity Earthwatch International for instance), which have enabled the project to endure. Such an account is beyond the scope of this chapter, although I have begun to tell aspects of this story elsewhere (Candea 2010). My aim here is more modestly to start from one particular object.

Observers at the KMP make use of a hand-held computer about the size and shape of a 1990s Nintendo 'Game Boy', which they refer to by its brand name as 'the Psion'. In the backpack that each of the volunteers pack every morning before they set off to observe a group of meerkats, the Psion jostles alongside a motley collection of other objects: a walkie-talkie, a radio, a plastic Tupperware box containing electronic scales carefully wrapped up in bubble wrap, a GPS device, a paper journal with a pen firmly attached with string and duck-tape, some boiled egg in a plastic bag, a water bottle fitted with a long, thin drinking spout of the kind one might find attached to the side of a hamster's cage. Each of these objects participates in its own way to the

Figure 30.1 The Psion. Photo by Matei Candea

growing collection of carefully indexed and solidly black-boxed behaviours, each has its own story and deploys its own possibilities and limitations. But let us focus on the Psion.

The Psion is heavy, a thick wodge of grey plastic that might seem just about indestructible to those who are used to more recent, slender machines; machines that are all screen and no buttons. The Psion plays it the other way: it has a small LCD (liquid crystal display) screen, which carries two lines of alphanumeric characters in dark grey on a light grey background, but is covered in buttons, providing a full keyboard for the thumbs. A solid plastic cover slides over the keys to protect them when the Psion sits in the bottom of the rucksack. A flap at the back reveals a slot for a good plain rectangular battery, the kind with two connectors on top, which, in my school at least, we used to dare each other to lick in the margins of science classes. And yet, despite its sturdy appearance, the Psion is intensively fretted over by volunteers. This is partly because many of these Psions are old and tired, having been deployed in the daily grind of field science in desert conditions for many years. Hinges do not always hinge and slides do not always slide as smoothly as they used to. Duck-tape holds cracked plastic and loose battery cover together. But mostly, extra care has to be taken with the Psions because they are now techno-logical orphans, disconnected from a once thriving life-support system.

Indeed, if we trace the KMP's 'Psions' beyond the field-site, they turn out to have a pretty exciting biography under the name Psion Organizer II. Although the Organizer II's makers, Psion Ltd, have now decidedly moved on and make no mention of the device on their website,[1] the machine has left other trails online, on the websites and wiki entries of enthusiasts. Zigzagging through broken links and long-defunct domain names, one occasionally comes across whole user manuals, lists of technical specifications painstakingly typed up, and a live forum with 600 members.[2] Practical patches, ideas for tinkering with hardware and software, solutions to technical problems, jostle with unattributed statements, undocumented facts and sad admissions of failure, floating on the web like messages in a bottle ('This Psion Organizer II web site is closed. [...]

I have asked for help from others but the continuation of this site in its current format has always been an issue. [...] So it is with great sadness that I am calling it a day.'[3]). But most of all, shining quite touchingly through these fragmentary trails is the love that is still out there for 'the grandfather of all handhelds', in the words of one forum contributor.[4]

The Organizer II, it seems, was first produced by Psion Ltd in 1986 as a versatile portable computer. It had a basic operating system and a number of inbuilt applications, which allowed it to be used as a diary or an alarm clock. Crucially, the Organizer II enabled users to create their own simple programs using Psion's own 'Organizer Programming Language'. It also had an external device slot that fitted a number of different hardware extensions, from a printer module to a 'comms-link' that allowed the Organizer II to talk to other devices via an RS-232 25-pin connector. Reportedly, over a million Organizer IIs were sold and used in a range of ways from retail through to government offices, from building sites through to scientific projects. It went out of production in the early 1990s and was replaced by a new range of clamshell devices. And yet, as a post from 2001 tells us, 'You'd be surprised how many of them still are doing their duty.'[5] The Organizer Programming Language, now renamed Open Programming Language, lives on as an open-source project,[6] and 'guerrilla' users have over the years created programs that allow Organizer IIs to be used as pollen counters, holiday memory logs, maze games and bike computers.[7] In sum, the Organizer II is a survivor: cut off from its official support system, it continues to live a multiple precarious and inventive life through an adopted international not-quite-community of users.

However, The KMP's Psions carry little of that sedimented and moving history, beyond a general sense that these superannuated machines need to be kept alive without outside support. Nor do they exhibit much of the versatility of which the web shows them to be capable. Neither diaries, alarm clocks, nor bike counters, and certainly not games machines, the KMP Psions sturdily 'do their duty' in one single, predictable way dictated by a user-generated program written in OPL, which was devised specifically for the project to collect behavioural data. The Psion enables the quick logging of observed behaviour in the following way: its program specifies a one-letter code for each of the behaviours that volunteers are tasked to collect (many Psions at the project have a printed sheet of paper sellotaped to the underside of the plastic cover, which lists the behaviours and their associated codes). For each behaviour entered, the program prompts users to specify the individual or individuals involved, each themselves identified by a one-letter code. The Psion logs the time of each entry and produces a set of lines of code, which are then transferred into the project's central database at the end of each field session via the comms-link port.

Self-control

The Psion could first of all be described as the nexus of a series of simplifications and constraints. It is itself simplified, its many potentialities constrained by the program into one specific set of input–output relations. This simplification in turn relies on and enables a simplification of the meerkats' multifarious and complex lives into a series of lines of code. In this sense, the Psion is a materialization of the principles of a particular sampling methodology articulated by behavioural biologists such as Jeanne Altman (1974; cf. Haraway 1989), and rehearsed in methodology manuals ever since (Lehner 1996; Dawkins 2007; Martin and Bateson 2007): animal behaviour is disaggregated into units, each of which is precisely defined *ahead of* the observation, in order to enable interobserver comparisons.

We have already seen Eileen Crist's analysis of this methodological shift as 'an intensification of the erasure of the [animal's] life-world' (Crist 1999:149). Unsurprisingly, however, this is not how behavioural biologists themselves would describe the logic of the practice.

A more ethnographic sense of what is in it for them, of the 'indigenous' logic and affect of these sampling practices can be garnered from the following striking observation by Marian Dawkins in her recent introduction to the methodology of observational studies of animal behaviour:

> [e]ven if we cannot control our animals as precisely as an experimentalist would like us to, we can, as Schneirla (1950) and Altman (1974) put it, control ourselves.
>
> *(Dawkins 2007:9)*

Drawing on Daston and Galison's excellent history of the many forms of objectivity that have shaped the scientific self over the centuries, one recognizes here the flavour of 'mechanical objectivity', in which the self that is being controlled is 'a projective self that overleap[s] its own boundaries, crossing the line between observer and observed' (Daston and Galison 2007:257). The Psion is a materialization and enabler of this self-control, constraining observers to record only those behaviours that the project has selected ahead of time as relevant. Unexpected behaviours, strange and exciting events and unknown individuals might well intrude into the observer's experience (and will of course be relayed back to the research station in the form of stories and accounts), but the Psion stops these from making it into the data proper.

The Psion thus constrains both the behaviour of humans and that of meerkats but, crucially, it does so in asymmetrical ways: it directly constrains the behaviour of human observers (what they are actually able to do), whereas it only constrains which aspects of those things the meerkats do get to count as behaviour in the database. In this respect, the Psion materializes an economy of knowledge that sets apart the constraints of observational field science from those of experimental laboratory science (Stengers, 2000:140–144; Despret, 1996). The laboratory maze or skinner box, to take two iconic examples, constrain the movements of rats or pigeons, subjecting them to a series of predefined choices: turn right, turn left, press this lever or that button. By contrast, the Psion is small and unobtrusive so as to stay out of the way of meerkats themselves, but it channels the observers through a series of 'if X, then Y' (if you want to describe a behaviour, then you must tell me which of these it is; if you have entered a behaviour, then you must tell me the individual involved; etc.). The Psion's effect on behaviour is intentionally asymmetrical: it aims to affect and channel the behaviour of human observers, without affecting that of meerkats. The Psion is, in other words, a maze for humans, rather than for meerkats.

Materializing knowledge

Equally, however, the Psion could be described not through what it constrains, but through what it enables; or rather, through what its constraints enable. To begin with the obvious, translating individuals and behaviours into one-letter codes greatly speeds up data entry. However, this takes work: each of the 200 or so meerkats studied at the project has a name (given by the volunteers themselves; cf. Candea 2010), as well as a unique 10-character number, enshrined in a chip the size of a grain of rice, which is embedded in the scruff of its neck, and another unique alphanumeric code which specifies its group, sex and other information and by which it is known in the central database. Typing any of these into the Psion would drastically slow down the process, which is why the program is configured to bind observation sessions to particular meerkat groups, within which meerkats carry a single one-letter code. The Psion then translates this one-letter 'group-relative' code into the long 'population-relative' code by which individuals are known in the general database.

The value of such materially enabled simplifications (see Strum and Latour 1987) emerges if we begin to place data entry within the process of observation as a whole. Taken literally, data

Figure 30.2   Juggling tools. Photo by Matei Candea

entry would be preceded by the following steps: recognizing the behaviour, checking its one-letter code, noting the individual's 'dye-marks' (the coordinated pattern of spots with which the researchers marked the meerkats in order to aid the recognition of individuals), relating the marks to the individual's contextual one-letter code with the help of the 'mark-sheet' (a small print-out that details the names, codes and distinctive markings of each of the animals in the group), and then actually typing the data into the Psion. All of this, while keeping an eye on the 15 or so other meerkats foraging in different directions!

During my first few outings with the volunteers, I simply could not understand how they were able to juggle all of these different procedures, and how some nevertheless managed to bring back up to 100 lines of data from a single field-session. In time, however, I came to see that as volunteers became more experienced, they progressively converted this set of successive steps into the near-immediate process of 'seeing' the behaviour of known individuals: 'there's Ningaloo going on guard again'. Learning to do this was partly about translating a set of abstract or arbitrary codes into personal, situated knowledge. During one of my first outings, for instance, I mistakenly identified an individual as bearing the dye-mark 'tail-base tail'. The volunteer I was accompanying, without missing a beat, told me there was no such mark in this group and briefly looking up, correctly identified the marking as 'left thigh, tail-base'. To the unfamiliar observer, matching dye-marks to an individual could be very tricky (a thigh-mark or shoulder-mark for instance, could easily be hidden on the side opposite the observer), not to mention the fact that the meerkats were constantly in motion, half buried as they dug for bugs, or weaving in and out of scrub. However, volunteers had learnt to instantly recognize meerkats in familiar groups as named individuals, by a combination of physical characteristics and dye-marks, and had memorized their one-letter codes. Aside from reducing the number of steps between seeing things and entering data, this kind of personalized knowledge brought with it a lot of information about each individual's antecedents, place in the group, habits and idiosyncrasies.

The same process of personalization of arbitrary codes applied to the behavioural units, for which volunteers had created a series of mnemotechnics on various levels of abstraction: C (guard up) for 'climb'; D (guard down) for 'down'; E for grooming, because E looks like a comb; Q for pup-feeds, because Q looks like a bottle. Learning these meant one avoided the need to check the code for any but the most unusual behaviours. But it also lent an uncontroversial solidity and uniqueness to the behavioural units themselves, which were as self-evidently 'out there' and distinct from one another as the keys on the key-pad. One came to know and recognize behaviours as one knew and recognized the meerkats themselves. Volunteers became attuned to what was likely and unlikely to happen, to the regularities of meerkat behaviour. Seasoned volunteers were able to spot the incipient signs of a 'pup-feed' or a 'guard up' just as they became skilled at recognizing particular individuals from a glimpsed body part alone. These kinds of familiarity crossed over onto each other, of course: knowing the meerkats was partly knowing how each *tended to* behave.

The Psion, with its simplifications and constraints, was thus one of a broader collective of objects, techniques and organisms that enabled the production of knowledgeable observers, known individual animals and plentiful data. Although I focus mostly on the program, the more obviously material qualities of the Psion were also an important factor here. As one volunteer pointed out, the clunky old-fashioned keypad had one distinct advantage over more recent touch-screen devices: it allowed experienced observers to touch-type lines of data without taking their eyes off the animals. In other words, the Psion both extended and constrained the abilities of the observers in specific embodied ways. It 'configured the users' (Woolgar 1991) as skilled field-based observers, just as it configured the meerkats as entities that could behave in a certain number of preset ways. It itself was configured as a usable and practical machine for logging behaviour, not only by the programmers, but also by the observers who knew how to use it and by the meerkats who did, after all, mostly behave roughly as expected.

Conclusion: the objectivity of behaviour and the behaviour of objectivity

So, in conclusion, what does a closer look at the Psion add to the three approaches to behaviour with which this chapter began? To Crist's focus on epistemological objectification, it adds, first of all, a sense of the materiality of the processes by which the distinction between action and behaviour is pinned down in practice. Crist characterizes objectivist accounts of behaviour as an ever-renewed and perhaps ultimately futile struggle against (the English) language's inbuilt propensity to attribute intention, and derives from this and other clues the lesson that the distinction between action and behaviour is 'neither a natural classification, nor an inbuilt one' (1999:222). But in the meantime, countless repeated measurements and inscriptions, enabled by the stable equipment of contemporary field and laboratory science, have helped to solidify this distinction in no uncertain way. This is perhaps why, in my ethnographic experience, concerns about excluding the language of intention in the way researchers speak to each other or to a broader public are little more than a side-show, devoid, for the researchers themselves, of the power to put in doubt that which the Psion and its kin show us to be objectively measurable. But the story of the Psion also adds a sense that the gulf is not as great as Crist's account occasionally implies, between 'personal knowledge' and the kind of knowledge that proceeds through abstracted, quantifiable units. Getting to know meerkats as individuals and getting to know behaviours goes hand in hand, and the Psion helps with both.

To Dawkins' account of behaviour as objective pattern-matching, this account adds the (eminently Latourian, and before him, 'Bachelardian'[8]) caveat that we need not only 'the computer in [the observers'] heads', but also the computer in their hands, to make sense of the solidity and objectivity of patterns of behaviour. This addition is not as trivial as it might first seem, because the Psion does not simply help to 'record' behaviour, but also teaches the eye to see it in a certain way. Volunteers at the KMP tune 'the computer in their heads' with the help of the computer in their hands, and the latter contributes something to the unequivocal solidity of the units of behaviour it is used to record. In Rheinberger's (1997) terminology, the Psion is one of the 'technical objects' that make up the 'experimental system' in which 'scientific objects' (the object of study, namely here meerkat behaviour), are embedded. Such technical objects, taken together '"contain" the scientific objects in the double sense of this expression: they embed them, and through that very embracement, they restrict and constrain them' (ibid.:29).

So far, however, the Psion merely yields yet another exemplification of a now canonical approach in science studies, which involves 'a shift of perspective from the actors' minds and interests to their objects of manipulation and desire' (Rheinberger 1997:1). But in what way if at all does my story add to or depart from this approach itself? Two things.

First, the constitutive asymmetry of the Psion raises an interesting albeit partial objection to an entrenched and ever-repeated lesson of this tradition in science studies (what one might term its central dogma), namely that of the identity of discovery and invention: the thought that facts are by definition (and indeed etymologically) made rather than found. The power of this argument has rested primarily on studies of laboratory science, the active experimental set-up of which lends itself easily to such a reformulation, although it has also been extended to the context of field science, notably through Latour's notion of 'circulating references' (1999:24–79). By pointing to the myriad things and practices that carefully, step by step, help scientists translate the world out there into the statement on the page, Latour aims to close the purported gap between 'nature' and its 'representation' by scientists, *or rather*, to redistribute it into a myriad of tiny gaps, tiny translations rather than one massive and mysterious effort of 'correspondence'.[9] What the Psion reminds us of is not to forget this 'or rather': the fact that the gap has not been closed, but simply redistributed. For there is still a crucial difference between saying that reality and representation are unattainable end points of a process which is all made of the same continuous 'stuff' (circulating reference, 'phenomenotechnique', etc.), and saying that a gap between reality and its representation inheres in every tiny step of that process.

What does this have to do with the Psion? As I wrote above, its crucial value is as an instrument that carefully constrains the behaviour of the humans but not that of the meerkats. Or in other words, while the Psion directly constrains what the humans can do in the field, it only constrains which aspects of what the meerkats do comes to *count as* behaviour in the database. That crucial distinction, which speaks to the difference between observing and transforming behaviour, is where, in this case, the gap reemerges. For all that this gap is small in physical size (fitting inside a Game-Boy-sized machine) this does not, pace Latour, make it any less of a metaphysical abyss.

More broadly, the Psion asks us to further unpack the overall description of behaviour as 'an inventive construction, a generative fact-fiction, put together by an intra-acting crowd of players that include people, organisms, and apparatuses' (Haraway 2008:211): to ask about the constitutive asymmetries and micro-abysses at the heart of this process.

Second, and more broadly, the story of the Psion highlights the fact that the science of behaviour introduces a kind of short-circuit between what Rheinberger terms 'scientific object' and 'technical objects'. Behaviour is both what the scientific object is made of, and also what the experimental system largely consists of: humans and objects 'behaving' in consistent and predictable ways. 'Predictable' is the key term here. The tradition of science studies that I am considering here has something of a tendency to background or 'redistribute' the predictability of behaviour. Thus, at times, Latour seems to argue that human and more broadly animal behaviour is inherently volatile and unpredictable, until it is stabilized and scaffolded by the 'steeliness' of objects (see for instance Latour 1996). As Maarten Derksen has pointed out, however, this strangely ignores the many ways in which people are able to act predictably, for instance, as scientific instruments (2010, see also Yarrow 2003).[10] At other times, Latour and others writing in this vein characterize the object precisely as that which 'objects', that which resists in some way, is refractory to complete stabilization, to complete 'black-boxing'. Objects are nebulous, fascinating, elusive entities that live in a kind of ontological *demi-monde*, between full, settled reality and complete inexistence (Daston 2000) and that vigorously push back against poorly conceived enquiry, thereby putting subjects to the test (Stengers 2000). This is why treating people (or animals) as objects, is (in this language) precisely about recognizing their recalcitrance, their fascination, their ability to 'object' to our questions (Latour 2005:255; Despret 2002). If anything, it is *people* who are too predictable, too willing to 'behave', too easily made to conform to what scientists expect of them. Occasionally in these writings, the achievements of sociology, psychology or ethology in showing the predictability of behaviour are redescribed as impositions of the power of the experimenter on hapless subjects who are too bemused by the authority of science to resist in the way the objects of physics or chemistry resist the probing enquiries of their scientists (Latour 2004, 2005; Stengers 2010; Despret 2002, 2004).

These authors' warnings about the need to ensure the objects of science really are able to 'object' express, albeit in a counterintuitive fashion, a concern that the practising scientists I have worked with would also recognize. Nevertheless it would be problematic to conclude that predictable behaviour is necessarily, or even typically, an effect of imposition. The constitutive asymmetry of the Psion's behaviour should once again give us pause in this respect: its aim is to (actively) enforce predictable behaviour amongst observers, but only to (passively) pick out predictable behaviour amongst meerkats.[11] That distinction suggests that the science of behaviour requires an account in which the active unpredictability of objects meets the objective predictability of actors.

Notes

1 www.Psion.com [accessed 4 September 2011].
2 http://forum.Psion2.org/YaBB.pl
3 http://archive.Psion2.org/org2/org2dead.htm
4 http://forum.Psion2.org/YaBB.pl?board=faq_general;action=display;num=100
5 http://forum.Psion2.org/YaBB.pl?board=faq_general;action=display;num=100
6 http://web.archive.org/web/20081119150450/http://www.allaboutpl.com/wiki
7 http://archive.Psion2.org/org2/links.htm; http://www.docsware.com/zschroff/Psion2/
8 My account of the Psion could be read as a story about the 'phenomenotechnique' of behavioural units (Latour and Woolgar, 1979:64, following Bachelard (1953)), recasting those millions of behaviours in the KMP's database as a reality 'which takes on the appearance of a phenomenon by its construction through material techniques' (ibid.).
9 'The immense abyss separating things and words can be found everywhere, distributed to many smaller gaps between the clods of earth and the cubes–cases–codes of the pedocomparator' (Latour 1999:51). Like the pedocomparator (ibid.:48–50), the Psion can be seen as one of those hybrid objects that helps translate world into word, the behaviour of meerkats into the 'behaviours/lines' in the database.
10 'In all his texts on technology and society, Latour argues that social relations lack solidity and permanence without the cement of material technology. People are prey to unpredictable passions and whims; purely human bonds are soft. Without material tools, our society would be as volatile as that of baboons, who need to re-establish the social order each morning. "It is always things – and I now mean this last word literally–which, in practice, lend their 'steely' quality to the hapless 'society'"(Latour 2005:68). This claim ignores the extent to which the fickleness of people is the object of intense social scientific work, rather than being the uncontested, established fact that Latour (curiously, given his approach to facts) takes it for. The point of social science in the manipulative paradigm is to establish to what extent and under what circumstances human actions are predictable. The success of such research is often limited, but in general it contradicts the idea of unpredictability as a fundamental trait of people' (Derksen 2010:6).
11 Of course, the Psion is only one part of a broader scientific set-up which also involves modifications of the meerkats' behaviour, primarily through habituation (Candea 2010). Crucially, however, there too the

researchers are concerned with isolating the aspects of the behaviour that they have modified from the ones they have not: but that is a different and more complex story (cf. Candea, Forthcoming).

Bibliography

Altman, J. (1974) 'Observational Study of Behavior: Sampling Methods'. *Behaviour*, **49(3/4)**, 227–267.

Bachelard, G. (1953) *Le matérialisme rationnel*, Paris: Presses universitaires de France.

Candea, M. (2010) '"I fell in love with Carlos the Meerkat": engagement and detachment in human–animal relations'. *American Ethnologist*, **37(2)**, 241–258.

—— (Forthcoming) 'Habituation and Counter-effectuation: Carefully Relating to Meerkats, Scientists and Philosophers'. *Theory, Culture and Society*.

Crist, E. (1999) *Images of animals: Anthropomorphism and animal mind*, Philadelphia: Temple University Press.

Daston, L. (2000) *Biographies of scientific objects*, Chicago: University of Chicago Press.

Daston, L. and Galison, P. (2007) *Objectivity*, New York Cambridge, MA: Zone Books; distributed by the MIT Press.

Dawkins, M. (2007) *Observing animal behaviour: Design and analysis of quantitative data*, Oxford and New York: Oxford University Press.

Derksen, M. (2010) 'People as Scientific Instruments'. *Spontaneous Generations: A Journal for the History and Philosophy of Science* 4:21–29.

Despret, V. (1996) *Naissance d'une théorie éthologique:la danse du cratérope écaillé*, Synthélabo, Le Plessis-Robinson [France].

—— (2002) *Quand le loup habitera avec l'agneau*, Paris: Les empêcheurs de penser en rond.

—— (2004) 'The Body We Care for: Figures of Anthropo-zoo-genesis'. *Body and Society*, **10**, 111–134.

Foucault, M. (1988) 'Technologies of the Self'. In *Technologies of the self. A seminar with Michel Foucault* (eds, Martin, L.H., Gutman, H. and Hutton, P.H.), Amherst: The University of Massachusetts Press.

Haraway, D. J. (1989) *Primate visions: Gender, race and nature in the world of modern science*, London: Routledge.

—— (2008) *When species meet*. Minneapolis: University of Minnesota Press,.

Latour, B. (1987) *Science in action: how to follow scientists and engineers through society*, Milton Keynes: Open University Press.

—— (1996) 'On Interobjectivity'. *Mind, Culture and Activity*, **3(4)**, 228–245.

—— (1999) *Pandora's hope: Essays on the reality of science studies*, Cambridge, MA: Harvard University Press.

—— (2004) 'How to Talk About the Body? The Normative Dimension of Science Studies'. *Body and Society*, **10(2–3)**, 205.

—— (2005) *Reassembling the social: An introduction to Actor-Network Theory*, Oxford: Oxford University Press.

Latour, B. and Woolgar, S. (1979) *Laboratory life: The social construction of scientific facts*, Beverly Hills and London: Sage Publications.

Lehner, P.N. (1996) *Handbook of ethological methods*, Cambridge and New York: Cambridge University Press.

Martin, P.R. and Bateson, P.P.G. (2007) *Measuring behaviour: An introductory guide*, Cambridge and New York: Cambridge University Press.

Rees, A. (2009) *The infanticide controversy: Primatology and the art of field science*, Chicago and London: University of Chicago Press.

Rheinberger, H.-J. (1997) *Toward a history of epistemic things: Synthesizing proteins in the test tube*, Stanford, CA: Stanford University Press.

Stengers, I. (2000) *The invention of modern science*, Minneapolis: University of Minnesota Press.

Stengers, I. (2010) *Cosmopolitics, vol. 2*, Minneapolis: University of Minnesota Press.

Strum, S. and Latour, B. (1987) 'Redefining the Social Link: From Baboons to Humans'. *Social Science Information*, **26(4)**, 783.

Woolgar, S. (1991) 'Configuring the User: The Case of Usability Trials'. In *A sociology of monsters*, (ed., Law, J.), London: Routledge, pp. 57–102.

Yarrow, T. (2003) 'Artefactual Persons: The Relational Capacities of Persons and Things in the Practice of Excavation'. *Norwegian Archaeological Review*, **36(1)**, 65–73.

31

Quantitative objects and qualitative things

Ethics and HIV biomedical prevention

Mike Michael and Marsha Rosengarten

Introduction

In this chapter, we make a case for an object-oriented ethics. By this, we mean, broadly speaking, an ethics that can be seen as partially constitutive of objects and, conversely, is itself enacted by and through objects. As such, an object-oriented ethics aims to address ethics and objects as coemergent. This entails a rethinking of the object that stresses its relationality, emergence, processuality, performativity and virtuality. As such, our position can be contrasted to a more conventional understanding of objects and ethics as distinct ontological and epistemological domains, where the domain of ethics is viewed as an activity external to the presence and operation of a material object. We thus trace the role of ethics in the production of a range of objects that contribute to, and emerge from, the assemblage of human immunodeficiency virus (HIV) and, in particular, the enactment of HIV through a particular preexposure prophylactic object (a 'pill'), PrEP, as it is clinically trialled in a number of offshore sites. What we aim to show is that a conventionally understood ethics, insofar as it mobilizes a series of standardized criteria by which to assess the 'ethicality' of the trials, performs the 'pill' in particular ways. Specifically, ethics serves in the 'reduction' of the 'pill's' multiplicity and complexity to what we shall call a 'quantitative' object. Against this, we contrast other enactments that acknowledge the multiplicity and complexity of the pill in ways that can affect (i.e. impact upon and change) not only the subjects of those trials, but also the practitioners (clinicians, policy analysts, etc.). In these cases, the 'pill' can be viewed as what we call a 'qualitative thing'. However, we also suggest that, ironically, the 'pill' as a thoroughly contingent 'qualitative' thing emerges in an assemblage made complex by the reductionist operations of ethics' quantitative objects.

HIV, PREP, RCTs, ethics

In global terms, an estimated 33 million people are currently living with HIV. Driving much of the scientific research for a biomedical prevention intervention is the continuing growth of the epidemic. Something in the order of 2.5 million new HIV infections occur a year (United Nations Programme on HIV/AIDS [UNAIDS] and World Health Organization [WHO] 2007). Often, it is noted that these infections occur despite, in principle, the high level of

95 per cent protection afforded by the male condom against sexual transmission and, similarly, the 100 per cent protection possible by using new needles and syringes when injecting intravenously. As a form of preexposure prophylaxis, PrEP uses HIV antiretroviral drugs now used to treat existing HIV infections, repackaged at present as a once-a-day pill for those at risk of becoming HIV infected, analogous in part to an antimalaria pill or the contraceptive pill. The risk/benefit assessment of PrEP by its developers is informed by its 'partial'-only protection against HIV infection; current estimates based on the iPrEX trial with men who have sex with men (MSM) and transgender women found efficacy at between 44 per cent and 73 per cent depending on dosing adherence (Australian Federation of AIDS Organisations 2010: 2; US Centers for Disease Control [CDC] cited 2010; Grant *et al.* 2010). In the absence of full protection, it is probable that new infections will occur and, in the presence of what is equivalent to a form of suboptimal drug therapy, this could lead to the development of drug-resistant viruses (AIDS Vaccine Advocacy Coalition [AVAC] 2008; Paxton *et al.* 2007: 89).

Here, we examine PrEP in terms of how it is partially constituted through ethics in ways that enact it as both a stable, delimited entity and one that is fluid and emergent. By tracing the work that goes into the performance of PrEP as 'partially efficacious' and as socially and medically challenging, we want to resituate ethics as complexly implicated in the configuration of such medical interventions. To put this another way, we show that by enacting ethics (specifically, in the guise of more or less formalized 'bioethics') as a set of practices that deal *with* 'a problem' (in this instance, the problem of PrEP and its clinical trialling), the problem becomes concretized in ways that exclude a more fruitful grasp of 'what matters ethically' and, thereby, medically, socially and politically.

By raising the notion of an 'object-oriented ethics', we thus aim to show how, on the one hand, the formal bioethics that informs trials serves in the particular enactment of the PrEP pill object, whereas on the other, the object 'PrEP', in its relations with other phenomena such as the virus, antibody testing and dosing adherence, entails emergent enactments of morality in relation to both the user's role in HIV prevention and for those involved in PrEP's development. Yet formal bioethics remains indifferent to these enactments of morality and, by doing so, gives legitimacy to processes that entail unnecessarily delimited reflexive consideration. One of the primary examples that can be offered here is of the person who is prescribed PrEP having been designated as someone engaging in high-risk practices: such designations are not innocent and can in the specific circumstances of the PrEP trial compound existing discrimination in relation to sexual orientation and sexual practices. Another example concerns the necessity of HIV antibody testing, which accompanies the initial prescription of PrEP (as well as forming part of the ongoing monitoring and represcribing of PrEP). Leaving aside cost considerations and the practicalities of making such testing available (and unlike the prevention capacities of condoms, which do not discriminate with regard to the serostatus of their user), PrEP is predicated on the user being HIV seronegative. To receive PrEP may thus function to repeatedly reinstate the belief in one's seronegative status, which in turn might change one's sexual practices (e.g., reduce the use of protection). However, it is possible, given PrEP's 'partial'-only capacity to protect against HIV infection, that this status may be altered, which contributes to raising the risks of sexual practices with an unprotected seronegative sexual partner. The bioethics typically used to assess trials remains silent on these matters; they do not fall within its technical purview, which includes such concerns as volunteer consent or clinical equipoise. And yet, as we have seen, an array of ethical issues have been precipitated by the introduction of PrEP. In sum, an object-oriented ethics allows us to explore how bioethics enacts an object like a PrEP pill, but also how that object (and its peculiar bioethical enactment) generates other connections, which have their own ethical implications.

Objects and events: qualitative and quantitative

In this chapter, we assume that objects such as PrEP emerge in particular events, such as clinical trials. These events entail a range of entities and relations; in addition to the pill itself, there are HIV-negative bodies, biomedical protocols, gendered relations, HIV viruses, dosing adherent individuals, bioethical accounts and so on and so forth, which come together to make the event of the trial. These are what Whitehead (1929) would call the 'prehensions' that 'concresce' to make the actual entity or actual occasion that is a particular version of PrEP. As we can see, ethics is one element in this process of concrescence of the object 'PrEP'.

Now, we need to specify our use of the 'event' in a little more detail, primarily through Mariam Fraser's (2010) discussion of the event in Whitehead and Deleuze. Fraser notes that in contrast to Whitehead, Deleuze's version of the event is a moment at which its component entities rather than simply 'being together' also 'become together'. In 'event-uation' (the making of an event), the constitutive elements do not simply 'interact', but change in the process of that interaction or concrescence (that is, they are *intra*-active, see Barad 2007). As such, the event can be characterized by a sort of mutual changing. In the process, she argues, what emerges is not 'solutions' but better or clearer problems; that is, the event should entail what Fraser calls 'inventive problem-making'. Analytically, and ontologically, we subscribe to a Deleuzian becoming-with model of the event. However, we are also aware that events incorporate their own narrations or, to draw on Deleuze and Guattari's (1988) assemblage terminology, their own 'enunciations' (also see Irwin and Michael, 2003). There is, in other words, an accounting of the event, which can enact it in terms of 'being-with': that the various elements come together to make the event but do not shape one another.

Our contention is that bioethics (as well as biomedical accounts) are just such an enunciation. As we shall trace below, the PrEP pill can emerge (eventuate) in the trial event through the coming together of an array of elements, some of which are enacted as remaining stable in relation to it. These are the elements of measurement. They affect, but are not affected by PrEP. We call this version of PrEP 'quantitative' because it is enacted along preexisting, externally validated criteria: criteria (which might include techniques for the assessment of effectiveness, or statistical validity, or principles for ethicality) that are standardized. PrEP can thus apparently only slide up or down stabilized 'scales' whether these be nominal, ordinal or interval.[1] For PrEP as a quantitative object, its eventfulness is delimited: the events in which it emerges have futures that are constrained because the 'nature' of PrEP is seemingly constrained by its enactment through such standardized scalings. Put another way, the problem space that can be convincingly associated with this quantitative eventualization of PrEP is in large part predetermined by these standardized enactments (see, for instance, Bowker and Star 1999).

In contrast to the quantitative object, we posit the qualitative thing. Here, the prehensions that comprise PrEP and the randomized clinical trial (RCT) event, change in the process of concrescence. In combining to 'make' PrEP there is an intra-active becoming together of the various components. In this preferred form of engagement with the trial event, bioethics in its guise as standardized quasi-metric might enunciate PrEP as a quantitative object. However, bioethics itself can also become an iterative reflection shaped in its intra-action with PrEP so that it can now serve in 'posing the problem clearly' (Stengers 1997; see below) or in 'inventive problem making' (Fraser 2010). Put another way, the problem space that can be associated with PrEP as a qualitative thing is open such that any scales along which PrEP might be enacted are themselves destabilized, rendered emergent.

This distinction between quantitative object and qualitative thing is, needless to say, ideal typical (and we are of course aware of the irony of classifying these processes of eventuation and emergence with such a crude dichotomy). On this score, and again drawing a parallel with Deleuze and Guattari's work (1988), in which the qualitative maps onto deterritorialization, and the quantitative onto re/territorialization, then these go chronically hand in hand. For example, as we detail below, qualifying PrEP can require recourse to quantitative versions of PrEP.

To summarize: although for biomedicine, policy and advocacy PrEP is primarily understood as an object-like pill (distinct from ethics and the bioethical practices that inform its development), we have proposed that it be viewed as a locus of ethics: an emergent, relational and virtual thing. However, we have also suggested that the character of this emergence, relationality and virtuality is variable. PrEP and its eventuation in RCTs emerges as more or less qualitative/quantitative. In what follows, we use this analytic schema to explore the ways in which PrEP's object-ness has been enacted in relation to the conduct of RCTs.

The events of ethics: the objects of prophylaxis

In previous publications on PrEP, we have noted how, despite the scientists' enactment of PrEP as a singular, stable object, their statements suggest that PrEP is a multiple entity, highly contingent on phenomena including but not limited to the everyday matter of dosing (Rosengarten and Michael 2009a; Rosengarten and Michael 2009b). From our perspective, taking together the various issues of efficacy, dosing and resistance noted above, we see that the PrEP pill is constituted by and in a heterogeneous assemblage that includes the capacities of bodies, human sexual practices, the adaptability of 'a' virus, policy and medical strategy, to name but the most obvious. Here we begin to gain glimpses of how PrEP is embroiled in heterogeneous relations that include the human and nonhuman, the individual and the collective, the actual and virtual.

We can now examine more closely the manner in which scientists deploy a number of devices in the quest for enacting PrEP as a singularized, stabilized entity for what is seen as necessary universal or near-universal application across HIV-affected populations. The most prominent of these is a series of statistical calculations directed toward establishing PrEP's efficacy and effectiveness derived from a clinical trial setting. Efficacy is the term used to refer to the capacity of the object under trial to achieve its goal; for PrEP, it refers to the capacity of the singularized pill-object to prevent HIV infection. However, efficacy measures cannot necessarily be extrapolated to the *effectiveness of* the technology. Both Kippax (2010) and Heise *et al.* (2011) raise issues that may affect the effective use of an intervention outside the trial conditions. In the case of PrEP, for instance, effectiveness depends on access to the drugs, consistency of dosing and a host of other phenomena that inform these practices and may affect their undertaking (Kippax 2010). Hence we can say that the trial (by design) externalizes phenomena that may be constitutive of effective practice and, moreover, will be likely to vary across HIV-affected populations. Heise *et al.* (2011: 11) also note that seemingly stable measures are products of a mix of variables that, in themselves, are not stable. For instance, when modellers assess *per-sex-act* efficacy for HIV risk, there may be variables (such as the probability that the partner is HIV infected, his level of viremia phase [amount of virus in bodily fluids, usually high at initial infection and in late stages of AIDS], and other sexually transmitted infections in either partner), which can increase the opportunity for transmission through bodily fluids. Kippax (2010) and also Heise *et al.*'s (2010) critique of research measures goes some way to revealing the sort of relationality we are getting at here.

Nevertheless, within the HIV field, a view of the variables (and their *objects*) as fixed rather than coaffective continues as researchers explore possibilities for the combining of technologies. For example, a recent trial that asked women to use a diaphragm with a condom in sexual intercourse found condom use was less likely than amongst women asked to use only condoms, with the result that the former face increased levels of risk. As Rosengarten *et al.* (2008) observe, combining prevention technologies changes the way they are used: the technologies and their associated modes of practice intra–act and become with another to produce a new, unforeseen event. In the enunciations of bioethics, each of these prophylactic objects is treated quantitatively, affording its respective and given amount of protection that can be added together with that of the other. The combination 'condom–and–diaphragm' simply increases protection: the ethics here is a simple additive one; it is proportionally more ethical to encourage the use of the combination. By contrast, a becoming–with eventualization would reflect on the intra–actions of these technologies (now conceptualized as qualitative things). The complex outcome noted above serves to trouble quantitative ethics: values cannot be enacted as a part of these objects, because the value of those values changes in the events in which those objects are enacted.

In the terms elaborated above, whether it is adjudged 'efficacious' within the clinical trial, or effective beyond, in the 'real world', we see how the quantitative object PrEP is routinely enacted along a nexus of preexisting, externally validated parameters. However, although the measures provide a basis for assessing whether to go ahead with the development of the PrEP object and enable a further process of public health planning, this scaling up of PrEP as a quantitative object at once elides and ironically eventuates the more complex and emergent processes of HIV exposure and prevention.

From quantitative objects to qualitative things

In this section, we offer a brief account of the first efforts to trial PrEP and the still–resonant claims that these trials were unethical. We are aware that by returning to an earlier phase, arguably superseded by recent modes of research conduct, our investigations may seem out of step with the current state of the art. However, it is precisely in the way that the early and highly contentious beginnings of PrEP took place that we can most clearly trace the work of a distinct, singular ethics and its rendering of PrEP as a quantitative object. Against this, we are able to juxtapose PrEP as a qualitative thing. In using the term 'thing' we simply wish to underline our previous discussion, adding emphasis to the emergent and immanent aspect of PrEP. We thus draw directly on Rheinberger's (1997) dichotomy of 'epistemic things' and 'technical objects'. Accordingly, epistemic things (the objects of scientific study) physical structures, chemical reactions, biological functions 'present themselves in a characteristic irreducible vagueness ... (because they) ... embody what one does not yet know' (1997: 28). To the epistemic thing, Rheinberger counterposes 'technical objects' operationally defined as 'a wider field of epistemic practices and material cultures, including instruments, inscription devices, model organisms, and the floating theorem or boundary concepts attached to them' (1997: 29).

Our use of the Rheinberger's schema draws attention to different aspects of object and thing. In the case of PrEP, as a quantitative object, it is stabilized and rendered knowable because, as noted above, it.is part of an array of mechanisms that measure it along a number of preexisting external parameters: efficacy, effectiveness, ethicality, etc. As a qualitative thing, PrEP becomes with the parameters themselves; as such, it is necessarily marked by the virtual insofar as it 'is' in process, emergent and novel.

The early phase of establishing PrEP trials show a reliance by both researchers and the researched on bioethical principles to mediate their different interests in HIV prevention research. These principles are intended to ensure that research on human subjects is sound in its aims and design and that it is carried out in a manner where, crucially, risks are minimized; those involved in the research are fully informed and consent to the known risks and compensation is available in the event of adverse effects. In other words, bioethics are rules of conduct that may or may not accompany the science (in this case the trialling of PrEP). However, as we show, the enunciation of bioethics as a guiding set of principles not only excludes a more relational account of the field but also institutes the quantification of the object in reductionist ways. Here, the enunciations of bioethics have a performative role in how the problem and hence the 'solutions' come to be posed, at the expense of 'inventive problem-making' (Fraser 2010).

Initially, in the early 2000s, PrEP trials were designed to target epidemiologically identified groups of people with high vulnerability to HIV infection. The Cambodian and Cameroon trials sought to recruit female sex workers. In Thailand, the trial targeted injecting drug users. In 2004, as the three trials (each conducted by different investigators and funded by different donors) were recruiting, claims were made that the trials were unethical. In Cambodia, it was said that the research participants did not receive accurate information on the trial in their native language of Khymer, arrangements for medical care for adverse events were not in place and no provision was made to provide antiretrovirals for those who became infected during the trial. Similar accusations were directed at the Cameroon trial. Both were eventually closed. The perceived unethicality of the Thai trial rested on the lack of clean needle and syringe provision. Availability would have afforded such levels of protection that there would effectively no longer be a 'research population.' Although scheduled for completion in 2012 according to a monitoring service by the AIDS Vaccine Advocacy Coalition (AVAC), called PrEP Watch, the trial continues as we go to print.

The scientists involved in the three trials have defended their work in various ways. Those involved in the Cambodian and Cameroon trials claim that they were planning to make provisions for adequate counselling and information on prevention. Importantly, at the time, the absence of follow-up treatment for those testing HIV positive at the recruitment stage or during the course of the trial would not have been deemed unethical by the then international standards (see WHO/UNAIDS 2004). In Thailand, the trial scientists defended their trial design by explaining that they were forbidden from providing clean needles and syringes by a combination of a US Congressional ruling that research funds cannot be spent on the provision of clean needles and syringes and by Thai Government Policy (International AIDS Society 2005: 17). Ethical grounds for proceeding with the trial were thus based on the provision of bleach for users to sterilize their needles for reuse and on the stated local availability of clean needles and syringes for purchase (Mills *et al.* 2005: 1404, 1405). In each defended case, the trial investigators made no reference to conditions contributing to HIV vulnerability. Notably, in Cambodia and Cameroon, women are drawn into sex work because of extreme poverty, and the occupation itself has no protection from violence. In Thailand, there had been a so-called 'war on drugs' by the government. A Human Rights Watch report (2004) states that, although government policy was supposedly targeting traffickers, sections of the police (who were paid accordingly) had, by 2004, killed over 2,000 people, many of whom were never proved to be involved in drugs, least of all trafficking. The same report notes that this created a culture of terror and many people still fear that purchasing needles could lead to accusations of trafficking and thus put their lives in danger.[2]

To echo previous remarks, the application of bioethics is a core part of the enactment of the quantitative object in clinical trials. Working in tandem with the presumptions of science as an appropriately disinterested activity, bioethics enables science to constitute its object (in this case PrEP eventuated in its trialling) as ethically legitimate. This is in part because bioethics entails an operation of selection and exclusion that cannot address whether its ethical standards are relevant, let alone applicable, in the events of different assemblages (for instance, in relation to grossly divergent socioeconomic conditions, with their dramatically varying levels of health and medical infrastructure).

As such, bioethics is integral simultaneously to the reductionist formulation of the issues around trialling and to the subsequent problems that arise through the complexity of the assemblage into which clinical trials are introduced. That is to say, the PrEP that is quantitatively adjudged an ethical object in trials becomes enacted as qualitative thing as it is remade through the particular eventuation of the trial, in the process, at least in principle, undercutting that which once constituted bioethics. For example, even if the concerns of the Cambodian and Cameroon protestors were addressed (as they have been in more recent trials), this would not have altered the problems now seen to arise with PrEP roll-out. These emergent issues, which can be seen to characterize PrEP, include: the risk of potential drug side-effects in otherwise healthy individuals; possible increases in HIV treatment drug resistance; 'risk compensation', whereby users and/or their sexual partners may assume that PrEP can replace, rather than contribute to, the protection offered by condoms; the resource implications of PrEP roll-out on an already inadequate local and national health infrastructure. The emphasis of ethics on gaining informed consent (as noted above) and thus ensuring community agreement for HIV prevention trials enacts PrEP as a quantitative object that emerges as a finite entity with specifiable properties. What is lost, and ironically precipitated, through such bioethical enactments (that is, their enunciations) are PrEP's multiple, constitutive relations: relations that enable particular effects and affects to come into being.

We have already pointed to some of the more proximal relations that make up PrEP: relations embodied in subject bodies and mediated through sexual and social conduct. However, these relations can take contorted and distal forms. For instance, for a population to be experimentally attractive (that is, to afford the generation of statistically significant results), it must be susceptible to sufficient numbers of infections. Populations in the UK and USA, for instance, are not suitable because they have access to treatment and prevention and, therefore, are not nearly as likely to become infected (WHO/UNAIDS 2004: 1). Such infections are not caused by the agent under trial; however, the relatively heightened likelihood of infection, by dint of poor healthcare infrastructure for instance, forms the ground (the material conditions of possibility) on which ethics comes to operate (MacQueen *et al.* 2007: 554). In sum, such ethical standards as consent, risk minimization and compensation provision, at once makes a PrEP trial 'quantifiable' in a highly delimited sense, peripheralizes a host of other relations and ironically can serve to precipitate the movement of those relations into the political limelight thus 'qualifying' PrEP.

Conclusion: it's a thing of quality ...

As a counterexample to the enactment of PrEP as quantitative object, we refer to an essay by Isabelle Stengers (1997) in which she celebrates a distinctive feature of the early phase of the HIV/AIDS epidemic. She explains that the 'AIDS Event,' as she calls that period, 'is characterized by the choice of not yielding to the urgency of the strictly medical problem, of resisting demagogic and security-seeking temptations, in other words of trying to actually *pose the problem clearly*' (1997: 216). Posing the problem *clearly*, in this context, meant enacting the combination, rather than the more usual separation, of technique and ethics. It meant instituting measures that were technically well formulated because they acted in the interests of those who were living with HIV (either already infected or at risk) to facilitate prevention. Such measures can be contrasted with the more common practices of identifying risk categories, instituting compulsory testing, identifying and isolating infected individuals, which would not have been effective. These latter proposed interventions were resisted early on because of their moralizing nature and the likelihood of creating a culture of denial. In countries where the resistance met with political success (e.g., Australia, Western Europe and Canada), growth of the epidemic was significantly less than, for instance, the USA.

The AIDS Event may stand as a remarkable moment in posing the problem clearly. Adapting Stengers, we might put it this way: the eventualization of the problem incorporated those to whom the solutions were addressed, enabling a becoming-with that redemarcated both the problem and the solutions. This has not been the case with PrEP. It has been and continues to be enacted as a quantitative object, situated along preset dimensions of medical and ethical parameters.

Importantly, the achievement of 'quantification' is not just driven by a scientific rationale that enacts the epidemic as comprised of two actors: fallible embodied subjects and lethal virus requiring mediation by a biomedical object and in this instance, a pill. It is also driven by a type of historical amnesia that fails to take into account, and potentially work with, the historical contingencies active in the everyday local enactment of PrEP. That is, by abstracting out the 'messiness' of science, it does not deal with what affects the occurrence of infections. For those protesting against the trials in Cambodia or Cameroon, there was more at stake than good information and provision of medical care for those who experienced side-effects or became infected within the duration of the trial. In place of a problem of high rates of HIV infection that transformed female sex workers into suitable research subjects, those involved in developing biomedical prevention might ask: How have these people come to be so HIV vulnerable? What relations would a biomedical prevention object have to embody in its design to tackle this vulnerability? Who might be able to contribute to answering these questions or refine such questions to make them more responsive to the interests of the vulnerable? Or, relatedly, what are the specificities of the extended assemblage that might be reworked in order to prevent HIV? These questions (which reflect responsiveness to local exigencies) are intended to show how the PrEP pill could also be enacted as a 'qualitative thing'. This would involve a recognition of the conditions that bring it into being and how it changes as its constituent relations change: relations that straddle and blur the ethical, technical, biomedical and political. Indeed, in the Thai situation, it would enable the inclusion of moves to legitimize free needle exchanges, elsewhere well shown to *prevent* HIV without medical or political risk (see for example Gibson *et al.* 2001; Hunter *et al.* 2000).[3]

In other words, what is required is giving up an intensely problematic enactment of PrEP as if its dimensions are predetermined rather than negotiable and emergent. In Stengers' (2005) cosmopolitical terms, we might say that the qualitative thing by virtue of its processual character is an 'event' in which multiple, heterogeneous actors come together to negotiate its character. However, within that event, those actors themselves are open to change; they become together, just as in Stengers' account of early HIV history, some governments found themselves changing insofar as, albeit contingently, they moved away from easy moralization (itself a form of quantification) to rearticulate the 'HIV problem'.

Notes

1 It should be clear that our version of the 'quantitative' includes more qualitative categories. Our key point is that such forms of standardization and measurement preexist their objects. As such this echoes the notion of qualqulation introduced by Franck Cochoy and developed, for example, by Callon and Law (2005).

2 Even as this article was going to press, Human Rights Watch was continuing to document cases of killing suspect drug dealers: http://www.hrw.org/en/news/2010/06/30/thailand-investigate-killing-handcuffed-drug-suspect retrieved 20 March 2012.

3 Although the HIV field is aware that clinical trials provide opportunities to address broader issues in prevention, capacity building, building of infrastructure, etc., our argument suggests that these opportunities will inevitably be delimited by the exclusionary activities of quantification (see for example, AVAC, 2008: 10).

Bibliography

Australian Federation of AIDS Organisations (2010) Briefing Paper, 25 November.

AIDS Vaccine Advocacy Coalition (AVAC) (2008) *Anticipating the Results of PrEP Trials*, New York: AVAC. http://www.avac.org/ht/a/GetDocumentAction/i/3120 retrieved 13 January 2010.

AVAC PrEP Watch http://www.avac.org/ht/d/sp/a/GetDocumentAction/i/3618 retrieved 13 January 2010.

Akrich, M. (1992) 'The de-scription of technical objects', in W.E. Bijker and J. Law (eds), *Shaping Technology/Building Society*, Cambridge, MA: MIT Press.

Akrich, M. and Latour, B. (1992) 'A summary of a convenient vocabulary for the semiotics of human and nonhuman assemblies', in W.E. Bijker and J. Law (eds), *Shaping Technology/Building Society*, Cambridge, MA: MIT Press.

Barad, K. (2007) *Meeting the Universe Halfway*, Durham, NC: Duke University Press.

Bennett, J. (2010) *Vibrant Matter*, Durham, NC: Duke University Press.

Bowker, G.C. and Star, S.L. (1999) *Sorting Things Out: Classification and its Consequences*, Cambridge, MA: MIT Press.

Callon, M. and Law, J. (2005) 'On qualculation, agency, and otherness', *Environment and Planning D: Society and Space*, 23: 717–33.

CDC (2010) Statement on Results of iPrEx Trial Examining Pre-Exposure Prophylaxis (PrEP) for HIV Prevention among Men Who Have Sex with Men http://www.cdc.gov/nchhstp/newsroom/iPrExMediaStatement.html retrieved 1 July 2011.

Deleuze, G. and Guattari, F. (1988) *A Thousand Plateaus: Capitalism and Schizophrenia*, London: Athlone Press.

Fraser, M. (2010) 'Facts, ethics and event', in C. Bruun Jensen and K. Rödje (eds), *Deleuzian Intersections in Science, Technology and Anthropology*, New York: Berghahn Press.

Gibson, D.R., Flynn, N.M. and Perales, D. (2001) 'Effectiveness of syringe exchange programs in reducing HIV risk behavior and HIV seroconversion among injecting drug users', *AIDS*, 15(11): 1329–41.

Grant, R., Lama, J., Anderson, P., McMahan, Liu A., Vargas, L. *et al.* (2010) 'Pre-exposure chemoprophylaxis for HIV prevention in men who have sex with men', *The New England Journal of Medicine*, 363: 2587–99.

Grant, R.M., Buchbinder, S., Cates, W., Clarke, E., Coates, T., Cohen, M.S., Delaney, M., Flores, G., Goicochea, P., Gonsalves, G., Harrington, M., Lama, J.R., MacQueen, K.M., Moore, J.P., Peterson, L., Sanchez, J., Thompson, M. and Wainberg, M.A. (2005) 'AIDS: promote HIV chemoprophylaxis research, don't prevent it', *Science*, 30, September: 2170–1.

Heise, L.L., Watts, C., Foss, A., Trussell, J., Vickerman, P., Hayes, R. and McCormack, S. (2011) 'Apples and oranges? Interpreting success in HIV prevention trials', *Contraception*, 83: 10–15.

Highmore, B. (2011) *Ordinary Lives: Studies in the Everyday*, London: Routledge.

Human Rights Watch Thailand (2004) 'Not enough graves: the war on drugs, HIV/AIDS, and violations of human rights', June 2004, Vol. 16, No. 8 (C).

Hunter, G.M., Stimson, G.V., Judd, A. *et al.* (2000) 'Measuring injecting risk behaviour in the second decade of harm reduction: a survey of injecting drug users', *Addiction*, 95: 1351–61.

International AIDS Society (IAS) (2005) 'Building collaboration to advance HIV prevention: global consultation on Tenofovir pre-exposure prophylaxis research', report of a consultation convened by the International AIDS Society on behalf of the Bill and Melinda Gates Foundation, US National Institutes of Health and US Centers for Disease Control and Prevention, September.

Irwin, A. and Michael, M. (2003) *Science, Social Theory and Public Knowledge*, Maidenhead, Berks: Open University Press/McGraw-Hill.

Kippax, S. (2010) 'Reasserting the social in a biomedical epidemic: the case of HIV-prevention', paper presented at Reframing the Social conference, London, UK, 5 March.

MacQueen, K., Namey, E., Chilongozl, D.A., Mtweve, S.P., Mlingo, M., Morar, N., Reid, C., Ristow, A., Sahay. S. and the HPTN 035 Standard of Care Assessment Team (2007) 'Community perspectives on care options for HIV prevention trial participants', *AIDS Care*, 19: 554–60.

Mills, E.J., Sing, S., Sing, J.A., Orbinski, J.J., Warren, M. and Upshur, R.E. (2005) 'Designing research in vulnerable populations: lessons from HIV prevention trials that stopped early', *British Medical Journal*, 331: 1404, 1405.

Paxton, L.A., Hope, T. and Jaffe, H.W. (2007) 'Pre-exposure prophylaxis for HIV infection: what if it works?' *Lancet*, 370: 89–93.

Rheinberger, Hans-Jörg (1997) *Toward a History of Epistemic Things: Synthesizing Proteins in the Test Tube*, Stanford: Stanford University Press.

Rosengarten, M. and Michael, M. (2009a) 'Rethinking the bioethical enactment of drugged bodies: on the paradoxes of using anti-HIV drug therapy as a technology for prevention', *Science as Culture*, 18: 183–99.

Rosengarten, M. and Michael, M. (2009b) 'The performative function of expectations in translating treatment to prevention: the case of HIV pre-exposure prophylaxis or PrEP', *Social Science and Medicine*, 69: 1049–55.

Rosengarten, M., Michael, M., Mykhalovskiy, E. and Imrie, J. (2008) 'The challenges of technological innovation in HIV', *Lancet*, 372: 357–8.

Stengers, I. (2005) 'The cosmopolitical proposal', in B. Latour and P. Webel (eds), *Making Things Public*, Cambridge, MA: MIT Press.

Stengers, I. (with Ralet, O.) (1997) 'Drugs: ethical choice or moral consensus', in I. Stengers *Power and Invention: Situating Science*, Minneapolis, London: University of Minneapolis Press.

UNAIDS and WHO (2007) 'AIDS epidemic update.' Report produced by Joint United Nations Programme on HIV/AIDS (UNAIDS) and World Health Organization (WHO).

Whitehead, A.N. (1929) *Process and Reality. An Essay In Cosmology*, New York: The Free Press.

WHO/UNAIDS (2004) 'Treating people with intercurrent infection in HIV prevention trials'. Report from a WHO/UNAIDS consultation, Geneva 17–18 July 2003, *AIDS*, 18(15): 1–12.

32

Potentialities and possibilities of needs assessment

Objects, memory and crystal images

Chris McLean

> The warnings issued by the Royal College of Psychiatrists about the fate of psychiatric services in the UK will ring true for mental health workers and patients alike. The huge pressures put on inpatient units, the shortage of beds and the often unnecessary and intrusive bureaucracy all contribute to lowering standards of care. This, combined with a reduction in the number of trainee psychiatrists and increasing difficulty in obtaining visas for overseas workers, spells gloom for the future of mental health. Ministers are being exhorted to act now, before this dreadful situation becomes irreversible. But what action should they take?'
>
> (Darian Leader, 21 June 2011, reproduced by permission of *The Guardian*)

You only need to glance through the newspapers and government reports, and listen to media stories and individuals' accounts of their experiences of mental health care, to be absorbed into a plethora of images, issues and controversies. These include concerns relating to the shift from 'asylum-based care' to 'care in the community' and increasing levels of bureaucracy and form filling, leaving less time for patient care. After the shift to 'community care', some claim a crisis of control or a greater risk to society and individuals, whereas others, in response to their individual experiences, call for changes in the way we manage and organize mental health care locally. These accounts are often reframed and aligned to specific 'problems', 'facts' and 'regimes of truth', such as questions of control, communication, cost, supervision, priorities, budgets and the process of risk and needs assessment.

The chapter focuses on a specific set of issues concerning the introduction of specific regimes and sets of 'truth'- and 'object'-making practices associated with the shift to 'community care', the process of needs assessment and the organization and management of mental health care. This involves examining how we conceptualize certain objects and relations by observing how the ordering of things (including what is considered to be the right thing to do, or the right way to understand a problem) is repeated into 'existence'. This process of repetition relates to the assembling of different actions, intensities and sets of relations which play a role in producing, at one and the same time, practices of regulation (e.g., specific standards, metrics and prompts) and instances of repetition through alterity (via different and non-standard forms). In other words, the chapter is concerned with reconsidering how standardization is viewed, not only in terms of the messy multitude of potentialities and possibilities, but also the performativity of materially relational scripts and orderings that underlie this process of managing and organizing 'community care' (e.g., needs assessment schedule [NAS]). This includes exploring the heterogeneity, localized practices and modes of organizing associated with certain cases of the needs assessment process; specific forms of repetition through difference, and how what counts as organizational 'facts', 'problems' and 'solutions' is performed and constructed through these practices and sets of relations.

My interest in these research issues developed during a long-term study of a National Health Service (NHS) mental health care trust and its implementation and audit of the Care Programme Approach (CPA). In particular, the study focused on the development of an NAS, which was seen as a fundamental aspect of the CPA[1] and a multidisciplinary team approach. The empirical research allowed an in-depth and detailed exploration of the different problems, relations and interconnections between specific controversies, regimes of truth-making and the different struggles and 'gaps' underlying everyday practice (Latour 2005). For example, evaluating how best to manage the care of the 'mentally ill' within the community setting, the trust focused on several different areas of concern. These included: how to assess the patient's past, current and potential status in terms of their needs and levels of risk (to themselves and others); ensuring, in a confidential manner, the 'effective' communication of 'reliable' information to all the parties involved; and providing 24-hour care and access to information for a wide range of service users. The process in and through which particular objects (such as the NAS) are made the basis for reorganizing how mental health care is ordered is thus fundamental to this process, especially in terms of the relation between practitioners and patients and negotiations over assessment and care.

The research was conducted within a mental health and social care trust, which has approximately 12,000 service users (around 3 per cent of the local population) within a region in the UK. It began with a two-year study based on an ethnographic style of investigation (e.g., participant and non-participant observation, informal chats, interviews, documentary evidence, etc.), which mainly focused on the implementation and audit of a CPA and the shift towards 'care in the community' (referred to in this chapter as Review One). A central theme underlying the CPA included greater levels of communication, coordination and control with regards to the care planning process (e.g., through multiagency team working, regular reviews and a specific role for a CPA coordinator[2] to liaise between different groups, assessing needs and risk, performing reviews, etc)[3]. During the first phase, I worked with the CPA coordinator to explore the introduction of the CPA within the trust, the CPA audit team, as well as interviewing and observing the practices of many different clinicians. This was followed by another period of research two years later, in which I returned to the department to study the introduction of a 'new' needs assessment form (NAS). This second phase of study (referred to in this chapter as Review Two) began with meetings with the designer of the form to discuss the role of a new assessment form and plans to develop it further. Between the first and second phase of research, there had been an increased amalgamation of social service and mental health care. This involved workers from different specialisms (community psychiatric nurses [CPNs], social workers, occupational health) being assembled together in Community Mental Health Teams under one roof. Furthermore, there were various changes in the organizational structure, geographical location and working practices of different clinicians. For instance, clinicians were required to complete new forms of documentation and follow different standardized practices within their new teams, and this was raising various issues and concerns.

One of the new forms of joint assessment within the trust was the NAS. The format of the NAS includes a header page with biographical information, a score sheet with a summary of the ratings (0–4) on the next page, and the following pages contain textual sections relating to the twenty areas of need. These different areas of need included self-care and diet, psychological health, safety to self and others, alcohol and drugs, employment, accommodation, social contacts, sexual expression, stigma and harassment. When first looking at a form such as the NAS, it is difficult to escape the feeling that such a 'standardized' form of assessment is going to play a significant and determining role in the practices of clinicians. The format of the form and the ratings on the score sheet lead to a feeling of objectivity, with a series of quantified numerical ratings alongside the qualitative textual responses within the form. Although this process seeks to instil an air of stability, continuity and standardization in the needs assessment process, discussions and observations of the everyday practice of clinicians highlighted the many qualitatively different events, variations, affects, potentialities and possibilities underlying this process of form filling and assessment. In order to examine the complexity underlying the needs assessment event, a greater understanding of the diverse sets of relations is required. This includes how different intensities and 'historical' traces are continually advancing and spreading in all directions and being assembled via specific acts of engagements, practices and memory traces (e.g., a patient's mental health history, his/her relationship with the clinician and mental health system, as well as the practices of organizing clinicians in their everyday work). It could also be seen as a kind of overspilling of both affect and relational intensity that the form cannot contain. Indeed, the shift towards a more user-led approach, which encouraged patients/users/clients to participate further in the process of assessment, was seen by many clinicians as a desirable aim. However, paradoxically, many described the problems with this form-filling process and raised concerns over how the process could end up marginalizing the complexity of the relational negotiation between the clinician and patient (e.g., in terms of assessing and recording the patient's most pressing needs). The desire for a needs–led approach was expressed by Paul, a Service Manager in the trust, who felt that this way of working was important and that:

> …. what we should be saying is 'why do they need a hospital bed'; do they need somewhere to stay because they have no accommodation, somewhere to titrate their medication or observation for 24 hours a day. These are things we should be assessing … We need to change the service away from the idea of service delivery and towards a needs–led approach which can adapt the services to these needs.
>
> *(Paul, Service Manager, Review One)*

This focus on user needs was also highlighted in my first meeting with the designer of a new NAS, when he talked about the importance of developing a relationship of trust through a conversational style of assessment and the notes attached to the NAS:

> The Care Schedule is not a standardised and specific measure of clients' needs or strengths. Negotiating issues at the client-worker level is a balance of user information and professional judgement, but if some discussion about the nature and severity of problems can be undertaken, and simple ratings made, certain things become possible. Firstly, care planning with clients becomes an open process in which the client has a clear, if not always final say. Secondly, programme fidelity is more likely – workers will be seen to be doing what they say they intend to do. Lastly, workers and clients have some evidence of the results of the work undertaken which both parties can rate and discuss, with a view to determining shortfall in resources, dissatisfaction, care plan changes, etc.
>
> *(NAS Explanatory Notes, Review One)*

Although the designer of the form points out that the NAS is not a standard form, it was clear that some clinicians viewed it as a way of standardizing care (both in a 'positive' and 'negative' sense).

---

1. ACCOMMODATION

Look for: Is client homeless? Does s/he like current accommodation? Are there any problems with neighbours, other tenants, landlord? Is home over-crowded, or under-furnished? Household amenities: bathroom, décor, heating, kitchen facilities. Are there any problems with wiring, lighting, plumbing, drains?

Note: how service user manages, strengths, views; other agencies/personnel involved; source(s)
Date and worker ID

Rating:

The designer also highlighted the problems of performing a holistic assessment, which covers the different areas such as social need, psychological/mental health need, and needs relating to occupational health. Although clinicians may have a wide range of experience in their areas of speciality, he believed that the NAS would help in providing more detailed assessments in those areas in which the worker may have less experience. The example of accommodation above shows the prompts under each heading relating to each area of need, and the textual and numerical spaces to be completed by the clinician in conversation with the client.

Depending on many factors that underlie the needs assessment event, many possibilities subsist: one relates to the creation of a series of ratings of the patient's needs. However, the rating does not exist either as some independent and objective thing 'out-there' (the obvious, self-evident 'truth' of the matter) nor is it simply a subjective interpretation or clinician's individual perspective. Rather, the rating is always in a state of 'becoming': a process that relies on various negotiated encounters emerging through relations between the virtual and actual; a relationship that produces many different actualized virtualities (Deleuze 1994).

Repeating needs through difference

This focus on the constant process of becoming (of subjects, objects and relations) is analytically useful because it brings to our attention the question of the relationship between 'virtuals' and 'actuals'. In this case, this includes the becoming of specific medical regimes of truth, patients, clinicians, needs, risk, trust, to name but a few. Central to this chapter is the need to overcome a representational approach, in which research objects are either viewed as existing in some discrete or substantive form 'out-there' or as nothing more than the different interpretations, perspectives and constructions in the researcher's 'mind'. There is also a need to avoid the reification of research objects into discrete analytical categories (e.g., 'culture'; 'structure'; 'individual') or in the case of this research, the unexamined concepts of an 'organization', a 'patient', an 'assessment', a 'diagnosis', etc. In other words, rather than taking for granted and black-boxing these categories of what is said to exist, what is most interesting is how these things are repeated into action as matters of fact or matters of concern (Latour 2005).

For Latour (2005), in addition to the image of 'sameness' and 'stability' relying on the assemblage of difference through a process of continual becoming; subsistence and endurance are provisional, because the performance of order is constantly under threat: revolt, resistance, breakdown, conspiracy and alternatives are everywhere.

Difference, in one sense, is the substantial side of things, what they have most in common and what makes them most different. One has to start from this difference and to abstain from trying to explain it, especially by starting with identity, as so many persons wrongly do. Because identity is a minimum and, hence, a type of difference, and a very rare type at that, in the same way as rest is a type of movement and the circle a type of ellipse. To begin with some primordial identity implies at the origin a prodigiously unlikely singularity, or else the obscure mystery of one simple being then dividing for no special reason.

(Tarde 1999:73 as cited in Latour 2002)

Although for Tarde 'to exist is to differ' and for Strathern (1991:37) 'to include is to alter', by recognizing the role of difference in repetition, both statements seek to question notions of representation associated with an idea of independent identities existing out-there or in the mind and endurance through sameness and inertia.[4] The focus is then on exploring the continual process of assemblage (acts of engagement in which different entities, intensities and possibilities coalesce) and mediation (including those acts and organizing practices involved in the constitution of facts). Rethinking difference and repetition in this way allows a wealth of concepts and terms to be drawn upon and reconsidered (e.g., objects, process, events, practices, relations, actions, materiality, potentiality, possibility, etc.).[5] This includes reflecting on the overflowing absences, discontinuities, displacements, and the different forces, intensities and sensations that are continuously folding, intersecting and producing further spaces and acts of engagement. For example, Cooper (1998:108) refers to this as the unknowable and excessive, which can provide the sources of energy and possibilities through a 'flux and flow of unfinished, heteromorphic organisms' (Law 2004:117). For Latour, modernity (or amodernity) grows out of the intersection between the purity of objective forms on the one hand and the inevitable proliferation of impurities, heterogeneities and hybrids on the other (Law 2004:82). With the desire for purity comes a host of hybrids (or with order comes mess). Underlying each of these approaches is a common thread that involves attending to how 'things' 'endure' via the many interlacing chains and traces of action that sustain them and how they require the support of many 'others' and heterogeneous acts of mediation to 'exist'.

In addition, rather than assuming that space and time are given in the order of things in some isotopic or isochronic form (Jones *et al.* 2004; Latour, 1997), Latour emphasizes the importance of studying the ways in which images of linearity, isotopy and isochrony are produced.[6] Such a shift towards non-representational modes of knowing (Thrift 1996; Crang and Thrift 2000)[7] requires a focus on associations, nests of relationships and difference; a lack of direct 'access' to the unknowable and otherness; researchers adopting a position that provides the 'modesty' suggested by both Nigel Thrift and Donna Haraway ('modest witness'); and the development of conceptual strategies that allow us to rethink relations, space and time in a productive manner. Along with this call to reduce an excessive desire for coherence and linearity in which stability and multiplicity cannot easily coexist or overlap, we also need to consider how this relates to how we study people and objects with regards to processes of standardization-through-repetition, and the situated unfolding of the experiences of space and time in terms of potentiality and possibilities.

Needs assessment and the crystal image

One way in which Deleuze (2009) can help in rethinking ideas of potentiality and possibility is through the crystal image: a way of reconsidering the relationship between the virtual and actual: an image in which the forces, energy, vitality, intensities and acts of engagements within the virtual coexist with the actual. Rather than a succession of presents existing in some discrete and independent form, this time-image avoids a reliance on a chronological ordering, because it allows us to consider the many possibilities associated with each and every event (e.g., needs assessment). Thus, what emerges as 'actual' is never inevitable in relation to the range of possibilities within the virtual, which are always in a state of becoming.

The crystal or time-image is not a site of chaos and indeterminacy, nor is the actual preformed.[8] In contrast, it is a way of exploring encounters such as the needs assessment process, as profound and intense interactions in which different 'memories' and experiences come forth. For example, in some cases, these may revitalize particular 'memories' of childhood, recent family or friendship relationships or emotional issues to do with money, work and home. Rather than memories existing in the mind or some original past, memory traces may emerge through specific material and semiotic dynamics and associations.[9] Furthermore, the script of the form and what it provokes may involve many different intensities and acts of engagement (e.g., via certain prompts, modes of ordering, ratings), which would otherwise not have been elicited. The form may also appear to take on a life of its own in terms of how it comes to order and reorder the possibilities of future action, as the following example shows. In particular, the example below highlights the role of certain events, assemblages, signs and objects (e.g., ratings and forms) in evoking certain decision-making arenas. Rather than being locked into the confines of linear and chronological time, the crystal image thus provides a way of examining the actual/virtual relationship and the assembling of specific intensities, material memory traces and complex sets of associations.

Ratings, memory traces and the allocation of caseloads

In certain settings, the NAS and the related ratings (along with other practices and objects) may become part of the process of allocating patients to different levels of case worker. During the allocation review meeting, the clinicians decide on how to allocate patients over the three levels of care: CPNs tend to have large caseloads and attend to clients with less complex or shorter-term needs; Continuing Support Services (CSS) workers are at the other end of the spectrum because they deal with small caseloads and clients with complex and intensive needs; finally, in the middle, there are Case Managers, who have medium caseloads and complexity/severity of need (e.g., lack of insight into mental health, problems with medication compliance, etc.).

> I'll tell you what I've found useful on the positive side – the sheet at the front where you're looking at the scoring. Cos what we do is, we move clients between the three levels of the service. I found that useful because I can actually say to people 'well this guy was scoring five on accommodation needs and that in effect means his score on psychological health was high, his engagement was bad, and his safety was at risk because he was homeless'. So someone who was scoring 4s and 5s all the way down gets accommodation and that immediately brought all the scores down. So I was able so go to the review meeting and say 'look this is where he was but the new accommodation has helped with all of these and he's now only scoring this ... So he's OK for a CPN service from now on. His needs can be dealt with by a CPN and not me.
>
> (*Jill, Case Manager, Review Two*)

Jill shows me the NAS score sheets and how she can easily flick through them to see how any patient's needs have shifted in terms of the ratings. This allows her to compare ratings over time and also provides a basis to discuss how they may shift the allocation of patients between levels of care. Although this may appear as a simple process of comparing figures on a sheet, it is important to consider the many negotiations that underlie such an event and how each event, in turn, relies on and produces different sets of relations and interactions. These occasions contribute to the creation of organizational 'facts' and clinical 'truths'. For example, in many cases, the ratings are taken as given and ordered in this way, whereas in others, detailed discussions ensue between the clinicians. There may be calls for further 'evidence' (e.g., patient's case notes and other assessments) and a debate over the 'ratings', 'appropriateness' and levels of care. Discussions may appear to shift between matters of 'fact' and matters of 'concern' (Latour 2005), with further questions and controversies. There may also be discussions concerning the history of the patient, their medication, the risk to themselves or others, and their housing or social conditions, and these may lead to further openings and closings (simplifications and amplifications) in terms of the organization of their care. What may be considered as the established 'clinical truth' or 'organizational fact', in certain situations, may be contested and reopened for further examination during other events.

Another example that shows the level of debate and the problems of defining needs emerged during a meeting between various clinicians relating to the introduction of the CPA and unmet needs. One of the clinicians began by describing a situation concerning an unmet accommodation need. He raised the question that if a patient was asking to be rehoused because his neighbours possessed negative feelings about him, could this be considered a 'real' unmet need? A consultant psychiatrist questioned the validity of this as an unmet real need of accommodation, because he suggested that these could be delusional feelings, requiring a change in medication. However, a social worker commented that such a request for rehousing could be seen as a 'real' need, especially if the neighbours had displayed signs of being uncomfortable with the individual's behaviour and were concerned about the behaviour of the individual in the future (i.e., they had made complaints about the individual). The social worker described how a relationship between the client and their neighbours can become strained in these situations and how certain incidents can lead to a 'real' need for rehousing. Even if they managed to stabilize the client's behaviour with medication, they highlighted that there may still be a real need in terms of moving the client to another house with new neighbours. Concerns over the issue of rating needs were also raised by Steve, a CSS worker. He was particular concerned with changing scores and what they reflect:

> If someone scores something and then two months later you ask them the same question and they score something different. It doesn't necessarily mean an improvement or deterioration. It could just mean it was scored differently the first time. There are so many reasons for that.
>
> (Steve, CSS, Review Two)

Not only did these differences and concerns underlie the construction of organizational and clinical facts and truths within the department and through different events, but also the continual need to negotiate, repair and fill any 'gaps' associated with the everyday practices of mental health care. Therefore, even while some may see the NAS as merely standardizing care, there is a continuous process of mediation that underlies these practices of assembling the 'truth' and the making of clinical or organizational 'facts'. This includes highly specific situated practices that may subvert certain 'rules' and forms of 'standardization' through different sets of relations and possibilities. For instance, when performing the needs assessment, the clinicians might take notes during the visit and then complete the form in the car or in the office. Alternatively, although they might take the form along to the visit, they may focus merely on those areas that they believe are relevant at that moment (e.g., ensuring their client's psychological health is stabilized may be prioritized or they may focus on certain social needs such as money, accommodation and/or relationships). This might involve them going against the recommended two-week completion period, especially for areas that are particularly difficult for that patient (e.g., sexuality). These variations were often linked to the importance of developing a therapeutic relationship of trust, as explained by Sam, a senior clinical nurse within the trust:

> The NAS is only a tool to use; it doesn't dictate care. It uses a way of measuring and getting some form of objective scoring, but it doesn't mean you're driven by the form itself. If you don't have a reasonable therapeutic relationship with the person, you won't get past first question anyway.
>
> *(Sam, Senior Clinical Nurse, Review Two)*

In fact, the clinicians described how they use different practices and techniques to ensure 'good' clinical practice, even though on occasions they may appear to go against 'good' management practice (Garfinkel 1967). Furthermore, whereas Sam felt that the form would not determine practice, various clinicians raised concerns about how certain aspects underlying the form affect everyday practice. This included problems such as fully completing the form within the given period in specific cases; the increased level of paperwork for some patients, who require a 'simpler' form of assessment (taking the clinician away from their 'real' work); the accountability of the clinician in terms of the completion of the form (e.g., record-keeping for management or possible future court cases), and how the patient may respond to the form. This highlights how clinicians are often faced with requirements to implement certain 'rules' or 'standards', while at the same time considering the needs of clinical and organizational practice: needs that on occasions can be contradictory. For instance, Jill described how you have to adapt the process of needs assessment to fit with the specific client:

> I don't think you can expect a person to talk spontaneously when you're trying to write it all down. A lot of my clients have a long history of mental health problems and they hate interviews and assessments ... For some of them, I have done it and they've not known I've been doing it. I've gone along with a few categories in my head and just talked through them and come back to the office and filled them in. The trouble was when the Care Schedule came in and we started using it, some of my clients knew me really well and if I'd started asking them some of the questions on the Care Schedule they'd said 'well you know all this, what are you asking me this for?' It would have sounded quite patronising ... Also when you first get to know a person, the response you get is not as accurate as you want it to be. You need to get to know people so that you can prompt them in the right areas.
>
> *(Jill, Case Manager, Review Two)*

Consequently, many different intensities are continually firing off in different directions and producing many possibilities through the mass of energy, forces and vitality within the virtual arena. As discussed earlier, this is neither a space of indeterminacy and chaos, nor a place in which entities exist *in potentia*, waiting to be realized. It is only through the relational nature of the actual/virtual (e.g., through specific performances and negotiations) that many possibilities transpire through various acts of engagement, and foldings, as well as discontinuities and displacements. In practice, this can involve a constant shifting between matters of 'concern' and matters of 'fact' within truth-making settings and events. This can raise serious difficulties for any clinician when attempting to decide on what 'matters' and how to proceed (e.g., in terms of assessment and care). The clinicians involved in mental health care clearly become 'experts' in considering the many possibilities and eventualities related to the care of patients with complex needs.

However, as you look more closely at specific examples of mental health care, it becomes interesting to reflect on the many different ways of making a difference, as well as the particular standards that seek to focus the process. By providing more in-depth studies of the organizing practices and processes that underlie clinical and organizational events, we can begin to explore the emergence of 'facts' and 'truths' in relation to the power of certain kinds of objects, like NASs. This includes the role they play in bringing about particular transformations of relations (e.g., between the patient, clinician and the service) and what is made to matter in future health care.

Finally, four specific areas of interest come to mind in relation to the study of standards, potentialities and possibilities: First, how can we explore the role of standards in relation to the notions of difference and repetition; stability and change; space and time given that there is never repetition of the same? Second, how do we understand the making of 'facts' and 'truths' in relation to standards and standardization; and how do the practices and processes associated with standardization produce on the one hand openings and opportunities, and on the other, closings, which in some cases can appear to stifle, limit or constrain localized and creative processes? Third, how can we encourage forms of standardizing that produce moments of adventure and experimenting that are seen as productive to those within the given settings? Finally, how can the ideas of the crystal image provide a way of rethinking memory that avoids a focus on some original form or merely an event of recovery in the mind; and how can we explore the different material memory traces that can play a significant role in the process of repetition through specific sets of relations and assemblages (e.g. NAS)? In conclusion, can we find ways of avoiding accounts that rely on problematic ideas of originating determinacy, sameness and representation, or become lost in the milieu of ambiguity and indeterminacy? In contrast, how do we reflect on ideas of possibilities and potentialities in relation to the issues of space and time; stability and change; and difference and repetition? For Whitehead, this would involve exploring the 'becoming of continuity' rather than a convergence on the 'continuity of becoming' (Whitehead 1978: 68–9). Such a move also involves a shift from being and identity to ideas of stability and change via multiplicity and discontinuities. Thus, when seeking to study 'problems' and controversies underlying mental health care and needs assessment, how can we draw on a radical empiricism (akin to the ideas of William James and developed further in the work of Deleuze, Latour and many other writers) that would help in providing a 'modest' rethinking of becoming objects, memory, spaces and times through concepts such as the crystal image?

Notes

1 The CPA was associated with a more systematic care planning through greater documentation, standardization, user involvement, regular reviews and multiagency working (e.g. encouraging greater coordination, and communication and information sharing between those involved in the care of the patient) (DOH, 1990; 2001).
2 A variety of clinical workers can take on the CPA coordinator role (e.g., Community Psychiatric Nurse [CPN], social workers, occupational health worker).
3 At the time of the research a patient would either be on an enhanced CPA if they are seen as having complex needs, or a standard CPA. However, this has changed and patients are either under the remit of the CPA or not (again depending on the complexity of their needs and the number of agencies involved in their care). There is no distinction between standard and enhanced.
4 Clearly, there is a wide and diverse literature on alterity within the anthropological literature especially relating to issues of culture otherness (e.g., Tausig's work on mimesis and alterity). This piece seeks to allude to the connections between difference and alterity with regards to those 'hidden' aspects that mediate and create further possibilities, inclusions and exclusions. However, this only scratches the surface of the many different issues and debates that underlie this area of concern.

5 For Deleuze (1994), complex repetitions are variable in the sense that they include difference within themselves. This difference and variability may be hidden and become distorted when forced to comply with limitations of representation in which difference is merely a negation of sameness. To actualize is to differentiate.

6 This raises the question of how we may understand intensities, interactions and shifting agencies, which are not always visible in the same time or place, do not exert pressure equally, are not homogeneous and can lead to different outcomes in terms of stability and multiplicity (Latour 2005).

7 Rather than a philosophy dominated by its 'object' (with a focus on a representational view in which we are searching for some correspondence with some truth 'out-there'), it is seized by what it speaks. This enables an opening to becoming Other, and a field of desire and differentiation in which twining and folding relationships are played out (Crang 2000:140).

8 Take for example, the description of the madeleine by Proust and how Deleuze (2008, 2009) develops this further in order to highlight how the biscuit dipped in the café in Paris did not relate to some original madeleine and Combray. Rather than becoming present through some memory in the mind, this concept of the crystal image provides a way of rethinking time and space as a process of becoming where times splits itself: one launched towards the future and another into the pure past (Deleuze 2009). It also explores the intercession of a 'sign event' with sensations and intensities folding and coalescing as they provide further opportunities for different possibilities. For Deleuze, this involves a 'new' Combray created as an event in its (or this) 'truth' as its internalized difference and repetition.

9 Rather than evoking some original memories contained in the mind of the patient or the form (such as uncovering something already there waiting in potential), these 'memory traces' involve many different semiotic and material traces assembling together afresh through each event. For example, different intensities relating to the introduction of the CPA, new practices of record keeping, the design of the form in terms of prompts, training, textual and ratings, new forms of community teams, risk assessment, accountability.

Bibliography

Ansell-Pearson, K. (2010) Deleuze on the Overcoming of Memory, in S. Radstone and B. Schwarz (eds.), *Memory: Histories, Theories, Debates*, Fordham University Press, pp. 61–77 and pp. 161–79.

Bergson, H. (2001) *Time and Free Will: An Essay on the Immediate Data of Consciousness*, Mineola: Dover.

Bogue, R. (2010) *Deleuzian Fabulation and the Scars of History*, Edinburgh: Edinburgh University Press.

Cooper, R. (1998) Assemblage Notes, in R. Chia (ed.), *Organized Worlds: Explorations in Technology and Organization*, London: Routledge.

Crang, M. (2000) Relics, Places and Unwritten Geographies in the Work of Michel De Certeau (1925–86), in Mike Crang and Nigel Thrift (eds.), *Thinking Space*, London: Routledge, pp. 136–153.

Crang, M. and Thrift, N. (2000) *Thinking Space*, London: Routledge.

De Certeau, M. (1983) The Madness of Vision. *Enclitic* 7(1): 24–31.

Delanda, M. (1998) *A Thousand Years of Nonlinear History*, New York: Zone Books.

Deleuze, G. (1988) *Bergsonism*, New York: Zone.

Deleuze, G. (1994) *Difference and Repetition*, London: Athlone.

Deleuze, G. (2008) *Proust and Signs*, London: Continuum.

Deleuze, G. (2009) *Cinema 2*, London: Continuum.

Department of Health (1990) Care Programme Approach. Circular HC(90)23/LASSL(90)11, London: Department of Health.

Department of Health (2001) *The Journey to Recovery – The Government's Vision for Mental Healthcare*, London: Department of Health.

Garfinkel, H. (1967) *Studies in Ethnomethodology*, Englewood Cliffs, NJ: Prentice-Hall.

The Guardian (2011) How Psychiatry Became a Damage Limitation Exercise. By Darian Leader. 21/6/2011 http://www.guardian.co.uk/commentisfree/2011/jun/21/ psychiatric-services-damage-limitation.

Jones, G., Mclean, C. and Quattrone, P. (2004) Spacing and Timing, Introduction to the Special Issue of *Organization* on Spacing and Timing, 11(6): 723–741.

Latour, Bruno (1997) Trains of Thought Piaget, Formalism and the Fifth Dimension. *Common Knowledge* 6(3).

Latour, B. (2001) Gabriel Tarde and the End of the Social, in Patrick Joyce (ed.), *The Social in Question. New Bearings in History and the Social Sciences*, London: Routledge, 117–132.

Latour, B. (2002) Gabriel Tarde and the End of the Social, in P. Joyce (ed.), *The Social and Its Problems*, London: Routledge.

Latour, B. (2005) *Reassembling the Social: An Introduction to Actor-Network Theory*, Oxford; New York: Oxford University Press.

Law, J. (2004) *After Method. Mess in Social Science Research*, London, New York: Routledge.

Linstead, S. and Thanem, T. (2007) Multiplicity, Virtuality and Organization: The Contribution of Gilles Deleuze. *Organization Studies* 28/10: 1483–1501.

Mol, A. (2002) *The Body Multiple: Ontology in Medical Practice*, Durham, North Carolina: Duke University Press.

Serres, M. and Latour, B. (1995) *Conversations on Science, Culture, and Time*, Ann Arbor, MI: University of Michigan Press.

Strathern, M. (1991) *Partial Connections*, Savage, MD: Rowman and Littlefield.

Thrift, N. (1996) *Spatial Formations*, London: Sage.

Whitehead, A.N. (1978) *Process and Reality*, New York: Free Press.

33

Digital traces and the 'print' of threat

Targeting populations in the war on terror

Alexandra Hall and Jonathan Mendel

Introduction

In the wake of the 9/11 terrorist attacks in Washington and New York (and subsequent attacks in London, Madrid and Mumbai), states have faced pressing questions about whether these attacks could have been prevented. The US 9/11 Commission, for example, accused security authorities of a 'failure of the imagination' and a failure to 'identify telltale indicators connected to the most dangerous possibilities' (Kean and Hamilton 2004: 346). A prominent theme of the war on terror ever since has been to 'connect the dots' of available information to avert security threats before they occur. Data and data analytics have become vital tools in international security efforts (Amoore and de Goede 2005; 2008).

In border security, in particular, the analysis of passenger data appears to solve the problem of how to target people who are threatening while facilitating the passage of bona fide travellers. In data-led border targeting programmes like the UK's e-Borders, the US Automatic Targeting System, and European Passenger Name Record programmes, personal passenger data are used to prescreen and risk-score passengers before travel. 'Smart' border programmes like e-Borders do not simply track arrivals and departures by scrutinizing conventional identification information from passports and visas, nor do they only chase known criminals or terrorists via watchlist checks. Rather, the analysis of passenger data promises to reveal the as-yet-unknown terrorist or criminal. Compared with crude racial or ethnic profiles, or established visual clues of 'suspicious behaviour', passenger data are heralded as an impartial way of targeting the risky subject via the digital traces that he or she leaves behind. Border security practitioners, in this way, are increasingly concerned with the digital residues of everyday life. As Detica (the security consultants responsible for the analytics for the UK e-Borders programme) put it, these data by-products form a 'digital footprint': 'a trail of ones and zeros that terrorists leave behind on the internet and in other electronic databases' (2008).

What kind of object is the 'digital footprint', and how is it related to targeting populations in contemporary security practice? The digital footprint is not an unmediated incriminating residue that is simply retrieved from mundane transactional data. It is an active, responsive abstraction, which, increasingly, is believed to provide an insight into a person's true identity and intention (see Amoore 2009; Amoore and Hall 2009). The data footprint has a particular temporal orientation to past and future. At the border, it is not used to reconstruct past events (although this is an important goal of other fields of data forensics). Nor is it an overview of an individual's life or actions, despite popular public concerns about all-encompassing border surveillance (Hayes 2009). The digital footprint, we argue, is oriented towards the unknown future. This chapter examines the digital footprint as a prominent new means of identifying populations and persons 'of interest' within border security programmes. It draws on the social and cultural history of conventional 'prints' of criminal forensic practice to show how the digital footprint is a dynamic data object, the apparent 'objectivity' of which conjures populations while ostensibly representing them, with uneven governmental effects.

The trace that 'cannot fail but be left behind'

Security consultants make frequent comparisons between the digital footprint of security practice and the prints of conventional criminal forensic investigation. Detica, for instance, refer to data traces as the 'digital DNA markers that change manifestly between law-abiding citizens and serious criminals' (Lewis 2008). Retrieving these data markers is presented as simply a matter of 'good old fashioned investigation work' augmented by new technological possibilities. Traditional forensic science is based on Edmond Locard's famous principle of exchange: 'every contact leaves a trace'. As the criminal body moves and acts, it cannot help but leave behind recoverable impressions and residues. These prints form a 'silent witness', Locard argued, which 'cannot be wrong' and which 'cannot be wholly absent' (cited in Chisum and Turvey 2000). The two most lauded forensic 'silent witnesses' (the fingerprint and the DNA profile) have locked irrefutable identity to the body (see Cole 2004; Sekula 1986; Williams and Johnson 2008). The whorls and ridges of the fingerprint, for instance, were once regarded as a 'God-given seal' of individuality and identity (Lynch *et al.* 2008: xii; Cole 2001; 2004). Nowadays, DNA is considered the indisputable body 'signature': not an impression of the body but actual somatic material, or body-data (Van der Ploeg 2003). DNA projects a 'transcendental evidential quality' within forensic criminal investigation, despite its problematic position in relation to pure, experimental science (Cole 2001; Lynch *et al.* 2008; Johnson and Williams 2007). As M'Charek (2008: 521) argues, the role for scientific intervention appears to be to simply make this forensic '"factual evidence" speak' and so retrieve 'the story of a criminal act' from inert material residues.

Locard's mantra of 'every contact leaves a trace' precisely describes the efforts made by security IT (information technology) experts to exploit potentially incriminating data by-products from everyday transactions. As security experts outline, the 'rare event' of terrorism can be seen as the culmination of a series of mundane 'mandatory' actions, purchases, communications and journeys (Agress *et al.* 2008: 171). So, although the 'threat from terrorists and criminals exploiting the information revolution is new and emerging, so too are the opportunities for detection and intervention' (Detica 2008). This is because *every action leaves a trace*. These digitized transactions and communications data form a crucial new frontier of security knowledge (Amoore and de Goede 2008). They are a new 'silent witness' which 'cannot be absent' and which 'cannot lie'. The UK e-Borders programme, for example, places centrally a passenger's data retrieved from a range of public and private databases. Data encoded in passports (Advanced Passenger Information [API]) are flushed through watchlist databases to identify *known* suspects before they travel: Is she wanted by the police? Does she have a record? Has he overstayed a visa? Has she previously claimed asylum? However, the battle to thwart the as-yet-unidentified terrorist requires a fuller picture of passengers, one that can delve beyond 'clean' appearances and 'identify terrorists and criminals attempting to blend into the travelling public' (Heyman 2011). Within international border targeting systems, analysis of the Passenger Name Record (PNR) has become a crucial means of generating this fuller picture.

The PNR is a commercial dataset generated on every occasion that someone flies. It might include credit card details for the ticketing purchase, travel agent information, travel companions and itineraries. The PNR contains data from which 'aspects of the passenger's history, conduct and behaviour can be deduced' (House of Lords 2007: 9). PNR augments the API identity check: it can be run against known risk criteria (unusual routes used for drug trafficking, last-minute third-party ticket purchases, frequent journeys to certain locations) to target suspicious people who are as yet unknown to the authorities. Developed within programmes such as the UK e-Borders, the US Computer-Assisted Passenger Prescreening System (CAPPS and CAPPS II), as well as the Automated Targeting System for Passengers (ATS-P) and the Transportation Security Administration's (TSA) troubled programme, Secure Flight, PNR data have become increasingly significant as a security resource. The UK, for instance, considers PNR data as 'an essential supply of data for the security, intelligence and law enforcement agencies … [it] is used for automated rules-based targeting in relation to unknowns; those potentially involved in terrorist and other criminal activity' (House of Commons 2011: 10). The analysis of passenger data (API and PNR) reenvisions the securitized border as a series of 'touchpoints' within a 'travel cycle': visa application, ticketing transaction, travel agent booking, airport check-in, passport swipe. Airport security screening is no longer 'something that happens at the security check-point', but is a continuum from reservation and check-in, to destination and departure again (House of Commons Home Affairs Committee 2010: 6).

Pixelated passengers

The security practitioners' claim for the usefulness of 'digital DNA markers' invokes the apparent neutrality, ubiquity and impartiality of forensic evidence: impossible not to leave, waiting to be discovered. Yet the securitized border touchpoint is more accurately the place where a passenger becomes pixelated into multiple transactions, journeys, associations and then recomposed. The digital footprint is not a single coherent recoverable trace, but a mutable data abstraction and visualization: the 'digitized dissection' of the subject into identifying traces, from which composite projections can be made (Amoore and Hall 2009). It is this abstraction (rather like the forensic abstractions of fingerprint, footprint or bite) that authoritatively 'stands for' the subject of interest. Fallible forms of identification at the border (appearances, names, documents) become augmented by, even replaced by, new abstracted identifiers: a suspicious lack of luggage, an unusual route, a missed return journey, a last-minute cash payment.

The data print can be seen as a contemporary iteration of a recurring desire to use the abstracted traces of life and bodies to discern the secrets of an individual's character. The history of the collection, measurement and interpretation of bodily metrics, markers, traces and residues (with which forensic practice is concerned, for instance) is part of a wider history of efforts to 'visibilize the invisible' (Stafford 1993: 17): to go beyond what is immediately apparent to the fallible human eye. History is replete with efforts to locate deviance, criminality and racial and gendered inequality in somatic abstractions. The 'digitized dissection', like all dissections, disintegrates a whole to generate 'reproducible and communicable traces' (Waldby 2000: 89, 94), whether it is fifteenth-century anatomy atlases or contemporary virtual body scans. Knowledge of a subject's interior life, of his or her destiny and inclinations, has constantly been sought by probing beneath surface appearances. More specifically, somatic diagnoses that 'simplify, abstract, isolate and detach segments of the body in order to calculate incongruity' (Stafford 1993: 116) are situated within (and productive of) social, moral and political taxonomies. We see this clearly, for instance, in Johann Lavater's eighteenth-century physiognomy, which sought to categorize character from distinctive features of the human anatomy, and in Josef Gall's phrenology, whereby intellect was discerned through the shape of the skull (Colbert 1997: xi). Early European anthropometry, as Stafford (1993: 103, 112) argues, was entangled with efforts to *compare* the human body and to align anatomy with intelligence within social, cultural, moral and imperial hierarchies.

More importantly for understanding the contemporary 'digital print', the early 'science' of biometrics was concerned with organizing knowledge of the habitual criminal recidivist through physical marks and prints. Francis Galton's nineteenth-century work on finger ridge analysis heralded the beginning of the systematic use of biometric technologies for criminal identification, but his interest in the fingerprint was part of a larger eugenic project to locate deviance in physical distinctiveness (Pick 1989; Rabinow 1993). The fingerprint, Galton believed, would 'benefit society by detecting rogues' and would 'give each human being an identity … which can be depended upon with certainty' (Galton, 1982 cited in Thomas 1994: 659, 660). The fingerprint, among other contemporaneous anthropometric practices, was initially a means of archiving knowledge of criminals in a context of rapid urbanization and bureaucratization, by linking records to a unique and reliable identifier. That is, the fingerprint could locate a given individual within a population of 'unfit' habitual criminals, whose propensity for social menace, it was believed, was written on their bodies (see Cole 2001; Sekula 1986). The print was an index of the subject's particularity, but also a way of uncovering a person's future inclinations before their full manifestation.

Nowadays it is the touchpointed data abstraction that betrays the dangerous subject ahead of time, in a context of unparalleled global mobility. A passenger's digital traces are subjected to rules-based targeting in order to 'divert' or 'flex' limited resources at the border in 'response to threats', as one e-Borders official put it (interview with e-Borders official, London, March 2009). Like Galton's nineteenth-century dream for the fingerprint, the digital print promises to reveal individuals with threatening and hidden intentions. The digital print of the pixelated traveller, then, is a specific, securitized medium through which the mobile subject is made comprehensible and governable. Like Galton's nineteenth-century criminals and Locard's suspect, the 'person of interest' is already leaving myriad data traces that can identify him or her.

Data objects

The attractiveness of PNR for the security agencies, then, is the way it reveals the suspicious suspect in advance. As the US Department of Homeland Security (DHS) explains, PNR data analysis can help identify individuals up to 72 hours before departure, 'including watchlisted individuals, non-watchlisted co-travelers, and terrorists or criminals adopting known illicit travel patterns' (Heyman 2011). DHS is able to link previously unknown terrorists and criminals to known terrorists or criminals by matching contact information, flight patterns, and other data. The rules about links, associations and connections in border security targeting programmes are vitally important and, as Amoore (2011) describes, are produced through offline discussion between software designers, police, immigration and customs. It is an iterative process that feeds back intelligence about new smuggling routes, or intelligence about an attack, or information about a suspect into the algorithmic rules: errors and false-positives are drawn into a constantly refined new model. Nigel Thrift (2005: 244) argues that software in the contemporary world is producing 'a new set of effectivities … to the business of life'. Software, he argues, is a kind of mechanical writing that directs the world, but which 'is deferred', in that it 'expresses the co-presence of different times, the time of its production and its subsequent dictation of future moments' (2005: 233; 240–1). Software is 'rarely considered anew' and it falls 'outside the phenomenal field of subjectivity' (Hansen 2000: 17, cited in Thrift 2005: 241). In the field of smart border security decisions, certainly, the complex algorithms recede in the screened resolution of the analytical process: a hit or match.

The data traces that terrorists and criminals cannot help but leave behind possess an aura of objectivity and authority. They appear as facts, in the same way that conventional forensic traces are facts. Traditional forensic science produces 'scientific objects' as 'objects of evidence', as Latour (2007) puts it, both of which 'emphasise the virtues of a disinterested and unprejudiced approach'. The objectivity of Western scientific practice, of course, is a historically layered concept, blending notions of 'asperspectivalism' with 'mechanical objectivity', the removal of subjective obtrusion and the technological augmentation of fallible apprehension (see Daston 1992; Daston and Galison 2007). The forensic trace as a 'scientific object' and 'object of evidence' projects an aura of objectivity because it is apparently disconnected from subjective, prejudicial judgement and because it appears to preexist the techniques for its extraction. However, on closer inspection, the factitity of the conventional forensic object dissolves. Cole (2008), for example, shows how the smeared crime scene print is an object of opinion and connoisseurship rather than 'absolute scientific certainty' (see Dror and Cole 2010). Similarly, the DNA profile, although it appears 'docile, singular and neutral' as an abstracted series of 'stripes and peaks on a laboratory computer screen' or a probability number in court, is more accurately viewed as an active, fluid configuration performed across time and space (M'Charek 2008: 521–3; Williams and Johnson 2008), 'infused with contingent judgements about the mundane meaning and significance of evidence' (Lynch *et al.* 2008: 23).

Similarly, the flagging of a suspicious 'digital footprint' at the touchpointed border is not the revealing of a coherent and incriminating data object that was always there. The 'digital footprint' is not lying ready to be discovered, but is a fleeting association of data fragments held together via algorithmic risk-scoring techniques that draw relationships between items of data (for example, *this* nationality with *that* length of stay with a last-minute cash payment; *this* itinerary with *that* age group with *this* credit card). The digital footprint, unlike the forensic print, must be reactive and flexible. It must hold together new data items, or arrange them in different ways, or make new links, to give a fresh abstraction. It must constantly be affected by 'the excitement of the moment' – new intelligence, fluctuating travel behaviours, a novel trend. Whereas the individual bits of data (a missed flight, a credit card transaction, an unused return ticket, a length of stay) remain static, the algorithmic rules that join them into the 'print' of a potential suspect only become 'self-evident on this particular day at this particular time, at this moment' (interview with e-Borders official, London, March 2009). As Amoore (2011: 29) argues, it is precisely the gaps between data items that are vital to producing the actionable picture of threat: it is the 'multiple decisions about what to select, how to isolate, what should be joined to what' that hold together the data dots (a cash payment, an itinerary, a seat choice) into something that becomes 'intelligence'. IBM Business Software Analytics, for instance, describe how their predictive data analytics are used to organize vehicle checks along the multiple land border crossings of what is referred to as 'a large country' (2010). These analytics draw owner record data and vehicle details (recalled via number plate recognition scans) into association with passport data and crossing histories to select vehicles for searches. Thus, a two-year-old SUV, driven by a man aged 17 to 24 years, making a same-day return journey, combined with multiple previous crossings at different checkpoints, might give a narcotics risk of 0.75, for instance, and an alert for firearms. The contingencies of local knowledge, and variations in weather, time of day, and day of the week allow a flexible (re)calibration of risk. In the wake of a spate of drugs seizures, for example, a new (previously irrelevant) data trace might be drawn into the calculation and a new abstraction will be used to identify the person warranting extra scrutiny.

The print of future threat

Whereas conventional security data analytics match new data with known patterns of criminal or terrorist activity, the future of border security data analytics promises a shift away from established targets and behaviours (Detica 2008: 5). The cutting edge of data analytics is a move towards predictive approaches or 'threat blueprints', as Detica term them. These 'threatprints' are 'the set of links between the digital footprints of possible terrorist activities' (2008: 6). They are the (speculated) associations between not yet existing data traces that might be used as a diagnostic tool for new data. The threatprint approach directly confronts the uncertainty of the future by projecting a range of future scenarios from which it is possible to look back and ask: What should we have seen in the data? How did the digital clues appear? Whose 'footprint' was suspicious? Who should we have searched? As an analytical approach, the threatprint takes small anomalies in the data (the digital DNA markers that differentiate criminals, as Detica put it) and then build a hypothesis about possible future events that have yet to happen.

In this way, the threatprint 'makes the future present' by bringing into being something that has not yet, or may never happen (see Massumi 2005; 2007). The aim is not accuracy of prediction. Rather, security programmes aim to generate a 'constant readiness to identify another possible way in which a radically different future may play out' (Anderson 2010: 782). This style of data analytics seeks to break future (possible, probable and improbable) threat events into 'component parts' so the first traces of a threat may be identified as it starts to materialize in the data: an apparently innocent but anomalous journey, a new pattern of consumption, an unusual ticketing transaction. The threatprint, then, moves security practice away from 'reality-based' evidence (see Suskind 2004). It alters what Jonas (2007) calls the 'predicates' upon which security investigations and inspections proceed. In searching for the print that threat is already leaving ahead of itself, no scenario has been overlooked. The threatprinted future and the appropriate response become cogenerated.

Brian Massumi describes the virtual as the future past of the present: it is 'a thing's destiny and condition of existence … The virtual is real and in reciprocal presupposition with the actual, but does not exist even to the extent that the actual could be said to exist. It *subsists* in the actual or is immanent to it' (1992: 36–7). Like Galton's nineteenth-century criminals (whose bodies contained indications of their future potential), the future pasts of threat are already in the data, waiting to be discerned: as Detica put it, 'we can, in principle, draw up millions of these patterns [threatprints] in advance' (Lewis 2008). If, as Massumi (1992) argues (after Deleuze and Guattari), the virtual is the mode of reality implicated in the emergence of new potentials, then the threatprint acts on this very potential and seeks to capture virtual potentialities. The virtual is 'called virtual in so far as … emission and absorption, creation and destruction, occur in a period of time shorter than the shortest continuous period imaginable; it is this very brevity that keeps [it] subject to a principle of uncertainty or indetermination' (Deleuze and Parnet 2002: 148). The threatprint style of data analysis intervenes on the very uncertainty and indeterminacy of the future, drawing small contingencies and deviations into 'patterns drawn up in advance' through which the future can be acted upon. More specifically, as Amoore (2011: 34) argues, the associative analysis of targeting systems does 'not aspire to virtuality at all, but to actuality and the actualization of an array of possibilities'; rather, the digital code of security risk analysis 'arrays alternatives' and 'renders calculable possible futures'. It scarcely matters whether a scenario corresponds to future reality: what matters is having already formulated a response. The desire to intervene 'before the terrorist or criminal has been radicalized or recruited in the first place' (Detica 2008) is thus not a proportionate response to an identified threat, but the actualization of a particular future.

Conclusion: targeted populations

We have argued that the digital footprint of security practice is a distinctive and novel abstraction of the subject's life, one that constantly shifts and responds. Certainly the invocation of the 'footprint' as inadvertent signature of threat occludes the myriad decisions and processes that are intrinsic to its production. The digital footprint (like the conventional criminal print on closer inspection) is not simply a factual, neutral, latent object: it is active, held together by rules and associations that draw into focus a constantly shifting population 'of interest'. Within border governance programmes like e-Borders, we can see the effort to modulate the uncertain future, which is intrinsic to liberal life (Foucault 2007; see Dean 2007; Rose 1999), become (via apparently neutral, objective targeting) productive of divisive and exclusionary power relations that divide populations in new ways. So, although an orthodox Muslim appearance is not an encoded risk criteria at the UK border, for instance, patterns of frequent flights to Pakistan associated with a specific duration of stay may well be. In order that the flows of people, money and objects that are vital to global order be maintained, some subjects will continually find themselves targeted in the name of security.

The data print can be seen as an actant, as Jane Bennett (after Latour) puts it: an 'intervener' within an assemblage that 'makes the difference, makes things happen' (2010: 9). The border security decisions that are taken (to arrest, search, detain, deport) become disconnected from specific border locales and become, instead, the outcomes of 'interfolding networks' and 'swarms of vitalities' (Bennett 2010: 31, 32) between human actors, mutable data forms and technological hardware, within and between targeting centres, border frontposts and dispersed touchpoints. What emerges is a 'transactional system' that augments, supersedes and transforms traditional active border vigilance (passport checks, frontline scrutiny) into data risk screening and automated responses; the danger is that the risk analysis puts people in a box when the data say no, as one e-Borders official put it (interview with e-Borders official, February 2011).

For passengers who (mistakenly or not) find themselves identified as 'of interest', the question becomes, how to contest the abstraction that has singled them out. How could a person called aside for airport questioning, for example, know the reasons for this scrutiny? How could a subject ever explain or contest a digital footprint that misrepresented him or her? Rules-based targeting claims to be indifferent to personal details: 'this is not about you or me, it's about whether you are looking at normal', as one software designer put it (interview with border security software designer, London, May 2009). The apparent facticity of the data threatens to irrevocably fold categories of gender, race and ethnicity into 'neutral' behavioural traces. In this sense, it is difficult to challenge programmes like the UK's e-Borders, for instance, under conventional antidiscrimination laws, because they do not work with criteria that are definitively based on race or ethnicity. The most prominent challenges to programmes like e-Borders are preoccupied with the collection, storage, sharing and protection of personal information (see, for example, Privacy International 2009). Yet the concern of activists, advocates and public bodies with protecting privacy and the rights of the data subject (although vital) find it difficult to confront the novel development of data analytics in security: the promise to definitively identify risk via a particular kind of mobile data abstraction or data derivative (Amoore 2011). Indeed, it is the claim that efficient 'fact-based data targeting' can *protect* the privacy of the majority of licit travellers that makes its rise so difficult to challenge, and thus insidious. When the political debate is mapped out across (albeit vital) issues of redress, transparency and 'purpose limitation' (crucial to conventional disputes about data protection), the circulation of bits and bytes of data in an attempt to identify the risky subject within a targeted approach may become 'the solution'.

What kind of population is being targeted here? The digital print and the threatprint as objects of security claim to simply represent or target a population already constituted. Yet the constant realignment of risk and the production of fresh data abstractions produce endlessly adjustable targets that may never fully emerge. Like the modern-day DNA profile, which 'assembles' and 'clusters' individuals within a population (M'Charek 2008: 524), the data print stands for the as-yet-unknown terrorist or criminal within a constantly refined population of risk, holding together the data bytes left behind with future potentials. Here, we might return to the organization of nineteenth-century knowledge around the habitual criminal population. Far from constituting a latent category, this group was 'made up' (Hacking 1990) via metric approaches to the body to differentiate between 'types' of offender and normal citizenry. The digital print of contemporary border security also 'makes up' specific populations of risk, orienting security attention in the moment to a specific population, conjured from a future that may never come.

The fingerprint, Francis Galton originally believed, would be able to detect criminals who were pretending to be someone they were not (Galton cited in Thomas 1994: 667), rather like the contemporary terrorist who tries to blend into the travelling public. Galton's great expectation was that the print could determine the 'true identity' of a person, and Galton's lasting regret, argues Rabinow (1993), was that these expectations were unfounded. The print gave no reliable indication of proclivity for criminality at all, despite clusters of similarities within certain population groups (see Cole 2001). Just as Galton's project to map the criminal body in order to decipher its latent threats proved unsuccessful, so current efforts to identify threats by the digital prints we leave behind constantly confront the potentialities of human life that will always exceed what can be 'held' or 'captured' within an abstracted recomposition. It is by showing the contingency of the apparently authoritative, fact-based, data-led 'finger of suspicion' and the risk-scored data objects that are said to identify us, that the security project to intervene 'before the terrorist or criminal has been radicalized' can be questioned.

Acknowledgements

This paper emerged from the Economic and Social Research Council (ESRC)-NWO (Netherlands Organisation for Scientific Research) funded project 'Data Wars: New Spaces of Governing in the War on Terror', RES-062 230594, led by Professor Louise Amoore (Durham University) and Professor Marieke de Goede (University of Amsterdam). This paper was presented at the CRESC (Centre for Research on Socio-Cultural Change) Annual Conference, *Objects – What Matters?*, September 2009. Thanks to conference participants and to the editors for their comments on this chapter.

Bibliography

Agress, R. *et al.* (2008) 'The case for use of a multi-method scientific approach for anticipating a rare event' in *Anticipating Rare Events (Multi-disciplinary White papers in support of counter-terrorism and counter WMD)*, Homeland Security Digital Library; https://www.hsdl.org.

Amoore, L. (2009) 'Lines of sight: on the visualisation of unknown futures', *Citizenship Studies* 13(1): 17–30.

Amoore, L. (2011) 'Data derivatives: on the emergence of a security risk calculus for our times', *Theory, Culture and Society* 28(6): 24–43.

Amoore, L. and de Goede, M. (2005) 'Governance, risk and dataveillance in the war on terror', *Crime, Law and Social Change* 43(2): 149–73.

Amoore, L. and de Goede, M. (2008) 'Transactions after 9/11: the banal face of the preemptive strike', *Transactions of the Institute of British Geographers* 33(2): 173–85.

Amoore, L. and Hall, A. (2009) 'Taking people apart: digitised dissection and the body at the border', *Environment and Planning D: Society and Space* 27(3): 444–64.

Anderson, B. (2010) 'Preemption, precaution, preparedness: anticipatory action and the future', *Progress in Human Geography* 34(6): 777–98.

Bennett, J. (2010) *Vibrant Matter: A Political Ecology of Things*, Durham, NC: Duke University Press.

Chisum, W.J. and Turvey, B. (2000) 'Evidence dynamics: Locard's exchange principle and crime reconstruction', *Journal of Behavioral Profiling* 1(1).

Colbert C. (1997) *A Measure of Perfection: Phrenology and the Fine Arts in America*, Chapel Hill and London: University of North Carolina Press.

Cole, S. (2001) *Suspect Identities: A History of Fingerprinting and Criminal Investigation*, Cambridge, MA: Harvard University Press.

Cole, S. (2004) 'Fingerprint identification and the criminal justice system: historical lessons for the DNA debate' in D. Lazer (ed.) *DNA and the Criminal Justice System: The Technology of Justice*, Cambridge, MA: MIT Press.

Cole, S. (2008) 'The "opinionization" of fingerprint evidence', *BioSocieties* 3(1): 105–13.

Daston, L. (1992) 'Objectivity and the escape from perspective', *Social Studies of Science* 22: 597–618.

Daston, L. and Galison, P. (2007) *Objectivity*, London: Zone Books.

Dean, M. (2007) *Governing Societies*, London: Sage.

Deleuze, G. and Parnet, C. (2002) 'The actual and the virtual', *Dialogues II*, London and New York: Continuum.

Detica (2008) *The Information Revolution and its Impact on Homeland Security*; available at http://www.detica. com/images/pdfs/detica_information_revolution_whitepaper.pdf, accessed 26 February 2009.

Dror, I. and Cole, S. (2010) 'The vision in "blind" justice: expert perception, judgment, and visual cognition in forensic pattern recognition', *Psychonomic Bulletin and Review* 17(2): 161–7.

Foucault, M. (2007) *Security, Territory, Population: Lectures at the College de France 1977–1978*, translated by G. Burchell, Basingstoke, Hants: Macmillan.

Hacking, I. (1990) *The Taming of Chance*, Cambridge: Cambridge University Press.

Hayes, B. (2009) *Neoconopticon: The EU Security-Industrial Complex*. Statewatch; available at http://www. statewatch.org/analyses/neoconopticon-report.pdf, accessed 13 September 2009.

Heyman, D. (2011) *Testimony of David Heyman, Assistant Secretary, Office of Policy, before the House Committee on Homeland Security Subcommittee on Counterterrorism and Intelligence*; available at http://www.dhs.gov/ ynews/testimony/20111005-heyman-info-sharing-privacy-travelers.shtm, accessed 13 June 2013.

House of Commons European Scrutiny Committee (2011) *Use of Passenger Name Records for Law Enforcement Purposes*, 21st Report of Session 2010–2011, London: The Stationary Office Limited.

House of Commons Home Affairs Committee (2010) *Counter-Terrorism Measures in British Airports*, 9th Report of Session 2009–2010, London: The Stationery Office Limited.

House of Lords European Union Committee (2007) *The EU/US Passenger Name Record (PNR) Agreement*, 21st Report of Session 2006–2007, London: The Stationery Office Limited.

House of Lords European Union Committee (2011) *The United Kingdom Opt-in to the Passenger Name Record Directive*, 11th Report of Session 2010–2011, London: The Stationery Office Limited.

IBM (2010) Public Safety: from 'Sense and Respond' to 'Predict and Act', IBM Business Analytics; available at ftp://public.dhe.ibm.com/common/ssi/ecm/en/ytw03024usen/YTW03024USEN.PDF, accessed 13 June 2013.

Johnson, P. and Williams, R. (2007) 'Internationalising new technologies of crime control: forensic DNA databasing and datasharing in the European Union', *Policing and Society* 17: 103–18.

Jonas, J. (2007) *Predicate-based Link Analysis: A Post 9/11 Analysis (1+1= 13)*; available at http://jeffjonas. typepad.com/jeff_jonas/2007/04/predicatebased_.html, accessed 13 June 2013.

Kean, T. and Hamilton, L. (2004) *The 9/11 Report: The National Commission on Terrorist Attacks upon the United States*, New York: St Martin's Press.

Latour, B. (2007) 'Scientific objects and legal objectivity', in A. Pottage and M. Mundy (eds.) *Law, Anthropology and the Constitution of the Social*, Cambridge: Cambridge University Press.

Lewis, H. (2008) 'Threatprints – Digital DNA Criminals Leave Behind', *Contingency Today*; available at http://www.contingencytoday.com/online_article/Threatprints---digital-DNA-criminals-leave-behind-/1620, accessed 13 June 2013.

Lynch, M., Cole, S., McNally, R. and Jordan, K. (2008) *Truth Machine: the Contentious History of DNA Fingerprinting*, Cambridge, MA: Harvard University Press.

M'Charek, A. (2008) 'Silent witness, articulate collective: DNA evidence and the inference of visible traits', *Bioethics* 22(9): 518–28.

Massumi, B. (1992) *A User's Guide to Capitalism and Schizophrenia*, Cambridge, MA: MIT Press.

Massumi, B. (2005) 'The future birth of the affective act', Conference Proceedings: Genealogies of Biopolitics; available at http://browse.reticular.info/text/collected/massumi.pdf, accessed 13 June 2013.

Massumi, B. (2007) 'Potential politics and the primacy of preemption', *Theory and Event* 10(2).

Pick, D. (1989) *Faces of Degeneration: A European Disorder, c. 1848–c. 1918*, Cambridge: Cambridge University Press.

Privacy International (2009) *Sharing the Misery: the UK's Strategy to Circumvent Data Privacy Protections*; available at http://www.privacyinternational.org/countries/uk/uk_data_sharing_report.pdf, accessed 15 December 2011.

Rabinow, P. (1993) 'Galton's regret and DNA typing', *Culture, Medicine and Psychiatry* 17: 59–65.

Rose, N. (1999) *Powers of Freedom: Reframing Political Thought*, Cambridge: Cambridge University Press.

Sekula, A. (1986) 'The Body and the archive', *October* 39 (Winter 1986): 3–64.

Stafford, B. (1993) *Body Criticism: Imaging the Unseen in Enlightenment Art and Medicine*, Cambridge, MA: MIT Press.

Suskind, R. (2004) 'Faith, certainty and the presidency of George W. Bush', *The New York Times*, 17 October.

Thomas, R. (1994) 'The fingerprint of the foreigner: colonising the criminal body in 1890s detective fiction and criminal anthropology', *ELH* 61(3): 655–83.

Thrift, N. (2005) 'Beyond mediation: three new material registers and their consequences', in D. Miller (ed.) *Materiality*, London: Duke University Press, pp. 231–56.

Van der Ploeg, I. (2003) 'Biometrics and the body as information: normative issues of the sociotechnical coding of the body', in D. Lyon (ed.) *Surveillance as Social Sorting*, London: Routledge.

Waldby, C. (2000) 'Virtual anatomy; from the body in the text to the body on the screen', *Journal of Medical Humanities* 21(2): 85–107.

Williams, R. and Johnson, P. (2008) *Genetic Policing: The Use of DNA in Criminal Investigations*, Devon: Willan Publishing.

34

Intangible objects

How patent law is redefining materiality

Mario Biagioli

> No right can exist without a substance to restrain it, and to which it is confined; it would otherwise be a right without any existence.
>
> *(Judge Joseph Yates, 1769)*

In this chapter, I look at how certain objects (patentable inventions) are construed at the intersection between technology and the law. The economic relevance of patents and the political controversies over the balance between proprietary and public knowledge are both extraordinarily important and well known, but are not my topic here. I focus instead on the peculiar nature of patentable inventions as constructs of both technoscientific practices and legal doctrine, and how the changing intersection of those two different agencies keeps reframing the meaning of 'invention.' For instance, a recent breed of patentable inventions look more like disembodied knowledge than physical entities, suggesting that the law is effectively redefining not only the boundaries of intellectual property but also the definition of technology.

Not all technological objects, even new ones, can lead to patents. Over the centuries, an increasingly complex legal discourse has developed around patentable subject matter and about the kind of entities (laws of nature, abstract ideas, mental processes, natural phenomena, etc.) that are instead excluded from intellectual property, and why. One necessary distinctive feature of patentable inventions is that they need to be artefactual, not natural: products of human ingenuity, not nature. In common parlance, they need to be inventions, not discoveries. The presence of 'abstract ideas' and 'mental processes' on the list of unpatentable matters given above points to another key feature of patentable inventions: materiality.

From popular literature to science and technology studies, patented inventions are typically presented as things: Edison's light bulb, Morse's telegraph and Bell's telephone. One may discover a natural principle or law, but can only patent a device that puts that principle to practical use, creating useful effects that were not known and practised before. That view holds for earlier periods as well. When one thinks of the key inventions of the eighteenth century, the images that come to mind are large, heavy steam engines, substantial textile machines, and the material goods they produced. Until recently, the law took the same position: in order to be patentable, an invention needed to have material features or material effects.

There is a tendency to explain the dramatic global increase in patenting activities as a consequence of the law's ability to construe new kinds of innovation (software, genetic sequences, etc.) in ways that conform to well-established legal concepts of patentable invention. But as new technologies produce new innovations, the concept of invention has undergone substantial qualitative change: the shape of the box has changed, not just its size (Pottage and Sherman 2011: 269). Redefinitions and expansions of what can be patented have typically involved the redrawing of distinctions between discovery and invention or between nature and artefact. The explosion of genetic patenting, for instance, relied on a conceptualization of genetic sequences not as purely natural entities but also partial products of human agency, at least to an extent sufficient to allow them to be moved from the category of discovery to that of invention. But the trend I discuss here is different, because it redraws the relation between patentability and the materiality of the invention.[1]

In 1997, Bernard Bilski and Rand Warsaw filed for a US patent for a simple and rather general price-hedging model, the use of which they then tied to the narrower field of energy commodity trading. The patent application concerned the model itself, not the software coding of that model or the computer running it. The application was denied by the Patent Office and by all courts that reviewed it thereafter, including the US Supreme Court. Strikingly, however, the Supreme Court's 2010 decision did not hinge on the immateriality of the invention, which it did not find to be a necessarily disqualifying factor. That was not an altogether surprising decision given that many other abstract methods and processes have been granted patent protection in the USA over the last two decades, like, for instance, the so-called Metabolite patent over a correlation between a certain level of homocysteine in bodily fluids and vitamin B deficiency. In the context of this discussion, the key claim of the Metabolite patent concerned:

> A method for detecting a deficiency of cobalamin or folate in warm-blooded animals comprising the steps of:
> (a) assaying a body fluid for an elevated level of total homocysteine; and
> (b) correlating an elevated level of total homocysteine in said body fluid with a deficiency of cobalamin or folate.[2]

It is important to notice that this claim does not cover any specific testing apparatus.[3] What is being patented is only the relation between two quantities: a linkage between a certain biomarker and a certain medical condition.

Transforming tangibility and intangibility

In the early modern period, patentable inventions were seen as things that performed useful tasks or yielded useful products. What mattered was not the 'idea,' but the ability of the material invention to produce useful material effects. Then, since about 1790 in both Europe and the USA, the law started to attribute an intangible dimension to the inventors' activities: the so-called inventive step or 'idea' of the invention (Biagioli 2006: 1132–4). However, the 'inventive step' had to be reduced to practice by embodying it into something material. The 1793 US Patent Act, for instance, required the inventor to describe 'the several modes in which [s/he] has contemplated the application of that principle or character.'[4]

Materiality has remained a central element of the legal notion of invention for the following two centuries. Modern US patent law states that: 'Whoever invents or discovers any new and useful process, machine, manufacture, or composition of matter, or any new and useful improvement thereof, may obtain a patent therefor.'[5] Machines, products ('manufacture') and chemical entities ('composition of matter') are obviously material. Moving to 'process' (not things but ways of doing things), this term, which used to be written as 'art' in older US patent law up to 1952, has been traditionally interpreted to mean activities and methods that produce useful effects through material transformations. Examples may include a process to cure rubber or a method to produce transgenic organisms (as distinct from the rubber products or the organisms themselves). In the USA, this conventional take on patentable processes has been recently formalized in the MORT (machine-or-transformation) test adopted by the Patent Office, defining patentable processes as those that are 'tied to a particular machine or apparatus or transform a particular article into a different state or thing.'[6] The logic of the test is that the invention must be material either in itself or in its effects, or both. This traditionally essential link between invention and materiality is now being radically challenged.

Over the years, intellectual property has expanded its boundaries by claiming the existence of intangibles within tangibles, or intangibles connected to tangibles. Both patent and copyright law has turned more and more kinds of things and activities into knowledge and property by attributing them some human-imposed immaterial feature: the inventor's 'inventive step' or the author's 'personal expression.' If you construe books or light bulbs or music recordings simply as tangible property, you cannot then prevent their buyers from copying and selling them. But if you say that a book is simply the material carrier of something intangible that is connected and yet distinct from the specific physical book that you have purchased and happily own, then copying that book is no longer an action allowed by property law but rather a violation of intellectual property law.

An intriguing feature of intellectual property is that although it articulates an increasingly complex discourse about intangibles and their protection, it does so not to protect intangibles per se but rather as proxies to control the copying, circulation and use of *tangibles*. We could say, metaphorically, that intellectual property has established an economy of 'souls': souls that it construed and then connected to bodies to distinguish them from other bodies. The soul is posited as intangible and yet it functions as a device to introduce essential (if invisible) distinctions between tangible bodies like, say, those of animals and humans. The trend exemplified by the Bilski case and subsequent ones fits the ongoing transformation of intellectual property toward the construction of more and more types of intangibles: in this case, abstract methods, processes and models. However, it adds a crucial new twist or transformation in the sense that whereas in the past the intangible was the inventor's contribution to an otherwise tangible invention, now it is the invention itself that is becoming intangible. We are witnessing a bit of 'category hopping' here, from the intangible that defines what an invention is to the invention as intangible. With information-based inventions like Bilski's price-hedging scheme or Metabolite's correlation between biomarkers and medical conditions, we are no longer grafting immateriality over materiality but perhaps doing away with materiality altogether.

This is a qualitatively different transformation not only because it goes from expanding forms of immateriality to rendering materiality unnecessary but because, in doing so, it breaks down the tangible/intangible distinction that has been fundamental to modern patent law and intellectual property law more generally. Traditionally, a crucial problem for intellectual property has been to establish a connection between intangibles and tangibles to control and restrict the use of tangibles by claiming control of the intangibles attached to them. If you think that the flat screen televisions that I produce and sell at electronics stores infringe on some patent of yours, you need to show how my screens incorporate your patent's intangible 'inventive step.' Abstract process patents have changed this not in the sense that invention has become 'purified' from its materiality (as if materiality were an accidental and thus disposable feature of invention), but rather because they seem to challenge the traditional and essentially dichotomous (tangible/ intangible) nature of invention.

Furthermore (and this is perhaps the most interesting conceptual consequence of this trend), these developments are modifying the very meaning of both tangibility and intangibility. Tangibility and intangibility are, I believe, impossible to define as separate freestanding concepts. In the past, intellectual property has managed this difficulty by defining the tangible and the intangible through a relationship of complementarily: saying, for instance, that the intangible idea is the 'form' that shapes tangible 'matter' into an invention (Pottage and Sherman 2011:269). Now, however, that dichotomous framework is being undone by inventions like Bilski's, which are casting the meaning of *both* tangibility *and* intangibility adrift.

Perhaps this is because the inventions instantiating this new trend are in one way or another about information and information processing. It is not clear where information stands in the spectrum that goes from materiality to immateriality, or whether that is even the right way to frame the question. Information can be thought of as something immaterial in the sense that its effects are not reducible to the materials on which information is carried, as indicated by the fact that there are typically different material substrata, formats, and modalities of coding that can hold and convey the same information. At the same time, information always relies on some material difference or trace to signify or 'carry' it: the binary setting of a computer's flip-flop register, different voltage levels, different wave frequencies and amplitudes, different markings on a piece of paper, wood, stone, etc.

The figure of the switch best captures the different ways in which information can be said to be both material and immaterial, or perhaps neither. From telephone switchboards to computer processors, the switch stands for binary information: open/closed, yes/no, 1/0, etc. But while the switch is obviously material, the difference that makes a difference is its *position*, its capacity to direct an *activity* or flow in one *direction* rather than another. The way a switch performs that task may be specific to the materiality of the flow, and yet the fact that we can have the same operations carried out by computers using different techniques and materials indicates that although information is tied to material differences, it is not tied to the specific materials instantiating those differences.

Information, then, can be said to incorporate the material–immaterial duality within its own definition. It does not solve that tension but rather internalizes it. Consequently, if in the past invention was defined as an intangible (the inventive step) connected to a tangible entity (the machine, the chemical compound, etc.), recent inventions involving abstract methods and processes fold the tangible–intangible relation within the inventive step itself because that step now involves information or information processing. Although this new kind of invention seems to have no materiality because they concern only methods (not things but ways of doing things), it may still be incorrect to say that inventions are becoming 'dematerialized' or 'immaterial.' What is new about these inventions is not their immateriality but the location where the nexus between tangible and intangible is articulated or activated: a nexus that is no longer *between* the idea of the invention and its material embodiment but *within* the idea itself. This changes the boundaries and meanings of the entities involved in the relation. It is not that the intangible inventive step becomes simultaneously tangible and intangible because that idea now amounts to information or to a manner of processing information. What happens is that the very meaning of 'tangible,' 'intangible,' 'material,' 'immaterial,' 'physical,' 'concrete,' 'abstract' and similar adjectives one finds in patent law and discourse are being profoundly modified by the destabilization of the relation between tangibility and intangibility.

An opposition remains, but the law redraws and reestablishes it between attributes of the invention other than tangibility and intangibility. Patent law may be translating (in the literal sense of relocating) its fundamental distinction between *tangible and intangible* to one between *specific and generic*.

Questioning material ontologies and political alignments

From the point of view of what I would call progressive knowledge politics, this may look like a bad story getting worse: a further expansion of the reach of the discursive magic of intellectual property through which it creates new and increasingly globalized forms of value and property by attaching ideas, souls, ghosts, flashes of genius and auras to material entities, or by turning tangible social relations into intangibles. It is possible that these undesirable consequences may indeed come to pass. Still, without in any way endorsing the trends exemplified by the Bilski case or others in the judicial pipeline, I think that they provide some excellent food for thought for anyone interested in the relation between knowledge and materiality.

The trend toward 'immaterial' invention may force us to reconsider the assumptions through which we have both conceptualized and criticized the way knowledge and property are produced. We tend to be comfortable with the notion of materiality, which has, for instance, become the keyword or buzzword of most science and technology studies for the last twenty years. Conversely, we are suspicious of transformations that claim to render material things immaterial. However, it could be that materiality is not (and has never been) as unproblematic a category as we now take it to be: at least not less problematic than the apparently stranger notion of intangibility.

In the USA, the required materiality or material effects of patentable processes and methods was traced to the Constitution, which states, in the article pertaining to intellectual property, that protection can be granted only to inventions that contribute to the 'progress of the useful arts.'[7] Until recently, the term 'useful arts' has been read to mean 'technological arts' or material technology, thus categorizing abstract methods as non-technological and thus potentially unpatentable. This is also the position upheld by the critics of the patenting of abstract methods, including several attorneys and scholars who wrote amicus briefs to the Supreme Court assailing the patentability of Bilski's invention. Based on the questions that they posed during the oral arguments in November 2009, the Court's more liberal justices seem to lean toward that position as well:

> JUSTICE BREYER: You know, I have a great, wonderful, really original method of teaching antitrust law, and it kept 80 percent of the students awake. They learned things –

> (Laughter.)

> JUSTICE BREYER: It was fabulous. And I could probably have reduced it to a set of steps, and other teachers could have followed it. That you are going to say is patentable, too?
> MR. JAKES [Bilski's counsel]: Potentially.[8]

Justice Sotomayor, another Democrat, sought a comical effect by addressing, and implicitly deriding, the implications of the trend exemplified by Bilski:

> JUSTICE SOTOMAYOR: So how do we limit [patents] to something that's reasonable? Meaning, if we don't limit [patents] to inventions or to technology, as some amici have, or to some tie or tether ... to the sciences, to the useful arts, then why not patent the method of speed dating?[9]

Conversely, those in favor of the patenting of abstract models (the financial industry among them) are arguing that 'technology' needs to be understood more broadly than what it meant during the Industrial Age. They say that, first of all, technology does not need to be limited to apparatuses but may include all sorts of structured human activities (a conceptual move not unlike what we have seen in the sociology of science and technology, where pretty much any way of doing things has become a 'technology').[10] Second, the supporters of abstract methods patents adopt a distinctly emergent notion of technology, also aligned with the position of contemporary science and technology studies. As Bilski's counsel put it during the oral arguments to the Supreme Court: '... today the raw materials [of invention] are just as likely to be information or electronic signals, and to simply root us in the industrial era because that's what we knew I think would be wrong and contrary to the forward-looking aspect of the patent laws.'[11] Technology started by producing material inventions, but then added immaterial ones to its repertoire: a development that could not have been envisaged by those who initially crafted patent law. They allowed for the patenting of processes and those processes happened to be material at first, but we should not now turn an accident of history into an ontology.

A few months later, in June 2010, the Supreme Court unanimously affirmed the position taken by the lower courts against the patentability of Bilski's invention. However, the justices failed to agree on the reasons for the decision, producing different opinions on the matter, pretty much along party lines. While deciding against Bilski, the Republican block has upheld, with virtual unanimity, the emergent view of technology put forward by Bilski's counsel, emphasizing the difference between inventions of the 'Industrial Age' and those of the 'Information Age.'[12] Attributing an equally emergent meaning to 'process,' they have concluded that processes do not necessarily need to be tied to a machine or physical transformation in order to be patentable. They have found Bilski's invention unpatentable, but have related their decision not to the immateriality of that invention but to the fact that it cannot not be classified as a 'process' even in the broad, emergent definition of the term they have come to adopt.[13]

The Democratic block has joined Justice Stevens, arguing that although they concur in the Court's judgment against Bilski, they disagree with its reasoning: Bilski is unpatentable because it is a business model, and 'methods of doing business are not, in themselves, covered by the statute.'[14] They may be processes but are not what the law defines as patentable processes. They are not part of the 'useful arts' mentioned in the Constitution and are not, consequently, a technology. The term 'process' should not be treated as an overly broad term comprising all sorts of practices or simple 'human activities,' but a legal term of art referring specifically to physical, material, or technological processes.[15] To assume a broad definition of 'process' amounts to including in it things that that notion was explicitly meant to exclude.

Sadly, the liberal critics put forward the kind of originalist argument that is typically the province of conservatives like Scalia and Thomas. They are effectively attempting to determine the true intent and meaning of two words in the Constitution ('useful arts'), thus ending up restricting the meaning of technology to the one it had circa 1800, when cast iron looked high-tech. Conversely, it is surprising and disturbing to see the Republican justices adopt a more fluid and less fundamentalist reading of that article of the Constitution, coupled with an equally non-essentialist (indeed emergent) notion of invention and patentability. Their notion of technology is in fact comparable with what we find in today's interpretive social sciences and humanities.

From materiality to specificity

As sharp and puzzling as the alignment between ontologies of invention and political orienta-tions may be, I have not sketched it to engage in a political sociology of the current discourse on patentability but rather to suggest that that kind of analysis would not be particularly rewarding. Because they rest on incompatible assumptions, the conceptual and philosophical differences between those who claim that patentable inventions must be material or induce material transformations and those who instead claim that new and useful immaterial inventions may be patentable too are, I believe, irresolvable, even more so when they are coupled with opposing views of capitalism and innovation like the emergent/laissez faire view of the Republican justices versus the more 'regulatory' stance of the Democratic ones. It may be more useful, therefore, to question the very divide between materiality and immateriality that structures these debates, so as to scramble both the conceptual and political stalemate: a reframing that may be particularly useful here given the fact that the 'good guys' seem to have the stodgy arguments, and vice versa.

Rather than accept that 'invention' is becoming immaterial or that it should never be anything but material, can we rethink invention as something that is neither material nor immaterial? The evidence from the Bilski case and others (coupled with strong evidence that the range of inventions involved in this trend is remarkably wide and widening precisely because of its disconnect from materiality) already points to interesting slippages and partial breakdowns in the dichotomy between materiality and immateriality. It is not at all clear that materiality is still the opposite of immateriality, or of abstractness.

Patent history indicates that the resistance to immaterial or abstract inventions was rooted in concerns with the size of the monopoly that would be created by allowing for the patenting of abstract principles, methods, or ideas. Still much-cited (and relevant to current debates over patentable subject matter) is the 1853 US Supreme Court decision against Samuel Morse's attempt to seek a patent on any electromagnetic technology for communicating printed messages. In Claim 8, Morse stated:

> I do not propose to limit myself to the specific machinery or parts of machinery described in the foregoing specification and claims; the essence of my invention being the use of the motive power of the electric or galvanic current, which I call electro-magnetism, however developed for marking or printing intelligible characters, signs, or letters, at any distances, being a new application of that power of which I claim to be the first inventor or discoverer.[16]

If Morse did not quite claim the whole of electromagnetism as his invention, he still claimed patent rights to all possible uses of electromagnetism for the purpose of 'marking or printing intelligible characters, signs, or letters, at any distances.' The extraordinary breadth of that claim was obviously connected to untethering his invention from any specific telegraphic apparatus: a move that enabled him not only to claim all presently conceivable uses of electromagnetism for telegraphy, but also the telegraphic applications of *future* knowledge about electromagnetism. By not limiting his patent claim to an apparatus (a claim that Morse could have clearly delineated by describing his apparatus in the text of the patent application), he would have secured a monopoly on something he had claimed but not disclosed, like saying 'I am the owner of vast new lands I have recently discovered out West,' without saying where exactly that property starts and ends. Furthermore, by claiming but not describing the 'motive power of the electric or galvanic current … for marking or printing intelligible characters, signs, or letters, at any distances,' Morse would have effectively obtained a patent also on future knowledge about the applications of electromagnetism to telegraphy. Wisely, the Court found that 'the claim is too broad, and not warranted by law.'[17]

Asking for the idea (the inventive step) to be connected to a machine was therefore a way to circumscribe the present and future scope of the inventor's monopoly. It functioned a bit like the lamp that contained and thus controlled Aladdin's genie. So, for instance, the landmark 1981 Supreme Court decision in Diamond v Diehr (which opened the door to software patenting) stated that although an abstract mathematical formula central to the invention could not be patented in and of itself, one could patent the software running that formula on a computer that was in turn embedded in a rubber–curing system: a system made new and better by the temperature control protocols enabled by said formula.[18] We see, therefore, that despite their superficial similarities, abstractness, immateriality and intangibility shared little as concepts. What related them was not conceptual similarity but the similarity of their effects, that is, that they could all enable large patent claims. Conversely, the materiality requirement (either the connection of the invention to a machine or to material transformations) was not a statement of the technological value of materiality per se ('only material inventions are good inventions') but rather a mobilization of materiality to limit the size of the patent claim.

I would add spatial location (a notion conceptually unrelated to materiality) to the list of monopoly-control strategies. Especially in the Renaissance and early modern period (when inventions were conceptualized as usefully performing machines rather than useful ideas embedded in a machine), it was common to find patents that limited the privilege on the use of an invention to a specific place: a windmill on a certain hill, a boat of a certain design on a given river, a certain industry at a certain distance from a city, etc.[19] Even if you grant broad patent *claims*, the effect of their monopoly is substantially limited by restricting the inventor's use of his/her patent[20] to a narrow place or jurisdiction, especially if that invention or its products were difficult to move around.

Not all these controlling or restricting techniques functioned equally well with all inventions, or notions of invention. The use of geographical restriction, for instance, could be effective in patent regimes that conceptualized inventions as soulless machines that may deserve protection within the legal jurisdiction of a given nation, but not in legal frameworks that, since about 1800, have cast them as ideas embedded in machines entitled to protection on an increasingly global scale. In the latter case, restricting the geographical scope of the patent would not control its effective scope. Because the 'soul' of the invention can, so to speak, leave the body behind and travel on, it can potentially enable the expansion of the patent monopoly elsewhere.

We could therefore say (but this is only a hypothesis) that whereas the effective breadth of the claims of pre-1800 inventions was controlled or curtailed by delimiting both the geographic location of the operation of the invention and the legal jurisdiction of the patent grant, post–1800 patent law pursued a comparable goal by imposing requirements about the materiality of the invention or of the transformations it produces. The former uses space, the latter matter.[21]

The differences between modern, post-1800 patenting scenarios and those produced by contemporary information-based inventions like Bilski and Metabolite may be a replay, mutatis mutandis, of those between inventions as things and inventions as materially embedded inventive ideas. Restrictions of a spatial nature could function relatively well to limit the effective claims of unstandardized and hard-to-blackbox inventions, the construction and operation of which required a great deal of local expertise and hands-on training for their construction and operation. However, that technique would not have performed well with inventions that could be expressed (and thus copied or disseminated) through a publicly accessible textual and pictorial specification of their 'inventive step.' The materiality requirement became the key legal technology for controlling the scope of the patent claim in that more modern regime.

However, when we move up to more recent information-based inventions, we quickly realize that the materiality requirement becomes either blunt or ineffective, or both. The immateriality of abstract inventions enables them to migrate widely: not only in the sense of being able to be easily pirated or licensed on a global scale (like most information-based products like texts, music, film), but in the more important sense of entailing indefinitely broad claims. Because of its abstractness, a hedging method can be applied to an indefinitely varied set of contexts, as in Pythagoras' theorem. But if the 1853 Supreme Court could control the scope of Morse's patent by invoking the materiality requirement to void his extraordinarily broad claim quoted above, that move would be fully ineffective with information-based inventions of the kind instantiated by Metabolite's claim to the correlation between homocysteine and vitamin B deficiency.

Even the broadest of Morse's claims had some distinctly material dimension to it: '… *marking or printing* intelligible characters, signs, or letters, at any distances.'[22] Metabolite's invention, instead, involves no material effect like marking or printing, only the establishment of a mental linkage between levels of homocysteine and vitamin B deficiency. Morse left unspecified the indefinitely many modes of the material embodiment of the invention in an attempt to claim all of them, even those he could not yet envisage. But the reason why the Metabolite patent lists no specific modes of embodiment is that they are all external to its main claim. The useful results enabled by Metabolite take place *in the diagnostician's mind*, not in things or material media external to the mind. Whereas Morse's claim listed no modes of the material embodiment of his invention in order to claim all of them, Metabolite claims none because it has none. Consequently, when applied to Metabolite, the materiality requirement that served well to curb Morse's expansionist claim would look like trying to catch the genie with a butterfly net.

One of course could follow Justice Stevens and his liberal colleagues in trying to simply rule abstract methods patents out of existence. However, doing that requires drawing essential and essentializing distinctions between what technology is and is not, and what materiality means. A more interesting alternative would be to rethink the material/immaterial dichotomy that has framed both modern patent law and its response to abstract methods. That rethinking is already immanent in patents like Metabolite's, in which specificity is coming to play the role that materiality or concreteness (or similarly 'solid' but actually remarkably vague adjectives) had played in traditional patent discourse. As already identified by some legal scholars, in information-based inventions the opposite of 'abstract' is no longer 'material' but 'specific.'[23]

For instance, what has been patented in Metabolite is not a general model the application of which is then narrowed down to a specific context (like Bilski's general hedging scheme, which is then restricted to energy commodities trading), but something that was never general and always specific to the two entities it connects: levels of homocysteine and vitamin B. Metabolite's invention was 'born local,' not born general and subsequently narrowed down to a particular context of use. Whereas Bilski's Claim 1 presents a 'method for managing the consumption risk costs of *a commodity*' (thus implying that this is a method applicable to a variety of entities of a certain kind), Metabolite talks about homocysteine: one specific entity, not a category of entities.[24] Metabolite has no other known contexts of application, at least at the time of the patent application. Although the meaning of 'applied' and 'specific' may seem similar, the invention claimed in Metabolite is indeed specific, but certainly not applied. If 'specific' and 'applied' sound similar by virtue of both being starkly different from 'abstract,' the analogy ends there. Yes, they are different from abstract, but in very different ways. In this context, to say that something is specific does not mean that it was something abstract that was then made material. Specificity is neither material nor immaterial.

We could say that the specificity of an immaterial invention like Metabolite creates effects comparable with the early modern spatial limitations imposed on the uses of some very material inventions: the windmills on hills scenario. Of course, specificity does not 'locate' an invention spatially, but it can be said to do so conceptually. It literally points to where the invention 'is' in the sense of what are the entities involved in the inventive step and what is the relation that produces the new and useful effects claimed by the patent: in this case the diagnostic relation between homocysteine and vitamin B, in whatever mammalian body those two entities might be found. The materiality or immateriality of the invention may be becoming less of a problem in this case; no longer a difference that makes a difference.

This does not mean, of course, that the trend exemplified by Metabolite is one that we should endorse or support, or that it will lead, as the founding fathers wished, to the 'progress of the useful arts.' The pros and cons of intellectual property are as debatable as ever, and the patenting of immaterial inventions (even intriguing ones like Metabolite) may in fact bring up some intractable problems within the larger framework of intellectual property law.[25] I hope to have shown, however, that while material ontologies (or the claim that almost everything can be treated as a 'technology') may sound sophisticated and perhaps even comforting in today's social sciences and humanities circles, they do not seem to capture the complexity of technological innovation, and are certainly not providing effective tools to limit the scope of patents of abstract methods and enlarge the knowledge commons many of us care about. What I have tried to show here is that there are in fact new notions or features of 'invention' (like specificity) that are being articulated or mobilized with the very emergent technologies they are trying to conceptualize. And although these new conceptualizations are embedded within esoteric contemporary debates about patenting, they are effectively redefining the meaning of technology, materiality, immateriality and their relation.

Notes

1 I wish to acknowledge the generous support of the Ministry of Education of the Russian Federation. I focus primarily on some of the issues that have emerged from the Bilski and Metabolite cases, but time and space constraints force me to skip the very recent, and important, Mayo Collaborative Services v. Prometheus Labs Inc. (2012).

2 US Patent #4,940,658 Robert H. Allen, Sally P. Stabler, John Lindenbaum (1986). Metabolite is not the patent's assignee, but its exclusive licensee.

3 Other claims of this patent do cover ways to assay homocysteine, but Claim 13 does not, focusing instead on the correlation itself.

4 US Patent Act 1793, Sec. 3.

5 35 U.S.C. 101.

6 USPTO, Interim Examination Instructions for Evaluating Subject Matter Eligibility under 35 U.S.C. § 101 – August 2009.

7 US Constitution, Article 1, Section 8: 'The Congress shall have Power To … promote the Progress of Science and useful Arts, by securing for limited Times to Authors and to Inventors the exclusive Right to their respective Writings and Discoveries.'

8 Official Transcript Proceedings Before the Supreme Court of the United States, Bernard L. Bilski and Rand A. Warsaw, Petitioners, v. David J. Kappos, Under Secretary of Commerce for Intellectual Property and Director USPTO, Case No. 08-964, November 9, 2009, p. 9.

9 Official Transcript Proceedings Before the Supreme Court of the United States, Bernard L. Bilski and Rand A. Warsaw, Petitioners, v. David J. Kappos, Under Secretary of Commerce for Intellectual Property and Director USPTO, Case No. 08-964, November 9, 2009, p. 7.

10 Consider for instance the title of Shapin's book 'Pump and Circumstance: Robert Boyle's Literary Technology' (Shapin 1984).

11 Official Transcript Proceedings Before the Supreme Court of the United States, Bernard L. Bilski and Rand A. Warsaw, Petitioners, v. David J. Kappos, Under Secretary of Commerce for Intellectual Property and Director USPTO, Case No. 08-964, November 9, 2009, p. 18.

12 Bilski v. Kappos – 561 U.S. 7 (2010), Opinion of the Court.

13 Bilski v. Kappos – 561 U.S. 2 (2010), Syllabus.

14 Bilski v. Kappos – 561 U.S. 47 (2010), Stevens, J. concurring in judgment.

15 The statute defines the term 'process' as a 'process, art or method [that] includes a new use of a known process, machine, manufacture, composition of matter, or material' §100(b). But, this definition is not especially helpful, given that it also uses the term 'process' and is therefore somewhat circular.' Bilski v. Kappos – 561 U.S. 11 (2010), Stevens, J. concurring in judgment.

16 US Patent 1617, Reissue # 117, June 3, 1848, Claim 8.

17 'While he shuts the door against inventions of other persons, the patentee would be able to avail himself of new discoveries in the properties and powers of electro-magnetism which scientific men might bring to light. For he says he does not confine his claim to the machinery or parts of machinery which he

specifies, but claims for himself a monopoly in its use, however developed, for the purpose of printing at a distance. New discoveries in physical science may enable him to combine it with new agents and new elements, and by that means attain the object in a manner superior to the present process and altogether different from it. And if he can secure the exclusive use by his present patent, he may vary it with every new discovery and development of the science, and need place no description of the new manner, process, or machinery upon the records of the patent office. And when his patent expires, the public must apply to him to learn what it is. In fine, he claims an exclusive right to use a manner and process which he has not described and indeed had not invented, and therefore could not describe when he obtained his patent. The court is of opinion that the claim is too broad, and not warranted by law.' O'Reilly v. Morse – 56 U.S. 113 (1853).

18 Diamond v. Diehr – 450 U.S. 175 (1981).

19 See for instance Prager (1946), Mandich (1960) and Mandich (1948).

20 It is anachronistic to talk about 'claims' of a patent prior to the modern regime of patent specification, but find the analogy productive in this specific discursive context.

21 This may seem surprising given that early modern inventions operated in a distinctly 'material regime' that focused on the invention as a usefully performing material device rather than an inventive step embodied in a machine. What I mean is that precisely because the early modern conceptualization of the invention construed it as a machine new and useful in a specific legal and political jurisdiction it effectively had few conceptual or legal tools to manage what later became the 'claim' of the invention because that claim was left largely undescribed and unspecified, folded within the material invention itself. In the absence of standardized discursive tools to assess and manage what the invention was (tools that would develop after 1800, in a radically different episteme of invention), the geographical restriction on the use and protection and use of an invention (still conceptualized as a material thing) functioned, therefore, as an indirect way to curtail the yet-unspecified claim. I would say, therefore, that the early modern regime conceptualized the invention as material and controlled its scope through spatial limitations, whereas the modern regime conceptualizes it largely in terms of its idea and then controls its scope through its material embodiments.

22 US Patent 1617, Reissue # 117, June 3, 1848, Claim 8, emphasis mine.

23 Lemley et al. (2011).

24 Bernard Bilski and Rand A. Warsaw patent application, April 10, 1997 (emphasis mine).

25 Brief for Amicus Curiae Law Professor Kevin Emerson Collins in Support of Neither Party, In re Bilski, 545 F.3d 943 (Fed. Cir. 2008) (No. 2007-1130).

Bibliography

Allen, R., Stabler, S. and Lindenbaum, J. (1986) US Patent #4,940,658 (filed Nov 20, 1986; issued July 10, 1990), Claim 13.

Biagioli, M. (2006) 'Patent Republic: Representing Inventions, Constructing Rights and Authors', *Social Research* 73, 2006, 1132–4.

Bilski, B. and Warsaw, Rand A.(1997) 'Patent Application,' April 10, 1997, Serial no. 08/833,892, Claim 1, Online at: http://www.uspto.gov/web/offices/com/sol/2007-1130bilski_joint_appendix.pdf, p. A–6.

Bilski, B. and Warsaw, R. v David J. Kappos, (2009) 'Official Transcript Proceedings Before the Supreme Court of the United States', Under Secretary of Commerce for Intellectual Property and Director USPTO, Case No. 08-964, November 9, 2009, p. 9.

Lemley, M., Risch, M., Sichelman, T. and Wagner, P. (2011) 'Life after Bilski', *Stanford Law Review*, 63, 2011, 1315–1347.

Mandich, G. (1948) 'Venetian Patents (1450–1550)', *Journal of the Patent Office Society* 30, 166–224.

—— (1960) 'Venetian Origins of Inventors' Rights', *Journal of the Patent Office Society* 42, 378–82.

Pottage, A. and Sherman, B. (2011) 'Kinds, Clones, and Manufactures', in M. Biagioli, P. Jaszi, and M. Woodmansee (eds) *Making and Unmaking Intellectual Property*, Chicago: University of Chicago Press, 2011, p. 269.

Prager, F. (1946) 'Brunelleschi's Patent', *Journal of the Patent Office Society*, 28, 1946, 109–35.

Shapin, S. (1984) 'Pump and Circumstance: Robert Boyle's Literary Technology', *Social Studies of Science* 14, 1984, 481–520.

Yates, Judge Joseph (1769) in Francis Hargrave (ed.), *Speeches or Arguments of the Judges of King's Bench in April 1769 in the Cause Millar Against Taylor* (Leith: Cooke, 1771), p. 56.

35

Thinking through place and late actor-network-theory spatialities

Robert Oppenheim

How do things make places, and how do places make the making of things more or less possible? For me, these have been productive naive questions that have structured inquiries in resonance, which I reexamine further below. Yet it is perhaps not entirely clear that one needs to think through place at all when considering 'object matters', or what the stakes are in choosing place as a focus over other spatializing categories. And so I begin by recounting a few nonexclusive qualities of an everyday sense of places, which I give more theoretical weight and conceptual precision as this chapter goes on.

Consider first an office, a prominent sort of place at which, ideally at least, 'things get done'. What it is as, if one will, a doing-things-place, is quite obviously dependent on other things found there: computers, files, co-workers, internet and telephone linkages. Connections and collections define its potential, and maybe even its identity, although of course, offices are not the kind of places usually thought of in terms of 'identity'. Nonetheless, anyone who has visited a suddenly emptied-out office, previously a hub of activity, can attest to its negative charge. It is weird and sad.

As an example, the office illuminates a sense of place as *situation*.[1] Yet an office is at the same time a misleading example, precisely because of the constant active engagement with its consti-tuting things that tends to be overemphasized (ask yourself: when is the last time you opened that book or report on the top shelf?). So consider also a street corner, where there is a shop that you have never entered. If one day you do, the place is now different, even though, of course, the shop is there as it always was. Furthermore, entering the shop may disclose geographies that you did not know about before, which may be different in shape and possibly logic from the geography that brought you to the encounter. If it is a musical instrument store that you encounter on your daily linear path (perhaps to the office of the first example), it may shunt you into the point map of piano teachers scattered throughout the city. Such disparate geographies may continue simply to overlap, or they may bleed into one another, affect one another, become intercalated. So if *situation* is basic to thinking about 'place with things', it is necessary but not sufficient. One must also have a language for talking about a *movement* within situation roughly equivalent to activa-tion, and the sort of *dimensionalities* that result from this movement.

This, then, is for me a minimum set of aspects of place that we might keep in mind as we move between different kinds of place theory, which indeed are central to the point of having any sort of theoretical language of place at all. The goal here is to consider how the category of place might be reconfigured for a post-social and post-representationalist anthropology of plural ontologies. Those who have advanced 'things' as a conceptual unit for such a programme over other options (like 'objects') prefer it precisely because of its vagueness, its 'vacuity' as a heuristic term (Henare *et al.* 2007: 5; Oppenheim 2008b: 6). It is tempting to treat place in the same manner, as likewise a heuristic category. Yet if 'place' is also a heuristic, it is also a different heuristic, of which we might ask something additional in tuning in sociospatioontological process. The intended effect of this minimum set is thus to preserve some of the common theoretical sense of place as a significant dimensional *where* that is a backdrop for the occurrence of things and action (not just a qualitatively uniform configuration of things and action themselves [see Casey 1997]) even while transporting anthropological place theory away from its most common emphases on deep contextual human embeddedness or social senses of place and towards the sort of relational ontological anthropology that is of central concern in this volume.

My interest in place has centred on its potentiating capacities. In line with the initial question of this chapter, I have focused on place as an 'orienting setting ... where some (other) things and actions become more possible' (Oppenheim 2008b: 12). Concretely, looking at a South Korean historic city, I have asked how this place, its array of things, and extant relations of spokesperson-ship some residents had with these things acted to domesticate and channel various aspects of a larger, national politics of history and development. Social anthropology offers one antecedent for this sort of consideration. If Alfred Gell's (1998: 7) central equation in *Art and Agency* can be paraphrased as 'agency in the vicinity of things', one might reverse Gell's formula and, in effect, seek to solve for vicinity: what is the 'place' of distributed agency? Another precursor stems from the figure of the laboratory in classical actor-network-theory (hereafter ANT), in which the laboratory appears as a made or engineered place-of-leverage for both the production of scientific results and the building of their social incontrovertibility (Latour 1983). Drawing in particular on this latter connection, I engage here in a two-pronged reading strategy. I examine some recent empirical anthropological and sociological studies of place that have sought to use ANT to reconfigure place theory, including my own Korean study that I introduced above. In alternation, I also consider the focus on spatiality that has come to the forefront in some recent 'late ANT'[2] theoretical writings, notably including Bruno Latour's (2005) *Reassembling the Social* and John Law's (2004) *After Method*, echoing an exegesis originally offered elsewhere (Oppenheim 2007). At the conjunction of these readings, I locate two questions that I pose as theoretical translations of the issue of how to do 'place with things', namely, what properties might a late ANT anthropological or sociological view of place have, and what might distinguish this 'ANTish theory of place' from an ANTish theory of anything else. A sufficient answer, I argue, reasserts the minimum set of place that I identified above for an ontological anthropology, in the process reiterating the necessity and value of place as a category itself.

A basic characteristic of empirical studies that have sought to draw on ANT literature to 'get back into place' (in Casey's [1993] felicitous phrase) is their attention to what I would call place's 'amongness'. This is to say that they tend to understand place not in terms of a singular and undifferentiated relation of contextual being possessed by those 'in place'('embeddedness', as I have glossed it above) but rather as a less dichotomous multiplicity of entanglements at a nexus of things of concern and situated engagement capacities.[3] Metaphors of depth, containment, 'withinness', and figure/ground relationality are more generally replaced by metaphors of intersection and connection. For example, in his study of Corsican place identity as constructed[4] among brush fires, scientific interventions, and tourists, Matei Candea (2008: 203) unpacks naturalized and essentialist understandings of insiderdom and outsiderdom and 'local knowledge' that have tended to populate both tourism research and postcolonially inflected studies of Corsican society encountering an encroaching technocratic rationality.[5] Candea's (2008: 205) alternative is to understand Corsican place as an 'assemblage' emergent through both human and 'non-human components ... intricately woven' together as matters of concern. Corsicans, tourists and researchers all care about the fires that sometimes ravage the island, but the different way in which fire mobilizes residents and the way in turn that residents reductively mobilize tourists as avatars of an uncaring or heedless outside becomes the ground for asserting a more essentialist place identity. For Candea (2008: 210–211), contingent modalities of connection give rise to notions of categorical difference, rather than the categorical quality of locals' leading to a different connectedness. Meanwhile, with a focus on the issue of platial potentiation that I have also regarded as central, the sociologists Harvey Molotch, William Freudenburg, and Krista E. Paulsen (2000: 803) have compared two southern Californian cities in relation to the twin issues of substantive, impactful place character and the structurations it imposes, the 'cumulating path adjacencies' that constitute and perpetuate the different characters of Santa Barbara and Ventura. Drawing on Law and Latour, Molotch and his coauthors ultimately understand place character as a 'lash-up', a 'mode of connection among unlike elements' (Molotch *et al.* 2000: 793, 816; see also Molotch 2005: 161–93). Here, then, is a strong, ANT-derived vision of place as an articulation of things and the concernful processes that make things matter. 'Surface similarities' of oil development and freeways arriving from the outside give rise to 'deeper differences' because of the way they are linked into existing arrangements and reinforce them (Molotch *et al.* 2000: 795).

My own empirical attempt to examine the mediation of place among things, to answer the questions of potentiation ('how things make place' and the other issues posed at the beginning of this chapter) occurred in the course of an examination of the changing conditions of ontological or technical politics in the South Korean 1990s (Oppenheim 2008b).[6] The culminating 'lash-up' examined in this book materialized the resolution of a development dispute involving competing proposed routings (and the possibility of outright cancellation) of South Korea's first high-speed rail line through the historic city of Kyŏngju, a site replete with ancient monuments, archaeological treasures known and unknown, and other matters of preservationist concern. A rupture of 1995, in which different, mutually incompatible routing plans jostled for attention, resolved by 1997 into a broadly if not universally agreed station and track location. The Kyŏngju high-speed rail segment that finally opened in 2010 runs according to this agreement, which occurred only through a subtle shifting of the object(s) of the project: what it was, what it encompassed, what it would do, what it redefined and redistributed.[7] This dispute over a highly consequential act of place-making brought together the remnants of authoritarian modes of technocratic politics, new expert actors, and various (sometimes incompatible) calls for democratic process or local self-determination. Yet I aim also to emphasize, per an aspect of 'classic' ANT that I am reluctant to give up easily, a more radically open-ended quality[8] of this politics as some participants engaged and lashed into the emergent ontological-political settlement of the railway dispute 'things' that had prior histories of being worked upon by a still wider range of Kyŏngju actors, notably resident historians, cultural groups, and citizens' organizations.[9]

These things were varied in nature. A mountain of special interest to resident religious and cultural groups, for example, became an obligatory standpoint (in a literal physical sense) from which a proper routing solution must be envisioned; the vista from the top of this mountain, transposed into photographs and other media, came to define a preservation zone from which the railway was excluded. *Tapsa*, 'field study', a word that can designate everything from engineers' site studies to historical field trips, but which had come to name both a national fad for heritage tourism and the constitutive ambulatory practice of Kyŏngju local history, a practice of visiting and studying historic monuments in the terrain alone or in small groups, was called for as a procedural necessity in the railway resolution. In part through the very semantic slippage of the term, this demand for *tapsa* guaranteed the participation of local historians in the 'on the ground' siting of the track routing. Even the widely agreed and apparently banal notion that the railway should be built in a way 'appropriate to Kyŏngju' (*Kyŏngju tapge*) drew its slogan from transformations of civic festivals in which 'Kyŏngju appropriateness' had been developed in a more concrete manner. In such ways, the heterogeneous 'unlike elements', the things lashed up in the railway controversy's solution, were also vehicles in which the agency of non-expert (one should say, 'differently expert') local actors was to some degree smuggled into a politics that did not make room for them of its own accord.

At first glance, these treatments of place by Candea, Molotch and his coauthors, and myself seem to suggest that an understanding of place as situation, to recall the initial thought exercise of this chapter, might be at the core of what would constitute an ontological, ANTish understanding of the category. Place would simply be a 'star-like' entity or actant not unlike other entities or actants in the late ANT purview (Latour 2005: 177), defined or given character not or not only through contrastive definition at the margins (as in many anthropological theories that derive ultimately from structuralist arguments) but through its 'fine internal array' of articulated entities often copresent elsewhere, the 'gathering and collusion' of things often themselves distributed or extensive in character (Oppenheim 2007: 486). Not for nothing have railways, *qua* paradigmatic thing present-here-present-in-other-places-simultaneously, been recurrently good to think with in ANT literature (cf. Latour 1993: 1). The place of the Kyŏngju railway itself, meanwhile, might be said to lie at the intersection of the mountain, grounded templates of appropriateness, and *tapsa* (as well, of course, as much else), just as we might imagine the place constituted by the average office as the intersection of humans with telephones, internet-enabled computers, and videoconference equipment, all on and humming.

Yet as already signalled, such a theorization of place for an ontological social science would seem partial, necessary but not sufficient, or at least desirous of further refinement. It would fail to address fully the 'minimum set' and thus to match an intuitive sense of place's aspects, and it would fail to distinguish ANTish place from any other ANTish actant, or place from things. I find this ironic, insofar as the central concern with spatiality in some recent late ANT writing resonates with a more nuanced understanding of place, and, reciprocally, place is a useful category for unfolding some of (late) ANT's 'sensibilit[ies] to materiality, relationality, and process' (Law 2004: 157).

In an earlier article, I presented a reading of late ANT and an argument for an expanded understanding of its relevance that was targeted most directly at certain ossified interpretations of this literature prevalent in its extant American anthropological appropriation (Oppenheim 2007). My most basic claim, that late ANT should be understood as 'among-ANT', a domain-independent ontology of association and enactment, was a response to still-prevalent shorthand 'about' and 'across' translations of ANT[10] that render it as a topically defined toolkit for writing on technoscience or at the borderlands of predefined domains of the social and technical, or for sprinkling in non-human agency. However, my more particular positive goal was to review late ANT's own attentiveness to spatial logics for anthropological consideration, and to note that its sensitivities to 'amongness' have been more complexly developed, if also differently in different works, than is often appreciated. Although 'place' is rarely an explicit category in these writings, here I will argue that in fact a more 'full-frontal' engagement with this literature is helpful for a reconstruction of the category of place for an ontological anthropology.

The article highlighted various images of dimensionality and dimensioning movement that late ANT provides as well as the question of its harmony with phenomenological spatial categories.

The aspect of dimensionality that is most apparent is indeed a concomitant of the classical ANT notion of 'star-like' actants reiterated by Latour in *Reassembling the Social* (2005: 177), the distributed stabilization of actor-nodes by connection to (articulation with, enrolment of) other actants accessed (and this is key) in and for their relational ontological difference. As movements that shift and scale other entities into support, such acts of connection are not simply mechanical but qualitatively transformative in the new ontological relations that they create. In the same book, moreover, there is a vibrant treatment of what I call Latour's dimensionality-sub-two, the qualitatively different dimensional relationship of the member nodes of a given actor-network to the 'vast outside' (or as he would prefer, 'in between') of the unconnected or 'not yet' connected: a 'plasma' characterized at once by absence, inattention, and nondetermination on the one hand and potentiality on the other (Latour 2005: 241–44; Oppenheim 2007: 479–80). Meanwhile, Law's *After Method* offers several rich dimensional vocabularies of its own. First, there is the irreducible articulateness or contoured quality of the enactment of presences through both manifest and occluded absence that Law (2004: 14, 161) suggests in taking the 'method assemblage' as his most basic unit. Second, in its concern with the fractionality and fractional coherence of objects simultaneously enacted within several overlapping but non-conformable method assemblages, the book (following notably on Law 2002 and Mol 2002) turns upon things themselves the analysis of different topological kinds, different coordinations of mobility and (im)mutability, which have featured in Law and Annemarie Mol's collaboration since the 1990s (Mol and Law 1994; Law and Mol 2001). On offer here is the possibility of talking about a genre of interaction and interference effects that are distinctively intertopological.

Taking stock of such qualitative dimensionalities leads me in turn to the position that (late) ANT writings on humans and things are in deep resonance with phenomenology in their ways of attending to interactive spatial movements and relations if not in the locations of action that they presume.[11] The most basic 'coordinates' of spatiality in (much) ANT as well as (much) phenomenology are orientation or directionality on the one hand and circumspective, attentive aroundness on the other, and the spatial movements that they tend to throw into sharpest relief are those of gathering and distancing (see Casey 1997: 247). To use a term that deserves wider circulation, they are all about deseverant process, the 'oriented bringing-close' of that which in some sense is already there, and its opposite (Casey 1997: 250). These coordinates unfold in phenomenological analyses of the qualities (the existence *for*) of objects that simply lie there versus those that announce themselves in their potential instrumental usefulness, those that disappear into their familiarity, and those that suddenly (re-)impinge upon consciousness in their failure. They also unfold in dimensional ANT distinctions between persons and things articulated into a given network, reality enactment, or method assemblage and Latour's plasma or Law's (2004: 7) 'flux' of the primitively out there that is otherwise unformatted.

Reading the attentiveness to dimensionality and phenomenology-like movements inherent to late ANT back into attempts to construct an ANTish theory of place leads, I would argue, to a more adequate overall treatment of the different conceptual 'moments' of place-making. To some degree, this is simply a matter of making the implicit explicit. As already hinted, one might start by highlighting the active and transformative aspect of Molotch's 'lash-ups'. Lash*ing*, as it were, is not merely an act of connection, but also a shifting-scaling, reorienting and dimensioning (and thus re-ontologizing) movement. In Candea's work, concern with fire and with tourists converge into a certain Corsican relation to outsiders, but it is not that there is a mechanical relation 'fire + tourists = damned tourists'. In being taken up by Corsican concern, in becoming an aspect of place identity on Corsica, tourists are rendered one-dimensionally precisely as heedless, uncaring, unconcernful oafs. My own work on Kyŏngju similarly sought to foreground the reformatting of things of concern in the act of articulation. *Tapsa* was twisted and stretched in being moved into the railway controversy solution: its localist significance was amplified, and blended into the expertise of engineers, whereas other aspects of its own prior articulateness were downplayed or forgotten. The practice genre came to interpellate a corps of local experts, whereas for some prior practitioners the point had been the openness of the category of expertise itself: that anyone could do *tapsa*, that anyone could eventually become knowledgeable and a leader through doing it. What is retained in accounts attentive to this aspect of lashing is not only a general sense of ontological place as process but a more specific evocation of the deseverant concernful spatialities of phenomenological action; as Casey (1997: 250) writes, 'place is not something we come across as something we *are simply in*; it is what we precipitate by the conjoint action of directing and desevering … there is no place without this intervention'.

The final step is to see that any given place is constituted by a multiplicity of such relationships, which in their multiple character define an overall circumstantial (i.e., 'standing around')[12] landscape with its own composite dimensionality. All the active connections of the situational lash-up that produce an office as a doing-things place coexist, if it is the average academic office, with a heterogeneous set of books on the top shelf ignored to date, each perhaps with its own distinct transformative capacity but sharing an aspect (and this is to be optimistic about one's future reading) as the 'not yet deseveres'. The unvisited music shop and pet store on the same corner would be differently disclosing, but are commonly undisclosed. To start a working definition of ontological place as 'a way in which many … dimensional, shifting-scaling relationships are collected or gathered' (Oppenheim 2008b: 14) recalls some of Mol and Law's (e.g., 1994) arguments and points to an inherently intertopological character of place as a (classically, but perhaps not necessarily, regional) co-location of connections and entities that are not themselves dependent on an identical (or a conformable) co-location. And this, in turn, leads to seeing such landscapes of actuality and potentiality, degrees or qualities of existence *for* that have become more clearly the subject of late ANT in its discussions of plasma and flux, as themselves part of the dimensional topology structure of platial terrains. In place-making in Kyŏngju, I adopted Law's (2004: 27–35) terminology of 'hinterlands' (highlighted in his rereading of Latour and Woolgar 1979) to name the dual character of the already-there that is also potentially a resource for some new stabilization (Oppenheim 2008b: 15). This was the governing concept of my central narrative of heterogeneous Kyŏngju things that, reoriented and rescaled, potentiated a resolution to the dispute over the high-speed railway routing. As noted above, the localist significance of *tapsa* was pre-present as one of its aspects, and it is this that made it a resource for the railway solution, even as it was transformed in being activated. The mountain that helped define the final routing, which acted as a locus to visualize a zone that must be preserved and from which the railway must be excluded, had a prior character as the centrepiece of a heterotopic imaginary for some residents, defined by its relegation 'off the map' of previous Kyŏngju development as well as its reappropriation as iconic of human-natural harmony and even as a concretization of Buddhist Pure Land. This character and this value were pulled forward, projected outward, and actualized on a wider scale by the railway resolution as the mountain was moved to become the logical pivot of future urban planning. It gave meaning to the 'alternative' character of the routing alternative.[13]

To retain and reconstruct the minimum set of place, I have contended, is to preserve intuition while giving theory its full due. This, then, is the sense of place, as a late ANT object of study or as a heuristic for an ontological anthropology, with which I conclude: a simultaneity of terrains of actuality and potentiality and of the intertopological movements that inextricably connect and collect them.

Notes

1 The concept has been developed by John Kelly (2010, see also 2003: 357–60), in particular in relation to the understanding of US power articulated by the nineteenth-century naval strategist Alfred Thayer Mahan.

2 So called in deference to the different attitudes towards the ANT label evinced by the authors in the works in question, i.e., the adoption of a 'post-ANT' designation by Law versus Latour's contingent and qualified reassertion (but reassertion nonetheless) of the 'actor-network-theory' triad, notwithstanding earlier attempts to 'recall' it (Latour 1999).

3 Embeddedness versus entanglement draws on Don Slater's interjection (2002: 242; building especially on Thomas 1991 and Callon 1998) into the debate between Michel Callon, Cécile Méadel, and Vololona Rabeharisoa (2002) and Daniel Miller (2002) on the ontology of the market in economic practice and anthropology.

4 Here as elsewhere in work influenced by science studies, 'construction' is a fine word so long as its basic meaning of 'built up of parts' is maintained, in antithesis to the more ethereal and singularly ideological relation that has attended many studies of 'discursive construction' or 'social construction' (Hacking 1999).

5 One may indeed find the same dichotomies more broadly in treatises on political epistemology (e.g., Scott 1998: 309–41).

6 On ontological politics, see Mol 1998, 2002 and Law 2004.

7 The delay in actual construction began with the Asian financial crisis of 1997–98; it is something of a long story.

8 For an interesting short text on the 'openness' of ANT, see Kelly's (2002) review of Riles 2000. This agenda was also a response to the area literature with which I am engaged: my determination to track 'mess' (à la Law 2004), to allow in the first instance an unranked multitude into the mix, and to offer the possibility of the mobility of centres of calculation was also a response to a strongly priorist 'we know what politics are important' (democracy, class, gender, but not the enactment of materialities) and 'we know what actors are important' (the state, Seoul in general, intellectuals, but not locals or amateurs) quality that is pronounced in much Korean studies research.

9 Reminiscent of Henare, Holbraad, and Wastell (2007), but without their theorization at hand, I presented 'things' in terms of an open-ended, nonexclusive cast of characters that included actual materialities (enmeshed within processes of matter-ing), organizational and conceptual templates, routines, and formattings of political subjectivity (Oppenheim 2008b: 6–11).

10 These are largely restrictively based on some combination of Latour and Woolgar 1979; Latour 1987, 1988, 1993; and sometimes also Law 1986 and Callon 1986: texts that tend to constitute the 'American standard version' of ANT.

11 For related debates, see Latour 2005: 60–62, 244; Ihde 2003. I implicitly focus on Heidegger here, for reasons of my relative familiarity with his writings (I claim no expertise) and, as Edward Casey (1997: 243) elaborates, because of Heidegger's relative non-reliance on the human body as the 'royal road' into the spatialities of being and worldhood.

12 The literality of this term is developed by Latour and Woolgar 1979: 239.

13 Intertopology also informed treatments of the 'prior' character of several of these things. The same Kyŏngju mountain that became the necessary standpoint for seeing the railway solution was also already a thing over which local amateur historians had a privileged spokespersonship and which conjointly produced their authority. It was this, I argue, because of its own internal topological multiplicity, a specific way in which it held together a dual character, as a token in a class of cultural sites and simultaneously as a unique depth object of 'local culture', in an oscillation of active and potential, of hinterlands energized and receding (Oppenheim 2008a, 2008b: 113–135).

Bibliography

Callon, M. (1986) 'Some Elements of a Sociology of Translation: Domestication of the Scallops and the Fishermen of St. Brieuc Bay', in J. Law (ed.) *Power, Action and Belief: A New Sociology of Knowledge?*, London: Routledge and Kegan Paul.

—— (ed.) (1998) *The Laws of the Markets*, Oxford: Blackwell.

Callon, M., Méadel, C. and Rabeharisoa, V. (2002) 'The Economy of Qualities', *Economy and Society* 31(2): 194–217.

Candea, M. (2008) 'Fire and Identity as Matters of Concern in Corsica', *Anthropological Theory* 8(2): 201–15.

Casey, E.S. (1993) *Getting Back into Place: Toward a Renewed Understanding of the Place-World*, Bloomington, IN: Indiana University Press.

—— (1997) *The Fate of Place: A Philosophical History*, Berkeley, CA: University of California Press.

Gell, A. (1998) *Art and Agency: An Anthropological Theory*, Oxford: Oxford University Press.

Hacking, I. (1999) *The Social Construction of What?*, Cambridge, MA: Harvard University Press.

Henare, A., Holbraad, M. and Wastell, S. (2007) 'Introduction: Thinking Through Things', in A. Henare, M. Holbraad and S. Wastell (eds) *Thinking Through Things: Theorising Artefacts Ethnographically*, London: Routledge.

Ihde, D. (2003) 'If Phenomenology is an Albatross, is *Post-Phenomenology* Possible?' in D. Ihde and E. Selinger (eds) *Chasing Technoscience: Matrix for Materiality*, Bloomington, IN: Indiana University Press.

Kelly, J.D. (2002) Review of A. Riles, *The Network Inside Out*, *American Ethnologist* 29(2): 468–70.

—— (2003) 'U.S. Power, After 9/11 and Before It: If Not an Empire, then What?' *Public Culture* 15(2): 347–69.

—— (2010) 'When in the Course of Human Events? Situating the Cold War', paper presented at the conference Cold War Cultures: Transnational and Interdisciplinary Perspectives, Austin, TX, October.

Latour, B. (1983) 'Give Me a Laboratory and I Will Raise the World', in K.D. Knorr-Cetina and M. Mulkay (eds) *Science Observed: Perspectives on the Social Study of Science*, London: Sage.

—— (1987) *Science in Action: How to Follow Scientists and Engineers through Society*, Cambridge, MA: Harvard University Press.

—— (1988) *The Pasteurization of France*, trans. A. Sheridan and J. Law, Cambridge, MA: Belknap Press of Harvard University Press.

—— (1993) *We Have Never Been Modern*, trans. C. Porter, Cambridge, MA: Harvard University Press.

—— (1999) 'On Recalling ANT', in J. Law and J. Hassard (eds) *Actor Network Theory and After*, Oxford: Blackwell.

—— (2005) *Reassembling the Social: An Introduction to Actor-Network-Theory*, Oxford: Oxford University Press.

Latour, B. and Woolgar, S. (1979) *Laboratory Life: The Construction of Scientific Facts*, Thousand Oaks, CA: Sage.

Law, J. (1986) 'On the Methods of Long-distance Control: Vessels, Navigation and the Portuguese Route to India', in J. Law (ed.) *Power, Action and Belief: A New Sociology of Knowledge?*, London: Routledge and Kegan Paul.

—— (2002) *Aircraft Stories: Decentering the Object in Technoscience*, Durham, NC: Duke University Press.

—— (2004) *After Method: Mess in Social Science Research*, London: Routledge.

Law, J. and Mol, A. (2001) 'Situating Technoscience: An Inquiry into Spatialities', *Environment and Planning D: Society and Space* 19: 609–21.

Miller, D. (2002) 'Turning Callon the Right Way Up', *Economy and Society* 31(2): 218–33.

Mol, A. (1998) 'Ontological Politics: A Word and Some Questions', *The Sociological Review* 46: 74–89.

—— (2002) *The Body Multiple: Ontology in Medical Practice*, Durham, NC: Duke University Press.

Mol, A. and Law, J. (1994) 'Regions, Networks and Fluids: Anaemia and Social Topology', *Social Studies of Science* 24(4): 641–71.

Molotch, H. (2005) *Where Stuff Comes From: How Toasters, Toilets, Cars, Computers, and Many Other Things Come to Be as They Are*, New York: Routledge.

Molotch, H., Freudenberg, W. and Paulsen, K.E. (2000) 'History Repeats Itself, But How? City Character, Urban Tradition, and the Accomplishment of Place', *American Sociological Review* 65(6): 791–823.

Oppenheim, R. (2007) 'Actor-network Theory and Anthropology after Science, Technology, and Society', *Anthropological Theory* 7(4): 471–93.

—— (2008a) 'Kyŏngju Namsan: Heterotopia, Place-Agency, and Historiographic Leverage', in T.R. Tangherlini and S. Yea (eds) *Sitings: Critical Approaches to Korean Geography*, Honolulu, HI: University of Hawaii Press.

—— (2008b) *Kyŏngju Things: Assembling Place*, Ann Arbor, MI: University of Michigan Press.

Riles, A. (2000) *The Network Inside Out*, Ann Arbor, MI: University of Michigan Press.

Scott, J.C. (1998) *Seeing Like a State: How Certain Schemes to Improve the Human Condition Have Failed*, New Haven, CT: Yale University Press.

Slater, D. (2002) 'From Calculation to Alienation: Disentangling Economic Abstractions', *Economy and Society* 31(2): 234–49.

Thomas, N. (1991) *Entangled Objects: Exchange, Material Culture, and Colonialism in the Pacific*, Cambridge, MA: Harvard University Press.

36

What documents make possible
Realizing London's Olympic legacy

Gillian Evans

Papier-mâché, in French, literally means chewed paper. It is more popularly understood to be a composite material (i.e., a material made out of two separate constituent materials; in this case paper and glue). The combination produces material properties unavailable from the individual constituent materials. Astonishing about papier-mâché, for example, as a composite material, is the way that rather flimsy stuff, such as paper, can be transformed, through a process of admixture with glue, into extremely hard and, therefore, durable object forms.

The earliest known use of papier-mâché was among ancient Egyptians, who used it to craft death masks. The mask was believed to strengthen the spirit of the mummified person and guard the soul from evil spirits on its way to the after-world. A composite material lends durability to fragile substance and preserves form through the process of shaping or moulding.

The two constituent materials of all composite materials are known technically as the matrix and the reinforcement and all engineered (i.e., man-made) composite materials must be formed to shape or moulded. In papier-mâché, for example, the reinforcement, which is the paper, could be made to take the form of the human face through the process of casting, which is made possible by first soaking the paper in a matrix material of glue that for a short time makes the paper malleable. Then, paper and glue partially meld together, set and solidify, taking the object form of whatever shape the papier-mâché was applied to (the face in the case of the death mask or a multitude of other kinds of objects) because papier-mâché can be applied to and produce moulds of virtually anything.

A balloon, for example, is often the first kind of papier-mâché object that children make at school in an art-and-craft lesson. What is fun about this is that children first have to blow the balloon up, filling it with air from their own lungs and thereby transforming flaccid rubber into a living, interactive, light-as-air shape, which endures only so long as the air remains, trapped within the balloon. One pinprick and the amazing form (and experience of what balloons are like to play with) literally explodes before the children's eyes. Using papier-mâché, children learn to make fragile forms, like balloons, endure. Children are taught to take newspapers, tear them into little strips, soak each strip in wallpaper glue and apply it when wet to the exterior surface of the balloon. Once the papier-mâché is set and solidified, the children experience the immense pleasure of popping the balloon – now encased in its moulding – and behold: the balloon does not lose its form with the loss of air. It now exists in a more durable material, transformed through the process of crafting into something other than itself, all the hot air, which formerly defined its possibility, now released. The lesson is that what is ephemeral (for example, an air-filled balloon or the memory of a deceased loved one's face) can to some extent be captured and preserved through a process of material transformation.

In the spirit of playing with paper, I want to use the analogy of papier-mâché to think about what kinds of objects documents are. In the context of urban development and in this case, the planning of London's Olympic legacy, I argue that documents are a reinforcement material relative to a matrix of relational glue that brings and endeavours to hold together, to 'lash-up' (Molotch 2003), as composite matter and flexible-for-a-while moulding material, a proliferating meshwork (Ingold 2008) of persons, papers, places and political promises. Documents, from this perspective, are a form of political technology, both a technology of persuasion (Evans forthcoming) (the means for envisioning and narrating ideas) and a technology of materialization: the first stage in a long process of realization, which here, is the attempt to bring into being, via the 2012 Olympic Games, a state-led project for the redevelopment of the post-industrial East End of London.

Ghost Milk

The document that I focus on here is an example of what author, psychogeographer and vehement anti-Olympic critic, Iain Sinclair, describes as 'Ghost Milk': a soup of images and text produced by Olympic legacy experts or what he calls 'the regiment of fixers parasitical on [the Grand Project of] the Olympics'.[1] I explain here what I understand Sinclair to mean by the concept of Ghost Milk and although, to some extent, I am in sympathy with his analysis, I critique it, offering an alternative explanation for the work that these kinds of Olympic legacy documents can do.

Describing his new book to a photographer friend, Sinclair explains that Ghost Milk refers to:

> CGI smears on the blue fence. Real juice from a virtual host. Embalming fluid. A soup of photographic negatives. Soul food for the dead. The universal element in which we sink and swim.
>
> *(2011: 338)*

By CGI smears on the blue fence, Sinclair means the computer-generated images, which until 2009, were plastered here and there on the outward facing side of the Olympic Park's eleven miles of blue fence: a construction site perimeter that depicted prospective visions of the landscape promised to emerge there in future. These images, which Iain Sinclair refers to as 'real juice from a virtual host' are, to him, the only evidence of a ghostly presence: an inaccessible, impenetrable, invisible body of people who are making changes happen in the East End of London. Sinclair's work forces the reader to question: Who are they, these change-makers? Where are they to be found? How has this land come to be assembled and enclosed, by force of the state, and made inaccessible? And what are the effects of these changes?

To be sure, the process of urban transformation appears to be at once dramatic and obscure (hidden behind a fence), which is alienating for people struggling either to understand what is going on in their own backyard or to navigate what were once familiar spaces that have now become no-go zones. The opaque blue, and now the see-through electric security fence that has replaced it, enclose the land-as-construction-site, obscure the action of change-makers and shut out those whose lives are supposed to be 'regenerated' by what so-called urban experts are doing to and imagining for London's East End neighbourhoods. Sinclair rails against the force of

Figure 36.1   Part of the perimeter of the Olympic Park showing a tiny part of the blue fence enclosing the site of Olympic Park construction work © Gillian Evans 2008

change and describes the Ghost Milk as embalming fluid because for him, as a new reality (the Olympic Park) struggles itself, to come to life, it signifies the death of something else. That death which is unspoken by the 'hopeful CGI smears on the blue fence' is, Sinclair argues, the suffocation of the cultural landscape that the Olympic Park is replacing: this is a post-industrial place ripe with the meaningful traces of both a long history of industry in the East End of London and, despite this once profoundly polluting economy, the determined perseverance of a distinctive and by now rather wild and much loved waterside ecology: the valley of the River Lea stretching from the shores of the Thames to the upper reaches of Hertfordshire.[2]

The Ghost Milk in Sinclair's account can only ever be soul food for the dead because the weight of the past, the alternative meanings of life in this space of the city, are obliterated by a vision of the future embodied in documents, which fail to properly recognize the history of what urban experts aim to transform. The Milk is a 'universal element in which we sink and swim' because the soup of photographic images stands always and can only ever stand, as I understand Sinclair's interpretation, for something other than itself: it is symbolic of the logic of the state in support of capitalism as it proceeds to acquire more territory and avariciously accrue unto itself (through processes of extraction) more and more value. Virtual hosts (the urban change-makers) from this perspective, are like vampires sucking the life blood out of the pieces of city that they aim to transform and offering in return, to dead places, milk fit for its ghosts to feed on, an aesthetic soup promising the sustenance of a future that Sinclair vehemently argues will never be materialized. The past is mobilized in this account as a haunting, a spectre that hangs over the Olympic Park and signifies impending doom.

Critical urbanism

Sinclair's demand for respect for, and recognition of, the cultural significance of post-industrial urban landscape is important and his preoccupations are shared by others who are invested in preserving either the architectural heritage of post-industrial city spaces or arguing for the value of retaining unregenerated sites as places of undefined possibility. Lara Almarcegui, for example, is a Spanish artist interested in the relationship between architecture and urban design who focuses on the abandoned, derelict or in-the-process-of-being-demolished spaces that are commonplace in contemporary cities and that reveal, relative to the hyperdesigned spaces of development, places of potential and freedom as well as traces of history that is to be lost. Almarcegui is also interested in the raw materiality of urban change, exhibiting in one installation, for example, all the exact, separate materials, like ingredients in a cooking demonstration, required to transform a particular urban space via the construction of a new building.[3] Lara's project on the post-industrial 'wastelands' of the Lower Lea Valley, before the preparation and enclosure of the 2012 Olympic site for construction, focused on '12 empty spaces awaiting the London Olympics'. The work was intended to be a polemic about the loss of wasteland that she perceives to be a necessary part of the urban fabric: spaces where sites of urban decay provide meaningful pauses relative to the fast pace of capitalist overdevelopment.

Lara's work, which was produced for an exhibition at the Barbican in 2009, entitled *Radical Nature: Art and Architecture for a Changing Planet*, relates to a broader, radical critique of urban development (Naik and Oldfield 2009, 2010), one aspect of which expresses an aesthetic nostalgia for the preservation of the post-industrial landscape as-it-is (a plea for the recognition of and a testament to the value of sites of decay), not as space necessarily crying out for development. As such Almarcegui's work complements well the work of photographer Stephen Gill (2007), who, in a book produced with Iain Sinclair, attempts to preserve and to conjure some trace of what is to be lost in the process of urban Olympic transformation.

All too often, however, the appeal of an aesthetic of post-industrial decay is separated from what characterized the industrial lifetime of these city spaces, which was an inseparable relationship between places and persons as particular kinds of industrial or manufacturing workers and inhabitants of work-related collectives/communities perhaps a hundred years in the making (Hart 1987, 2008). Research literature and photographic work that does use a focus on post-industrial ruins to conjure a social world of discarded labour (Bluestone *et al.* 2003; High and Lewis 2007; Dubowitz 2010) achieves, I would argue, a more radical critique than the visualizations and critiques of Sinclair, Almarcegui or Gill. This is because it still uses the emotive force of photography to reveal an aesthetic of decay, but refuses to separate this from oral testimonies of workers and local inhabitants whose stories require of readers that they reflect on these places pragmatically, as former sites of production and, therefore, as contemporary spaces of social and economic decline for certain kinds of populations. The recent work of High and Lewis (2007), for example, depicts the political economy of American post-industrialization; it is at once a beautiful book of post-industrial architectural photography and an outcry against how badly corporations behave when they suddenly abandon places of work/working class livelihood and how democratic governments also collude in this. This foregrounding of persons as workers-abandoned, rather than on post-industrial places as simply good-to-look-at sites of ruin and decay for the pleasure of an aesthetically sensitive urban middle class, leads inevitably to a contemporary concern to want to know and to understand how those people affected by and who are perhaps still inhabiting the landscapes of post-1980s deindustrialization (e.g., in the USA and the UK, such as the post-industrial Docklands of the East End) are coping now. How is a formerly working-class population living and working or not, either in a new service economy or a service economy now in recession? What does it mean, for example, in the case of cities like Detroit, for an abandoned working-class population to inhabit what might be described as a dying city (Moore 2010; Marchand and Meffre 2010; Edwards *et al.* 2012)? And if, and when, governments attempt, finally, to intervene and to promote the 'regeneration' of post-industrial neighbourhoods twenty or thirty years after social and economic decline has set in, how, exactly, do they proceed? What new kinds of relations does the state forge with corporations and local residents and what difference do these schemes of transformation hope to make, in the here and now, and in the future? The complexity of the political imperative in post-industrial cities is described by Savitch (1988), who makes visible the task facing the state as it tries to harness the power of strategic planning and seduce the creative potential of capital the flow of which has long ago abandoned and left stagnant, urban neighbourhoods in need of change.

Urban planners and their documents

Undertaking an odyssey in reverse to the one that Iain Sinclair has journeyed through, I have for the past three years been conducting an ethnographic study of the Olympic Park Legacy Company, and am writing a book-length account, which tells a rather more sophisticated story about the people and practices behind urban development in the East End of London, than the one that Iain Sinclair relates.

The Olympic Park Legacy Company[4] is a not-for-profit limited company, created as a 'special purpose vehicle' (SPV)[5] in 2009, which was jointly owned and funded until May 2012 by the Mayor of London and the national government[6] and has now transformed into a Mayoral Development Corporation. The task of the Legacy Company is to design and deliver an Olympic Legacy in the form of a new piece of city, which is to be the transformation or regeneration of post-industrial East London out of 2.4 square kilometres of land especially assembled through compulsory purchase order to become the newly created Olympic Park. This is the beginning of an ambitious process of large-scale urban change planned to take place during the twenty to thirty years after the Games in 2012.

As I understand it, in Iain Sinclair's analysis, regeneration professionals of all kinds can only ever be the dupes of the state in collusion with capitalism, an economic system so self-evidently morally vacuous that there is no need to study processes of regeneration from the inside out. Paradoxically then, Sinclair records and provides the means for valuable critical reflection on the absenting, the killing off, the ghosting of the cultural landscape of the East End of London, restoring it, in some important, but extremely partial measure, to life, but he simultaneously produces, in his writing, the world of the change-makers as little more than a phantasmagoric show: a staged exhibition of optical effects and ghostly illusions. His own work, as a particular kind of document also produced, by his own admission, from a 'parasitical feeding on the Grand Project of the Olympics' is, then, a kind of Ghost Milk too, soul food for the hosts.

Following anthropologist Annelise Riles, and inspired by her 2006 edited collection of essays about documents as highly specific kinds of collectively produced ethnographic artefacts, I do not assume in advance that documents are institutional tools for the disciplining and objectification of modern subjects. Nor do I buy wholesale Sinclair's idea that Olympic legacy documents necessarily stand for nothing other than themselves. Rather, I am interested to think ethnographically about the generative capacities of documents as particular kinds of objects. I argue that the kinds of documents produced by the Olympic Park Legacy Company, such as vision statements, are most usefully thought of as at the very least, fivefold technologies; they are propositional statements; technologies of persuasion; organizational building matter; surfacing materials and scaling devices.

As propositional statements, legacy documents materialize, attribute value to and declare as statements of truth the visions, narratives of and arguments for a new imagining of the East End of a post-industrial city, which when seen from a strategic London-wide vantage point, is in desperate need of socioeconomic regeneration. Part of the original impetus for the London Games, inspired by the spatial reworking of the city achieved by a socialist city leadership via the 1992 Olympic Games, was the reorientation of Barcelona towards the waterfront. This made it possible for the city to achieve in five years urban plans that would otherwise have taken thirty years to achieve; this was not without controversy, however, and the displacement of poor people living on the waterfront remains a bone of political contention in Barcelona (Marshall 2004) as does the displacement of small businesses, residents and allotment holders in London. Nevertheless, the potential was made clear for other cities to also use the hosting of the Games as a catalyst for the acceleration of city-level strategic objectives. Richard Sumray, the person behind the drive to develop London's Olympic bid (Evans forthcoming) was determined to follow suit and make the transformation of East London's post-industrial brownfield sites, the centre of the bid for London's Games. In addition, Richard Sumray also learned from London's rival, Manchester, which had twice bid for the Games and, in a desperate attempt to survive the 1980s Thatcherite assault on public spending, had developed an assertive, entrepreneurial rhetoric around sports-focused regeneration of the run-down and poverty stricken East End of the city (Evans forthcoming; Ward and Peck 2002).

Important about these precedents and an analysis of the evolution of London's Olympic bid (Evans forthcoming) is that they were strategic, state-led attempts to deliver pragmatically focused urban change. They may not have led to ideal consequences, for example in terms of population displacement in Barcelona or an overemphasis on housing-led regeneration in Manchester, but they were certainly not cynical attempts by the state to suck the life blood out of the city and particularly those areas characterized by post-industrial decline. On the contrary, they were pragmatic and perhaps idealist projects of transformation which raise a more interesting political question than straightforward state oppression or capitalist collusion could convey: how it is that so many people who appear to be so determined to realize beneficial transformation to urban areas in post-industrial decline nevertheless struggle to deliver the promised benefits of change in the living conditions of the poor? This is an age-old question, addressed most famously by Scott (1998) and pertaining not just to urban regeneration initiatives, but also to 'development' projects the world over. The failures of the state or other top-down institutions (Ferguson 1994) are never straightforward questions to do with 'us' and 'them' dichotomies between 'the people' and 'the powers that be'. It seems to me that a more interesting and important task, rather than dismissing the state and asserting categorically that its projects, by definition, can never be realized, is to study what it is that the state thinks it is doing when it acts in the urban context and how it goes about executing the plans for the city that it hopes might make a difference to the future of the inhabitants it has been elected to serve. The point is that an aesthetic appeal for the preservation of the post-industrial spaces of the city is important, but it must be brought into conversation with both a broader, deeper sense of the history of these places as sites of industrial production and habitation, and city-wide, strategic and political demands for contemporary solutions to the social and economic abandonment of industrial working class populations. This is not to say that Olympic Games-focused regeneration is the solution, but at least state-led projects such as London 2012 recognize, are attempting to draw attention to and trying to do something about the urban living conditions of what are classified as the most deprived areas of the capital city.

The Queen Elizabeth Olympic Park

In October 2010, after more than a year of transition and uncertainty,[7] the Olympic Legacy Company launched, for the first time, its vision for the future of the Olympic Park. This was an important moment for various reasons: the launch event, held on the top of the BT Tower, overlooking London, was successful in the sense that, for the first time, the Company was able, proactively, to generate top-level media coverage about itself and its activities; it was also an opportunity to convince senior-level politicians, stakeholders and interested parties at both national and city level, of the credibility and viability of the Company and the scope of its ambitions. The event was, then, as much a declaration of the existence of the Company as it was a statement of its aims and objectives. After a difficult 18 months internally, the vision launch was as significant for Olympic Legacy Company staff as it was for interested external parties. Here at last was evidence of the Company's emerging self-confidence, a sign that it really existed, was going to endure and had a clear purpose to fulfil.

Centre stage at the vision launch featuring Olympic legacy leaders and political partners at central and London government level, was a document entitled Queen Elizabeth Olympic Park, known by Company insiders as 'the pink brochure'. This was especially produced for and distributed at the launch event; it was a snazzy product reflecting the aspirational style and visual leadership flair of a recently appointed Executive Director of Marketing and Communications (Comms) who had been brought on board to lend some 'Olympic sparkle' to the Legacy Company. The brochure looked more like the output of a cool architectural practice than a public sector organization and it created a much-needed sense of excitement in the 'Comms team', giving them a sense that they really were part of something worthwhile and that the ball was finally rolling after months of struggle and hiatus. For them, this felt like the Legacy Company's take-off moment.

As a statement, the pink brochure dared to declare as given, the world or state of affairs in which its proposition was true. This is a typical narrative device of proposal documents and visuals are an essential part of the document's rhetorical equipment, part of the forceful imaging of a future state of affairs. Their propositional force is part of what marks the shameless bravado of these kinds of documents (Evans forthcoming). And the people who produced this document (the Communications and Marketing team of the Legacy Company) know full well that each and every 'public-facing' document invites either affirmation or denial of the new state of reality that the documents propose. The success of each document is measured, then, by the extent to which the intended audience for any document appears to be persuaded of the veracity of the claims made. Crucially, however, success is also given by the degree to which the document convinces the Company itself that it can deliver what the proposition promises. The Company gains in existence, then, through the continuous production of documents, which propose and circulate the Company's proposition for and expertise in engineering and delivering urban change. Deniers of this competence, like Iain Sinclair, and a critical press and public are fully expected to want to shoot the proposition of every legacy-focused document down. In the 'oh yes we can' 'oh no you can't' pantomime that is the reality play of the Olympic legacy, every aspect of every document is therefore carefully crafted, every line, every message, every image and the overall look and feel are considered before the document goes to print.

The pink brochure was a 'top-line' document, which means that it was visual heavy, text thin and lacking in operational detail or explanation of political context. It stated aims, but was thin on objectives or potential obstacles. Any credible member of the audience would have noticed this at once, but without necessarily immediately jumping to undermine the project. In 2010, it was still OK for people to feel that the Legacy Company had time to prove itself. The document and its launch event was, if you like, a showcase, a way to whet the appetite of interested parties, but without yet containing a sense of the full process of production to follow. Central to the pages of the brochure was the linking of particular political actors (e.g. the Mayor of London and Legacy Company leaders) with the project as it pertains to a particular time line (2012–2030) and space of transformation: the Olympic Park and its particular features, 15 minutes from the City of London, proximal to the vibrant cultural diversity of the East End surroundings, 2.4 square kilometres of Olympic Park, 250 acres of open space, five new neighbourhoods, 6.5 km of waterways, five Olympic sporting venues, 11,000 new homes, 35 per cent affordable housing, 40 per cent family homes, community facilities, employment spaces, transport connectivity to city, nation and Europe, etc.

The pink brochure, as a document, substantiated, therefore, and attempted to objectify, both the emerging claims of the Olympic Park Legacy Company about the new piece of city it imagined itself creating and the sets of relations that constituted the Company as a particular kind of organizational entity in its own right. As a scaling device, the document was the means for the Legacy Company to attract to itself and then further substantiate, as a set of partnerships, various kinds of supportive and productive relationships that would increase its influence and distribute its slowly gathering propositional force through a range of interests city-wide and in the wider world. The brochure can be understood then, as a technology of persuasion (Evans forthcoming), the means to recruit allies to its cause (Latour 1993). Documents are, therefore, both surfacing materials (the means for the Legacy Company to make itself manifest in the world, to mould, materialize and transform what the Company is perceived to be all about both inside and out) and the means for making and remaking the interface through which the Company forges relations with existing and new partners in the project of trying to materialize and make real its plans for an Olympic legacy.[8]

This brings me back, finally, to the analogy of the papier-mâché. The ideas of the Legacy Company about what it wants to do in the East End of London are, for Iain Sinclair, nothing more than hot air, but a focus of the processes through which ephemeral ideas are materialized in paper form as a reinforcement and then made composite with a matrix of relational glue, shows that ideas about cities can gain in strength and durability, appear to take on more reality and finally become a future form of the land that they model. Sometimes ideas can mobilize enough reputational capital and a sufficiently dense network of allies that something exceptional happens: fragile pieces of paper can become the reinforcement to a relational matrix that is made more durable as plans become contracts and contracts become actions on the ground. And then, against all the odds hopes are raised that London might become the first city in history to deliver some kind of Olympic legacy, a transformative use value for its Park and at least some of its venues, and, as a result, produce a potentially catalytic effect for transformed living conditions and long-term regional socioeconomic change.[9] This reminds us that although we love to and must continue to shoot them down, we desperately need propositions for change in the post-industrial cities of Britain. Nostalgia for the past is not a sufficient future.

Notes

1 Quoted verbatim from a keynote speech given by Iain Sinclair at the conference in Manchester in September 2011 of the Centre for Research on Socio-Cultural Change (CRESC) entitled 'Framing the City'.
2 Most symbolic of the cultural vitality of what has been displaced from the land are the Manor Garden Allotments, which were cultivated by East End families for three generations, over a hundred-year time span. The four-and-a-half acre site was gifted to them in 1900 by Major Arthur Villiers, an old Etonian and former director of Barings Bank. The displacement of the Manor Gardens Allotment Society caused

a fierce resistance movement, which culminated, after a protracted struggle, in the legal requirement of the Olympic authorities to relocate the allotments on the Olympic Park after the Games are over.

3 http://www.friezefoundation.org/commissions/detail/lara_almarcegui/

4 On 1 April 2012, the Olympic Park Legacy Company became a Mayoral Development Company entitled London Legacy Development Corporation http://www.londonlegacy.co.uk/

5 An SPV or Special Purpose Vehicle is a company created to transfer assets and debt liability from the balance sheet of one entity (in this case the LDA [London Development Agency]) to another (in this case the Olympic Park Legacy Company). The aim was to create an organization whose sole remit was to focus on the planning and delivery of Olympic legacy, thereby removing the responsibility for legacy from the LDA, which was later abolished as part of mayoral devolution initiatives.

6 Government departments with a vested interest in the Olympic legacy are the DCMS (Department of Culture, Media and Sport) and CLG (Department of Communities and Local Government).

7 This was the transition from the Olympic Legacy Directorate at the LDA to the SPV and then Olympic Park Legacy Company (OPLC) under a new leadership team, which needed to establish the Company, review the direction of travel and set a course at the same time as navigating a political process leading to an eventual change of government.

8 As just one example of how many of such propositions are becoming reality, consider the 2011 OPLC achievement of securing post-Games contracts with operators to make the Aquatic Centre and Multi-Use Arena live and fully functional for both elite sport and community use after the Park reopens. This is just one of a long list of 'delivery' targets that have been met in advance of the Games and that makes London historic in terms of its pre-Games legacy achievements.

9 The Host Boroughs Unit has been in charge of working with OPLC and the London and national governments to craft the 'Convergence Agenda', which aims to ensure that the long-term legacy of the Games is to bring the East End to a point of matching the West End of London in terms of socioeconomic indicators within 20 years of the end of the Olympics 2012.

Bibliography

Bluestone B., Cowie J. and Heathcott J. (2003) *Beyond the Ruins: the meaning of deindustrialisation*. NY: Cornell University Press.

Dubowitz D. (2010) *Wastelands*. Stockport: Dewi Lewis Publishing.

Edwards J., Evans G. and Smith K. (2012) *Class Community and Crisis in Britain. Focaal, Journal of Historical Anthropology*, 62.

Evans G. (forthcoming, 2014) *London's Olympic Legacy*. London: Palgrave Macmillan.

Ferguson J. (1994) *The Anti-Politics Machine: development, depoliticization and bureacractic power in Lesotho*. MN: University of Minnesota Press.

Gill S. and Sinclair I. (2007) *Archaeology in Reverse*. London: Nobody Books.

Hart E. (1987) Paintresses and potters: work, skill and social relations in a pottery factory in Stoke-on-Trent, 1981–1984. PhD diss., University of London.

Hart E. (2008) An ethnographic study of industrial decline and regeneration in the UK potteries: Full Research Report. ESRC End of Award Report, RES-000-22-1945. Swindon.

High S. and Lewis D. W. (2007) *Corporate Wasteland*. NY: Cornell University Press, Ithica.

Ingold T. (2008) When ANT meets SPIDER: social theory for Arthropods, in Carl Knappett and Lambros Malafouris (eds.) *Material Agency: towards a non-anthropocentric approach*, New York: Springer Science and Media, pp. 209–216.

Latour B. (1993) *The Pasteurisation of France*. MA: Harvard University Press.

Marchand Y. and Meffre R. (2010) *The Ruins of Detroit*. London: Steidl.

Marshall T. (ed.) (2004) *Transforming Barcelona: the renewal of a European metropolis*. London: Routledge.

Molotch H. (2003) *Where Stuff Comes From: how toilets, toasters, cars and many other things come to be as they are*. NY: Routledge.

Moore A. (2010) *Detroit Disassembled*. NY; LA: Damiani.

Naik D. and Oldfield T. (2009) *Critical Cities: ideas, knowledge and agitation from emerging urbanists: 1*. London: Myrdle Court Press.

Naik D. and Oldfield T. (2010) *Critical Cities: ideas, knowledge and agitation from emerging urbanists: 2*. London: Myrdle Court Press.

Riles A. (ed.) (2006) *Documents: artifacts of modern knowledge*. MI: University of Michigan Press.

Savitch H.V. (1988) *Post-Industrial Cities*. NJ: Princeton University Press.

Sinclair I. (2011) *Ghost Milk: calling time on the grand project*. London: Hamish Hamilton.

Scott J. (1998) *Seeing Like a State: how certain schemes to improve the human condition have failed*. CT: Yale University Press.

Ward K. and Peck J. (2002) *City of Revolution: restructuring Manchester*. Manchester: University of Manchester Press.

Index